Cambridge
International AS and A Level

Geography

Garrett Nagle & Paul Guinness

AN HACHETTE UK COMPANY

To Angela, Rosie, Patrick and Bethany for their support and good humour.

Hachette UK's policy is to use papers that are natural, renewable and recyclable products and made from wood grown in sustainable forests. The logging and manufacturing processes are expected to conform to the environmental regulations of the country of origin.

Orders: please contact Bookpoint Ltd, 130 Milton Park, Abingdon, Oxon OX14 4SB.
Telephone: (44) 01235 827720. Fax: (44) 01235 400454. Lines are open 9.00–5.00, Monday to Saturday, with a 24-hour message answering service. Visit our website at www.hoddereducation.co.uk

First published in 2011 by
Hodder Education, a Hachette UK company,
338 Euston Road
London NW1 3BH

Impression number   9 8 7 6
Year   2017 2016 2015

Cover photo by Chris Guinness
Illustrations by Philip Allan Updates
Typeset in Garamond Light 9/12 by Philip Allan Updates
Printed in Dubai

A catalogue record for this title is available from the British Library

ISBN 978 1 4441 2316 6

Contents

Paper 1: Core Geography
Physical Core

Contents

Contents

Paper 3: Advanced Human Geography Options

Contents

Student's CD contents

Geographical skills: Graphs and charts and Maps

Key terms

Topic summaries

Additional work

Suggested websites

Interactive tests

Introduction

The aim of this book is to enable you to achieve your potential. In doing so, we hope to help you gain:

- an awareness of the usefulness of geographical analysis to understand and solve contemporary human and environmental problems
- a sense of relative location, including an appreciation of the complexity and variety of natural and human environments
- an understanding of the principal processes operating within physical and human geography
- an understanding of the causes and effects of change on the natural and human environments.

Any study of Geography includes a number of aspects, including:

- elements of physical and human geography and the inter-relationships between these components
- processes operating at different scales within physical and human geography
- a sense of relative location, including an appreciation of the complexity and variety of natural and human environments
- demonstration and explanation of the causes and effects of change over space and time on the natural and human environments.

In addition, you will use many skills, including:

- exploring primary (fieldwork) sources and secondary sources (e.g. statistical data)
- interpreting a range of map and diagram techniques displaying geographical information
- assessing methods of enquiry and considering the limitations of evidence
- demonstrating skills of analysis and synthesis
- using geographical understanding to develop your own explanations and hypotheses.

In addition to this book there is a student's CD-ROM, which enables you to revise and test your knowledge and to practise key skills. It includes key terms, topic summaries, additional work, suggested websites and interactive multiple-choice tests. There is also a supporting teacher's CD-ROM containing all the student's CD-ROM material, plus selected illustrations from the textbook and annotated sample suggested examination answers at three levels.

Structure of the syllabus

Cambridge International A and AS Level Geography (syllabus code 9696)

- Candidates for Advanced Subsidiary (AS) certification take Paper 1 only.
- Candidates who already have AS certification and wish to achieve the full Advanced Level qualification may carry their AS marks forward and take just Papers 2 and 3 in the exam session in which they require certification.
- Candidates taking the complete Advanced Level qualification take all three papers.

Paper 1: Core Geography
3 hours

Physical Core

- Hydrology and fluvial geomorphology
- Atmosphere and weather
- Rocks and weathering

Human Core

- Population
- Migration
- Settlement dynamics

Candidates answer questions in three sections. In Section A, they must answer five of six questions on the Physical and Human Core topics for a total of 50 marks. In each of Sections B and C, candidates answer one of three structured questions based on the Physical (Section B) and Human (Section C) Core topics, for a total of 25 marks in each section.

100% of total marks at AS Level 50% of marks at A Level

Paper 2: Advanced Physical Geography Options
1 hour 30 minutes

- Tropical environments
- Coastal environments
- Hazardous environments
- Arid and semi-arid environments

Candidates answer two structured essay questions, each on a different optional topic, from a total of eight questions based on the Advanced Physical Geography Options syllabus, for a total of 50 marks.

25% of marks at A Level

Paper 3: Advanced Human Geography Options
1 hour 30 minutes

- Production, location and change
- Environmental management
- Global interdependence
- Economic transition

Candidates answer two structured essay questions, each on a different optional topic, from a total of eight questions based on the Advanced Human Geography Options syllabus, for a total of 50 marks.

25% of marks at A Level

1 Hydrology and fluvial geomorphology

1.1 The drainage basin system

The hydrological cycle refers to the cycle of water between atmosphere, lithosphere and biosphere (Figure 1.1). At a local scale – the drainage basin (Figure 1.2) – the cycle has a single input, precipitation (PPT), and two major losses (outputs): evapotranspiration (EVT) and runoff. A third output, leakage, may also occur from the deeper subsurface to other basins. The drainage basin system is an **open system** as it allows the movement of energy and matter across its boundaries.

Water can be stored at a number of stages or levels within the cycle. These stores include vegetation, surface, soil moisture, groundwater and water channels.

Human modifications are made at every scale. Good examples include large-scale changes of channel flow and storage, irrigation and land drainage, and large-scale abstraction of groundwater and surface water for domestic and industrial use.

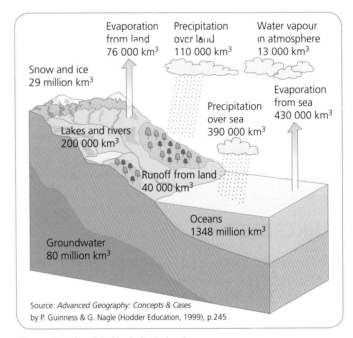

Source: *Advanced Geography: Concepts & Cases*
by P. Guinness & G. Nagle (Hodder Education, 1999), p.245

Figure 1.1 The global hydrological cycle

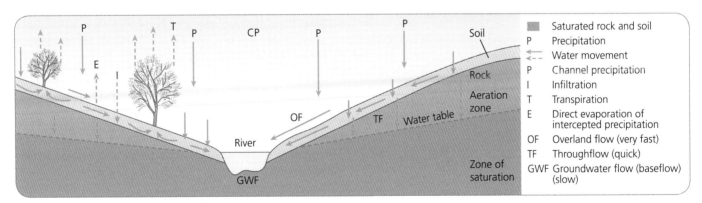

Figure 1.2 The drainage basin hydrological cycle

Precipitation

Precipitation includes all forms of rainfall, snow, frost, hail and dew. It is the conversion and transfer of moisture in the atmosphere to the land. Precipitation is considered in more detail in Section 2.3 (pages 40–48). Here it is important to mention the main characteristics that affect local hydrology. These are:

- the total amount of precipitation
- intensity
- type (snow, rain, etc.)
- geographic distribution and
- variability.

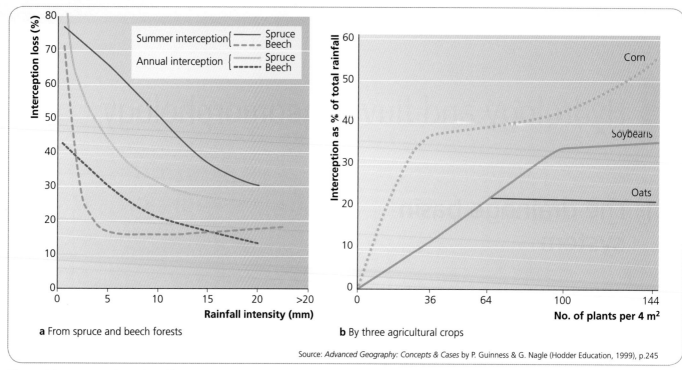

a From spruce and beech forests

b By three agricultural crops

Source: *Advanced Geography: Concepts & Cases* by P. Guinness & G. Nagle (Hodder Education, 1999), p.245

Figure 1.3 Interception losses for different types of vegetation

Interception

Interception refers to water that is caught and stored by vegetation. There are three main components:

- **interception loss** – water that is retained by plant surfaces and which is later evaporated away or absorbed by the plant
- **throughfall** – water that either falls through gaps in the vegetation or which drops from leaves, twigs or stems
- **stemflow** – water that trickles along twigs and branches and finally down the main trunk.

Interception loss varies with different types of vegetation (Figure 1.3). Interception is less from grasses than from deciduous woodland owing to the smaller surface area of the grass shoots. From agricultural crops, and from cereals in particular, interception increases with crop density. Coniferous trees intercept more than deciduous trees in winter, but this is reversed in summer.

Evaporation

Evaporation is the process by which a liquid or a solid is changed into a gas. It is the conversion of solid and liquid precipitation (snow, ice and water) to water vapour in the atmosphere. It is most important from oceans and seas. Evaporation increases under warm, dry conditions and decreases under cold, calm conditions. Evaporation losses are greater in arid and semi-arid climates than in polar regions.

Factors affecting evaporation include meteorological factors such as temperature, humidity, and wind speed. Of these, temperature is the most important factor. Other factors include the amount of water available, vegetation cover, and colour of the surface (albedo or reflectivity of the surface).

Evapotranspiration

Transpiration is the process by which water vapour escapes from a living plant, principally the leaves, and enters the atmosphere. The combined effects of evaporation and transpiration are normally referred to as evapotranspiration (EVT). EVT represents the most important aspect of water loss, accounting for the loss of nearly 100 per cent of the annual precipitation in arid areas and 75 per cent in humid areas. Only over ice and snow fields, bare rock slopes, desert areas, water surfaces and bare soil will purely evaporative losses occur.

Potential evapotranspiration (P.EVT)

The distinction between actual EVT and P.EVT lies in the concept of **moisture availability**. Potential evapotranspiration is the water loss that would occur if there was an unlimited supply of water in the soil for use by the vegetation. For example, the actual evapotranspiration rate in Egypt is less than 250 mm, because there is less than 250 mm of rain annually. However, given the high temperatures experienced in Egypt, if the rainfall was as high as 2000 mm, there would be sufficient heat to evaporate that water. Hence the potential evapotranspiration rate there is 2000 mm. The factors affecting evapotranspiration include all those that affect evaporation. In addition, some plants, such as cacti, have adaptations to help them reduce moisture loss.

Infiltration

Infiltration is the process by which water soaks into or is absorbed by the soil. The **infiltration capacity** is the maximum rate at which rain can be absorbed by a soil in a given condition.

Infiltration capacity decreases with time through a period of rainfall until a more or less constant value is reached (Figure 1.4). Infiltration rates of 0–4 mm/hour are common on clays whereas 3–12 mm/hour are common on sands. Vegetation also increases infiltration. This is because it intercepts some rainfall and slows down the speed at which it arrives at the surface. For example, on bare soils where rainsplash impact occurs, infiltration rates may reach 10 mm/hour. On similar soils covered by vegetation, rates of between 50 and 100 mm/hour have been recorded. Infiltrated water is chemically rich as it picks up minerals and organic acids from vegetation and soil.

Table 1.1 Influence of ground cover on infiltration rates

Ground cover	Infiltration rate (mm/hour)
Old permanent pasture	57
Permanent pasture: moderately grazed	19
Permanent pasture: heavily grazed	13
Strip-cropped	10
Weeds or grain	9
Clean tilled	7
Bare, crusted ground	6

Infiltration is inversely related to overland runoff and is influenced by a variety of factors, such as duration of rainfall, antecedent soil moisture (pre-existing levels of soil moisture), soil porosity, vegetation cover (Table 1.1), raindrop size and slope angle (Figure 1.5). In contrast, **overland flow** is water that flows over the land's surface.

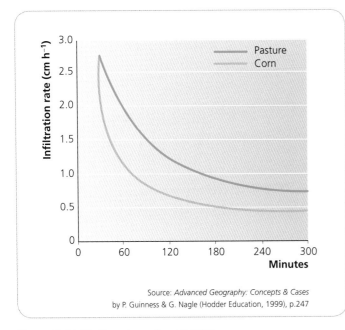

Source: *Advanced Geography: Concepts & Cases* by P. Guinness & G. Nagle (Hodder Education, 1999), p.247

Figure 1.4 Infiltration rates under vegetation

Section 1.1 Activities

1 Define the following hydrological characteristics:
   a interception
   b evaporation
   c infiltration.

2 Study Figure 1.2.
   a Define the terms *overland flow* and *throughflow*.
   b Compare the nature of water movement in these two flows.
   c Suggest reasons for the differences you have noted.

3 Figure 1.3 shows interception losses from spruce and beech trees and from three agricultural crops. Describe and comment on the relationship between the number of plants and interception and the type of plants and interception.

4 Figure 1.5 shows the relationship between infiltration, overland flow (surface runoff) and six factors. Write a paragraph on each of the factors, describing and explaining the effect it has on infiltration and overland runoff.

5 Comment on the relationship between ground cover and infiltration, as shown in Table 1.1.

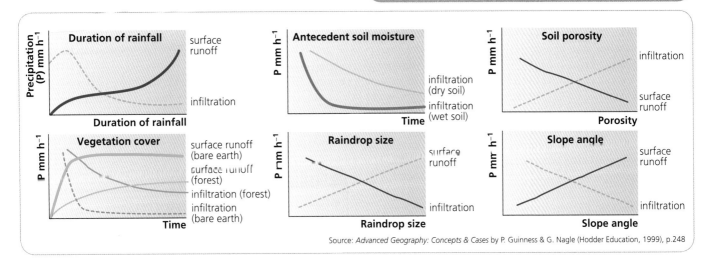

Source: *Advanced Geography: Concepts & Cases* by P. Guinness & G. Nagle (Hodder Education, 1999), p.248

Figure 1.5 Factors affecting infiltration and surface runoff

Soil moisture

Soil moisture refers to the subsurface water in the soil. **Field capacity** refers to the amount of water held in the soil after excess water drains away – that is, saturation or near saturation. **Wilting point** refers to the range of moisture content in which permanent wilting of plants occurs. They define the approximate limits to plant growth.

Throughflow refers to water flowing through the soil in natural pipes and **percolines** (lines of concentrated water flow between soil horizons).

Groundwater

Groundwater refers to subsurface water. Water moves slowly downwards from the soil into the bedrock – this is known as percolation. Depending on the permeability of the rock, this may be very slow, or in some rocks, such as Carboniferous limestone and chalk, it may be quite fast, locally. The permanently saturated zone within solid rocks and sediments is known as the phreatic zone. The upper layer of this is known as the **water table**. The water table varies seasonally. It is higher in winter following increased levels of precipitation. The zone that is seasonally wetted and seasonally dries out is known as the aeration zone. Most groundwater is found within a few hundred metres of the surface but has been found at depths of up to 4 km beneath the surface (Figure 1.6). **Baseflow** refers to the part of a river's discharge that is provided by groundwater seeping into the bed of a river. It is a relatively constant flow although it increases slightly following a wet period.

Groundwater is very important. It accounts for 96.5 per cent of all freshwater on the Earth. However, while some soil moisture may be recycled by evaporation into atmospheric moisture within a matter of days or weeks, groundwater may not be recycled for as long as 20 000 years. **Recharge** refers to the refilling of water in pores where the water has dried up or been extracted by human activity. Hence, in some places, where **recharge** is not taking place, groundwater is considered a non-renewable resource.

Aquifers (rocks that contain significant quantities of water) provide a great reservoir of water. Aquifers are permeable rocks such as sandstones and limestones. The water in aquifers moves very slowly and acts as a natural regulator in the hydrological cycle by absorbing rainfall which otherwise would reach streams rapidly. In addition, aquifers maintain stream flow during long dry periods. Where water flow reaches the surface (as shown by the discharge areas in Figure 1.6) **springs** may be found. These may be substantial enough to become the source of a stream or river.

Groundwater recharge occurs as a result of:
- infiltration of part of the total precipitation at the ground surface
- seepage through the banks and bed of surface water bodies such as ditches, rivers, lakes and oceans
- groundwater leakage and inflow from adjacent rocks and aquifers

a In humid regions

b In semi-arid regions

Source: *Advanced Geography: Concepts & Cases* by P. Guinness & G. Nagle (Hodder Education, 1999), p.248

Figure 1.6 Groundwater and aquifer characteristics

- artificial recharge from irrigation, reservoirs, etc.

Losses of groundwater result from:
- evapotranspiration particularly in low-lying areas where the water table is close to the ground surface
- natural discharge by means of spring flow and seepage into surface water bodies
- groundwater leakage and outflow through aquicludes and into adjacent aquifers
- artificial abstraction; for example, the water table near Lubbock on the High Plains of Texas (USA) has declined by 30–50 m in just 50 years, and in Saudi Arabia the groundwater reserve in 2010 was 42 per cent less than in 1985.

Section 1.1 Activities

1 Define the terms *groundwater* and *baseflow*.

2 Outline the ways in which human activities have affected groundwater.

1.2 Rainfall–discharge relationships within drainage basins

A **river regime** is the annual variation in the flow of a river. Stream flow occurs as a result of overland runoff, groundwater springs, from lakes and from meltwater in mountainous or subpolar environments. The character or **regime** of the resulting stream or river is influenced by several variable factors:

- the amount and nature of precipitation
- the local rocks, especially porosity and permeability
- the shape or morphology of the drainage basin, its area and slope

- the amount and type of vegetation cover
- the amount and type of soil cover.

On an annual basis the most important factor determining stream regime is climate. Figure 1.7 shows generalised regimes for Europe. Notice how the regime for the Shannon at Killaloe (Ireland) has a typical temperate regime, with a clear winter maximum. By contrast, Arctic areas such as the Gloma in Norway and the Kemi in Finland have a peak in spring associated with snowmelt. Others, such as the Po near Venice, have two main maxima – autumn and winter rains (Mediterranean climate) and spring snowmelt from Alpine tributaries.

Figure 1.8a shows a simple regime, based upon a single river with one major peak flow. By contrast, Figure 1.8b shows a complex regime for the River Rhine. It has a number of large tributaries which flow in a variety of environments, including alpine, Mediterranean and temperate. By the time the Rhine has travelled downstream it is influenced by many, at times contrasting, regimes.

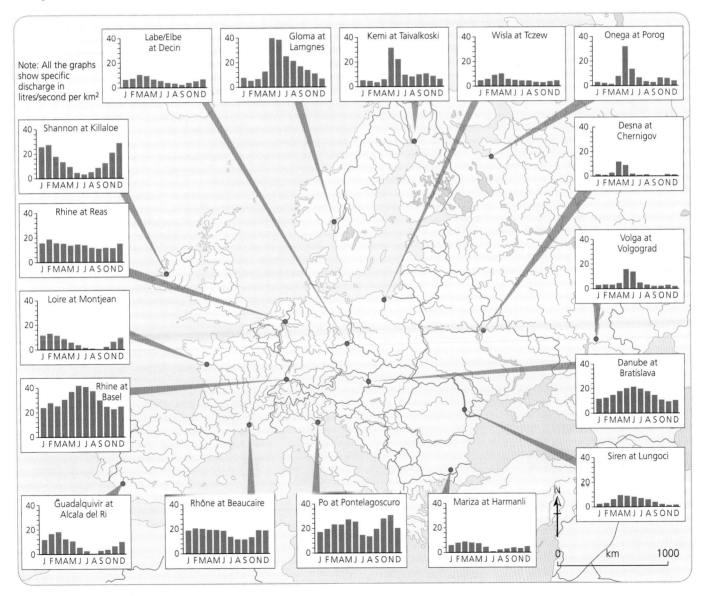

Figure 1.7 River regimes in Europe

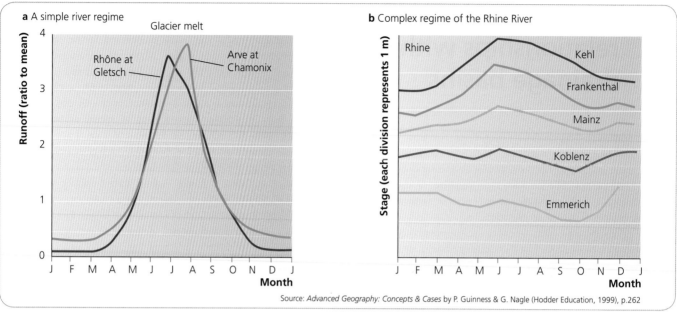

Figure 1.8 Simple and complex river regimes

Table 1.2 Precipitation and runoff data for a storm on the Delaware River, New York

Date	Time	Duration of rainfall	Total (cm)
29 September	6a.m.	12 hours	0.1
29 September	6p.m.	12 hours	0.9
30 September	6p.m.	24 hours	3.7
30 September	12p.m.	6 hours	0.1
		Total	*4.8*

Date	Stream runoff (m³/sec)
28 September	28.3 (baseflow)
29 September	28.3 (baseflow)
30 September	339.2
1 October	2094.2
2 October	1330.1
3 October	594.3
4 October	367.9
5 October	254.2
6 October	198.1
7 October	176.0
8 October	170.0
9 October	165.2 (baseflow)

Section 1.2 Activities

1 Compare the river regimes of the Gloma (Norway), Shannon (Ireland) and Rhine (Switzerland). Suggest reasons for their differences.

2 The data in Table 1.2 show precipitation and runoff data for a storm on the Delaware River, New York. Using this data, plot the storm hydrograph for this storm. Describe the main characteristics of the hydrograph you have drawn.

Flood hydrographs

A **flood hydrograph** shows how the discharge of a river varies over a short time (Figure 1.9). Normally it refers to an individual storm or group of storms of not more than a few days in length. Before the storm starts the main supply of water to the stream is through groundwater flow or **baseflow**. This is the main supplier of water to rivers. During the storm some water infiltrates into the soil while some flows over the surface as overland flow or runoff. This reaches the river quickly as **quickflow**. This causes the rapid rise in the level of the river. The **rising limb** shows us how quickly the flood waters begin to rise whereas the **recessional limb** is the speed with which the water level in the river declines after the peak. The **peak flow** is the maximum discharge of the river as a result of the storm and the **time lag** is the time between the height of the storm (not the start or the end) and the maximum flow in the river.

Figure 1.9 A simple hydrograph

Table 1.3 Factors affecting storm hydrographs

Factor	Influence on flood hydrograph
Precipitation type and intensity	Highly intensive rainfall is likely to produce overland flow and a steep rising limb and high peak flow. Low-intensity rainfall is likely to infiltrate into the soil and percolate slowly into the rock, thereby increasing the time lag and reducing the peak flow. Precipitation that falls as snow sits on the ground until it melts. Sudden, rapid melting can cause flooding and lead to high rates of overland flow, and high peak flows.
Temperature and evapotranspiration	Not only does temperature affect the type of precipitation, it also affects the evaporation rate (higher temperatures lead to more evaporation and so less water getting into rivers). On the other hand, warm air can hold more water so the potential for high peak flows in hot areas is raised.
Antecedent moisture	If it has been raining previously and the ground is saturated or nearly saturated, rainfall will quickly produce overland flow and a high peak flow and short time lag.
Drainage basin size and shape	Smaller drainage basins respond more quickly to rainfall conditions. For example, the Boscastle (UK) floods of 2004 drained an area of less than 15 km². This meant that the peak of the flood occurred soon after the peak of the storm. In contrast, the Mississippi River is over 3700 km long – it takes much longer for the lower part of the river to respond to an event that might occur in the upper course of the river. Circular basins respond more quickly than linear basins, where the response is more drawn out.
Drainage density	Basins with a high drainage density, such as urban basins with a network of sewers and drains, respond very quickly. Networks with a low drainage density have a very long time lag.
Porosity and impermeability of rocks and soils	Impermeable surfaces cause more water to flow overland. This causes greater peak flows. Urban areas contain large areas of impermeable surfaces. In contrast, rocks such as chalk and gravel are permeable and allow water to infiltrate and percolate. This reduces the peak flow and increases the time lag. Sandy soils allow water to infiltrate whereas clay is much more impermeable and causes water to pass overland.
Slopes	Steeper slopes create more overland flow, shorter time lags and higher peak flows.
Vegetation type	Broad-leafed vegetation intercepts more rainfall, especially in summer, and so reduces the amount of overland flow and peak flow and increases time lag. In winter, deciduous trees lose their leaves and so intercept less.
Land use	Land uses that create impermeable surfaces, or reduce vegetation cover, reduce interception and increase overland flow. If more drainage channels are built (sewers, ditches, drains) the water is carried to rivers very quickly. This means that peak flows are increased and time lags reduced.

The effect of urban development on hydrographs is to increase peak flow and decrease time lag (Figure 1.10). This is due to an increase in the proportion of impermeable ground in a drainage basin as well as an increase in the drainage density. Storm hydrographs also vary with a number of other factors (Table 1.3) such as basin shape (Figure 1.11), drainage density, and gradient.

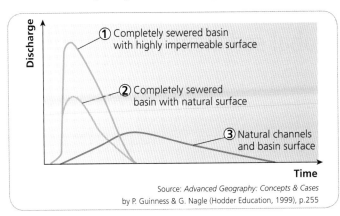

Source: *Advanced Geography: Concepts & Cases* by P. Guinness & G. Nagle (Hodder Education, 1999), p.255

Figure 1.10 The effects of urban development on flood hydrographs

Section 1.2 Activities

1 Define the terms *river regime* and *flood hydrograph*.

2 Study Figure 1.10 which shows the impact of urbanisation on flood hydrographs. Describe and explain the differences in the relationship between discharge and time.

1.3 River channel processes and landforms

Transport

The load is transported downstream in a number of ways:
- The smallest particles (silts and clays) are carried in suspension as the **suspended load**.
- Larger particles (sands, gravels, very small stones) are transported in a series of 'hops' as the **saltated load**.
- Pebbles are shunted along the bed as the **bed** or **tracted load**.
- In areas of calcareous rock, material is carried in solution as the dissolved load.

The load of a river varies with discharge and velocity. The **capacity** of a stream refers to the largest amount of debris that a stream can carry, while the **competence** refers to the diameter of the largest particle that can be carried. The **critical erosion velocity** is the lowest velocity at which grains of a given size can be moved. The relationship between these variables is shown by means of a **Hjulstrom curve** (Figure 1.11). For example, sand can be moved more easily than silt or clay, as fine-grained particles tend to be more cohesive. High velocities are required to move gravel and cobbles because of their large size. The critical velocities tend to be an area rather than a straight line on the graph.

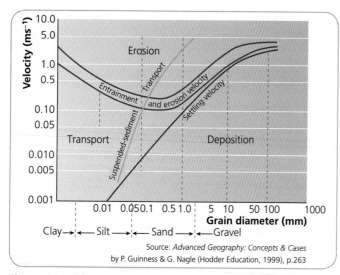

Figure 1.11 Hjulstrom curve

There are three important features on Hjulstrom curves:

- The smallest and largest particles require high velocities to lift them. For example, particles between 0.1 mm and 1 mm require velocities of around 100 mm/sec to be entrained, compared with values of over 500 mm/sec to lift clay (0.01 m) and gravel (over 2 mm). Clay resists entrainment due to its cohesion, gravel due to its weight.
- Higher velocities are required for entrainment than for transport.
- When velocity falls below a certain level (settling or fall velocity), those particles are deposited.

Section 1.3 Activities

Study Figure 1.11.

1 Describe the work of the river when sediment size is 1 mm.

2 Comment on the relationship between velocity, sediment size and river process when the river is moving at 0.5 m/sec^{-1}.

Deposition

There are a number of causes of deposition such as:
- a shallowing of gradient which decreases velocity and energy
- a decrease in the volume of water in the channel
- an increase in the friction between water and channel.

Erosion

Abrasion (or **corrasion**) is the wearing away of the bed and bank by the load carried by a river. It is the mechanical impact produced by the debris eroding the bed and banks of the stream. In most rivers it is the principal means of erosion. The effectiveness of abrasion depends on the concentration, hardness and energy of the impacting particles and the resistance of the bedrock. Abrasion increases as velocity increases (kinetic energy is proportional to the square of velocity).

Attrition is the wearing away of the load carried by a river. It creates smaller, rounder particles.

Hydraulic action is the force of air and water on the sides of rivers and in cracks. It includes the direct force of flowing water, and **cavitation**, the force of air exploding. As fluids accelerate, pressure drops and may cause air bubbles to form. Cavitation occurs as bubbles implode and evict tiny jets of water with velocities of up to 130 m/sec. These can damage solid rock. Cavitation is an important process in rapids and waterfalls, and is generally accompanied by abrasion.

Corrosion or **solution** is the removal of chemical ions, especially calcium. The key factors controlling the rate of corrosion are bedrock, solute concentration of the stream water, discharge and velocity. Maximum rates of corrosion occur where fast-flowing, undersaturated streams pass over soluble rocks – humid zone streams flowing over mountain limestone.

There are a number of factors affecting rates of erosion. These include:

- **load** – the heavier and sharper the load the greater the potential for erosion
- **velocity** – the greater the velocity the greater the potential for erosion (Figure 1.11)
- **gradient** – increased gradient increases the rate of erosion
- **geology** – soft, unconsolidated rocks such as sand and gravel are easily eroded
- **pH** – rates of solution are increased when the water is more acidic
- **human impact** – deforestation, dams and bridges interfere with the natural flow of a river and frequently end up increasing the rate of erosion.

Erosion by the river will provide loose material. This eroded material (plus other weathered material that has moved downslope from the upper valley sides) is carried by the river as its load.

Global sediment yield

It is possible to convert a value of mean annual sediment and solute load to an estimate of the rate of land surface lowering by fluvial denudation. This gives a combined sediment and solute load of 250 tonnes/km^2/year – that is, an annual rate of lowering of the order of 0.1 mm/year. There is a great deal of variation in sediment yields. These range from 10 tonnes/km^2/year in such areas as northern Europe and parts of Australia to in excess of 10 000 tonnes/km^2/year in certain areas where conditions are especially conducive to high rates of erosion (Figure 1.12). These include Taiwan, South Island New Zealand and the Middle Yellow river basin in China. In the first two cases steep slopes, high rainfall and tectonic instability are major influences, whilst in the last case the deep loess deposits and the almost complete lack of natural vegetation cover are important. Rates of land surface lowering vary from less than 0.004 mm per year to over 4 mm per year. The broad pattern of global suspended sediment is shown in the diagram and it reflects the influence of a wide range of factors, including climate, relief, geology, vegetation cover and land use.

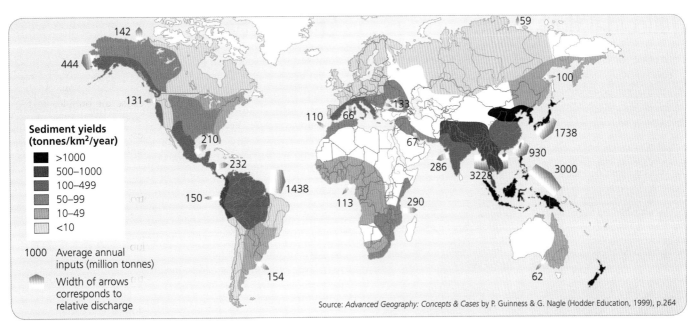

Figure 1.12 Global sediment yield

Stream flow

Stream flow and associated features of erosion are complex. The velocity and energy of a stream are controlled by:

- the gradient of channel bed
- the volume of water within the channel, which is controlled largely by precipitation in the drainage basin (for example, 'bankfull' gives rapid flow whereas low levels give lower flows)
- the shape of the channel
- channel roughness, including friction.

Manning's Equation

$$Q = (AR^{2/3} S^{1/2})/n$$

where Q = discharge, A = cross-sectional area, R = hydraulic radius, S = channel slope (as a fraction), n = coefficient of bed roughness (the rougher the bed the higher the value).

If bed roughness increases, velocity and discharge decrease; if the hydraulic radius and or slope/gradient increase, the velocity and discharge increase.

Manning's 'n'

Mountain stream, rocky bed	0.04–0.05
Alluvial channel (large dunes)	0.02–0.035
Alluvial channel (small ripples)	0.014–0.024

There are three main types of flow: laminar, turbulent and helicoidal. For **laminar flow** a smooth, straight channel with a low velocity is required. This allows water to flow in sheets, or laminae, parallel to the channel bed. It is rare in reality and most commonly occurs in the lower reaches. However, it is more common in groundwater and in glaciers when one layer of ice moves another.

Turbulent flow occurs where there are higher velocities and complex channel morphology such as a meandering channel with alternating pools and riffles. Turbulence causes marked variations in pressure within the water. As the turbulent water swirls (eddies) against the bed or bank of the river, air is trapped in pores, cracks and crevices and put momentarily under great pressure. As the eddy swirls away, pressure is released; the air expands suddenly, creating a small explosion which weakens the bed or bank material. Thus turbulence is associated with hydraulic action (cavitation).

Vertical turbulence creates hollows in the channel bed. Hollows may trap pebbles which are then swirled by eddying, grinding at the bed. This is a form of vertical corrasion or abrasion and given time may create potholes (Figure 1.13). Cavitation and vertical abrasion may help to deepen the channel, allowing the river to down cut its valley. If the downcutting is dominant over the other forms of erosion (vertical erosion exceeds lateral erosion) then a gulley or gorge will develop.

Figure 1.13 Potholes as seen by the areas occupied by water (dark patches)

Helicoidal flow

Horizontal turbulence often takes the form of **helicoidal flow**, a 'corkscrewing' motion. This is associated with the presence of alternating pools and riffles in the channel bed, and where the river is carrying large amounts of material. The erosion and deposition by helicoidal flow creates meanders (Figure 1.14).

Figure 1.14 Meander formation

Channel types

Sinuosity is the length of a stream channel expressed as a ratio of the valley length. A low sinuosity has a value of 1.0 (i.e. it is straight) whereas a high sinuosity is above 4.4. The main groupings are **straight channels** (<1.5) and **meandering** (>1.5). Straight channels are rare. Even when they do occur the thalweg (line of maximum velocity) moves from side to side. These channels generally have a central ridge of deposited material, due to the water flow pattern.

Braiding occurs when the channel is divided by islands or bars (Figure 1.15). Islands are vegetated and long-lived whereas bars are unvegetated, less stable and often short-term features. Braided channels are formed by various factors, for example:
- a steep channel gradient
- a large proportion of coarse material
- easily erodable bank material
- highly variable discharge.

Figure 1.15 A braided river, Myrdalsjokull, Iceland

Braiding tends to occur when a stream does not have the capacity to transport its load in a single channel, whether it is straight or meandering. It occurs when river discharge is very variable and banks are easily erodable. This gives abundant sediment. It is especially common in periglacial and semi-arid areas.

Braiding begins with a mid-channel bar which grows downstream. As the discharge decreases following a flood, the coarse bed load is first to be deposited. This forms the basis of bars that grow downstream and as the flood is reduced, finer sediment is deposited. The upstream end becomes stabilised with vegetation. This island localises and narrows the channel in an attempt to increase the velocity to a point where it can transport its load. Frequently, subdivision sets in.

Surgery

How are meanders formed?

Meanders are complex (Figure 1.14). There are a number of relationships, although the reasons are not always very clear. However, they are *not* the result of obstructions in the floodplain. Meandering is the normal behaviour of fluids and gases in motion. Meanders can occur on a variety of materials, from ice to solid rock. Meander development occurs in conditions where channel slope, discharge and load combine to create a situation where meandering is the only way that the stream can use up the energy it possesses equally throughout the channel reach. The wavelength of the meander is dependent upon three main factors: channel width, discharge, and the nature of the bed and banks.

Why are meanders so special?

Meanders have an asymmetric cross-section (Figure 1.14b). They are deeper on the outside bank and shallower on the inside bank. In between meanders they are more symmetrical. They begin with the development of pools and riffles in a straight channel and the thalweg begins to flow from side to side. Helicoidal flow occurs whereby surface water flows towards the outer banks, while the bottom flow is towards the inner bank. This causes the variations in the cross-section and variations in erosion and deposition. These variations give rise to **river cliffs** on the outer bank and **point bars** on the inner bank.

How are pools and riffles formed?

Pools and riffles are formed by turbulence. Eddies cause the deposition of coarse sediment (riffles) at high velocity points and fine sediment (pools) at low velocity. Riffles have a steeper gradient than pools which leads to variations in subcritical and supercritical flow, and therefore erosion and deposition.

What are the relationships between meanders and channel characteristics?

- Meander wavelengths are generally 6–10 times channel width and discharge.
- Meander wavelengths are generally 5 times the radius of curvature.
- The meander belt (amplitude) is generally 14–20 times the channel width.
- Riffles occur at about 6 times the channel width.
- Sinuosity increases as depth of channel increases in relation to width.
- Meandering is more pronounced when the bed load is varied
- Meander wavelength increases in streams that carry coarse debris.
- Meandering is more likely on shallow slopes.
- Meandering best develops at or near bankfull state.

Natural meanders are rarely 'standard'. This is due, in part, to variations in bed load – where the bed load is coarse, meanders are often very irregular.

What causes meanders?

There is no simple explanation for the creation of meanders, and a number of factors are likely to be important.

1 Friction with the channel bed and bank causes turbulence, which makes stream flow unstable. This produces bars along the channel, and a helicoidal flow (corkscrew motion), with water being raised on the outer surfaces of pools, and the return flow occurring at depth.
2 Sand bars in the channel may cause meandering.
3 Sinuosity is best developed on moderate angles. There is a critical minimum gradient below which straight channels occur. At very low energy (low gradient), helicoidal flow is insufficient to produce alternating pools and ripples. In addition, high-velocity flows in steep gradient channels are too strong to stop cross-channel meandering and the development of alternating pools and ripples. In such circumstances, braided channels are formed.
4 Helicoidal flow (corkscrewing) causes the line of fastest flow to move from side to side within the channel. This increases the amplitude of the meander.

How do meanders change over time?

There are a number of possibilities:

- Meanders may migrate downstream and erode **river cliffs**.
- They may migrate laterally (sideways) and erode the floodplain.
- They may become exaggerated and become cutoffs (ox-bow lakes).
- Under special conditions they may become intrenched or ingrown.

What are intrenched and ingrown meanders?

The term **incised meanders** describes meanders that are especially well developed on horizontally bedded rocks, and form when a river cuts through alluvium and into underlying bedrock. Two main types occur – intrenched and ingrown meanders. Intrenched meanders are symmetrical, and occur when downcutting is fast enough to offset the lateral migration of meanders. This frequently occurs when there is a significant fall in base level (generally sea level). The Goosenecks of the San Juan in the USA is a classic example of intrenched meanders. Ingrown meanders are the result of lateral meander migration. They are asymmetric in cross-section – examples can be seen in the lower Seine in France.

Section 1.3 Activities

Study Figure 1.14b.

1 Compare the main characteristics of river cliffs with those of point bars.
2 Briefly explain the meaning of the term *helicoidal flow*.
3 Describe and explain the role of pools and riffles in the development of meanders in a river channel.

Features of erosion and deposition

Waterfalls and gorges

Waterfalls occur where the river spills over a sudden change in gradient, undercutting rocks by hydraulic impact and abrasion, thereby creating a waterfall (Figure 1.16). There are many reasons for this sudden change in gradient along the river:

- a band of resistant strata such as the resistant limestones at Niagara Falls
- a plateau edge such as Victoria Falls on the Zimbabwe–Zambia border
- a fault scarp such as at Gordale, Yorkshire (UK)
- a hanging valley such as at Glencoyne, Cumbria in the UK
- coastal cliffs.

① undercutting before collapse
② weight of water causes pressure on the unsupported Whin Sill
③ pieces of Whin Sill – hard, igneous rock – are used to erode the limestone
④ hydraulic action by force of falling water
⑤ organic-rich waters help dissolve the limestone

Whin Sill – tough igneous rock

brown, peaty waters of the River Tees

waterfall gradually recedes

softer limestones

boulder-strewn gorge

Source: Goudie, A. and Gardner, R., *Discovering Landscapes in England and Wales*, Unwin 1985

Figure 1.16 Waterfall formation

The undercutting at the base of the waterfall creates a precarious overhang which will ultimately collapse. Thus a waterfall may appear to migrate upstream, leaving a gorge of recession downstream. The Niagara Gorge is 11 km long due to the retreat of Niagara Falls.

Gorge development is common for example where the local rocks are very resistant to weathering but susceptible to the more powerful river erosion. Similarly, in arid areas where the water necessary for weathering is scarce, gorges are formed by periods of river erosion. A rapid acceleration in downcutting is also associated when a river is rejuvenated, again creating a gorge-like landscape. Gorges may also be formed as a result of:

- antecedent drainage (Rhine Gorge)
- glacial overflow channelling (Newtondale, UK)
- collapse of underground caverns in carboniferous limestone areas
- surface runoff over limestone during a periglacial period
- retreat of waterfalls (Niagara Falls).

Case Study

Niagara Falls

Most of the world's great waterfalls are the result of the undercutting of resistant cap rocks, and the retreat or recession that follows. The Niagara River flows for about 50 km between Lake Erie and Lake Ontario. In that distance it falls just 108 m, giving an average gradient of 1:500. However, most of the descent occurs in the 1.5 km above the Niagara Falls (13 m) and at the Falls themselves (55 m). The Niagara River flows in a 2 km wide channel just 1 km above the Falls, and then into a narrow 400 m wide gorge, 75 m deep and 11 km long. Within the gorge the river falls a further 30 m.

The course of the Niagara River was established about 12 000 years ago when water from Lake Erie began to spill northwards into Lake Ontario. In doing so, it passed over the highly resistant dolomitic (limestone) escarpment. Over the last 12 000 years the Falls have retreated 11 km, giving an average rate of retreat of about 1 m/year. Water velocity accelerates over the Falls, and decreases at the base of the Falls. Hydraulic action and abrasion have caused the development of a large plunge pool at the base of the Falls, while the fine spray and eddies in the river help to remove some of the softer rock underneath the resistant dolomite. As the softer rocks are removed the dolomite is left unsupported and the weight of the water causes the dolomite to collapse. Hence the waterfall retreats, forming a gorge of recession.

In the nineteenth century rates of recession were recorded at 1.2 m/year. However, now that the amount of water flowing over the Falls is controlled (due to the construction of hydro-electric power stations), rates of recession have been reduced. In addition, engineering works in the 1960s reinforced parts of the dolomite that were believed to be at risk of collapse. The Falls remains an important tourist attraction and local residents and business personnel did not want to lose their prized asset!

Section 1.3 Activities

Draw a labelled diagram to show the formation of a waterfall.

Alluvial fans and cones

Many types of deposition are found along the course of a river. In general, as a river carries its load, the load is eroded by attrition. This results in the load getting rounder and smaller downstream. **Piedmont alluvial fans and cones** are found in semi-arid areas where swiftly flowing mountain streams enter a main valley or plain at the foot of the mountains (Figure 1.17). There is a sudden decrease in velocity, causing deposition. Fine material is spread out as an alluvial fan with a nearly flat surface – under 1° angle. By contrast, coarse material forms a relatively small, steep-sided alluvial cone, with a slope angle of up to 15°. They are also common therefore in glaciated areas at the edges of major troughs, particularly at the base of hanging valleys. However, they are much smaller than their semi-arid counterparts.

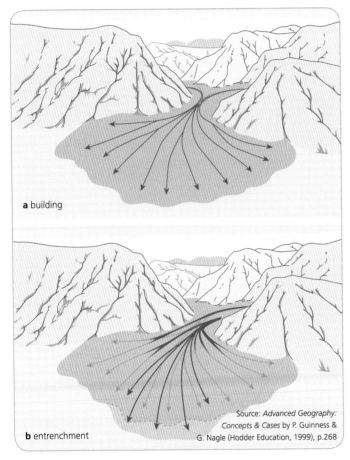

Source: *Advanced Geography: Concepts & Cases* by P. Guinness & G. Nagle (Hodder Education, 1999), p.268

Figure 1.17 Phases of alluvial fan formation

Riffles

Riffles are small ridges of material deposited where the river velocity is reduced midstream, in between pools (the deep parts of a meander – see Figure 1.14 on page 10). If many such ridges are deposited, the river is said to be 'braided'. A braided river channel consists of a number of interconnected shallow channels separated by alluvial and shingle bars (islands). These may be exposed during low flow conditions. They are formed in rivers that are heavily laden with sediment and have a pronounced

seasonal flow. There are excellent examples on the Eyra Fjordur in northern Iceland.

Levees and floodplains

Levees and floodplain deposits are formed when a river bursts its banks over a long period of time. Water quickly loses velocity, leading to the rapid deposition of coarse material (heavy and difficult to move a great distance) near the channel edge. These coarse deposits build up to form embankments called **levees**. The finer material is carried further away to be dropped on the **floodplain**, sometimes creating **backswamps**. Old floodplains may be eroded – the remnants are known as terraces. At the edge of the terrace is a line of relatively steep slopes known as **river bluffs** (Figure 1.18).

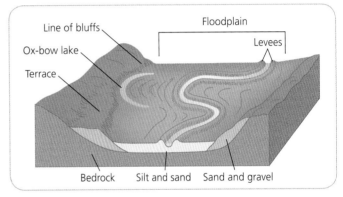

Figure 1.18 Floodplains, levees and bluffs

Deltas

Deltas are river sediments deposited when a river enters a standing body of water such as a lake, a lagoon, a sea or an ocean (Figure 1.19). They are the result of the interaction of fluvial and marine processes. For a delta to form there must be a heavily laden river, such as the Nile or the Mississippi, and a standing body of water with negligible currents, such as the Mediterranean or the Gulf of Mexico. Deposition is enhanced if the water is saline, because salty water causes small clay particles to flocculate or adhere together. Other factors include the type of sediment, local geology, sea-level changes, plant growth and human impact.

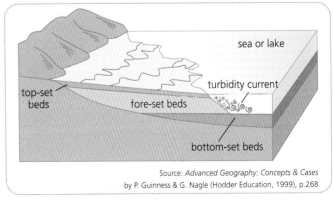

Source: *Advanced Geography: Concepts & Cases* by P. Guinness & G. Nagle (Hodder Education, 1999), p.268

Figure 1.19 Model of a simple delta

The material deposited as a delta can be divided into three types:

- **Bottomset beds** – the lower parts of the delta are built outwards along the sea floor by turbidity currents (currents of water loaded with material). These beds are composed of very fine material.
- **Foreset beds** – over the bottomset beds, inclined/sloping layers of coarse material are deposited. Each bed is deposited above and in front of the previous one, the material moving by rolling and saltation. Thus the delta is built seaward.
- **Topset beds** – composed of fine material, they are really part of the continuation of the river's floodplain. These topset beds are extended and built up by the work of numerous distributaries (where the main river has split into several smaller channels).

The character of any delta is influenced by the complex interaction of several variables (Figure 1.20):

- the rate of river deposition
- the rate of stabilisation by vegetation growth
- tidal currents
- the presence (or absence) of longshore drift
- human activity (deltas often form prime farmland when drained).

There are many types of delta, but the three 'classic' ones are:

- **Arcuate delta**, or fan-shaped – these are found in areas where regular longshore drift or other currents keep the seaward edge of the delta trimmed and relatively smooth in shape, such as the Nile and Rhône deltas.
- **Cuspate delta** – pointed like a tooth or cusp, for example the Ebro and Tiber deltas, shaped by regular but opposing gentle water movement.
- **Bird's-foot delta** – where the river brings down enormous amounts of fine silt, deposition can occur in a still sea area, along the edges of the distributaries for a very long distance offshore, such as the Mississippi delta.

Deltas can also be formed inland. When a river enters a lake it will deposit some or all of its load, so forming a **lacustrine delta**. As the delta builds up and out, it may ultimately fill the lake basin. The largest lacustrine deltas are those that are being built out into the Caspian Sea by the Volga, Ural, Kura and other rivers.

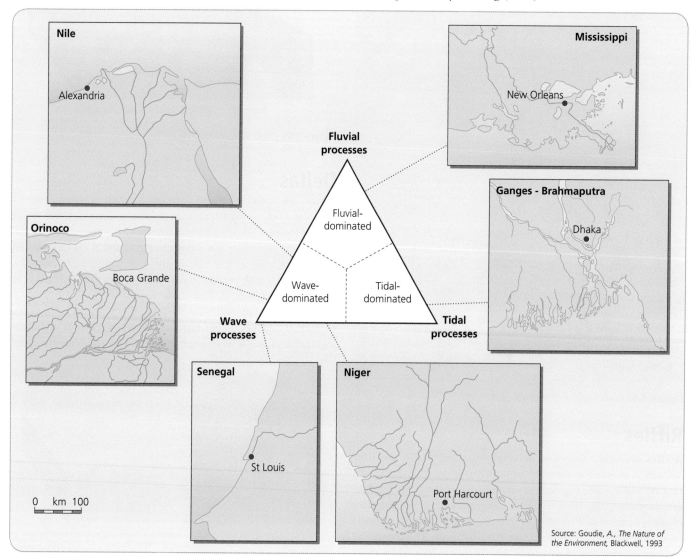

Source: Goudie, A., *The Nature of the Environment*, Blackwell, 1993

Figure 1.20 River delta shapes related to river, wave and tidal processes

The future of the Nile delta

The Nile delta is under threat from rising sea levels. Without the food it produces, Egypt faces much hardship. The delta is one of the most fertile tracts of land in the world. However, coastal erosion is steadily eroding it in some places at a rate of almost 100 m a year. This is partly because the annual deposits from the Nile floods – which balanced coastal erosion – no longer reach the delta, instead being trapped behind the Aswan High Dam. However, erosion of the delta continues, and may be increasing, partly as a result of global warming and rising sea levels. The delta is home to about 50 million people, living at densities of up to 4000 people per km^2.

In 2007 the Intergovernmental Panel on Climate Change declared Egypt's Nile delta to be among the top three areas most vulnerable to a rise in sea level. Even a small temperature increase will displace millions of Egyptians from one of the most densely populated regions on Earth.

The delta stretches out from the northern stretches of Cairo into 25 000 km^2 of farmland fed by the Nile's branches. It is home to two-thirds of the country's rapidly growing population, and responsible for more than 60 per cent of its food supply. About 270 km of the delta's coastline is at a dangerously low level and a 1 m rise in the sea level would drown 20 per cent of the delta.

The delta is also suffering from a number of environmental crises, including flooding, coastal erosion, salinisation, industrial/agricultural pollution and urban encroachment. Egypt's population of 83 million is set to increase to more than 110 million in the next two decades. More people in the delta means more cars, more pollution and less land to feed them all on, just at a time when increased crop production is needed most.

Saltwater intrusion is destroying crops. Coastal farmland has always been threatened by salt water, but salinity has traditionally been kept at bay by plentiful supplies of fresh water flushing out the salt. It used to happen naturally with the Nile's seasonal floods; after the construction of Egypt's High Dam, these seasonal floods came to an end, but a vast network of irrigation canals continued to bring enough fresh water to ensure salinity levels remained low.

Today, however, Nile water barely reaches the end of the delta. A growing population has extracted water supplies upstream, and what water does make it downriver is increasingly polluted with toxins and other impurities.

The impact of climate change is likely to be a 70 per cent drop in the amount of Nile water reaching the delta over the next 50 years, due to increased evaporation and heavier demands on water use upstream. The consequences for food production are ominous: wheat and maize yields could be down 40 per cent and 50 per cent respectively, and farmers could lose around $1000 per hectare for each degree rise in the average temperature.

While politicians, scientists, and community workers are trying to educate Egyptians about the dangers of climate change, there is confusion over whether the focus should be on promoting ways to combat climate change, or on accepting climate change as inevitable and instead encouraging new forms of adaptation to the nation's uncertain future.

Egypt's contribution to global carbon emissions is just 0.5 per cent – nine times less per capita than for the USA. However, the consequences of climate change are disproportionate and potentially disastrous.

The scale of the crisis – more people, less land, less water, less food – is overwhelming. As a result, many now believe that Egypt's future lies far away from the delta, in land newly reclaimed from the desert. Since the time of the pharaohs, when the delta was first farmed, Egypt's political leaders have tried to harness the Nile. The Egyptian government is creating an array of canals and pumping stations that draw water from the Nile into sandy valleys to the east and west, where the desert is slowly being turned green. The Nile delta may well become history – as a landform and for the people who live and work there.

Section 1.3 Activities

1 Outline the main conditions needed for delta formation.
2 Suggest reasons for the variety of deltas, as shown in Figure 1.20.
3 a Outline the natural and human processes that are operating on the Nile delta.
  b Comment on the advantages and disadvantages for people living in the delta.

1.4 The human impact

The influence of human activity on the hydrological cycle

Precipitation

There are a number of ways in which human activity affects precipitation. Cloud seeding has probably been one of the more successful. Rain requires either ice particles or large water droplets on which to form. Seeding introduces silver iodide, solid carbon dioxide (dry ice) or ammonium nitrate to attract water droplets. The results are somewhat unclear. In Australia and the USA, seeding has increased precipitation by 10–30 per cent on a small scale and on a short-term basis. However, the increase in precipitation in one place might decrease precipitation elsewhere. In urban and industrial areas precipitation is often increased by up to as much as 10 per cent due to increased cloud frequency and amount and because of the addition of pollutants, the heat island effect and turbulence.

Evaporation and evapotranspiration

The human impact on evaporation and evapotranspiration is relatively small in relation to the rest of the hydrological cycle but is nevertheless important. There are a number of impacts:

- **Dams** – there has been an increase in evaporation due to the construction of large dams. For example, Lake Nasser behind the Aswan Dam loses up to a third of its water due to evaporation. Water loss can be reduced by using chemical sprays on the water, by building sand-fill dams and by covering the dams with some form of plastic.
- **Urbanisation** leads to a huge reduction in evapotranspiration due to the lack of vegetation. There may also be a slight increase in evaporation because of higher temperatures and increased surface storage (see Figure 1.21).

Urbanising influence	Potential hydrological response
Removal of trees and vegetation	Decreased evapotranspiration and interception; increased stream sedimentation
Initial construction of houses, streets and culverts	Decreased infiltration and lowered groundwater table; increased storm flows and decreased base flows during dry periods
Complete development of residential, commercial and industrial areas	Decreased porosity, reducing time of runoff concentration, thereby increasing peak discharges and compressing the time distribution of the flow; greatly increased volume of runoff and flood damage potential
Construction of storm drains and channel improvements	Local relief from flooding; concentration of floodwaters may aggravate flood problems downstream

Figure 1.21 Potential hydrological effects of urbanisation

Interception

Interception is determined by vegetation, density and type. Most vegetation is not natural but represents some disturbance by human activity. In farmland areas, for example, cereals intercept less than broad leaves. Row crops, such as wheat or corn,

leave a lot of soil bare. For example, in the Mississippi basin, if sediment yields in woodland areas are just 1 unit, sediment from soil covered by pasture produces 30 units and areas under corn produce 350 units of sediment. Deforestation leads to:

- a reduction in evapotranspiration
- an increase in surface runoff
- a decline of surface storage
- a decline in time lag.

Afforestation is believed to have the opposite effect, although the evidence does not necessarily support it. For example, in parts of the Severn catchment sediment loads increased four times after afforestation. Why was this? The result is explained by a combination of an increase in overland runoff, little ground vegetation, young trees, access route for tractors, and fire- and wind-breaks. All of these allowed a lot of bare ground. However, after only five years the amount of erosion declined.

Infiltration and soil water

Human activity has a great impact on infiltration and soil water. Land use changes are important. Urbanisation creates an impermeable surface with compacted soil. This reduces infiltration and increases overland runoff and flood peaks (Figure 1.22).

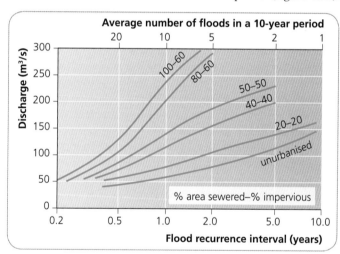

Figure 1.22 Flood frequency and urbanisation

Infiltration is up to five times greater under forest compared with grassland. This is because the forest trees channel water down their roots and stems. With deforestation there is reduced interception, increased soil compaction and more overland flow. Land use practices are also important. Grazing leads to a decline in infiltration due to compaction and ponding of the soil. By contrast, ploughing increases infiltration because it loosens soils. Waterlogging and salinisation are common if there is poor drainage. When the water table is close to the surface, evaporation of water leaves salts behind and may form an impermeable crust. Human activity also has an increasing impact on surface storage. There is increased surface storage due to the building of large-scale dams. These dams are being built in increasing numbers, and they are also larger in terms of general size and volume. This leads to:

- increased storage of water
- decreased flood peaks
- low flows in rivers
- decreased sediment yields (clear-water erosion)
- decreased losses due to evaporation and seepage leading to changes in temperature and salinity of the water
- increased flooding of the land
- triggering of earthquakes
- salinisation – for example, in the Indus Valley in Pakistan, 1.9 million hectares are severely saline and up to 0.4 million hectares are lost per annum to salinity
- large dams can cause local changes in climate.

In other areas there is a decline in the surface storage, for example in urban areas water is channelled away very rapidly over impermeable surfaces into drains and gutters.

Section 1.4 Activities

Study Figure 1.22. Describe and explain the changes in flood frequency and flood magnitude that occur as urbanisation increases.

Changing groundwater

Human activity has seriously reduced the long-term viability of irrigated agriculture in the High Plains of Texas. Before irrigation development started in the 1930s, the High Plains groundwater system was stable, in a state of dynamic equilibrium with long-term recharge equal to long-term discharge. However, groundwater is now being used at a rapid rate to supply **centre-pivot irrigation schemes**. In under fifty years, the water level has declined by 30–50 m in a large area to the north of Lubbock, Texas. The aquifer has narrowed by more than 50 per cent in large parts of certain counties, and the area irrigated by each well is contracting as well as yields are falling.

By contrast, in some industrial areas, recent reductions in industrial activity have led to less groundwater being taken out of the ground. As a result, groundwater levels in such areas have begun to rise, adding to the problem caused by leakage from ancient, deteriorating pipe and sewerage systems. Such a rise has numerous implications including:

- increase in spring and river flows
- re-emergence of flow from 'dry springs'
- surface water flooding
- pollution of surface waters and the spread of underground pollution
- flooding of basements
- increased leakage into tunnels
- reduction in stability of slopes and retaining walls
- reduction in bearing capacity of foundations and piles
- swelling of clays as they absorb water
- chemical attack on building foundations.

There are various methods of recharging groundwater resources, provided that sufficient surface water is available. Where the materials containing the aquifer are permeable (as in some alluvial fans, coastal sand dunes or glacial deposits), water-spreading (a form of infiltration and seepage) is used. By contrast, in sediments with impermeable layers such water-spreading techniques are not effective, and the appropriate method may then be to pump water into deep pits or into wells. This method is used extensively on the heavily settled coastal plain of Israel, both to replenish the groundwater reservoirs when surplus irrigation water is available, and in an attempt to diminish the problems associated with saltwater intrusions from the Mediterranean.

Case Study
Changing hydrology of the Aral Sea

The Aral Sea began shrinking in the 1960s when Soviet irrigation schemes took water from the Syr Darya and the Amu Darya rivers. This greatly reduced the amount of water reaching the Aral Sea. By 1994, the shorelines had fallen by 16 m, the surface area had declined by 50 per cent and the volume had been reduced by 75 per cent (Figure 1.23). By contrast, salinity levels had increased by 300 per cent.

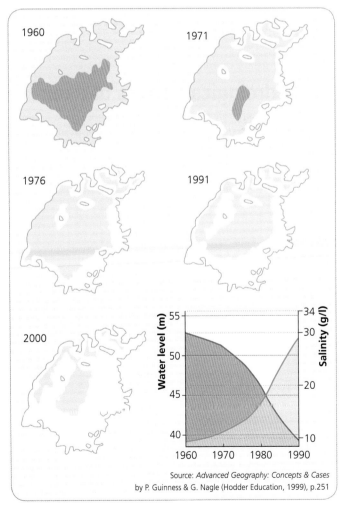

Source: *Advanced Geography: Concepts & Cases* by P. Guinness & G. Nagle (Hodder Education, 1999), p.251

Figure 1.23 The changing geography of the Aral Sea

Increased salinity levels killed off the fishing industry. Moreover, ports such as Muynak are now tens of kilometres from the shore. Salt from the dry seabed has reduced soil fertility and frequent dust storms are ruining the region's cotton production. Drinking water has been polluted by pesticides and fertilisers and the air has been affected by dust and salt. There has been a noticeable rise in respiratory and stomach disorders and the region has one of the highest infant mortality rates in the former Soviet Union.

Section 1.4 Activities

Study Figure 1.23.

1 Why do you think the former Soviet Union (FSU) embarked on such a programme of large-scale irrigation? Use an atlas to produce detailed information.

2 Why have salinity levels increased so much?

3 What problems does the shrinking of the Aral Sea cause for towns such as Aralsk and Muynak?

4 What is the likely effect of the irrigation scheme on the two rivers in terms of velocity, erosion, sediment transport and deposition?

The hydrological effects of dams

The number of large dams (more than 15 m high) that is being built is increasing rapidly and is reaching a level of almost two completions every day (Figure 1.24).

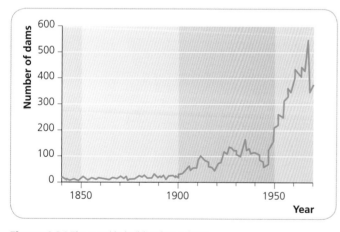

Figure 1.24 The trend in building large dams

The advantages of dams are numerous, as the following examples from the Aswan High Dam on the River Nile, Egypt, show:

- flood and drought control – dams allow good crops in dry years as, for example, in Egypt in 1972 and 1973
- irrigation – 60 per cent of water from the Aswan Dam is used for irrigation and up to 4000 km of the desert are irrigated

- hydro-electric power – this accounts for 7000 million kW hours each year
- improved navigation
- recreation and tourism.

It is estimated that the value of the Aswan High Dam is about $500 million to the Egyptian economy each year.

On the other hand, there are numerous disadvantages. For example:

- water losses – the dam provides less than half the amount of water expected
- salinisation – crop yields have been reduced on up to one-third of the area irrigated by water from the Aswan Dam, due to salinisation
- groundwater changes – seepage leads to increased groundwater levels and may cause secondary salinisation
- displacement of population – up to 100 000 Nubian people have been removed from their ancestral homes
- drowning of archaeological sites – Ramases II and Nefertari at Abu Simbel had to be removed to safer locations – however, the increase in the humidity of the area has led to an increase in the weathering of ancient monuments
- seismic stress – the earthquake of November 1981 is believed to have been caused by the Aswan Dam; as water levels in the Dam decrease so too does seismic activity increase
- deposition within the lake – infilling is taking place at about 100 million tonnes each year
- channel erosion (clear-water erosion) beneath the channel – lowering the channel by 25 mm over 18 years, a modest amount
- erosion of the Nile delta – this is taking place at a rate of about 2.5 cm each year
- loss of nutrients – it is estimated that it costs $100 million to buy commercial fertilisers to make up for the lack of nutrients each year
- decreased fish catches – sardine yields are down 95 per cent and 3000 jobs in Egyptian fisheries have been lost
- diseases have spread – such as schistosomiasis (bilharzia).

Section 1.4 Activities

1 Study Figure 1.24. Describe the pattern shown and suggest reasons to explain the trend.

2 Evaluate the effectiveness of large dams.

Floods

Floods are one of the most common of all environmental hazards. This is because so many people live in fertile river valleys and in low-lying coastal areas. For much of the time rivers act as a resource. However, extremes of too much water – or too little – can be considered a hazard (Figure 1.25). In addition, extreme events occur infrequently. Many urban areas are designed to cope with floods that occur on a regular basis, perhaps annually or once in a decade. Most are ill-equipped to deal with the low-

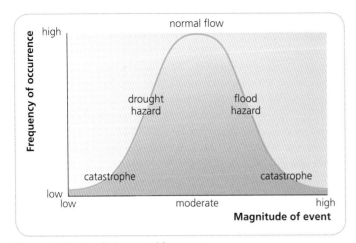

Figure 1.25 River discharge and frequency

frequency/high-magnitude event that may occur once every 100 years or every 500 years (Figure 1.26). The **recurrence interval** refers to the regularity of a flood of a given size. Small floods may be expected to occur regularly. Larger floods occur less often. A 100-year flood is the flood that is expected to occur, *on average*, once every 100 years. Increasingly larger floods are less common, but more damaging.

The nature and scale of flooding varies greatly. For example, less than 2 per cent of the population of England and Wales and in Australia live in areas exposed to flooding, compared with 10 per cent of the US population. The worst problems occur in Asia where floods damage about 4 million hectares of land each year and affect the lives of over 17 million people. Worst of all is China where over 5 million people have been killed in floods since 1860.

Some environments are more at risk than others. The most vulnerable include the following:

- Low-lying parts of active floodplains and river estuaries. For example, in Bangladesh 110 million people living on the floodplain of the Ganges and Brahmaputra rivers are relatively unprotected. Floods caused by the monsoon regularly cover 20–30 per cent of the flat delta. In very high floods up to half of the country may be flooded. In 1988 46 per cent of the land was flooded and more than 1500 people were killed.
- Small basins subject to flash floods. These are especially common in arid and semi-arid areas. In tropical areas some 90 per cent of lives lost through drowning are the result of intense rainfall on steep slopes.
- Areas below unsafe dams. In the USA there are about 30 000 large dams and 2000 communities are at risk from dams. Following the 2008 Sichuan earthquake in China, some 35 quake dams were created by landslides blocking river routes. These were eventually made safe by engineers and the Chinese military.
- Low-lying inland shorelines such as along the Great Lakes and the Great Salt Lake in the USA.

In most more economically developed countries (MEDCs) the number of deaths from floods is declining while in contrast the economic cost of flood damage has been increasing. In less economically developed countries (LEDCs), on the other hand, the death rate due to flooding is much greater, although the economic cost is not as great. It is likely that the hazard in LEDCs will increase over time as more people migrate and settle in low-lying areas and river basins. Often newer migrants are forced into the more hazardous zones.

Since the Second World War there has been a change in the understanding of the flood hazard, in the attitude towards floods, and the policy towards reducing the flood hazard. The response to hazards has moved away from physical control (engineering structures) towards reducing vulnerability through non-structural approaches.

Figure 1.26 Urban land use and flood risk

Causes of flooding

A flood is a high flow of water which overtops the bank of a river. The main causes of floods are climatic forces whereas the flood-intensifying conditions tend to be drainage basin specific (Figure 1.27). Most floods in the UK, for example, are associated with deep depressions (low pressure systems) which are both long-lasting and cover a wide area. By contrast, in India up to 70 per cent of the annual rainfall occurs in three months during the summer monsoon. In Alpine and Arctic areas, melting snow is responsible for widespread flooding.

Flood-intensifying conditions cover a range of factors which alter the drainage basin response to a given storm (Figure 1.28). The factors that influence the storm hydrograph determine the response of the basin to the storm. These factors include topography, vegetation, soil type, rock type, and characteristics of the drainage basin.

The potential for damage by floodwaters increases exponentially with velocity. The physical stresses on buildings are increased even more when rough, rapidly flowing water contains debris such as rocks, sediment and trees.

Other conditions that intensify floods include changes in land use. Urbanisation, for example, increases the magnitude and frequency of floods in at least three ways:

- creation of highly impermeable surfaces, such as roads, roofs, pavements
- smooth surfaces served with a dense network of drains, gutters and underground sewers increase drainage density

- natural river channels are often constricted by bridge supports or riverside facilities reducing their carrying capacity.

Deforestation is also a cause of increased flood runoff and a decrease in channel capacity. This occurs due to an increase in deposition within the channel. However, the evidence is not always conclusive. In the Himalayas, for example, changes in flooding and increased deposition of silt in parts of the lower Ganges-Brahmaputra is due to the combination of high monsoon rains, steep slopes, and the seismically unstable terrain. These ensure that runoff is rapid and sedimentation is high irrespective of the vegetation cover.

Forecasting and warning

During the 1980s and 1990s flood forecasting and warning had become more accurate and these are now among the most widely used measures to reduce the problems caused by flooding. Despite advances in weather satellites and the use of radar for forecasting, over 50 per cent of all of unprotected dwellings in England and Wales have less than six hours of flood warning time. In most LEDCs there is much less effective flood forecasting. An exception is Bangladesh. Most floods in Bangladesh originate in the Himalayas, so authorities have about 72 hours' warning.

According to the United Nations Environment Programme's publication *Early Warning and Assessment* there are a number of things that could be done to improve flood warnings. These include:

- improved rainfall and snow pack estimates, and better and longer forecasts of rainfall

Causes of flood

- Climatological
  - Rain
  - Ice melt
  - Snow melt
- Part-Climatological
  - Estuarine interactions between stream flow and tidal conditions
  - Coastal storm surges
- Other
  - Earthquake
  - Landslide
  - Dam failure

Source: *Access to Geography: Rivers and Water Management* by G. Nagle (Hodder Education, 2003), p.64

Figure 1.27 The causes of floods

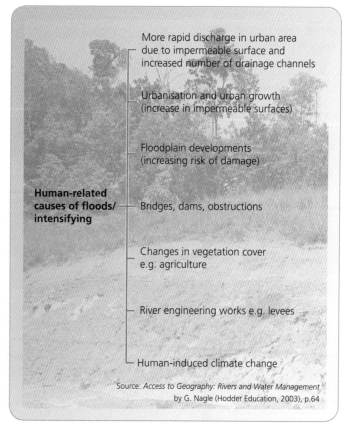

Human-related causes of floods/ intensifying

- More rapid discharge in urban area due to impermeable surface and increased number of drainage channels
- Urbanisation and urban growth (increase in impermeable surfaces)
- Floodplain developments (increasing risk of damage)
- Bridges, dams, obstructions
- Changes in vegetation cover e.g. agriculture
- River engineering works e.g. levees
- Human-induced climate change

Source: *Access to Geography: Rivers and Water Management* by G. Nagle (Hodder Education, 2003), p.64

Figure 1.28 Flood-intensifying conditions

- better gauging of rivers, collection of meteorological information and mapping of channels
- better and current information about human populations and infrastructure, elevation and stream channels need to be incorporated into flood risk assessment models
- better sharing of information is needed between forecasters, national agencies, relief organisations and the general public
- more complete and timely sharing of information of meteorological and hydrological information is needed among countries within international drainage basins
- technology should be shared among all agencies involved in flood forecasting and risk assessment both in the basins and throughout the world.

Prevention and amelioration of floods

Economic growth and population movements throughout the twentieth century have caused many floodplains to be built on. However, in order for people to live on floodplains there needs to be flood protection. This can take many forms, such as loss-sharing adjustments and event modifications.

Loss-sharing adjustments include disaster aid and insurance. **Disaster aid** refers to any aid, such as money, equipment, staff and technical assistance that are given to a community following a disaster. In MEDCs **insurance** is an important loss sharing strategy. However, not all flood-prone households have insurance and many of those that are insured may be underinsured.

Event modification adjustments include environmental control and hazard-resistant design. Physical control of floods depends on two measures: flood abatement and flood diversion.

Flood abatement involves decreasing the amount of runoff, thereby reducing the flood peak in a drainage basin. There are a number of ways of reducing flood peaks. These include:
- reforestation
- reseeding of sparsely vegetated areas to increase evaporative losses
- treatment of slopes such as by contour ploughing or terracing to reduce the runoff coefficient
- comprehensive protection of vegetation from wildfires, overgrazing, and clear-cutting of forests
- clearance of sediment and other debris from headwater streams
- construction of small water- and sediment-holding areas
- preservation of natural water storage zones, such as lakes.

Flood diversion measures, by contrast, include the construction of levees, reservoirs, and the modification of river channels (Figures 1.29 and 1.30). **Levees** are the most common form of river engineering. They can also be used to divert and restrict water to low-value land on the floodplain. Over 4500 km of the Mississippi River has levees. Channel improvements such as channel enlargement will increase the carrying capacity of the river. **Reservoirs** store excess rainwater in the upper drainage basin. However, this may only be appropriate in small drainage networks. It has been estimated that some 66 billion m^3 of storage is needed to make any significant impact on major floods in Bangladesh!

1 Flood embankments with sluice gates. The main problem with this is that it may raise flood levels up and down.

2 Channel enlargement to accommodate larger discharges. One problem with such schemes is that as the enlarged channel is only rarely used it becomes clogged with weed.

3 Flood relief channels. This is appropriate where it is impossible to modify the original channel due to cost, e.g. the flood relief channels around Oxford.

4 Intercepting channels. These are in use during times of flood, diverting part of the flow away, allowing flow for town and agricultural use, e.g. the Great Ouse Protection Scheme in the Fenlands

5 Flood storage reservoirs. This solution is widely used, especially as many reservoirs created for water-supply purposes may have a secondary flood control, e.g. the intercepting channels along the Loughton Brook.

6 The removal of settlements. This is rarely used because of cost, although many communities were forced to leave as a result of the 1993 Mississippi floods.

Source: *Access to Geography: Rivers and Water Management* by G. Nagle (Hodder Education, 2003), p.65

Figure 1.29 Channel diversions

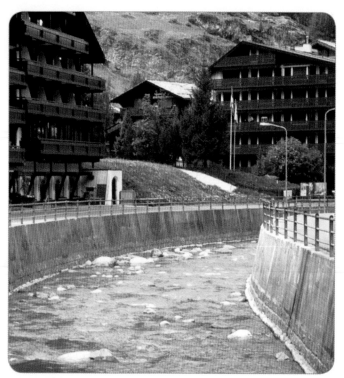

Figure 1.30 Flood relief channel, Zermatt, Switzerland

Hazard-resistant design

Floodproofing includes any adjustments to buildings and their contents, which help reduce losses. Some are temporary, such as:
- blocking up entrances
- sealing doors and windows
- removal of damageable goods to higher levels
- use of sandbags.

By contrast, long-term measures include moving the living spaces above the likely level of the floodplain. This normally means building above the flood level, but could also include building homes on stilts.

Land use planning

Most land use zoning and land use planning has been introduced since the Second World War. In the USA land use management has been effective in protecting new housing developments from 1 in 100 year floods (that is, the size of flood that we would expect to occur once every century).

One example where partial urban relocation has occurred is at Soldier's Grove on the Kickapoo River in south-western Wisconsin, USA. The town experienced a series of floods in the 1970s, and the Army Corps of Engineers proposed building two levees and moving part of the urban area. Following floods in 1978 they decided that relocation of the entire business district would be better than just flood damage reduction. Although levees would have protected the village from most floods, they would not have provided other opportunities. Relocation allowed energy conservation and an increase in commercial activity in the area.

Section 1.4 Activities

1 Outline the natural and man-made causes of floods.

2 Compare and contrast methods of flood management.

3 To what extent can flood frequency and magnitude be predicted?

Drought

A large proportion of the world's surface experiences dry conditions. Semi-arid areas are commonly defined as having a rainfall of less than 500 mm per annum, while arid areas have less than 250 mm, and extremely arid areas less than 125 mm per annum. In addition to low rainfall, dry areas have **variable rainfall**. As rainfall total decreases, variability increases. For example, areas with a rainfall of 500 mm have an annual variability of about 33 per cent. This means that in such areas rainfall could range between 330 mm and 670 mm. This variability has important consequences for vegetation cover, farming and the risk of flooding.

Defining drought

Drought is an extended period of dry weather leading to conditions of extreme dryness. Absolute drought is a period of at least 15 consecutive days with less than 0.2 mm of rainfall. Partial drought is a period of at least 29 consecutive days during which the average daily rainfall does not exceed 0.2 mm.

Case Study

Europe's drought of 2003

Estimates for the death toll from the French heatwave in 2003 were as high as 30 000. Harvests were down by between 30 per cent and 50 per cent on 2002. France's electricity grid was also affected, as demand for electricity soared because people turned up their air conditioning and fridges. At the same time, nuclear power stations, which generate around 75 per cent of France's electricity, were operating at a much reduced capacity because there was less water available for cooling. Portugal declared a state of emergency after the worst forest fires for 30 years. Temperatures reached 43 °C in Lisbon in August 2003 – 15 °C hotter than the average for the month. Over 1300 deaths occurred in that country in the first half of August, and up to 35 000 ha of forest, farmland and scrub were burned. Some fires were, in fact, deliberately started by arsonists seeking insurance or compensation money. More than 70 people were arrested.

The prolonged heatwave left some countries facing their worst harvests since the end of the Second World War. Some countries that usually export food were forced to import it for the first time in decades. Across the European Union, wheat production was down by 10 million tonnes – about 10 per cent.

Arid conditions

Arid conditions are caused by a number of factors:

- The main cause is the global atmospheric circulation. Dry, descending air associated with the **subtropical high-pressure belt** is the main cause of aridity around at 20–30 °N.
- In addition, distance from sea, or **continentality**, limits the amount of water carried across by winds.
- In some areas, such as the Atacama and Namib deserts, **cold offshore currents** limit the amount of condensation in the overlying air.
- Some places are affected by intense **rainshadow effects**, as air passes over mountains. This is true of the Patagonian desert.
- A final cause, or range of causes, are human activities. Many of these have given rise to the spread of desert conditions into areas previously fit for agriculture. This is known as desertification, and is an increasing problem.

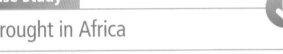

Case Study

Drought in Africa

In 2003 parts of southern Ethiopia experienced the longest drought anyone had known. The world's largest emergency food aid programme was in operation, but it proved inadequate. Because of a sixth poor rainy season in three years, 20 million people needed help (Tables 1.4 and 1.5). The situation was worse than the 1984 famine, when only 10 million people needed food.

Table 1.4 Africa's 'at risk' population

Country	People seen as under threat of famine in Africa (millions, 2003)
Ethiopia	20.0
Zimbabwe	7.0
Malawi	3.2
Sudan	2.9
Zambia	2.7
Angola	1.9
Eritrea	1.0
plus around 7.3 million across Swaziland, Congo, Uganda, Congo-Brazzaville, Lesotho and Mozambique	

Table 1.5 Adjustments to drought suggested by peasant farmers in Tanzania and northern Nigeria

Adjustment	Tanzania	Northern Nigeria
Change location	Nothing permanent	Nothing permanent
Change use	Drought-resistant crops, irrigation	Nothing
Prevent effects	More thorough weeding; cultivate larger areas; work elsewhere; tie ridging; plant on wet places; send cattle to other areas; sell cattle to buy food; staggered planting	Store food for next year; seek work elsewhere temporarily; seek income by selling firewood, crafts, or grass; expand fishing activity; plant late cassava; plant additional crop
Modify events	Employ rainmakers; pray	Consult medicine men; pray for end of drought
Share	Send children to kinsmen; government relief; store crops; move to relative's farm; use savings	Turn to relatives; possible government relief
No change	Do nothing	Suffer and starve; pray for support

Section 1.4 Activities

1 Define the term *drought*.

2 Compare the impact of drought in MEDCs and LEDCs.

3 To what extent can drought be managed?

2 Atmosphere and weather

2.1 Local energy budgets

An energy budget refers to the amount of energy entering a system, the amount leaving the system, and the transfer of energy within the system. Energy budgets are commonly considered at a global scale (macro-scale) and at a local scale (micro-scale). However, the term 'microclimate' is sometimes used to describe regional climates, such as those associated with large urban areas, coastal areas and mountainous regions.

Figure 2.1 shows a classification of climate and weather phenomena at a variety of spatial and temporal scales. Phenomena vary from small-scale turbulence and eddying (such as dust devils) which cover a small area and last for a very short time, to large-scale anticyclones (high pressure zones) and jet streams which affect a large area and may last for weeks. The jet stream that carried volcanic dust from underneath the Eyjafjallsjokull glacier in Iceland to northern Europe in 2010 is a good example of jet stream activity (Figure 2.2).

Flights over northern Europe were disrupted after a cloud of volcanic ash from Iceland's Eyjafjallsjokull volcano – drifting from 6000 to 11000 metres high – closed airports and caused flights to be cancelled.

Figure 2.2 Jet stream activity and the transfer of dust from Eyjafjallsjokull, Iceland

These different scales should not be considered as separate scales but as a hierarchy of scales in which smaller phenomena may exist within larger ones. For example, the temperature surrounding a building will be affected by the nature of the building and processes that are taking place within the building. However, it will also be affected by the wider synoptic (weather) conditions, which are affected by latitude, altitude, cloud cover and season, for example.

Daytime energy budget

There are six components to the daytime energy budget:
- incoming solar radiation (insolation)
- reflected solar radiation
- surface absorption
- sensible heat transfer
- long-wave radiation (Figure 2.3)
- latent heat (evaporation).

Figure 2.1 Classification of climate and weather phenomena at a variety of spatial and temporal scales

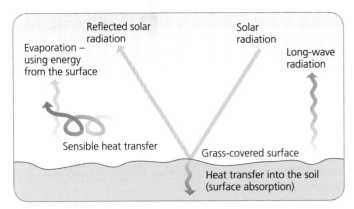

Figure 2.3 Local energy budget – daytime

These influence the gain or loss of energy for a point at the Earth's surface. The daytime energy budget assumes a horizontal surface with grass-covered soil. The daytime energy budget can be expressed by the formula:

energy available at the surface = incoming solar radiation – (reflected solar radiation + surface absorption + sensible heat transfer + long-wave radiation + latent heat transfers)

Incoming solar radiation

Incoming solar radiation (insolation) is the main energy input and is affected by latitude, season and cloud cover (see pages 31–32 and 35). Figure 2.4 shows how the amount of insolation received varies with the angle of the Sun and with cloud type. For example, with strato-cumulus clouds (like those in Figure 2.5) when the Sun is low in the sky, about 23 per cent of the total radiation transmitted is received at the Earth's surface – about 250 watts per m². When the Sun is high in the sky, about 40 per cent is received, just over 450 watts per m². The less cloud cover there is, and/or the higher the cloud, the more radiation reaches the Earth's surface.

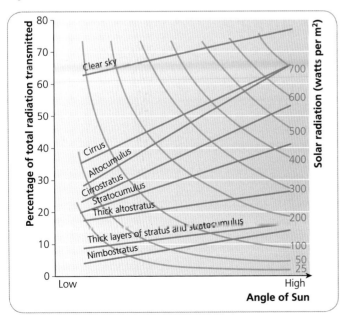

Figure 2.4 Energy, cloud cover/type and the angle of the Sun

Figure 2.5 Strato-cumulus clouds

Reflected solar radiation

The proportion of energy that is reflected back to the atmosphere is known as the albedo. The albedo varies with colour – light materials are more reflective than dark materials (Table 2.1). Grass has an average albedo of 20–30 per cent, meaning that it reflects back about 20–30 per cent of the radiation it receives.

Table 2.1 Selected albedo values

Surface	Albedo (%)
Water (Sun's angle over 40°)	2–4
Water (Sun's angle less than 40°)	6–80
Fresh snow	75–90
Old snow	40–70
Dry sand	35–45
Dark, wet soil	5–15
Dry concrete	17–27
Black road surface	5–10
Grass	20–30
Deciduous forest	10–20
Coniferous forest	5–15
Crops	15–25
Tundra	15–20

Section 2.1 Activities

1 The model for the daytime energy budget assumes a flat surface with grass-covered soil. Suggest reasons for this assumption.

2 Study Table 2.1.
   a What is meant by the term *albedo*?
   b Why is albedo important?

Surface absorption

Energy that reaches the Earth's surface has the potential to heat it. Much depends on the nature of the surface. For example, if the surface can conduct heat to lower layers, the surface will remain cool. If the energy is concentrated at the surface, the surface warms up. (Rock is a poor conductor of heat – this is why in hot desert areas, exfoliation may occur as repeated heating and cooling of the rock surface results in stresses at the surface, and eventual peeling or flaking – see pages 63–64.)

Sensible heat transfer

Sensible heat transfer refers to the movement of parcels of air into and out from the area being studied. For example, air that is warmed by the surface may begin to rise (convection) and be replaced by cooler air. This is known as a convective transfer. It is very common in warm areas in the early afternoon.

Long-wave radiation

Long-wave radiation refers to the radiation of energy from the Earth (a cold body) into the atmosphere and, for some of it, eventually into space. There is, however, a downward movement of long-wave radiation from particles in the atmosphere. The difference between the two flows is known as the net radiation balance. During the day, the outgoing long-wave radiation transfer is greater than the incoming long-wave radiation transfer, so there is a net loss of energy from the surface.

Latent heat transfer (evaporation)

When liquid water is turned into water vapour, heat energy is used up. In contrast, when water vapour becomes a liquid, heat is released. Thus when water is present at a surface, a proportion of the energy available will be used to evaporate it, and less energy will be available to raise local energy levels and temperature.

Night-time energy budget

The night-time energy budget consists of four components – long-wave Earth radiation, latent heat transfer (condensation), absorbed energy returned to Earth (sub-surface supply), and sensible heat transfer (Figure 2.6).

Long-wave radiation

During a cloudless night there is a large loss of long-wave radiation from the Earth. There is very little return of long-wave radiation from the atmosphere, due to the lack of clouds. Hence there is a net loss of energy from the surface. In contrast, on a cloudy night the clouds return some long-wave radiation to the surface, hence the overall loss of energy is reduced. Thus in hot desert areas, where there is a lack of cloud cover, the loss of energy at night is maximised. In contrast, in cloudy areas the loss of energy (and change in daytime and night-time temperatures) is less noticeable.

Latent heat transfer (condensation)

During the night, water vapour in the air close to the surface can condense to form water, since the air has been cooled by the cold surface. When water condenses, latent heat is released. This affects the cooling process at the surface. In some cases evaporation may occur at night, especially in areas where there are local sources of heat.

Sub-surface supply

The heat transferred to the soil and bedrock during the day may be released back to the surface at night. This can partly offset the night-time cooling at the surface.

Sensible heat transfer

Cold air moving into an area may reduce temperatures whereas warm air may supply energy and raise temperatures.

Temperature changes close to the surface

Ground-surface temperatures can vary considerably between day and night. During the day, the ground heats the air by radiation, conduction (contact) and convection. The ground radiates energy and as the air receives more radiation than it emits, the air is warmed. Air close to the ground is also warmed through conduction. Air movement at the surface is slower due to friction with the surface, so there is more time for it to be heated. The combined effect of radiation and conduction is that the air becomes warmer, and rises as a result of convection.

At night the ground is cooled as a result of radiation. Heat is transferred from the air to the ground. The air in contact with the ground loses most heat.

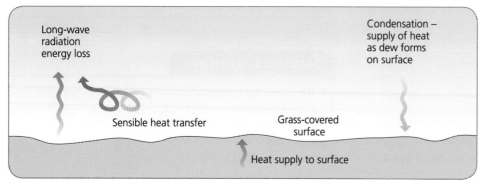

Figure 2.6 Night-time energy budget

Humidity

Absolute humidity refers to the amount of water in the atmosphere. For example, there may be 8 grams of water in a cubic metre of air. **Relative humidity** refers to the water vapour present expressed as a percentage of the maximum amount air at that temperature can hold. For example, air at 20 °C can hold up to 17.117 g cm^{-3} of water vapour. If it contains only 8.5585 g cm^{-3}, its relative humidity is 8.5585/17.117 × 100 per cent or 50 per cent relative humidity (RH).

Saturated air is air with a relative humidity of 100 per cent. As air temperature rises if there is no increase in water vapour in the air, its relative humidity decreases. For example, air at 5 °C may be saturated with as little as 6.8 g of water. As the air is warmed the amount of moisture it can hold increases. However, if none is added to the air, the amount it contains compared with the amount it can hold decreases. Hence, as the air is warmed to 10 °C its relative humidity drops to 71 per cent, at 15.5 °C its RH drops to 51 per cent and at 32 °C its RH is down to 19 per cent.

Mist and fog

Mist and fog are cloud at ground level. According to the Met Office, mist occurs when visibility is between 1000 m and 5000 m and relative humidity is over 93 per cent. In contrast, fog occurs when visibility is below 1000 m. Dense fog occurs when the visibility is below 200 m.

Air can hold a certain amount of moisture. Once this level is reached the air is said to be saturated and the vapour turns into liquid. The amount of vapour that air can hold depends on its temperature – warm air can hold more moisture than cold air.

For mist and fog to form, condensation nuclei, such as dust and salt, are needed. These are more common in urban areas and coastal areas, so mist and fog are more common there.

Fog is common in many areas, for example the North Sea coast of the UK in summer, the Grand Banks of Newfoundland, and coastal Peru. Fog is basically a suspension of small water droplets in the lower atmosphere. It occurs when condensation of moist air cools below its dew point. The most common types are radiation fog (Figure 2.7) and advection fog.

For fog to occur, condensation must take place near ground level. Condensation can take place in two major ways:
- air is cooled
- more water is added to the atmosphere.

The cooling of air as we have seen is quite common (orographic, frontal and convectional uplift). By contrast the addition of moisture to the atmosphere is relatively rare. However, it does occur over warm surfaces such as the Great Lakes in North America or over the Arctic Ocean. Water evaporates from the relatively warm surface and condenses into the cold air above to form fog. Calm high pressure conditions are required to avoid the saturated air being mixed with drier air above. In addition, contact cooling at a cold ground surface may produce saturation. As warm moist air passes over a cold surface it is chilled, condensation takes

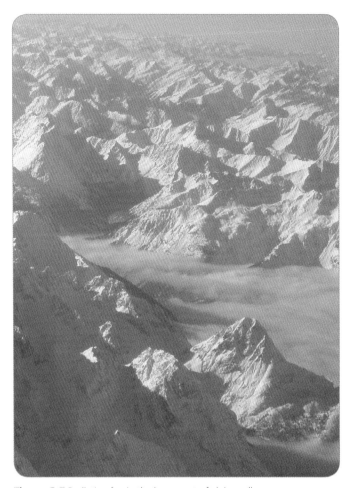

Figure 2.7 Radiation fog in the lower part of alpine valleys

place as the temperature of the air is reduced and the air reaches dew point (temperature at which relative humidity is 100 per cent). When warm air flows over a cold surface, **advection fog** is formed. For example, air from the North Atlantic Drift blowing over cold surfaces in Devon and Cornwall in the UK will often form a fog. Similarly, near the Grand Banks off Newfoundland, warm air from the Gulf Stream passes over the waters of the Labrador Current. This is 8–11 °C cooler, since it brings with it meltwater from the disintegrating pack-ice further north. This forms dense fog on 70–100 days/year. This also occurs 40 days a year at the Golden Gate Bridge, San Francisco, because of warm air moving over the cold offshore currents. With fairly light winds, the fog forms close to the water surface, but with stronger turbulence the condensed layer may be uplifted to form a low stratus sheet. **Radiation fog** occurs when the ground loses heat at night by long-wave radiation. This occurs during high pressure conditions associated with clear skies.

Fog is a major environmental hazard – airports may be closed for many days and road transport is hazardous and slow. Freezing fog is particularly problematic. Large economic losses result from fog but the ability to do anything about it is limited. This is because it would require too much energy (and hence cost) to warm up the air or to dry out the air to prevent condensation.

Dew

Dew refers to condensation on a surface. The air is saturated, generally because the temperature of the surface has dropped enough to cause condensation. Occasionally, condensation occurs because more moisture is introduced, for example by a sea breeze, while the temperature remains constant.

Dew may be very useful. In the Negev desert it provides much of the annual rainfall. On the other hand, it may cause some areas to become too damp for cultivation, and may cause some soils to be wet and cold.

Temperature inversions

Maximum solar radiation occurs at noon, but this is not the hottest part of the day. There is a time lag between the ground being heated and it, in turn, heating the air above. The heating takes place as a result of long-wave radiation, conduction, sensible heat transfer and latent heat transfer. During the night the Earth's surface loses the energy it has absorbed during the day. The air also loses energy that it has absorbed. Since air is a less efficient absorber or conductor of energy, it loses it more slowly than the Earth's surface. Consequently, the surface cools more quickly than the air. Some of the energy from the air is re-absorbed by the surface but is quickly emitted again. By the end of the night, the surface is very cold and the layer of air above it is very cold. However, air above this layer is not as cold as it has not been affected by conduction with the surface. It has only cooled as a result of radiation. Thus it is the opposite of what happens in the day. This relative increase in temperature with height in the lower part of the atmosphere is known as a temperature inversion (or radiation- or nocturnal-inversion) (Figure 2.8). This happens when there are relatively calm conditions and little mechanical

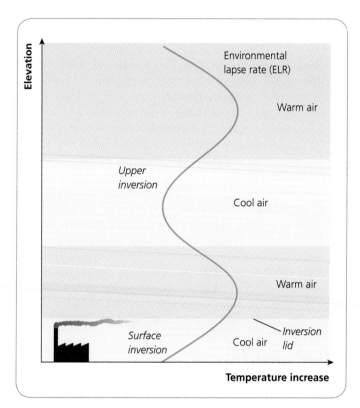

Figure 2.8 Temperature inversion

turbulence from the wind causing the air to mix. As the cold air at the surface is dense, it will tend to stay at the surface. During the longer nights of winter there is even more time for the air near the surface to cool. During calm, high pressure conditions the band of cooled air may extend for a few metres before the warmer air is reached. If the air contains moisture, when the dew point is reached the moisture will condense, releasing latent heat, and off-setting the cooling process.

Figure 2.9 The effects of temperature inversion

Temperature inversions are important as they influence air quality. Under high pressure conditions and limited air movement, a temperature inversion will act like a lid on pollutants causing them to remain in the lower atmosphere next to the Earth's surface (Figure 2.9). Only when the surface begins to heat up and in turn warms the air above it, will the warm air be able to rise and with it any pollutants that it may contain.

Temperature inversions are common in depressions and valleys. Cold air may sink to the bottom of the valley and be replaced by warmer air aloft. In some cases, the inversion can be so intense that frost hollows develop. These can reduce growth of vegetation, so are generally avoided by farmers. Urban areas surrounded by high ground are also vulnerable, such as Mexico City and Los Angeles, as cold air sinks from the mountain down to lower altitudes.

Section 2.1 Activities

Figure 2.8 shows some of the conditions that promote temperature inversions.

1 Define the term *temperature inversion*.

2 Explain why temperature inversions occur.

3 Describe the problems associated with temperature inversions.

Case Study

Annual surface energy budget of an Arctic site – Svalbard, Norway

The annual cycle of the surface energy budget at a high-arctic permafrost site on Svalbard shows that during summer, the net short-wave radiation is the dominant energy source (Figure 2.10). In addition, sensible heat transfers and surface absorption in the ground lead to a cooling of the surface. About 15 per cent of the net radiation is used up by the seasonal thawing of the active layer in July and August (the active layer is the layer at the top of the soil that freezes in winter and thaws in summer). During the polar night in winter, the net long-wave radiation is the dominant energy loss channel for the surface, which is mainly compensated by the sensible heat transfer and, to a lesser extent, by the ground heat transfer, which originates from the refreezing of the active layer. The average annual sensible heat transfer of $-6.9\,Wm^{-2}$ is composed of strong positive transfers in July and August, while negative transfers dominate during the rest of the year. With $6.8\,Wm^{-2}$, the latent heat transfer more or less compensates the sensible heat transfer in the annual average. Strong evaporation occurs during the snowmelt period and particularly during the snow-free period in summer and autumn. When the ground is covered by snow, latent heat fluxes through sublimation of snow are recorded, but are insignificant for the average surface energy budget.

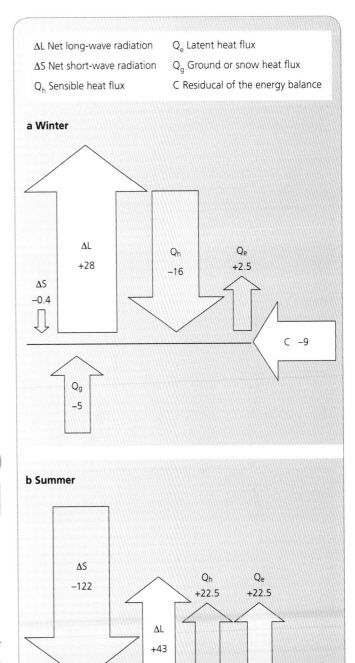

ΔL Net long-wave radiation Q_e Latent heat flux

ΔS Net short-wave radiation Q_g Ground or snow heat flux

Q_h Sensible heat flux   C Residucal of the energy balance

a Winter

ΔL +28

Q_h −16

Q_e +2.5

ΔS −0.4

C −9

Q_g −5

b Summer

ΔS −122

Q_h +22.5

Q_e +22.5

ΔL +43

C +22

Q_g +12

The area of the arrows is proportional to the relative importance in the energy budget. Arrows pointing away from the surface indicate positive fluxes. The flux values are given in Wm^{-2}.

Figure 2.10 Energy budgets for Svalbard

Section 2.1 Activities

1 With reference to Figure 2.10, draw the likely **night-time** energy budgets for Svalbard in summer and in winter.

2 Figure 2.11 shows rural and urban energy budgets for Washington DC (USA) during daytime and night-time. The figures represent the proportions of the original 100 units of incoming solar radiation dispersed in different directions.

  a How does the amount of insolation received vary between the rural area and the urban area?

  b How does the amount of heat lost through evaporation vary between the areas? Justify your answer.

c Explain the difference between the two areas in terms of short-wave radiation reflected to the atmosphere.

d What are the implications of the answers to **b** and **c** for the heating of the ground by conduction?

e Compare the amount of heat given up by the rural area and the urban area by night. Suggest two reasons for these differences.

f Why is there more long-wave radiation by night from the urban area than from the rural area?

a Rural surface

b Urban surface

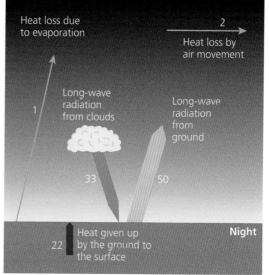

The figures represent the proportions of the original 100 units of incoming solar radiation dispersed in different directions.

Source: University of Oxford, 1989, Entrance examination for Geography

Figure 2.11 Day-time and night-time energy budgets for Washington DC

2.2 The global energy budget

Atmospheric energy

The atmosphere is an open energy system receiving energy from both Sun and Earth. Although the latter is very small, it has an important local effect, as in the case of urban climates. **In**coming **sol**ar radi**ation** is referred to as **insolation**.

The atmosphere constantly receives solar energy yet until recently the atmosphere was not getting any hotter. Therefore there has been a balance between inputs (insolation) and outputs (re-radiation) (Figure 2.12). Under 'natural' conditions the balance is achieved in three main ways:

- radiation – the emission of electromagnetic waves such as X-ray, short- and long-wave; as the Sun is a very hot body, radiating at a temperature of about 5700 °C, most of its radiation is in the form of very short wavelengths such as ultraviolet and visible light
- convection – the transfer of heat by the movement of a gas or liquid
- conduction – the transfer of heat by contact.

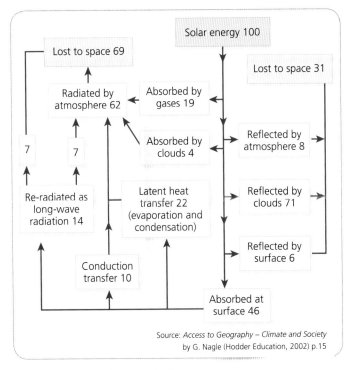

Source: *Access to Geography – Climate and Society* by G. Nagle (Hodder Education, 2002) p.15

Figure 2.12 The Earth's energy budget

Of incoming radiation, 17 per cent is absorbed by atmospheric gases, especially oxygen and ozone at high altitudes, and carbon dioxide and water vapour at low altitudes. Scattering accounts for a net loss of 6 per cent, and clouds and water droplets reflect 23 per cent. In fact, clouds can reflect up to 80 per cent of total

Latitude

Areas that are close to the equator receive more heat than areas that are close to the poles. This is due to two reasons:

1 incoming solar radiation (insolation) is concentrated near the equator, but dispersed near the poles.

2 insolation near the poles has to pass through a greater amount of atmosphere and there is more chance of it being reflected back out to space.

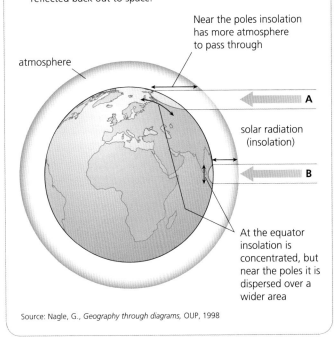

Source: Nagle, G., *Geography through diagrams*, OUP, 1998

Figure 2.13 Latitudinal contrasts in insolation

insolation. Reflection from the Earth's surface (known as the **planetary albedo**) is generally about 7 per cent. About 36 per cent of insolation is reflected back to space and a further 17 per cent is absorbed by atmospheric gases. So only about 47 per cent of the insolation at the top of the atmosphere actually gets through to the Earth's surface.

Energy received by the Earth is re-radiated at long wavelength. (Very hot bodies such as the Sun emit short-wave radiation whereas cold bodies, such as the Earth, emit long-wave radiation.) Of this, 8 per cent is lost to space. Some energy is absorbed by clouds and re-radiated back to Earth. Evaporation and condensation account for a loss of heat of 23 per cent. There is also a small amount of condensation (carried up by turbulence). Thus heat gained by the atmosphere from the ground amounts to 39 per cent of incoming radiation.

The atmosphere is largely heated from below. Most of the incoming short-wave radiation is let through, but some outgoing long-wave radiation is trapped by greenhouse gases. This is known as the greenhouse principle or greenhouse effect.

There are important variations in the receipt of solar radiation with latitude and season (Figure 2.13). The result is an imbalance: a positive budget in the tropics, a negative one at the poles (Figure 2.14). However, neither region is getting progressively hotter or colder. To achieve this balance the horizontal transfer of energy from the equator to the poles takes place by winds and ocean currents. This gives rise to an important second energy budget in the atmosphere: the horizontal transfer between low latitudes and high latitudes to compensate for differences in global insolation.

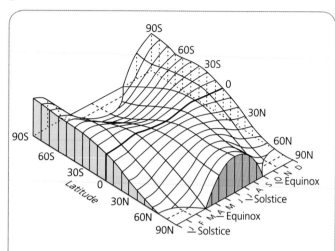

The variations of solar radiation with latitude and season for the whole globe, assuming no atmosphere. This assumption explains the abnormally high amounts of radiation received at the poles in summer, when daylight lasts for 24 hours each day.

Source: Barry, R. and Chorley, R., *Atmosphere, Weather and Climate*, Routledge, 1998

Figure 2.14 Contrasts in insolation by season and latitude

Section 2.2 Activities

1 Outline the main thermal differences between short-wave and long-wave radiation.

2 Study Figures 2.13 and 2.14. Comment on latitudinal differences in the receipt of solar radiation.

Annual temperature patterns

There are important large-scale east–west temperature zones (Figure 2.15). For example, in January highest temperatures over land (above 30 °C) are found in Australia and southern Africa. By contrast the lowest temperatures (less than –40 °C) are found over parts of Siberia, Greenland and the Canadian Arctic. In general there is a decline in temperatures northwards from the Tropic of Capricorn, although there are important anomalies, such as the effect of the Andes in South America, and the effect of the cold current off the coast of Namibia. By contrast, in July maximum temperatures are found over the Sahara, Near East, northern India and parts of southern USA and Mexico. By contrast, areas in the southern hemisphere are cooler than in January.

These patterns reflect the general decrease of insolation from the equator to the poles. There is little seasonal variation at the equator, but in mid or high latitudes large seasonal differences

occur, due to the decrease in insolation from the equator to the poles, and changes in the length of day. There is also a time lag between the overhead Sun and the period of maximum insolation – up to two months is some places – largely because the air is heated from below, not above. The coolest period is after the winter solstice (the shortest day), since the ground continues to lose heat even after insolation has resumed. Over oceans the lag time is greater than over the land, due to differences in their specific heat capacities.

Section 2.2 Activities

Describe the differences in temperature as shown in Figure 2.15. Suggest reasons for these contrasts.

Pressure variations

Pressure is measured in millibars (mb) and is represented by isobars, which are lines of equal pressure. On maps pressure is adjusted to mean sea level (MSL), therefore eliminating elevation as a factor. MSL pressure is 1013 mb, although the mean range is from 1060 mb in the Siberian winter high pressure system to 940 mb (although some intense low pressure storms may be much lower). The trend of pressure change is more important than the actual reading itself. Decline in pressure indicates poorer weather, and rising pressure better weather.

Surface pressure belts

Sea-level pressure conditions show marked differences between the hemispheres. In the northern hemisphere there are greater seasonal contrasts whereas in the southern hemisphere (SH) much simpler average conditions exist (Figure 2.16 on page 34). The differences are largely related to unequal distribution of land and sea, because ocean areas are much more equable in terms of temperature and pressure variations.

One of the more permanent features is the subtropical high pressure (STHP) belts, especially over ocean areas. In the SH these are almost continuous at about 30° latitude, although in summer over South Africa and Australia they tend to be broken. Generally pressure is about 1026 mb. In the northern hemisphere, by contrast, at 30° the belt is much more discontinuous because of the land. High pressure only occurs over the ocean as discrete cells such as the Azores and Pacific highs. Over continental areas such as south-west USA, southern Asia and the Sahara, major fluctuations occur: high pressure in winter, and summer lows because of overheating.

Over the equatorial trough, pressure is low – 1008–1010 mb. The trough coincides with the zone of maximum insolation. In the northern hemisphere (July) it is well north of the equator (25 °C over India), whereas in the SH (January) it is just south of the equator because landmasses in the SH are not of sufficient size to displace it southwards. 'The doldrums' refers to the equatorial trough over sea areas, where slack pressure gradients have a becalming effect on sailing ships.

Source: Briggs, D et al., *Fundamentals of the physical environment*, Routledge, 1997

Figure 2.15 Seasonal temperature patterns

a
Northern
hemisphere

July

January

b
Southern
hemisphere

July

January

Source: Barry, R. and Chorley, R., *Atmosphere, weather and climate*, Routledge, 1998

Figure 2.16 Variations in pressure

In temperate latitudes pressure is generally less than in subtropical areas. The most unique feature is the large number of depressions (low pressure) and anticyclones (high pressure) which do not show up on a map of mean pressure. In the northern hemisphere there are strong winter low pressure zones over Icelandic and oceanic areas, but over Canada and Siberia there is high pressure, due to the coldness of the land. In summer, high pressure is reduced. In polar areas pressure is relatively high throughout the year, especially over Antarctica, owing to the coldness of the land mass.

Section 2.2 Activities

Describe the variations in pressure as shown on Figure 2.16.

Surface wind belts

Winds between the Tropics converge on a line known as the **intertropical convergence zone** (ITCZ) or equatorial trough (Figure 2.17). This convergence zone is a few hundred kilometres wide, into which winds blow inwards and subsequently rise (thereby forming an area of low pressure). The rising air releases vast quantities of latent heat, which in turn stimulates convection.

Source: Linacre, E. and Geerts, B., *Climates and Weather Explained*, Routledge, 1997

Figure 2.17 Surface winds

- - - **ITCZ**   Intertropical Convergence Zone
· · · · · **ZAB**   Zaïre Air Boundary
- - - **SPCZ** South Pacific Convergence Zone
        H   Centre of high pressure
———   Equator

Latitudinal variations in the ITCZ occur as a result of the movement of the overhead Sun. In June the ITCZ lies further north, whereas in December it lies in the southern hemisphere. The seasonal variation in the ITCZ is greatest over Asia, owing to its large landmass. By contrast, over the Atlantic and Pacific Oceans its movement is far less. Winds at the ITCZ are generally light (the doldrums), occasionally broken by strong westerlies, generally in the summer months.

Low-latitude winds between 10° and 30° are mostly easterlies – that is, they flow towards the west. These are the reliable trade winds; they blow over 30 per cent of the world's surface. The weather in this zone is fairly predictable – warm, dry mornings and showery afternoons, caused by the continuous evaporation from tropical seas. Showers are heavier and more frequent in the warmer summer season.

Occasionally there are disruptions to the pattern; easterly waves are small-scale systems in the easterly flow of air. The flow is greatest not at ground level but at the 700 mb level. Ahead of the easterly wave air is subsiding, hence there is surface divergence. At the easterly wave there is convergence of air, and descent – as in a typical low pressure system. Easterly waves are important for the development of tropical cyclones (pages 282–86).

Westerly winds dominate between 35° and 60° of latitude, which accounts for about a quarter of the world's surface. However unlike the steady trade winds, these contain rapidly evolving and decaying depressions.

The word *monsoon* means 'reverse'; the monsoon is reversing wind systems. For example, the south-east trades from the SH cross the equator in July. Owing to the Coriolis effect these south-east trades are deflected to the right in the northern hemisphere and become south-west winds. The monsoon is induced by Asia – the world's largest continent – which causes winds to blow outwards from high pressure in winter but pulls the southern trades into low pressure in the summer.

The monsoon is therefore influenced by the reversal of land and sea temperatures between Asia and the Pacific during the summer and winter. In winter, surface temperatures in Asia may be as low as –20 °C. By contrast the surrounding oceans have temperatures of 20 °C. During the summer the land heats up quickly and may reach 40 °C. By contrast the sea remains cooler at about 27 °C. This initiates a land/sea breeze blowing from the cooler sea (high pressure) in summer to the warmer land (low pressure), whereas in winter air flows out of the cold landmass (high pressure) to the warm water (low pressure). The presence of the Himalayan Plateau also disrupts the strong winds of the upper atmosphere, forcing winds either to the north or south and consequently deflecting surface winds.

The uneven pattern shown in Figure 2.17 is the result of seasonal variations in the overhead Sun. Summer in the southern hemisphere means that there is a cooling in the northern hemisphere, thereby increasing the differences between polar and equatorial air. Consequently high level westerlies are stronger in the northern hemisphere in winter.

Section 2.2 Activities

Describe the main global wind systems shown in Figure 2.17.

Explaining variations in temperature, pressure and winds

Latitude

On a global scale latitude is the most important factor determining temperature (Figure 2.13). Two factors affect the temperature: the angle of the overhead Sun, and the thickness of the atmosphere. At the equator the overhead Sun is high in the sky, so the insolation received is of a greater quality or intensity. At the poles, the overhead Sun is low in the sky, so the quality of energy received is poor. Secondly, the thickness of the atmosphere affects temperature. Energy has more atmosphere to pass through at A, so more energy is lost, scattered or reflected by the atmosphere than at B – therefore temperatures are lower at A than at B. In addition, the albedo (reflectivity) is higher in polar regions. This is because snow and ice are very reflective, and low-angle sunlight is easily reflected from water surfaces. However, variations in length of day and season partly offset the lack of intensity in polar and arctic regions. The longer the Sun shines the greater the amount of insolation received, which may overcome in part the lack of intensity of insolation in polar regions. (On the other hand, the long polar nights in winter lose vast amounts of energy.)

Specific heat capacity

The specific heat capacity is the amount of heat needed to raise the temperature of a body by 1 °C. There are important differences between the heating and cooling of water. Land heats and cools more quickly than water. It takes five times as much heat to raise the temperature of water by 2 °C as it does to raise land temperatures.

Water heats more slowly because:
- it is clear, so the Sun's rays penetrate to great depth, distributing energy over a wider area
- tides and currents cause the heat to be further distributed.

Therefore a larger volume of water is heated for every unit of energy than of land, so water takes longer to heat up. Distance from the sea has an important influence on temperature. Water takes up heat and gives it back much more slowly than the land. In winter, in mid latitudes sea air is much warmer than the land air, so onshore winds bring heat to the coastal lands. By contrast, during the summer coastal areas remain much cooler than inland sites. Areas with a coastal influence are termed **maritime** or **oceanic** whereas inland areas are called **continental**.

The effect of an ocean current depends upon whether it is a warm current or a cold current. Warm currents move away from the equator, whereas cold currents move towards it. The cold Labrador Current reduces the temperatures of the western side of the Atlantic, while the warm North Atlantic Drift raises temperatures on the eastern side.

Source: Nagle, G., *Geography through diagrams*, OUP, 1998

Figure 2.18 The effects of the North Atlantic Drift/Gulf Stream

Sea currents

Surface ocean currents are caused by the influence of prevailing winds blowing steadily across the sea. The dominant pattern of surface ocean currents (known as gyres) is roughly circular flow. The pattern of these currents is clockwise in the northern hemisphere and anti-clockwise in the southern hemisphere. The main exception is the circumpolar current that flows around Antarctica from west to east. There is no equivalent current in the northern hemisphere because of the distribution of land and sea there. Within the circulation of the gyres water piles up into a dome. The effect of the rotation of the Earth is to cause water in the oceans to push westward; this piles up water on the western edge of ocean basins – rather like water slopping in a bucket. The return flow is often narrow, fast-flowing currents such as the Gulf Stream. The Gulf Stream in particular transports heat northwards and then eastwards across the North Atlantic; the Gulf Stream is the main reason why the British Isles have mild winters and relatively cool summers (Figure 2.18).

The effect of ocean currents on temperatures depends upon whether the current is cold or warm. Warm currents from equatorial regions raise the temperature of polar areas (with the aid of prevailing westerly winds). However, the effect is only noticeable in winter. For example, the North Atlantic Drift raises the winter temperatures of north-west Europe. By contrast, other

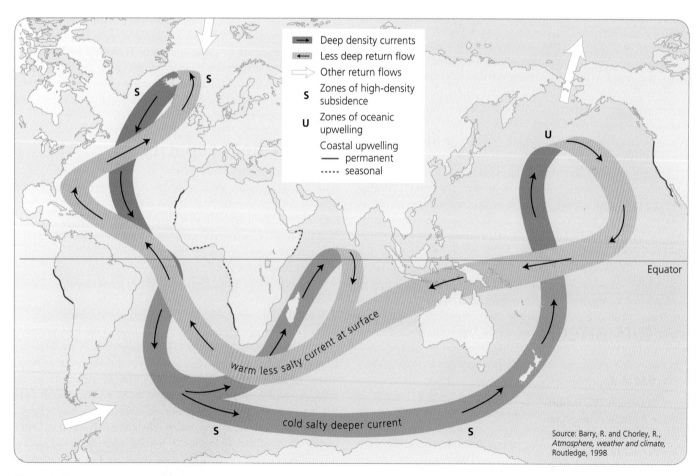

Figure 2.19 The ocean conveyor belt

Source: Barry, R. and Chorley, R., *Atmosphere, weather and climate*, Routledge, 1998 areas are made colder by ocean currents. Cold currents such as the Labrador Current off the north-east coast of North America may reduce summer temperatures, but only if the wind blows from the sea to the land.

In the Pacific Ocean there are two main atmospheric states. The first is warm surface water in the west with cold surface water in the east; the other is warm surface water in the east with cold in the west. In both cases the warm surface causes low pressure. As air blows from high pressure to low pressure there is a movement of water from the colder area to the warmer area. These winds push warm surface water into the warm region, exposing colder deep water behind them and maintaining the pattern.

The ocean conveyor belt

In addition to the transfer of energy by wind and the transfer of energy by ocean currents there is also a transfer of energy by deep sea currents. Oceanic convection movement is from polar regions where cold salty water sinks into the depths and makes its way towards the equator (Figure 2.19). The densest water is found in the Antarctic, where sea water freezes to form ice at a temperature of around about −2 °C. The ice is fresh water, so the sea water that is left behind is much saltier and therefore denser. This cold dense water sweeps around Antarctica at a depth of about 4 km. It then spreads into the deep basins of the Atlantic, the Pacific and the Indian Oceans. In the oceanic conveyor belt model, surface currents bring warm water to the North Atlantic from the Indian and Pacific Oceans. These waters give up their heat to cold winds which blow from Canada across the North Atlantic. This water then sinks and starts the reverse convection of the deep ocean current. The amount of heat given up is about a third of the energy that is received from the Sun. The pattern is maintained by salt: because the conveyor operates in this way, the North Atlantic is warmer than the North Pacific, so there is proportionally more evaporation there. The water left behind by evaporation is saltier and therefore much denser, which causes it to sink. Eventually the water is transported into the Pacific where it picks up more water and its density is reduced.

Section 2.2 Activities

Outline the main factors affecting global and regional temperatures.

Factors affecting air movement

Pressure and wind

Vertical air motion is important on a local scale whereas horizontal motion (wind) is important at many scales, from small-scale eddies to global wind systems. The basic cause of air motion is the unequal heating of the Earth's surface. The major equalising factor is the transfer of heat by air movement. Variable heating of the Earth causes variations in pressure and this in turn sets the air in motion. There is thus a basic correlation between winds and pressure.

Pressure gradient

The driving force is the **pressure gradient** – that is, the difference in pressure between any two points. Air blows from high pressure to low pressure (Figure 2.20). Globally very high pressure conditions exist over Asia in winter due to the low temperatures. Cold air contracts, leaving room for adjacent air to converge at high altitude, adding to the weight and pressure of the air. By contrast the mean sea-level pressure is low over continents in summer. High surface temperatures produce atmospheric expansion and therefore a reduction in air pressure. High pressure dominates at around 25–30° latitude. The highs are centred over the oceans in summer and over the continents in winter – whichever is cooler.

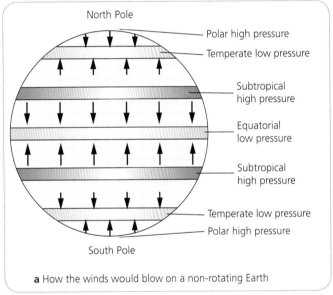

a How the winds would blow on a non-rotating Earth

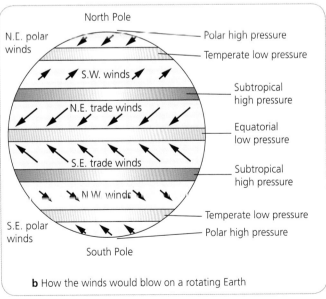

b How the winds would blow on a rotating Earth

Figure 2.20 Pressure gradient winds

The **Coriolis effect** is the deflection of moving objects caused by the easterly rotation of the Earth (Figure 2.21). Air flowing from high pressure to low pressure is deflected to the right of its path in the northern hemisphere and to the left of its path in the southern hemisphere. The Coriolis force is at right angles to wind direction.

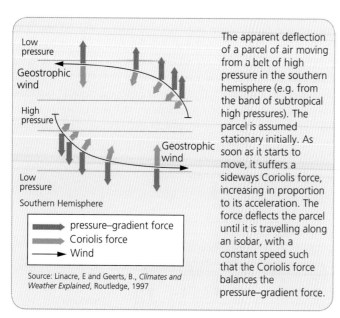

The apparent deflection of a parcel of air moving from a belt of high pressure in the southern hemisphere (e.g. from the band of subtropical high pressures). The parcel is assumed stationary initially. As soon as it starts to move, it suffers a sideways Coriolis force, increasing in proportion to its acceleration. The force deflects the parcel until it is travelling along an isobar, with a constant speed such that the Coriolis force balances the pressure–gradient force.

Source: Linacre, E and Geerts, B., *Climates and Weather Explained*, Routledge, 1997

Figure 2.21 The Coriolis force

Every point on the Earth completes one rotation every 24 hours. Air near the equator travels a much greater distance than air near the poles. Air that originates near the equator is carried towards the poles, taking with it a vast momentum. The Coriolis force deflects moving objects to the right of their path in the northern hemisphere and to the left of their path in the southern hemisphere.

The balance of forces between the pressure gradient force and the Coriolis force is known as the **geostrophic balance** and the resulting wind is known as a **geostrophic wind**. The geostrophic wind in the northern hemisphere blows anti-clockwise around the centre of low pressure and clockwise around the centre of high pressure.

This **centrifugal force** is the outward force experienced when you drive around a corner. The centrifugal force acts at right angles to the wind, pulling objects outwards, so for a given pressure air flow is faster around high pressure (because the Coriolis and centrifugal forces work together rather than in opposite directions).

The drag exerted by the Earth's surface is also important. **Friction** decreases wind speed, so it decreases the Coriolis force, hence areas more likely to flow towards low pressure.

Section 2.2 Activities

Briefly explain the meaning of the terms **a** *pressure gradient force* and **b** *Coriolis force*.

General circulation model

In general:
- warm air is transferred polewards and is replaced by cold air moving towards the equator
- air that rises is associated with low pressure whereas air that sinks is associated with high pressure
- low pressure produces rain, high pressure produces dry conditions.

Any circulation model must take into account the meridional (north/south) transfer of heat, and latitudinal variations in rainfall and winds. (Any model is descriptive and static – unlike the atmosphere.) In 1735 George Hadley described the operation of the Hadley cell, produced by the direct heating over the equator. The air here is forced to rise by convection, travels polewards and then sinks at the subtropical anticyclone (high pressure belt). Hadley suggested that similar cells might exist in mid latitudes and high latitudes. William Ferrel suggested that Hadley cells interlink with a mid latitude cell, rotating it in the reverse direction, and these cells in turn rotate the polar cell.

There are very strong differences between surface and upper winds in tropical latitudes. Easterly winds at the surface are replaced by westerly winds above, especially in winter. At the ITCZ, convectional storms lift air into the atmosphere, which increases air pressure near the tropopause, causing winds to diverge at high altitude. They move out of the equatorial regions towards the poles, gradually losing heat by radiation. As they contract more air moves in and the weight of the air increases the air pressure at the subtropical high pressure zone (Figure 2.22). The denser air sinks, causing subsidence (stability). The north/south component of the Hadley cell is known as a meridional flow.

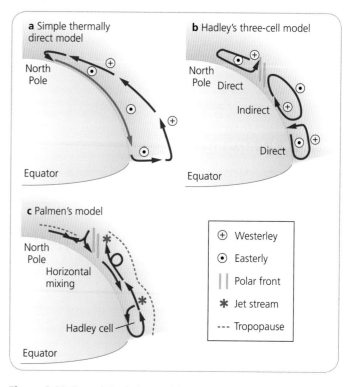

Figure 2.22 General circulation model

The zonal flow (east–west) over the Pacific was discovered by Gilbert Walker in the 1920s. The Southern Oscillation Index (SOI) is a measure of how far temperatures vary from the 'average'. A high SOI is associated with strong westward trades (because winds near the equator blow from high pressure to low pressure and are unaffected by the Coriolis effect). Tropical cyclones are more common in the South Pacific when there is an El Niño Southern Oscillation warm episode.

The polar cell is found in high latitudes. Winds at the highest latitudes are generally easterly. Air over the North Pole continually cools, and being cold it is dense and therefore it subsides, creating high pressure. Air above the polar front flows back to the North Pole, creating a polar cell. In between the Hadley cell and the polar cell is an indirect cell, the Ferrel cell, driven by the movement of the other two cells, rather like a cog in a chain.

In the early twentieth century researchers investigated patterns and mechanisms of upper winds and clouds at an altitude of between 3 and 12 km. They identified large-scale fast-moving belts of westerly winds, which follow a ridge and trough wave-like pattern known as Rossby waves or planetary waves (Figure 2.23). The presence of these winds led to Rossby's 1941 model of the atmosphere. This suggested a three-cell north/south (meridional) circulation with two thermally direct cells and one thermally indirect cell. The thermally direct cell is driven by the heating at the equator (the Hadley cell) and by the sinking of cold air at the poles (the polar cell). Between them lies the thermally indirect cell whose energy is obtained from the cells to either side by the mixing of the atmosphere at upper levels. The jet streams are therefore key locations in the transfer of energy through the atmosphere. Further modifications of Rossby's models were made by Palmen in 1951.

New models change the relative importance of the three convection cells in each hemisphere. These changes are influenced by jet streams and Rossby waves:

- Jet streams are strong, regular winds which blow in the upper atmosphere about 10 km above the surface; they blow between the poles and tropics (100–300 km/h).
- There are two jet streams in each hemisphere – one between 30° and 50°, the other between 20° and 30°. In the northern hemisphere the polar jet flows eastwards, and the subtropical jet flow westwards.
- Rossby waves are 'meandering rivers of air' formed by westerly winds. There are three to six waves in each hemisphere. They are formed by major relief barriers such as the Rockies and the Andes, by thermal differences and uneven land–sea interfaces.
- The jet streams result from differences in equatorial and sub-tropical air, and between polar and sub-tropical air. The greater the temperature difference, the stronger the jet stream.

Rossby waves are affected by major topographic barriers such as the Rockies and the Andes. Mountains create a wave-like pattern, which typically lasts six weeks. As the pattern becomes more exaggerated (Figure 2.23b) it leads to blocking anticyclones (blocking highs) – prolonged periods of unusually warm weather.

Jet streams and Rossby waves are an important means of mixing warm and cold air.

Section 2.2 Activities

1 Describe and explain how the Hadley cell operates.

2 Define the term *Rossby wave*. Suggest how an understanding of Rossby waves may help in our understanding of the general circulation.

Figure 2.23 Rossby waves

2.3 Weather processes and phenomena

Moisture in the atmosphere

Atmospheric moisture exists in all three states – vapour, liquid and solid (Figure 2.24). Energy is used in the change from one phase to another, for example between a liquid and a gas. In evaporation, heat is absorbed. It takes 600 calories of heat to change 1 gramme of water from a liquid to a vapour. Heat loss during evaporation passes into the water as latent heat (of vaporisation). This would cool 1 kg of air by 2.5 °C. By contrast, when condensation occurs, latent heat locked in the water vapour is released, causing a rise in temperature. In the changes between vapour and ice, heat is released when vapour is converted to ice (solid), for example rime at high altitudes and high latitudes. In contrast, heat is absorbed in the process of sublimation, for example when snow patches disappear without melting. When liquid water turns to ice, heat is released and temperatures drop. In contrast, in melting ice heat is absorbed and temperatures rise.

Figure 2.24 Atmospheric moisture – condensation

Factors affecting evaporation

Evaporation occurs when vapour pressure of a water surface exceeds that in the atmosphere. Vapour pressure is the pressure exerted by the water vapour in the atmosphere. The maximum vapour pressure at any temperature occurs when the air is saturated (Figure 2.25). Evaporation aims to equalise the pressures. It depends on three main factors:

- initial humidity of the air – if air is very dry then strong evaporation occurs; if it is saturated then very little occurs
- supply of heat – the hotter the air the more evaporation that takes place
- wind strength – under calm conditions the air becomes saturated rapidly.

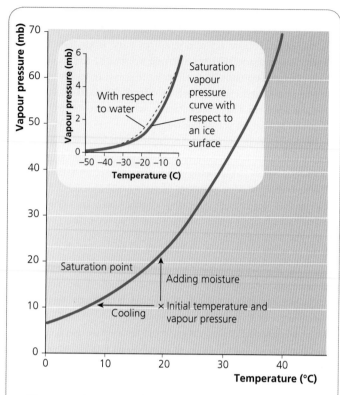

The curves demonstrate how much moisture the air can hold for any temperature. Below 0 °C the curve is slightly different for an ice surface than for a supercooled water droplet.

Source: Briggs et al., *Fundamentals of the physical environment*, Routledge, 1997

Figure 2.25 Maximum vapour pressure

Factors affecting condensation

Condensation occurs when either (a) enough water vapour is evaporated into an air mass for it to become saturated or (b) when the temperature drops so that dew point (the temperature at which air is saturated) is reached. The first is relatively rare, the second common. Such cooling occurs in three main ways:

- radiation cooling of the air
- contact cooling of the air when it rests over a cold surface
- adiabatic (expansive) cooling of air when it rises.

Condensation is very difficult to achieve in pure air. It requires some tiny particle or nucleus onto which the vapour can condense. In the lower atmosphere these are quite common, such as sea salt, dust and pollution particles. Some of these particles are hygroscopic – that is, water-seeking – and condensation may occur when the relative humidity is as low as 80 per cent.

Humidity and precipitation

The properties of *absolute humidity* and *relative humidity* are described on page 27.

The term *precipitation* refers to all forms of deposition of moisture from the atmosphere in either solid or liquid states. It includes rain, hail, snow and dew. Because rain is the most common form of precipitation in many areas, the term is sometimes applied to rainfall alone. For any type of precipitation to form, clouds must first be produced.

When minute droplets of water are condensed from water vapour, they float in the atmosphere as clouds. If droplets coalesce they form large droplets which, when heavy enough to overcome by gravity an ascending current, they fall as rain. Therefore cloud droplets must get much larger to form rain. There are a number of theories to suggest how raindrops are formed.

The Bergeron theory suggests that for rain to form, water and ice must exist in clouds at temperatures below 0 °C. Indeed, the temperature in clouds may be as low as −40 °C. At such temperatures, water droplets and ice droplets form. Ice crystals grow by condensation and become big enough to overcome turbulence and cloud updrafts, so they fall. As they fall, crystals coalesce to form larger snowflakes. These generally melt and become rain as they pass into the warm air layers near the ground. Thus, according to Bergeron, rain comes from clouds that are well below freezing at high altitudes, where the coexistence of water and ice is possible. The snow/ice melts as it passes into clouds at low altitude where the temperatures are above freezing level.

Other mechanisms must also exist as rain also comes from clouds that are not so cold. Mechanisms include:
- condensation on extra-large hygroscopic nuclei
- coalescence by sweeping, whereby a falling droplet sweeps up others in its path
- the growth of droplets by electrical attraction.

Adiabatic processes (lapse rates)

Adiabatic processes are those that relate to the rising and sinking of air. This means that the temperature of the air is changed internally, without any other influence. It is the rising (expanding and cooling) and sinking (contracting and warming) of air that causes it to change temperature. As air rises in the atmosphere it is cooled and there may be condensation. Air may rise for four reasons:
- convection (caused by the heating of the ground below)
- orographic barriers (air forced to rise over hills or mountains)
- turbulence (in the air flow)
- at frontal systems.

When air rises from one elevation to another, the temperature changes. The decrease of pressure with height allows the rising parcel of air to expand. As it expands it uses up energy from within the air parcel (since air is a poor conductor of heat it will not gain any heat from the surrounding atmosphere). Likewise, when air is sinking it gains heat by contraction. Therefore adiabatic heating and cooling is an internal mechanism without any heat exchange. By contrast, diabatic processes involve the physical mixing of air. Normal or **environmental lapse rate** (ELR) is the actual temperature decline with height, on average 6 °C/km.

Adiabatic cooling and warming in dry (unsaturated) air occurs at a rate of approximately 10 °C/km. This is known as the **dry adiabatic lapse rate** (**DALR**). Air in which condensation is

occurring cools at the lower **saturated adiabatic lapse rate** (**SALR**) of between 4 °C and 9 °C/km. This is because latent heat released in the condensation process partly offsets the temperature loss from cooling. The rate varies according to the amount of latent heat released. It will be less for warm saturated (4 °C/km) air than cold saturated air (9 °C/ km). For example, an air mass of 27 °C may contain so much water vapour, and therefore release so much latent heat, that the SALR may be as low as 4 °C/km. In a very cold air mass, on the other hand, there may be so little water vapour that very little latent heat is released and so the SALR differs very little from the DALR. However, an average of 5 °C/km is generally accepted for the SALR.

Lapse rates can be shown on a temperature/height diagram (Figure 2.26). For example, an air temperature of 20 °C may have a dew point of 10 °C. At first when the air is lifted it cools at the DALR. When it reaches dew point (the temperature at which air is saturated and condensation occurs), it cools at the SALR. Saturation level is the same as the condensation level. This marks the base of the cloud. Air continues to rise at the SALR until it reaches the same temperature and density as the surrounding air. This marks the top of the cloud development. Thus the changes in lapse rates can be used to show the lower and upper levels of cloud development in a cumulus cloud (see Figure 2.5).

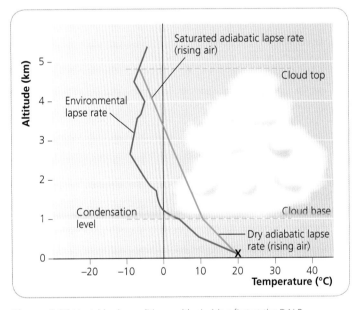

Figure 2.26 Unstable air conditions, with air rising first at the DALR and then at the SALR. Ascent ceases when the rising air has the same temperature and density as the surrounding air.

A very noticeable effect of adiabatic processes is the föhn effect, in the European Alps (Figure 2.27). Winds approach the mountains as very warm moist air streams, rise, quickly reach condensation level, and therefore are cooling at the SALR. At the summit, most moisture is already lost. Hence, on descent, winds warm up at the DALR. They reach the plains/valleys as hot winds with low relative humidity, and can have a drastic effect by clearing snow very rapidly.

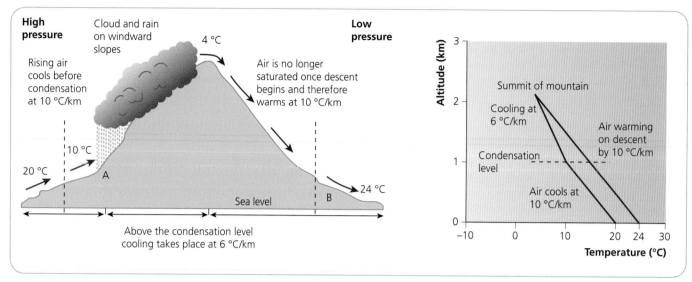

Figure 2.27 Air flow on a mountain – the fohn effect

Atmospheric stability and instability

Air stability and instability refers to the buoyancy characteristics of air:

- **Instability** – instability occurs when a parcel of air is warmer and therefore less dense than the air above, causing rising and expansion. There is uplift and adiabatic cooling of moist air. This is the result of instability and is the main cause of precipitation. Air is unstable if the ELR is greater than the DALR, as on Figure 2.28. If a parcel of air is lifted, it rises at the DALR and immediately becomes warmer and lighter than its surroundings. It therefore continues to rise. Unstable air

tends to occur on very hot days when the ground layers are heated considerably. If the air is moist enough, there will be strong vertical cloud development.

- **Stability** – stable air conditions (stability) exist when the ELR is greater than the DALR and the SALR. If a parcel of air is displaced upwards, it immediately gets cooler and denser and sinks (Figure 2.29). Uplift cannot be sustained. Conditions in an anticyclone (high pressure) with subsiding air are usually stable. The only time when stable air can rise is when it is forced upwards, such as over high ground.

- **Conditional instability** – when the ELR lies between the SALR and DALR, moist saturated air will rise whereas dry unsaturated air will sink. Air is therefore stable in respect to the dry rate and would normally sink to its original level. But if air should then become saturated because it is forced to rise to higher elevations, it may become warmer than the surrounding air and would continue to rise of its own accord. Thus the air is unstable, if it is saturated.

Figure 2.28 Instability

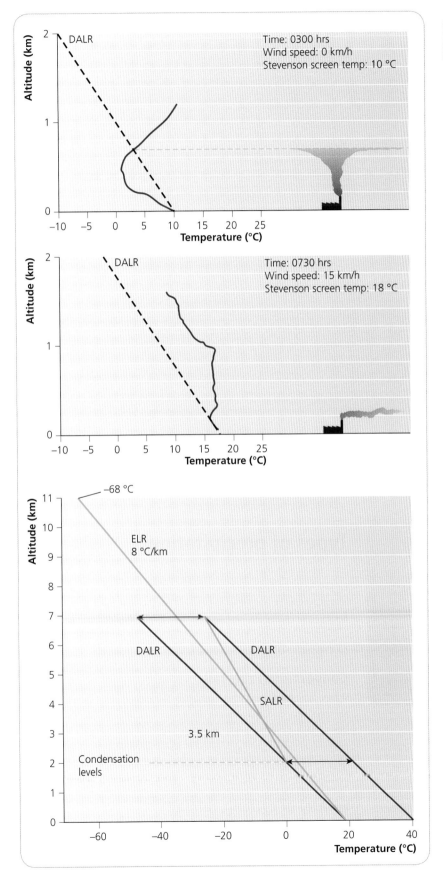

Weather phenomena

A fundamental distinction can be made between atmospheric stability and instability, and associated weather phenomena. Stability (or stable conditions) means that air does not rise. On a global scale it produces the great high pressure belts such as those in the subtropical high pressure belt. On a local scale stability can lead to the formation of fog, mist and frost. Under clear skies, temperatures may drop enough to form frost. Where there is moisture present, the cooling of air at night may be sufficient to produce mist and fog. Instability, on the other hand, produces unstable or rising air. This produces clouds and is the mechanism for the formation of rain. So cloud formation, and the formation of rain and snow, is dependent on there being unstable air (instability) causing the rising of air and subsequent condensation.

Clouds

Clouds are formed of millions of tiny water droplets held in suspension. They are classified in a number of ways, the most important being:

- form or shape, such as stratiform (layers) and cumuliform (heaped type)
- height, such as low (<2000 m), medium or alto (2000–7000 m) and high (7000–13 000 m).

There are a number of different types of clouds (Figure 2.30). High clouds consist mostly of ice crystals. Cirrus are wispy clouds, and include cirrocumulus (mackerel sky) and cirrostratus (halo effect around Sun or Moon). Alto or middle-height clouds generally consist of water drops. They exist at temperatures lower than 0 °C. Low clouds indicate poor weather. Stratus clouds are dense, grey and low-lying (Figure 2.31). Nimbostratus are those that produce rain (*nimbus* means 'storm'). Stratocumulus are long cloud rolls, and a mixture of stratus and cumulus (see Figure 2.5).

Vertical development suggests upward movement. Cumulus clouds are flat-bottomed and heaped. They indicate bright brisk weather. Cumulonimbus clouds produce heavy rainfall and often thunderstorms.

Figure 2.29 Stability and conditional instability

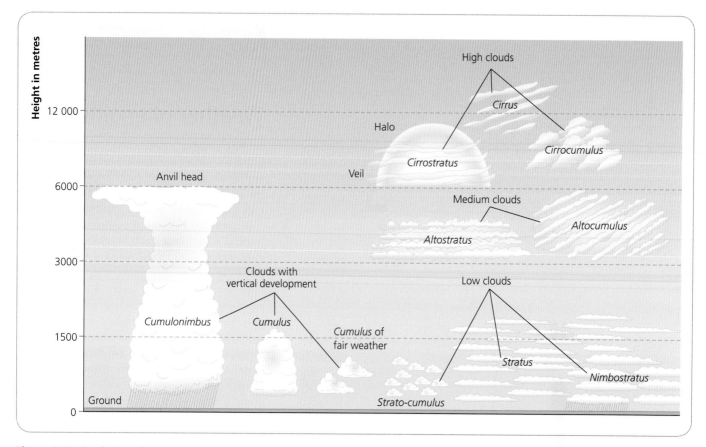

Figure 2.30 Classification of clouds

Figure 2.31 Stratus clouds

The important facts to keep in mind:
- In unstable conditions the dominant form of uplift is convection and this may cause cumulus clouds.
- With stable conditions stratiform clouds generally occur.
- Where fronts are involved a variety of clouds exist.
- Relief or topography causes stratiform or cumuliform clouds, depending on the stability of the air.

Banner clouds

These are formed by orographic uplift (that is, air forced to rise, over a mountain for example) under stable air conditions. Uplifted moist air streams reach condensation only at the very summit, and form a small cloud. Further downwind the air sinks, and the cloud disappears. Wave clouds reflect the influence of the topography on the flow of air.

Types of precipitation

The Bergeron theory relates mostly to snow making. **Snow** is a single flake of frozen water. Rain and drizzle are found when the temperature is above 0 °C (drizzle has a diameter of < 0.5 mm). **Sleet** is partially melted snow.

There are three main types of rainfall – convectional, frontal (depressional) and orographic (relief) (Figure 2.32).

Convectional rainfall

When the land becomes very hot it heats the air above it. This air expands and rises. As it rises, cooling and condensation take place. If it continues to rise rain will fall. It is very common in tropical areas (Figure 2.33) and is associated with the permanence of the ITCZ (see page 34). In temperate areas, convectional rain is more common in summer.

Frontal or cyclonic rainfall

Frontal rain occurs when warm air meets cold air. The warm air, being lighter and less dense, is forced to rise over the cold, denser air. As it rises it cools, condenses and forms rain. It is most common in middle and high latitudes where warm tropical air and cold polar air converge.

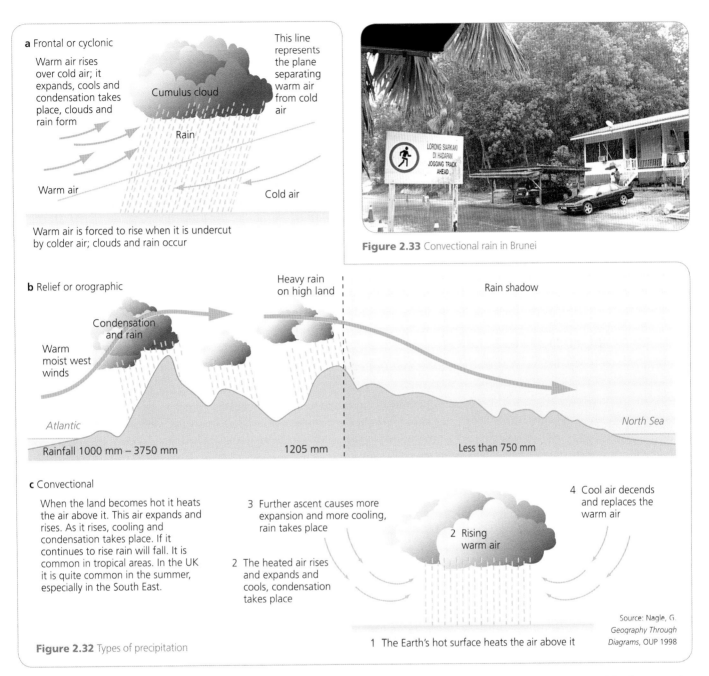

a Frontal or cyclonic

Warm air rises over cold air; it expands, cools and condensation takes place, clouds and rain form

Cumulus cloud

This line represents the plane separating warm air from cold air

Rain

Warm air

Cold air

Warm air is forced to rise when it is undercut by colder air; clouds and rain occur

Figure 2.33 Convectional rain in Brunei

b Relief or orographic

Heavy rain on high land

Rain shadow

Condensation and rain

Warm moist west winds

Atlantic

North Sea

Rainfall 1000 mm – 3750 mm

1205 mm

Less than 750 mm

c Convectional

When the land becomes hot it heats the air above it. This air expands and rises. As it rises, cooling and condensation takes place. If it continues to rise rain will fall. It is common in tropical areas. In the UK it is quite common in the summer, especially in the South East.

3 Further ascent causes more expansion and more cooling, rain takes place

2 The heated air rises and expands and cools, condensation takes place

2 Rising warm air

4 Cool air decends and replaces the warm air

1 The Earth's hot surface heats the air above it

Source: Nagle, G. *Geography Through Diagrams*, OUP 1998

Figure 2.32 Types of precipitation

Relief or orographic rainfall

Air may be forced to rise over a barrier such as a mountain. As it rises it cools, condenses and forms rain. There is often a rainshadow effect whereby the leeward slope receives a relatively small amount of rain. Altitude is important, especially on a local scale. In general, there are increases of precipitation up to about 2 km. Above this level rainfall decreases because the air temperature is so low.

Hail

Hail is alternate concentric rings of clear and opaque ice, formed by raindrops being carried up and down in vertical air currents in large cumulonimbus clouds. Freezing and partial melting may occur several times before the pellet is large enough to escape from the cloud. As the raindrops are carried high up in the cumulonimbus cloud they freeze. The hailstones may collide with droplets of supercooled water, which freeze on impact with and form a layer of opaque ice around the hailstone. As the hailstone falls, the outer layer may be melted but may freeze again with further uplift. The process can occur many times before the hail finally falls to ground, when its weight is great enough to overcome the strong updraughts of air.

Section 2.3 Activities

Using diagrams, explain the meaning of the terms **a** *convectional rainfall*, **b** *orographic rainfall* and **c** *frontal rainfall*.

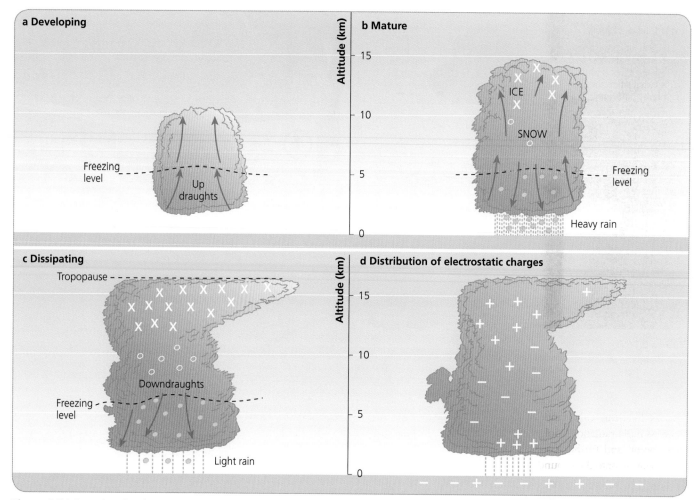

Figure 2.34 Stages in a thunderstorm

Thunderstorms

These are special cases of rapid cloud formation and heavy precipitation in unstable air conditions. Absolute or conditional instability exists to great heights causing strong updraughts to develop within cumulonimbus clouds. Thunderstorms are especially common in tropical and warm areas where air can hold large amounts of water. They are rare in polar areas.

Several stages can be identified (Figure 2.34):

1. Developing stage: updraught caused by uplift; energy (latent heat) is released as condensation occurs; air becomes very unstable; rainfall occurs as cloud temperature is greater than 0 °C; the great strength of uplift prevents snow and ice from falling.

2. Mature stage: sudden onset of heavy rain and maybe thunder and lightning; rainfall drags cold air down with it; upper parts of the cloud may reach the tropopause; the cloud spreads, giving the characteristic anvil shape.

3. Dissipating stage: downdraughts prevent any further convective instability; the new cells may be initiated by the meeting of cold downdraughts from cells some distance apart, triggering the rise of warm air in between.

Lightning occurs to relieve the tension between different charged areas, for example between cloud and ground or within the cloud itself. The upper parts of the cloud are positive whereas the lower parts are negative. The very base of the cloud is positively charged. The origin of the charges is not very clear, although they are thought to be due to condensation and evaporation. Lightning heats the air to very high temperatures. Rapid expansion and vibration of the column produces thunder.

Snow

Snow is frozen precipitation. Snow crystals form when the temperature is below freezing and water vapour is converted into a solid. However, very cold air contains a limited amount of moisture, so the heaviest snowfalls tend to occur when warm moist air is forced over very high mountains or when warm moist air comes into contact with very cold air at a front.

Frost

Frost is a deposit of fine ice crystals on the ground or on vegetation (Figure 2.35). It occurs on cloud-free nights when there has been radiation cooling to below freezing point. Water vapour condenses directly onto these surfaces by sublimation. Black ice is a solid sheet of ice found on a road, and is caused by raindrops falling through a layer close to the surface with below freezing temperatures. On vegetation it is called glazed frost.

Figure 2.35 Frost – here ice crystals have lifted some soil and a small pebble

Dew

Dew is the direct deposition of water droplets onto a surface. It occurs in clear, calm anticyclonic conditions (stability) where there is rapid radiation cooling by night. The temperature reaches dew point, and further cooling causes condensation and direct precipitation onto the ground and vegetation (Figure 2.36).

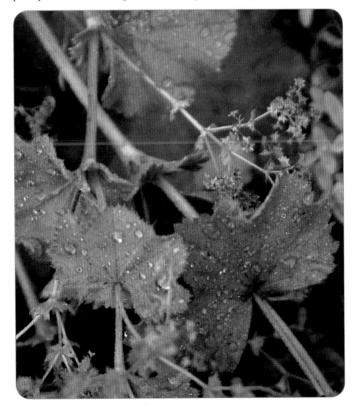

Figure 2.36 Dew – direct condensation onto vegetation

Fog

Fog is cloud at ground level. **Radiation fog** (Figure 2.37) is formed in low-lying areas during calm weather, especially during spring and autumn. The surface of the ground, cooled rapidly at night by radiation, cools the air immediately above it. This air then flows into hollows by gravity and is cooled to **dew point** (the temperature at which condensation occurs). Ideal conditions include a surface layer of moist air and clear skies, which allow rapid **radiation cooling**.

The decrease in temperature of the lower layers of the air causes air to go below the dew point. With fairly light winds, the fog forms close to the water surface, but with stronger turbulence the condensed layer may be uplifted to form a low stratus sheet.

Figure 2.37 Fog in the Wicklow mountains, Ireland

As the Sun rises, radiation fog disperses. Under cold anti-cyclonic conditions in late autumn and winter, fog may be thicker and more persistent, and around large towns smog may develop under an inversion layer. An inversion means that cold air is found at ground level whereas warm air is above it – unlike the normal conditions in which air temperature declines with height. In industrial area emissions of sulphur dioxide act as condensation nuclei and allow fog to form. Along motorways the heavy concentration of vehicle emissions does the same. By contrast, in coastal areas the higher minimum temperatures means that condensation during high pressure conditions is less likely.

Fog commonly occurs over the sea in Autumn and Spring because the contrast in temperature between land and sea is significant. Warm air from over the sea is cooled when it moves on land during anticyclonic conditions. In summer, the sea is cooler than the land so air is not cooled when it blows onto the land. By contrast, in winter there are more low pressure systems, causing higher winds and mixing the air.

Fog is more common in anticyclonic conditions. Anticyclones are stable high pressure systems characterised by clear skies and low wind speeds. Clear skies allows maximum cooling by night. Air is rapidly cooled to dew point, condensation occurs and fog is formed.

Advection fog is formed when warm moist air flows horizontally over a cooler land or sea surface. **Steam fog** is very localised. Cold air blows over much warmer water. Evaporation from the water quickly saturates the air and the resulting condensation leads to steaming. It occurs when very cold polar air meets the surrounding relatively warm water.

Section 2.3 Activities

1 Distinguish between *radiation fog* and *advection fog*.

2 Under which atmospheric conditions (stability or instability) do mist and fog form? Briefly explain how fog is formed.

3 Under which atmospheric conditions do thunder and lightning form? Briefly explain how thunder is created.

2.4 The human impact

Global warming

The role of greenhouse gases

Greenhouse gases are essential for life on Earth. The Moon is an airless planet which is almost the same distance from the Sun as is the Earth. Average temperatures on the Moon are about –18 °C compared with about 15 °C on Earth. The Earth's atmosphere therefore raises temperatures by about 33 °C. This is due to the greenhouse gases – such as water vapour, carbon dioxide, methane, ozone, nitrous oxides and chlorofluorocarbons (CFCs). They are called greenhouse gases because, as in a greenhouse, they allow short-wave radiation from the Sun to pass through them, but they trap outgoing long-wave radiation, thereby raising

the temperature of the lower atmosphere (Figure 2.38). The greenhouse effect is both natural and good – without it there would be no human life on Earth. On the other hand, there are concerns about the enhanced greenhouse effect.

The enhanced greenhouse effect is built up of certain greenhouse gases as a result of human activity. **Carbon dioxide** (CO_2) levels have risen from about 315 ppm in 1950 to 355 ppm and are expected to reach 600 ppm by 2050. The increase is due to human activities – burning fossil fuels (coal, oil and natural gas) and deforestation. Deforestation of the tropical rainforest is a double blow – not only does it increase atmospheric CO_2 levels, it also removes the trees that convert CO_2 into oxygen.

Methane is the second largest contributor to global warming, and is increasing at a rate of between 0.5 and 2 per cent per annum. Cattle alone give off between 65 and 85 million tonnes of methane per year. Natural wetland and paddy fields are another important source – paddy fields emit up to 150 million tonnes of

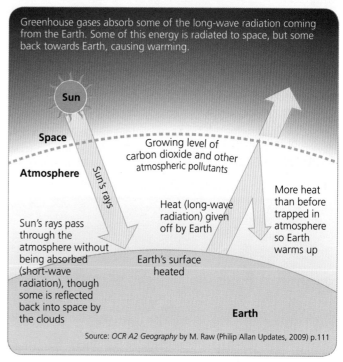

Greenhouse gases absorb some of the long-wave radiation coming from the Earth. Some of this energy is radiated to space, but some back towards Earth, causing warming.

Source: *OCR A2 Geography* by M. Raw (Philip Allan Updates, 2009) p.111

Figure 2.38 The greenhouse effect

Table 2.2 Properties of key greenhouse gases

	Average atmospheric concentration (ppmv)	Rate of change (% per annum)	Direct global warming potential (GWP)	Lifetime (years)	Type of indirect effect
Carbon dioxide	355	0.5	1	120	None
Methane	1.72	0.6–0.75	11	10.5	Positive
Nitrous oxide	0.31	0.2–0.3	270	132	Uncertain
CFC-11	0.000255	4	3400	55	Negative
CFC-12	0.000453	4	7100	116	Negative
CO				Months	Positive
NO$_x$					Uncertain

methane annually. As global warming increases, bogs trapped in permafrost will melt and release vast quantities of methane. **Chlorofluorocarbons** (CFCs) are synthetic chemicals that destroy ozone, as well as absorb long-wave radiation. CFCs are increasing at a rate of 6 per cent per annum, and are up to 10 000 times more efficient at trapping heat than CO_2.

As long as the amount of water vapour and carbon dioxide stay the same and the amount of solar energy remains the same, the temperature of the Earth should remain in equilibrium. However, human activities are upsetting the natural balance by increasing the amount of carbon dioxide in the atmosphere, as well as the other greenhouse gases.

How human activities add to greenhouse gases

Much of the evidence for the greenhouse effect has been taken from ice cores dating back 160 000 years. These show that the Earth's temperature closely paralleled the levels of CO_2 and methane in the atmosphere. Calculations indicate that changes in these greenhouse gases were part, but not all, of the reason for the large (5°–7°) global temperature swings between ice ages and interglacial periods.

Accurate measurements of the levels of CO_2 in the atmosphere began in 1957 in Hawaii. The site chosen was far away from major sources of industrial pollution and shows a good representation of unpolluted atmosphere. The trend in CO_2 levels shows a clear annual pattern, associated with seasonal changes in vegetation, especially those over northern hemisphere. By the 1970s there was a second trend, one of a long-term increase in CO_2 levels, superimposed upon the annual trends.

Studies of cores taken from ice packs in Antarctica and Greenland show that the level of CO_2 between 10 000 years ago and the mid-nineteenth century was stable at about 270 ppm. By 1957 the concentration of CO_2 in the atmosphere was 315 ppm and it has since risen to about 360 ppm. Most of the extra CO_2 has come from the burning of fossil fuels, especially coal, although some of the increase may be due to the disruption of the rainforests. For every tonne of carbon burned, 4 tonnes of CO_2 are released.

By the early 1980s 5 gigatonnes (5000 million tonnes, or 5 Gt) of fuel were burned every year. Roughly half the CO_2 produced is absorbed by natural sinks, such as vegetation and plankton.

Other factors have the potential to affect climate, too. For example, a change in the albedo (reflectivity of the land brought about by desertification or deforestation) affects the amount of solar energy absorbed at the Earth's surface. Aerosols made from sulphur, emitted largely in fossil fuel combustion, can modify clouds and may act to lower temperatures. Changes in ozone in the stratosphere due to CFCs may also influence climate.

Since the Industrial Revolution the combustion of fossil fuels and deforestation have led to an increase in 26 per cent of CO_2 concentration in the atmosphere (Figure 2.39). Emissions of CFCs used as aerosol propellants, solvents, refrigerants and foam blowing agents are also well know. They were not present in the atmosphere before their invention in the 1930s. The sources of methane and nitrous oxides are less well known. Methane concentrations have more than doubled because of rice production, cattle rearing, biomass burning, coal mining and ventilation of natural gas. Also fossil fuel combustion may have also contributed through chemical reactions in the atmosphere which reduce the rate of removal of methane. Nitrous oxide has increased by about 8 per cent since preindustrial times, presumably due to human activities. The effect of ozone on climate is strongest in the upper troposphere and lower stratosphere.

- The increasing carbon dioxide in the atmosphere since the pre-industrial era, from about 280 to 382 ppmv (parts per million by volume), makes the largest individual contribution to greenhouse gas radiative forcing 1.56 W/m^2 (watts per square metre).
- The increase of methane (CH_4) since pre-industrial times (from 0.7 to 1.7 ppmv) contributes about 0.5 W/m^2.
- The increase in nitrous oxide (NO_x) since pre-industrial times from about 275 to 310 ppbv[3] contributes about 0.1 W/m^2.
- The observed concentrations of halocarbons, including CFCs, have resulted in direct radiative forcing of about 0.3 W/m^2.

Figure 2.39 Changes in greenhouse gases since pre-industrial times

Arguments surrounding global warming

There are many causes of global warming and climate change. Natural causes include:
- variations in the Earth's orbit around the Sun
- variations in the tilt of the Earth's axis
- changes in the aspect of the poles from towards the Sun to away from it
- variations in solar output (sunspot activity)
- changes in the amount of dust in the atmosphere (partly due to volcanic activity)
- changes in the Earth's ocean currents as a result of continental drift.

All of these have helped cause climate change, and may still be doing so, despite anthropogenic forces.

Complexity of the problem

Climate change is a very complex issue for a number of reasons:
- Scale – it includes the atmosphere, oceans, and landmasses across the world.
- Interactions between these three areas are complex.
- It includes natural as well as anthropogenic forces.
- There are feedback mechanisms involved, not all of which are fully understood.
- Many of the processes are long-term and so the impact of changes may not yet have occurred.

Figure 2.40 The effects of global warming

The effects of increased global temperature change

The effects of global warming are varied (see Table 2.3). Much depends on the scale of the changes. For example, some impacts could include:

- a rise in sea levels, causing flooding in low-lying areas such as the Netherlands, Egypt and Bangladesh – up to 200 million people could be displaced
- 200 million people at risk of being driven from their homes by flood or drought by 2050
- 4 million km² of land – home to one-twentieth of the world's population – threatened by floods from melting glaciers
- an increase in storm activity such as more frequent and intense hurricanes (owing to more atmospheric energy)
- changes in agricultural patterns, for example a decline in the USA's grain belt, but an increase in Canada's growing season

Table 2.3 Some potential effects of a changing climate in the UK

Positive effects	Negative effects
• An increase in timber yields (up to 25% by 2050) especially in the north (with perhaps some decrease in the south).	• Increased damage effects of increased storminess, flooding and erosion on natural and human resources and human resource assets in coastal areas.
• A northward shift of farming zones by about 200–300 km per °C of warming, or 50–80 km per decade, will improve some forms of agriculture, especially pastoral farming in the north-west.	• An increase in animal species, especially insects, as a result of northward migration from the continent and a small decrease in the number of plant species due to the loss of northern and montane (mountain types).
• Enhanced potential for tourism and recreation as a result of increased temperatures and reduced precipitation in the summer, especially in the south.	• An increase in soil drought, soil erosion and the shrinkage of clay soils.

- reduced rainfall over the USA, southern Europe and the Commonwealth of Independent States (CIS) (Figure 2.40)
- 4 billion people could suffer from water shortages if temperatures rise by 2 °C
- a 35 per cent drop in crop yields across Africa and the Middle East expected if temperatures rise by 3 °C
- 200 million more people could be exposed to hunger if world temperatures rise by 2 °C, 550 million if temperatures rise by 3 °C
- 60 million more Africans could be exposed to malaria if world temperatures rise by 2 °C
- extinction of up to 40 per cent of species of wildlife if temperatures rose by 2 °C.

The Stern Review

The Stern Review (2006) was a report by Sir Nicholas Stern analysing the financial implications of climate change. The report has a simple message:

- Climate change is fundamentally altering the planet.
- The risks of inaction are high.
- Time is running out.

The effects of climate change vary with the degree of temperature change (Figure 2.41). The Report states that climate change poses a threat to the world economy and it will be cheaper to address the problem than to deal with the consequences. The global warming argument seemed a straight fight between the scientific case to act, and the economic case not to. Now, economists are urging action.

The Stern Review says doing nothing about climate change – the business-as-usual (BAU) approach – would lead to a reduction in global per capita consumption of at least 5 per cent now and for ever. According to the Stern Review, global warming could deliver an economic blow of between 5 and 20 per cent of GDP to world economies because of natural disasters and the creation of hundreds of millions of climate refugees displaced by sea-level rise. Dealing with the problem, by comparison, will cost just 1 per cent of GDP, equivalent to £184 billion.

Figure 2.41 Projected impacts of climate change, according to the Stern Review

Main points

- Carbon emissions have already increased global temperatures by more than 0.5 °C.
- With no action to cut greenhouse gases, we will warm the planet by another 2–3 °C within 50 years.
- Temperature rise will transform the physical geography of the planet and the way we live.
- Floods, disease, storms and water shortages will become more frequent.
- The poorest countries will suffer the earliest and the most.
- The effects of climate change could cost the world between 5 and 20 per cent of GDP.
- Action to reduce greenhouse gas emissions and the worst of global warming would cost 1 per cent of GDP.
- With no action, each tonne of carbon dioxide we emit will cause at least $85 (£45) of damage.
- Levels of carbon dioxide in the atmosphere should be limited to the equivalent of 450–550 ppm.
- Action should include carbon pricing, new technology and robust international agreements.

International policy to protect climate

The first world conference on climate change was held in Geneva in 1979. The Toronto Conference of 1988 called for the reduction of carbon dioxide emissions by 20 per cent of the 1988 levels by 2005. Also in 1988, UNEP and the World Meteorological Organisation established the Intergovernmental Panel on Climate Change (IPCC).

'The ultimate objective is to achieve ... stabilisation of greenhouse gas concentrations in the atmosphere at a level that would prevent dangerous anthropogenic interference with the climate system.'

The Kyoto Protocol (1997) gave all MEDCs legally binding targets for cuts in emissions from the 1990 level by 2008–12. The EU agreed to cut emissions by 8 per cent, Japan 7 per cent and the USA by 6 per cent.

Section 2.4 Activities

1 Figure 2.41 shows some of the projected impacts related to global warming.

   a Describe the potential changes as a result of a 3 °C rise in temperature.

   b Explain why there is an increased risk of hazards in coastal cities.

   c Outline the ways in which it is possible to manage the impacts of global warming.

   d Evaluate the potential impacts of global warming.

2 Figure 2.42 shows variations in mean air temperature between 1880 and 2000.

   a i Identify the reason why the temperature in the early 1960s fell below 15 °C.

     ii Describe the impact of Pinatubo on global climate in the 1990s.

   b Outline the natural sources of greenhouse gases.

   c Using an annotated diagram, explain what is meant by the term *the greenhouse effect*.

   d Outline the benefits of the greenhouse effect.

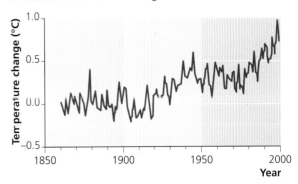

Figure 2.42 Variations in mean air temperature between 1880 and 2000

Urban climates

Urban climates occur as a result of extra sources of heat released from industry, commercial and residential buildings as well as from vehicles, concrete, glass, bricks, tarmac – all of these act very differently from soil and vegetation. For example, the albedo (reflectivity) of tarmac is about 5–10 per cent while that of concrete is 17–27 per cent. In contrast, that of grass is 20–30 per cent. Some of these – notably dark bricks – absorb large quantities of heat and release them slowly by night (Figure 2.43). In addition, the release of pollutants helps trap radiation in urban areas. Consequently, urban microclimates can be very different from rural ones. Greater amounts of dust mean an increasing concentration of hygroscopic particles. There is less water vapour, but more carbon dioxide and higher proportions of noxious fumes owing to combustion of imported fuels. Discharge of waste gases by industry is also increased.

Urban heat budgets differ from rural ones. By day the major source of heat is solar energy, and in urban areas brick, concrete and stone have high heat capacities. A kilometre of an urban area contains a greater surface area than a kilometre of countryside, and the greater number of surfaces in urban areas allow a greater area to be heated. There are more heat-retaining materials with lower albedo and better radiation-absorbing properties in urban areas than in rural ones.

In urban areas there is relative lack of moisture. This is due to:
- a lack of vegetation
- a high drainage density (sewers and drains) which removes water.

Thus there are decreases in relative humidity in inner cities due to the lack of available moisture and higher temperatures there. However, this is partly countered in very cold, stable conditions by early onset of condensation in low-lying districts and industrial zones.

Nevertheless, there are more intense storms, particularly during hot summer evenings and nights, owing to greater instability and stronger convection above built-up areas. There is a higher incidence of thunder (due to more heating and instability) but less snowfall (due to higher temperatures), and any snow that does fall tends to melt rapidly.

Figure 2.43 Processes in the urban heat island

Figure 2.44 The urban heat island (Chester, UK)

There is greater scattering of shorter-wave radiation by dust, but much higher absorption of longer waves owing to the surfaces and to carbon dioxide. Hence there is more diffuse radiation, with considerable local contrasts owing to variable screening by tall buildings in shaded narrow streets. There is reduced visibility arising from industrial haze.

There is a higher incidence of thicker cloud cover in summer because of increased convection, and radiation fogs or smogs in winter because of air pollution. The concentration of hygroscopic particles accelerates the onset of condensation. Daytime temperatures are, on average, 0.6 °C higher.

The contrast between urban and rural areas is greatest under calm high pressure conditions. The typical heat profile of an urban heat island shows a maximum at the city centre, a plateau across the suburbs and a temperature cliff between the suburban and rural areas (Figure 2.44). Small-scale variations within the urban heat island occur with the distribution of industries, open spaces, rivers, canals and so on.

The heat island is a feature that is delimited by isotherms (lines of equal temperature), normally in an urban area. This shows that the urban area is warmer than the surrounding rural area, especially by dawn during anticyclonic conditions (Figure 2.45). The heat island effect is caused by a number of factors:

- heat produced by human activity: a low level of radiant heat can be up to 50 per cent of incoming energy in winter
- changes of energy balance: buildings have a high thermal capacity in comparison to rural areas – up to six times greater than agricultural land
- the effect on air flow: turbulence of air may be reduced overall, although buildings may cause funnelling effects

Hence little energy is used for evapotranspiration, so more is available to heat the atmosphere. This is in addition to the man-made sources of heating such as industries, cars, and people.

At night the ground radiates heat and cools. In urban areas the release of heat by buildings offsets the cooling process, and some industries, commercial activities and transport networks continue to release heat throughout the night.

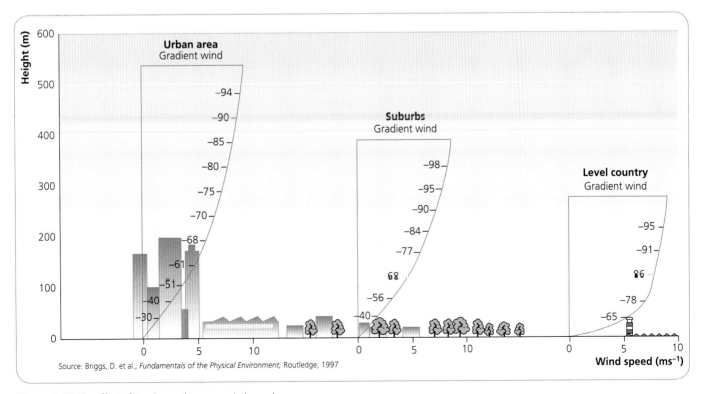

Figure 2.45 The effect of terrain roughness on wind speed

- there are fewer bodies of open water, so less evaporation and fewer plants, therefore less transpiration
- the composition of the atmosphere: the blanketing effect of smog, smoke or haze.
- reduction in thermal energy required for evaporation and evapotranspiration due to the surface character, rapid drainage, and generally lower wind speeds
- reduction of heat diffusion due to changes in airflow patterns as a result of urban surface roughness.

Air flow over an urban area is disrupted, winds are slow and deflected over buildings (Figure 2.45). Large buildings can produce eddying. Severe gusting and turbulence around tall buildings causes strong local pressure gradients from windward to leeward walls. Deep narrow streets are much calmer unless they are aligned with prevailing winds to funnel flows along them – the 'canyon effect'.

The nature of urban climates is changing (Table 2.4). With the decline in coal as a source of energy there is less sulphur dioxide pollution and so fewer hygroscopic nuclei, there is therefore less fog. However, the increase in cloud cover has occurred for a number of reasons:

- greater heating of the air (rising air, hence condensation)
- increase in pollutants
- frictional and turbulent effective air flow
- changes in moisture.

Table 2.4 Average changes in climate caused by urbanisation

Factor		Comparison with rural environments
Radiation	Global	2–10% less
	Ultraviolet, winter	30% less
	Ultraviolet, summer	5% less
	Sunshine duration	5–15% less
Temperature	Annual mean	1 °C more
	Sunshine days	2–6 °C more
	Greatest difference at night	11 °C more
	Winter maximum	1.5 °C more
	Frost free season	2–3 weeks more
Wind speed	Annual mean	10–20% less
	Gusts	10–20% less
	Calms	5–20% more
Relative humidity	Winter	2% less
	Summer	8–10% less
Precipitation	Total	5–30% more
	Number of rain days	10% more
	Snow days	14% less
Cloudiness	Cover	5–10% more
	Fog, winter	100% more
	Fog, summer	30% more
	Condensation nuclei	10 times more
	Gases	5–25 times more

Source: J. Tivy, *Agricultural Ecology*, Longman 1990 p.372

Section 2.4 Activities

1 Describe and account for the main differences in the climates of urban areas and their surrounding rural areas.

2 What is meant by the *urban heat island*?

3 Describe **one** effect that atmospheric pollution may have on urban climates.

4 Explain how buildings, tarmac and concrete can affect the climate in urban areas.

5 Why are microclimates, such as urban heat islands, best observed during high pressure (anticyclonic) weather conditions?

3 Rocks and weathering

3.1 Elementary plate tectonics

The Earth's interior

The theory of plate tectonics states that the Earth is made up of a number of layers (Figure 3.1). On the outside there is a very thin crust, and underneath is a mantle that makes up 82 per cent of the volume of the Earth. Deeper still is a very dense and very hot core. In general these concentric layers become increasingly

Table 3.1 A comparison of oceanic crust and continental crust

Examples	Continental crust	Oceanic crust
Thickness	35 to 70 km on average	6 to 10 km on average
Age of rocks	Very old, mainly over 1500 million years	Very young, mainly under 200 million years
Colour and density of rocks	Lighter with an average density of 2.6; light in colour	Heavier with an average density of 3.0; dark in colour
Nature of rocks	Numerous types – many contain silica and oxygen, granitic is the most common	Few types, mainly basaltic

Figure 3.1 The Earth's internal structure

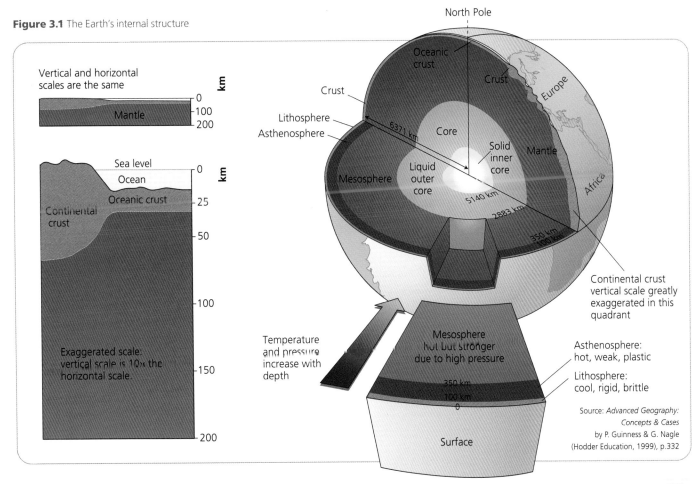

Source: *Advanced Geography: Concepts & Cases* by P. Guinness & G. Nagle (Hodder Education, 1999), p.332

more dense towards the centre. The density of these layers is controlled by temperature and pressure. Temperature softens or melts rocks.

Close to the surface rocks are mainly solid and brittle. This upper surface layer is known as the **lithosphere**, which includes the **crust** and the upper **mantle**, and is about 70 km deep. The Earth's crust is commonly divided up into two main types: **continental crust** and **oceanic crust** (Table 3.1). In continental areas silica and aluminium are very common. When combined with oxygen they make up the most common type of rock, granitic. By contrast, below the oceans the crust consists mainly of basaltic rock in which silica, iron and magnesium are most common.

The evidence for plate tectonics

In 1912 Alfred Wegener proposed the idea of continental drift. Others, such as Francis Bacon in 1620, had commented on how the shape of the coast of Africa was similar to that of South America. Wegener proposed that the continents were slowly drifting about the Earth. He suggested that, starting in the Carboniferous period some 250 million years ago, a large single continent, Pangaea, broke up and began to drift apart, forming the continents we

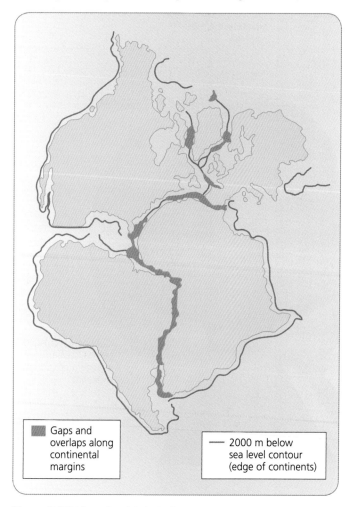

Gaps and overlaps along continental margins

— 2000 m below sea level contour (edge of continents)

Figure 3.2 Evidence for plate tectonics

know today. Wegener's theory provoked widespread debate initially, but with the lack of a mechanism to cause continental drift, his theory failed to receive widespread support.

In the mid-twentieth century the American Harry Hess suggested that convection currents would force molten rock (magma) to well up in the interior and to crack the crust above and force it apart. In the 1960s research on rock magnetism supported Hess. The rocks of the Mid Atlantic Ridge were magnetised in alternate directions in a series of identical bands on both sides of the ridge. This suggested that fresh magma had come up through the centre and forced the rocks apart. In addition, with increasing distance from the ridge the rocks were older. This supported the idea that new rocks were being created at the centre of the ridge and the older rocks were being pushed apart.

In 1965 a Canadian geologist J. Wilson linked together the ideas of continental drift and seafloor spreading into a concept of mobile belts and rigid plates, which formed the basis of plate tectonics.

The evidence of plate tectonics includes:
- the past and present distribution of earthquakes
- changes in the Earth's magnetic field
- the 'fit' of the continents: in 1620 Francis Bacon noted how the continents on either side of the Atlantic could be fitted together like a jigsaw (Figure 3.2)
- glacial deposits in Brazil match those in West Africa
- the fossil remains in India match those of Australia
- the geological sequence of sedimentary and igneous rocks in parts of Scotland match those found in Newfoundland
- ancient mountains can be traced from east Brazil to west Africa, and from Scandinavia through Scotland to Newfoundland and the Appalachians (eastern USA)
- fossil remains of a small aquatic reptile, Mesosaurus, which lived about 270 million years ago, are found only in a restricted part of Brazil and in south-west Africa. It is believed to be a poor swimmer!

Plate boundaries

The zone of earthquakes around the world has helped to define six major plates and a number of minor plates (Figures 3.3 and 3.4). The boundaries between plates can be divided into three main types: spreading plates, colliding plates and conservative plates. Spreading ridges where new crust is formed are mostly in the middle of oceans (Figure 3.5a). These ridges are zones of shallow earthquakes (less than 50 km below the surface). Where two plates converge, the deep-sea trench may be formed and one of the plates is **subducted** (forced downwards) into the mantle. In these areas fold mountains are formed and chains of island arcs may be formed (Figure 3.5b). Deep earthquakes, up to 700 km below the surface, are common. Good examples include the trenches off the Andes and the Aleutian Islands that stretch out from Alaska. If a thick continental plate collides with an ocean plate a deep trench develops. The partial melting of the descending ocean plate causes volcanoes to form in an arc-shaped chain of islands, such as in the Caribbean.

Figure 3.3 Thingvellir, Iceland

Source: *Advanced Geography: Concepts & Cases* by P. Guinness & G. Nagle (Hodder Education, 1999), p.334

Figure 3.4 Plate boundaries

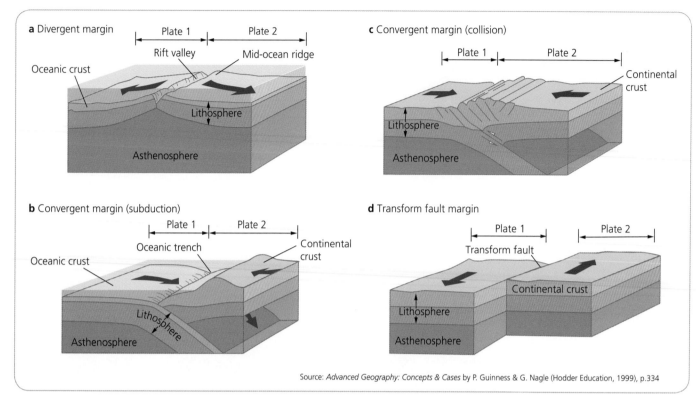

Source: *Advanced Geography: Concepts & Cases* by P. Guinness & G. Nagle (Hodder Education, 1999), p.334

Figure 3.5 Types of plate boundary

Along some plate boundaries plates slide past one another to create a transform fault (fault zone) without colliding or separating (Figure 3.5c). Again these are associated with shallow earthquakes, such as the San Andreas Fault in California. Where continents embedded in the plates collide with each other there is no subduction but crushing and folding may create young fold mountains such as the Himalayas and the Andes (Figure 3.5d).

The movement of plates

There are three main theories about movement.

1 The convection current theory – this states that huge convection currents occur in the Earth's interior. Magma rises through the core to the surface and then spreads out at mid-ocean ridges. The cause of the movement is radioactive decay in the core.

2 The dragging theory – plates are dragged or subducted by their oldest edge which have become cold and heavy. Plates are hot at the mid ocean ridge but cool as they move away. Complete cooling takes about a million years. As cold plates descend at the trenches, pressure causes the rock to change and become heavier.

3 A hotspot is a plume of lava which rises vertically through the mantle. Most are found near plate margins and they may be responsible for the original rifting of the crust. However, the world's most abundant source of lava, the Hawaiian Hotspot, is not on the plate margin. Hotspots can cause movement – the outward flow of viscous rock from the centre may create a drag force on the plates and cause them to move.

Section 3.1 Activities

1 Briefly outline the evidence for plate tectonics.

2 What is a convection current? How does it help explain the theory of plate tectonics?

3 What happens at **a** a mid-ocean ridge and **b** a subduction zone?

Sea-floor spreading

It was not until the early 1960s that R.S. Dietz and H.H. Hess proposed the mechanism of sea-floor spreading to explain continental drift. They suggested that continents moved in response to the growth of oceanic crust between them. Oceanic crust is thus created from the mantle at the crest of the mid-ocean ridge system.

Confirmation of the hypothesis of sea-floor spreading came with the discovery by F.J. Vine and D.H. Matthews that magnetic anomalies across the Mid-Atlantic Ridge were symmetrical on either side of the ridge axis (Figure 3.6). The only acceptable explanation for these magnetic anomalies was in terms of sea-floor spreading and the creation of new oceanic crust. When lava cools on the sea floor, magnetic grains in the rock acquire the direction of the Earth's magnetic field at the time of cooling. This is known as paleomagnetism.

Figure 3.6 Sea-floor spreading and paleomagnetism

The anomalies found across the Mid-Atlantic Ridge could, moreover, be matched with similar anomalies that had been discovered in Iceland and other parts of the world where young volcanic rocks could be dated.

The reason why the ridges are elevated above the ocean floor is that they consist of rock that is hotter and less dense than the older, colder plate. Hot mantle material wells up beneath the ridges to fill the gap created by the separating plates; as this material rises it is decompressed and undergoes partial melting.

Spreading rates are not the same throughout the mid-ocean ridge system but vary considerably from a few millimetres per year in the Gulf of Aden to 1 cm per year in the North Atlantic near Iceland and 6 cm per year for the East Pacific Rise. This variation in spreading rates appears to influence the ridge topography. Slow-spreading ridges, such as the Mid-Atlantic Ridge, have a pronounced rift down the centre. Fast-spreading ridges, such as the East Pacific Rise, lack the central rift and have a smooth topography. In addition, spreading rates have not remained constant through time.

The main reason for the differences in spreading rates is that the slow-spreading ridges are fed by small and discontinuous magma chambers, thereby allowing for the eruption of a comparatively wide range of basalt types. Fast-spreading ridges have large, continuous magma chambers that generate comparatively similar magmas. Because of the higher rates of magma discharge, sheet lavas are more common.

Although mid-ocean ridges appear at first sight to be continuous features within the oceans, they are all broken into segments by transverse fractures (faults) that displace the ridges by tens or even hundreds of kilometres. Fractures are narrow, linear features that are marked by near-vertical fault planes.

Section 3.1 Activities

Briefly explain what is meant by **a** *paleomagnetism* and **b** *sea-floor spreading*.

Mid-ocean ridges

The longest linear, uplifted features of the Earth's surface are to be found in the oceans. They are giant submarine mountain chains with a total length of more than 60 000 km, they are between 1000 and 4000 km wide, and have crests that rise 2–3 km above the surrounding ocean basins, which are 5 km deep. The average depth of water over their crests is thus about 2500 m. These features are the mid-ocean ridges, famous now not only for their spectacular topography, but because it was with them, in the early 1960s, that the theory of ocean-floor spreading, the precursor of plate tectonic theory, began. We now know that it is at these mid-ocean ridges that new lithosphere is created.

Similar ridges occur at the margins of oceans; the East Pacific Rise is an example. There are other spreading ridges behind the volcanic arcs of subduction zones. These are usually termed *back-arc spreading centres*. The first ridge to be discovered, the Mid-Atlantic Ridge, was found during attempts to lay a submarine cable across the Atlantic in the mid-nineteenth century.

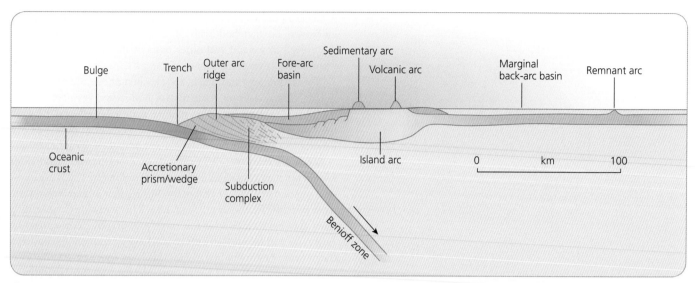

Figure 3.7 Ocean–ocean subduction zone

Subduction zones

Subduction zones form where an oceanic lithospheric plate collides with another plate – whether **continental** or **oceanic** (Figure 3.7). The density of the oceanic plate is similar to that of the **aesthenosphere**, so it can be easily pushed down into the upper mantle. Subducted (lithospheric) oceanic crust remains cooler, and therefore denser than the surrounding mantle, for millions of years, so once initiated subduction carries on, driven, in part, by the weight of the subducting crust. As the Earth has not grown significantly in size – not enough to accommodate the new crustal material created at mid-ocean ridges – the amount of subduction roughly balances the amount of production at the constructive plate margins.

Subduction zones dip mostly at angles between 30° and 70°, but individual subduction zones dip more steeply with depth. The dip of the slab is related inversely to the velocity of convergence at the trench, and is a function of the time since the initiation of subduction. The older the crust the steeper it dips. Because the downgoing slab of lithosphere is heavier than the plastic aesthenosphere below, it tends to sink passively; and the older the lithosphere, the steeper the dip.

The evidence for subduction is varied:
- the existence of certain landforms such as deep-sea trenches and folded sediments – normally arc-shaped and containing volcanoes
- the Benioff zone – a narrow zone of earthquakes dipping away from the deep-sea trench
- the distribution of temperature at depth – the oceanic slab is surrounded by higher temperatures.

At the subduction zone, deep-sea **trenches** are found. Deep-sea trenches are long, narrow depressions in the ocean floor with depths from 6000 m to 11 000 m. Trenches are found adjacent to land areas and associated with island arcs worldwide. They are more numerous in the Pacific Ocean. The trench is usually asymmetric, with the steep side towards the landmass. Where a

trench occurs off a continental margin, the turbidites (sediments) from the slope are trapped, forming a hadal plain on the floor of the trench.

Benioff zone

A large number of events take place on a plane that dips on average at an angle of about 45° away from the underthrusting oceanic plate. The plane is known as the Benioff (or Benioff-Wadati) zone, after its discoverer(s), and earthquakes on it extend from the surface, at the trench, down to a maximum depth of about 680 km. For example, shallow, intermediate and deep-focus earthquakes in the south-western Pacific occur at progressively greater distances away from the site of underthrusting at the Tonga Trench.

> **Section 3.1 Activities**
>
> Describe the main characteristics of **a** mid-ocean ridges and **b** subduction zones.

Island arcs

Island arc systems are formed when oceanic lithosphere is subducted beneath oceanic lithosphere. They are consequently typical of the margins of shrinking oceans such as the Pacific, where the majority of island arcs are located. They also occur in the western Atlantic, where the Lesser Antilles (Caribbean) and Scotia arcs are formed at the eastern margins of small oceanic plates. The Lesser Antilles (Eastern Caribbean) Arc shows all the features of a typical island arc. Ocean–ocean subduction zones tend to be simpler than ocean–continental subduction zones. In a typical ocean–ocean subduction zone there are a number of characteristic features (Figure 3.8):

Figure 3.8 Island arcs in the Caribbean

Volcanic activity, Montserrat

- Ahead of the subduction zone there is a low bulge on the sea floor (known as the **trench outer rise**) caused by the bending of the plate as it subducts. One of the most well-known features is the trench which marks the boundary between the two plates. In the Eastern Caribbean, the trench associated with the subduction zone is largely filled with sediment from the Orinoco River. These sediments, more than 20 km thick, have been deformed and folded into the Barbados Ridge, which emerges above the sea at Barbados.
- The **outer slope** of the trench is generally gentle, but broken by faults as the plate bends. The floor of the trench is often flat and covered by sediment (turbidites) and ash. The trench **inner slope** is steeper and contains fragments of the subducting plate, scraped off like shavings from a carpenter's plane. The **subduction complex** (also known as **accretionary prisms**) is the slice of the descending slab and may form significant landforms – for example in the Lesser Antilles, the islands of Trinidad, Tobago and Barbados are actually the top of the subduction complex.
- Most subduction zones contain an **island arc**, located parallel to a trench on the overriding plate. Typically they are found some 150–200 km from the trench. Volcanic island arcs such as those in the Caribbean, including the islands from Grenada to St Kitts, are island arcs above sea level.

Section 3.1 Activities

1 Describe the main features of an island arc system.

2 Briefly explain how island arcs are formed.

Mountain building

Plate tectonics is associated with mountain building. Linear or arcuate chains – sometimes called orogenic mountain belts – are associated with convergent plate boundaries, and formed on land. Where an ocean plate meets a continental plate, the lighter, less dense continental plate may be folded and buckled into fold mountains, such as the Andes. Where two continental plates meet, both may be folded and buckled, as in the case of the Himalayas, formed by the collision of the Eurasian and Indian plates. Mountain building is often associated with crustal thickening, deformation and volcanic activity, although in the case of the Himalayas, volcanic activity is relatively unimportant.

The Indian subcontinent moved rapidly north during the last 70 million years, eventually colliding with the main body of Asia. A huge ocean (Tethys) has been entirely lost between these continental masses. Figure 3.9a shows the situation just prior to the elimination of the Tethys Ocean by subduction beneath Asia. Note the volcanic arc on the Asian continent (rather like the Andes today).

In Figure 3.9b the Tethys Ocean has *just* closed. The leading edge of the Indian subcontinent and the sedimentary rocks of its continental shelf have been thrust beneath the edge of the Asian continent.

Finally, in Figure 3.9c the Indian subcontinent continues to move north-eastward relative to the rest of Asia. In the collision zone the continental crust is thickened because Asia overrides India, and it is this crustal thickening that results in the uplift of the Himalayan mountain range. The red lines show the many locations in the collision zone where thrust faults are active to accommodate the deformation and crustal thickening.

Figure 3.9 Formation of the Himalayas

Figure 3.10 Fold mountains

In contrast the Andes were formed as a result of the subduction of oceanic crust under continental crust. The Andes are the highest mountain range in the Americas with 49 peaks over 6000 m high. Unlike the Himalayas, the Andes contains many active volcanoes.

Before about 250 million years ago, the western margin of South America was a passive continental margin. Sediments accumulated on the continental shelf and slope. With the break-up of Pangaea, the South American plate moved westward, and eastward-moving oceanic lithosphere began subducting beneath the continent.

As subduction continued, rocks of the continental margin and trench were folded and faulted and became part of an accretionary wedge along the west coast of South America (Figure 3.10). Subduction also resulted in partial melting of the descending plate, producing andesitic volcanoes at the edge of the continent.

The Andes Mountains comprise a central core of granitic rocks capped by andesitic volcanoes. To the west of this central core along the coast are the deformed rocks of the accretionary wedge. And to the east of the central core are sedimentary rocks that have been intensely folded. Present-day subduction, volcanism and seismicity indicate that the Andes Mountains are still actively forming.

Section 3.1 Activities

Compare and contrast the formation of the Andes and the formation of the Himalayas.

3.2 Weathering and rocks

Weathering is the **decomposition** and **disintegration** of rocks *in situ*. Decomposition refers to chemical weathering and creates altered rock substances, such as kaolinite (china clay) from granite. By contrast, disintegration or mechanical weathering produces smaller, angular fragments of the same rock, such as scree. A third type, **biological** weathering, has been identified, whereby plants and animals chemically alter rocks and physically break rocks through their growth and movement. Biological weathering is not a separate type of weathering, but a form of disintegration and decomposition. It is important to note that these processes are **interrelated** rather than operating in isolation.

Weathering is central to landscape evolution, as it breaks down rock and enables erosion and transport. A number of key features can be recognised:

- Many minerals are formed under high pressure and high temperatures in the Earth's core. As they cool they become more stable.
- Weathering produces irreversible changes in a rock. Some rocks change from a solid state to a fragmented or **clastic** state, such as scree. Others are changed to a pliable or **plastic** state, such as clay.
- Weathering causes changes in volume, density, grain size, surface area, permeability, consolidation and strength.
- Weathering forms new minerals and solutions.
- Some minerals such as quartz may resist weathering.
- Minerals and salts may be removed, transported, concentrated or consolidated.
- Weathering prepares rocks for subsequent erosion and transport.
- New landforms and features are produced.

Mechanical/physical weathering

There are four main types of mechanical weathering: freeze–thaw (ice crystal growth), salt crystal growth, disintegration and pressure release. Mechanical weathering operates at or near the Earth's surface, where temperature changes are most frequent.

Freeze–thaw (also called ice crystal growth or frost shattering) occurs when water in joints and cracks freezes at 0 °C. It expands by about 10 per cent and exerts pressure up to a maximum of 2100 kg/cm^2 at −22 °C. These pressures greatly exceed most rocks' resistance (Table 3.2). However, the average pressure reached in freeze–thaw is only 14kg/cm^2.

Freeze–thaw is most effective in environments where moisture is plentiful and there are frequent fluctuations above and below freezing point. Hence it is most effective in periglacial and alpine regions. Freeze–thaw is most rapid when it operates in connection with other processes, notably pressure release and salt crystallisation.

Salt crystallisation causes the decomposition of rock by solutions of salt. There are two main types of **salt crystal growth**. First, in areas where temperatures fluctuate around 26–28 °C sodium sulphate (Na_2SO_4) and sodium carbonate (Na_2CO_3) expand by about 300 per cent. This creates pressure on joints, forcing them to crack. Second, when water evaporates, salt crystals may be left behind. As the temperature rises, the salts expand and exert pressure on rock. Both mechanisms are frequent in hot desert regions where low rainfall and high temperatures cause salts to accumulate just below the surface. It may also occur in polar areas when salts are deposited from snowflakes.

Experiments investigating the effectiveness of saturated salt solutions have shown a number of results.

1. The most effective salts are sodium sulphate, magnesium sulphate and calcium chloride.
2. Chalk decomposes fastest, followed by limestone, sandstone and shale.
3. The rate of disintegration of rocks is closely related to porosity and permeability.
4. Surface texture and grain size control the rate of rock breakdown. This diminishes with time for fine materials and increases over time for coarse materials.
5. Salt crystallisation is more effective than insolation weathering, hydration, or freeze–thaw. However, a combination of freeze–thaw and salt crystallisation produces the highest rates of breakdown.

Disintegration is found in hot desert areas where there is a large diurnal temperature range. In many desert areas daytime temperatures exceed 40 °C whereas night-time ones are little above freezing. Rocks heat up by day and contract by night. As rock is a poor conductor of heat, stresses occur only in the outer layers. This causes peeling or **exfoliation** to occur. Griggs (1936) showed that moisture is essential for this to happen. In the absence of moisture, temperature change alone did not cause the rocks to break down. The role of salt in insolation weathering has also been studied. The expansion of many salts such as sodium, calcium, potassium and magnesium has been linked with the exfoliation. However, some geographers find little evidence to support this view.

Pressure release is the process whereby overlying rocks are removed by erosion. This causes underlying rocks to expand and fracture parallel to the surface. The removal of a great weight, such as a glacier, has the same effect. Rocks are formed at very high pressure in confined spaces in the Earth's interior. The **unloading** of pressure by the removal of overlying rocks causes cracks or joints to form at right-angles to the unloading surface. These cracks are lines of weakness within the rock. For example, if overlying pressure is released, horizontal **pseudo-bedding planes** will be formed. By contrast, if horizontal pressure is released, as on a cliff face, vertical joints will develop. The size and spacing of cracks varies with distance from the surface: with

Table 3.2 Resistance to weathering

Rock	Resistance (kg/cm²)
Marble	100
Granite	70
Limestone	35
Sandstone	7–14

increasing depth the cracks become smaller and further apart. Hence the part of the rock that is broken the most is the part that is most subjected to denudation processes, namely at the surface.

Chemical weathering

Water is the key medium for chemical weathering. Unlike mechanical weathering, chemical weathering is most effective sub-surface since percolating water has gained organic acids from the soil and vegetation. Acidic water helps to break down rocks such as chalk, limestone and granite. The amount of water is important as it removes weathered products by solution. Most weathering therefore takes place above the water table since weathered material accumulates in the water and saturates it. There are four main types of chemical weathering: carbonation-solution, hydrolysis, hydration and oxidation.

Carbonation-solution occurs on rocks with calcium carbonate, such as chalk and limestone. Rainfall combines with dissolved carbon dioxide or organic acid to form a weak carbonic acid.

$$CO_2 + H_2O \leftrightarrow H_2CO_3 \text{ (carbonic acid)}$$

Calcium carbonate (calcite) reacts with an acid water and forms **calcium bicarbonate** (also termed calcium hydrogen carbonate), which is soluble and removed by percolating water:

$$CaCO_3 + H_2CO_3 \rightarrow Ca(HCO_3)_2$$
calcite + carbonic acid → calcium bicarbonate

The effectiveness of solution is related to the pH of the water. For example, iron is highly soluble when the pH is 4.5 or less, and alumina (Al_2O_3) is highly soluble below 4.0 or above 9.0 but not in between.

Hydrolysis occurs on rocks with orthoclase feldspar, notably granite. Feldspar reacts with acid water and forms **kaolin** (also termed kaolinite or china clay), silicic acid and potassium hydroxyl:

$$2KAlSi_3O_8 + 2 H_2O \rightarrow Al_2Si_2O_5 (OH)_4 + K_2O + 4 SiO_2$$

orthoclase feldspar + water → kaolinite + potassium hydroxyl + silicic acid

The acid and hydroxyl are removed in the solution leaving **kaolin** behind as the end product. Other minerals in the granite, such as quartz and mica, remain in the kaolin. Hydrolysis also involves solution as the potassium hydroxyl is carbonated and removed in solution.

Hydration is the process whereby certain minerals absorb water, expand and change. For example, anhydrite is changed to gypsum. Although it is often classified as a type of chemical weathering, mechanical stresses occur as well. When anhydrite ($CaSO_4$) absorbs water to become gypsum ($CaSO_4.2H_2O$) it expands by about 0.5 per cent. More extreme is the increase in volume of up to 1600 per cent by shales and mudstones when clay minerals absorb water.

Oxidation occurs when iron compounds react with oxygen to produce a reddish-brown coating. Dissolved oxygen in the soil or the atmosphere affects iron minerals. Oxidation is most common in areas that are well drained. FeO is oxidised to Fe_2O_3. This is soluble only under extreme acidity (pH < 3.0). Hence it remains in soils and accounts for the red colour in many rocks and soils, especially in tropical areas. By contrast, **reduction** of ferric iron to ferrous iron allows iron oxides to be removed from solution. This typically occurs in waterlogged, marshy areas and forms blue-grey clays associated with anaerobic (oxygen deficient) conditions.

Controls of weathering

Climate

In the simplest terms, the type and rate of weathering vary with climate (Figure 3.11). But it is very difficult to isolate the exact relationship, at any scale, between climate type and rate of process. Peltier's diagrams (1950) show how weathering is related to moisture availability and average annual temperature

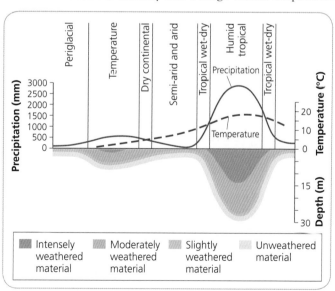

Figure 3.11 Depth of weathering profile and climate

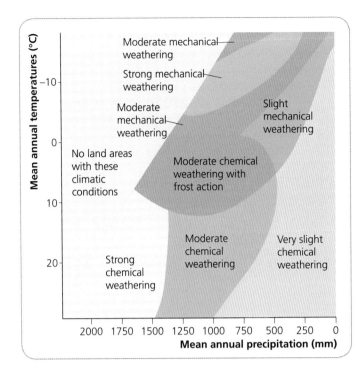

Figure 3.12 Peltier's diagram showing variations of chemical and mechanical weathering with climate

to a maximum temperature of 60 °C). The efficiency of freeze–thaw, salt crystallisation and insolation weathering is influenced by:

- critical temperature changes
- frequency of cycles
- diurnal and seasonal variations in temperature.

Geology

Rock type and rock structure influence the rate and type of weathering in many ways due to:

- chemical composition
- the nature of cements in sedimentary rock
- joints and bedding planes.

For example, limestone consists of calcium carbonate and is therefore susceptible to carbonation-solution. By contrast granite is prone to hydrolysis because of the presence of feldspar. In sedimentary rocks, the nature of the cement is crucial. Iron-oxide based cements are prone to oxidation whereas quartz cements are very resistant. The effect of rock structure varies from large-scale folding and faulting to localised patterns of joints and bedding planes. Joint patterns exert a strong control on water movement. These act as lines of weakness thereby creating **differential resistance** within the same rock type. Similarly, grain size influences the speed with which rocks weather. Coarse-grained rocks weather quickly owing to a large void space and high permeability (Table 3.4). On the other hand, fine-grained rocks offer a greater surface area for weathering and may be highly susceptible to weathering. The importance of individual minerals was stressed by Goldich in 1938. Rocks formed of resistant minerals, such as quartz, muscovite and feldspar in granite, will

(Figure 3.12; see also Table 3.3). In general, frost-shattering increases as the number of freeze–thaw cycles increases. By contrast, chemical weathering increases with moisture and heat. According to **Van't Hoff's Law**, the rate of chemical weathering increases 2–3 times for every increase of temperature of 10 °C (up

Table 3.3 Generalised weathering characteristics in four climatic regions

Climatic region	Characteristics	Examples – rates of weathering (mm yr^{-1})
Glacial/ Periglacial	Frost very important. Susceptibility to frost increases with increasing grain size. *Taiga*: fairly high soil leaching, low rates organic matter decomposition. *Tundra*: low precipitation, low temperatures, permafrost – moist conditions, slow organic production and breakdown. May have slower chemical weathering. Algal, fungal, bacterial weathering may occur. Granular disintegration occurs. Hydrolytic action reduced on sandstone, quartzite, clay, calcareous shales, phyllites, dolerites. Hydration weathering common due to high moisture.	Narvik 0.001 Spitzbergen 0.02–0.2 Alaska 0.04
Temperate	Precipitation and evaporation generally fluctuate. Both mechanical weathering and chemical weathering occur. Iron oxides leached and redeposited. Carbonates deposited in drier areas, leached in wetter areas. Increased precipitation, lower temperatures, reduced evaporation. Organic content moderate to high, breakdown moderate. Silicate clays formed and altered. *Deciduous* forest areas: abundant bases, high nutrient status, biological activity moderate to high. *Coniferous areas*: acidic, low biological activity, leaching common.	Askrigg 0.5–1.6 Austria 0.015–0.04
Arid/ semi-arid	Evaporation exceeds precipitation. Rainfall low. Temperatures high, seasonal. Organic content low. Mechanical weathering, salt weathering, granular disintegration, dominant in driest areas. Thermal effects possible. Low organic input relative to decomposition. Slight leaching produces $CaCO_3$ in soil. Sulphates and chlorides may accumulate in driest areas. Increased precipitation and decreased evaporation toward semi-arid areas and steppes yield thick organic layers, moderate leaching and $CaCO_3$ accumulation.	Egypt 0.0001–2.0 Australia 0.6–1.0
Humid tropical	High rainfall often seasonal. Long periods of high temperatures. Moisture availability high. Weathering products (a) removed or (b) accumulate to yield red and black clay soils, ferruginous and aluminous soils (lateritic), calcium-rich soils. Calcareous rocks generally heavily leached where silica content is high, soluble weathering products removed and parent silica in stable products are sandy. Where products remain, iron and aluminium are common. Usually intense deep weathering, iron and alumina oxides and hydroxides predominate. Organic content high but decomposition high.	Florida 0.005

resist weathering (Figure 3.13). By contrast, rocks formed of weaker minerals will weather rapidly. The interrelationship of geology and climate on the development of landforms is well illustrated by limestone and granite.

Table 3.4 Average porosity and permeability for common rock types

Rock type	Porosity (%)	Relative permeability
Granite	1	1
Basalt	1	1
Shale	18	5
Sandstone	18	500
Limestone	10	30
Clay	45	10
Silt	40	–
Sand	35	1 100
Gravel	25	10 000

Source: D. Brunsden, 'Weathering processes' in C. Embleton and J. Thornes (eds) *Processes in Geomorphology*, Edward Arnold 1979

Stability	Dark-coloured minerals	Light-coloured minerals	Susceptibility
Least stable	Olivine		Least susceptible
		Lime plagioclase	
	Augite		
		Lime soda plagioclase	
	Hornblende	Soda lime plagioclase	
	Olivine	Soda plagioclase	
	Biotite		
Most stable	Orthoclase	Muscovite Quartz	Most susceptible

Figure 3.13 Goldich's weathering system

Section 3.2 Activities

1 a Define the terms *porosity* and *permeability*.
  b Choose a suitable method to show the relationship between porosity and permeability.
  c Describe the relationship between porosity and permeability.
  d What are the exceptions, if there are any, to this relationship?

2 Describe and explain how the type and intensity of mechanical weathering varies with climate.

3 Describe and explain how the type and intensity of chemical weathering varies with climate.

4 How useful are mean annual temperature and mean annual rainfall as a means of explaining variations in the type and intensity of weathering processes?

5 How do **a** evaporation and **b** leaf fall affect the type and rate of weathering?

Limestone scenery

Limestone scenery is unique on account of its:
- permeability
- solubility in rain and groundwater.

Variations exist between the different types of limestone on account of their hardness, chemical composition, jointing and bedding planes.

Limestone consists mainly of calcium carbonate ($CaCO_3$) and is known as a calcareous or base-rich rock. It is formed of the remains of organic matter, notably plants and shells. Owing to its permeability, limestone areas are often dry on the surface and are known as karst areas (from the Yugoslav *krs* meaning dry). Karst features are best developed on carboniferous limestone on account of its greater strength, and its lower porosity and permeability compared with other limestones.

Carboniferous limestone has a distinctive bedding plane and joint pattern, described as being **massively jointed**. These joints act as weaknesses allowing water to percolate into the rock and to dissolve it. One of the main processes to affect limestone is carbonation-solution. The process is reversible, so under certain conditions calcium carbonate can be deposited in the form of **speleothems** (cave deposits such as stalactites and stalagmites) and **tufa** (calcium deposits around springs). Limestone is also affected by freeze–thaw, fluvial erosion, glacial erosion and mass movements.

The ability of water to dissolve calcium carbonate is known as its **aggressivity**. Water containing carbon dioxide can dissolve limestone and is termed 'aggressive'. It can continue to dissolve limestone until it reaches **saturation point**. After this the river is described as **non-aggressive**. If the water is **over-saturated**

For example, water with a temperature of 30 °C and a CO_2 content of 50 mg/l can absorb 250 ppm $CaCO_3$.

The two most important factors for the solution of limestone are:
- **temperature** – CO_2 diffuses faster with lower temperatures
- **speed** and **turbulence** of water movement.

C If saturated water is cooled, it can dissolve more limestone
W If water is warmed, it will deposit more limestone
H If it comes in contact with air with more CO_2, it will take in CO_2 and dissolve more limestone
L If it comes in contact with air with less CO_2, it will lose CO_2 and precipitate calcium carbonate

Figure 3.14 Trombe's curves of limestone solution

calcium carbonate is likely to be precipitated. Mixing of streams and changes in temperature cause changes in aggressivity and saturation. This can lead to changes in solution and precipitation of calcium carbonate (Figure 3.14).

Factors controlling the amount and rate of limestone solution

The amount and rate of limestone solution is affected by:
- the amount of carbon dioxide in the atmosphere, soil and groundwater
- the amount of water in contact with the limestone
- water temperature (carbon dioxide is more soluble at low temperatures)
- the turbulence of the water
- the presence of organic acids
- the presence of lead, iron sulphides, sodium or potassium in the water.

In the Burren, western Ireland, the average depth of solution is 8 cm on bare ground, 10 cm under soil and 22 cm underground. This has taken place over the last 10 000 years, representing an average of 15 cm in 10 000 years or 0.015 mm per year.

Accelerated solution occurs under certain conditions:
- Impermeable rocks join limestone – waters from non-karstic areas have aggressive waters and will cause above-average rates of solution.
- Solution by rivers: intense solution takes place by water which passes through alluvium and morainic sands and gravels.
- Solution by mixture: this occurs when waters of different hardness mix.
- At the margins of snow and ice fields, snow meltwater is able to dissolve more limestone than rainwater.
- Solution of limestone increases as annual rainfall and runoff increase.
- Limestone weathers more quickly under soil cover than on bare surfaces.

Surface features

As the joints and cracks are attacked and enlarged over thousands of years, limestone's permeability increases. **Clints** and **grikes** develop on the surface of the exposed limestone (Figure 3.15). Large areas of bare exposed limestone are known as limestone pavements. The processes involved include carbonation-solution, freeze–thaw and ice action. The last stripped away horizontal bedding planes and the overlying soil. **Karren** or **lapies** are small-scale solution grooves, only a few centimetres deep, caused by runoff and solution on limestone.

Dolines are large depressions formed by the solution or collapse of limestone. Frequently they are covered by glacial deposits. Depressions can range from small-scale sinks to large **uvaalas** up to 30 m in diameter. **Swallow holes** (or **sinks**) are smaller depressions in the landscape, also caused by the solution of limestone. They can also be formed by the enlargement of a grike system, by carbonation or fluvial activity, or by the collapse of a cavern. Often a river disappears down the hole, hence the term 'sink'. **Resurgent streams** arise when the limestone is underlain by an impermeable rock, such as clay.

Other important surface features include dry valleys. A dry valley is a river valley without a river and is a common feature on chalk and limestone. A number of ideas have been put forward to explain their origin.

1 Carboniferous limestone is initially impermeable, but becomes increasingly permeable owing to carbonation over a long time period of, say, 100 000 to 1 million years. Therefore river systems that developed on the impermeable limestone will tend to disappear as it becomes more permeable.

2 Alternatively, dry valleys could be formed by the collapse of a cave system.

3 Climatic change and decreased levels of precipitation since the creation of the valley have left it dry.

4 The periglacial hypothesis argues that limestone became temporarily impermeable during a cold periglacial phase (as water in the limestone was frozen to become permafrost). Surface melting of snow would have produced torrents of

Figure 3.15 Limestone scenery

Figure 3.16 Harrisons Cave, Barbados

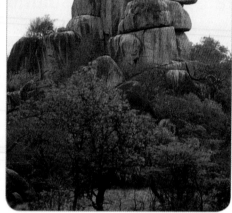

Figure 3.17 The Holy Family tor, Zimbabwe

water that were able to carve valleys in the cold phase. When temperatures rose, the permafrost melted and the limestone became permeable once more.

The idea that different processes can create the same end-product or landform is known as **equifinality.**

The term **karst** refers to well-developed features on dry limestone (without surface drainage). Underground features include caves and tunnels formed by carbonation-solution and erosion by rivers. Carbonation is a reversible process. When saturated, calcium-rich water drips from the ceiling it leaves behind calcium in the form of **speleothems**. These are cave deposits formed by the precipitation of dissolved calcium carbonate. **Tufa** is formed by the precipitation of dissolved calcium carbonate, usually found at springs or in streams and often around algae and mosses. It is a soft porous rock and forms features such as tufa dams, mounds and waterfall curtains. **Stalactites** develop from the top of the cave whereas **stalagmites** are formed on the base of the cave (Figure 3.16). Rates of deposition are slow, about 1 mm/100 years (thickness of a coat of paint). The speed at which water drips from the cave ceiling appears to have some influence on whether stalactites (slow drip) or stalagmites (fast drip) are formed.

Section 3.2 Activities

1 What are the main processes affecting limestone?

2 Explain the formation of swallow holes.

3 Account for the formation of caves in limestone.

4 What are the factors necessary for dolines to develop?

5 How do dolines developed on chalk differ from those on carboniferous limestone?

Granite

Granite is an igneous, crystalline rock. It has great physical strength and is very resistant to erosion. There are many types of granite but all share certain characteristics. They contain quartz, mica and feldspar. These are resistant minerals. The main processes of weathering at work on granite are freeze–thaw and hydrolysis.

Characteristic granite landscapes include exposed large-scale **batholiths**, which form mountains. **Tors** are isolated masses of bare rock which can be up to 20 m high. One example is the Holy Family tor, Zimbabwe (Figure 3.17) – some of the boulders of the mass are attached to part of the bedrock, others merely rest on the top.

Because of granite's resistance to weathering, there is only a thin, gritty soil cover in these regions. Such soils are generally infertile, so rough grazing is the dominant land use. Granite is an impermeable rock and many marshy hollows at the heads of the valleys indicate the limited downward movement of water.

Equifinality: the formation of tors

Linton (1955) argued that the well-developed jointing system (of irregular spacing) was chemically weathered. This occurred under warm humid conditions during warm wet periods of the Tertiary era. Decomposition was most rapid along joint planes. Where the distance between the joint planes was largest, masses of granite remained relatively unweathered. These core stones were essentially embryonic tors. Subsequent denudation, perhaps under periglacial conditions, has removed the residue of weathering. This left the unweathered blocks standing out as tors (Figure 3.18a).

An alternative theory, proposed by Palmer and Neilson (1962) also relates tor formation to the varied spacing of joints within the granite. However, they believe that frost action under periglacial conditions was the dominant process involved. This led to the removal of the more closely jointed portions of the rock. The evidence tends to support their idea, as the amount of kaolin in the joints is limited. So too is the amount of rounding that has occurred. Both of these would be expected to be dominant if chemical weathering were the main process in operation. Palmer and Neilson suggest that intense frost-shattering under periglacial conditions, followed by removal of material – first soil and then weathered **growan** – by solifluction took away the finer material and left the tors remaining (Figure 3.18b).

Tors are a good example of **equifinality**. This means that different processes can produce the same end result. Hence, whether tors are formed by chemical weathering or mechanical weathering, or indeed by a combination of the two, is highly debatable. What is clear, however, is that the joints and bedding planes, and the great physical strength and resistance of the rocks, have determined the distribution of tors on the landscape.

Section 3.2 Activities

1 The sketch plan in Figure 3.19 shows the distribution of joints in an area of unweathered granite.
  a Which parts of the rock are likely to produce resistant tors? Justify your answer.
  b How might the type of weathering differ between an alpine area and a subtropical region?
  c Explain your answer to part **b**.

2 Evaluate the role of rock type and climate in the development of granite tors.

a Formation according to Linton

1 Deep chemical weathering followed by stripping

Original surface

Joints

2

Deeply weathered material (growan)

Weathering greater where joints are closely spaced

Growan removed

3

Tor

b Formation according to Palmer and Neilson

Frost action during periglacial periods

Soft and weathered material

Decomposed granite   Joints

Summit tor   Frost action in well-jointed areas loosens blocks

Weathered material collects in valleys   Solifluction   Blocks moved downslope

Clitter

Permafrost

Figure 3.18 The development of tors

Figure 3.19 Joints in unweathered granite

0   m   100

3.3 Slope processes and development

Section 3.3 Activities

1 Refer to Figure 3.20. What is an 'open system'?
2 Explain how slopes can be described as open systems.

Introduction and definitions

The term *slope* refers to:
- an inclined surface or **hillslope**
- an angle of inclination or **slope angle**.

Slopes therefore include any part of the solid land surface, including level surfaces of 0°. These can be **sub-aerial** (exposed) or **sub-marine** (underwater), **aggradational** (depositional), **degradational** (erosional), **transportational** or any mixture of these. Given the large scope of this definition, Geographers generally study the **hillslope**. This is the area between the **watershed** (or drainage basin divide) and the base. It may or may not contain a river or stream.
- Slope **form** is the shape of the slope in cross-section.
- Slope **processes** are the activities acting on the slopes.
- Slope **evolution** is the development of slopes over time.

Slopes can be seen as **natural systems** in which processes, forms and factors of development can be related. Clark and Small (1982) regard slopes as the outcome of 'active' **processes** shaping 'passive' **materials**. Form depends on the time during which the processes have operated. Slopes are examples of **open systems**. Inputs to the slopes include energy, such as insolation, and mass, such as water and sediment. Outputs from the system also include energy (reradiated heat) and mass (water, regolith). The profile of the slope creates a store of potential energy. This is due to the difference in height between the crest and the base of the slope. This potential energy is converted into kinetic energy (energy of movement) through mass movement and erosion (Figure 3.20).

Slope controls

Many slopes vary with **climate**. In humid areas, slopes are frequently rounder, due to chemical weathering, soil creep and fluvial transport. By contrast, in arid regions slopes are jagged or straight owing to mechanical weathering and sheetwash. **Climatic geomorphology** is a branch of geography that studies how different processes operate in different climatic zones, and produce different slope forms or shapes (see Table 3.3).

However, although generalisations are made about slopes and climate, slope form is so variable that climate is rarely the main factor. Nevertheless, climate affects the type and rate of processes that operate in a region, and when they occur. For example, in the humid tropics accelerated chemical weathering dominates. This is due to the hot, wet conditions and the availability of organic acids. Deep clays are produced favouring low-angle slopes.

Geological structure is another important control on slope development. This includes faults, angle of dip and vulcanicity. These factors influence the strength of a rock and create lines of potential weakness within it. In addition, rock type and character affect vulnerability to weathering and the degree of resistance to downslope movement.

Geological structure has an important bearing on slope development. Faulting may produce steep valley sides, as in a rift valley, and folding can produce either steep or gentle slopes depending on the angle of the dip. Another structural control is vulcanicity. The Great Whin Sill is an example of an igneous intrusion. It is a harder and more resistant rock than the surrounding dolomite, and so has produced a steep slope.

Geological structure can also influence the occurrence of landslips. Slopes composed of many different types of rock are often more vulnerable to landslides due to differential erosion – that is, softer rocks are worn away and can lead to the undermining of harder rocks.

Rock type and character influence whether a rock is affected by weathering, and to what extent it can resist the downslope force of mass movement. Resistance is largely physical resistance. Regular jointing may increase the risk of movement, as well as increase the amount of water that enters a rock.

The **regolith** is the superficial and unconsolidated material found

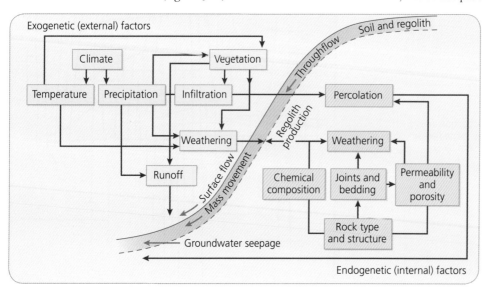

Figure 3.20 The slope as an open system

at the Earth's surface. It includes soil, scree, weathered bedrock and deposited material. Its unconsolidated nature makes it prone to downslope movement. The extra weight of a deep regolith will increase the likelihood of instability. Clay-rich regoliths are particularly unstable because of their ability to retain water. By contrast, susceptibility to slope failure is reduced where the regolith has a high percentage of sand particles, as seen in landslides in Hong Kong (see page 75 and Figure 3.30 on page 76).

Soil can be considered as part of the regolith. Its structure and texture will largely determine how much water it can hold. Clay soils can hold more water than sandy soils. A deep clay on a slope where vegetation has been removed will offer very little resistance to mass movement.

Aspect refers to the direction in which a slope faces. In some areas, past climatic conditions varied depending on the direction a slope faced. During the cold periglacial period in the northern hemisphere, the south slope, which faced north, remained in the shade. Temperatures rarely rose above freezing. By contrast, the north slope, facing south, was subjected to many more cycles of freeze–thaw. Solifluction and overland runoff lowered the level of the slope, and streams removed the debris from the valley. The result was an asymmetric valley.

Vegetation can decrease overland runoff through the interception and storage of moisture. Deforested slopes are frequently exposed to intense erosion and gullying. However, vegetation can also increase the chance of major landslips. Dense forests reduce surface wash, causing a build-up of soil between the trees, thus deepening the regolith and increasing the potential for failure.

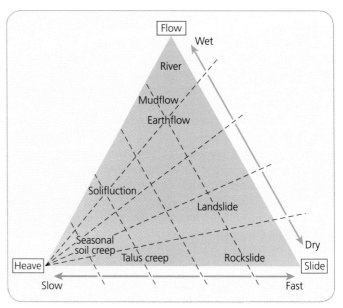

Figure 3.21 A classification of mass movements

The **types of processes** can be classified in a number of different ways:
- speed of movement (Figure 3.22)
- water content
- type of movement: flows, slides, slumps
- material.

Section 3.3 Activities

1 Briefly describe **two** ways in which climate affects slope development. What does the term *climatic geomorphology* mean?

2 Briefly describe **two** ways in which geology affects slope development. How would you expect slopes developed on chalk to differ from those developed on granite?

Mass movements

Mass movements include any large-scale movement of the Earth's surface that are not accompanied by a moving agent such as a river, glacier or ocean wave. They include:
- very slow movements, such as soil creep
- fast movement, such as avalanches
- dry movement, such as rockfalls
- very fluid movements such as mudflows (Figure 3.21).

A range of slope processes occur which vary in terms of magnitude, frequency and scale. Some are large and occur infrequently, notably rockfalls, whereas others are smaller and more continuous, such as soil creep.

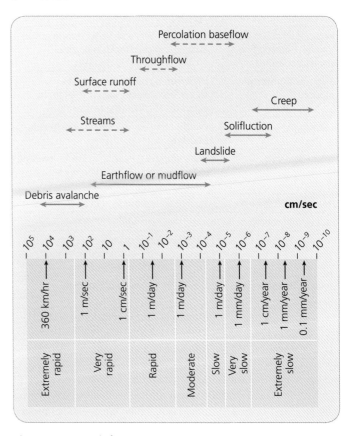

Figure 3.22 Speed of mass movements

Causes of mass movements

The likelihood of a slope failing can be expressed by its safety factor. This is the relative strength or resistance of the slope, compared with the force that is trying to move it. The most important factors that determine movement are gravity, slope angle and pore pressure.

Gravity has two effects. First it acts to move the material downslope (a slide component). Second it acts to stick the particle to the slope (a stick component). The downslope movement is proportional to the weight of the particle and slope angle. Water lubricates particles and in some cases fills the spaces between the particles. This forces them apart under pressure. Pore pressure will greatly increase the ability of the material to move. This factor is of particular importance in movements of wet material on low-angle slopes.

Shear strength and shear resistance

Slope failure is caused by two factors:

1 a reduction in the internal resistance, or shear strength, of the slope, or
2 an increase in shear stress, that is the forces attempting to pull a mass downslope.

Both can occur at the same time.

Table 3.5 Increasing stress and decreasing resistance

Factor	Example
Factors that contribute to increased shear stress	
Removal of lateral support through undercutting or slope steepening	Erosion by rivers and glaciers, wave action, faulting, previous rockfalls or slides
Removal of underlying support	Undercutting by rivers and waves, subsurface solution, loss of strength by extrusion of underlying sediments
Loading of slope	Weight of water, vegetation, accumulation of debris
Lateral pressure	Water in cracks, freezing in cracks, swelling (especially through hydration of clays), pressure release
Transient stresses	Earthquakes, movement of trees in wind
Factors that contribute to reduced shear strength	
Weathering effects	Disintegration of granular rocks, hydration of clay minerals, dissolution of cementing minerals in rock or soil
Changes in pore-water pressure	Saturation, softening of material
Changes of structure	Creation of fissures in shales and clays, remoulding of sand and sensitive clays
Organic effects	Burrowing of animals, decay of tree roots

Increases in shear stress can be caused by a multitude of factors (Table 3.5). These include material characteristics, weathering processes and changes in water availability. Weaknesses in rocks include joints, bedding planes and faults. Stress may be increased by:

- steepening or undercutting of a slope
- addition of a mass of regolith
- dumping of mining waste
- sliding from higher up the slope
- vibrational shock
- earthquakes.

Weathering may reduce cohesion and resistance. Consequently, material may be more susceptible to movement on slopes even though the original material was stable.

Water can weaken a slope by increasing shear stress and decreasing shear resistance. The weight of a potentially mobile mass is increased by:

- an increase in the volume of water
- heavy or prolonged rain
- a rising water table
- saturated surface layers.

Moreover, water reduces the cohesion of particles by saturation. Water pressure in saturated soils (pore water pressure) decreases the frictional strength of the solid material. This weakens the slope. Over time the safety factor for a particular slope will change. These changes may be gradual, for example percolation carrying away finer material. By contrast, some changes are rapid.

There are a number of ways that downslope movement can be opposed:

- **Friction** will vary with the weight of the particle and slope angle. Friction can be overcome on gentle slope angles if water is present. For example, solifluction can occur on slopes as gentle as 3°.
- **Cohesive forces** act to bind the particles on the slope. Clay may have high cohesion, but this may be reduced if the water content becomes so high that the clay liquefies, when it loses its cohesive strength.
- **Pivoting** occurs in the debris layers which contain material embedded in the slope.
- **Vegetation** binds the soil and thereby stabilises slopes. However, vegetation may allow soil moisture to build up and make landslides more likely (see pages 74–75).

Section 3.3 Activities

1 a Define the term *mass movement*.
  b Suggest how mass movements can be classified.
2 Define the terms *strength* and *shear stress*.
3 With the use of examples, explain why mass movements occur.

Types of mass movement

Surface wash occurs when the soil's infiltration capacity is exceeded. In the UK this commonly occurs in winter as water drains across saturated or frozen ground, following prolonged or heavy downpours or the melting of snow. It is also common in arid and semi-arid regions where particle size limits percolation.

Sheetwash is unchannelled flow of water over a soil surface. On most slopes sheetwash breaks into areas of high velocity separated by areas of lower velocity. It is capable of transporting material dislodged by rainsplash. Sheetwash occurs in the UK on footpaths and moorlands. For example, during the Lynmouth floods of 1952, sheetwash from the shallow moorland peat caused gullies 6 m deep to form. In the semi-arid areas of the south-west USA it lowers surfaces by 2–5 mm/year compared with 0.01 mm/year on vegetated slopes in a temperate climate.

Throughflow refers to water moving down through the soil. It is channelled into natural pipes in the soil. This gives it sufficient energy to transport material, and added to its solute load, may amount to a considerable volume.

Heave or **creep** is a slow, small-scale process which occurs mostly in winter. It is one of the most important slope processes in environments where flows and slides are not common. **Talus creep** is the slow movement of fragments on a scree slope.

Individual soil particles are pushed or heaved to the surface by (a) wetting, (b) heating or (c) freezing of water (Figure 3.23). About 75 per cent of the soil creep movement is induced by moisture changes and associated volume change. Nevertheless freeze–thaw and normal temperature-controlled expansion and contraction are important in periglacial and tropical climates.

Particles move at right-angles to the surface (2) as it is the zone of least resistance. They fall under the influence of gravity (5) once the particles have dried, cooled, or the water has thawed. Next movement is downslope.

Figure 3.23 Soil creep

Rates of soil creep are slow, 1–3 mm/year in temperate areas and up to 10 mm/year in tropical rainforest. They form terracettes. In well vegetated humid temperate areas soil creep can be ten times more important than slope wash. In periglacial areas it can be as much as 300 mm per year. By contrast, in arid environments slope wash is more important. Small-scale variations in slope,

compaction, cohesion and vegetation will have a significant effect on the rate of creep.

Observation of soil creep is difficult. Traditional qualitative evidence such as bent trees (Figure 3.24) is misleading and now largely discredited. The slow rate of movement may mean that measurement errors are serious.

Figure 3.24 The evidence for soil creep

Rainsplash erosion

Raindrops can have an erosive effect on hillslopes (Figure 3.25). On a 5° slope about 60 per cent of the movement is downslope. This figure increases to 95 per cent on a 25° slope. The amount of erosion depends upon the rainfall intensity, velocity and raindrop distribution. It is most effective on slopes of between 33° and 45° and at the start of a rainfall event when the soil is still loose.

On flat surfaces (a) raindrops compact the soil and dislodge particles equally in all directions. On steep slopes (b) the downward component is more effective than the upward motion due to gravity. Erosion downslope increases with slope angle.

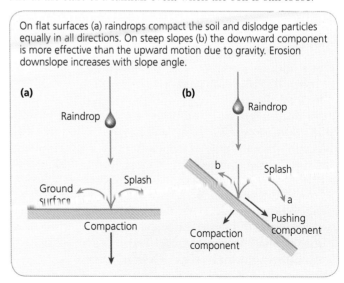

Figure 3.25 Rainsplash erosion

Falls

Falls occur on steep slopes (greater than 40°), especially on bare rock faces where joints are exposed. The initial cause of the fall may be weathering, such as freeze–thaw or disintegration, or erosion prising open lines of weakness. Once the rocks are detached they fall under the influence of gravity (Figure 3.26). If the fall is short it produces a relatively straight scree. If it is long, it forms a concave scree. Falls are significant in producing the retreat of steep rock faces and in providing debris for scree slopes and talus slopes.

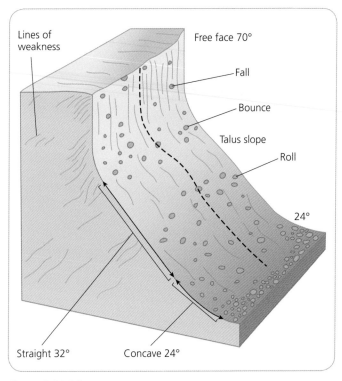

Figure 3.26 Falls

Slides

Slides occur when an entire mass of material moves along a slip plane. These include:

- rockslides and landslides of any material, rock, or regolith
- rotational slides, which produce a series of massive steps or terraces.

Slides commonly occur where there is a combination of weak rocks, steep slopes and active undercutting. Slides are often caused by a change in the water content of a slope or by very cold conditions. As the mass moves along the slip plane it tends to retain its shape and structure until it hits the bottom of a slope (Figure 3.27). Slides range from small-scale slides close to roads, to large-scale movements killing thousands of people. One of the classic examples of a slide is the Vaiont Dam in Italy where more than 2000 people died on 9 October 1963.

Slip planes occur for a variety of reasons:

- at the junction of two layers
- at a fault line
- where there is a joint
- along a bedding plane
- at the point beneath the surface where the shear stress becomes greater than the shear strength.

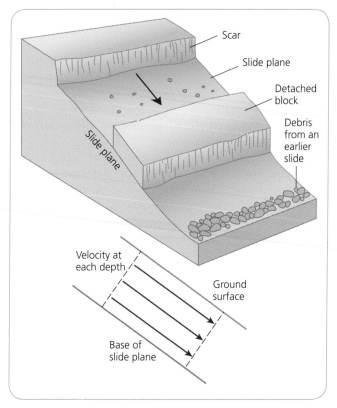

Figure 3.27 Slides

Weak rocks such as clay have little shear strength to start with and are particularly vulnerable to the development of slip planes. The slip plane is typically a concave curve and as the slide occurs the mass will be rotated backwards.

Rockslides

In 1959 the sixth strongest earthquake ever to affect the USA occurred in Montana. Close to the epicentre of the earthquake, in the Madison River valley, a slope of schists and gneiss with slippery mica and clay was supported by a base of dolomite. The earthquake cleanly broke the dolomite. A huge volume of rock, 400 m high and 1000 m long, slid into the valley. Eighty million tonnes of material moved in less than a minute! The Madison River was dammed and a lake 60 m deep and 8 km long was created.

Landslides

Loose rock, stones and soil all have a tendency to move downslope. They will do so whenever the downward force exceeds the resistance produced by friction and cohesion. When the material moves downslope as a result of shear failure at the boundary of the moving mass, the term *landslide* is applied. This may include a flowing movement as well as straightforward sliding. Landslides are very sensitive to water content. This reduces the strength of the material by increasing the water pressure. This effectively pushes particles apart, thereby weakening the links between them. Moreover, water adds weight to the mass, increasing the downslope force.

Case Study

The Hong Kong landslides

In June 1966 rainstorms triggered massive landslides which killed 64 people. Over 2500 people were made homeless and a further 8000 were evacuated. Rainfall had been high for the first ten days in June. Over 300 mm had fallen compared with 130 mm in a normal year. On 11 and 12 June over 400 mm fell – nearly a third of this occurred in just one hour! By 15 June the area had received over 1650 mm of rain. Over 700 landslides were recorded in Hong Kong that month!

Vegetation intensified the problem. The plants held back many of the smaller landslides and allowed the larger ones to build up. The main form of landslide was a **washout**. These are large-scale, deep-seated landslides which involve some rotational movement. They were accompanied by the emergence of subsurface water which helped to erode the slopes below. Other forms of landslides were sheetflows, debris avalanches and rockslides.

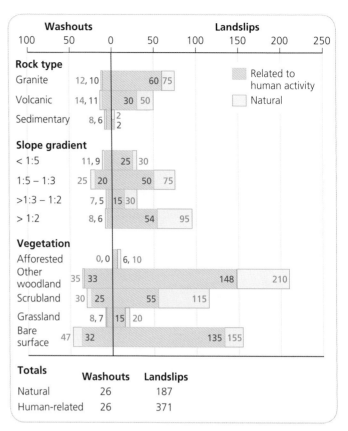

Figure 3.29 Mass movements in Hong Kong data:

	Washouts (Human, Natural)	Landslips (Human, Natural)
Rock type		
Granite	12, 10	60, 75
Volcanic	14, 11	30, 50
Sedimentary	8, 6	2, 2
Slope gradient		
< 1:5	11, 9	25, 30
1:5 – 1:3	25, 20	50, 75
>1:3 – 1:2	7, 5	15, 30
> 1:2	8, 6	54, 95
Vegetation		
Afforested	0, 0	6, 10
Other woodland	35, 33	148, 210
Scrubland	30, 25	55, 115
Grassland	8, 7	15, 20
Bare surface	47, 32	135, 155

Key: Related to human activity / Natural

Totals	Washouts	Landslips
Natural	26	187
Human-related	26	371

Figure 3.29 Mass movements in Hong Kong

Figure 3.28 Hong Kong landscape

Section 3.3 Activities

1 Compare and contrast the characteristics of falls and slides.

2 Study Figures 3.28 and 3.29, which show the relationship between mass movements in Hong Kong and rock type, gradient and vegetation. Using the data, describe and explain the relationship between mass movements and:

a rock type
b gradient
c vegetation.

Slumps and flows

Slumps occur on weaker rocks, especially clay, and have a rotational movement along a curved slip plane (Figure 3.30). Clay absorbs water, becomes saturated, and exceeds its liquid limit. It then flows along a slip plane. Frequently the base of a cliff has been undercut and weakened by erosion, thereby reducing its strength. By contrast, flows are more continuous, less jerky, and are more likely to contort the mass into a new form (Figure 3.31). Material is predominantly of a small size, such as deeply weathered clays. Particle size involved in flows is generally small, for example sand-sized and smaller.

Figure 3.30 Slumps

Figure 3.31 Flows

The speed of a flow varies – mudflows are faster and more fluid than earthflows, which tend to be thicker and deeper. A higher water content will enable material to flow across gentle angles.

Earthflows and mudflows can occur on the saturated toe (end) of a landslide, or may form a distinctive type of mass movement in their own right. Small flows may develop locally whereas others may be larger and more rapid. In theory, mudflows give way to sediment-laden rivers – but the distinction is very blurred.

Case Study

Sidoarjo mudflow

Since May 2006 more than 50 000 people in Porong District, Indonesia, have been displaced by hot mud flowing from a natural well. Gas and hot mud began spewing out when a drill penetrated a layer of liquid sediment. The amount of material spilling out peaked at 135 000 m³/day in September 2006. By 2010, the main thoroughfare in Porong was raised 80 cm to avoid further mudflows. The Sidoarjo mudflow is an ongoing eruption of gas and mud.

Avalanches

Avalanches are rapid movements of snow, ice, rock or earth down a slope. They are common in mountainous areas: newly fallen snow may fall off older snow, especially in winter (a dry avalanche), while in spring partially melted snow moves (a wet avalanche), often triggered by skiers (Figure 3.32). Avalanches

Figure 3.32 Avalanches

frequently occur on steep slopes over 22°, especially on north-facing slopes where the lack of sun inhibits the stabilisation of snow. Debris avalanches are a rapid mass movement of sediments, often associated with saturated ground conditions.

Case Study

The Abbotsford landslide, Dunedin, New Zealand

The landslide that took place in East Abbotsford, South Island, New Zealand is a very good example of how human and physical factors can interact to produce a hazardous event. It also shows clearly how such hazards can be managed.

From 1978 several families in Abbotsford noticed hairline cracks were appearing in their homes – in the brickwork, concrete floors and driveways. During 1979 workmen discovered that a leaking water main had been pulled apart. Geologists discovered that water had made layers of clay on the hill soft, and the sandstone above it was sliding on this slippery surface.

As a result of this, an early warning system was put in place. A civil defence emergency was declared on 6 August, although the situation wasn't thought to be urgent as geologists believed that landslip would continue to move only slowly. However, on 9 August a 7 ha section of Abbotsford started down the hill at a rate of over 3 m a minute (Figure 3.33), with houses and 17 people on board. No-one was killed, although 69 homes were destroyed or

damaged and over 200 people were displaced. The total cost from the destruction of the homes, infrastructure and relief organisation amounted to over £7 million. An insurance scheme designed to cope with such disasters, and government and voluntary relief measures, meant that many of the residents were compensated for their loss. However, other costs such as depressed house prices in the surrounding area, psychological trauma and the expense of a prolonged public enquiry, were not immediately appreciated.

The landslide was essentially a block slide of sandstone resting on a bed of weaker clay. Displacement of 50 m took place in about 30 minutes, leaving a small rift 30 m deep at the head of the slope. Such geological conditions – in which a permeable hard rock rests on an impermeable soft rock – are commonly associated with landslides. In addition, the slope was dipping at an angle of 7°. Water collected in the impermeable clay, reduced its strength and cohesion, and caused the sandstone to slip along the boundary of the two rocks.

The landslide involved 5.4 million m³ of material. At first the land moved as a slow creep, followed by a rapid movement with speeds of 1.7 m/minute. Rapid sliding lasted for about 30 minutes. An area of about 18 ha was affected.

However, other factors are also believed to have made a contribution. Deforestation in the area, even over a century before, had reduced evapotranspiration in the area and there was less binding of the soil by plant roots. Urbanisation in the previous forty years had modified the slopes by cutting and infilling, and had altered surface drainage (speeding up the removal of surface water). Quarrying of material at the toe of the slope in the 1960s and 1970s had removed support from the base of the slope. The trigger of the landslide is believed to have been a combination of leaking water pipes and heavy rainfall.

A number of lessons can be learnt from the Abbotsford landslide:
- Dangerous landslides can occur on relatively gentle slopes if the right conditions exist.
- Attention to early warning can help preparedness and reduce the loss of life.
- Human activity can destabilise slopes.
- Low-frequency, high-magnitude events may be hard to predict, but mapping and dating of old hazards may indicate areas of potential risk – a regional landslide hazard assessment should be made where there is evidence of previous landslide activity.
- A landslide insurance scheme eased the cost of the event – however, money was available only after the event rather than beforehand, and the insurance only covered houses, not land damage.

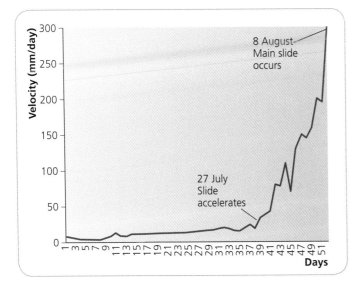

Figure 3.33 Abbotsford landslide, New Zealand

Case Study

Mexican landslides, 2010

In October 2010 mud buried part of a remote town in the southern Mexican state of Oaxaca when a large chunk of a nearby mountain collapsed after three days of relentless rain. Initially it was thought that the landslide had caused a massive tragedy with up to 1000 people killed. However, the number of deaths was believed to be less than ten. The landslide happened at about 4 am in the morning. The authorities were unsure how many houses had been buried because it was dark, so they estimated.

The rescue progress along the unpaved mountain road was hampered by smaller landslides and a collapsed bridge. Heavy cloud cover prohibited helicopters from getting a clear view of the situation on the ground. When the first rescue workers and soldiers eventually reached the town, they found considerable destruction in one relatively small part of the town. Two houses were completely interred, two partially buried, and thirty more in serious danger because they lay within the path of the still unstable mudflow.

In 2010 Mexico experienced one of the most intense rainy seasons on record with large areas under water in lowland regions of Oaxaca as well as in other southern states. Landslides are a major danger in mountainous parts of the country – particularly those, such as Oaxaca, that have long suffered from severe deforestation.

Section 3.3 Activities

1 Study Figure 3.29 which provides details on landslides in Hong Kong.
- **a** Using the data, describe and explain the relationship between mass movements and **i** rock type, **ii** gradient and **iii** vegetation.
- **b** What type of mass movement was most common in Hong Kong?
- **c** What do you think is the difference between a washout and a landslip? Give reasons for your answer.
- **d** Which type of rock was most affected by **a** washouts and **b** landslips?
- **e** What type of mass movement most affected **a** granite and **b** volcanic rocks? How do you explain these differences?
- **f** What is the relationship between gradient and mass movement? Give reasons for your answer.
- **g** What impact does vegetation have on the type and number of mass movements? Briefly explain your answer.
- **h** Briefly discuss the impact of human activity on mass movements. Use the evidence in Figure 3.29 to support your answer.

2 Explain the effect of **a** climate and **b** rock type on slope development.

3 With the use of examples, explain how mass movements take place.

3.4 The human impact

There are very few areas of human activity that do not have an impact on environments and landforms. Landforms can be created by constructional activities (tipping, excavation, hydrological interference, farming). Hillsides have been terraced in many parts of the world for centuries.

Landscape-forming processes are a product of geological structure, time and geomorphological processes over different scales of time and space. It is only the geomorphological processes that can be modified significantly by human activity. Geomorphological processes are largely climatically determined, such as weathering, or gravity controlled, such as mass movement. Hence, they are not readily controllable.

Changes in landforms caused by people can be deliberate or unintentional. Artificial valleys can be created by road or rail cuttings, and drainage systems may be constructed to control the hydrology of an area. New land may be created by the infill of marshes or lagoons, or may be generated by estuarine deposition of excess sediment load carried by rivers as a result of high levels of soil erosion. Hollows may be excavated for mineral extraction or may result from land subsidence due to mining or land drainage.

The shape of the Earth's surface has had a major impact upon human activity. Many ancient settlements, such as Iron Age hill forts, are located on hilltops. Lines of communication are strongly influenced by the shape of the land, and so is the siting of many towns and settlements. In recent decades, the siting of airports and nuclear plants have been heavily influenced by physical geography.

Figure 3.34 Oxford Castle mound

The shape of the land may also impose opportunities and restraints upon towns and cities. The influence of the shape is not restricted to urban environments. Slope geometry is important in relation to soil control. Slope angles have been modified by terracing and the surface has also been affected by mining and quarrying. A number of landforms are the direct result of human activity, such as mounds, embankments and cuttings (Figure 3.34).

Our ability to affect the natural environment has increased as technology has developed. In spite of all the activity, actual changes to the shape of the land surface have been small relative to the scale of the natural landforms. Indirect human activities are often difficult to recognise but they may lead to acceleration of natural processes. The indirect modification of process and form is one of the most crucial aspects of human activity. For example, removing natural vegetation cover through cutting, burning and grazing can lead to increased erosion and sedimentation. Human activity can often set into effect the train of events. For example, attempts to protect coastal areas in one part may lead to increased erosion elsewhere.

Weathering

Weathering is the breakdown of rock on the spot. Weathering processes can be intensified by changes in local climate as shown by increased chemical weathering in urban areas. Changes in the nature and rate of weathering are closely linked to air quality. Increased emissions of sulphur dioxide (from the burning of fossil fuels) has led to higher levels of sulphuric acid. Chemical reactions with sulphur dioxide can create salts, such

Figure 3.35 The effects of weathering on limestone at Worcester College, Oxford, UK

as calcium sulphate and magnesium sulphate. These are able to chemically weather rocks (Figure 3.35). Similarly, as atmospheric levels of carbon dioxide have risen, the potential for carbonation increases. Carbonation is the process whereby atmospheric carbon dioxide combines with water to form a weak carbonic acid. This chemically attacks rocks, especially those with calcium carbonate such as limestones and chalk. Thus, as levels of atmospheric carbon dioxide rise, so too does the potential for increased weathering.

Human activity has many impacts on the nature and rate of limestone denudation:

- The burning of fossil fuels and deforestation has increased atmospheric levels of carbon dioxide, so the weathering of limestone might increase.
- There are increasing levels of acidity in rainwater due to sulphur dioxide and nitrogen oxides in the atmosphere (see pages 83–6).
- Agriculture and forestry are affecting soil acidity and carbon dioxide contents.
- Increased lighting in caves allows plants to grow and biological weathering has increased in some cases due to increased levels of organic acids.

Mass movement

Mass movement is the movement under gravity of material on a slope. The rate and nature of such movement varies with the nature of the material, the topography, the climate and the vegetation. It can be very slow (creep) or very rapid (slides and slumps). Rates of mass movement can be altered by building or excavation, drainage or agriculture. Mass movements can be accelerated by destabilising slopes. Local erosion can be intensified by footpath trampling in recreational areas. Some mass movements are created by humans piling up waste soil and rock into unstable accumulations that move without warning. Landslides can be created by undercutting or overloading. As well as causing mass movements, human activities can reduce them (Table 3.6, overleaf).

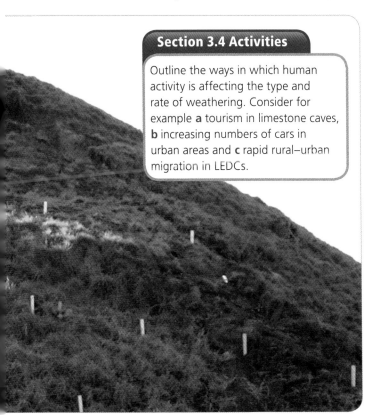

Section 3.4 Activities

Outline the ways in which human activity is affecting the type and rate of weathering. Consider for example **a** tourism in limestone caves, **b** increasing numbers of cars in urban areas and **c** rapid rural–urban migration in LEDCs.

Table 3.6 Examples of methods of controlling mass movement

Type of movement	Method of control
Falls	Flattening the slope
	Benching the slope
	Drainage
	Reinforcement of rock walls by grouting with cement, anchor bolts
	Covering of wall with steel mesh
Slides and flows	Grading or benching to flatten the slope
	Drainage of surface water with ditches
	Sealing surface cracks to prevent infiltration
	Subsurface drainage
	Rock or earth buttresses at foot
	Retaining walls at foot
	Pilings through the potential slide mass

Source: Goudie, 1993

Slopes

Most changes to slopes caused by human activities have been very minor in relation to the scale of the natural land surface. Human interference of slopes tends to have been most effective in speeding up naturally occurring processes rather than creating new features.

In urban areas the intensity of slope modification is often very high, given the need for buildings and roads to be constructed safely, using sound engineering principles. Almost all buildings with foundations cause some modification to the natural slope of the land, and even on flat sites, large modern buildings generally involve the removal of material to allow for proper foundations. Slope modification tends to increase as a construction moves on to steeper slopes. In these conditions, in order to provide a horizontal base plus reasonable access a cut-and-fill technique is often used (Figure 3.36), thereby creating a small level terrace with an over-steepened slope at both ends. The steep slopes, devoid of soil and vegetation, are potentially much less stable than the former natural slope and are, in times of intense rainfall, susceptible to small but quite damaging landslips.

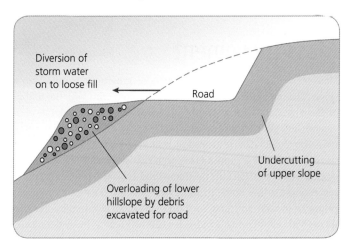

Diversion of storm water on to loose fill

Road

Undercutting of upper slope

Overloading of lower hillslope by debris excavated for road

Figure 3.36 Slope instability caused by road building

Pollution

Pollution is defined as the contamination of the Earth/atmosphere system to such an extent that normal environmental processes are adversely affected. Polluted elements are disagreeable, noxious, toxic, harmful and/or objectionable. Pollution can be natural, such as from volcanic eruptions, as well as human in origin. It can be deliberate or it may be accidental.

The costs of pollution are widespread: death, decreased levels of health, declining water resources, reduced soil quality, and poor air quality. Thus it is vital to control and manage pollution. To be effective pollution must be treated at its source. However, unless point sources can be targeted it may be impossible to treat pollution effectively.

Mineral workings

Materials that are mined are normally classified in four groups:
- metals such as iron ore and copper
- industrial minerals such as lime and soda ash
- construction materials such as sand and gravel
- energy minerals such as coal, oil and natural gas.

The environmental impacts of mining are diverse (Table 3.7). Habitat destruction is widespread, especially if opencast or strip mining is used. Open cast mining is a form of extensive excavation in which the overlying material (overburden) is removed by machinery, revealing the seams or deposits below. In the USA it is referred to as strip mining. Disposal of waste rock and 'tailings'

Table 3.7 Environmental problems associated with mining

Problem	Type of mining operation			
	Open pit and quarrying	Opencast (as in coal)	Underground	Dredging (as in tin or gold)
Habitat destruction	X	X	–	X
Dump failure/ erosion	X	X	X	–
Subsidence	–	–	X	–
Water pollution	X	X	X	X
Air pollution*	X	X	X	–
Noise	X	X	–	–
Air/blast/ ground vibration	X	X	–	–
Visual intrusion	X	X	X	X
Dereliction	X	–	X	X

X Problem present

– Problem unlikely

* Can be associated with smelting which may not be at the site of ore/ mineral extraction

Source: N. Middleton, *The Global Casino*, Edward Arnold 1995 (the impurities left behind after a mineral has been extracted from its ore) may destroy whole ecosystems. Copper mining is especially polluting: to produce 9 million tonnes of copper (world production levels in the 1990s) creates about 990 million tonnes of waste rock. Even the production of 1 tonne of china clay (kaolin) creates 1 tonne of mica, 2 tonnes of undecomposed rock, and 6 tonnes of quartz sand. Smelting causes widespread deforestation. The Grande Carajas project in Brazil removes up to 50 000 ha of tropical forest each year.

Moreover, there is widespread pollution from many forms of mining. This results from the extraction, transport and processing of the raw material, and affects air, soil and water. Water is affected by heavy metal pollution, acid mine drainage, eutrophication and deoxygenation. Dust can also be an important local problem. The use of mercury to separate fine gold particles from other minerals in riverbed sediments leads to contamination in many rivers. In Brazil up to 100 tonnes of mercury have been introduced into rivers by gold prospectors. Mercury is highly toxic and accumulates in the higher levels of the food chain, and can enter the human food chain.

Derelict land that results from extraction produces landforms of different size, shape and origin. A major subdivision is between excavations and heaps. Spoil heaps are large unconsolidated mounds of waste materials extracted in the process of obtaining an ore. Heaps can be visually intrusive and have a large environmental impact. Heaps include those composed of blast furnace slag, fly-ash from power stations, as well as spoils of natural materials (overmatter) such as the white cones associated with china clay workings, oil shale wastes in Lothian, and colliery spoil heaps.

Damaged areas can be rehabilitated and managed. In many cases forward planing is the most useful method of cleaning. Proper site surveys, replacement of topsoil after excavation, and reseeding with original species all help to restore mined areas. Alternatively, spoil heaps can be stabilised with vegetation, reduced in height or landscaped. Waste materials can be used for landfill, as long as it is economic to transport it. Legislative controls, such as Environmental Impact Assessments, enable planners to work out the environmental costs of developments, and to assess whether the benefits of any plan outweigh the costs. In many cases it is a matter of time. Many of the wetlands of lowland England result from flooded sand and gravel quarries. The pollution caused was temporary – but the consequences may have lasted decades.

Many former sand and gravel pits have been converted into recreational lakes for angling, watersports and nature reserves.

Case Study

Bauxite mining in Cockpit Country, Jamaica

Cockpit Country is an area of outstanding ecological and cultural significance. It is an island-within-an-island and contains especially adapted plants and animals found nowhere else in the world. Cockpit Country's biodiversity is of global significance. It is the largest remaining intact primary wet limestone forest in Jamaica and is the home to the endangered Giant Swallowtail butterfly. Many of Jamaica's threatened birds are found there, including the endangered Jamaican blackbird, and 95 per cent of the black-billed parrot population.

Cockpit Country is also of historical significance. It is renowned in Jamaican history as the refuge of the fiercely independent Maroons, descendants of the earliest slaves who were freed by the Spanish settlers around the time of the British conquest in 1655. After almost a century of resistance to British rule in the 'Land of Look Behind', the Maroons forced the British into signing a peace treaty in 1739.

Cockpit Country is now threatened by bauxite mining. Although 22 327 ha of Cockpit Country is a designated Forest Reserve, prospecting or mining bauxite can be done within the Forest Reserve. Alcoa Minerals of Jamaica and Clarendon Alumina Production applied for the renewal of a Special Exclusive Prospecting Licence, which was first granted in May 2004. This allowed them to exclusively prospect for bauxite within a specified area in Cockpit Country. In November 2006, the Minister of Agriculture renewed Alcoa's licence. The public outcry that ensued prompted the Minister to suspend the licences almost immediately.

The impacts of mining

During the exploration or prospecting phase considerable damage can be done because roads are needed to bring in drilling equipment. In the mining phase a more extensive road network would be needed, and all the vegetation on the surface of the land where bauxite deposits occur would be removed. This would cause increased surface runoff and possibly impede infiltration to the groundwater.

Because the water resources are based on underground caves and tunnels, underground streams in the region are very prone to damage through in-filling, siltation, and accumulation of solid waste. These result in reduced flow and reduced water quality downstream, and flooding upstream. Mining could lead to flooding of previously safe areas and a reduction in the volume of major rivers flowing from Cockpit Country, reducing the water supplies for the western half of Jamaica's north coast.

Furthermore, deforestation due to bauxite mining in the Cockpit Country would contribute to greenhouse gas emissions. Bauxite mining itself is energy-intensive and most of the energy comes from fossil fuels, further adding to greenhouse gases.

It is clear that no matter what approach is taken to the reclamation of mined lands, the biological diversity would be lost for ever. And if bauxite mining were allowed even on the edges of Cockpit Country, the region would soon be opened up to logging and limestone quarrying on a massive scale.

Coal mining

The mining of coal has a number of environmental impacts (Table 3.8). Where the overburden is shallow (less than 15 m) small depressions are formed over the mined area. These may develop for up to fifty years after the mining has stopped. There is also a considerable impact on water resources and quality. Up to 17 litres of water are needed for each tonne of coal mined. Underground mining uses 63–120 l/tonne and a further 33 l/tonne for surface waste disposal.

Table 3.8 Major direct environmental impacts of coal use (excluding human health)

Impact	Characteristics
Accumulation of carbon dioxide in the atmosphere	Effects potentially global but unpredictable spatially and temporally. Resistant to technical amelioration.
Acid precipitation from sulphur dioxide and nitrogen oxides; acid mine drainage	Regional damage (often across international boundaries) to forest productivity and freshwater fisheries. Emission control of gases feasible.
Land use for mining operations	Local to regional scale. May be only temporary if reclamation is practised; technology for this is available.
Consumptive water use for conversion plants, opencast mining and reclamation	Regional impacts on agricultural and other ecosystems where water is scarce. 'Mining' of aquifers is possible. Resistant to technical amelioration.

Source: I. Simmons, *Changing the Face of the Earth: Culture, Environment, History*, Blackwell, 1989

Table 3.9 Effluents from a coal-fired power station

Type of effluent	Tonnes per GW(e) per year
Airborne effluents	
Particulates	3×10^3
Sulphur oxides	11×10^4
Nitrogen oxides	2.7×10^4
Carbon monoxide	2×10^3
Hydrocarbons	400
Liquid effluents	
Organic material	66.2
Sulphuric acid	82.5
Chlorides	26.3
Phosphates	41.7
Boron	331
Suspended solids	497
Solid waste (ash)	3.6×10^5

GW(e) = Gigawatt of energy

Source: I. Simmons, *Changing the Face of the Earth: Culture, Environment, History*, Blackwell, 1989

Section 3.4 Activities

1 Using a dictionary, explain the meaning of the term *technical amelioration*.

2 Study Table 3.9, which shows effluents from a coal-fired station.
 a Which is the largest emission from the station?
 b Why is a table a better way of showing this data than a pie chart?

3 Briefly outline some of the environmental implications of the data shown in Figure 3.37 (such as pollution, subsidence, flooding: try to link cause with result).

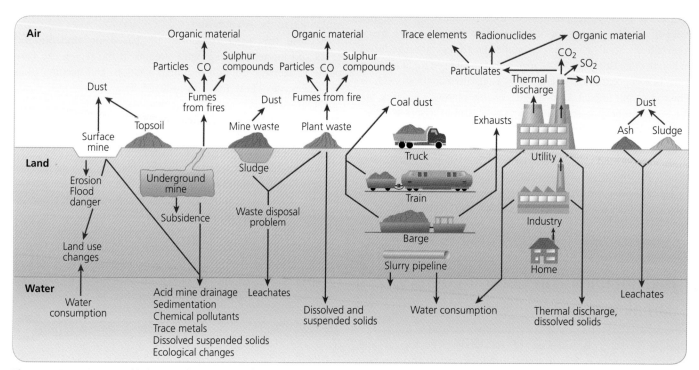

Figure 3.37 Environmental linkages in the extraction of coal

Case Study

Opencast mining in West Virginia, USA

America's second largest coal producer, Arch Coal, has been blasting away mountaintops and dumping the spoil in the valleys below. One ongoing conflict has been at Pigeonroost Hollow, West Virginia. Eleven families once lived in Pigeonroost Hollow. Most families sold their homes rather than endure the dynamiting, noise and dust, as the company prepares the land while waiting for a permit to start a strip-mining operation known as mountaintop removal.

Pigeonroost Hollow is a nature lover's paradise, with large butterflies, humming birds, and trout in the brook. One local resident filed a lawsuit against the state and federal governments for granting permits that allow companies to decapitate mountaintops and deposit tons of debris in the valleys. These huge waste disposal areas violate the Surface Mining Act and the Clean Water Act, so the permits should never have been issued.

Mountaintop removal mining (MTR), also known as **mountaintop mining (MTM)**, is a form of surface mining that involves the mining of the summit or summit ridge of a mountain. Mountaintop removal – lopping 5000 m from the top of a mountain – involves little human labour and the use of gigantic £63 million machines called draglines wielding 53-cubic-yard scoops. Once the trees are cut and the topsoil removed, the rock above the coal seams is blasted away. The debris is removed by trucks and draglines. Coal companies claim that mountaintop removal is the least destructive and most efficient way to extract a vital resource. Entire coal seams are removed from the top of a mountain, hill or ridge by removing the overburden above them, and restacking the overburden back on the ridge to reflect the approximate original contour of the mountain. The land is then smoothed over, and grass and trees planted. The excess amounts of overburden that cannot be placed on the ridge top are moved into neighbouring valleys.

West Virginia, one of America's poorest states, possesses great beauty, rivers that are a whitewater-rafter's dream, and lush mountains. It is also blessed – and cursed – with coal. Coal has brought jobs, but the rapacity of coal companies has fermented conflict with the unions, notably the Battle of Blair Mountain in 1921 when 7000 workers fought 2000 government troops. West Virginia coal is prized, as the southern mountains contain low-sulphur coal which burns efficiently and produces less pollution than other coal. The 1990 Clean Air Act made West Virginia a favourite site with coal companies because the law fed demand for such coal.

Since 1995 West Virginia's division of environmental protection has permitted at least 38 new mountaintop removal mines, covering 12 000 ha. Governor Cecil Underwood, a former coal executive, previously appointed two coal executives in sequence as the state's environmental protection director!

Arch Coal wants to remove several mountaintops, extract coal, and dump 150 million cubic yards of rock into five valley fills. If work begins in earnest, Pigeonroost Hollow will become part of a 1255 ha strip-mine, the largest in the state's history. If the mining continues unabated, environmentalists predict that by 2020 half of the peaks of southern West Virginia will disappear.

In 2007 The Army Corps of Engineers approved a permit in 2007 to blast 120 m off the hilltops here to expose the rich coal seams, disposing of the debris in the upper reaches of six valleys, including Pigeonroost Hollow. However, the Environmental Protection Agency under the Obama administration, in a break with President George W. Bush's more coal-friendly approach, has threatened to halt or sharply scale back the project known as Spruce 1.

Studies show that mountaintop mining has serious environmental impacts, including loss of biodiversity, which mitigation practices cannot successfully address. There are also adverse human health impacts which result from contact with affected streams or exposure to airborne toxins and dust.

Acidification

Sulphur dioxide (SO_2) and nitrogen oxides (NO_x) are emitted from industrial complexes, vehicles and urban areas. Some of these oxides fall directly to the ground as **dry deposition** (dry particles, aerosols and gases) close to the source (Figure 3.38). By contrast, the longer the sulphur dioxide and nitrogen oxides remain in the air the greater the chance they will be oxidised, forming sulphuric acid (H_2SO_4) and nitric acid (HNO_3). These acids dissolve in cloud droplets (rain, snow, mist, hail) and reach the ground as **wet deposition**. This can be carried thousands of kilometres from the source. The dissolved acids consist of sulphate ions (SO_4^{2-}), nitrate ions (NO^{3-}) and hydrogen ions (H^+). These ions form **acid rain**.

The pH scale is logarithmic – this means that pH 6.0 is ten times more acid than pH 7.0, natural rainwater of pH 5.6 is about twenty-five times more acidic than distilled water (neutral water) of pH 7.0. Natural rain is acidic, largely due to the presence of carbon dioxide in the atmosphere, and combined with rainwater it forms a weak carbonic acid. Acid rain is frequently more than twenty times more acidic than natural rainwater. Rain over Scandinavia commonly has a pH of 4.2–4.3.

The direct effects of sulphur oxides and nitrogen oxides in the air include damage to human health, damage to plants, and atmospheric corrosion. The worst-hit areas used to include Sweden, Norway, eastern North America, Germany, Belgium, the Netherlands, Scotland, the former Yugoslavia, Austria and Denmark (Figure 3.39). Future trends are likely to see increased sulphur emissions in NICs (newly industrialising countries) such as China, India and Brazil. The worst-hit areas have a number of features in common:

- industrialised belts
- downwind of dense concentration of fossil fuel power stations, smelters and large cities

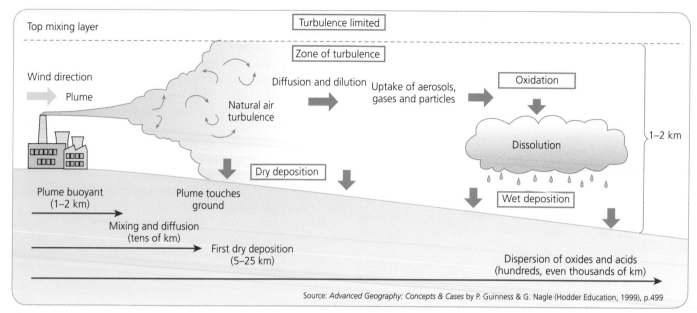

Figure 3.38 Types of acid deposition

- upland areas
- high rainfall
- they contain lots of forest, streams and lakes
- they have thin soils.

The effects of acid rain are to create acid surges and acid flushes, especially after snowmelts and after droughts. A surge may also occur when dry deposits are flushed through a system, perhaps during floods. There are also natural causes of acidification: bog moss secretes acid, heather increases acidity and conifer plantations acidify soils – so the increasing acidification might not necessarily be due to acid rain.

The first effects of acid rain were noted in Scandinavian lakes in the 1960s. Over 18 000 lakes in Sweden are acidified, 4000 of which are seriously affected. Fish stocks in about 9000 Swedish lakes, mostly in the south and the centre of the country, are also badly affected. The most important health effect of acid water is due to its ability to flush trace metals from soil and pipes. Some wells in Sweden have aluminium levels of up to 1.7 mg/l compared with the WHO safe limit of 0.2 mg/l. High levels of metal mercury in fish can cause serious health problems when they are eaten by people.

Trees and forests are severely affected by acid rain. Sulphur dioxide interferes with the process of photosynthesis. Coniferous trees seem to be most at risk from acid rain because they do not shed their needles at the end of year year. On a healthy conifer, needles can be traced back for up to seven years but trees affected by acid rain often have needles from only the last two or three years. If a tree loses over 65 per cent of its needles, it will probably die.

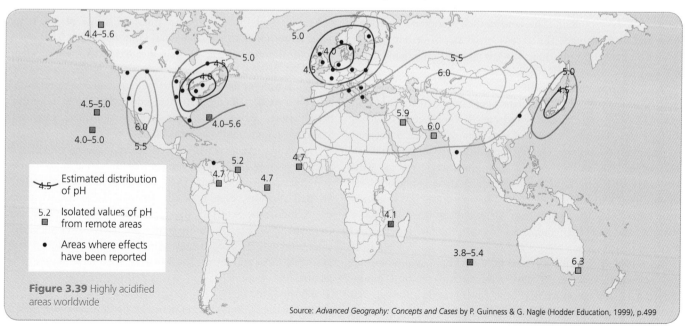

Figure 3.39 Highly acidified areas worldwide

Source: *Advanced Geography: Concepts and Cases* by P. Guinness & G. Nagle (Hodder Education, 1999), p.499

Young trees in soils affected by acid rain often show abnormally rapid growth. This is because the nitrogen in the pollutants acts as a fertiliser. However, the root systems do not develop as well as in trees that have to collect their nutrients from a larger area, and the trees are more easily blown over. Also, they are short of other vital nutrients and the wood can be very soft, making the trees more prone to attacks from insects.

Damaged coniferous trees can be recognised because the extremities of the trees die, especially the crown which is most exposed. Needles drop and leave the tree looking very thin. Branches on some trees droop. In most cases acid rain does not kill the tree. It is one more pressure on the tree which becomes stressed and more likely to suffer damage from insects, fungi, frost, wind and drought. Although deciduous trees generally do not suffer as much, research is showing that their growth is also affected.

Farming and forestry can also increase acidification. When plants grow they take up nutrients from the soil and it becomes more acid. When they die and rot back into the soil the nutrients are replaced and the soil becomes less acid. In farming and forestry the plants are harvested, not left to rot back into the soil, which gradually becomes more acid. The removal of a whole tree, including the branches and roots, can be equivalent to the accumulation of 60 years of acid rain. Only taking the trunks reduces this to the equivalent of 20 years of acid rain.

Acidified lakes are characterised by:
- an impoverished species structure
- visibility in the water being several times greater than normal
- white moss spreading across the bottom of the lake
- metals such as cadmium, copper, aluminium, zinc and lead becoming more soluble and more easily available to plants and animals.

It is the extreme pH values that cause most damage to plants and animals. Very often organisms are exposed to extremely low pH levels during the most sensitive part of their life cycle (for fish this may be the fry stage). These short periods coincide with snowmelt and the accompanying acid surge. At these times the water also has a high metal content.

When plants absorb nutrients from the soil they release hydrogen ions, thereby acidifying the soil. However, decomposition of plants returns nutrients to the soil and offsets the acidification process. In arable areas plants are not left to rot on the land but are removed for consumption. Hence a natural buffering mechanism is removed. In addition, the use of nitrogenous fertilisers causes acidification.

The low pH of soil and the presence of metals may cause damage to root filaments (they are used by the tree to absorb nutrients). The tree loses vitality, growth is retarded, there is an inability to cope with stress (such as frost, drought and pests), and the tree becomes susceptible to injury. Needles turn brown and fall off, and eventually whole branches snap away. In parts of Germany more than 50 per cent of the spruce trees are dead or damaged.

Sulphur deposition damages plants and corrodes materials, including steel, zinc, copper, nickel, aluminium, plastics, paper, leather, textiles, plaster, electrical contacts, sandstones and limestones. Acid rain corrodes metal and stonework, making the maintenance of buildings more costly. The major threats are to older historic buildings (Figure 3.40).

As the land becomes more acid, it is less suitable for growing crops and yields can be reduced. The crops themselves can be damaged, for example pollen on maize affected by acid rain does not germinate so well and cannot fertilise the female plant.

The effect on humans is to increase morbidity and mortality. The elderly are especially vulnerable, and those with a heart problem or respiratory problems.

Some environments are able to neutralise the effects of acid rain – this is referred to as the buffering capacity. Chalk and limestone areas are very alkaline and can neutralise acids very effectively. However, the underlying rocks over much of Scandinavia, Scotland and northern Canada are granite. They are naturally acid, and have a very low buffering capacity. It is in these areas that there is the worst damage from acid rain.

Acid waters can be neutralised by adding lime. This causes the aluminium ions to be fixed and precipitated to the lake bed. However, this may poison species that live on the lake bed. The simplest way to reduce sulphur emissions is to:
- make more use of low-sulphur fuels
- desulphurise oil (which is possible, and relatively cheap, whereas desulphurisation of coal is not as effective)
- fix sulphur to lime (a fluidised bed does not involve much additional expense)

Figure 3.40 The effects of acid rain on buildings

- cut down emissions of nitrogen oxides
- apply flue gas desulphurisation
- burn less oil and coal.

Since the 1960s sulphur concentrations in precipitation have remained fairly constant. However, it is likely that dry deposition has increased (the more acid the air the more difficult it is for sulphur dioxide to become sulphuric acid).

Acidification is largely related to human activity, but problems related to its effects on lakes, groundwater, soils and vegetation are diverse. There are environmental, social, economic and medical implications. It is said to be a 'post-industrial form of ruination, which pays little heed to international boundaries'. Many countries produce acid rain and some, like the UK, export it.

Nevertheless there are variations within these areas: some storms produce more acid rain depending on the source of the airmass movement in relation to the source of the oxides; and lime-rich soils and rocks have a large buffering capacity. Moreover, some active volcanoes acidify rainfall through their release of sulphur – the impact of acid rain on the Soufrière Hills in Montserrat is related to volcanic activity there (Figure 3.41).

Figure 3.41 Natural acid rain

Management: prevention or cure?

Repairing the damage caused by acid rain may include liming – but this is not really sustainable. There are a number of options for prevention:

- Burn less fossil fuel (this requires a government initiative in order to switch to nuclear power or HEP).
- Switch to low-sulphur fuel (oil/gas plus high-grade coal).
- Remove sulphur before combustion (an expensive process).
- Reduce sulphur oxides released on combustion (fluidised bed technology – FBT).
- Burn coal in the presence of crushed limestone in order to reduce acidification.
- Remove sulphur from waste gases after combustion (FGD).

Both FBT and FGD are well developed and effective but they are very expensive.

Most nitrogen oxides in the UK come from power stations (46 per cent) and vehicle exhausts (28 per cent). Emissions from power stations can be reduced by FGD and the use of different types of boiler, which reduce the amounts of air present at combustion. Car exhaust gases can be reduced by different types of engine or exhaust, lower speed limits and the provision of more public transport.

Section 3.4 Activities

1 a Outline the natural and man-made causes of acidification.
  b Describe the effects of acidification.
  c In what ways is it possible to manage the effects of acidification?

2 Study Figure 3.42. Identify two ways in which human activities have altered the natural landscape.

3 Outline the environmental impacts of *either* mining *or* quarrying.

4 'The human impact upon the natural environment is largely negative.' Discuss this statement, using examples to support your case.

5 To what extent is the human impact on rocks and weathering sustainable?

Figure 3.42 Some human impacts in southern England

1 Population

1.1 Natural increase as a component of population change

Early humankind

The first hominids appeared in Africa around 5 million years ago, on a planet that is generally accepted to be 4600 million years old. They differed from their predecessors, the apes, in the fact that they walked on two legs and did not use their hands for weight-bearing. During most of the period of early humankind, the global population was very small, reaching perhaps some 125 000 people a million years ago. It has been estimated that 10 000 years ago, when people first began to domesticate animals and cultivate crops, world population was no more than 5 million. Known as the Neolithic Revolution, this period of economic change significantly altered the relationship between people and their environments. But even then the average annual growth rate was less than 0.1 per cent per year – extremely low compared with contemporary trends. This figure represents a rate of **natural increase** of one per thousand (1/1000). Natural increase (or decrease) is the difference between the birth rate and the death rate.

However, as a result of technological advances the **carrying capacity** of the land improved and population increased. By 3500BC global population had reached 30 million and by the time of Christ this had risen to about 250 million (Figure 1.1).

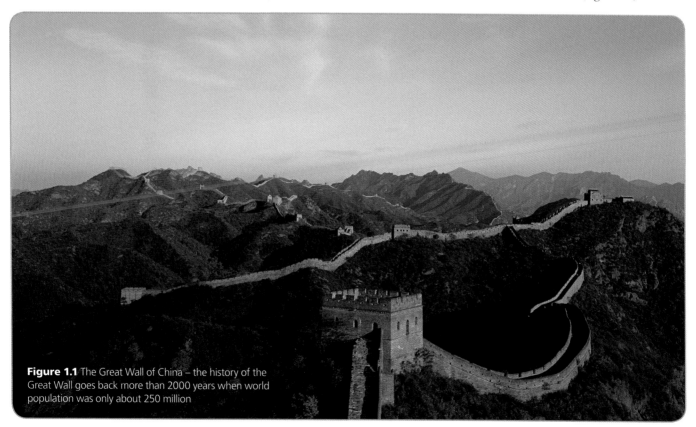

Figure 1.1 The Great Wall of China – the history of the Great Wall goes back more than 2000 years when world population was only about 250 million

Demographers estimate that world population reached 500 million by about 1650. From this time population grew at an increasing rate. By 1800 global population had doubled to reach 1 billion (Figure 1.2). Table 1.1 shows the time taken for each subsequent billion to be reached, with the global total reaching 6 billion in 1999. It had taken only 12 years for world population to increase from 5 billion to 6 billion – the same time span required for the previous billion to be added. It is estimated that the time taken for future billions to be reached will be 12 years until 7 billion is reached in 2011 and a further 13 years until 8 billion is reached in 2024.

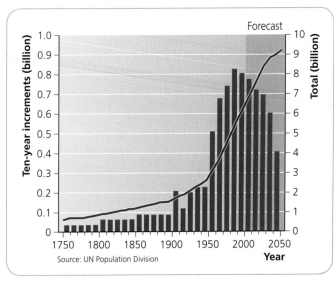

Figure 1.2 World population growth, 1750–2050

Table 1.1 World population growth by each billion

Each billion	Year	Number of years to add each billion
1st	1800	All of human history
2nd	1930	130
3rd	1960	30
4th	1974	14
5th	1987	13
6th	1999	12
7th	2011	12
8th	2024	13

Recent demographic change

Figure 1.3 shows that both total population and the rate of population growth are much higher in the less economically developed countries (LEDCs) than in the more economically developed countries (MEDCs). However, only since the Second World War has population growth in the LEDCs overtaken that in the MEDCs. The MEDCs had their period of high population growth in the nineteenth and early twentieth centuries, while for the LEDCs high population growth has occurred since 1950.

The highest ever global population growth rate was reached in the early to mid-1960s when population growth in the LEDCs

peaked at 2.4 per cent a year. At this time the term 'population explosion' was widely used to describe this rapid population growth. But by the late 1990s the rate of population growth was down to 1.8 per cent. However, even though the rate of growth has been falling for three decades, **population momentum** meant that the numbers being added each year did not peak until the late 1980s (Figure 1.4).

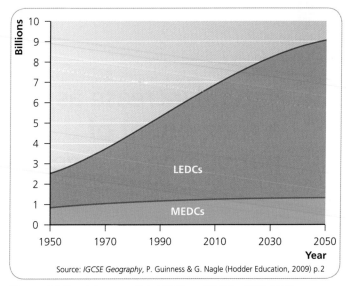

Source: *IGCSE Geography*, P. Guinness & G. Nagle (Hodder Education, 2009) p.2

Figure 1.3 Population growth in MEDCs and LEDCs, 1950–2050

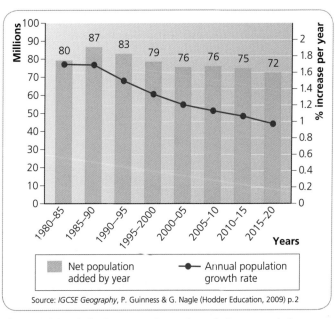

Source: *IGCSE Geography*, P. Guinness & G. Nagle (Hodder Education, 2009) p.2

Figure 1.4 Population increase and growth rate in five-year periods, 1980–2020

The demographic transformation, which took a century to complete in MEDCs, has occurred in a generation in some LEDCs. Fertility has dropped further and faster than most demographers foresaw two or three decades ago, except in Africa and the Middle East, where in over 30 countries families of at least five children are the norm and population growth is still over 2.5 per cent – this is a very high rate of natural increase.

The components of population change

Figure 1.5 illustrates the components of population change for world regions and smaller areas. In terms of the planet as a whole, natural change accounts for all population increase. Natural change is the balance between births and deaths, while net migration is the difference between immigration and emigration. The corrugated divide on Figure 1.5 indicates that the relative contributions of natural change and net migration can vary over time within a particular country as well as between countries at any one point in time. The model is a simple graphical alternative to the population equation:

$$P = (B - D) \pm M$$

where P = population, B = births, D = deaths and M = migration.

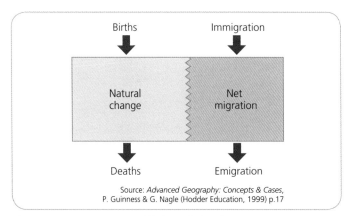

Source: *Advanced Geography: Concepts & Cases,*
P. Guinness & G. Nagle (Hodder Education, 1999) p.17

Figure 1.5 Input–output model of population change

Natural change can be stated in absolute or relative terms. Absolute natural change gives the actual change in population as a result of the difference between the number of births and deaths, for example, 200 000. Relative natural change is expressed as a rate per thousand, for example 3/1000. Table 1.2 shows natural change by world region for 2010.

Table 1.2 Birth rate, death rate and rate of natural change by world region, 2010

Region	Birth rate	Death rate	Rate of natural change
World	20	8	12
MEDCs	11	10	1
LEDCs	22	8	14
Africa	37	13	24
Asia	19	7	12
Latin America/ Caribbean	19	6	13
North America	13	8	6
Oceania	18	7	11
Europe	11	11	0

Source: Population Reference Bureau, *2010 World Population Data Sheet*

Section 1.1 Activities

1 Define the term *natural increase*.

2 Describe the change in world population since 1750 illustrated by Figure 1.2.

3 Describe and explain the trends shown in Figure 1.4.

4 Discuss the global variations in birth rate, death rate and rate of natural change shown in Table 1.2.

The factors affecting levels of fertility

Fertility varies widely around the world. According to the 2010 World Population Data Sheet the **crude birth rate**, the most basic measure of fertility, varied from a high of 52/1000 in Niger to a low of 7/1000 in Monaco. The word 'crude' means that the birth rate applies to the total population, taking no account of gender and age. The crude birth rate is heavily influenced by the age structure of a population. The crucial factor is the percentage of young women of reproductive age, as these women produce most children.

For more accurate measures of fertility, the 'fertility rate' and the 'total fertility rate' are used. The **fertility rate** is the number of live births per 1000 women aged 15–49 years in a given year. The **total fertility rate** is the average number of children that would be born alive to a woman (or group of women) during her lifetime, if she were to pass through her childbearing years conforming to the age-specific fertility rates of a given year. The total fertility rate varies from a high of 7.4 in Niger to a low of 1.0 in China (Macao) and China (Hong Kong). Table 1.3 shows the variations in total fertility rate by world region alongside data for the percentage of women using contraception for each region. The latter is a major factor influencing fertility. Figure 1.6 shows in detail how the fertility rate varies by country around the world.

Table 1.3 Variations in total fertility rate and the percentage of women using contraception by world region, 2010

Region	Total fertility rate	% of women using contraception (all methods)
World	2.5	62
MEDCs	1.7	71
LEDCs	2.7	60
Africa	4.7	29
Asia	2.2	66
Latin America/ Caribbean	2.3	73
North America	2.0	78
Oceania	2.5	82
Europe	1.6	70

Source: Population Reference Bureau, *2010 World Population Data Sheet*

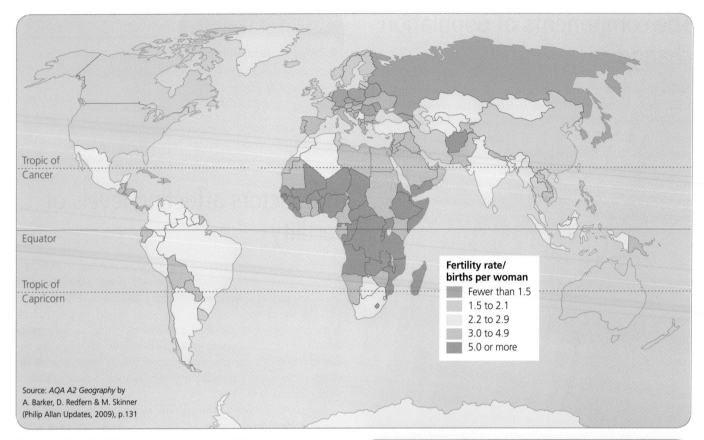

Source: *AQA A2 Geography* by
A. Barker, D. Redfern & M. Skinner
(Philip Allan Updates, 2009), p.131

Figure 1.6 Total fertility rate by country, around 2008

The factors affecting fertility can be grouped into four main categories:

- **Demographic**: other population factors, particularly mortality rates, influence fertility. Where infant mortality is high, it is usual for many children to die before reaching adult life. In such societies, parents often have many children to compensate for these expected deaths.
- **Social/Cultural**: in some societies, particularly in Africa, tradition demands high rates of reproduction. Here the opinion of women in the reproductive years may have little influence weighed against intense cultural expectations. Education, especially female literacy, is the key to lower fertility (Figure 1.7). With education comes a knowledge of birth control, greater social awareness, more opportunity for employment, and a wider choice of action generally. In some countries religion is an important factor. For example, the Muslim and Roman Catholic religions oppose artificial birth control. Most countries that have population policies have been trying to reduce their fertility by investing in birth control programmes. Within LEDCs it is usually the poorest neighbourhoods that have the highest fertility, due mainly to a combination of high infant mortality and low educational opportunities for women.
- **Economic**: in many LEDCs children are seen as an economic asset because of the work they do and also because of the support they are expected to give their parents in old age.

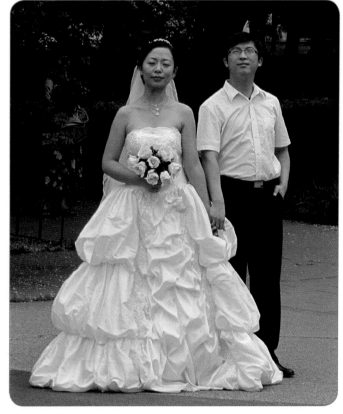

Figure 1.7 The average age of marriage in a country is an important factor affecting fertility

In MEDCs the general perception is reversed and the cost of the child dependency years is a major factor in the decision to begin or extend a family. Economic growth allows greater spending on health, housing, nutrition and education, which is important in lowering mortality and in turn reducing fertility. Also, the nature of employment can have an impact on fertility. Many companies, particularly in MEDCs, do not want to lose valuable female workers and therefore may provide workplace childcare and offer the opportunity of flexible working time.

- **Political**: there are many examples in the past century of governments attempting to change the rate of population growth for economic and strategic reasons. During the late 1930s Germany, Italy and Japan all offered inducements and concessions to those with large families. In more recent years Malaysia has adopted a similar policy. However, today, most governments that are interventionist in terms of fertility still want to reduce population growth.

The above factors do not affect fertility directly; they influence another set of variables that determine the rate and level of childbearing. Figure 1.8 shows these 'intermediate variables'. These factors operate in every country, but their relative importance can vary from one country to another.

Fertility decline

A study by the United Nations published in 2007 predicted that global population would peak at 9.2 billion in 2050. This contrasts with a report published in 1996 which forecast that

Fecundity
- Ability to have intercourse
- Ability to conceive
- Ability to carry a pregnancy to term

Sexual unions*
- The formation and dissolution of unions
- Age at first intercourse
- Proportion of women who are married or in a union
- Time spent outside a union (separated, divorced or widowed, for example)
- Frequency of intercourse
- Sexual abstinence (religious or cultural customs, for example)
- Temporary separations (military service, for example)

Birth control
- Use of contraceptives
- Contraceptive sterilisation
- Induced abortion

*Includes marriage as well as long-term and casual relationships

Figure 1.8 The intermediate variables that affect fertility

the world's population would peak at 10.6 billion in 2080. The global peak population has been continually revised downwards in recent decades. This is in sharp contrast to warnings in earlier decades of a population 'explosion'. The main reason for the slowdown in population growth is that fertility levels in most parts of the world have fallen faster than was previously expected.

In the second half of the 1960s, after a quarter-century of increasing growth, the rate of world population growth began to slow down. Since then some LEDCs have seen the speediest falls in fertility ever known and thus earlier population projections did not materialise.

A fertility rate of 2.1 children per woman is **replacement level fertility**, below which populations eventually start falling. According to the 2010 World Population Data Sheet there are already 87 countries with total fertility rates at or below 2.1. This number is likely to increase. The movement to replacement level fertility is undoubtedly one of the most dramatic social changes in history, enabling many more women to work and children to be educated.

Section 1.1 Activities

1 a Define the terms *fertility rate* and *total fertility rate*.
  b Why is the fertility rate a better measure of fertility than the crude birth rate?

2 a Describe and explain the differences in fertility by world region shown in Table 1.3.
  b Describe and attempt to explain the more detailed pattern of global fertility shown by Figure 1.6.

3 How can **a** government policies and **b** religious philosophy influence fertility?

4 Why is replacement level fertility an important concept?

5 Discuss the importance of three of the intermediate variables shown in Figure 1.8.

The factors affecting mortality

Like crude birth rate, **crude death rate** is a very generalised measure of mortality. It is heavily influenced by the age structure of a population. For example, the crude death rate for the UK is 9/1000 compared with 6/1000 in Brazil. Yet life expectancy at birth in the UK is 80 years compared with 73 years in Brazil. Brazil has a much younger population than the UK, but the average quality of life is significantly higher in the latter.

In 2010 the crude death rate varied around the world, from a high of 20/1000 in Zambia to a low of 1/1000 in Qatar. Table 1.4 shows variations by world region and also includes data for infant mortality and life expectancy at birth. The **infant mortality rate** and **life expectancy** are much more accurate measures of mortality. The infant mortality rate is an age-specific rate – that is, it applies to one particular year of age.

Table 1.4 Death rate, infant mortality rate and life expectancy at birth by world region, 2010

Region	Crude death rate	Infant mortality rate	Life expectancy at birth
World	8	46	69
MEDCs	10	6	77
LEDCs	8	50	67
Africa	13	76	55
Asia	7	41	70
Latin America/Caribbean	6	22	74
North America	8	6	78
Oceania	7	21	76
Europe	11	6	76

Source: Population Reference Bureau, *2010 World Population Data Sheet*

The causes of death vary significantly between the MEDCs and LEDCs (Figure 1.9; and see also Figure 1.10). In LEDCs, infectious and parasitic diseases account for over 40 per cent of all deaths. They are also a major cause of disability and social and economic upheaval. In contrast, in MEDCs these diseases have a relatively low impact. In these countries heart disease and cancer are the big killers. Epidemiology is the study of diseases. As countries develop, the ranking of major diseases tends to change from infectious to degenerative. This change is known as the epidemiological transition.

Apart from the challenges of the physical environment in many LEDCs, a range of social and economic factors contribute to the high rates of infectious diseases. These include:

- poverty
- poor access to healthcare
- antibiotic resistance
- evolving human migration patterns
- new infectious agents.

When people live in overcrowded and insanitary conditions, communicable diseases such as tuberculosis and cholera can spread rapidly. Limited access to healthcare and medicines means that otherwise treatable conditions such as malaria and tuberculosis are often fatal to poor people. Poor nutrition and deficient immune systems are also key risk factors involved in many deaths from conditions such as lower respiratory infections, tuberculosis and measles.

Within most individual countries variations in mortality occur due to:

- social class
- ethnicity
- place of residence
- occupation
- age structure of the population.

As Table 1.4 shows, there is a huge contrast in infant mortality by world region. Africa has the highest rate (76/1000) and Europe and North America (6/1000) the lowest rate. The variation among individual countries is even greater. In 2010 the highest infant mortality rates were in Afghanistan (155/1000) and Chad (130/1000). In contrast the lowest rate was in Hong Kong (1.7/1000). The infant mortality rate is frequently considered to be the most sensitive indicator of socio-economic progress, being heavily influenced by fundamental improvements in the quality of life such as improvements in water supply, better nutrition, and improved healthcare. Once children survive the crucial first year, their life chances improve substantially. Infant mortality in today's rich countries has changed considerably over time. In 1900, infant mortality in the USA was 120/1000. In 2009 it was down to 6.4/1000.

Table 1.4 shows that the lowest average life expectancy by world region is in Africa (55 years), with the highest average figure in northern America (78 years). Rates of life expectancy at birth have converged significantly between MEDCs and LEDCs during the last 50 years or so, in spite of a widening wealth gap. These increases in life expectancy have to a certain extent offset the widening disparity between per capita incomes in MEDCs

Figure 1.9 Contrasts in the causes of death between MEDCs and LEDCs

Figure 1.10 Drinking and dangerous driving warning to motorists in Mongolia: a significant cause of death among young men

and LEDCs. However, it must not be forgotten that the ravages of AIDS in particular has caused recent decreases in life expectancy in some countries in sub-Saharan Africa. It is likely that the life expectancy gap between MEDCs and LEDCs will continue to narrow in the future.

Section 1.1 Activities

1 Define the terms **a** *crude death rate*, **b** *infant mortality rate* and **c** *life expectancy*.

2 Why is crude death rate a very limited measure of mortality?

3 Using Figure 1.9, describe and explain the contrast in the causes of death between MEDCs and LEDCs.

4 To what extent does infant mortality vary around the world?

5 Discuss the main reasons for such large variations in infant mortality.

6 Describe the global variations in life expectancy.

The interpretation of age/ gender pyramids

The most studied aspects of **population structure** are age and gender (Figure 1.11). Other aspects of population structure that can also be studied include race, language, religion, and social/ occupational groups.

Figure 1.11 Young children outside a *ger* in central Asia

Age and gender structures are conventionally illustrated by the use of **population pyramids**. Pyramids can be used to portray either absolute or relative data. Absolute data show the figures in thousands or millions, while relative data show the numbers involved in percentages. The latter is most frequently used as it allows for easier comparison of countries of different population sizes. Each bar represents a five-year age-group, apart from the uppermost bar which illustrates the population of a certain age and older, such as 85 or 100. The male population is represented to the left of the vertical axis with females to the right.

Population pyramids change significantly in shape as a country progresses through demographic transition (Figure 1.12).

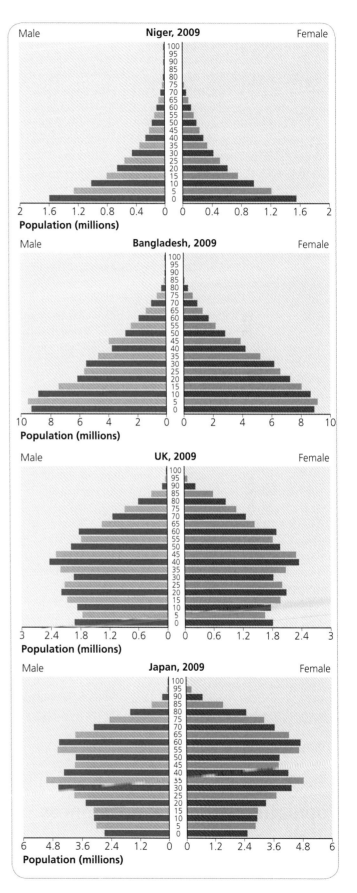

Figure 1.12 Four population pyramids

- The wide base in Niger's pyramid reflects extremely high fertility. The birth rate in Niger is 53/1000, the highest in the world. The marked decrease in width of each successive bar indicates relatively high mortality and limited life expectancy. The death rate at 14/1000 is high, particularly considering how young the population is. The infant mortality rate is a very high 88/1000. Life expectancy in Niger is 53 years; 49 per cent of the population is under 15, with only 3 per cent aged 65 or more. Niger is in stage 2 of demographic transition.
- The base of the second pyramid, showing the population structure of Bangladesh, is narrower, reflecting a considerable fall in fertility after decades of government-promoted birth control programmes. The almost equal width of the youngest three bars is evidence of recent falls in fertility. The birth rate is currently 23/1000. Falling mortality and lengthening life expectancy is reflected in the relatively wide bars in the teenage and young adult age groups. The death rate at 7/1000 is almost half that of Niger. The infant mortality rate is 48/1000. Life expectancy in Bangladesh is 65 years; 32 per cent of the population are under 15, while 4 per cent are 65 or over. Bangladesh is an example of a country in stage 3 of demographic transition.
- In the pyramid for the UK much lower fertility still is illustrated by narrowing of the base. The birth rate in the UK is only 13/1000. The reduced narrowing of each successive bar indicates a further decline in mortality and greater life expectancy compared with Bangladesh. The death rate in the UK is 9/1000, with an infant mortality rate of 4.6/1000. Life expectancy is 79 years; 18 per cent of the population are under 15, while 16 per cent are 65 or over. The UK is in stage 4 of demographic transition.
- The final pyramid (Japan) has a distinctly inverted base reflecting the lowest fertility of all four countries. The birth rate is 9/1000. The width of the rest of the pyramid is a consequence of the lowest mortality and highest life expectancy of all four countries. The death rate is 9/1000 with infant mortality at 2.6/1000. Life expectancy is 83 years. Japan has only 13 per cent of its population under 15, with 23 per cent at 65 or over. With the birth rate and the death rate in balance Japan is on the boundary of stages 4 and 5 of demographic transition.

Figure 1.13 provides some useful tips for understanding population pyramids. A good starting point is to divide the pyramid into three sections:
- the young dependent population
- the economically active population
- the elderly dependent population.

Population structure: differences within countries

In countries where there is strong rural to urban migration, the population structures of the areas affected can be markedly different. These differences show up clearly on population

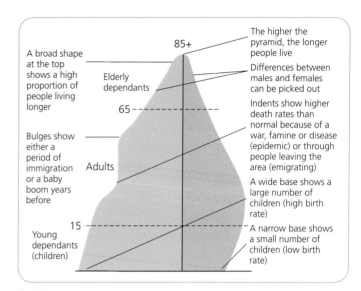

Figure 1.13 An annotated population pyramid

pyramids. Out-migration from rural areas is age-selective with single young adults and young adults with children dominating this process. Thus, the bars for these age groups in rural areas affected by out-migration will indicate fewer people than expected in these age groups. In contrast, the population pyramids for urban areas attracting migrants will show age-selective in-migration, with substantially more people in these age groups than expected. Such migrations may also be sex-selective. If this is the case it should be apparent on the population pyramids.

Sex structure

The **sex ratio** is the number of males per 100 females in a population. Male births consistently exceed female births, for a combination of biological and social reasons. For example, more couples decide to complete their family on the birth of a boy than on the birth of a girl. In the UK 105 boys are born for every 100 girls. However, after birth the gap generally begins to narrow until eventually females outnumber males, as at every age male mortality is higher than female mortality. This process happens most rapidly in the poorest countries where infant mortality is markedly higher among males than females. Here the gap may be closed in less than a year. In the UK it is not until the 45–59 age group that females outnumber males. In the age group 85 and over, females make up 74 per cent of the population.

However, there are anomalies to the picture just presented. In countries where the position of women is markedly subordinate and deprived, the overall sex ratio may show an excess of males. Such countries often exhibit high mortality rates in childbirth. For example, in India there are 107 males per 100 females for the population as a whole.

A report published in China in 2002 recorded 116 male births for every 100 female births due to the significant number of female foetuses aborted by parents intent on having a male child. Even within countries there can be significant differences in the sex ratio. In the USA, Alaska has the highest ratio at 103.2, while Mississippi has the lowest at 92.2.

The dependency ratio

Dependants are people who are too young or too old to work. The **dependency ratio** is the relationship between the working or economically active population and the non-working population. The formula for calculating the dependency ratio is:

$$\text{Dependency ratio} = \frac{\text{\% population aged 0–14 + \% population aged 65 and over}}{\text{\% population aged 15–64}} \times 100$$

A dependency ratio of 60 means that for every 100 people in the economically active population there are 60 people dependent on them. The dependency ratio in MEDCs is usually between 50 and 75. In contrast, LEDCs typically have higher ratios which may reach over 100. In LEDCs, children form the great majority of the dependent population. In contrast, in MEDCs there is a more equal balance between young and old dependants. Calculations of the **youth dependency ratio** and the **elderly dependency ratio** can show these contrasts more clearly.

$$\text{Youth dependency ratio} = \frac{\text{\% population aged 0–14}}{\text{\% population aged 15–64}} \times 100$$

$$\text{Elderly dependency ratio} = \frac{\text{\% population aged 65 and over}}{\text{\% population aged 15–64}} \times 100$$

For any country or region the dependency ratio is equal to the sum of the youth dependency ratio and the elderly dependency ratio.

The dependency ratio is important because the economically active population will in general contribute more to the economy in income tax, VAT and corporation tax. In contrast, the dependent population tend to be bigger recipients of government funding, particularly for education, healthcare and public pensions. An increase in the dependency ratio can cause significant financial problems for governments if it does not have the financial reserves to cope with such a change.

The dependency ratio is an internationally agreed measure. Partly because of this it is a very crude indicator. For example:

- In MEDCs, few people leave education before the age of 18 and a significant number will go on to university and not get a job before the age of 21. In addition, while some people will retire before the age of 65, others will go on working beyond this age. Also, a significant number of people in the economically active age group do not work for various reasons, such as parents staying at home to look after children (Figure 1.14). The number of people in this situation can vary considerably from one country to another.
- In LEDCs a significant proportion of children are working full or part-time before the age of 15. In some LEDCs there is very high unemployment and underemployment within the economically active age group.

Figure 1.14 Early Learning Centre: this shop caters for the needs of young dependants, creating economic demand and jobs

However, despite its limitations the dependency ratio does allow reasonable comparisons between countries (Table 1.5). It is also useful to see how individual countries change over time. Once an analysis using the dependency ratio has been made, more detailed research can look into any apparent anomalies.

Table 1.5 Dependency ratio calculations

Country	% population		Dependency ratio
	<15 years	**65 and over**	
USA	20	13	
Japan	13	23	
Germany	14	20	
UK	18	16	
Russia	15	14	
Brazil	27	6	
India	32	5	
China	18	8	
Nigeria	43	3	
Bangladesh	32	4	
Egypt	33	4	
Bolivia	37	4	

Source: Population Reference Bureau, *2010 World Population Data Sheet*

1.2 Demographic transition

Changes in birth rate and death rate over time: the demographic transition model

Birth and death rates change over time. Although the birth and death rates of no two countries have changed in exactly the same way, some broad generalisations can be made about population growth since the middle of the eighteenth century. These generalisations are illustrated by the model of **demographic transition** (Figure 1.15) which is based on the experience of north-west Europe, the first part of the world to undergo such changes as a result of the significant industrial and agrarian advances which occurred during the eighteenth and nineteenth centuries.

No country as a whole retains the characteristics of stage 1, which applies only to the most remote societies on Earth, such as isolated tribes in New Guinea and the Amazon which have little or no contact at all with the outside world. All the MEDCs of the world are now in stages 4 or 5, most having experienced all of the previous stages at different times. The poorest of the LEDCs (for example Bangladesh, Niger, Bolivia) are in stage 2 but are joined in this stage by a number of oil-rich Middle East nations where increasing affluence has not been accompanied by a significant fall in fertility. Most LEDCs that have registered significant social and economic advances are in stage 3 (for example Brazil, China, India) while some of the newly industrialised countries such as South Korea and Taiwan have entered stage 4. With the passage of time there can be little doubt that more countries will attain the demographic characteristics of the final stages of the model. The basic characteristics of each stage are as follows.

The high fluctuating stage (stage 1): The crude birth rate is high and stable while the crude death rate is high and fluctuating due to the sporadic incidence of famine, disease and war. The use of the word 'crude' means that the birth and death rates are based on the total population and as such they are very generalised, with clear limitations. In this stage population growth is very slow and there may be periods of considerable decline. Infant mortality is high and life expectancy low (see Figure 1.16). A high proportion of the population is under the age of 15. Society is pre-industrial with most people living in rural areas, dependent on subsistence agriculture.

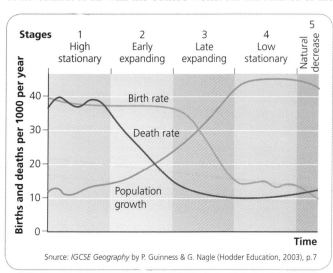

Source: *IGCSE Geography* by P. Guinness & G. Nagle (Hodder Education, 2003), p.7

Figure 1.15 Model of demographic transition

Figure 1.16 A graveyard dating from the eighteenth century in the UK. Inscriptions show that life expectancy at that time was very low.

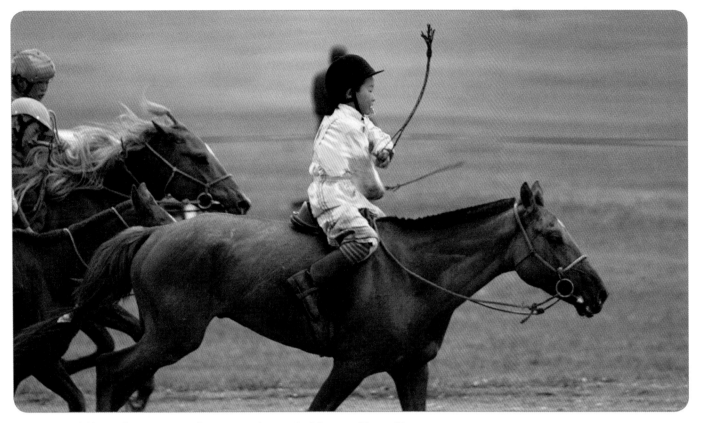

Figure 1.17 Children on horses in Mongolia – a country in stage 3 of demographic transition

The early expanding stage (stage 2): The death rate declines significantly. The birth rate remains at its previous level as the social norms governing fertility take time to change. As the gap between the two vital rates widens, the **rate of natural change** increases to a peak at the end of this stage. Infant mortality falls and life expectancy increases. The proportion of the population under 15 increases. Although the reasons for the decline in mortality vary somewhat in intensity and sequence from one country to another, the essential causal factors are: better nutrition; improved public health, particularly in terms of clean water supply and efficient sewerage systems; and medical advance. Considerable rural-to-urban migration occurs during this stage. However, for LEDCs in recent decades urbanisation has often not been accompanied by the industrialisation that was characteristic of the MEDCs during the nineteenth century.

The late expanding stage (stage 3): After a period of time social norms adjust to the lower level of mortality and the birth rate begins to decline. Urbanisation generally slows and average age increases. Life expectancy continues to increase and infant mortality to decrease. Countries in this stage usually experience lower death rates than nations in the final stage, due to their relatively young population structures (Figure 1.17).

The low fluctuating stage (stage 4): Both birth and death rates are low. The former is generally slightly higher, fluctuating somewhat due to changing economic conditions. Population growth is slow. Death rates rise slightly as the average age of the population increases. However, life expectancy still improves as age-specific mortality rates continue to fall.

The natural decrease stage (stage 5): In an increasing number of countries the birth rate has fallen below the death rate, resulting in **natural decrease**. In the absence of net migration inflows these populations are declining. Most countries in this stage are in eastern or southern Europe.

Criticisms of the model

Critics of the demographic transition model see it as too Eurocentric as it was based on the experience of Western Europe. It is therefore not necessarily relevant to the experience of other countries. Critics argue that many LEDCs may not follow the sequence set out in the model. It has also been criticised for its failure to take into account changes due to migration.

The model presumes that all countries will eventually pass through all stages of the transition, just as the MEDCs have done. Because these countries have achieved economic success and enjoy generally high standards of living, completion of the demographic transition has come to be associated with socio-economic progress.

This raises two major questions:
- Can LEDCs today hope to achieve either the demographic transition or the economic progress enjoyed by the MEDCs which passed through the transition at a different time and under different circumstances?
- Is the socio-economic change experienced by MEDCs a prerequisite or a consequence of demographic transition?

Demographic transition in LEDCs

There are a number of important differences in the way that LEDCs have undergone population change compared with the experiences of most MEDCs. In LEDCs:

- Birth rates in stages 1 and 2 were generally higher. About a dozen African countries currently have birth rates of 45/1000 or over. Twenty years ago many more African countries were in this situation.
- The death rate fell much more steeply and for different reasons. For example, the rapid introduction of Western medicine, particularly in the form of inoculation against major diseases, has had a huge impact in reducing mortality. However, AIDS has caused the death rate to rise significantly in some countries, particularly in sub-Saharan Africa.
- Some countries had much larger base populations and thus the impact of high growth in stage 2 and the early part of stage 3 has been far greater. No countries that are now classed as MEDCs had populations anywhere near the size of India and China when they entered stage 2 of demographic transition.
- For those countries in stage 3 the fall in fertility has also been steeper. This has been due mainly to the relatively widespread availability of modern contraception with high levels of reliability.

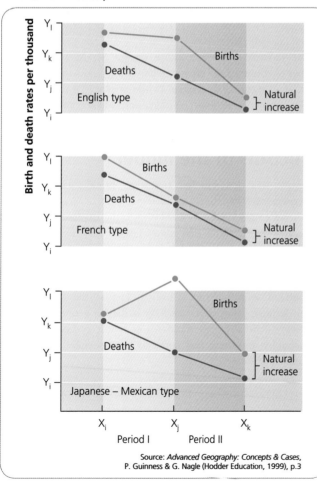

Source: *Advanced Geography: Concepts & Cases,*
P. Guinness & G. Nagle (Hodder Education, 1999), p.3

Figure 1.18 Types of demographic transition

- The relationship between population change and economic development has been much more tenuous.

Different models of demographic transition

Although most countries followed the classical or UK model of demographic transition illustrated above, some countries did not. The Czech demographer Pavlik recognised two alternative types of population change, shown in Figure 1.18. In France the birth rate fell at about the same time as the death rate and there was no intermediate period of high natural increase. In Japan and Mexico the birth rate actually increased in stage 2 due mainly to the improved health of women in the reproductive age range.

Section 1.2 Activities

1 What is a geographical model (such as the model of demographic transition)?

2 Explain the reasons for declining mortality in stage 2 of demographic transition.

3 Why does it take some time before fertility follows the fall in mortality (stage 3)?

4 Suggest why the birth rate is lower than the death rate in some countries (stage 5).

5 Discuss the merits and limitations of the model of demographic transition.

6 Why has the death rate in LEDCs fallen much more steeply over the last 50 years, compared with the fall in the death rate in earlier times in MEDCs?

Issues of ageing populations

According to the United Nations, 'Population ageing is unprecedented, without parallel in human history and the twenty-first century will witness even more rapid ageing than did the century just past.' In western Europe in 1800, less than 25 per cent of men would live to the age of 60. Today, more than 90 per cent do.

The world's population is ageing significantly. **Ageing of population** (demographic ageing) is a rise in the median age of a population. It occurs when fertility declines while life expectancy remains constant or increases.

The following factors have been highlighted by the United Nations:

- The global average for life expectancy increased from 46 years in 1950 to nearly 65 in 2000. It is projected to reach 74 years by 2050.
- In LEDCs the population aged 60 years and over is expected to quadruple between 2000 and 2050.
- In MEDCs the number of older people was greater than that of children for the first time in 1998. By 2050 older people in MEDCs will outnumber children by more than two to one.

- The population aged 80 years and over numbered 69 million in 2000. This was the fastest-growing section of the global population which is projected to increase to 375 million by 2050.
- Europe is the 'oldest' region in the world. Those aged 60 years and over currently form 20 per cent of the population. This should rise to 35 per cent by 2050.
- Japan is the oldest nation with a median age of 41.3 years, followed by Italy, Switzerland, Germany and Sweden (Figure 1.19).
- Africa is the 'youngest' region in the world, with the proportion of children accounting for 43 per cent of the population today. However, this is expected to decline to 28 per cent by 2050. In contrast the proportion of older people is projected to increase from 5 per cent to 10 per cent over the same time period.

Figure 1.20 A 60th birthday party with three generations present

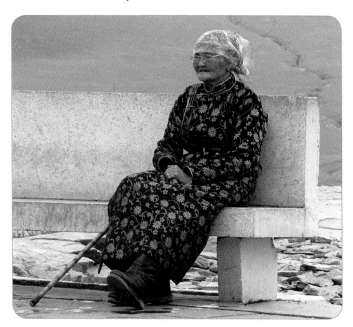

Figure 1.19 An elderly woman – demographic ageing is a worldwide phenomenon

Table 1.6 shows that 8 per cent of the world's population are aged 65 years and over. On a continental scale this varies from only 3 per cent in Africa to 16 per cent in Europe. Population projections show that the world population in the age group 65 years and over will rise to 10 per cent in 2025, and to 16 per cent by 2050.

Table 1.6 The percentage of total population aged 65 years and over, 2010

World	8
Africa	3
North America	13
Latin America/Caribbean	7
Asia	7
Europe	16
Oceania	11

Source: Population Reference Bureau, *2010 World Population Data Sheet*

The problem of demographic ageing has been a concern of MEDCs for some time, but it is now also beginning to alarm LEDCs. Although ageing has begun later in LEDCs it is progressing at a faster rate. This follows the pattern of previous demographic change, such as declining mortality and falling fertility where change in LEDCs was much faster than that previously experienced by MEDCs.

Demographic ageing will put healthcare systems, public pensions, and government budgets in general, under increasing pressure (Figure 1.20). Four per cent of the USA's population was 65 years of age and older in 1900. By 1995 this had risen to 12.8 per cent and by 2030 it is likely that one in five Americans will be senior citizens. The fastest-growing segment of the population is the so-called 'oldest-old': those who are 85 years or more. It is this age group that is most likely to need expensive residential care. The situation is similar in other MEDCs.

Some countries have made relatively good pension provision by investing wisely over a long period of time. However, others have more or less adopted a pay-as-you-go system, as the elderly dependent population rises. It is this latter group who will be faced with the biggest problems in the future.

For much of the post-1950 period the main demographic problem has been generally perceived as the 'population explosion', a result of very high fertility in LEDCs. However, greater concern is now being expressed about demographic ageing in many countries where difficult decisions about the reallocation of resources are having to be made. At present very few countries are generous in looking after their elderly. Poverty amongst the elderly is a considerable problem but technological advance might provide a solution by improving living standards for everyone. If not, other less popular solutions, such as increased taxation, will have to be examined.

However, some demographers argue that there needs to be a certain rethinking of age and ageing, with older people adopting healthier and more adventurous lifestyles than people of the same age only one or two generations ago. Sayings such as '50 is the new 40' have become fairly commonplace. They argue that we should not just think of chronological age, but also of prospective age – the remaining years of life expectancy people have (Table 1.7).

It is of course easy to underestimate the positive aspects of ageing:

- Many older people make a big contribution to childcare by looking after their grandchildren.
- Large numbers of older people work as volunteers, for example in charity shops.

Table 1.7 Remaining life expectancy among French women, 1952 and 2005

Year	Years lived	Remaining life expectancy (years)
1952	30	44.7
2005	30	54.4

Source: *Population Bulletin* Vol.63 No.4 2008

Section 1.2 Activities

1 Describe the variations shown in Table 1.6.

2 Why is a large elderly dependent population generally viewed as a problem?

3 Discuss the possible benefits of a large elderly population.

4 Briefly explain the data shown in Table 1.7.

Case Study

Population ageing in Japan

Japan has the most rapidly ageing population in the history of the world:

- One in five Japanese are over the age of 60.
- Nearly 2 million Japanese are now over 80 years of age.
- The country's population peaked in 2005 at 128 million (Figure 1.21). The most extreme population projection predicts a decline of 50 million by the end of this century.
- Fertility has declined substantially and the total fertility rate is an extremely low 1.3.
- No other country has a lower percentage of its population under 15.

A high elderly dependency ratio presents considerable economic and social challenges to the country, not least in terms of pensions, healthcare and long-term care. Japan's workforce peaked at 67.9 million in 1998 and has been in decline since. This presents an increasing economic burden on the existing workforce. However, it must be noted that there is a high labour force participation rate among the elderly. Japanese men work an average of five years after mandatory retirement.

Japan has a long tradition of positive attitudes towards older people. Every year, National Respect the Aged Day is a public holiday. However, while there is a strong tradition of elderly people being looked after by their families, the number of old people living in care homes or other welfare facilities is steadily rising. The cost of care is shared between the elderly person, their family and the government. As the number of people in

this situation increases, more pressure is placed on the country's economy. Social changes are also occurring, for example the emergence of ageing as a theme in films and books.

Younger workers are at a premium and there is considerable competition to recruit them. One solution is for manufacturers to set up affiliated companies in China or other countries, but past results have been mixed. The possibility of expanding immigration to help reduce the rising dependency ratio appears to be politically unacceptable in Japan. Foreigners make up only 1 per cent of Japan's labour force. Legal immigration is practically impossible (except for highly skilled ethnic Japanese workers) and illegal immigration is strictly suppressed.

The UN predicts that, by 2045, for every four Japanese aged 20–64 there will be three people aged 65 or over. The key question is what is a socially acceptable level of provision for the elderly in terms of the proportion of the country's total GDP? This is a question many other countries are going to have to ask themselves as well. Pension reforms have been implemented, with later retirement and higher contributions from employers. However, it is likely that further changes will be required as the cost of ageing rises.

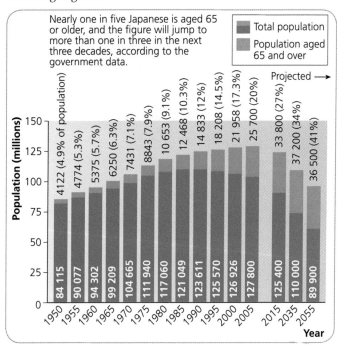

Figure 1.21 Population trends in Japan

Section 1.2 Activities

1 Describe the changes in Japan's population shown in Figure 1.21.

2 Why does Japan have a rapidly ageing population?

3 Suggest why this trend may contribute to changing attitudes towards the elderly.

The link between population and development

Development, or improvement in the quality of life, is a wide-ranging concept. It includes wealth, but it also includes other important aspects of our lives. For example, many people would consider good health to be more important than wealth. People who live in countries that are not democracies and where freedom of speech cannot be taken for granted often envy those who do live in democratic countries. Development occurs when there are improvements to the individual factors making up the quality of life. For example, development occurs in a low-income country when:

- the local food supply improves due to investment in machinery and fertilisers
- the electricity grid extends outwards from the main urban areas to rural areas
- a new road or railway improves the accessibility of a remote province
- levels of literacy improve throughout the country
- average incomes increase above the level of inflation.

There has been much debate about the causes of development. Detailed studies have shown that variations between countries are due to a variety of factors:

Physical geography

- Landlocked countries have generally developed more slowly than coastal ones.
- Small island countries face considerable disadvantages in development.
- Tropical countries have grown more slowly than those in temperate latitudes, reflecting the cost of poor health and unproductive farming in the former. However, richer non-agricultural tropical countries, such as Singapore, do not suffer a geographical deficit of this kind.
- A generous allocation of natural resources has spurred economic growth in a number of countries.

Economic policies

- Open economies that welcomed and encouraged foreign investment have developed faster than closed economies.
- Fast-growing countries tend to have high rates of saving and low spending relative to GDP.
- Institutional quality in terms of good government, law and order and lack of corruption generally result in a high rate of growth.

Demography

- Progress through demographic transition is a significant factor, with the highest rates of economic growth experienced by those nations where the birth rate has fallen the most.

In 1990 the **Human Development Index (HDI)** was devised by the United Nations to indicate levels of development in countries. The HDI contains three variables:

- life expectancy

- educational attainment (adult literacy and combined primary, secondary and tertiary enrolment)
- GDP per capita (PPP$).

One of the three variables used in the HDI is therefore a key demographic factor. The actual figures for each of these three measures are converted into an index (Figure 1.22) which has a maximum value of 1.0 in each case. The three index values are then combined and averaged to give an overall Human Development Index value. This also has a maximum value of 1.0. Every year the United Nations publishes the *Human Development Report* which uses the Human Development Index (HDI) to rank all the countries of the world in terms of their level of development.

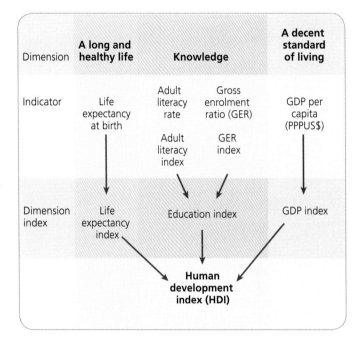

Figure 1.22 Constructing the Human Development Index

Various academic studies have concluded that there is no straightforward relationship between population and economic growth. Thus some economies with a low level of economic growth may not be hugely affected by population growth, but are more affected by other factors such as political instability and lack of investment. On the other hand, some economies that achieve a high level of economic growth may not have done so mainly because of declining population growth, but due to other factors.

Table 1.8 shows the top 25 countries listed in the *Human Development Report* for 2009. All 25 countries are in stage 4 (or stage 5) of demographic transition, suggesting a very strong link between the rate of population growth and the level of economic development (Figure 1.23). Two first-generation newly industrialised countries (NICs) are on the list – Singapore and Hong Kong. In both of these countries the rate of natural increase declined as economic growth progressed. Of course, the debate is – which comes first? Does economic growth lead to lower natural increase, or vice versa? Or is there a more complex relationship between the two variables?

Table 1.8 Top 25 countries in the *Human Development Report 2009*

HDI rank		HDI value 2007	Life expectancy at birth (years) 2007	Adult literacy rate (% aged 15 and above) 1999–2007	Combined gross enrolment ratio in education (%) 2007	GDP per capita (PPPUS$) 2007	Life expectancy index 2007	Education index 2007	GDP index 2007	GDP per capita rank minus HDI rank 2007
1	Norway	0.971	80.5	–	98.6	53 433	0.925	0.989	1.000	4
2	Australia	0.970	81.4	–	114.2	34 923	0.940	0.993	0.977	20
3	Iceland	0.969	81.7	–	96.0	35 742	0.946	0.980	0.981	16
4	Canada	0.966	80.6		99.3	35 812	0.927	0.991	0.982	14
5	Ireland	0.965	79.7	–	97.6	44 613	0.911	0.985	1.000	5
6	Netherlands	0.964	79.8	–	97.5	38 694	0.914	0.985	0.994	8
7	Sweden	0.963	80.8	–	94.3	36 712	0.930	0.974	0.986	9
8	France	0.961	81.0	–	95.4	33 674	0.933	0.978	0.971	17
9	Switzerland	0.960	81.7	–	82.7	40 658	0.945	0.936	1.000	4
10	Japan	0.960	82.7	–	86.6	33 632	0.961	0.949	0.971	16
11	Luxembourg	0.960	79.4	–	94.4	79 485	0.906	0.975	1.000	–9
12	Finland	0.959	79.5	–	101.4	34 526	0.908	0.993	0.975	11
13	USA	0.956	79.1	–	92.4	45 592	0.902	0.968	1.000	–4
14	Austria	0.955	79.9	–	90.5	37 370	0.915	0.962	0.989	1
15	Spain	0.955	80.7	97.9	96.5	31 560	0.929	0.975	0.960	12
16	Denmark	0.955	78.2	–	101.3	36 130	0.887	0.993	0.983	1
17	Belgium	0.953	79.5	–	94.3	34 935	0.908	0.974	0.977	4
18	Italy	0.951	81.1	98.9	91.8	30 353	0.935	0.965	0.954	11
19	Liechtenstein	0.951	–	–	86.8	85 382	0.903	0.949	1.000	–18
20	New Zealand	0.950	80.1	–	107.5	27 336	0.919	0.993	0.936	12
21	UK	0.947	79.3	–	89.2	35 130	0.906	0.957	0.978	–1
22	Germany	0.947	79.8	–	88.1	34 401	0.913	0.954	0.975	2
23	Singapore	0.944	80.2	94.4	–	49 704	0.920	0.913	1.000	–16
24	Hong Kong (China)	0.944	82.2	–	74.4	42 306	0.953	0.879	1.000	–13
25	Greece	0.942	79.1	97.1	101.6	28 517	0.902	0.981	0.944	6

Source: *Human Development Report 2009*

Figure 1.23 The Waterfront, San Francisco – the USA has a very high level of human development

Figure 1.24 shows the variation in human development in 2007. Countries are divided into three categories – high, medium and low human development. The 'high' category also includes those countries with 'very high' human development shown in Table 1.9, which shows the human development index values for each category. The countries with low human development invariably have high rates of population growth and most are in stage 2 of demographic transition. The more advanced LEDCs are generally in stage 3 of demographic transition. This includes countries such as Brazil, Mexico, India and Malaysia. However, again it must be stated that the development process is complex and is the result of the interaction of a wide range of factors.

Table 1.9 Human Development Index values

Level of human development	HDI value	Number of countries 2007
Very high	0.900 and over	38
High	0.800–0.899	45
Medium	0.500–0.799	75
Low	Below 0.500	24

Source: *Human Development Report 2009*

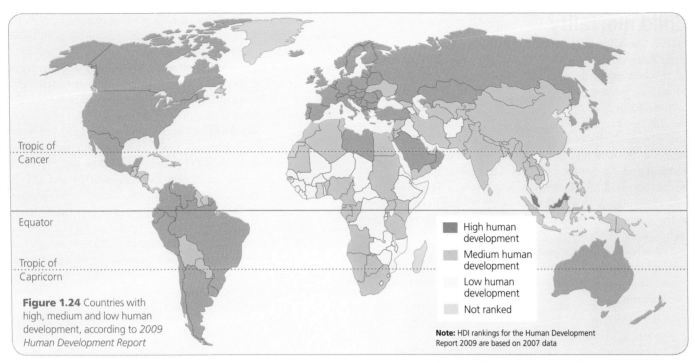

Figure 1.24 Countries with high, medium and low human development, according to *2009 Human Development Report*

High human development

Medium human development

Low human development

Not ranked

Note: HDI rankings for the Human Development Report 2009 are based on 2007 data

Changes in demographic indices over time

Fertility and mortality

Figure 1.25 illustrates change in birth and death rates in England and Wales between 1700 and 2000. The birth and death rates in stages 1, 2 and 3 broadly correspond to those in many poorer societies today. For example, infant mortality in England fell from 200/1000 in 1770 to just over 100/1000 in 1870. Today the average infant mortality for the developing world as a whole is 50/1000. Only the very poorest countries in the world today have infant mortality rates over 100/1000. Infant mortality is regarded as a key measure of socio-economic development. Figure 1.25 identifies a range of important factors that influenced birth and death rates in England and Wales during the time period concerned.

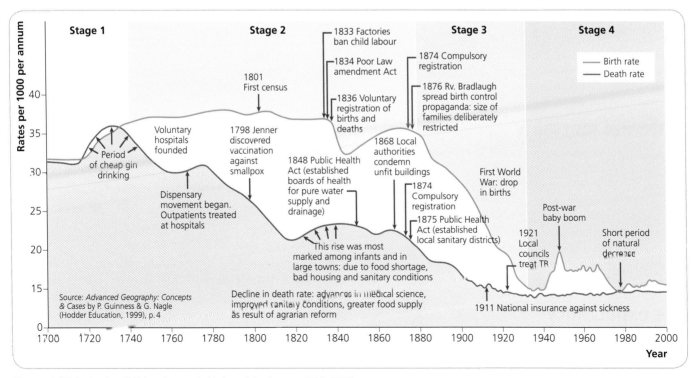

Figure 1.25 England and Wales: changes in birth and death rates, 1700–2000

Child mortality

Figure 1.26 shows how **child mortality** rates have changed around the world between 1990 and 2006. Globally, the number of children under 5 years who died in 2006 dropped below 10 million for the first time. Unicef estimated the total at 9.7 million, down from almost 13 million in 1990. The main reasons for the decline included measles vaccinations, mosquito nets and increased rates of breast-feeding. In some countries such as Morocco, Vietnam and the Dominican Republic, the number of children under 5 dying dropped by a third. The majority of child deaths occurred in sub-Saharan Africa (4.8 million) and south Asia (3.1 million). In Vietnam the steep fall has been attributed to the training of 30 000 health workers to treat people in their own villages.

Unicef argues that the majority of the remaining child deaths are preventable. In 2007 Unicef called on the global community to invest another $5 billion to help the UN achieve its Millennium Development Goals.

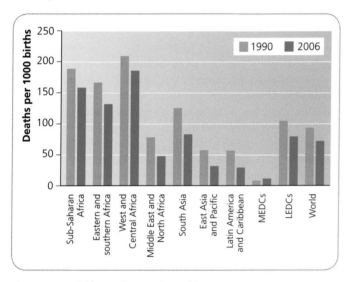

Figure 1.26 Child mortality rates by world region, 1990–2006

Maternal mortality

Reducing **maternal mortality** is one of the UN's eight Millennium Development Goals. There is a huge contrast in maternal mortality between the MEDCs and LEDCs. Globally, 1 in 92 women die from pregnancy-related causes. However, in MEDCs the risk is only 1 in 6000 compared with 1 in 22 in sub-Saharan Africa. Major influencing factors in maternal mortality are the type of pre-natal care available, and the type of attendance at birth. These factors depend to a very significant extent on how much a country can afford to invest in its health services.

Life expectancy

The decline in levels of mortality and the increase in **life expectancy** has been the most important reward of economic and social development. On a global scale 75 per cent of the total improvement in longevity has been achieved in the twentieth

century and the early years of the twenty-first century. In 1900 the world average for life expectancy is estimated to have been about 30 years but by 1950–55 it had risen to 46 years. By 1980–85 it had reached a fraction under 60 years. The current global average is 68 years. Here there is a three-year gap between males and females (67 and 70 years). The gender gap is wider in MEDCs (74 and 81 years) than in LEDCs (65 and 68 years).

Table 1.4 shows that the lowest average life expectancy by world region is in Africa (55 years), with the highest average figure in northern America (78 years). Rates of life expectancy at birth have converged significantly between MEDCs and LEDCs during the last fifty years or so, in spite of a widening wealth gap. These increases in life expectancy have to a certain extent offset the widening disparity between per capita incomes in MEDCs and LEDCs. However, it must not be forgotten that the ravages of AIDS in particular has caused recent decreases in life expectancy in some countries in sub-Saharan Africa. It is likely that the life expectancy gap between MEDCs and LEDCs will continue to narrow in the future (Figure 1.27).

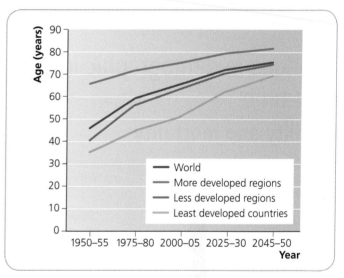

Figure 1.27 Life expectancy at birth: world and development regions, 1950–2050

Section 1.2 Activities

1 a What is *development*?
 b Give three examples of how development occurs.

2 Discuss the demographic and other factors that influence development.

3 Describe the data presented in Table 1.8.

4 With reference to Figure 1.24, analyse the global distribution of human development.

5 Comment on the variations in birth and death rates for England and Wales over time, shown in Figure 1.25.

6 Describe and explain the variations and changes in child mortality shown in Figure 1.26.

7 Discuss the changes in life expectancy shown in Figure 1.27.

1.3 Population–resource relationships

Carrying capacity

Carrying capacity is the largest population that the resources of a given environment can support. Carrying capacity is not a fixed concept as advances in technology can significantly increase the carrying capacity of individual regions and the world as a whole. For example, Abbé Raynal (*Révolution de l'Amérique*, 1781) said of the USA: 'If ten million men ever manage to support themselves in these provinces it will be a great deal.' Yet today the population of the USA is over 300 million and hardly anyone would consider the country to be overpopulated.

Resources can be classed as either natural or human. The traditional distinction is between renewable or flow resources and non-renewable or stock resources. However, the importance of aesthetic resources is being increasingly recognised. Further subdivision of the non-renewable category is particularly relevant to both fuel and non-fuel minerals. Renewable resources can be viewed as either critical or non-critical. The former are sustainable if prudent resource management is employed, while the latter can be seen as everlasting.

The relationship between population and resources has concerned those with an understanding of the subject for thousands of years. However, the assumptions made by earlier writers were based on very limited evidence, as few statistical records existed more than two centuries ago.

The enormous growth of the global economy in recent decades has had a phenomenal impact on the planet's resources and natural environment (Figure 1.28). Many resources are running out and waste sinks are becoming full. The remaining natural world can no longer support the existing global economy, much less one that continues to expand. The main responsibility lies with the rich countries of the world. The world's richest 20 per cent accounted for 76.6 per cent of the world's private consumption in 2005, while the world's poorest 20 per cent were responsible for only 1.5 per cent of global consumption.

Climate change will have an impact on a number of essential resources for human survival, increasing the competition between countries for such resources. An article in the British newspaper *The Times* (9 March 2009) about this global situation was entitled 'World heading for a War of the Resources'. In the same month an article appeared in *The Guardian* newspaper (20 March 2009) entitled 'Deadly crop fungus brings famine threat to developing world'. It reported that leading crop scientists had issued a warning that a deadly airborne fungus could devastate wheat harvests in poor countries and lead to famines and civil unrest over significant regions of central Asia and Africa. A further article in *The Times* (14 May 2009) was entitled 'Russia warns of war within decade over hunt for oil and gas'.

The **ecological footprint** has arguably become the world's foremost measure of humanity's demands on the natural environment. It was conceived in 1990 by M. Wackernagel and W. Rees at the University of British Columbia. The concept of ecological footprints has been used to measure natural resource consumption, how it varies from country to country, and how it has changed over time. The ecological footprint (Figure 1.29) for a country has been defined as 'the sum of all the cropland, grazing land, forest and fishing grounds required to produce the food, fibre

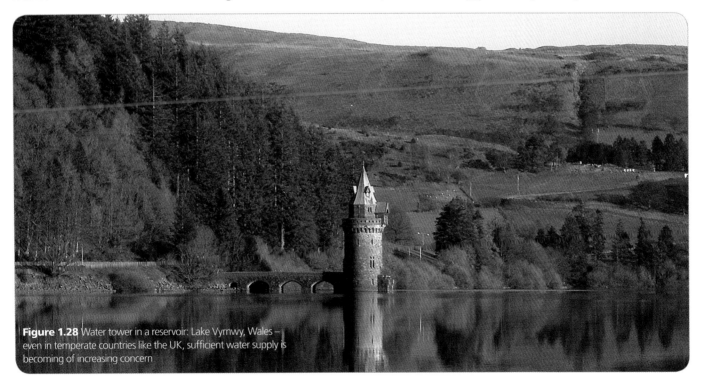

Figure 1.28 Water tower in a reservoir: Lake Vyrnwy, Wales – even in temperate countries like the UK, sufficient water supply is becoming of increasing concern

and timber it consumes, to absorb the wastes emitted when it uses energy, and to provide space for its infrastructure' (*Living Planet Report 2008*). Thus the ecological footprint, calculated for each country and the world as a whole, has six components (Figure 1.29):

- built-up land
- fishing ground
- forest
- grazing land
- cropland
- carbon footprint.

In previous years an additional component reflecting the electricity generated by nuclear power plants was included in ecological footprint accounts. This component is no longer used because the risks and demands of nuclear power are not easily expressed in terms of **biocapacity**.

The ecological footprint is measured in **global hectares**. A global hectare is a hectare with world-average ability to produce resources and absorb wastes. In 2005 the global ecological footprint was 17.5 billion global hectares (gha) or 2.7 gha per person. This can be viewed as the demand side of the equation. On the supply side, the total productive area, or biocapacity of the planet, was 13.6 billion gha, or 2.1 gha per person. With demand greater than supply, the Earth is living beyond its environmental means.

Figure 1.29 shows the ecological footprint of countries with the highest per capita figures and how the footprint of each country is made up. The United Arab Emirates, the USA, Kuwait and Denmark have the highest ecological footprints in the world. All four countries have figures above 8 global hectares per person. Nations at different income levels show considerable disparities in the extent of their ecological footprint. The lowest per capita figures were attributed to Bangladesh, Congo, Haiti, Afghanistan and Malawi. All these countries have an ecological footprint of about 0.5 gha per person. Footprint and biocapacity figures for individual countries are calculated annually by Global Footprint Network.

In many of the countries illustrated in Figure 1.29 the **carbon footprint** is the dominant element of the six components that comprise the ecological footprint, but in others like Australia, Uruguay and Sweden other aspects of the ecological footprint are more important. In Uruguay, the demand on grazing land is by far the dominant component of the ecological footprint. In Sweden, the demands on its forests is the country's major impact on the natural environment. In general the relative importance of the carbon footprint declines as the total ecological footprint of countries falls. In many sub-Saharan African countries the contribution of carbon to the total ecological footprint is extremely low.

The ecological footprint is strongly influenced by the size of a country's population. The other main influences are the level of demand for goods and services in a country (the standard of living), and how this demand is met in terms of environmental impact. International trade is taken into account in the calculation of a country's ecological footprint. For each country its imports are added to its production while its exports are subtracted from its total.

The expansion of world trade has been an important factor in the growth of humanity's total ecological footprint. In 1961, the first year for which full datasets are available, global trade accounted for 8 per cent of the world's ecological footprint. By 2005, this had risen to more than 40 per cent.

The ecological footprint includes only those aspects of resource consumption and waste production for which the Earth has regenerative capacity, and where data exist that allow this demand to be expressed in terms of productive area. For example, toxic releases do not figure in ecological footprint accounts. Ecological footprint calculations provide snapshots of past resource demand and availability. They do not:

- attempt to predict the future
- indicate the intensity with which a biologically productive area is being used
- evaluate the social and economic dimensions of sustainability.

Assessing human pressure on the planet is a vital starting point. The ecological footprint can be calculated at the full range of scales from the individual to the total global population. Knowing

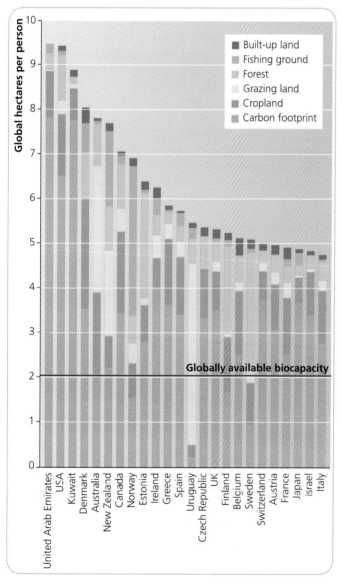

Figure 1.29 Ecological footprint per person for the highest footprint countries

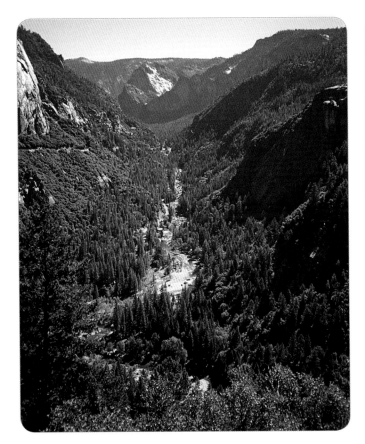

Figure 1.30 Forested landscape, western USA – depletion of forest resources is part of the ecological footprint

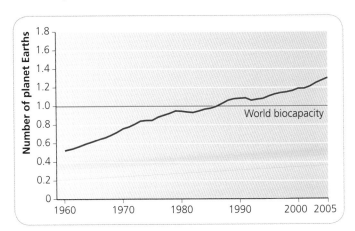

Figure 1.31 Global ecological footprint, 1961–2005

Figure 1.32 Fishing boats off the coast of Tunisia – fish are an important resource

deforestation, water shortages, declining biodiversity and climate change are putting the future development of all countries at risk.

Human demand on the Earth has more than doubled over the past 45 years due to a combination of population growth and rising living standards which has involved greater individual consumption (Figure 1.32). In 1961, most countries in the world had more than enough biocapacity to meet their own demand. But by the mid-1980s humankind's ecological footprint had reached the Earth's biocapacity. Since then humanity has been in ecological '**overshoot**' with annual demand on resources each year exceeding the Earth's regenerative capacity. The WWF calculates that it now takes the Earth one year and four months to regenerate what the global population uses in a year. This is a very significant threat to both the well-being of the human population and the planet as a whole.

Section 1.3 Activities

1 Define the term *carrying capacity*.

2 a What is the ecological footprint?
b How is it calculated?

3 Describe the variations in the ecological footprint for the countries illustrated in Figure 1.29.

4 Present a brief analysis of Figure 1.31.

The causes and consequences of food shortages

About 800 million people in the world suffer from hunger. The problem is mainly concentrated in Africa but also affects a number of Asian and Latin American countries. In early 2006 the UN's Food and Agriculture Organisation warned that 27 sub-Saharan countries could need food assistance. Food shortages can occur because of both natural and human problems. The natural problems that can lead to food shortages include:

• soil exhaustion
• drought

the extent of human pressure on the natural environment helps us to manage ecological assets more wisely on both an individual and a collective basis (Figure 1.30). It is an important tool in the advancement of sustainable development.

Figure 1.31 shows how humanity's ecological footprint increased from 1961 to 2005. According to the *Living Planet Report 2008*, the global ecological footprint now exceeds the planet's regenerative capacity by about 30 per cent. This global excess is increasing and as a result ecosystems are being run down and waste is accumulating in the air, land and water. The resulting

- floods
- tropical cyclones
- pests
- disease.

However, economic and political factors can also contribute to food shortages. Such factors include:

- low capital investment
- rapidly rising population
- poor distribution/transport difficulties
- conflict situations.

The impact of such problems has been felt most intensely in LEDCs, where adequate food stocks to cover emergencies affecting food supply usually do not exist. However, MEDCs have not been without their problems. In 2007, the USA faced its worst summer drought since the Dust Bowl years in the 1930s. Other MEDCs such as Australia have also experienced major drought problems. Thus MEDCs are not immune from the physical problems that can cause food shortages. However, they invariably have the human resources to cope with such problems, so actual food shortages do not generally occur.

The effects of food shortages are both short-term and longer-term. Malnutrition can affect a considerable number of people, particularly children within a relatively short period when food supplies are significantly reduced. With malnutrition people are less resistant to disease and more likely to fall ill. Such diseases include beri-beri (vitamin B1 deficiency), rickets (vitamin D deficiency) and kwashiorkor (protein deficiency). People who are continually starved of nutrients never fulfil their physical or intellectual potential. Malnutrition reduces people's capacity to work, so the land may not be properly tended and other economic activities may not be pursued to their full potential. This is threatening to lock parts of the developing world into an endless cycle of ill-health, low productivity and underdevelopment.

Case Study

Sudan

In recent years there have been severe food shortages in Sudan (Figure 1.33), Africa's largest country. The long civil war and drought there have been the main reasons for famine in Sudan, but there are many other associated factors (Figure 1.34). The civil war, which has lasted for over 20 years, is between the government in Khartoum and rebel forces in the western region of Darfur and in the south. A Christian Aid document in 2004 described Sudan as 'a country still gripped by a civil war that has been fuelled, prolonged and part-financed by oil'. One of the big issues between the two sides in the civil war is the sharing of oil wealth between the government-controlled north, and the south of the country where much of the oil is found. The United Nations has estimated that up to 2 million people have been displaced by the civil war and more than 70 000 people have died from hunger and associated diseases. At times, the UN World Food Programme has stopped deliveries of vital food supplies because the situation has been considered too dangerous for the drivers and aid workers.

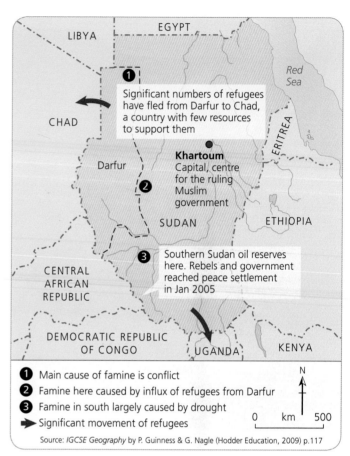

Source: *IGCSE Geography* by P. Guinness & G. Nagle (Hodder Education, 2009) p.117

Figure 1.33 Sudan

Economic/political factors
- High dependency on farming (70% of labour force; 37% of GDP)
- Dependency on food imports (13% of consumption 1998–2000) whilst exporting non-food goods, e.g. cotton
- Limited access to markets to buy food or infrastructure to distribute it
- Debt and debt repayments limit social and economic spending
- High military spending

Agricultural factors
- Highly variable per capita food production; long-term the trend is static
- Static (cereals and pulses) or falling (roots and tubers) crop yields
- Low and falling fertiliser use (compounded by falling export receipts)
- Lack of a food surplus for use in crisis

Social factors
- High population growth (3%) linked to use of marginal land (overgrazing, erosion)
- High female illiteracy rates (65%)
- Poor infant health
- Increased threat of AIDS

Physical factors
- Long-term decline of rainfall in southern Sudan
- Increased rainfall variability
- Increased use of marginal land leading to degradation
- Flooding

Figure 1.34 Summary of causes of famine in Sudan

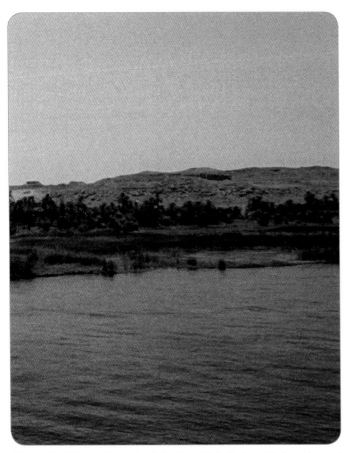

Figure 1.35 The fertile banks of the River Nile in Sudan with desert beyond

Conflict in Darfur reduces food production and distribution

Conflict in Darfur reduces food production and distribution

Shorter-term factors leading to increased Sudanese food insecurity and famine

Both reduce food availability in Sudan and inflate food prices

Situation compounded by:
- Lack of government political will
- Slow donor response
- Limited access to famine areas
- Regional food shortages

Drought in southern Sudan compounds low food intake; any remaining surpluses quickly used

Source: *IGCSE Geography* by P. Guinness & G. Nagle (Hodder Education, 2009) p.118

The role of technology and innovation in resource development

The global use of resources has changed dramatically over time. Such changes can be illustrated with reference to the UK. Technological advance has been the key to:

- the development of new resources
- the replacement of less efficient with more efficient resources.

The combination of the many advances in technology during the Industrial Revolution brought about a huge increase in resource use and considerable changes in the demand for different resources. Such changes included the following:

- The replacement of water power by steam power which resulted in the rapid development of the UK's coalfields from the mid-1700s. Steam power was the fundamental invention of the Industrial Revolution.
- The invention of the Gilchrist-Thomas process in the iron and steel industry in 1878. This made it possible to smelt iron from phosphoric iron ores for the first time, leading to the development of the Jurassic iron ore fields of Lincolnshire and the East Midlands. Before 1878 these ores had no economic use. The mining of the Jurassic iron ores led to the construction of steelworks in the region and the expansion of urban settlements.

In more recent times:

- The intense pressure on food supplies during the Second World War resulted in the ploughing-up of large areas of chalk downland for the first time. Advances in agricultural science made it possible to obtain reasonable crop yields with the application of the correct fertiliser mix. Prior to this understanding, the economic use of the chalk downlands was almost totally for sheep farming.
- The development of the nuclear power industry in the UK and other countries found a new use for uranium which significantly increased its price.
- The railway system, which was once totally steam-driven, was electrified.
- North Sea oil and gas was exploited – the location of oil and gas in the deeper parts of the North Sea was established some time before production from these areas began. What was required was (a) higher oil prices to justify the costs of deepwater production and (b) advances in deep-sea oil production technology (oil had never been produced in such deep waters before). Experience gained in the North Sea has been invaluable in drilling for oil in other deepwater locations around the world.
- Renewable energy technology, particularly the construction of offshore wind farms, is now beginning to utilise flow resources in a significant way.
- Recycling has increased considerably in importance over the last decade, involving a much wider range of materials and products.

As society has changed, attitudes to certain resources and their use have also changed. For example, the demand for organic food is much higher today than it was even ten years ago and this strong upward trend is expected to continue. Some power companies provide 'green energy' options which are attracting an increasing number of customers. Attitudes to plastic bags and the packaging of goods in general are changing, too. More and more people are questioning the environmental credentials of the companies from which they purchase goods and services.

Food production: the Green Revolution

Innovation in food production has been essential to feeding a rising global population. The package of agricultural improvements generally known as the **Green Revolution** was seen as the answer to the food problem in many LEDCs. India was one of the first countries to benefit when a high-yielding variety seed programme (HVP) commenced in 1966–67. In terms of production it was a turning point for Indian agriculture, which had virtually reached stagnation. The HVP introduced new hybrid varieties of five cereals: wheat, rice, maize, sorghum and millet. All were drought-resistant with the exception of rice, were very responsive to the application of fertilisers, and they had a shorter growing season than the traditional varieties they replaced. Although the benefits of the Green Revolution are clear, serious criticisms have also been made. The two sides of the story can be summarised as follows:

Advantages
- Yields are twice to four times greater than of traditional varieties.
- The shorter growing season has allowed the introduction of an extra crop in some areas.
- Farming incomes have increased, allowing the purchase of machinery, better seeds, fertilisers and pesticides.
- The diet of rural communities is now more varied.
- Local infrastructure has been upgraded to accommodate a stronger market approach.
- Employment has been created in industries supplying farms with inputs.
- Higher returns have justified a significant increase in irrigation.

Disadvantages
- High inputs of fertiliser and pesticide are required to optimise production. This is costly in both economic and environmental terms. In some areas rural indebtedness has risen sharply.
- High-yielding varieties (HYVs) require more weed control and are often more susceptible to pests and disease.
- Middle- and higher-income farmers have often benefited much more than the majority on low incomes, thus widening the income gap in rural communities. Increased rural-to-urban migration has often been the result.
- Mechanisation has increased rural unemployment.

- Some HYVs have an inferior taste.
- The problem of salinisation has increased along with the expansion of the irrigated areas.
- HYVs can be low in minerals and vitamins. Because the new crops have displaced the local fruits, vegetables and legumes that traditionally supplied important vitamins and minerals, the diet of many people in LEDCs is now extremely low in zinc, iron, vitamin A and other micronutrients.

Perennial crops: the next agricultural revolution?

The answer to many of the world's current agricultural problems may lie in the development of **perennial crops**. Today's annual crops die off once they are harvested and new seeds have to be planted before the cycle of production can begin again. The soil is most vulnerable to erosion in the period between harvesting and the next planting. Perennial crops would protect the soil from erosion and also offer other advantages. Over the next few years, plant biologists hope to breed plants that closely resemble domestic crops but retain their perennial habit. Classical crossing methods have been proved to work in the search for perennial crop plants but the process is slow. Some plant breeders aim to speed up the process by using genetic engineering. The objective is to find the genes that are linked to domestication and then insert these into wild plants.

Section 1.3 Activities

1 Describe three ways in which technological development has changed resource use in the UK.

2 Discuss one way in which major technological advance might change resource use in the future.

3 Discuss the advantages and disadvantages of the Green Revolution.

4 How might perennial crops lead to a new agricultural revolution?

The role of constraints in sustaining populations

There are a significant number of potential constraints in developing resources to sustain changing populations. Figure 1.36 illustrates the factors affecting the development of a particular resource body. The factors included in the diagram are those which operate in normal economic conditions and thus do not include war or other types of conflict which can greatly increase the constraints operating on resource development.

War is a major issue for development. It significantly retards development and the ability of a country to sustain its population. Major conflict can set back the process of development by decades. In many conflicts water, food and other resources are deliberately destroyed to make life as difficult as possible for the

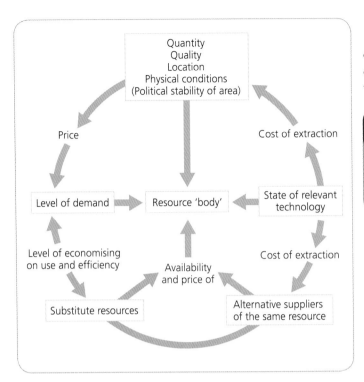

Figure 1.36 Factors affecting the development of a particular resource body

opposing population. Conversely, where development succeeds, countries become progressively safer from violent conflict, making subsequent development easier.

Trade barriers are another significant constraint. Many LEDCs complain that the trade barriers (tariffs, quotas and regulations) imposed by many MEDCs are too stringent. This reduces the export potential of poorer countries and hinders their development.

Climatic and other hazards in the short term, and climate change in the medium and long term, have a serious impact on the utilisation of resources. For example:

- Tropical storms are a major hazard and an impediment to development in a number of LEDCs such as Bangladesh and the countries of Central America and the Caribbean.
- Regions at significant risk of flooding, due to tropical storms and other factors, are often deprived of investment in agriculture and other aspects of development because of the potential losses involved.
- Drought has a considerable impact on the ability to sustain changing populations in many parts of the world. Desertification is reducing the agricultural potential of many countries, for example those in the Sahel region in Africa.
- Volcanic eruptions can devastate large areas, covering farmland with lava, burying settlements and destroying infrastructure. A major eruption on the island of Montserrat in the Caribbean in 1995 has had a huge impact on the development of the island. The southern third of the island had to be evacuated and all public services had to be removed to the north of the island.
- Earthquakes can have a significant impact on resource development, adding considerably to the costs of

development because of the costly construction techniques required to mitigate the consequences of this hazard.

Climate change has the potential to increase the frequency of extreme events in many parts of the world. In some regions there will be wide ranging implications for human health.

Section 1.3 Activities

1 How can technology and innovation affect resource development?

2 Explain the role of constraints in sustaining changing populations.

Overpopulation, optimum population and underpopulation

The idea of **optimum population** has been mainly understood in an economic sense (Figure 1.37). At first, an increasing population allows for a fuller exploitation of a country's resource base, enabling living standards to rise. However, beyond a certain level rising numbers place increasing pressure on resources, and living standards begin to decline. The highest average living standard marks the optimum population, or more accurately the **economic optimum**. Before that population is reached, the country or region can be said to be **underpopulated**. As the population rises beyond the optimum, the country or region can be said to be **overpopulated**.

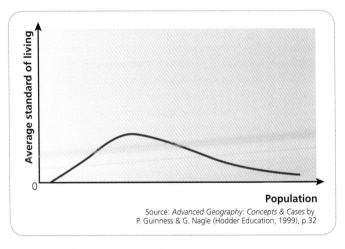

Source: *Advanced Geography: Concepts & Cases* by P. Guinness & G. Nagle (Hodder Education, 1999), p.32

Figure 1.37 The optimum population

There is no historical example of a stationary population having achieved appreciable economic progress, although this may not be so in the future. It is not coincidental that in the past, periods of rapid population growth have paralleled eras of technological advance which have increased the carrying capacity of countries and regions. Thus we are led from the idea of optimum population as a static concept to the dynamic concept of **optimum rhythm of growth** (Figure 1.38) whereby population growth responds to substantial technological advances.

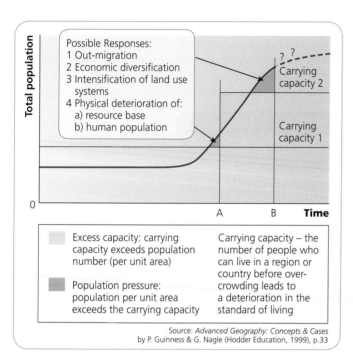

Possible Responses:
1 Out-migration
2 Economic diversification
3 Intensification of land use systems
4 Physical deterioration of:
 a) resource base
 b) human population

Excess capacity: carrying capacity exceeds population number (per unit area)	Carrying capacity – the number of people who can live in a region or country before over-crowding leads to a deterioration in the standard of living
Population pressure: population per unit area exceeds the carrying capacity	

Source: *Advanced Geography: Concepts & Cases* by P. Guinness & G. Nagle (Hodder Education, 1999), p.33

Figure 1.38 Optimum rhythm of growth

The most obvious examples of **population pressure** are to be found in LEDCs, but the question here is: are these cases of absolute overpopulation, or the results of underdevelopment that can be rectified by adopting remedial strategies over time?

The ideas of Thomas Malthus

The Rev. Malthus (1766–1834) produced his *Essay on the Principle of Population* in 1798. He said that the crux of the population problem was 'the existence of a tendency in mankind to increase, if unchecked, beyond the possibility of an adequate supply of food in a limited territory'. Malthus thought that an increased food supply was achieved mainly by bringing more land into arable production. He maintained that while the supply of food could, at best, only be increased by a constant amount in arithmetical progression (1 - 2 - 3 - 4 - 5 - 6), the human population tends to increase in geometrical progression (1 - 2 - 4 - 8 - 16 - 32), multiplying itself by a constant amount each time. In time, population would outstrip food supply until a catastrophe occurred in the form of famine, disease or war. War would occur as human groups fought over increasingly scarce resources. These limiting factors maintained a balance between population and resources in the long term. In a later paper Malthus placed significant emphasis on 'moral restraint' as an important factor in controlling population.

Clearly Malthus was influenced by events in and before the eighteenth century and could not have foreseen the great advances that were to unfold in the following two centuries which have allowed population to grow at an unprecedented rate alongside a huge rise in the exploitation and use of resources. There have been many advances in agriculture since the time of Malthus that have contributed to huge increases in agricultural production. These advances include: the development of artificial fertilisers and pesticides, new irrigation techniques, high-yielding varieties

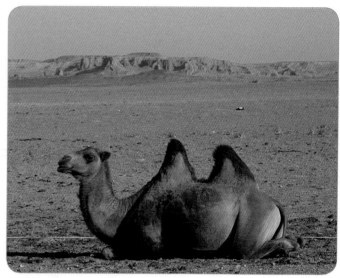

Figure 1.39 The Gobi desert in central Asia – the process of desertification has been spreading in recent decades

of crops, cross-breeding of cattle, greenhouse farming, and the reclamation of land from the sea.

However, nearly all of the world's productive land is already exploited. Most of the unexploited land is either too steep, too wet, too dry or too cold for agriculture (Figure 1.39). In Asia, nearly 80 per cent of potentially arable land is now under cultivation.

Figure 1.40 summarises the opposing views of the **neo-Malthusians** and the resource optimists such as Esther Boserup (1910–99). Neo-Malthusians argue that an expanding population will lead to unsustainable pressure on food and other resources. In recent years neo-Malthusians have highlighted:

- the steady global decline in the area of farmland per person
- the steep rise in the cost of many food products in recent years

There are two opposing views of the effects of population growth:

Source: *Advanced Geography: Concepts & Cases* by P. Guinness & G. Nagle (Hodder Education, 1999), p.35

Figure 1.40 The opposing views of the neo-Malthusians and the anti-Malthusians

- the growing scarcity of fish in many parts of the world
- the already apparent impact of climate change on agriculture in some world regions
- the switchover of large areas of land from food production to the production of biofuels, helping to create a food crisis in order to reduce the energy crisis
- the continuing increase in the world's population
- the global increase in the level of meat consumption as incomes rise in newly industrialised countries in particular.

The **anti-Malthusians** or resource optimists believe that human ingenuity will continue to conquer resource problems, pointing to many examples in human history where, through innovation or intensification, humans have responded to increased numbers. Resource optimists highlight a number of continuing advances which include:

- the development of new resources
- the replacement of less efficient with more efficient resources
- the rapid development of green technology with increasing research and development in this growing economic sector
- important advances in agricultural research
- stabilising levels of consumption in some MEDCs.

Figure 1.41 S-shaped growth curve

Figure 1.42 J-shaped growth curve

shows an S-shaped growth curve for a yeast colony in a constant but limited supply of nutrient:

- Over the first few days the colony grows slowly as it begins to multiply (the lag phase).
- This is followed by a phase of rapid growth due to a plentiful supply of nutrient. This is known as the exponential phase.
- Later the population size stabilises because only a set number of yeast cells can survive on the limited resources available (the stationary phase). The population has stabilised at the carrying capacity of the environment.

The pattern of growth in an S-shaped growth curve is consistent with density-dependent limiting factors. Here the effects of limiting factors increase with greater population size.

J-curves (Figure 1.42) illustrate a 'high growth and collapse' pattern:

- The population initially grows exponentially.
- Then the population suddenly collapses. Such collapses are known as 'diebacks'. Often the population exceeds the carrying capacity (overshoot) before the collapse occurs.

J-shaped growth curves have been observed in populations of microbes, invertebrates, fish and small mammals.

S- and J-shaped curves are viewed as conceptual situations, with many animal populations showing a combination of the characteristics of both curves.

The growth of the human population has been slowing since the latter part of the 1960s as it is predicted that global population is reaching or has reached the carrying capacity of the global environment. Will the future of the human population follow:

- the S-shaped curve
- the J-shaped curve
- a combination of the two curves?

Section 1.3 Activities

1 Explain the following:
  a *underpopulation*, **b** *overpopulation* and **c** *optimum population*.

2 Study Figure 1.38.
  a Suggest why the population initially started to increase.
  b What could account for the increases in carrying capacity at Times A and B?
  c Why can Figure 1.38 be described as a dynamic model while Figure 1.37 is a static model?

3 With the aid of Figure 1.40, explain the opposing views of the neo-Malthusians and the resource optimists.

The concept of a population ceiling and population adjustments over time

Studies of the growth of animal and fungus populations show that population numbers may either crash after reaching a high level or reach an equilibrium around the carrying capacity. These contrasting scenarios are represented by S- and J-growth curves. Both incorporate the concept of a population ceiling beyond which a population cannot grow because of the influence of limiting factors such as lack of food, limited space and disease.

S-curves (Figure 1.41) begin with exponential growth, but beyond a certain population size the growth rate gradually slows, eventually resulting in a stable population. Research shows that population growth reduces more in larger populations. Figure 1.41

Section 1.3 Activities

1 What do you understand by the term *population ceiling*?

2 Describe and explain the differences between S- and J-shaped population curves.

3 What is the relevance of studying animal populations in terms of predicting future trends in human population?

1.4 The management of natural increase

Population policy encompasses all of the measures explicitly or implicitly taken by a government aimed at influencing population size, growth, distribution or composition. Population policies generally evolve over time and are clearly documented in writing.

Such policies may promote large families (**pro-natalist policies**) or immigration to increase population size, or encourage limitation of births (**anti-natalist policies**) to decrease it. A population policy may also aim to modify the distribution of the population over the country by encouraging migration or by displacing populations. Population policies that narrow people's choices are generally very controversial.

A significant number of governments have officially stated positions on the level of the national birth rate. However, forming an opinion on demographic issues is one thing, but establishing a policy to do something about it is much further along the line. Thus not all nations stating an opinion on population have gone as far as establishing a formal policy.

Most countries that have tried to control fertility have sought to curtail it. For example, in 1952 India became the first LEDC to introduce a policy designed to reduce fertility and to aid development, with a government-backed family planning programme. Rural and urban birth control clinics rapidly increased in number. Financial and other incentives were offered in some states for those participating in programmes, especially for **sterilisation**. In the mid-1970s the sterilisation campaign became increasingly coercive, reaching a peak of 8.3 million operations in 1977. **Abortion** was legalised in 1972 and in 1978 the minimum age of marriage was increased to 18 years for females and 21 years for males. The birth rate fell from 45/1000 in 1951–61 to 41/1000 in 1961–71. By 1987 it was down to 33/1000, falling further to 29/1000 in 1995. By 2008 it had dropped to 24/1000. It was not long before many other LEDCs followed India's policy of government investment to reduce fertility. The most severe anti-natalist policy ever introduced has been in operation in China since 1979.

Vietnam is planning to return to a two-child policy to limit population growth. This policy was introduced in the 1960s, but stopped in 2003. However, with a current population of 86 million and two-thirds of the population aged under 35, the government is concerned that high population growth will hinder economic growth and put education and health services under too much strain. A spokesperson for the government's population and family planning office said that 'the demographic boom is damaging the country's sustainable development'. The UN Population Fund is puzzled by the reintroduction of the two-child policy as fertility levels have already fallen below replacement rates. However, population momentum means that the population will continue increasing for some time even with the recently reduced fertility levels.

What is perhaps surprising is the number of countries that now see their fertility as too low. Such countries are concerned about:
- the socio-economic implications of population ageing
- the decrease in the supply of labour
- the long-term prospect of population decline.

Russia has seen its population drop considerably since 1991. Alcoholism, AIDS, pollution and poverty are among the factors reducing life expectancy and discouraging births. In 2008 Russia began honouring families with four or more children with a Paternal Glory medal. The government has urged Russians to have more children, sometimes suggesting it is a matter of public duty.

Section 1.4 Activities

1 Define the term *population policy*.

2 What is the difference between a pro-natalist policy and an anti-natalist policy?

3 Suggest why the governments of some countries want to reduce their fertility while others want to increase it.

4 Why does the management of natural increase focus on fertility as opposed to mortality?

Case Study

Managing natural increase in China

China, with a population in excess of 1.3 billion, has been operating the world's most strict **family planning programme** since 1979. Known as the one-child policy, it has drastically reduced population growth, but also brought about a number of adverse consequences, including:

Figure 1.43 The central business district of Beijing

- demographic ageing
- an unbalanced sex ratio
- a generation of 'spoiled' only children
- a social divide as an increasing number of wealthy couples 'buy their way round' the legislation.

Chinese demographers say that the one-child policy has been successful in preventing at least 300 million births, and has played a significant role in the country's economic growth.

Although it is the third largest country in the world in terms of land area, 25 per cent of China is infertile desert or mountain and only 10 per cent of the total area can be used for arable

Table 1.10 China's administrative regions by population

Rank	Administrative division, China	Population	Comparable country (country rank worldwide)
	CHINA	*1 358 650 000*	India (1.2 billion) or combined populations of western Europe, North America and South America
1	Guangdong	95 440 000	Mexico (11)
2	Henan	94 290 000	Ethiopia (15) + Guatemala (66)
3	Shandong	94 170 000	Vietnam (13) + Sierra Leone (107)
4	Sichuan	81 380 000	Germany (14)
5	Jiangsu	76 770 000	Egypt (16)
6	Hebei	69 890 000	Iran (18)
7	Hunan	63 800 000	Thailand (21)
8	Anhui	61 350 000	UK (22)
9	Hubei	57 110 000	Italy (23)
10	Zhejiang	51 200 000	Myanmar (24)
11	Guangxi	48 160 000	South Korea (26)
12	Yunnan	45 430 000	Spain (28)
13	Jiangxi	44 000 000	Colombia (29)
14	Liaoning	43 150 000	Sudan (31)
15	Heilongjiang	38 250 000	Argentina (33)
16	Guizhou	37 930 000	Kenya (32)
17	Shaanxi	37 620 000	Poland (34)
18	Fujian	36 040 000	Algeria (35)
19	Shanxi	34 110 000	Canada (36)
20	Chongqing	28 390 000	Nepal (40)
21	Jilin	27 340 000	Uzbekistan (45)
22	Gansu	26 280 000	Saudi Arabia (45)
23	Inner Mongolia	24 140 000	North Korea (47)
	Taiwan Province (Republic of China)	22 980 000	Texas state, USA
24	Xinjiang	21 310 000	Mozambique (51)
25	Shanghai	18 880 000	Cameroon (58)
26	Beijing	16 950 000	Netherlands (61)
27	Tianjin	11 700 000	Greece (73)
28	Hainan	8 540 000	Austria (92)
29	Hong Kong	7 000 000	Tajikistan (98)
30	Ningxia	6 180 000	Paraguay (102)
31	Qinghai	5 540 000	Denmark (108)
32	Tibet	2 870 000	Kuwait (136)
33	Macau	540 000	Solomon Islands (164)

farming. Most of the best land is in the east and south, reflected in the extremely high population densities found in these regions. Table 1.10 ranks China's administrative regions by population size and shows a comparable country in terms of total population for each region. For example, Guangdong, with over 95 million people, equivalent to the population of Mexico, has the largest population in China. Anhui has a population similar to that of the UK, and seven Chinese provinces have populations higher than the UK.

The balance between population and resources has been a major cause of concern for much of the latter part of the twentieth century, although debate about this issue can be traced as far back in Chinese history as Confucius (Chinese philosopher and teacher of ethics, 551–479 BC). Confucius said that excessive population growth reduced output per worker, depressed the level of living and produced strife. He discussed the concept of optimum numbers, arguing that an ideal proportion between land and numbers existed and any major deviation from this created poverty. When imbalance occurred, he believed the government should move people from overpopulated to underpopulated areas.

Table 1.11 shows key demographic changes in China's population between 1950 and 2005, during which time the total population increased from 555 million to 1.316 billion. In 1950 the population growth rate was 1.87 per cent. This increased to 2.61 per cent in 1965, declining thereafter. By 2005 the population growth rate had fallen to 0.65 per cent. Figure 1.44 shows changes in the birth and death rates for the same period and beyond. Between 1950 and 2005 the crude birth rate fell from 43.8/1000 to 13.6/1000. China's birth rate is now at the level of many MEDCs such as the UK. The impact of the one-child policy is very clear to see on the table and graph.

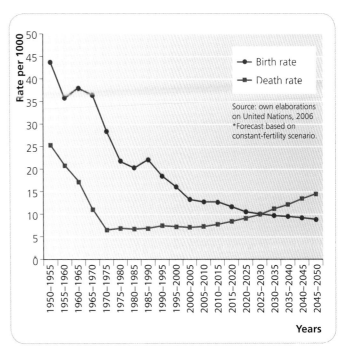

Figure 1.44 Birth and death rates, 1950–2050

Table 1.11 Demographic changes in China, 1950–2005

Indicators	1950–55	1955–60	1960–65	1965–70	1970–75	1975–80	1980–85	1985–90	1990–95	1995–2000	2000–05
Population (thousands)	554 760	609 005	657 492	729 191	830 675	927 808	998 877	1 070 175	1 155 305	1 219 331	1 273 979
Population growth rate (%)	1.87	1.53	2.07	2.61	2.21	1.48	1.38	1.53	1.08	0.88	0.65
Crude birth rate (per 1000 popn)	43.8	36.1	38.0	36.6	28.6	21.5	20.4	22.1	18.3	16.0	13.6
Crude death rate (per 1000 popn)	25.1	20.7	17.1	10.9	6.3	6.7	6.6	6.7	7.3	7.0	6.8
Total fertility rate (children per woman)	6.22	5.59	5.72	6.06	4.86	3.32	2.55	2.46	1.92	1.78	1.70
Infant mortality rate (per 1000 births)	195.0	178.7	120.7	80.8	61.1	52.0	52.0	50.0	47.1	41.5	34.7
Life expectancy at birth, both genders combined (years)	40.8	44.6	49.5	59.6	63.2	65.3	66.6	67.1	68.1	69.7	71.5

For people in the West it is often difficult to understand the all-pervading influence over society that a government can have in a **centrally planned economy**. In the aftermath of the communist revolution in 1949, population growth was encouraged for economic, military and strategic reasons. Sterilisation and abortion were banned and families received a benefit payment for every child. However, by 1954 China's population had reached 600 million and the government was now worried about the pressure on food supplies and other resources. Consequently, the country's first birth control programme was introduced in 1956. This was to prove short-lived, for in 1958 the 'Great Leap Forward' began. The objective was rapid industrialisation and modernisation. The government was now concerned that progress might be hindered by labour shortages and so births were again encouraged. But by 1962 the government had changed its mind, heavily influenced by a catastrophic famine due in large part to the relative neglect of agriculture during the pursuit of industrialisation. An estimated 20 million people died during the

Figure 1.45 Crowds at the Forbidden City, Beijing – China's population was only about 75 million when the Forbidden City was built in the early 15th century

famine. Thus a new phase of birth control ensued in 1964. Just as the new programme was beginning to have some effect, a new social upheaval – the Cultural Revolution – got underway. This period, during which the birth rate peaked at 45/1000, lasted from 1966 to 1971.

With order restored, a third family planning campaign was launched in the early 1970s with the slogan 'Late, sparse, few'. However, towards the end of the decade the government felt that its impact might falter and in 1979 the controversial one-child policy was imposed. The Chinese demographer Liu Zeng calculated that China's optimum population was 700 million, and he looked for this figure to be achieved by 2080. Some organisations, including the UN Fund for Population Activities, have praised China's policy on birth control. Many others see it as a fundamental violation of **civil liberties**.

Ethnic minorities were exempt from parts of the policy, which applied mainly to the Han ethnic majority which makes up more than 90 per cent of the total population. China's policy is based on a reward and penalty approach. Rural households that obey family planning rules get priority for loans, materials, technical assistance, and social welfare. The slogan in China is, 'shao sheng kuai fu' – 'fewer births, quickly richer'. The one-child policy has been most effective in urban areas where the traditional bias of couples wanting a son has been significantly eroded. However, the story is different in rural areas where the strong desire for a male heir remains the norm. In most provincial rural areas, government policy has relaxed so that couples can now have two children without penalties.

The policy has had a considerable impact on the sex ratio which at birth in China is currently 119 boys to 100 girls. This compares with the natural rate of 106:100. In some provinces it is estimated the figure may be as high as 140. A paper published in 2008 estimated that China had 32 million more men aged under 20 than women. The imbalance is greatest in rural areas because women are 'marrying out' into cities. This is already causing social problems which are likely to multiply in the future. **Selective abortion** after pre-natal screening is a major cause of the wide gap between the actual rate and the natural rate. But even if a female child is born, her lifespan may be sharply curtailed by infanticide or deliberate neglect. Feminist writers in China see 'son preference' as a blatant form of gender discrimination and gender-based violence. However, this is an issue that affects other countries as well as China.

The significant gender imbalance means that a very large number of males will never find a female partner, which could result in serious social problems as significant numbers of males are unable to conform to the basic **social norms** of society which revolve around marriage and parenthood. Such unmarried men are known as 'bare branches'!

In recent years, reference has been made to the 'Four-Two-One' problem whereby one adult child is left with having to provide support for two parents and four grandparents. Care for the elderly is clearly going to become a major problem for the Chinese authorities, since the only social security system for most of the country's poor is their family.

In July 2009, newspapers in the UK and elsewhere reported that dozens of babies had been taken from parents who had breached China's one-child policy and sold for adoption abroad. In the cities, the fines for having a second child can be up to 200 000 yuan (£20 000). This is meant to reflect the schooling and healthcare costs of additional children. However, an increasing number of affluent parents are prepared either to pay these fines outright or to travel to Hong Kong where no permit for a second child is needed.

Figure 1.46
The metro in Beijing

SECOND CHILD NOT RIGHT POPULATION RECIPE

Chen Weihua

Shanghai's announcement on encouraging couples who have no siblings to have a second child is sending a wrong signal.

By claiming the city is suffering from an increasingly aging population and a possible shortage of workforce 40 years from now, these officials seem to talk as if Shanghai were an independent 'republic'.

This, of course, has no basis. If you count the 6.4 million people, mostly young, residing and working in Shanghai without a local *hukou*, or permanent residence permit, Shanghai's greying threat would not look that gloomy. These people actually make up a third of the city's 19 million.

Since Shanghai has long been a top destination in China for both young professionals and migrant rural workers, it would be near-sighted to examine the population problem from the viewpoint of the *hukou*-holding people, while ignoring those without a *hukou*.

With 1.3 billion people, China is the world's most populous country that would be surpassed by India in 2028, according to a recent study by the South Korea National Statistical Office.

The achievement of China moving towards becoming the second most populous country may be attributed to the last 30 years of family planning work, which translated into 300 to 400 million fewer births.

However, China still gives birth each year to some 8 million children.

Population pressure has long been an impediment to social and economic progress, despite the benefit China has reaped from its population dividend – the rise in the economic growth rate due to a rising share of working-age people.

On the employment side, China is still fighting a tough battle to create jobs for an estimated 10 million people entering the workforce each year. In addition, some 200 million surplus rural laborers are also in need of jobs.

It is true that the increasing graying population will and should be a matter of great concern. Yet that problem cannot be solved by ignoring the pressure from an even larger population – as a result of encouraging couples to have a second child.

There are other ways of dealing with this problem. Key among them is to build an effective social security system and better community service system offering good care to the elderly both in urban and rural areas.

While having one more child might mean more attention for the elderly, it is by no means a guarantee.

The real problem we are facing now or in the future is not a shortage of people, but an excess of people who don't have access to proper education and medical resources, especially in the vast rural areas. We are challenged by a rural labor force that lacks proper training, and a rural population which still counts on more children for old age security. And that vicious cycle will continue if we choose to ignore the issues.

The right approach to the population problem is to divert more resources, such as in education and medical care, to the countryside.

Having fewer, yet healthy and well-educated children is a policy that should be encouraged.

It was only 60 years ago that China's population was around 450 million. If we had that number of people today, we would have faced fewer problems.

Figure 1.47 Extract from *China Daily*, 28 July 2009

Figure 1.47 shows that there is a certain level of debate within China about the one-child policy. The article highlights Shanghai's concerns about its ageing population. To counteract this trend the city government wants to encourage couples who have no siblings to have a second child. However, this view has drawn considerable criticism, as the columnist Chen Weihua explains. Even with the low birth rate of today, there are still 8 million births in China every year.

Another consequence of the one-child rule has been the creation of a generation of so-called 'little emperors' – indulged and cosseted boy children who are often overweight, arrogant and lacking in social skills.

Although many Chinese couples would undoubtedly have more children if allowed by the government, in urban areas a new class of city workers has arisen with a Western-style reluctance to have more than one child, because they want to preserve their rising standard of living.

Section 1.4 Activities

1 Write a brief bullet-point summary of the main changes in Chinese fertility policy since 1949.

2 Look at Table 1.11 and Figure 1.44.

   a Describe the changes in the birth rate between 1950 and 2005.

   b How did the total fertility rate change over the same period?

   c Comment on the changes in the death rate between 1950 and 2005.

   d What impact did these changes have on the population growth rate?

3 a Describe the changes in the infant mortality rate in China between 1950 and 2005.

   b How did this help most people to accept the one-child policy?

2 Migration

2.1 Migration as a component of population change

Movements of populations: definitions

Migration is more volatile than fertility and mortality, the other two basic demographic variables. It can react very quickly indeed to changing economic, political and social circumstances. However, the desire to migrate may not be achieved if the constraints imposed on it are too great.

Migration is defined as the movement of people across a specified boundary, national or international, to establish a new permanent place of residence (Figure 2.1). The United Nations defines 'permanent' as a change of residence lasting more than one year. Movements with a time scale of less than a year are termed 'circulatory movements'.

It is customary to subdivide the field of migration into two areas: **internal migration** and **international migration**. International migrants cross international boundaries; internal migrants move within the frontiers of one nation. The terms **immigration** and **emigration** are used with reference to international migration. The corresponding terms for internal movements are **in-migration** and **out-migration**. Internal migration streams are usually on a larger scale than their international counterparts. **Net migration** is the number of migrants entering a region or country less the number of migrants who leave the same region or country. The balance may be either positive or negative.

Migrations are embarked upon from an area of **origin** and are completed at an area of **destination.** Migrants sharing a common origin and destination form a **migration stream**. For every migration stream a **counterstream** or reverse flow at a lower volume usually results as some migrants dissatisfied with their destination return home. Push and pull factors (Figures 2.2 and 2.3) encourage people to migrate. **Push factors** are the observations that are negative about an area in which the individual is presently living, while **pull factors** are the perceived better conditions in the place to which the migrant wishes to go. Once strong links between a rural and an urban area are established the phenomenon of **chain migration** frequently results. After one or a small number of pioneering migrants have led the way, others from the same rural community follow. In some communities the process of **relay migration** has been identified, whereby at different stages in a family's life cycle different people take responsibility for migration in order to improve the financial position of the family. Another recognisable process is **step migration** whereby the rural migrant initially heads for a familiar small town and then after a period of time moves on to a larger urban settlement. Over many years the migrant may take a number of steps up the urban hierarchy.

Figure 2.1 Chinatown in San Francisco – the Chinese community has been long established in this city

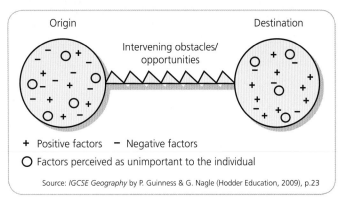

Origin   Destination

Intervening obstacles/opportunities

+ Positive factors   – Negative factors
O Factors perceived as unimportant to the individual

Source: *IGCSE Geography* by P. Guinness & G. Nagle (Hodder Education, 2009), p.23

Figure 2.2 Push and pull factors

The most basic distinction drawn by demographers is between voluntary and forced migration (Figure 2.4). **Voluntary migration** is where the individual or household has a free choice about whether to move or not. **Forced migration** occurs when the individual or household has little or no choice but to move. This may be due to environmental or human factors. Figure 2.4 shows that there are barriers to migration. In earlier times the physical dangers of the journey and the costs involved were major obstacles. However, the low real cost of modern transportation and the high level of safety have reduced these barriers considerably. In the modern world it is the legal restrictions that countries place on migration that are the main barriers to international migration. Most countries now have very strict rules on immigration, and some countries restrict emigration.

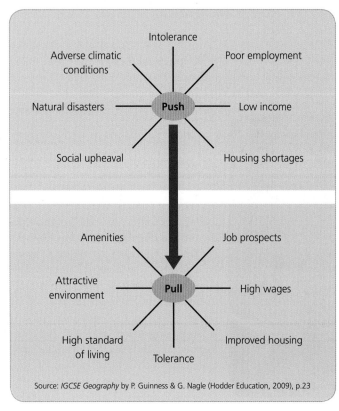

Intolerance

Adverse climatic conditions

Poor employment

Natural disasters —— **Push** —— Low income

Social upheaval

Housing shortages

Amenities

Job prospects

Attractive environment —— **Pull** —— High wages

High standard of living

Improved housing

Tolerance

Source: *IGCSE Geography* by P. Guinness & G. Nagle (Hodder Education, 2009), p.23

Figure 2.3 Push and pull factors

1 Define *migration*.

2 Distinguish between **a** *immigration* and *emigration* and **b** *in-migration* and *out-migration*.

3 Explain the terms **a** *origin* and *destination* and **b** *stream* and *counterstream*.

4 Briefly describe each of the following:
  a chain migration
  b relay migration
  c step migration.

5 Discuss three push factors and three pull factors shown in Figure 2.3.

6 Write a brief summary to explain Figure 2.4.

Causes of migration

Various attempts to classify migration have helped improve understanding of its causes. In 1958 W. Peterson noted the following five migratory types: primitive, forced, impelled, free, and mass.

- The nomadic pastoralism and shifting cultivation practised by the world's most traditional societies are examples of primitive migration. Physical factors such as seasonal rainfall and the limits of soil fertility govern such migratory practices.
- The abduction and transport of Africans to the Americas as slaves was the largest forced migration in history. In the seventeenth and eighteenth centuries 15 million people were shipped across the Atlantic Ocean as slaves. The expulsion of Asians from Uganda in the 1970s, when the country was under the dictatorship of Idi Amin, and the forcible movement of people from parts of the former Yugoslavia under the policy of 'ethnic cleansing', are much more recent examples. Migrations may also be forced by natural disasters (volcanic eruptions, floods, drought etc.) or by environmental catastrophe such as nuclear contamination in Chernobyl.
- Impelled migrations take place under perceived threat, either human or physical, but an element of choice lacking in forced migrations remains. Arguably the largest migration under duress in modern times occurred after the partition of India in 1947, when 7 million Muslims fled India for the new state of Pakistan and 7 million Hindus moved with equal speed in the opposite direction. Both groups were in fear of their lives but they were not forced to move by government, and minority groups remained in each country.
- The distinction between free and mass migration is one of magnitude only. The movement of Europeans to North America was the largest mass migration in history.

Within each category Peterson classed a particular migration as either innovating or conservative. In the former the objective of the move was to achieve improved living standards while in the latter the aim was just to maintain present standards.

Source: *IGCSE Geography* by P. Guinness & G. Nagle (Hodder Education, 2009), p.23

Figure 2.4 Voluntary and forced migration

E.S. Lee (1966) produced a series of Principles of Migration, in an attempt to bring together all aspects of migration theory at that time. Of particular note was his origin-intervening obstacles – destination model which emphasised the role of push and pull factors (Figures 2.2 and 2.3). Here he suggests there are four classes of factors that influence the decision to migrate:

1 those associated with the place of origin
2 those associated with the place of destination
3 intervening obstacles which lie between the places of origin and destination
4 a variety of personal factors that moderate 1, 2 and 3.

Each place of origin and destination has numerous positive, negative and neutral factors for the individual. What may constitute a negative factor at destination for one individual – a very hot climate, say – may be a positive factor for another

Figure 2.5 A severe winter in Mongolia forces people to leave the countryside for the capital city, Ulaanbaatar

person. Lee suggested that there is a difference in the operation of these factors at origin and destination as the latter will always be less well known, 'There is always an element of ignorance or even mystery about the area of destination, and there must always be some uncertainty with regard to the reception of a migrant in a new area'. This is particularly so with international migration. Another important difference noted by Lee between the factors associated with area of origin and area of destination related to stages of the life cycle. Most migrants spend their formative years in the area of origin enjoying the good health of youth with often only limited social and economic responsibilities. This frequently results in an overvaluation of the positive elements in the environment and an undervaluation of the negative elements. Conversely, the difficulties associated with assimilation into a new environment may create in the newly arrived a contrary but equally erroneous evaluation of the positive and negative factors at destination. The intervening obstacles between origin and destination include distance, the means and cost of transport and legal restraints (mainly in the form of immigration laws).

Akin Mabogunje, in his analysis of rural–urban migration in Africa, attempted to set the phenomenon in its economic and social context as part of a system of interrelated elements (Figure 2.6). The systems approach does not see migration in over-simplified terms of cause and effect, but as a circular, interdependent and self-modifying system.

In Mabogunje's framework the African rural–urban migration system is operating in an environment of change. The system and the environment act and react upon each other continuously. For example, expansion in the urban economy will stimulate migration from rural areas, while deteriorating economic conditions in the larger urban areas will result in a reduction of migration flows from rural areas.

If the potential migrant is stimulated to move to an urban area by the positive nature of the environment, he/she then comes under the influence of the 'rural control subsystem'. Here the attitudes of the potential migrant's family and local community

Environment
Economic conditions — wages, prices, consumer preferences,
degrees of commercialisation and industrial development

Urbanite

Urban
adjustment
mechanism

Environment

Social welfare,
development

Education,
health,
etc.

Urban
control
sub-systems

Environment

Technology

Transportation,
communication,
mechanisation,
etc.

Urban
subsystem

Positive
feedback
channels

Negative
feedback
channels

Migration
channels

Rural
adjustment
mechanism

Potential
migrant

Rural
control
subsystem

Environment
Governmental policies, agricultural practices,
marketing organisations, population movement, etc.

Source: *Access to Geography: Migration* by P. Guinness (Hodder Education, 2002), p.18

Figure 2.6 A systems approach to migration

come into strong play, either encouraging or restraining movement. If movement occurs, the migrant then comes under the influence of the 'urban control subsystem'. The latter will determine, by means of the employment and housing opportunities it offers, the degree to which migrants assimilate.

In addition there are adjustment mechanisms. For example, at the rural point of origin a positive adjustment resulting from out-migration might be increased income per head for the remaining villagers. The most likely negative adjustment will be the reduced level of social interaction between the out-migrants and their families. At the urban destination the in-migrant may benefit from the receipt of regular wages for the first time but as a result may be drawn into the negative aspects of lower-income urban life such as gambling, excessive drinking and prostitution.

The flow of information between out-migrants and their rural origin is an important component of the system. Favourable reports from the new urban dwellers will generally increase the migration flow while negative perceptions will slow down the rate of movement (Figure 2.7).

Figure 2.7 The trans-Siberian railway – an important routeway for people moving between the European and Asiatic regions of Russia

Section 2.1 Activities

1 What is meant by *primitive migration*?

2 What is the difference between *forced migration* and *impelled migration*?

3 With reference to Figure 2.2:
  a Explain the terms *origin*, *destination* and *intervening obstacles*.
  b Suggest how intervening obstacles between origin and destination have changed over time.

4 Look at Figure 2.6.
  a What do you understand by a systems approach to migration?
  b Suggest how the 'rural control subsystem' might affect a potential migration decision.
  c Outline three ways in which the urban subsystem can have an impact on rural–urban migration.
  d Explain the influence of positive and negative feedback channels on new potential migrants.

Recent approaches to migration

Figure 2.8 summarises the main differences to the most recent approaches to migration, each of which is briefly discussed below.

The Todaro model: the cost–benefit approach

In the post-1950 period there has been a huge movement of population from rural to urban areas in LEDCs. For many migrants it appeared that they had just swapped rural poverty for urban poverty. The simplistic explanation put forward was that many rural dwellers had been attracted by the 'bright lights' of the large urban areas without any clear understanding of the real deprivation of urban life for those at or near the bottom of the socio-economic scale. They had migrated due to false perceptions picked up from the media and other sources. The American economist Michael Todaro challenged this view, arguing that migrants' perceptions of urban life were realistic, being strongly based on an accurate flow of information from earlier migrants from their rural community. Potential migrants carefully weighed up the costs and benefits of moving to urban areas, including the 'anticipated income differential'. They were very aware that in the short term they might not be better off, but weighing up the odds the likelihood was that their socio-economic standing would improve in the long term. Thus people were willing to endure short-term difficulties in the hope of better prospects eventually, if not for themselves then for their children. Expected wages were discounted against the prospects of remaining unemployed for any length of time.

Figure 2.9 summarises the typical net-income stream of a young rural–urban migrant. While at school the young rural dweller's net income is zero. At A_1 he migrates to a large urban area but is initially unable to find work because of the intense competition for employment and the limited nature of his contacts. His net income is negative as he has no option but to live on savings or borrowed money. However, in time, as his knowledge of the city improves and his contact base widens, he finds employment and his net income becomes positive (A_2), rising to a peak and then decreasing with age as his productivity begins to fall.

Stark's 'new economics of migration'

Stark, in what is often referred to as the 'new economics of migration', has extended the Todaro model by replacing the individual with the household as the unit of analysis. Stark, along with others, argued that insufficient attention had been paid to the institutions that determine migration. For example, in the Todaro model it is assumed that migrants act individually according to a rationality of economic self-interest. However, migration, according to Stark, is seen as a form of economic diversification by families whereby the costs and rewards are shared. It is a form of risk spreading. She asserts that 'even though the entities that engage in migration are often individual agents, there is more to labour migration than an individualistic optimising behaviour. Migration by one person can be due to, fully consistent with, or undertaken by a group of persons, such as the family.'

So often the initial cost of establishing the rural migrant in an urban area is carried by the family in the expectation of returns in the form of remittances. The migrant also has expectations in maintaining the link, for example in the form of inheritance. A number of studies have described how families invest in the education of one member of the family, usually the firstborn son, for migration to the urban formal sector. The expectation is that the remittances received will be crucial to the up-bringing of the remaining children and have an important effect on the general standard of living of the family.

The Stark model also takes account of: incomplete and imperfect information, imperfections in rural capital markets and transaction costs; and stresses the importance in migration decisions of relative deprivation in the local income distribution rather than absolute deprivation.

Marxist/structuralist theory

Some writers, often in the tradition of Marxist analyses, see labour migration as inevitable in the transition to capitalism (Figure 2.10). Migration is the only option for survival after alienation from the land. Structuralist theory draws attention to the advantages of migrant labour for capitalist production and emphasises the control

Determinants of migration	Effects	Unit of analysis		
		Individual	Household/family	Institutions
Economic	Positive	Todaro Push–pull	Stark and others; 'new economics' of migration	
	Negative			Marxism Structuralism
Sociological/ anthropological		← Structuration theory → ← Gender analyses →		

Figure 2.8 Recent approaches to migration studies

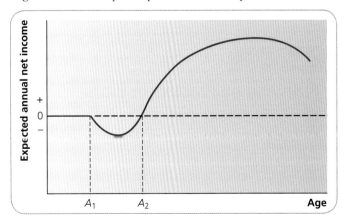

Figure 2.9 A typical net income stream

123

that capitalism has over migrant labour. For example, employers in destinations do not bear the cost of their workers' reproduction as the latter maintain ties with their rural communities, and employers use migrant labour to reduce the bargaining power of local labour. In the international arena migration is seen as a global movement in which labour is manipulated in the interest of MEDCs to the detriment of LEDCs. According to Rubenstein remittances are 'a minor component of surplus labour extraction, a small charge to capital in a grossly unequal process of exchange between core and peripheral societies'.

Figure 2.10 East European food shop in London – the population of East Europeans in the UK has increased rapidly since Poland and other East European countries joined the EU in 2004

Structuration theory

Structuration theory incorporates both individual motives for migration and the structural factors in which the migrants operate. It stresses that rules designed to regulate behaviour also provide opportunity and room for manoeuvre for those they seek to constrain. This approach also builds in an awareness of cultural factors.

Gender analyses

In recent decades gender has come to occupy a significant place in migration literature. According to Arjan de Haan, 'There is now much more emphasis on the different migration responses by men and women, which themselves are context dependent, and on gender discrimination in returns to migrant labour.'

Case Study

Push and pull factors in Brazil

While recognising that individuals can react differently to similar circumstances, it is still important to consider the negative factors that act to 'push' people from rural areas of origin, and the positive influences that 'pull' them towards towns and cities. In Brazil the push factors responsible for rural–urban migration can be summarised as follows:

- The mechanisation of agriculture has reduced the demand for farm labour in most parts of the country.

- Farms and estates have been amalgamated, particularly by agricultural production companies. In Brazil, as elsewhere in Latin America, the high incidence of landlessness has led to a much greater level of rural–urban migration than in most parts of Africa and Asia.
- Conditions of rural employment are generally poor. Employers often ignore laws relating to minimum wages and other employee rights.
- There is desertification in the north-east and deforestation in the north.
- Unemployment and underemployment are significant.
- Social conditions are poor, particularly in terms of housing, health and education.

The pull factors for internal migrants in Brazil revolve around individuals wanting to better their own and their children's lives. Within the larger urban areas such as São Paulo, Rio de Janeiro, Belo Horizonte and Brasilia migrants hope to find particular advantages:

- A greater likelihood of paid employment – many people will be unable to find work in the formal sector, but opportunities in the informal sector, even if only part-time, may be available. Developing skills in the informal sector may open the way to work in the formal sector at a later date. Paid employment provides the opportunity to save money, even if the amounts initially are very small.
- Greater proximity to health and education services – this factor is particularly important for migrants with children. There is a clear urban/rural divide in standards for both health and education.
- Most migrants end up in favelas or corticos (deteriorating formal inner city housing). However, even favela housing may be better than that found in some rural areas. Many favelas show substantial signs of upgrading over time and develop an important sense of community.
- Greater access to retail services than in rural areas – competition in the urban retail services sector can result in lower prices, enabling the individual/household to purchase a wider range of goods.
- The cultural and social attractions of large cities may be viewed as important factors in the quality of life.
- Access to internet services is often lacking in rural areas. This is often an important factor for younger migrants.

The role of constraints, obstacles and barriers

Brief reference has already been made to factors that can either prevent migration or make it a difficult process. Here a distinction has to be made between internal and international migration. In most countries there are no legal restrictions on internal migration. Thus the main constraints are distance and cost. In contrast, immigration laws present the major barrier in international migration.

The cost of migration can be viewed in three parts.

- 'Closing up' at the point of origin – this will vary considerably according to the assets owned by an individual or household. In LEDCs the monetary value may be small, although the personal value may be high. In MEDCs costs such as those of estate agents and legal fees for selling a house, selling possessions that cannot be transported at below market value, and other associated costs, can be substantial.
- The actual cost of movement itself will depend on the mode of transport used and the time taken on the journey. Costs may involve both personal transport costs and the freight costs of transporting possessions.
- The costs of 'opening up' at the point of destination – many MEDCs impose a 'stamp duty' on the purchase of a house above a certain value. This is in addition to estate agents' and legal fees. Other legal costs may also be required to begin life at the destination. If the migration is linked to employment, costs may be paid by an employer. In poorer countries such costs may appear low in monetary value, but may be substantial for the individuals concerned because of their very low income.

The consideration of distance usually involves the dangers associated with the journey. Such dangers can be subdivided into physical factors and human factors. Physical factors include risks such as flood, drought, landslide and crossing water bodies (Figure 2.11). Human factors centre around any hostility from other people that may be encountered on the journey, and the chances of an accident while travelling. For example, in recent years people fleeing Zimbabwe for South Africa have encountered bandits on both sides of the border, waiting at these locations to rob them. Ethnic tensions along a migration route may also result in significant danger.

In terms of international migration, government attitudes in the form of immigration laws usually present the most formidable barrier to prospective migrants. A number of reasonably distinct periods can be recognised in terms of government attitudes to immigration:

Figure 2.11 Iguaçu Falls, Brazil – the physical environment is much less of a barrier to migration than it once was

- Prior to 1914 government controls on international migration were almost non-existent. For example, the USA allowed the entry of anybody who was not a prostitute, a convict, a lunatic and, after 1882, Chinese. Thus the obstacles to migration at the time were cost and any physical dangers that might be associated with the journey.
- Partly reflecting security concerns, migration was curtailed between 1914 and 1945. During this period many countries pursued immigration policies that would now be classed as overtly racist.
- After 1945 many European countries, facing labour shortages, encouraged migrants from abroad. In general, legislation was not repealed but interpreted very liberally. The West Indies was a major source of labour for the UK during this period. The former West Germany attracted 'guest workers' from many countries but particularly from Turkey.
- In the 1970s slow economic growth and rising unemployment in MEDCs led to a tightening of policy which, by and large, has remained in force. However, in some countries immigration did increase again in the 1980s and early 1990s, spurring the introduction of new restrictions.

Thus over time the legal barriers to immigration have generally become more formidable. Most countries favour immigration applications from people with skills that are in short supply and from people who intend to set up businesses and create employment.

Migration data

There are three principal sources of migration data: censuses, population registers and social surveys. For all three, moves are recorded as migration when an official boundary used for data collection is crossed. Moves that do not cross a boundary may go unrecorded even though they may cover longer distances. This is one of the major problems encountered by the researcher in the study of migration.

Population censuses are important sources of information because they are taken at regular intervals and cover whole countries. The two sorts of data generally provided are

- birthplaces of the population
- period migration figures (movement over a particular period of time).

Birthplace data tells us a great deal about the broad picture of migration but it is not without its deficiencies. For example, there is no information about the number of residential moves between place of birth and present residence. In terms of period migration, recent British censuses have asked for place of residence a year before as well as place of birth. When these are compared with the present addresses of people at the time of the census we can begin to trace migration patterns. However, again, intervening moves during the one-year period and between censuses (every ten years in the UK) will go unrecorded.

Japan and a number of European countries (including Norway, Sweden and Switzerland) collect 'continuous data' on migration through *population registers*. Inhabitants are required to register an address with the police or a civic authority and to notify all changes of residence. Population registers aim to record every move, rather than just those caught by the rather arbitrary administrative and period framework of the census. In the UK and many other countries only partial registers exist to record movements for some parts of the population. Examples are electoral rolls, tax registers and school rolls. Social researchers have argued for the introduction of population registers in countries like the UK but strong opposition has focused on possible infringements of individual liberties. Thus it was only under the exceptional circumstances of the Second World War and its immediate aftermath that a national register operated in the UK.

Specific *social surveys* can do much to supplement the sources of data discussed above. An example from the UK is the International Passenger Survey, a sample survey carried out at seaports and airports. It was established to provide information on tourism and the effect of travel expenditure on the balance of payments, but it also provides useful information on international migration. The annual General Household Survey of 15 000 households also provides useful information, as does the quarterly Labour Force Survey. Questionnaire-based surveys are perhaps the only means by which the relationship between attitudes and behaviour in the migration process can be fully analysed.

Even when all the available sources of information are used to analyse migration patterns the investigator can be left in no doubt that a large proportion of population movements go entirely unrecorded and even in those countries with the most advanced administrative systems there is only partial recording of migrants and their characteristics.

Conclusion

Migration has been a major process in shaping the world as it is today. Its impact has been economic, social, cultural, political and environmental. Few people now go through life without changing residence several times. Through the detailed research of geographers, demographers and others we have a good understanding of the causes and consequences of the significant migrations of the past, which should make us better prepared for those of the future whose impact may be every bit as great. We can only speculate about the locations and causes of future migrations. Causal factors may include the following: continuing socio-economic disparity between rich and poor nations, global warming and all its implications, nuclear catastrophe, civil wars, and pandemics due to current and new diseases.

Section 2.1 Activities

1 Briefly discuss the cost–benefit approach of the Todaro model.

2 What are the main elements of Stark's new economics of migration?

3 Discuss the principal sources of migration data.

2.2 Internal migration (within a country)

Distance, direction and patterns

Figure 2.12 provides a comprehensive classification of population movements in LEDCs, covering distance, direction and patterns. The 'distance continuum' ranges from relatively limited local movements to very long-distance movements, often crossing international frontiers. The majority of the movements shown in Figure 2.12 are internal migrations. In terms of settlement size, the following movements are included:

- rural–rural
- rural–urban
- urban–rural
- urban–urban.

In this section particular consideration will be given to **rural–urban migration** in LEDCs and urban–rural movements in MEDCs (Figure 2.13).

As Parnwell states in relation to Figure 2.12, 'Distance provides a useful basis for differentiating between types of movement and types of mover, because the distance over which a person travels can also be used as a proxy for other important variables'. As cost is a significant factor in the distance over which migration takes place, the relative distance of movements may have a filtering effect upon the kinds of people who are moving between different areas. There is also a broad relationship between social/cultural change and distance. A change of dialect or differences in the social organisation

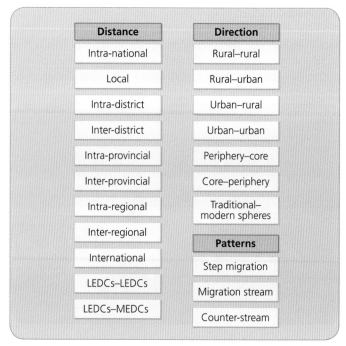

Figure 2.12 Spatial dimensions of population movements in LEDCs

Figure 2.13 Rural depopulation in northern Spain as a result of out-migration

of groups may make the migrant seem an obvious 'outsider'. To avoid such changes the prospective migrant may decide on a shorter-distance movement. Long-distance movement may also involve entry into areas with different ethnicity, colour or religion, which may all hinder the process of assimilation.

In terms of direction the most prevalent forms of migration are from rural to urban environments and from peripheral regions to economic core regions. Thus the main migration streams are from culturally traditional areas to areas where rapid change, in all its manifestations, is taking place. In LEDCs the socio-economic differences between rural and urban areas are generally of a much greater magnitude than in MEDCs. This may necessitate some quite fundamental forms of adaptation by rural–urban migrants in the poorer nations of the world.

Although of a lesser magnitude, rural–rural migration is common in LEDCs for a variety of reasons, including employment, family reunion and marriage. In some instances governments have encouraged the agricultural development of frontier areas such as the Amazon basin in Brazil.

Movements between urban areas consist in part of **step migration** up the urban hierarchy as migrants improve their knowledge base and financial position, adding to a range of other urban–urban migrations for reasons such as employment and education. Urban–rural migration is dominated by counterstream movement – that is, urbanites who are returning to their rural origins. Very few people, apart from the likes of government officials, teachers and doctors, move to the countryside for the first time to live or work. Apart from perhaps Brazil and a few other more affluent developing nations, **counterurbanisation** has yet to gain any kind of foothold in LEDCs.

Section 2.2 Activities

1 What is *internal migration*?

2 Provide a brief explanation of Figure 2.12.

3 Define **a** *step migration* and **b** *counterurbanisation*.

The causes of internal migration

The reasons why people change their place of permanent residence can be viewed at three dimensions of scale: macro-level, meso-level and micro-level.

The macro-level

This dimension highlights socio-economic differences at the national scale, focusing particularly on the **core–periphery** concept. The development of core regions in many LEDCs had its origins in the colonial era, which was characterised by the selective and incomplete opening-up of territories, supporting development in a restricted range of economic sectors. At this time migration was encouraged to supply labour for new colonial enterprises and infrastructural projects, such as the development of ports and the construction of transport links between areas of raw material exploitation and the ports through which export would take place.

The introduction of capitalism, through colonialism, into previously non-capitalist societies had a huge influence on movement patterns. The demand for labour in mines, plantations and other activities was satisfied to a considerable extent by restricting native access to land and by coercing people into migration to work either directly through forced labour systems or indirectly through taxation. The spread of a cash economy at the expense of barter into peripheral areas further increased the need for paid employment which, on the whole, could only be found in the economic core region (Figure 2.14).

In the post-colonial era most LEDCs have looked to industrialisation as their path to a better world, resulting in disproportionate investment in the urban-industrial sector and the relative neglect of the rural economy. Even where investment in agriculture has been considerable, either the objective or the

Figure 2.14 The Ger district in Ulaanbaatar, Mongolia, which is expanding rapidly due to high levels of rural–urban migration

end result was to replace labour with machinery, adding further to rural out-migration.

The macro-level perspective provides a general explanation of migration patterns in LEDCs. However, this approach has two weaknesses:

- it fails to explain why some people migrate and others stay put when faced with very similar circumstances in peripheral areas
- it offers no explanation as to why not all forms of migration occur in the direction of economic core regions.

The meso-level

The meso-level dimension includes more detailed consideration of the factors in the origin and destination that influence people's migration decisions. E. S. Lee's **origin-intervening obstacles-destination** model, which was discussed in the previous section, is a useful starting point in understanding this level of approach, which looks well beyond economic factors and recognises the vital role of the perception of the individual in the decision-making process.

Lee argues that migration occurs in response to the prevailing set of factors both in the migrant's place of origin and in one or a number of potential destinations. However, what is perceived as positive and what is viewed as negative at origin and destination may vary considerably between individuals, as may the intervening obstacles. As Lee states, 'It is not so much the actual factors at origin and destination as the perception of these factors which result in migration'. Lee stressed the point that the factors in favour of migration would generally have to outweigh considerably those against, due to the natural reluctance of people to uproot themselves from established communities.

High population growth is often cited as the major cause of rural–urban migration. However, in itself population growth is not the main cause of out-migration. Its effects have to be seen in conjunction with the failure of other processes to provide adequately for the needs of growing rural communities. Even when governments focus resources on rural development, the volume of out-migration may not be reduced. The irony in many LEDCs is that people are being displaced from the countryside because in some areas change is too slow to accommodate the growing size and needs of the population, or because in other areas change is too quick to enable redundant rural workers to find alternative employment in their home areas. In such circumstances out-migration does indeed provide an essential 'safety valve'.

The evidence in Table 2.1 and in other similar studies is that the economic motive underpins the majority of rural–urban movements. During the 1960s most demographers cited the higher wages and more varied employment opportunities of the cities as the prime reason for internal migration. It was also widely held that the level of migration was strongly related to the rate of urban unemployment. However, while rural/urban income differentials are easy to quantify, they do not take into account the lower cost of living in the countryside and the fact that non-cash income often forms a significant proportion of rural incomes.

Table 2.1 Reasons for migration from rural areas in Peru and Thailand

PERU

Reason	% respondents citing reason
To earn more money	39
To join kin already working	25
No work in the villages	12
Work opportunities presented themselves	11
Dislike of village life	11
To be near the village and family	11
To support nuclear and/or extended family	9
Poor	8
To pay for education	7

Source: J. Laite 'The migrant response in central Peru', in J. Gugler (ed.) *The Urbanization of the Third World*, OUP 1988

NORTH-EAST THAILAND

Principal reason	No. respondents citing reason	% respondents citing reason
To earn more money for the household	138	52.9
To earn more money for self	57	21.8
To earn more money for parents	31	11.9
To further education	12	4.6
To earn money to build a house	10	3.8
To earn money to invest in farming	4	1.5
For fun	3	1.1
To earn money to purchase land/land title	2	0.8
To earn money to repay a debt	1	0.4
To earn money to pay for hired labour	1	0.4
To see Bangkok	1	0.4
To earn money to get married	1	0.4
Total	261	100.0

Source: M. Parnwell, *Population Movements and the Third World*, Routledge, 1993

In the 1970s, as more and more cities in LEDCs experienced large-scale in-migration in spite of high unemployment, demographers began to reappraise the situation. Michael Todaro was one of the first to recognise that the paradox of urban deprivation on the one hand and migration in pursuit of higher wages on the other could be explained by taking a long-term view of why people move to urban areas. As the more detailed consideration of the Todaro model in the previous section explains, people are prepared to ensure urban hardship in the short term in the likelihood that their long-term prospects will be much better in the city than in the countryside. Apart from employment prospects the other perceived advantages of the cities are a higher standard of accommodation, a better education for migrants' children, improved medical facilities, the conditions of infrastructure often lacking in rural areas, and a wider range of consumer services. The most fortunate migrants find jobs in the formal sector. A regular wage then gives some access to the other advantages of urban life. However, as the demand for jobs greatly outstrips supply, many can do no better than the uncertainty of the informal sector.

Of all the factors that migrants take into account before arriving at a decision, the economic perspective invariably dominates the decision to leave the countryside. However, all the evidence shows that other factors, particularly the social environment, have a very strong influence on the direction that the movement takes. This largely explains why capital cities, with their wide range of social opportunities, attract so many rural migrants.

The micro-level

The main criticisms of the macro- and meso-level explanations of migration are that:

- they view migration as a passive response to a variety of stimuli
- they tend to view rural source areas as an undifferentiated entity.

The specific circumstances of individual families and communities in terms of urban contact are of crucial importance in the decision to move, particularly when long distances are involved. The alienation experienced by the unknown new migrant to an urban area should not be underestimated and is something that will be avoided if at all possible. The evidence comes from a significant number of sample surveys and of course from the high incidence of 'area of origin' communities found in cities. For example:

- A sample survey of rural migrants in Mumbai found that more than 75 per cent already had one or more relatives living in the city, from whom 90 per cent had received some form of assistance upon arrival.
- A survey of migration from the Peruvian Highlands to Lima found that 90 per cent of migrants could rely on short-term accommodation on arrival in the city, and that for about half their contacts had managed to arrange a job for them.

The importance of established links between urban and rural areas frequently results in the phenomenon of 'chain migration'. After one or a small number of pioneering migrants have led the way, subsequent waves of migration from the same rural community follow. The more established a migrant community becomes in the city, the easier it appears to be for others in the rural community to take the decision to move and for them to assimilate into urban society.

Apart from contact with, and knowledge of urban locations, differentiation between rural households takes the following forms:

- level of income
- size of land holding
- size of household
- stage in the life cycle
- level of education
- cohesiveness of the family unit.

All of these factors have an influence on the decision to migrate (Figure 2.15). Family ties and commitments may determine whether or not someone is able to migrate, and may also influence who from a family unit is most likely to take on the responsibility of seeking employment in the city. Here the stage in the life cycle is

crucial and it is not surprising that the great majority of migrants in LEDCs are aged between 15 and 25 years. In some communities the phenomenon of 'relay migration' has been identified whereby at different stages in a family's life cycle, different people take responsibility for migration.

It is only by examining all three dimensions – macro, meso and micro – that the complexity of the migration process can be fully understood. As elsewhere in geographical analysis there is a tendency to over-simplify. This is often useful in the early stages of enquiry but unless we are careful the understandable generalisation may mask essential detail.

Figure 2.15 Migrants from North East Brazil farming a smallholding in the Amazon basin

Section 2.2 Activities

1 Why is it important to consider different dimensions of scale when examining internal migration?

2 Produce a brief summary of the information in Table 2.1.

The impacts of internal migration

Socio-economic impact

Figure 2.16 provides a useful framework for understanding the costs and returns from migration. It highlights the main factors that determine how rural areas are affected by migration – namely the two-way transfers of labour, money, skills and attitudes. However, while all of the linkages seem fairly obvious, none is easy to quantify. Therefore, apart from very clear-cut cases, it is often difficult to decide which is greater – the costs or benefits of migration.

Figure 2.16 The costs and returns from migration

The first question is the least problematic. The importance of pull factors in explaining both national and international movements is widely accepted. Clearly migrants do move in reaction to newly developed opportunities. However, a number of recent studies have shown that people in the poorest areas of LEDCs do not exhibit the highest levels of out-migration. In such regions levels of literacy and skill may be so low that access to even very menial urban jobs can be difficult.

It is in many ways ironic that development in rural areas of origin often acts as a stimulus to out-migration. In China the development of rural enterprises appears to increase rates of out-migration. In the Punjab, the Green Revolution witnessed both high rates of out-migration by the resident population and in-migration from a number of poorer Indian states. Development often acts as an important stimulus, widening the horizons of a significant number among the rural population.

There is some evidence that internal migration in LEDCs is beneficial for receiving regions. The fact that rural migrants are often the most dynamic young adults from their communities should be of benefit to the receiving urban areas, providing enough opportunities are available for most to gain reasonable employment. However, newcomers can place a massive burden on over-stretched urban amenities and services, particularly if large numbers are unemployed.

The impact of out-migration on areas of origin is not at all clear. The traditional view has been that by reducing unemployment and underemployment, and providing inputs such as remittances and newly acquired skills, migration promotes development in rural areas of origin, narrows regional disparities and eventually makes migration unnecessary. However, recent research on this issue has in some respects been contradictory and the possibility of such mobility having an adverse effect on the economy of labour-exporting areas cannot be ruled out. Lipton, with reference to the Indian Village Studies Programme, emphasised the inequality-increasing effects of rural–urban migration in areas of origin. High emigration from a village was strongly related to the unequal distribution of resources, usually land. Migration frequently involved both the richest and poorest households in the village. Richer potential migrants were 'pulled' towards fairly firm job prospects in the formal sector whereas the poor were 'pushed' by rural poverty and labour-replacing methods. The much higher remittances from rich migrants compared with those from poorer migrants from the same community acted to increase inequalities in villages and between villages in the same region.

An important issue is the impact of out-migration on local agriculture. In some cases out-migration undoubtedly causes a shortage of labour, although in other instances it clearly alleviates unemployment and underemployment. In some areas large numbers of women now perform agricultural tasks that were once the preserve of men. This 'new' work is frequently in addition to an existing heavy household workload. Although remittances help, they are often too low to hire-in labour. There is also a tendency for land to become concentrated in the hands of migrant families, who gradually turn into non-farmers resulting in a fall in agricultural production.

Remittances from internal migration are even more difficult to estimate than those arising from international migration. Thus it is not surprising that research has produced a fairly wide range of conclusions, of which the following are but a sample:

- Williamson (1988) put urban–rural remittances at 10–13 per cent of urban incomes in Africa.
- Reardon (1997) noted that in rural areas in Africa not close to major cities, migrant earnings accounted for only 20 per cent of total non-farm earnings, whereas it reached as high as 75 per cent of total non-farm earnings in areas close to major cities.
- Adepoju and Mbugua (1997) note that migrants often remit up to 60 per cent of their income.

However, it is important to note that the flow of money and support in general is not always one-way. Some studies have highlighted village-to-town remittances to support education or the search for employment.

Helweg (1983) studied the changing use of remittances over time, noting three stages: initially they are spent on family maintenance and improving land productivity; in the following stage spending tends to be on 'conspicuous' consumption; in the third and final stage remittances are also invested to start commercial, non-agricultural activities.

The relationship between migration and development is complex and still the subject of much debate. The four questions that have been the subject of much research are:

1 How does development in areas of destination affect migration?
2 How does development in the area of origin affect migration?
3 How does migration affect development in areas of destination?
4 How does migration affect development in areas of origin?

Whether the impact of out-migration on agriculture is positive or negative depends on the complex interaction of a range of social and economic factors which may be subject to change over time.

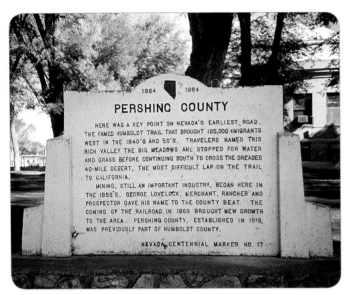

Figure 2.17 Lovelock, Nevada – on the historic Humboldt Trail

Political impact

Internal migration at a significant scale can have considerable political repercussions. For example:

- Where migration results in **depopulation**, the reduced number of people in a region can reduce the 'political voice' of the community. A lower population can also result in decreased funding from central government. Such a downward spiral may result in a region becoming more and more peripheral to its country as a whole.
- In contrast, where population is growing rapidly, partly at least as a result of in-migration, the political voice of such regions will become more important. In some LEDCs in particular, capital cities have grown rapidly, attaining an increasingly dominant political and economic role. Such economic and political primacy may be of considerable benefit to the residents of the capital city, but to the detriment of the rest of that country.
- Internal migration can significantly change the ethnic composition of a region or urban area, which may result in tension. In the Niger Delta many local people feel that most jobs go to members of the country's majority ethnic groups – the Igbo, Yoruba, Hausa and Fulani, who traditionally come from elsewhere in Nigeria. The local ethnic groups, whose numbers are small in national terms, feel that they have been largely overlooked by the government. This has resulted in a high level of resentment and is certainly one cause of the development of armed groups which have become a major threat to the large oil industry in the region.

Tibet's changing ethnic balance

In some countries governments have been accused of deliberately using internal migration to change the ethnic balance of a region. Tibet is an example where the in-migration of large numbers of Han Chinese has had a huge impact. Prior to the Chinese occupation of Tibet in 1950, very few Chinese lived in what is now the Tibetan Autonomous Region (TAR). This has changed completely, with Chinese migrants now in the majority in some parts of Tibet. In the capital Lhasa there are 200 000 Chinese and 100 000 Tibetans. If the present influx continues, Tibetans could become the minority population within a few decades. Most Tibetans see this as an immense threat to the survival of their culture and identity. The Dalai Lama, Tibet's exiled spiritual leader, has stated that this policy of 'demographic aggression' has led to 'cultural genocide'.

Most in-migrants to Tibet are Han Chinese, by far the largest ethnic group in China. They fall into two general groups:

- government officials and technical experts who can be thought of as involuntary migrants
- economic migrants – miners, construction workers, retail and other service workers.

Incentives provided by the government for Han Chinese to go to Tibet include tax incentives, allowances, higher wages and better housing.

In 2006, the world's highest railway, the Qinghai–Tibet line, was opened. It runs from Golmud to Lhasa (Figure 2.18). China says the 1140 km line will bring economic opportunities to Tibet. However, many Tibetans fear it will encourage even more in-migration.

Figure 2.18 The Qinghai–Tibet railway

Environmental impact

Large-scale rural–urban migration has led to the massive expansion of many urban areas in LEDCs (Figure 2.19) which has swallowed up farmland, forests, floodplains and other areas of ecological importance. In turn, the increased impact of these enlarged urban areas is affecting environments even further afield, in a variety of different ways. These include:

- deforestation due to the increasing demand for firewood
- increasing demands on regional water supplies and other resources
- the expansion of landfill sites
- air and water pollution from factories, households, power stations, transportation and other sources.

Internally displaced people and refugees can have a considerable impact on the environment. They often concentrate in marginal and vulnerable environments where the potential for environmental degradation is high. Apart from immediate problems concerning sanitation and the disposal of waste, long-term environmental damage may result from deforestation associated with the need for firewood and building materials. Increased pressure on the land can result in serious soil degradation.

A study of high in-migration into the coastal areas of Palawan in the Philippines found that the historical social processes which helped maintain reasonable patterns of environmental use had been overwhelmed by the rapid influx of migrants. The newcomers brought in new resource extraction techniques which were more efficient, but also more destructive than those previously employed by the established community. The study concluded that high in-migration had caused severe environmental damage to the coastal environment.

Impact on population structures

The age-selective (and often gender-selective) nature of migration can have a very significant impact on both areas of origin and destination. This is no more so than in rural areas of heavy out-migration and urban areas where heavy in-migration is evident.

Population pyramids for rural areas in LEDCs frequently show the loss of young adults (and their children) and may also show a distinct difference between the number of males and females in the young adult age group, due to a higher number of males than females leaving rural areas for urban destinations. However, in some rural areas female out-migration may be at a higher level than male out-migration, as Figure 2.20 illustrates. In contrast, urban population pyramids show the reverse impact, with age-selective in-migration.

In Figure 2.20, women aged 20 to 35 years in Grant County comprise just 4.3 per cent of the population. This is a mainly rural area. The county's ageing population lowers the birth rate and increases the death rate. Here out-migration has caused depopulation – an actual fall in the population. In contrast in Orange County, Florida, 12 per cent of the population are women aged 20 to 35 years. Orange County is a predominantly urban area.

Figure 2.19 Cairo has expanded rapidly due to both high in-migration and high natural increase

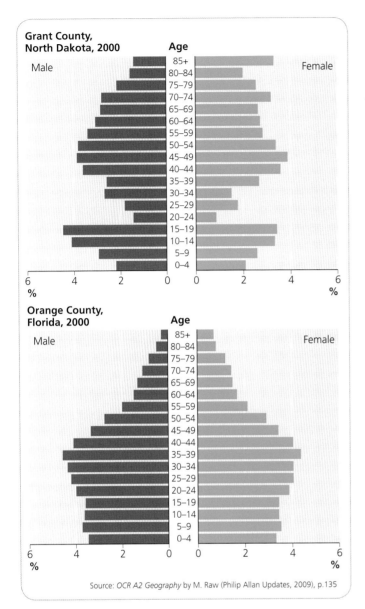

Figure 2.20 Population pyramids for Grant County, North Dakota and Orange County, Florida

Source: *OCR A2 Geography* by M. Raw (Philip Allan Updates, 2009), p.135

Section 2.2 Activities

1 With reference to Figure 2.16:
  a Give two reasons for rural–urban migration.
  b To what extent and why is rural–urban migration selective?
  c Discuss the 'support costs' flowing from village to city.
  d What are *remittances*? Suggest how remittances are used in rural areas.

2 In what ways can internal migration have a political impact?

3 Describe how internal migration can have an impact on the environment.

4 Explain how rural–urban migration can have an impact on population structures.

Stepped migration and urban–urban movements

A number of analyses of internal migration, for example in Nigeria, have recognised a stepped structure to such movements, with migrants from rural areas often moving to a local town before later making a move further up the urban hierarchy. Figure 2.21 shows three ways **stepped migration** might occur in an LEDC.

During the initial move from a rural environment to a relatively small urban area, migrants may develop skills and increase their knowledge of and confidence in urban environments. They may become aware of better employment opportunities in larger urban areas and develop the personal contacts that can be so important in the migration process. For those working in the formal sector, a move up the urban hierarchy may be linked to a promotion within the company in which they work, or a transfer linked to public sector employment.

Figure 2.21 Stepped migration

Another important form of urban–urban migration is from towns and cities in economic periphery areas to urban areas in the economic core. An example is Brazil, with significant movement in the past 50 years from urban areas in the relatively poor North East such as Fortaleza, Natal, Recife and Salvador to the more prosperous cities of the South East, such as São Paulo, Rio de Janeiro and Belo Horizonte. Greater employment opportunities and higher average wages have been the main reason for such movements, but many of the other push and pull factors discussed earlier have also been significant.

Causes and impacts of intra-urban movements

Demographic analysis shows that movements of population within cities are closely related to stages in the **family life cycle**, with the available housing stock being a major determinant of where people live at different stages in their life. Studies in Toronto show a broad concentric zone pattern (Figure 2.22). Young adults frequently choose housing close to the CBD, while older families occupy the next ring out. Middle-aged families are more likely to reside at a greater distance from the central area; and farther out still, in the newest suburban areas, young families dominate. This simplified model applies particularly well to a rapidly growing metropolis like Toronto where an invasion and succession process evolves over time.

Source: *Toronto in Transition*, City of Toronto Planning and Development Dept. Policy and Research Division, April 1980, p. 21

Figure 2.22 Toronto – changing social structure in a growing city

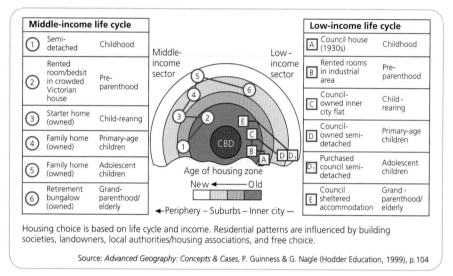

Housing choice is based on life cycle and income. Residential patterns are influenced by building societies, landowners, local authorities/housing associations, and free choice.

Source: *Advanced Geography: Concepts & Cases*, P. Guinness & G. Nagle (Hodder Education, 1999), p.104

Figure 2.23 Middle- and low-income models of the family life cycle in the UK

Toronto's inner city has a much higher percentage of rented and small unit accommodation than the outer regions which, along with the stimulus of employment and the social attractions of the central area, has attracted young adults to the area. Most housing units built in the inner area in recent decades have been in the form of apartments.

Studies in the UK have highlighted the spatial contrasts in life cycle between middle- and low-income groups (Figure 2.23). With life cycle and income being the major determinants of where people live, residential patterns are also influenced by a range of organisations, foremost of which are local authorities, housing associations, building societies and landowners. On top of this is the range of choice available to the household. For those on low income this is frequently very restricted indeed. As income rises the range of choice in terms of housing type and location increases.

Counterurbanisation

According to G.J. Lewis 'counterurbanisation involves a series of fundamental changes in the redistribution of population including a population shift out of core industrial regions and into the

peripheral regions as well as movements down the urban hierarchy'. Changes in telecommunications in particular have helped to diversify many non-metropolitan economies so that they are now viable locations for employers and residents in search of less congestion, lower costs and a better quality of life.

The general consensus is that counterurbanisation first became clearly evident in the USA in the 1970s and that since then most countries of western Europe as well as Australia, New Zealand, Canada and Japan have followed suit. However, this is not to say that evidence of counterurbanisation could not be found to some degree before 1970 in various parts of the developed world. It seems the starting point of counterurbanisation was the transformation of the most accessible rural settlements within the metropolitan hinterland into commuter communities. As a 'rural' lifestyle became more popular amongst urbanites, its spatial impact gradually diffused into more remote regions.

In all the countries affected, the movement of urbanites into rural areas has reduced differences in culture, lifestyle and population composition. There has been much debate about the causes of counterurbanisation. The most plausible explanations are as follows:

- The 'period' explanation emphasises the role of the peculiar economic and demographic circumstances of the 1970s. The energy crisis, periods of recession, the sharp growth in retirees and the impact of the post-war baby boom combined to weaken metropolitan growth. In metropolitan areas push factors had never been stronger, while – perhaps for the first time – rural location was a viable alternative for many. This perspective viewed counterurbanisation as a very temporary phenomenon which would subside once economic and demographic conditions returned to 'normal'.

- The 'regional restructuring' explanation emphasises the role of the new organisation of production, the changing spatial division of labour and the increasing importance of service industries. All these factors stimulated a greater spread of activities and population towards smaller places and the rural periphery.

- The 'de-concentration' explanation highlights the lowering of institutional and technological barriers to rural location. Long-standing preferences for lower-density environments are now much less constrained than in the past and an increasing number of businesses and households have felt free to leave the metropolitan areas, confident that their prospects were more likely to improve rather than diminish. The key factor here is the convergence, across size and place, in the availability of amenities that were previously accessible only in larger places.

While all three explanations have their merits, it would appear from the literature on the subject that the third argument is viewed as the most important.

2.3 International migration

Voluntary migration

International migration is a major global issue. In the past it has had a huge impact on both donor and receiving nations. In terms of the receiving countries the consequences have generally been beneficial. But today few countries favour a large influx of outsiders, for a variety of reasons.

In terms of **voluntary migration** it is useful to differentiate between *independent* and *dependent* movements. In independent movements the decision to move to a new location is made by the individual whereas in dependent movements the decision is taken collectively by the household. In the latter case the individual concerned may or may not have a significant say in the final decision, often depending on the age and gender of the prospective migrant.

Currently, one in every 35 people around the world is living outside the country of their birth. This amounts to about 175 million people, higher than ever before. Recent migration data shows that:

- With the growth in the importance of labour-related migration and international student mobility, migration has become increasingly temporary and circular in nature. For example in 2006/07 there were 583 000 foreign students in the USA. The international mobility of highly skilled workers increased substantially in the 1990s and 2000s.
- The spatial impact of migration has spread, with an increasing number of countries affected either as points of origin or destination. While many traditional migration streams remained strong, significant new streams have developed.
- The proportion of female migrants has steadily increased (now over 47 per cent of all migrants). For some countries of origin, for example The Philippines, Sri Lanka, Thailand and Indonesia, women now make up the majority of contract workers.

- The great majority of international migrants from MEDCs go to other affluent nations. Migration from LEDCs is more or less equally split between MEDCs and LEDCs (Figure 2.24). However, there is an important qualification here in that the movement between LEDCs is usually from weaker to stronger economies.
- MEDCs have reinforced controls, in part in response to security issues, but also to combat illegal immigration and networks that deal in trafficking and exploitation of human beings.

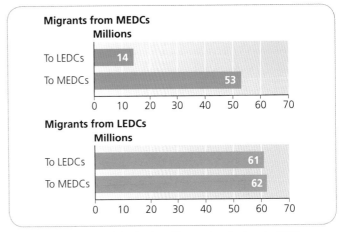

Figure 2.24 Origin and destination of international migrants, 2005

Globalisation in all its aspects has led to an increased awareness of opportunities in other countries. With advances in transportation and communication and a reduction in the real cost of both, the world's population has never had a higher level of potential mobility (Figure 2.25). Also, in various ways, economic and social development has made people more mobile and created the conditions for emigration.

Each receiving country has its own sources, the results of historical, economic and geographical relationships. Earlier generations of migrants form networks that help new ones to overcome legal and other obstacles. Today's tighter rules tend to confine immigration to family members of earlier 'primary' migrants.

Figure 2.25 The development of air transport (Air China) has been a significant factor in high levels of international migration in recent decades

Forced migration

In the historical writings on migration in LEDCs, there is an emphasis on the forced recruitment of labour. The abduction and transport of Africans to the Americas as slaves was the largest forced migration in history. In the seventeenth and eighteenth centuries 15 million people were shipped across the Atlantic Ocean as slaves.

Even in recent times the scale of involuntary movement in LEDCs is considerably higher than most people think. However, giving due consideration to such movements should not blind us to the increasing scale of free labour migration that has occurred in recent decades. Here the focal points have been the most dynamic economies of the LEDCs which have sucked in labour from more laggard neighbouring countries.

In the latter part of the twentieth century and the beginning of the twenty-first century, some of the world's most violent and protracted conflicts have been in the LEDCs, particularly in Africa and Asia. These troubles have led to numerous population movements of a significant scale. Not all have crossed international frontiers to merit the term '**refugee**' movements. Instead many have involved **internal displacement**. This is a major global problem which is showing little sign of abatement.

A number of trends appear to have contributed to the growing scale and speed of forced displacement:
- the emergence of new forms of warfare involving the destruction of whole social, economic and political systems
- the spread of light weapons and land mines, available at prices that enable whole populations to be armed
- the use of mass evictions and expulsions as a weapon of war and as a means of establishing culturally and ethnically homogeneous societies – the term 'ethnic cleansing' is commonly used to describe this process.

Spiralling global conflicts and worldwide instability have forced millions of people to leave their homes and seek refuge either abroad or in their own countries. The latest figures do not include the wars in Sri Lanka and Pakistan's Swat valley, which have displaced thousands more

 Countries with high IDPs

People displaced around the world **42 million**

○ **Asylum seeker**
Has left their own country and seeks protection in another. In the UK – a person who has made an official claim for asylum and is waiting for a decision on their claim

○ **Refugee**
Recognised under the UN 1951 Convention on Refugees as having a well-founded fear of persecution, has been forced to flee their own country and is unable to return

○ **Internally displaced person (IDP)**
Forced to flee their home because their life was in danger but, unlike a refugee, did not cross international borders

○ **Stateless person**
Someone who, under national laws, does not enjoy citizenship or nationality – the legal bond between a state and an individual – with any country

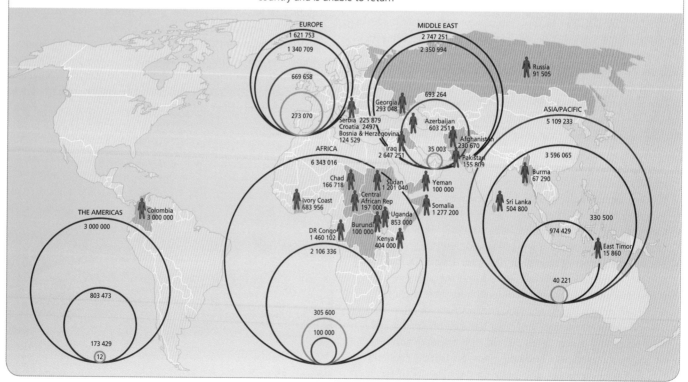

Figure 2.26 Global human displacement, June 2009

KENYA–SOMALIA: DADAAB GRAPPLING WITH DRAMATIC REFUGEE SITUATION

7 August 2009

NAIROBI – The UN Refugee Agency (UNHCR) is to support livelihood and environmental protection programmes for local Kenyan communities in Dadaab, says a senior UN official.

The Dagahaley, Hagadera and Ifo camps in Dadaab comprise the largest refugee site in the world. As of 5 July, the site hosted an estimated 284 306 refugees, mainly from Somalia. This number was triple the designated capacity.

"We have witnessed in the recent months arrivals [in] the region [of] 5000 per month, creating a situation that is extremely dramatic," the UN High Commissioner for Refugees, António Guterres, said.

Relations between refugees and the surrounding host population often sour with increasing insecurity and environmental degradation being blamed on the refugee influx, aid workers say.

Dadaab, some 90 km from the Kenya–Somalia border, has seen a large number of asylum-seekers fleeing years of conflict in Somalia.

Guterres said there was a need to adequately screen people coming into Dadaab to improve safety for the refugees and locals, and to address Kenya's security concerns.

"UNHCR is preparing a comprehensive strategy for decongestion, rehabilitation and security in Dadaab," he said, adding that immediate priorities were in health, water and sanitation.

A measles outbreak was reported in Hagadera camp in July. Earlier, a cholera outbreak had been reported.

In a briefing note, UNHCR said the inability to provide adequate shelter for refugees had exposed them to exploitation by their hosts. For example, cases of sexual- and gender-based violence reported this year had increased by 30 per cent.

To decongest Dadaab, UNHCR plans to move some refugees to Kakuma in the northwest, along the border with Sudan, and hopes to secure additional land in Dadaab. Kakuma already hosts some 45 017 refugees and has inadequate shelter.

The first group of 12 900 refugees from Dadaab is expected to go to Kakuma – about 1000 km away – before the rainy season. "As soon as the minimum logistic and reception conditions are established, the movement to Kakuma can start," Guterres said.

Figure 2.27 Somalian refugees in Kenya

In a number of locations around the world, whole 'neighbourhoods of states have become affected by interlocking and mutually reinforcing patterns of armed conflict and forced displacement, for example in the Caucasus and Central Africa. The United Nations High Commission for Refugees (UNHCR) is responsible for guaranteeing the security of refugees in the countries where they seek asylum and aiding the governments of these nations in this task. The UNHCR has noted a growing number of situations in which people are repeatedly uprooted, expelled or relocated within and across state borders, forcing them to live a desperately insecure and nomadic existence. The UNHCR has observed that 'the forced displacement of minorities, including depopulation and repopulation tactics in support of territorial claims and self-determination, has become an abominable characteristic of the contemporary world'. Figure 2.26 shows that a total of 42 million people were classed as displaced in 2009, with the largest numbers being in Africa and the Asia/Pacific region.

Three refugee camps in Dadaab, Kenya comprise the largest refugee site in the world, with an estimated 284 000 refugees (Figure 2.27). The impact on the region has been immense. The countries most affected by the refugee problem are the poorest in the world. Refugee populations are dominated by women and children. Adult males tend to be heavily under-represented because they are engaged in other activities.

Many LEDCs are prone to natural disasters. Because poor nations do not possess the funds to minimise the consequences of natural disaster, forced migration is often the result. Some areas have been devastated time and time again, often eliciting only a minimal response from the outside world. Ecological and environmental change are a common cause of human displacement. Much of Central Asia is affected by problems such as soil degradation and desertification, a situation created by decades of agricultural exploitation, industrial pollution and overgrazing. The worst situation is in and around the Aral Sea, a large lake located between Kazakstan and Uzbekistan. In a large-scale effort to increase cotton production in the region, most of the river water flowing into the Aral Sea was siphoned off for irrigation. Since 1960 the surface area of the sea has been reduced by half. Dust from the dried-up bed of the sea, containing significant amounts of agricultural and industrial chemicals, is carried long distances by the wind, adding further to the pollution, salinisation and desertification of the land. Agricultural production has fallen sharply and food has increased in price, the fishing industry has been almost totally destroyed, and local people are plagued by significant health problems. It has been estimated that more than 100 000 people have left the Aral Sea area since 1992 because of these problems.

Semipalatinsk in Kazakhstan, where almost 500 nuclear bombs were exploded between 1949 and 1989, 150 of them above ground, is another environmental disaster zone. Here 160 000 people decided to leave, due to concerns about the consequences of nuclear radiation. Around half of these people moved to other parts of Kazakhstan, with the remainder going to a number of other former Soviet states. Tackling environmental degradation in this region will not be an easy task. The problem is so deep-rooted and was kept hidden for so long under Soviet rule that it may in some instances be too late for effective remedial action to be taken.

Increasingly large numbers of people have been displaced by major infrastructural projects and by the commercial sector's huge appetite for land. In LEDCs the protests of communities in the way of 'progress' are invariably ignored for reasons of 'national interest' or pure greed. The World Bank and other international organisations have been heavily criticised in recent decades for financing numerous large-scale projects without giving sufficient consideration to those people directly affected.

It is predicted that climate change will force mass migrations in the future. In 2009 the International Organisation for Migration estimated that worsening tropical storms, desert droughts and rising sea levels will displace 200 million people by 2050.

Section 2.3 Activities

1 What is the difference between a *refugee* and an *internally displaced person*?

2 Describe the extent of global human displacement shown in Figure 2.26.

3 Briefly describe the refugee situation in Kenya (Figure 2.27).

4 Suggest how climate change may cause forced migrations in the future.

The impacts of international migration

Socio-economic impact

Recent international migration reports have stressed the sharp rise in the number of people migrating to the world's richest countries for work, although the 2008/10 global recession has had a considerable impact on this trend. Such movement is outpacing family-related and humanitarian movements in many countries. The rise in labour-related migration has been for both temporary and permanent workers and across all employment categories – skilled workers, seasonal employees, trainees, working holiday-makers, transfers of staff within transnational corporations, and cross-border workers. Of the major industrial economies, only Japan has not had a significant influx of migrant workers.

While the inflow of skilled labour remains the priority for MEDCs, some countries also welcome less skilled workers, particularly in agriculture (e.g. USA, Australia, Spain and Greece), construction, care for the elderly and other business and household services (e.g. the UK, Italy, Portugal). The distribution of immigrants in receiving countries is far from uniform, with significant concentration in economic core regions. Factors that influence the regional destination of immigrants into OECD (Organisation for Economic Cooperation and Development) countries are:

- the extent of economic opportunities
- the presence of family members or others of the same ethnic origin

- the point of entry into the country.

The socio-economic status of OECD immigrants was frequently low. Immigrants were more likely to:

- be unemployed compared to nationals – in most European countries unemployment rates for foreigners are twice as high as for native workers
- have '3D' jobs – that is jobs that were 'dirty, dangerous and dull/difficult'
- be over-represented in construction, hospitality and catering, and in household services.

Although many migrants rely on family contacts and migrant networks, others may have little choice but to use a labour broker who will try to match a potential migrant to a job in a richer country. For example, in Bangladesh workers can pay up to $2000 to a broker for a job in Saudi Arabia.

Some international labour migration takes the form of commuting. Examples include:

- workers travelling daily from Malmo in Sweden to Copenhagen, the Danish capital city
- German, French and Belgium 'frontaliers' commuting daily into Luxembourg, where they account for a quarter of the labour force.

The World Bank estimates that international remittances totalled $397 billion in 2008, of which $305 billion went to LEDCs, involving some 190 million migrants or 3.0 per cent of world population. Figure 2.28 shows how much remittances have increased since 1990. The graph also compares the value of remittances with official development assistance, foreign direct investment, and private debt and portfolio equity. Figure 2.29 shows (a) the top recipients of remittances by value in 2007 and (b) countries where remittances formed the highest percentage of GDP in 2006. Research in a number of countries has linked rising remittance payments to reduced levels of poverty. For example, Figure 2.30 shows the relationship between remittances and poverty in Nepal.

Some economists argue that remittances are the most effective source of financing in LEDCs. Although foreign direct investment

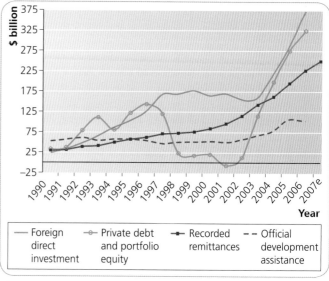

Figure 2.28 Recorded remittances, 1990–2007e

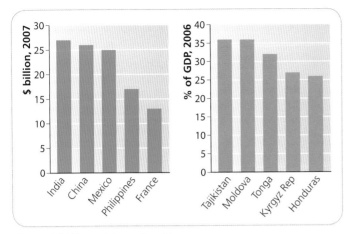

Figure 2.29 Top recipients of remittances

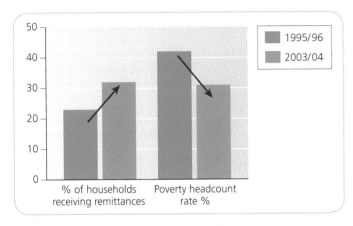

Figure 2.30 Remittances and poverty in Nepal

Figure 2.31 Moneygram sign – remittances are an important element of international migration

All three forms of economic benefit mentioned above combine to form a positive **multiplier effect** in donor countries.

In the past the perceived major disadvantage of emigration has been that it will lead to a 'brain drain' in which countries will lose their best workers. However, the direct and indirect effects of remittances may more than compensate for this. For some countries the proportion of graduates working overseas is high – 25 per cent for Iran, 26 per cent for Ghana, 10 per cent for the Philippines, 6 per cent for South Korea. It has been estimated that about $60 billion worth of LEDC investment in tertiary education has been 'drained' to OEDC countries. However, it should be noted that some LEDCs have more graduates in some areas than they need.

Social assimilation usually follows on the back of economic assimilation, although the speed and degree to which it is achieved tends to be strongly related to the socio-political maturity of the host society as well as to the degree of difference between an immigrant community and the host society. Racial differences create the greatest barrier to social assimilation but differences in language, religion and culture can also be important. As social barriers decline, the benefits that different cultures can bring to society as a whole become more apparent. One of the great attractions of cities such as London and New York is their multiculturalism. The social impact on the donor country can also be considerable. This tends to occur in two stages. The first stage is the initial loss of many of its most dynamic individuals. The second stage occurs as new ideas from the adopted country filter back to the home country, often clashing with traditional values.

is larger it varies with global economic fluctuations. Remittances exceed considerably the amount of official aid received by LEDCs (Figure 2.28). Remittances have been described as 'globalisation bottom up'. Migration advocates stress that these revenue flows:

- help alleviate poverty
- spur investment
- cushion the impact of global recession when private capital flows decrease.

The major sources of remittances are the USA, Western Europe and the Gulf (Figure 2.31). The number of foreigners working in these areas is rising significantly. About 1.3 million migrants settle in the USA annually, around one-third of them illegally. The top destinations of remittances are India, China, Mexico and the Philippines. The 20 million people who make up the Indian **diaspora** are scattered over 135 countries. In 2007 they sent back to India $27 billion – a source of foreign exchange that exceeds revenues generated by India's software industry. The Indian state of Kerala has nearly 1 million 'Gulf wives' living apart from their husbands.

Apart from the money that migrants send directly to their families, their home communities and countries also benefit from:

- donations by migrants to community projects
- the purchase of goods and services produced in the home country by migrants working abroad
- increased foreign exchange reserves.

Section 2.3 Activities

1 Comment on the socio-economic status of immigrants in OECD countries.

2 Describe the trend in international remittances shown in Figure 2.28.

3 Produce tables to present the data shown in Figure 2.29.

4 Analyse the data shown in Figure 2.30.

The cultural impact

Migration has played a major role in shaping the global cultural map. The phenomenon is essentially a series of exchanges between places. The impact of migration on population change has been greatest where mass migrations have overwhelmed relatively small indigenous populations, as exemplified by the demographic histories of the Americas and of Australia and New Zealand. In turn the old colonial powers have relatively cosmopolitan populations compared with most of their non-colonial counterparts, as significant numbers of people from former colonies have sought a higher standard of living in the 'mother' country. The Afro-Caribbean and Asian elements of the British population are a reflection of this process. In countries such as the UK, France, Germany, Italy and the USA there is a considerable difference in ethnic composition between the large metropolitan areas and rural regions as most immigrants invariably head for large urban areas where the greatest concentration of employment opportunities can be found.

Significant diaspora populations have been established in many MEDCs resulting in growing cultural hybridity. A recent example is the enlargement of the European Union in 2004 to include Eastern European countries such as Poland. A considerable number of Polish workers migrated to the UK. In areas such as London and Reading where the Polish community concentrated, shops providing goods and services to the expanding Polish community opened up and a number of Catholic churches began offering a weekend mass conducted in the Polish language. The building industry and hotels, pubs and catering attracted particularly large numbers of Polish workers. High immigration from Poland and a number of other countries increased the birth rate in the UK and widened the range of first languages spoken by children in schools. This placed considerable demands on many education authorities.

In the USA the large inflow of migrants from Latin America has resulted in a substantial increase in the proportion of Spanish speakers in the country. Many areas in the southern part of the USA, in states such as California, New Mexico, Texas and Florida, are effectively bilingual. Many other traits of Latin American culture are also evident in the region. In turn, the contact that migrant workers have with their families and communities elicits a certain reverse flow of cultural traits as workers relate their experiences and send money home.

The political impact

Significant levels of international migration can have a considerable political impact both within and between countries. In many countries there is a clear trend of immigrants being more likely to vote for parties of the centre and the left as opposed to political parties to the right of centre. In MEDCs immigrants tend to head for economic core regions and to inner city areas within these regions. Such concentrations can have a big impact on voting patterns.

Over time, immigrants gradually assimilate into host societies. In general, economic assimilation comes first, followed by social assimilation and then political assimilation. When immigrant groups reach a certain size and standing they begin to develop their own politicians as opposed to voting for politicians from the host society.

This process is more likely to happen in mature democracies where there is a long history of immigration. The UK and the USA are examples of countries where this process has been evident.

High levels of international migration between one country and another can lead to political tension. The high level of Mexican migration into the USA, both legal and illegal, has created tensions between the US and Mexican governments. In recent years the USA has greatly increased the size of its Border Patrol. Critics refer to the 'militarisation of the Mexican border' which is costing $3 billion a year.

In a number of EU countries immigration from Muslim countries over the last 50 years or so has resulted in sizeable Muslim communities. Some people and politicians have become worried about this trend, referring to the 'Islamisation of Europe'. One of the big concerns is the number of Muslims who favour introducing Sharia Law into European countries.

Many LEDCs are looking to MEDCs to adopt a more favourable attitude to international migration. The subject is brought up regularly at international conferences. This political pressure is known as 'the pro-migration agenda of developing nations'.

Living within a new political system can also affect the attitudes of immigrant communities to what goes on back in their home country. The harshest critics of authoritarian governments in the Middle East and Asia are invariably exiles living in other countries.

The environmental impact

In an article entitled 'The Environmental Argument for Reducing Immigration to the United States', Winthrop Staples and Philip Cafaro argue that 'a serious commitment to environmentalism entails ending America's population growth by implementing a more restrictive immigration policy. The need to limit immigration necessarily follows when we combine a clear statement of our main environmental goals – living sustainably and sharing the landscape generously with other species – with uncontroversial accounts of our current demographic trajectory and of the negative environmental effects of U.S. population growth, nationally and globally.'

Staples and Cafaro explain how population growth contributes significantly to a host of environmental problems in the USA. They also argue that a growing population increases America's large environmental footprint beyond its borders and creates a disproportionate role in stressing global environmental systems.

There have been growing environmental concerns about immigration in other countries too as the concept of sustainability has become understood in a more detailed way. However, some critics see such arguments as a disingenuous way of attempting to curtail immigration.

Section 2.3 Activities

1 With brief reference to one country, describe the cultural impact of international migration.
2 Give two examples of the way international migration can have a political impact.
3 How can international migration have an impact on the environment?

Case Study

Diasporas in London

London is undoubtedly the most cosmopolitan city in Europe (Figure 2.32). Some commentators go further and view London as the most multiracial city in the world. The diverse **ethnicity** of the capital is exemplified by the fact that over 200 languages are spoken within its boundaries. The lobby group Migration Watch estimate that two-thirds of immigration into the UK since the mid-1990s has been into London. Within the UK the process of **racial assimilation** is much more advanced in London than anywhere else. Almost 30 per cent of people in London were born outside the UK compared with 2.9 per cent in north-east England. In 2000 16 per cent of all new solicitors in London were black or Asian, and a third of London's doctors are now non-white. London has the highest proportion of each ethnic minority group apart from Pakistanis, of whom there is a higher proportion in Yorkshire.

Figure 2.32 An Indian pub in Southall – the largest Indian community in the UK

Figure 2.33 Percentage population non-white ethnic group in London, and the highest proportion of particular ethnic groups in England and Wales

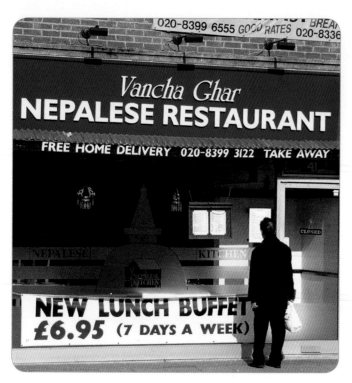

Figure 2.34 A Nepalese restaurant in South London

Just over 50 per cent of London's population described themselves as white British in the 2001 census. A further 14 per cent are either white Irish or white Other (Europeans, Americans, Australians, New Zealanders etc.). There are now more ethnically African residents (8 per cent) in London than black Caribbean. The largest Asian community is Bangladeshis (5 per cent).

London's non-white population – 28.8 per cent of the capital's total – is the largest of any European city. Demographers at the Greater London Authority predict that, due to continuing immigration, this will rise to a third of London's population within the next ten years. The biggest growth will be in London's Asian communities, which still have relatively large families, and also black Africans, due mainly to migration. It is also likely that the number of British-born children of Afro-Caribbean and mixed parentage will increase at a significant rate.

The highest proportion of most ethnic groups in the UK can be found in one London borough or another (Figure 2.33). A range of factors affect ethnic concentration (Figure 2.34):

- There is a tendency for more recent immigrants to live in wards with a high ethnic minority concentration.
- Those who are not fluent in English are more likely to live in areas with a high ethnic minority concentration.
- Those in the highest social classes live in areas with a lower concentration of ethnic minority communities.
- Higher levels of qualification are also associated with lower levels of ethnic minority concentration.
- The more paid workers there are in a household, the less likely they are to live in areas with a high concentration of ethnic minority population.

Ethnic villages

The concept of ethnic villages often appears in newspapers, magazines and academic journals. **Ethnic villages** to a greater or lesser extent show clear evidence of the groups residing within their areas in terms of shops, places of worship, schools, cinemas, newspapers, social facilities, advertising and, of course, street presence. The following list of ethnic villages in London comes from a variety of recent publications including *The Economist* and various articles in the *London Evening Standard*:

- Arabs in Bayswater
- West Indians in Brixton
- Punjabis in Southall
- Bangladeshis in Tower Hamlets
- Algerians and Moroccans in Finsbury Park
- Kosovans and Albanians in Enfield and Newham
- Iraqis in Barnet
- Congolese in Croydon
- Germans in Richmond
- Brazilians in Bayswater
- Turks in Hackney and Haringey
- Chinese in Soho
- Koreans in New Malden (Figure 2.35).

Figure 2.35 There are many Korean businesses in New Malden, which has the largest concentration of Koreans in the UK

Section 2.3 Activities

1 Define the terms **a** *diaspora*, **b** *ethnicity* and **c** *racial assimilation*.

2 Summarise the information presented in Figure 2.33.

3 Discuss the concept of ethnic villages in relation to London.

2.4 A case study of international migration

Mexicans to the USA: a major migration stream

One of the largest international migration streams in the world over the past 40 years has been from Mexico to the USA, a rare example where an MEDC borders an LEDC. This significant movement of people has been primarily **a labour migration** and has largely been the result of a very large gap in:

- average income: the income gap has been a powerful stimulus to movement and emigration has tended to surge during periods of wage decline in Mexico
- unemployment rates: weak growth in Mexico's labour demand has resulted in high levels of unemployment and **underemployment**
- the growth of the labour force: with significantly higher population growth in Mexico compared with the USA
- the overall quality of life: for virtually every aspect of the quality of life conditions are better in the USA than in Mexico.

About 30 per cent of legal immigrants in the USA and an estimated half of all unauthorised foreigners in the country are from Mexico. The ties between the two countries go back to the 1800s, when what is now the south-western USA was part of Mexico. However, there was only very limited movement across the US/Mexican border until the twentieth century. In fact most migration has taken place in the last three decades. Although previous surges occurred in the 1920s and 1950s, persistent **mass migration** between the two countries did not take hold until the late twentieth century. Table 2.2 summarises the main push and pull factors influencing migration from Mexico to the USA. Mexico is Latin America's major emigration country, sending up to 500 000 people – half of its net population increase – to the USA each year. Most emigrants make unauthorised entries.

Early and mid-twentieth century migration

In the early part of the twentieth century the American government allowed the recruitment of Mexican workers as **guest workers**. Young Mexican men known as *braceros* were allowed into the USA legally between 1917 and 1921, and then later between 1942 and 1964. Both guest worker programmes began when US farms faced a shortage of labour during periods of war. US farmers were strong supporters of allowing the entry of Mexican labour, as the increased supply of labour kept wages low and this contributed to higher land prices. Trade unions and many religious groups were against the programmes. Congress agreed with what was then a common view in the USA – that the inflow of Mexican workers was holding down the wages of US farm workers – and ended the programme.

The end of the *bracero* programme saw farm wages rise along with the increasing mechanisation of US agriculture. Re-adjusting the labour market in America after several decades of significant dependence on Mexican workers was not easy. On the other side, the loss of US jobs and wages was a difficult adjustment for many Mexican workers. Under the *bracero* programme American farmers were required to pay for the transportation of Mexican workers from the US/Mexican border. This was an incentive for many Mexicans to move to the border area in the hope of being selected for work in the USA. When the programme ended they returned to border communities in Mexico where unemployment was extremely high.

The establishment of maquiladoras

The US and Mexican governments made changes to their trade laws to allow the establishment of ***maquiladoras***. These were factories in Mexico that import components and use Mexican labour to assemble them into goods such as televisions for export to the USA. The logical location for the *maquiladoras* was in towns just over the border in Mexico so that they were as close to their US markets as possible. As the number of factories grew, more Mexicans migrated from other parts of the country to the border towns, putting them in competition with returning *braceros* for jobs. The establishment of *maquiladoras* only solved the returning *bracero* problem to a certain extent, as many of the jobs in the factories went to women.

Table 2.2 Factors encouraging migration from Mexico, by type of migrant

Type of migrant	Demand-pull	Supply-push	Network/other
Economic	Labour recruitment (guest workers)	Unemployment or underemployment; low wages (farmers whose crops fail)	Job and wage information flows
Non-economic	Family unification (family members join spouse)	Low income, poor quality of life, lack of opportunity	Communications; transport; assistance organisations; desire for new experience/ adventure

Note: All three factors may encourage a person to migrate. The relative importance of pull, push and network factors can change over time.

Source: *Population Bulletin* Vol.63 No.1 2003

The increase in illegal migration

Figure 2.36 US Border Patrol

Although many rural Mexicans had become dependent on US employment, there was very little illegal migration from Mexico to the USA in the 1960s and 1970s. However, high population growth and the economic crisis in the early 1980s resulted in a considerable increase in illegal migration across the border. Networks were soon established between Mexican communities and US employers. At this time there were no penalties placed on American employers who knowingly hired illegal migrants. During this period Mexican workers spread out more widely in the USA than ever before. They were employed mainly in agriculture, construction, various manufacturing industries and in low-paid services jobs. The US Border Patrol was responsible for apprehending illegal workers, but their numbers were limited and they only had a modest impact on the spread of illegal workers (Figure 2.36). Figure 2.37 shows the number of Mexican immigrants to the USA between 1966 and 1999.

As attitudes in America again hardened against illegal workers, Congress passed the Immigration Reform and Control Act (IRCA) of 1986. This imposed penalties on American employers who knowingly hired illegal workers. The objective was to discourage Mexicans from illegal entry. Much of the opposition of the unions to guest workers was because they saw the process creating 'bonded workers' with very limited rights.

However, the Act also legalised 2.7 million unauthorised foreigners. Of this number, 85 per cent were Mexican. The legalisation substantially expanded network links between Mexican workers and US employers.

The formation of the North American Free Trade Agreement (NAFTA) lowered barriers to trade and investment flow between Mexico, the USA and Canada. At the time the Mexican government expected Mexico's export trade to increase and Mexico–USA migration to fall due to NAFTA. However, this proved not to be the case and migration from Mexico to the USA increased. Labour migration continued at a high rate even after economic and employment growth in Mexico improved in the late 1990s.

Table 2.3 shows the number of Mexican guest workers in the USA under H-2 visas from 1998 to 2006. The H-2 programme was created in the 1980s to revise the guest worker programme. The H-2A visa is granted for agricultural work, and the H-2B visa for non-agricultural work.

Table 2.3 Mexican guest workers in the USA under H-2 visas, 1998–2006

	1998	1999	2000	2001	2002	2003	2004	2005	2006
H-2A	21 594	26 069	27 172	21 569	12 846	9 924	17 218	1 282	40 283
H-2B	10 727	18 927	27 755	41 852	52 972	65 878	56 280	89 184	89 184
Total	32 321	44 996	54 927	63 421	65 818	75 802	73 498	90 466	129 467

Source: www.globalworkers.org

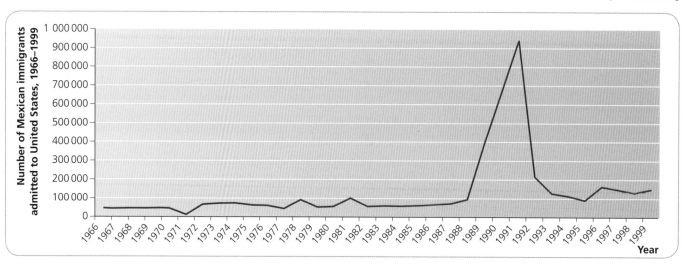

Figure 2.37 Number of Mexican immigrants admitted to the USA, 1966–99

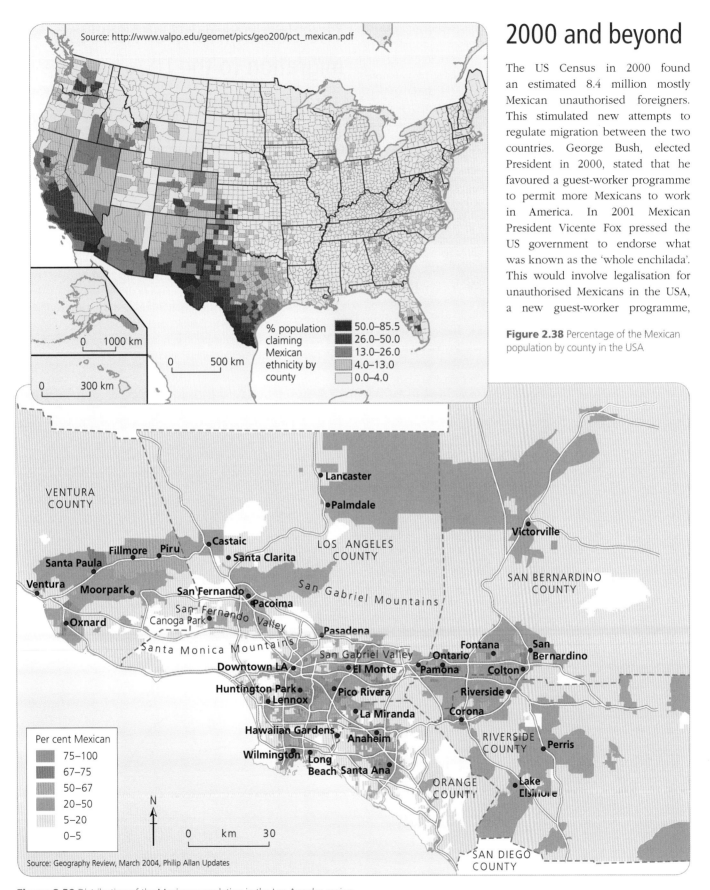

Source: http://www.valpo.edu/geomet/pics/geo200/pct_mexican.pdf

1000 km

500 km

300 km

% population claiming Mexican ethnicity by county

- 50.0–85.5
- 26.0–50.0
- 13.0–26.0
- 4.0–13.0
- 0.0–4.0

2000 and beyond

The US Census in 2000 found an estimated 8.4 million mostly Mexican unauthorised foreigners. This stimulated new attempts to regulate migration between the two countries. George Bush, elected President in 2000, stated that he favoured a guest-worker programme to permit more Mexicans to work in America. In 2001 Mexican President Vicente Fox pressed the US government to endorse what was known as the 'whole enchilada'. This would involve legalisation for unauthorised Mexicans in the USA, a new guest-worker programme,

Figure 2.38 Percentage of the Mexican population by county in the USA

VENTURA COUNTY

Lancaster
Palmdale
Victorville

Fillmore Piru Castaic
Santa Paula Santa Clarita
LOS ANGELES COUNTY
SAN BERNARDINO COUNTY
Ventura Moorpark San Fernando
Oxnard Pacoima San Gabriel Mountains
Canoga Park San Fernando Valley
Santa Monica Mountains Pasadena
San Gabriel Valley Fontana San Bernardino
Downtown LA El Monte Ontario Pamona Colton
Huntington Park Pico Rivera Riverside
Lennox Corona
La Miranda
Hawaiian Gardens Anaheim RIVERSIDE COUNTY Perris
Wilmington Long Beach Santa Ana ORANGE COUNTY Lake Elsinore
SAN DIEGO COUNTY

Per cent Mexican
- 75–100
- 67–75
- 50–67
- 20–50
- 5–20
- 0–5

N

0 km 30

Source: Geography Review, March 2004, Philip Allan Updates

Figure 2.39 Distribution of the Mexican population in the Los Angeles region

145

improved conditions along the border, and exempting Mexico from immigrant visa ceilings. These discussions were halted by the 11 September 2001 terrorist attacks.

Legal and illegal migration from Mexico continued as before. By 2006 there were an estimated 12 million Mexican-born people living in the USA. This amounted to around 11 per cent of living people born in Mexico. With their children also taken into account, the figure increased to more than 20 million. This was equivalent to almost a fifth of the population of Mexico. The next four leading countries of origin were the Philippines, India, China and Vietnam, with between 1.1 and 1.6 million people each. This illustrates the size and impact of Mexican immigration into the USA. In 2005 the median income for Mexicans in the USA was $21 000, a little more than half that for US-born workers. However, it was still far in excess of the median income in Mexico itself.

Figure 2.38 shows the distribution of the Mexican population in the USA by county. Counties are subdivisions of states in the USA. There is a very strong concentration of the US Mexican population in the four states along the Mexican border – California, Arizona, New Mexico and Texas. The concentration is particularly strong in California and Texas. Other western states including Washington, Oregon, Colorado, Nevada and Idaho, also have above-average concentrations. The main reasons for this spatial distribution are:

- proximity to the border
- the location of demand for immigrant farm workers
- urban areas where the Mexican community is long-established.

Figure 2.39 illustrates the distribution of the Mexican population in the Los Angeles region. Within the urban area itself the Mexican population is concentrated in areas of poor housing and low average income. In more peripheral areas the Mexican population is concentrated in low-cost housing areas where proximity to farm employment is an important factor.

Mexican culture has had a sustained impact on many areas in the USA, particular urban areas close to the border. As a result many Mexican migrants find reassuring similarities between the two countries. One study on labour migration from Mexico to the USA stated: 'Many Mexicans find adapting to Los Angeles as easy as navigating Mexico City.'

There is no doubt that the Mexican population in the USA has undergone a process of **assimilation** over time. There are three facets to assimilation:

- economic
- social
- political.

Assimilation tends to occur in the order presented above, with economic assimilation occurring first. While most migrants from Mexico would be in the low skills category, their children and grandchildren usually aspire to, and gain, higher qualifications and skills. Such economic mobility inevitably results in greater social contact with the mainstream population. Eventually more people from migrant populations get involved in politics and the migrant community gains better political representation.

The demography of Mexican migration to the USA

In an article entitled 'The demography of Mexican migration to the US', G.H. Hanson and C. McIntosh highlight the fact that with the US baby boom peaking in 1960, the number of US native born people coming of working age actually declined in the 1980s. In contrast high levels of fertility continued in Mexico in the 1960s and 1970s. The sharp increase in Mexico–USA relative labour supply coincided with the stagnation of Mexico's economy in the 1980s, after significant economic progress in the 1960s and 1970s. This created ideal conditions for an emigration surge.

However, the conditions behind recent emigration from Mexico are unlikely to be sustained. Today Mexico's labour supply growth is converging to US levels. Between 1965 and 2000, Mexico's **total fertility rate** fell from 7.0 to 2.5, close to the US rate of 2.1. Thus, labour supply pressures for emigration from Mexico peaked in the late 1990s and are likely to fall in coming years.

Figure 2.40 is a simulation of migration from Mexico to the USA based on differences in labour supply and wage differentials

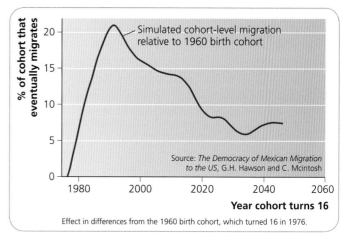

Figure 2.40 Labour supply pressures for Mexican migration to the USA

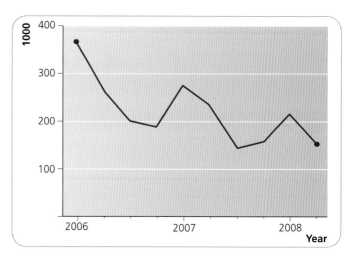

Figure 2.41 Declining emigration from Mexico

between the two countries. Population projections are used to estimate future labour supply. Hanson and McIntosh's analysis correlates with recent census data published by the Mexican government (Figure 2.41) which showed 226 000 fewer people emigrating from Mexico during the year that ended in August 2008 than during the previous year – a decline of 25 per cent. All but a very small fraction of emigration from Mexico is to the USA.

Opposition to Mexican migration into the USA

In the USA the Federation for American Immigration Reform (FAIR) argues that unskilled newcomers:
- undermine the employment opportunities of low-skilled US workers
- have negative environmental effects
- threaten established US cultural values.

The recent global economic crisis saw unemployment in the USA rise to about 10 per cent, the worst job situation for 25 years. Immigration always becomes a more sensitive issue in times of high unemployment. FAIR has also highlighted the costs to local taxpayers of illegal workers in terms of education, emergency medical care, detention and other costs that have to be borne.

Those opposed to FAIR see its actions as uncharitable and arguably racist. Such individuals and groups highlight the advantages that Mexican and other migrant groups have brought to the country.

An ethnographic case study

A. Mountz and R. Wright (1996) presented an interesting **ethnographic** account of the transnational migrant community of San Agustin, a village in the Mexican state of Oaxaca, and Poughkeepsie, a city in New York state. The link between the two communities began with the migration of a lone Oaxacan to Poughkeepsie in the early 1980s. In classic network fashion the Mexican population of Poughkeepsie, predominantly male, grew to well over a thousand over the next decade. Most Oaxacans found employment as undocumented workers in hotels, restaurants, shops and as building workers and landscapers. Their **remittances** transformed village life in their home community.

What struck Mountz and Wright most was the high level of connectedness between San Agustin and Poughkeepsie, with the migrant community keeping in daily contact with family and friends via telephone, fax, camcorders, videotape and VCRs – communications technology that was rapidly being introduced to San Agustin. Rapid migration between the two communities was facilitated by jet travel and systems of wiring payments. In effect the community of San Agustin had been geographically extended to encompass the Oaxacan enclave in Poughkeepsie. This is a classic example of **time–space distanciation** – the stretching of social systems across space and time.

Migrant remittances were used not only to support the basic needs of families but also for home construction, the purchase of consumer goods and financing fiestas. The last provided an important opportunity for migrants to display continued village membership. However, as out-migration became more established, tensions began to develop between some migrants and the home community. The main point of conflict was over the traditional system of communal welfare that requires males to provide service and support to the village. Where this could not be done in terms of time, a payment could be substituted. This was increasingly resented by some migrants who saw 'their money as their own'. The traditionalists in the village cited migration as the major cause of the decline of established values and attitudes.

The researchers found that a **migrant culture** had now become established in San Agustin, as it had in so many other Mexican communities, for four main reasons:
- economic survival
- rite of passage for young male adults
- the growing taste for consumer goods and modern styles of living
- the enhanced status enjoyed by migrants in the home community.

What started out as an exception was now well on the way to becoming the rule for San Agustin's young males.

The impact on Mexico

Sustained large-scale labour migration has had a range of impacts on Mexico, some of them clear and others debatable. Significant impacts include:
- the high value of remittances, which totalled $25 billion in 2008 – as a national source of income this is only exceeded by oil exports
- reduced unemployment pressure as migrants tend to leave areas where unemployment is particularly high
- lower pressure on housing stock and public services as significant numbers of people leave for the USA
- changes in population structure with emigration of young adults, particularly males
- loss of skilled and enterprising people
- migrants returning to Mexico with changed values and attitudes.

Section 2.4 Activities

1 With reference to Table 2.2, discuss the factors that encourage migration from Mexico by type of migrant.

2 Draw a graph to represent the data shown in Table 2.3

3 Describe the distribution of the Mexican population in Los Angeles shown in Figure 2.39.

4 Describe and explain the information presented in Figure 2.40.

5 Analyse the trends shown in Figure 2.41.

3 Settlement dynamics

3.1 Changes in rural settlements

Rural settlements form an essential part of the human landscape. However, such settlements in both MEDCs and LEDCs have undergone considerable changes in recent decades. This has happened for a number of reasons which include:

- rural–urban migration
- urban–rural migration
- the consequences of urban growth
- technological change
- rural planning policies
- the balance of government funding between urban and rural areas.

Changing rural environments in the UK

In the past, **rural** society was perceived to be distinctly different from urban society. The characteristics upon which this idea was based are shown in Figure 3.1. However, rapid rural change over the past fifty years or so in Britain and other MEDCs has seen the idea of a rural–urban divide superseded by the notion of a rural–urban continuum. The latter is a wide spectrum which runs from the most remote type of rural settlement to the most highly urbanised. A number of the intermediate positions exhibit both rural and urban characteristics. Paul Cloke (1979) used 16 variables including population density, land use and remoteness to produce an 'index of rurality' for England and Wales (Figure 3.2). Urban areas now make substantial demands on the countryside, the evidence of which can be found in even the most remote areas.

Rural areas are dynamic spatial entities. They constantly change in response to a range of economic, social, political and environmental factors. In recent years the pace of change has been more rapid than ever before. The UK reflects many of the changes occurring in rural areas in other MEDCs.

The economy of rural areas is no longer dominated by farmers and landowners. As agricultural jobs have been lost, new employers have actively sought to locate in the countryside. Manufacturing, high technology and the service sector have led this trend. Most of these firms are classed as SMEs – small and medium-sized enterprises. In fact in recent decades employment has been growing faster in rural than in urban areas. Other significant new users of rural space are recreation, tourism and environmental conservation. The **rural landscape** has evolved into a complex multiple-use resource and as this has happened the **rural population** has changed in character.

These economic changes have fuelled social change in the countryside with the in-migration of particular groups of people. To quote Brian Ilbery, a leading authority on rural geography, 'The countryside has been repopulated, especially by middle-class groups … who took advantage of relatively cheap housing in the 1960s and 1970s to colonize the countryside'. Once they are significant in number, the affluent newcomers exert a strong influence over the social and physical nature of rural space. In many areas newcomers have dominated the housing market,

1. Close-knit community with everybody knowing and interacting with everyone else.

2. Considerable homogeneity in social traits: language, beliefs, opinions, mores, and patterns of behaviour.

3. Family ties, particularly those of the extended family, are much stronger than in urban society.

4. Religion is given more importance than in urban society.

5. Class differences are less pronounced than in urban society. Although occupational differentiation does exist, it is not as pronounced as in towns and cities. Also the small settlement size results in much greater mixing which in turn weakens the effects of social differentiation.

6. There is less mobility than in urban society, both in a spatial sense (people do not move house so frequently) and in a social sense (it is more difficult for a farm labourer to become a farmer or farm manager than for a factory worker to become a manager).

Source: *The Geography of Rural Resources*
by C. Bull, P. Daniel and M. Hopkinson, Oliver & Boyd, 1984

Figure 3.1 Principal characteristics of traditional rural society

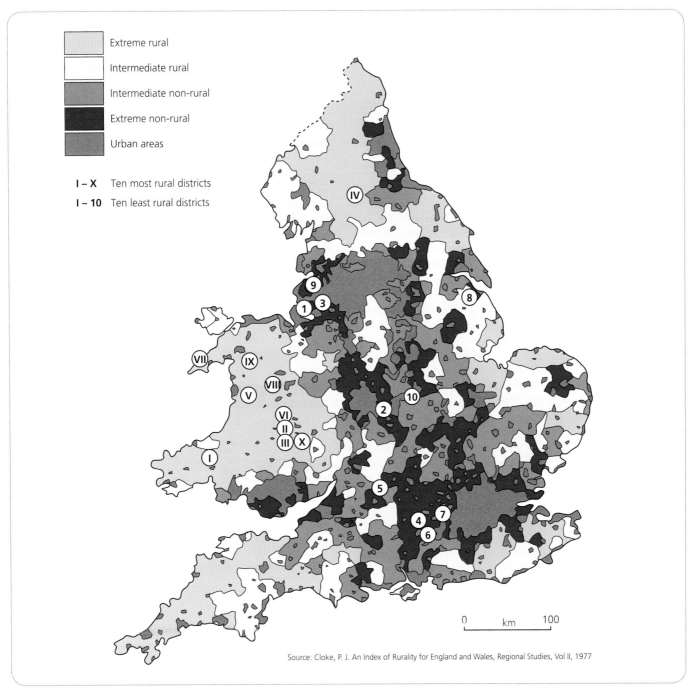

Figure 3.2 An index of rurality for England and Wales

Source: Cloke, P. J. An Index of Rurality for England and Wales, Regional Studies, Vol II, 1977

to the detriment of the established population in the locality. Increased demand has pushed up house prices to a level beyond the means of many original families who then have no option but to move elsewhere.

Gentrification is every bit as evident in the countryside as it is in selected inner city areas. However, the increasing mobility of people, goods and information has eroded local communities. A transformation that has been good for newcomers has been deeply resented by much of the established population.

In the post-war period the government has attempted to contain expansion into the countryside by creating **green belts** and by the allocation of housing to urban areas or to large **key villages**. Rural England has witnessed rising owner-occupation and low levels of local authority housing. The low level of new housing development in smaller rural communities has been reflected in higher house prices and greater social exclusivity.

Such social and economic changes have increased the pressure on rural resources so that government has had to re-evaluate policies for the countryside. Regulation has become an important element in some areas, notably in relation to sustainability and environmental conservation.

Changing agriculture

The countryside in Britain and other MEDCs has been affected by major structural changes in agricultural production. Although agricultural land forms 73 per cent of the total land area of the UK, less than 2 per cent of the total workforce are now employed in agriculture. This is down from 6.1 per cent in 1950 and 2.9 per cent in 1970. Even in the most rural of areas, agriculture and related industries rarely account for more than 15 per cent of the employed population.

At the same time, the size of farms has steadily increased (Figure 3.3). Such changes have resulted in a significant loss of hedgerows, which provide important ecological networks. Agricultural wages are significantly below the national average and as a result farmers are among the poorest of the working poor. As many farmers have struggled to make a living from traditional agricultural practices, a growing number have sought to diversify both within and outside agriculture (Figure 3.4). However, while diversification may initially halt job losses, if too many farmers in an area opt for the same type of diversification, a situation of over-supply can result in a further round of rural decline.

Figure 3.3 Large-scale farming in southern England

TOURIST AND RECREATION
Tourism
Self-catering
Serviced accommodation
Activity holidays
Recreation
Farm visitor centre
Farm museum
Restaurant/tea room

VALUE-ADDED
By marketing
Pick your own
Home delivered products
Farm-gate sales
By processing
Meat products – patés, etc.
Horticultural products to jam
Farmhouse cider
Farmhouse cheese

Potential farm diversification

UNCONVENTIONAL PRODUCTS
Livestock
Sheep for milk
Goats
Snails
Crops
Borage
Evening primrose
Organic crops

ANCILLARY RESOURCES
Buildings
For craft units
For homes
For tourist accommodation
Woodlands
For timber
For game
Wetlands
For lakes
For game

Source: Slee, 1987

Figure 3.4 Areas of potential farm diversification

Section 3.1 Activities

1 With reference to Figure 3.1, outline the principal characteristics of traditional rural society.
2 Briefly describe the pattern of rural areas shown in Figure 3.2.
3 What impact has agricultural change had on the rural landscape?
4 Why does the potential for farm diversification vary from region to region?

Counterurbanisation and the rural landscape

In recent decades **counterurbanisation** has replaced urbanisation as the dominant force shaping settlement patterns. It is a complex and multifaceted process which has resulted in a 'rural population turnaround' in many areas where depopulation had been in progress. Green belt restrictions have limited the impact of counterurbanisation in many areas adjacent to cities. But, not surprisingly, the greatest impact of counterurbanisation has been just beyond green belts where commuting is clearly viable. Here rural settlements have grown substantially and been altered in character considerably.

Figure 3.5 shows the changing morphology of metropolitan villages identified by Hudson (1977). Stage 1 is characterised by the conversion of working buildings into houses with new building mainly in the form of infill. However, some new building might occur at the edge of the village. The major morphological change in stage 2 is ribbon development along roads leading out of the village. Stage 3 of the model shows planned additions on a much larger scale of either council or private housing estates at the edge of villages. Clearly, not all metropolitan villages will have evolved in the same way as the model, particularly those where green belt restrictions are in place. Nevertheless, the model provides a useful framework for reference.

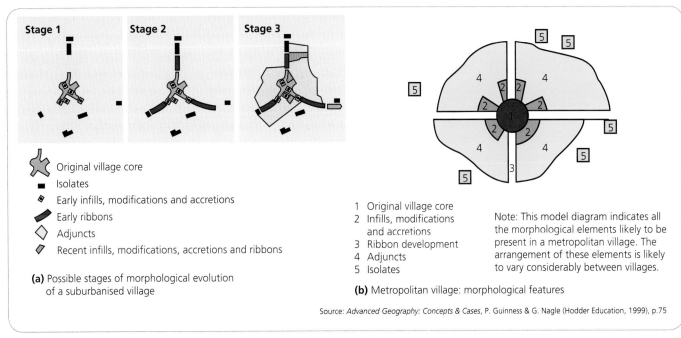

Original village core

Isolates

Early infills, modifications and accretions

Early ribbons

Adjuncts

Recent infills, modifications, accretions and ribbons

(a) Possible stages of morphological evolution of a suburbanised village

1 Original village core
2 Infills, modifications and accretions
3 Ribbon development
4 Adjuncts
5 Isolates

Note: This model diagram indicates all the morphological elements likely to be present in a metropolitan village. The arrangement of these elements is likely to vary considerably between villages.

(b) Metropolitan village: morphological features

Source: *Advanced Geography: Concepts & Cases*, P. Guinness & G. Nagle (Hodder Education, 1999), p.75

Figure 3.5 Morphology of metropolitan villages

Rural depopulation

Because of the geographical spread of counterurbanisation since the 1960s or so, the areas affected by **rural depopulation** have diminished. Depopulation is now generally confined to the most isolated areas of the country but exceptions can be found in other areas where economic conditions are particularly dire. Figure 3.6 is a simple model of the depopulation process.

The issue of rural services

Services – access to shops and post offices, healthcare, activities – are the basis for any community, creating and enhancing a feeling of belonging and a sustainable future for the area. However, rural services have been in decline for a number of decades, with a significant impact on the quality of life of many people, particularly those without a car. A major report published in 2008 revealed that nearly half of communities have seen the loss of key local services in the previous four years. The Oxford University study warned that poorer people in the countryside 'form a forgotten city of disadvantage'. It found that residents of the village of Bridestowe on Dartmoor had the fewest amenities while the village of Wrotham, in Kent, had suffered the greatest loss of services since 2004 and was the most excluded community in the South East of the UK.

Critics accused the government of masterminding the 'near certain death of the village post office' with its plans to close 2500 branches by the end of the year. One in 13 rural primary schools has closed since 1997, and more are under threat as new Whitehall rules mean schools could lose funding by failing to fill their places. Existing village GP surgeries are also at risk as the government promotes its new 'polyclinics'.

The Commission for Rural Committees warned that 233 000 people are living in 'financial service deserts' – areas with no post office within 1.25 miles, or no bank, building society or cashpoint for 2.5 miles.

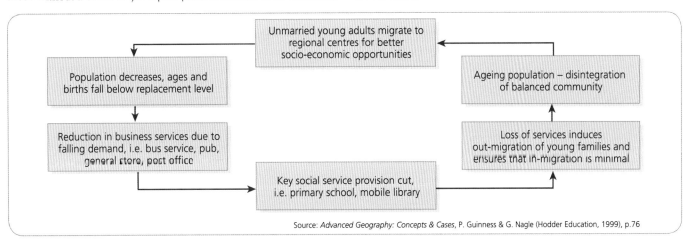

Source: *Advanced Geography: Concepts & Cases*, P. Guinness & G. Nagle (Hodder Education, 1999), p.76

Figure 3.6 Model of rural depopulation

ACRE (Action with Communities in Rural England) highlights the following reasons for rural service decline:

- the effect of market forces and, in some cases, the arrival of supermarkets in local areas, making local services no longer competitive
- the changing pattern of rural population, with more mobile residents with different shopping and consumer patterns becoming a greater part of the rural pattern of life
- a change in expectations of rural residents themselves, no longer prepared to make do with relatively poor and expensive services and, in many cases, with the means and opportunity to access better services.

Key villages

Between the 1950s and 1970s the concept of key settlements was central to rural settlement policy in many parts of Britain, particularly where depopulation was occurring (Figure 3.7). The concept relates to central place theory and assumes that focusing services, facilities and employment in one selected settlement will satisfy the essential needs of the surrounding villages and hamlets. The argument was that with falling demand, dispersed services would decline rapidly in vulnerable areas. The only way to maintain a reasonable level of service provision in such an area was to focus on those locations with the greatest accessibility and the best combination of other advantages. In this way threshold populations could be assured and hopefully the downward spiral of service decline would be halted.

Devon introduced a key settlement policy in 1964 to counter the impact of:

- rural depopulation
- the changing function of the village in relation to urban centres
- the decline in agricultural employment
- the contraction of public transport.

The selection of key settlements in Devon was part of a wider settlement policy involving sub-regional centres, suburban towns and coastal resorts. The criteria used for selecting key settlements were as follows:

- existing services
- existing employment other than agriculture in or near the village
- accessibility by road
- location in relation to current bus (and possibly rail) services
- location in relation to other villages which would rely on them for some services
- the availability of public utilities capable of extension for new development
- the availability and agricultural value of land capable of development
- proximity to urban centres (key settlements would not flourish too close to competing urban areas).

Sixty-eight key settlements were selected initially, reduced to 65 in 1970. Although it has been difficult to measure the effectiveness of the policy with precision, depopulation in north and mid-Devon did fall considerably after the introduction of the policy. And in many areas the decline in service provision was slower than the predictions before the policy was implemented.

The rural transport problem

The considerable increase in car ownership in recent decades has had a devastating effect on public transport (Figure 3.8). While this has not disadvantaged rural car owners very much, it has considerably increased the isolation of the poor, the elderly and the young. The lack of public transport puts intense pressure on low-income households to own a car, a large additional expense that many could do without. Recent increases in the price of fuel have exacerbated this problem.

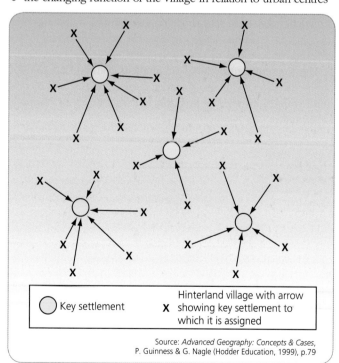

Source: *Advanced Geography: Concepts & Cases*, P. Guinness & G. Nagle (Hodder Education, 1999), p.79

Figure 3.7 Key settlement concept

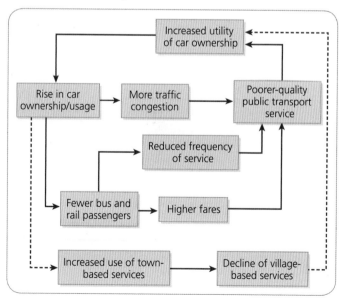

Figure 3.8 Car ownership and public transport

Advantages

1 Bring new employment opportunities to areas previously dependent upon a contracting agricultural economy (e.g. building trade, gardening and domestic staff).

2 Local restaurants, shops and garages derive new business and additional profits (which may be essential to year-round economic survival).

3 Specialised shops opened to cater for second-home owners also benefit local residents.

4 Property taxes imposed on second homes increase the finances of the local community.

5 Second-home owners make fewer demands on local services since education and other community facilities are not required.

6 Renovation of old buildings improves the appearance of the rural area.

7 Rural residents have the opportunity to sell-off surplus land and buildings at a high price.

8 Contacts with urban-based second-home owners can benefit local residents by exposing them to national values and information, broadening outlooks or stimulating self-advancement via migration.

Disadvantages

1 Concentrations of second homes may require installation of costly sewerage schemes, extension of water and electricity lines to meet peak season demand, and more frequent maintenance of rural roads, with the costs being partly borne by local people.

2 Demand for second homes by urbanites pushes up house prices to the disadvantage of local people.

3 Future schemes for farm enlargement or agricultural restructuring may be hindered by inflated land prices.

4 Fragmentation of agricultural land.

5 Destruction of the 'natural' environment (e.g. soil erosion and stream pollution).

6 Visual degradation may result from poorly constructed or inappropriately located second homes.

7 Second-home construction may distract the local workforce from ordinary house building and maintenance.

8 The different values and attitudes of second-home families disrupt local community life.

Source: *Advanced Geography: Concepts & Cases*, P. Guinness & G. Nagle (Hodder Education, 1999), pp.80–1

Figure 3.9 The second homes debate

There has been continuing concern that Britain's remaining rural railway lines are under threat in a repeat of the 'Beeching cuts' of the 1960s. The new fears about government intentions towards rural rail closures were first awakened in 1998 when the transport minister said branch lines in sparsely populated areas might be replaced by buses. It would be possible to convert track beds into guided busways, and then for buses to divert into towns and villages. However, one study of replacing trains with buses found that at most, only half of former rail passengers used the bus replacements. With one in five rural households lacking a car and a low level of bus service in many country areas, the train is essential for many.

The rural housing problem

The lack of affordable housing in village communities has resulted in a large number of young people having to move to market towns or larger urban centres. Only 12 per cent of rural housing is subsidised, compared with 25 per cent in urban areas. The 1995 White Paper on Rural Development sought to improve the rural housing situation by exempting villages with fewer than 3000 inhabitants from the right-to-buy for housing association tenants. This is to prevent such housing disappearing on to the open market and being bought up at prices local people cannot afford. The government also announced plans to speed up the disposal of Ministry of Defence (MoD) housing. It estimated that there were 13 000 empty MoD homes in the UK, many of them in rural areas. Rural households would also be encouraged to take in lodgers through the rent-a-room scheme.

The issue of second homes has become increasingly contentious. Figure 3.9 indicates that some advantages might accrue from second home development. However, recent debate on the issue has centred firmly on the problems created.

Section 3.1 Activities

1 Explain the morphological changes in metropolitan villages illustrated by Figure 3.5.

2 Examine the causes and consequences of rural depopulation.

3 a Outline two reasons for the decline of rural services.
   b Which sections of the rural population see their quality of life decline the most when rural services are lost?

4 Explain the logic of the key settlement concept.

5 Write a brief explanation of Figure 3.8.

6 Discuss the main issues relating to rural housing.

Contemporary issues in rural settlements in LEDCs

The main process affecting rural settlements in LEDCs has been rural–urban migration. The impact of such migration has varied considerably across rural communities in LEDCs (Figure 3.10). In some areas it has been considered advantageous by providing a safety valve in:

- reducing rural population growth and pressure on food, water and other resources
- helping to limit unemployment and underemployment
- providing a valuable source of income through the remittances of migrants.

However, in some rural communities the scale of rural–urban migration has been so great that it has resulted in:

- rural depopulation and an ageing population
- the closure of services, both public and private as population declines

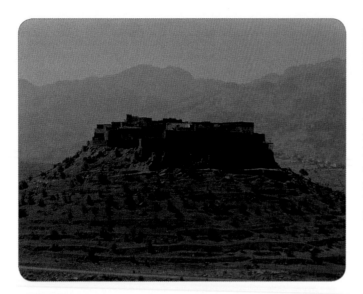

Figure 3.10 Hilltop rural settlement in Morocco

- insufficient labour to maintain agricultural production at its former levels.

In southern African countries such as Botswana and Lesotho the devastating impact of AIDS has resulted in rural depopulation in many areas.

Rural poverty accounts for over 60 per cent of poverty worldwide, reaching 90 per cent in some LEDCs like Bangladesh. In the countries of sub-Saharan Africa rural poverty makes up between 65 and 90 per cent of national totals. In almost all countries, the conditions in terms of personal consumption and access to education, healthcare, potable water and sanitation, housing, transport, and communication faced by the rural poor are far worse than those faced by the urban poor. Much urban poverty is created by the rural poor's efforts to get out of poverty by moving to cities.

An analysis of rural poverty in LEDCs by the International Monetary Fund highlighted the following factors in creating and perpetuating rural poverty:
- political instability and civil strife
- systemic discrimination on the basis of gender, race, ethnicity, religion, or caste
- ill-defined property rights or unfair enforcement of rights to agricultural land and other natural resources
- high concentration of land ownership and asymmetrical tenancy arrangements
- corrupt politicians and rent-seeking public bureaucracies
- economic policies that discriminate against or exclude the rural poor from the development process and accentuate the effects of other poverty-creating processes
- large and rapidly growing families with high dependency ratios
- market imperfections owing to high concentration of land and other assets and distortionary public policies
- external shocks owing to changes in the state of nature (for example, climatic changes) and conditions in the international economy.

Case Study

Rural Mongolia

There are very few parts of the world that remain completely untouched by interactions with the outside world, but there are a number where such interaction has been very limited. The people living in such areas can be considered to be non-globalised societies. An example of such a non-globalised society is the majority of rural Mongolia (apart from areas close to the capital, Ulaanbaatar and a few other urban areas) which is characterised by:
- traditional family structures with a strong emphasis on the extended family
- the importance of local customs and hospitality
- populations living at extremely low densities, equalling the lowest in the world
- a heavy reliance on agricultural activities, particularly herding (Figure 3.11)
- difficult environmental conditions in both summer and winter
- traditional housing in the form of *gers*, often involving changes of location as herds are moved in search of fodder
- relative inaccessibility, with most parts of the country lacking paved roads; movement by horseback is common and only 4 × 4 vehicles can make progress in many areas
- low incomes and limited material possessions – repair and re-use have long been important strategies to make possessions last
- very limited service provision reflected in lower health and education standards in many provinces compared with the capital city
- low levels of personal contact with other countries.

Figure 3.11 *Gers* and cattle with rock outcrop background in rural Mongolia

About a third of the population live as nomadic herders on sparsely populated grasslands. Most live in very isolated locations. This is a major factor in their non-globalised status. In recent years, droughts and unusually cold and snowy winters have devastated livestock, destroying the livelihoods of hundreds of thousands of households. Many have moved to Ulaanbaatar where they live in impoverished conditions, mainly on the periphery of the city. This exemplifies the concept of **the urbanisation of poverty**.

According to 2006 census data, there are 170 700 herding households in Mongolia of which 40 per cent live below of the poverty line. Since 1996 the poverty of herding households has not decreased. A more detailed survey examined the livelihood conditions of rural herding households and found over 60 per cent in the lowest of four income categories (Table 3.1).

Table 3.1 Livelihood conditions of rural herding households

% poor	% low-middle income	% middle income	% upper-middle income
60.7	33.7	5.4	0

Government programmes that have been set up to improve the lives of herders have focused on:

- livestock insurance to protect herders from losses incurred in the extreme winters that occur every few years
- expansion of cell phone coverage throughout the countryside
- the expansion of rural education.

Section 3.1 Activities

1 Why has rural–urban migration benefited some rural areas in LEDCs, but caused problems in other rural areas?

2 Describe the main characteristics of the rural landscape in Mongolia.

Case Study

The Isle of Purbeck: issues in rural settlement

Location and historical development

The Isle of Purbeck forms the south-eastern part of Purbeck District in Dorset (Figure 3.12). It is an area of about 200 km² bounded by the sea to the south and east, and by the River Frome and Poole Harbour to the north.

The Isle of Purbeck is classed as a remote rural district. Here the rural settlement is concentrated in clustered villages, with Corfe Castle being the largest (Figure 3.13). Although these villages are set in a network of isolated farms and houses, there

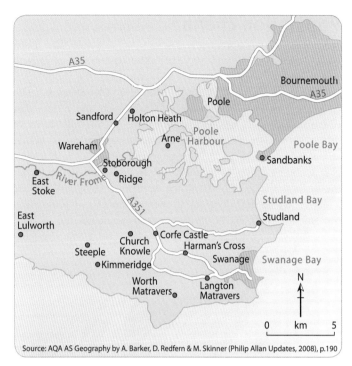

Source: AQA AS Geography by A. Barker, D. Redfern & M. Skinner (Philip Allan Updates, 2008), p.190

Figure 3.12 The Isle of Purbeck

Figure 3.13 Village pub at Corfe Castle

are relatively few hamlets in the region. Lower order urban services are provided by the towns of Swanage and Wareham with higher order urban services being found in the Bournemouth-Poole conurbation, as it has increasingly become known in the region. The growth of the Bournemouth-Poole conurbation, with a population now approaching half a million people, has had an increasing influence on the rural settlement of the Isle of Purbeck, with the region developing an important dormitory function. The resulting commuter traffic at peak periods presents particular problems in the peninsula.

Population change

The population of Purbeck District as a whole has risen consistently over the past 40 years, although the rate of growth has varied by parish. Figure 3.14 compares the population structure of Purbeck District with the UK average. The population of Purbeck District is considerably older than that of the country as a whole, mainly because of the popularity of the area for retirement. However, the out-migration of young adults in search of wider economic opportunities and lower-cost accommodation is also a factor. In 2001, the birth rate for the district was 10.1/1000 and the death rate 11.9/1000, leaving a significant natural decrease in the population. In some rural settlements such as Corfe Castle and Studland the natural decrease was considerably higher.

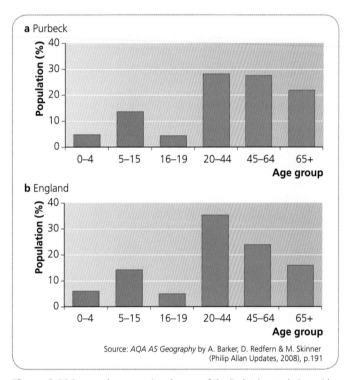

Source: *AQA AS Geography* by A. Barker, D. Redfern & M. Skinner (Philip Allan Updates, 2008), p.191

Figure 3.14 Bar graphs comparing the age of the Purbeck population with the average for England, 2001

The rural housing problem

House prices in the area have risen at a rate above the national average over the last decade or so. This has been due largely to competition from a number of different groups of people:

- out-of-area commuters
- retirees
- second-home owners
- in-migrants.

This high level of competition for a limited number of available properties has pushed the cost of housing to a level well beyond the reach of most local people. The problem is compounded by the fact that local employment opportunities are limited and wages are low. The right-to-buy local authority housing has reduced the potential stock of moderately priced rented properties. This,

combined with the inability of many in the established population to compete with newcomers, has led to significant fragmentation of some local communities.

Rural service decline

Dorset County Council sees access to services as a key issue in the county. Service decline can have a huge impact on rural populations. This is an issue that has affected virtually all rural areas in Britain in recent decades. The Dorset Rural Facilities Survey 2002 found a continuing decline in rural services in the Isle of Purbeck and throughout Dorset. Some services had declined more than others in the previous decade. The survey noted a 'dramatic decline in the number of shops selling general produce, whether they are incorporated within a post office, garage or as a stand-alone general store'. In particular the Survey noted that for Dorset as a whole:

- three out of four villages had no general store
- 38 rural post offices had closed since 1991
- eight villages had lost their only pub over the previous decade
- 35 rural petrol stations had closed since 1991
- four villages with a population of over 500 had no general store.

However, the Survey also noted some service gains. Six village doctors' surgeries had opened since 1991 and there had been no rural school closures in the previous decade. The village church, or chapel, continued to be the facility most available in rural Dorset.

Rural settlements are constantly in fear of losing services such as a post office or the one remaining pub. Privately-owned services are lost more quickly than public services because for the latter the decision to remain open is not purely an economic one – social and political considerations are also important. Service decline makes people more reliant on transport, both public and private, to gain access to basic services.

Table 3.2 shows the services located in each rural settlement in 2004. Corfe Castle had by far the best level of service provision, partly due to its tourist function and partly due to its location on the A351 halfway between Swanage and Wareham. Although Langton Matravers has a similar population to Corfe Castle, it is very close to Swanage and suffers from a 'service shadow' effect.

In terms of causal factors for rural service decline, the Dorset Rural Facilities Survey pointed in particular to:

- the increased competition from urban supermarkets that can undercut the prices and provide a greater range of produce than small rural retail outlets (Figure 3.15)
- the increasing personal mobility of most of the rural population as the proportion of people who have access to a private vehicle has risen over the years – this enables most of the rural population to shop weekly and in bulk.

It is now the policy of Dorset's District Councils not to permit the change of use of public houses in rural settlements unless it can be demonstrated that:

- there is no local need for the facility
- the retention is not economically viable and that there is no reasonable likelihood of an alternative facility being economically viable.

Table 3.2 Rural facilities in the Isle of Purbeck, 2004

District	Population	Church/chapel	Village hall	Village school	Post office & shop	Post office	General store	Food shop	Other shop	Petrol station & shop	Petrol station	Bank	GP surgery	Public house	Library	Recreation area	Cash point	Mobile library	Bus service*
Arne	20	Yes																	
Church Knowle	120	Yes	1											1				1	W
Coombe Keynes	60		1															1	D
Corfe Castle	980	Yes	1	1		1	1	2	13		1		1	4	1	1	1		D
East Holme	30	Yes																	W
East Stoke	60																		W
East Lulworth	170	Yes												1		1		1	D
Furzebrook	60		1																W
Harmans Cross	340	Yes	1			1					1						1	1	D
Kimmeridge	70	Yes	1															1	W
Kingston	100	Yes												1					D
Langton Matravers	910	Yes	1	1	1									2		1		1	D
Ridge	290																	1	W
Steeple	30	Yes																	W
Stoborough	800		1	1	1								1	1		1			D
Stokeford	180		1											1					D
Studland	540	Yes	1		1									1				1	D
West Lulworth	770	Yes	1	1	1									2		1	1	1	D
Wool	1970	Yes		2	1			2	9	2			1	2	1	1	1		D
Worth Matravers	240	Yes	1		1									1					D

Source: Dorset County Council, 2004
*W = weekly, D = daily

Figure 3.15 Post office and general store in Studland

There have been some high-profile cases over the last decade or so where the local community has fought to save their village pub, sometimes with success but not always.

The decline of public transport

Public transport in the Isle of Purbeck is limited. It exists in the form of the 150 bus from Poole to Swanage via the Sandbanks/Studland ferry and the 142/143/144 via Holton Heath, Sandford, Wareham, Corfe and variously Kingston, Langton Matravers, Worth Matravers and Harman's Cross to Swanage. There is extra minibus coverage through volunteer schemes but this is also limited in extent. The decline in public transport in rural areas usually becomes a vicious cycle.

In terms of rail transport, Wareham Station is on the London-Waterloo to Weymouth line. The line between Wareham and Swanage was cut in 1972, along with many other rural railway lines around the country. A connection from Wareham to Furzebrook was however maintained to serve the railhead for the oil-well at Wytch Farm. Swanage does boast a steam railway but this is basically a tourist facility. The Swanage Railway currently operates on the six miles of track between Swanage and Norden, passing the ruins of Corfe Castle. However, a prime objective of the Swanage Railway Trust is to restore the rail link between Swanage and Wareham, re-establishing a daily service to connect with mainline trains.

Rural deprivation

Deprivation in terms of housing is particularly acute in high-priced housing counties such as Dorset.

Opportunity deprivation – the lack of opportunity in health and social services, education and retail facilities also affects disadvantaged people, particularly those living in the most isolated rural areas.

Mobility deprivation is also evident, as public transport is very limited on the Isle of Purbeck. As a result many low-income households have no choice but to spend a high proportion of their income on running a car, which means that even less money is left available for other needs. In the Isle of Purbeck, hospital access is often dependent on voluntary organisations. Deprivation is concentrated in the long-established population. Those who have migrated into the area generally have a significantly higher level of income.

Fieldwork: case study of a rural settlement

For this section, 'Changes in rural settlements', the syllabus states: 'A case study of a rural settlement (village or hamlet) or a rural area illustrating some of the issues of its development and growth (or decline) and evaluating the responses'. The confines of space prevent coverage of both options in this book, but the study of an individual rural settlement offers an excellent (and relatively straightforward) fieldwork opportunity.

Select a rural settlement within reasonable travelling distance and attempt the following:

- Find a map showing the location of the settlement.
- Gather census data illustrating population change.
- Draw a map showing the functions of the settlement (shop, place of worship etc.) and their location.
- Find out how the number and nature of functions have changed over time. What have been the reasons for these changes?
- Is the settlement linked by public transport? If yes, how has public transport provision changed over time?
- How are people in the settlement employed? How has the nature of employment changed over time?
- How much employment is local to the settlement and how much involves commuting or other forms of movement?

- What have been the main problems facing the settlement in recent decades and what has been done to attempt to solve these problems?
- Any other relevant information.

Now write up your case study using the title 'A case study of (settlement name): issues of its development, growth and management'. Limit yourself to 1000 words.

Section 3.1 Activities

1 Describe the location of the Isle of Purbeck.

2 With reference to Figure 3.14, describe and explain the differences between the population structures of the Isle of Purbeck and the UK as a whole.

3 Discuss the main issues affecting the rural population on the Isle of Purbeck.

3.2 Urban trends and issues of urbanisation

The development of the urban environment

The first cities

Gordon Childe used the term '**urban revolution**' to describe the change in society marked by the emergence of the first cities some 5500 years ago. The areas which first witnessed this profound social-economic change were:

- Mesopotamia – the valleys of the Tigris and Euphrates rivers
- the lower Nile valley
- the plains of the river Indus.

Later, urban civilisations developed around the Mediterranean, in the Yellow River valley of China, in South East Asia and in the Americas. Thus the first cities mainly emerged in areas that are now considered to be LEDCs.

The catalyst for this period of rapid change was the Neolithic Revolution which occurred about 8000BC. This was when sedentary agriculture, based on the domestication of animals and cereal farming, steadily replaced a nomadic way of life. As farming advanced, irrigation techniques were developed. Other major advances which followed were the ox-drawn plough, the wheeled cart, the sailing boat and metallurgy. However, arguably the most important development was the invention of writing about 4000BC, for it was in the millennium after this that some of the villages on the alluvial plains between the Tigris and Euphrates rivers increased in size and changed in function so as to merit the classification of urban.

Considerably later than the first cities, trading centres began to develop. The Minoan civilisation cities of Knossos and Phaistos, which flourished in Crete during the first half of the second millennium BC, derived their wealth from maritime trade. Next it was the turn of the Greeks and then the Romans to develop urban and trading systems on a scale larger than ever before. For example, the population of Athens in the fifth century BC has been estimated at a minimum of 100 000. The fall of the Roman Empire in the fifth century AD led to a major recession in urban life in Europe which did not really revive until medieval times.

The medieval revival was the product of population growth and the resurgence of trade, with the main urban settlements of this period located at points of greatest accessibility. While there were many interesting developments in urban life during the medieval period, it required another major technological advance to set in train the next urban revolution.

The urban industrial revolution

The second 'urban revolution', based on the introduction of mass production in factories, began in Britain in the late eighteenth century. This was the era of the Industrial Revolution when industrialisation and urbanisation proceeded hand in hand. The key invention, among many, was the steam engine, which in Britain was applied to industry first and only later to transport. The huge demand for labour in the rapidly growing coalfield towns and cities was satisfied by the freeing of labour in agriculture through a series of major advances. The so-called 'Agricultural Revolution' had in fact begun in the early seventeenth century.

By 1801 nearly one-tenth of the population of England and Wales was living in cities of over 100 000 people. This proportion doubled in 40 years and doubled again in another 60 years. The 1801 census recorded London's population at 1 million, the first city in the world to reach this figure. By 1851 London's population had doubled to 2 million. However, at the global scale fewer than 3 per cent of the population lived in urban places at the beginning of the nineteenth century.

As the processes of the Industrial Revolution spread to other countries the pace of urbanisation quickened. The change from a population of 10–30 per cent living in urban areas of 100 000 people or more took about 80 years in England and Wales; 66 years in the USA; 48 years in Germany; 36 years in Japan; and 26 years in Australia.

The initial urbanisation of many LEDCs was restricted to concentrations of population around points of supply of raw materials for the affluent MEDCs. For example, the growth of São Paulo was firmly based on coffee; Buenos Aires on mutton, wool and cereals; and Kolkata on jute.

By the beginning of the most recent stage of urban development in 1950, 27 per cent of people lived in towns and cities, with the vast majority of urbanites still living in MEDCs. In fact, in MEDCs the cycle of urbanisation was nearing completion.

The post-1945 urban 'explosion' in LEDCs

Throughout history **urbanisation** and significant economic progress have tended to occur together. In contrast, the rapid

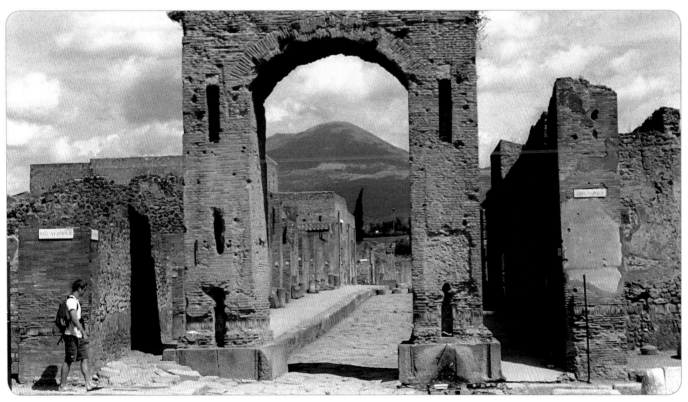

Figure 3.16 Remains of the Roman city of Pompeii, with Mt Vesuvius in the background

urban growth of LEDCs in the latter part of the twentieth century has in general far outpaced economic development, creating huge problems for planners and politicians (Figure 3.17). Because urban areas in LEDCs have been growing much more quickly than the cities of MEDCs did in the nineteenth century, the term 'urban explosion' has been used to describe contemporary trends.

However, the clear distinction between urbanisation and urban growth should be kept in mind as some of the least urbanised countries, such as China and India, contain many of the world's largest cities and are recording the fastest rates of growth.

An approach known as dependency theory has been used by a number of writers to explain the urbanisation of LEDCs, particularly the most recent post-1950 phase. According to this approach, urbanisation in LEDCs has been a response to the absorption of countries and regions into the global economy. The capitalist global economy induces urbanisation by concentrating production and consumption in locations that:

- offer the best economies of scale and agglomeration
- provide the greatest opportunities for industrial linkage
- give maximum effectiveness and least cost in terms of control over sources of supply.

Thus urban development is one of the spatial outcomes of the capitalist system. Transnational corporations (TNCs) are the major players in this economic process, which enables and encourages people to cluster in geographical space. The actions of TNCs encourage urbanisation directly in response to localised investment. However, TNCs also influence urbanisation indirectly through their impact on traditional patterns of production and employment. For example, the advance of export-oriented agriculture at the expense of traditional food production has reduced employment opportunities in the countryside and encouraged rural–urban migration.

Other factors that have encouraged urbanisation in LEDCs include:

- the investment policies of central governments which have generally favoured urban over rural areas, often in an attempt to enhance their prestige on the international stage
- higher wage rates and better employment protection in cities
- greater access to healthcare and education
- the decline in the demand for locally produced food as consumers increasingly favour imported food.

The combined result of these factors has been 'backwash urbanisation', destroying the vitality of rural areas and placing enormous pressure on cities. In the longer term, the rate of urban growth should eventually slow as a result of falling fertility rates and a deceleration in the urbanisation process itself, as a growing share of the population becomes urbanised.

Current patterns

Current levels of urbanisation, as in the past, vary considerably across the globe (Figure 3.18). The most urbanised regions are North America, Europe, Oceania and Latin America. The lowest levels of urbanisation are in Africa and Asia. In contrast, **urban growth** is highest in Asia and Africa as these regions contain the fastest-growing urban areas. By 2025 (Figure 3.19) half of the populations of Asia and Africa will live in urban areas and 80 per cent of urban dwellers will live in LEDCs. In MEDCs levels of urbanisation peaked in the 1970s and have declined since then due to the process of counterurbanisation.

Table 3.3 shows the largest cities in the world in 1960 and 2008. If you look on the internet you will see that the rank order can change according to the source of information. Different sources can use different criteria to define urban boundaries. Table 3.3 shows three urban areas with populations over 20 million: Tokyo–Yokohama (34.4 million), New York (20.3 million), and Seoul–Inchon (20.1 million).

Table 3.3 The world's ten largest cities in 1960 and 2008

Rank	1960	Population (millions)	2008	Population (millions)
1	New York	14.2	Tokyo–Yokohama	34.4
2	London	10.7	New York	20.3
3	Tokyo	10.7	Seoul–Inchon	20.1
4	Shanghai	10.7	Jakarta	19.9
5	Beijing	7.3	Mumbai	19.4
6	Paris	7.2	São Paulo	19.1
7	Buenos Aires	6.9	Mexico City	18.4
8	Los Angeles	6.6	Delhi	17.6
9	Moscow	6.0	Osaka–Kobe–Kyoto	17.2
10	Chicago	6.0	Manila	17.0

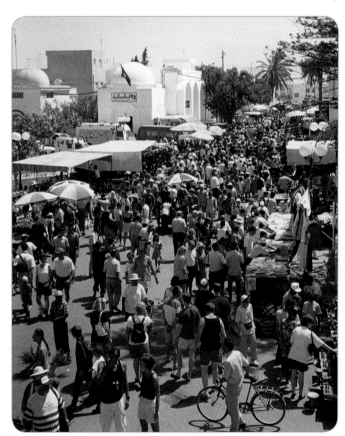

Figure 3.17 Street market in Nabul, Tunisia

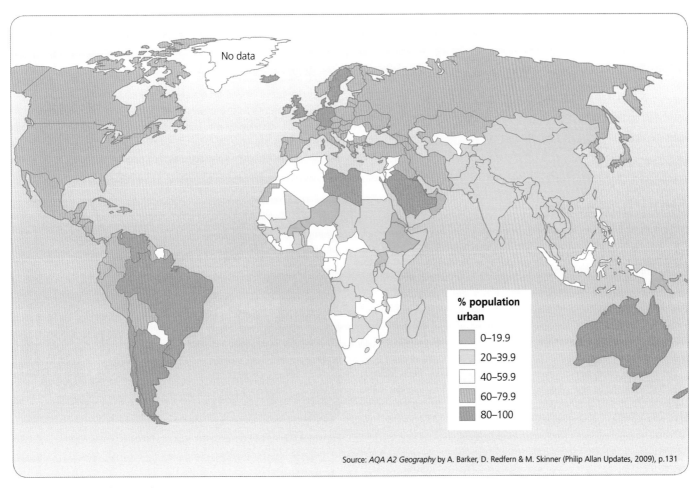

Figure 3.18 World urban population, 2005

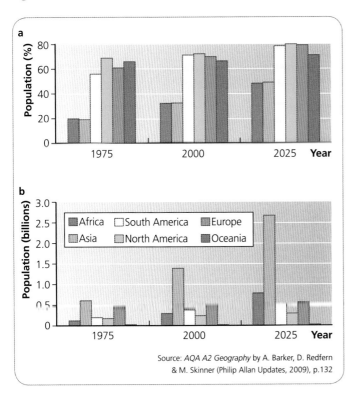

Source: *AQA A2 Geography* by A. Barker, D. Redfern & M. Skinner (Philip Allan Updates, 2009), p.132

Figure 3.19 Predicted patterns of urbanisation, 1975–2025

Section 3.2 Activities

1 a When did the first and second urban revolutions occur?
   b What were the reasons for each of these major changes in human settlement?

2 Distinguish between urbanisation and urban growth.

3 Describe and explain the variations shown in Figure 3.18.

4 Comment on the changes shown in Figure 3.19.

5 Compare the locations of the world's ten largest cities in 1960 and 2008 (Table 3.3).

The cycle of urbanisation

The development of urban settlement in the modern period can be seen as a sequence of processes known as the **cycle of urbanisation** (Figure 3.20). The key processes and their landscape implicatons are: **suburbanisation**, **counterurbanisation** and **reurbanisation**. In Britain suburbanisation was the dominant process until the 1960s. From this decade counterurbanisation increasingly had an impact on the landscape. Reurbanisation of some of the largest cities, beginning in the 1990s, is the most recent phenomenon.

Source: *Edexcel AS Geography* by S. Warn, C. Dunn,
S. Oakes, B. Hordern et al. (Philip Allan Updates, 2008), p.147

Figure 3.20 The cycle of urbanisation

Suburbanisation

Although the urban Industrial Revolution in Britain began in the late eighteenth century, it was not really until the 1860s that urban areas began to spread out significantly. The main factor in this development was the construction of suburban railway lines. Each railway development spurred a rapid period of house building. Initially the process of suburbanisation was an almost entirely middle-class phenomenon. It was not until after the First World War, with the growth of public housing, that working-class suburbs began to appear.

In the interwar period about 4.3 million houses were built in the UK, mainly in the new suburbs. Just over 30 per cent were built by local authorities (councils). The reasons for such a rapid rate of suburban growth were:

- government support for house-building
- the willingness of local authorities to provide piped water and sewerage systems, and gas and electricity
- the expansion of building societies
- low interest rates
- development of public transport routes
- improvements to the road network.

Figure 3.21 describes the development of Stoneleigh, an outer suburb in south-west London (Figure 3.22). In the latter half of the twentieth century suburbanisation was limited by the creation of Green Belts and the introduction of general planning controls.

Figure 3.22 Stoneleigh: an outer suburb in south-west London

STONELEIGH: A RAILWAY SUBURB

By the end of the 1930s developments were taking place on the rural–urban fringe. Stoneleigh acquired a railway station in 1932 and witnessed spectacular growth thereafter. The Stoneleigh Estate consisted of three farms. These had been offered for building development in the early 1900s but by the end of the 1920s only a few dozen houses had been built. However, following the arrival of the railway, development intensified. By 1933 a 3500 acre site for 3000 homes existed, and the area had a complete set of drains and sewers. By 1937 all farmland and woodland within a 1 mile radius of the railway station had been destroyed.

The housing density at Stoneleigh was low at eight houses per acre. As well as the railway there was a good bus service to Epsom, Surbiton and Kingston. Further developments followed quickly:

- a block of 18 shops (by 1933);
- a sub-post office (1933) and a bank (1934);
- Stoneleigh's first public house (1934);
- a cinema (1937);
- a variety of churches (1935 onwards);
- schools (from 1934);
- recreational grounds at Nonsuch Park and Cuddington.

Stoneleigh benefited from a strong and dynamic residents' association. The residents were aggrieved that nearby working-class areas in Sutton and Cheam were reducing their own land values. They canvassed successfully for boundaries to be redrawn, raising the values of their properties. There were many social activities too, including dances, whist-drives, cricket, children's parties, choral societies, cycling and tennis. This went a long way to creating a sense of community. The chairman of the residents' association was also the editor of a local newspaper, which helped the residents in their aims.

By 1939 Stoneleigh was a model railway suburb. Over 3000 people used the railway each day for commuting to work and it was also useful for reaching the south coast. However, the railway also split the community in two. There were problems for buses and cars trying to move from one side of the town to the other. Socially, it also split the community.

The development of Stoneleigh shows many similarities with other suburbs:

- a variety of housing styles, reflecting the different building companies;
- a somewhat chaotic road layout;
- complete destruction of the former farming landscape;
- ponderous shopping parades;
- the claim by some that it is dull and soulless.

Yet because of its poor road layout, in particular the lack of railway crossings, and its housing developments right up to the railway line, it does not have the worst trappings of modern suburban development.

Source: *Geography Review*, September 1998

Figure 3.21 Stoneleigh – a railway suburb

Counterurbanisation

Urban deconcentration is the most consistent and dominant feature of population movement in most cities in MEDCs today, in which each level of the settlement hierarchy is gaining people from the more urban tiers above it but losing population to those below it. However, it must be remembered that the net figures hide the fact that there are reasonable numbers of people moving in the opposite direction. There has been a consistent loss of population for metropolitan England in terms of net within-UK migration. It does not, however, mean an overall population decline of this magnitude, because population change is also affected by natural increase and international migration. London is the prime example of the counterbalancing effect of these last two processes.

Around London, where central rents are particularly high, much office employment has diffused very widely across south-east England. Between 20 and 30 decentralisation centres can be identified in the Outer Metropolitan Area, between 20 and 80 km from central London, especially along the major road and rail corridors. Examples include Dorking, Guildford and Reigate.

Reurbanisation

In very recent years British cities have, to a limited extent so far, reversed the population decline that has dominated the post-war period. Central government finance, for example the millions of pounds of subsidies poured into London's Docklands, Manchester's Hulme wastelands and Sheffield's light railway, has been an important factor in the revival. New urban design is also playing a role. The rebuilding of part of Manchester's city centre after a massive IRA bomb has allowed the planners to add new pedestrian areas, green spaces and residential accommodation.

The reduction in urban street crime due to the installation of automated closed-circuit surveillance cameras has significantly improved public perception of central areas (Figure 3.23). Rather than displacing crime to nearby areas, as some critics have claimed, a Home Office study found that, on the contrary, the installation of cameras had a halo effect, causing a reduction in crime in surrounding areas.

Is the recent reurbanisation just a short-term blip or the beginning of a significant trend, at least in the medium term? Perhaps the most important factor favouring the latter is the government's prediction in the late 1990s of the formation of

Figure 3.23 Reurbanisation in the central area of Reading, UK

4.4 million extra households over the next two decades. Sixty per cent of these new households will have to be housed in existing urban areas because there is such fierce opposition to the relaxation of planning restrictions in the countryside. Also, as many of the new households will be single-person units, the existing urban areas may well be where most of them would prefer to live.

Case Study

The rejuvenation of inner London

For the first time in about 30 years London stopped losing population in the mid-1980s and has been gaining people ever since, due to net immigration from overseas and natural increase. Perhaps the most surprising aspect of this trend is the rejuvenation of inner London where the population peaked at 5 million in 1900, but then steadily dropped to a low of 2.5 million by 1983. The subsequent rise, forecast by the Department of the Environment to reach 3 million by 2011, will subside thereafter. Young adults now form the predominant population group in inner London, whereas in the 1960s all the inner london boroughs exhibited a mature population structure. Inner London is seen as a vibrant and attractive destination by young migrants from both the UK and abroad.

Section 3.2 Activities

1 What is the cycle of urbanisation?

2 With reference to Figure 3.21, describe the process of suburbanisation.

3 What is counterurbanisation and when did it begin?

4 a Define reurbanisation.

   b Explain the reasons for the occurrence of this process.

Competition for land

All urban areas exhibit competition for land to varying degrees. Such competition varies according to location, and the level of competition can change over time. The best measures of competition are the price of land and the rents charged for floorspace in buildings. However, planning measures such as **land use zoning** and other restrictions can complicate the free market process to a considerable degree. Bid-rent theory does much to explain how competition for land can result in functional variation – this is discussed in more detail in the next section. Space does not usually stay idle for long in the sought-after parts of urban areas. However, there are areas of some cities where dereliction has been long-standing. Here the land may be unattractive for both residential and business purposes and it may require substantial investment from government to bring the area back into active use again.

Renewal and redevelopment

Urban redevelopment involves complete clearance of existing buildings and site infrastructure and constructing new buildings, often for a different purpose, from scratch. In contrast, **urban renewal** keeps the best elements of the existing urban environment (often because they are safeguarded by planning regulations) and adapts them to new usages. Simple examples are where a bank has been turned into a restaurant, keeping the former's façade, but altering the inside of the building to suit its new purpose. Urban renewal helps to maintain some of the historic character of urban areas.

In cities in various countries where damage was extensive as a result of the Second World War (1939–45), large-scale redevelopment took place in the subsequent decades. The general model was to completely clear the land (redevelopment) and build anew. However, from the 1970s renewal gained increasing acceptance and importance in planning circles. In more recent years the term **urban regeneration** has become increasingly popular. This involves both redevelopment and renewal.

In the UK, urban development corporations were formed in the 1980s and early 1990s to tackle large areas of urban blight in major cities around the country. The establishment of the London Docklands Development Corporation in 1981 set in train one of the largest urban regeneration projects ever undertaken in Europe. An important part of this development was the construction of Canary Wharf which extended London's central business district (CBD) towards the east. The regeneration of the Lower Lea Valley is a more recent development stimulated by the granting of the Olympic Games to London for 2012.

The Lower Lea Valley is home to one of the most deprived communities in the country and is seen as the largest remaining regeneration opportunity in inner London. Unemployment is high and the public health record poor. At present this run-down environment with an industrial history suffers from a lack of **infrastructure**. Most of the existing industry provides only low-density employment. Flytipping has been a major problem here for many years. The area is one of the most ethnically diverse in the UK. It has a negative image both within East London and in the capital city as a whole. It is hoped that the Olympic Games will transform the Lower Lea Valley, bringing permanent prosperity to the area through the process of **cumulative causation**. The development that the Olympics will bring will be dovetailed with the existing regeneration framework. The total investment in the area is expected to exceed £6 billion. Plans to develop the Lower Lea Valley have been around for some time – the development role of the Olympic Games will be to speed up this process.

Gentrification: reshaping social geography

There are small areas of striking affluence in the inner cities of most urban areas within MEDCs. There are two main reasons for clusters of high socio-economic status in the inner city. Some areas have always been fashionable for those with money. In London areas such as St John's Wood and Chelsea are only a short distance from the City and West End and are pleasantly laid out with a good measure of open space. The original high quality of housing has been maintained to a very good standard.

Other fashionable areas have become so in recent decades through the process of **gentrification**. Gentrification is marked by the occupation of more space per person than the original occupants from lower socio-economic groups. The low-income areas that are most likely to undergo this process usually have some distinct advantages, such as:

- an attractive park
- larger than average housing
- proximity to a station.

Evidence of gentrification is:

- many houses being renovated – skips, scaffolding etc.
- house prices rising faster than in comparable areas
- 'trendier' shops and restaurants opening in the area.

Because the demand for housing in London exceeds the supply, many parts of the city have been gentrified since the 1960s.

The term 'gentrification' was first coined in 1963 by the sociologist Ruth Glass to describe the changes occurring in the social structure and housing market in parts of inner London. The process involved:

- the physical improvement of the housing stock (Figure 3.24)
- a change in housing tenure from renting to owning
- an increase in house prices
- the displacement or replacement of the working class by the new middle class.

Figure 3.24 Gentrification of terraced housing in inner London

Lower-income migrants move into deteriorated housing (previously owned by middle-income groups)

Lower-income groups gradually move up the housing scale

CBD

Gentrification: upper-middle-income groups move to old housing

Older housing occupied by lower-income groups

Better housing occupied by middle-income groups

Best housing occupied by upper-middle-income groups

Expansion: new houses built for upper-middle-income groups

Filtering occurs as housing deteriorates and it moves downwards through the social groups.

Gentrification reverses this process as middle-income groups upgrade older city properties by renovating them.

Source: *Advanced Geography: Concepts & Cases* by P. Guinness & G. Nagle (Hodder Education, 1999), p.114

Figure 3.25 The process of filtering and gentrification

According to Professor C. Hamnett, 'the importance of gentrification in dramatically reshaping the social geography of inner London over the last 30–40 years cannot be overestimated'. Much of inner London in the 1950s and 1960s was dominated by a large working-class population. Since then gentrification has changed much of the inner city in terms of both social structure and housing tenure. As the middle classes have expanded in the inner city, the remaining working-class population has been squeezed into smaller and smaller areas. Gentrification is particularly concentrated in a relatively small number of major cities where:

- the change from an industrial to a post-industrial economy has been rapid
- the professional and managerial classes have expanded significantly
- there is an attractive old nineteenth or early twentieth century inner city housing stock suitable for renovation and conversion.

Gentrification not only results in a considerable upgrading of the housing stock, but also significant changes to other aspects of the urban environment (Figure 3.25). For example, the nature of retailing in areas that have been gentrified often undergoes a profound change as pubs, restaurants, clothes shops and other retail outlets go 'upmarket' due to the increased purchasing power of people in the area.

The shortage of housing, illustrated by extremely high house prices has caused young professional people increasingly to seek homes in areas that were once considered undesirable. The types of change that could be observed in Fulham, Paddington and Battersea in the 1960s and 1970s have recently been occurring in Hackney, Brixton and Shepherd's Bush.

Although the overall borough statistics still show a pronounced inner London/outer London contrast, gentrification has intensified the **residential mosaic** of inner London, with affluent areas often not far from deprived inner city estates. The poverty in London's worst housing estates is extreme. The boroughs of Hackney, Southwark and Tower Hamlets all contain a hundred or more estates officially classed as deprived, accounting between them for a fifth of the national total.

Changing accessibility and lifestyle

As cities have spread outwards with the development of new suburbs, many people have enjoyed a higher quality of life in such locations. The suburban lifestyle is an ambition for many more people around the world. However, the flip-side has been increasingly long journeys to work.

More than two-thirds of all journeys to work in the UK are now by car, up from about 50 per cent in 1980. Over the same period the average commuting journey has risen by 50 per cent. At the same time all other types of journey have become more car intensive. Increasing personal mobility is an important factor in improving the quality of life of people. However, it comes at a cost – congestion and pollution. As more people can afford to spend money on transportation, public and private, levels of **accessibility** rise, at least in theory. However, significant investment in transport infrastructure is required to ensure that congestion does not reduce travel times.

The perceived wisdom now is that building new roads may cause people to undertake trips they would otherwise not have attempted. Traffic almost always rises over time to exceed highway capacity. In terms of the environment there is concern that the growth in vehicle miles will overwhelm any improvements in vehicle emissions. The reasons for the increase in urban car use in most cities include:

- rising real incomes which have enabled more and more households to purchase vehicles
- decentralisation, which has resulted in people living further from their places of work now than in the past
- the growth in the number of households, which has generated more trips
- the growing proportion of households with two earners of working age, which also generates more trips
- the perceived high cost and low quality of public transportation which limits its appeal as an alternative to the car
- the increasing proportion of journeys to school taken by car.

The fastest rates of motor vehicle increase are in the cities of LEDCs. One of the first things people buy as soon as they can is a car.

Figure 3.26 Public transport in Vienna, Austria

This is the major reason why the quality of the environment in most cities in LEDCs continues to deteriorate. In so many instances population increase (and car usage) outstrips investment in urban infrastructure and environmental improvement. It is not just an issue of aesthetics; recent research has stressed the economic cost of pollution.

The increase in environmental problems in cities in LEDCs has been paralleled by a rise in local anxiety about them. Environmental lobby groups have grown substantially in number; some are offshoots of world organisations established in MEDCs, such as Friends of the Earth and Greenpeace, while others are local organisations. As concern has increased politicians have been forced to act.

The best way to counter the pollution problem is to plan the growth of cities more carefully, particularly to avoid widespread urban sprawl which encourages car use. The UN has pointed to Curitiba in Brazil as an example of effective urban planning. Here urban growth has been channelled along five corridors stretching out from the city centre, each served by a road with exclusive lanes for high-speed buses. Rates of car ownership in Curitiba are high due to its relative affluence, but it has cleaner air and lower petrol consumption than other Brazilian cities of a comparable size, mainly because so many people use public transport.

In Vienna the combination of high-quality, heavily subsidised public transport, high petrol taxes and parking fees, and strictly regulated on-street parking has succeeded in keeping the streets relatively uncongested (Figure 3.26).

The most effective measure would be to upgrade public transportation to a much better standard than it is at present.

However, because of the high cost involved it is unlikely that enough will ever be done in most countries to attract significant numbers away from their cars.

Section 3.2 Activities

1 Why is there often intense competition for land in urban areas?

2 How can the competition for urban land be measured?

3 Distinguish between *urban redevelopment* and *urban renewal*.

4 Define *infrastructure*.

5 a Define *gentrification*.
  b How has gentrification affected London?

6 Explain the factors that result in changes in accessibility in urban areas.

Global (world) cities

A global (world) city is one that is judged to be an important nodal point in the global economic system. The term 'global city' was first introduced by Saskia Sassen in her book *The Global City* published in 1991. Initially referring to New York, London and Tokyo, Sassen described global cities as ones that play a major role in global affairs in terms of politics, economics and culture. The number of global cities has increased significantly

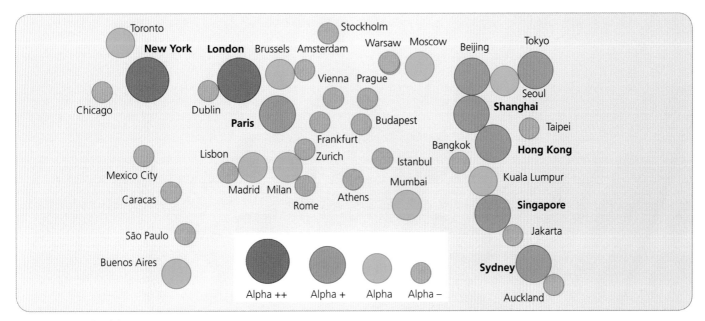

Figure 3.27 Alpha global cities

in recent decades as the process of globalisation has deepened. Global cities are defined by influence rather than size. Which large cities in terms of population do not appear on Figure 3.27? For example, in the USA, Los Angeles is larger in population size than Chicago, but while Chicago has Alpha status, Los Angeles does not merit an Alpha ranking.

The Globalisation and World Cities (GaWC) Research Network at Loughborough University has identified various levels of global city. Figure 3.27 shows what are termed the 'Alpha' cities in 2008, which are subdivided into four categories. Only New York and

London are placed in the highest Alpha++ category under this classification. Beijing (Figure 3.28) is in the Alpha+ category along with Shanghai, Hong Kong and Tokyo in the East Asia geographical region. The remaining cities in this category are Paris, Singapore and Sydney. The GaWC analysis also recognises four lower levels of urban area around the world. The next two levels in the global city hierarchy, the Beta and Gamma levels, are shown in Table 3.4. The results are based upon the office networks of 175 advanced producer service firms in 526 cities in 2008.

Table 3.4 Beta and gamma global cities

Beta+	Beta	Beta–	Gamma+	Gamma	Gamma–
Melbourne	Bangalore	Sofia	Panama City	Guadalajara	Edinburgh
Barcelona	Jeddah	Dusseldorf	Casablanca	Antwerp	Porto
Los Angeles	Kuwait	Houston	Chennai	Rotterdam	Tallinn
Johannesburg	Luxembourg	Beirut	Brisbane	Lagos	San Salvador
Manila	Munich	Guangzhou	Quito	Philadelphia	St Petersburg
Bogotá	Kiev	Nicosia	Stuttgart	Perth	Port Louis
New Delhi	Dallas	Karachi	Denver	Amman	San Diego
Atlanta	Lima	Montevideo	Vancouver	Manchester (UK)	Calgary
Washington	Boston	Rio de Janeiro	Zagreb	Riga	Almaty
Tel Aviv	Miami	Nairobi	Guatemala City	Detroit	Birmingham (UK)
Bucharest		Bratislava	Cape Town	Guayaquil	Islamabad
San Francisco		Montreal	San Jose (Costa Rica)	Wellington	Doha
Helsinki		Ho Chi Minh City	Ljubljana	Portland	Vilnius
Berlin			Minneapolis		Colombo
Dubai			Santo Domingo		
Oslo			Seattle		
Geneva			Manama		
Riyadh			Shenzhen		
Copenhagen					
Hamburg					
Cairo					

Source: Globalisation and World Cities (GaWC) Research Network, Loughborough University

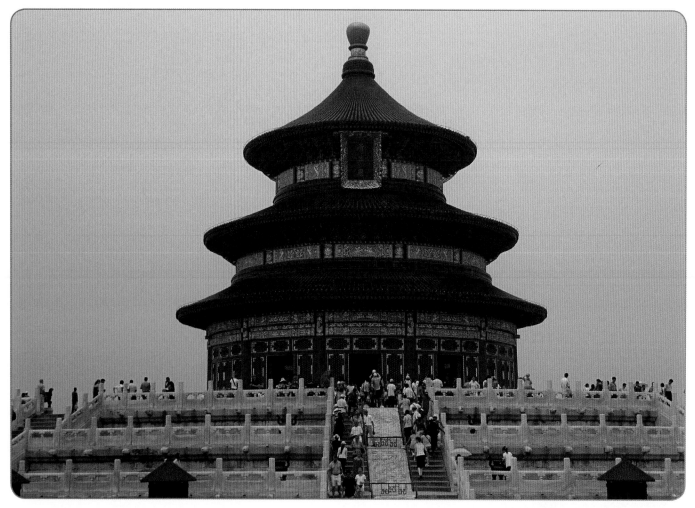

Figure 3.28 Beijing – a world city

In 2008, the American journal *Foreign Policy* published its Global Cities Index. The rankings are based on 24 measures over five areas:
- business activity
- human capital
- information exchange
- cultural experience
- political engagement.

Foreign Policy noted that 'the world's biggest, most interconnected cities help set global agendas, weather transnational dangers, and serve as the hubs of global integration. They are the engines of growth for their countries and the gateways to the resources of their regions.'

The growth of global cities has been due to:
- demographic trends: significant rates of natural increase and in-migration at different points in time for cities in MEDCs and LEDCs – large population clusters offer potential in terms of both workforce and markets
- economic development: the emergence of major manufacturing and service centres in national and continental space, along with the development of key transport nodes in the global trading system

- cultural/social status: the cultural facilities of large cities are an important element of their overall attraction to foreign direct investment and tourism
- political importance: many global cities are capital cities, benefiting from particularly high levels of investment in infrastructure.

There will undoubtedly be many changes in the hierarchy of global cities as the years unfold. The rapid development of many newly industrialised countries will have a significant impact on the rankings. Africa is so far unrepresented on the Alpha list but cities such as Johannesburg, Cairo and Lagos may well get there in the not too distant future. In contrast, other established global cities may decline in importance.

Section 3.2 Activities

1 What is a *global city*?

2 Describe the levels and distribution of global cities shown in Figure 3.27.

3 On an outline map of the world show the locations of the Beta global cities shown in Table 3.4.

4 Suggest how global cities can rise and fall in terms of their level or grading.

3.3 The changing structure of urban settlements

Functional zonation

The patterns evident and the processes at work in large urban areas are complex but by the beginning of the twentieth century geographers and others interested in urban form were beginning to see more clearly than before the similarities between cities as opposed to laying stress on the uniqueness of each urban entity. The first generalisation about urban land use to gain widespread recognition was the concentric zone model emanating from the so-called 'Chicago School'.

The concentric zone model

Figure 3.29 The CBD of Chicago

Published in 1925, and based on American Mid-Western cities, particularly Chicago (Figure 3.29), E.W. Burgess's model (Figure 3.30) has survived much longer than perhaps its attributes merit as it has only limited applicability to modern cities. However, it did serve as a theoretical foundation for others to investigate further.

The main assumptions upon which the model was based are:

- a uniform land surface
- free competition for space
- universal access to a single-centred city
- continuing in-migration to the city, with development taking place outward from the central core.

Burgess concluded that the city would tend to form a series of concentric zones. The model's basic concepts were drawn from ecology, with the physical expansion of the city occurring by invasion and succession, with each of the concentric zones expanding at the expense of the one beyond.

Business activities agglomerated in the central business district (CBD) which was the point of maximum accessibility for the urban area as a whole. Surrounding the CBD was the '**zone in transition**' where older private houses were being subdivided into flats and bed-sitters or converted to offices and light industry. Newcomers to the city were attracted to this zone because of the concentration of relatively cheap, low-quality rented accommodation. In-migrants tended to group in ethnic ghettos and areas of vice could be recognised (Figure 3.31). However, as an ethnic group assimilated into the wider community – economically, socially and politically – its members would steadily move out to zones of better housing, to be replaced by the most recent arrivals. Beyond the zone in transition came the 'zone of working-men's homes' characterised by some of the oldest housing in the city and stable social groups. Next came the 'residential zone' occupied by the middle classes with its newer and larger houses. Finally, the commuters' zone extended beyond the built-up area.

Burgess observed in his paper that 'neither Chicago nor any other city fits perfectly into this ideal scheme. Complications are introduced by the lake front, the Chicago River, railroad lines, historical factors in the location of industry, the relative degree of the resistance of communities to invasion, etc.'

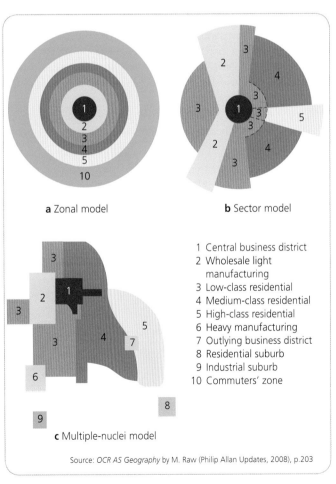

a Zonal model

b Sector model

c Multiple-nuclei model

1 Central business district
2 Wholesale light manufacturing
3 Low-class residential
4 Medium-class residential
5 High-class residential
6 Heavy manufacturing
7 Outlying business district
8 Residential suburb
9 Industrial suburb
10 Commuters' zone

Source: *OCR AS Geography* by M. Raw (Philip Allan Updates, 2008), p.203

Figure 3.30 Concentric zone, sector and multiple-nuclei models

Figure 3.31 Subway graffiti, the Bronx – inner city New York

Bid-rent theory

Alonso's theory of urban land rent (1964), generally known as **bid-rent theory**, also produces a concentric zone formation, determined by the respective ability of land uses to pay the higher costs of a central location (Figure 3.32). The high accessibility of land at the centre, which is in short supply, results in intense competition among potential land users. The prospective land use willing and able to bid the most will gain the most central location. The land use able to bid the least will be relegated to the most peripheral location.

Alonso explained the paradox of poorer people living on expensive land in inner areas and more affluent people living on cheaper land further out as follows:

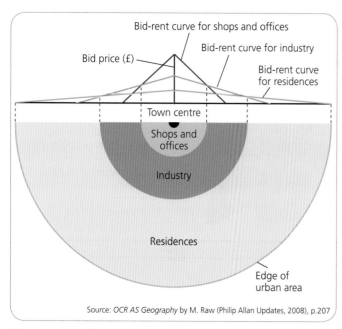

Source: *OCR AS Geography* by M. Raw (Philip Allan Updates, 2008), p.207

Figure 3.32 The bid-rent model

- With poor personal mobility, low-income groups prefer to reside in inner locations. They overcome the problem of land costs by living at high densities, each household buying or renting only a small amount of space.
- The more affluent, desiring a large house and garden, seek out cheaper land in the low-density suburbs where they can realise their 'dreams'. Being highly mobile they trade off space against accessibility to the CBD.

The assumptions upon which the theory is based and the criticisms of it are similar to the Burgess model.

The sector model

Homer Hoyt's **sector** model (1939) was based on the study of 142 cities in the USA (Figure 3.30). Following Burgess, Hoyt placed the business district in a central location for the same reason – maximum accessibility. However, he observed that once variations arose in land uses near to the centre, they tended to persist as the city expanded. High-income housing usually developed where there were distinct physical or social attractions, with low-income housing confined to the most unfavourable locations. Middle-income groups occupied intermediate locations. Major transport routes often played a key role in influencing sectoral growth, particularly with regard to industry. As new land was required by each sector it was developed at the periphery of that sector. However, medium- and high-class housing near the centre – the oldest housing in each case – was subject to suburban relocation by its residents, leading to deterioration, subdivision and occupation by low-income groups.

The multiple-nuclei model

C.D. Harris and E. Ullman (1945) argued that the pattern of urban land use does not develop around a single centre but around a number of discrete nuclei (Figure 3.30). Some nuclei may be long established, for example old villages that have been incorporated into the city by urban expansion. Others, such as industrial estates for light manufacturing, are much newer. Similar activities group together, benefiting from agglomeration, while some land uses repel others. Middle- and high-income house buyers can afford to avoid residing close to industrial areas which become the preserve of the poor. A very rapid rate of urban expansion may result in some activities being dispersed to new nuclei, such as a new out-of-town shopping centre.

A British urban land use model

P. Mann based his land use model for a typical British city on the theories of both Burgess and Hoyt (Figure 3.33), which he tried to apply to Sheffield, Nottingham and Huddersfield. The outcome was very much a compromise between the two models, which he regarded as being complementary. Identifying four residential sectors from middle class to lower working-class, he noted the influence of prevailing winds on the location of industry and the most expensive housing. He also allowed for local authority house building (the influence of planning), particularly towards the periphery of the urban area, and for commuter villages.

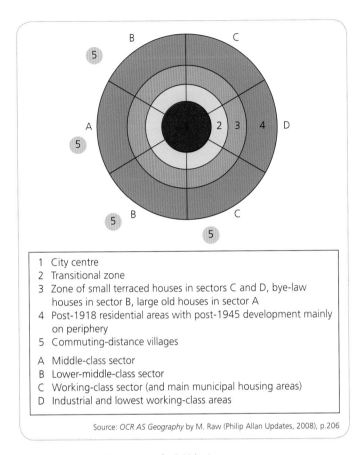

1. City centre
2. Transitional zone
3. Zone of small terraced houses in sectors C and D, bye-law houses in sector B, large old houses in sector A
4. Post-1918 residential areas with post-1945 development mainly on periphery
5. Commuting-distance villages

A. Middle-class sector
B. Lower-middle-class sector
C. Working-class sector (and main municipal housing areas)
D. Industrial and lowest working-class areas

Source: *OCR AS Geography* by M. Raw (Philip Allan Updates, 2008), p.206

Figure 3.33 Mann's structure of a British city

Source: *Advanced Geography: Concepts & Cases*, P. Guinness & G. Nagle (Hodder Education, 1999), p.92

Figure 3.34 The spatial structure of the post-industrial American city

A model of the modern North American city

Another model which incorporates aspects of both Burgess and Hoyt was produced by David Clark (Figure 3.34) in his book *Post-Industrial America*, although similar diagrams have also been produced by others. Here the CBD is subdivided into a core and a frame. Outside the low-income inner city are three suburban rings divided into sectors of lower middle, middle and high income. Important elements in the commercial hierarchy are included, along with industrial and office parks. Thus decentralisation is a key element of this model. The central city boundary shows the legal limits of the main city which once contained the whole urban area. In the twentieth century the city has sprawled way beyond its legal limits to incorporate other legal entities. The Standard Metropolitan Statistical Area (SMSA) also includes the rural sections of counties that form part of the wider urban area.

Models of cities in LEDCs

Although the development of urban land use models has favoured Western cities, some interesting contributions relating to cities in LEDCs and socialist cities have appeared at various points in time.

Griffin and Ford's model, upon which Figure 3.35 is based, summarises many of the characteristics that they noted in modern Latin American cities:

- Central areas, which had changed radically from the colonial period to now, exhibit most of the characteristics of modern Western CBDs.
- The development of a commercial spine, extending outwards from the CBD, is enveloped by an elite residential sector.
- There is a tendency for industries, with their need for urban services such as power and water, to be near the central area.
- The model includes a 'zone of maturity' with a full range of services containing both older, traditional-style housing and more recent residential development. The traditional housing, once occupied by higher-income families who now reside in the elite sector, has generally undergone subdivision and deterioration. A significant proportion of recent housing is self-built of permanent materials and of reasonable quality.
- Also included is a zone of '*in situ* accretion', with a wide variety of housing types and quality but with much still in the process of extension or improvement. Urban services tend to be patchy in this zone with typically only the main streets having a good surface. Government housing projects are often a feature of this zone (Figure 3.36).
- There is a zone of squatter settlements, which are the place of residence of most recent in-migrants. Services in this zone are at their most sparse, with open trenches serving as sewers and communal taps providing water. Most housing is

Source: *OCR AS Geography* by M. Raw (Philip Allan Updates, 2008), p.205

Figure 3.35 Latin American city model

Figure 3.36 Low-cost government housing: Manaus, Brazil

Figure 3.37 High-rise apartment blocks in the inner area of São Paulo

of the 'shanty' type, constructed of wood, flattened oil-cans, polythene and any other materials available at the time of construction. The situation is dynamic and there is evidence of housing at various stages of improvement.

Urban density gradients

Contrasting functional zones within urban areas characteristically vary in residential population density. Examination of population density gradients, termed gradient analysis, shows that for most cities densities fall with increasing distance from the centre (Figure 3.37). Gradient analysis of cities in MEDCs over time (Figure 3.38a) shows the following trends:

- the initial rise and later decline in density of the central area
- the outward spread of population and the consequent reduction in overall density gradient over time.

In contrast, analysis of density gradients in LEDCs shows:

- a continuing increase in central area densities (Figure 3.38b)
- the consequent maintenance of fairly stable density gradients as the urban area expands.

Figure 3.38 Changes in urban density gradients through time

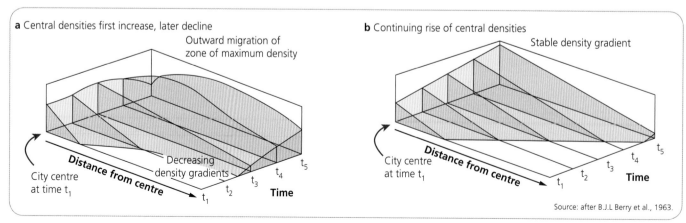

a Central densities first increase, later decline

Outward migration of zone of maximum density

Distance from centre

City centre at time t_1

Decreasing density gradients

t_1 t_2 t_3 t_4 t_5

Time

b Continuing rise of central densities

Stable density gradient

Distance from centre

City centre at time t_1

t_1 t_2 t_3 t_4 t_5

Time

Source: after B.J.L Berry et al., 1963.

In cities in LEDCs both personal mobility and the sophistication of the transport infrastructure operate at a considerably lower level. Also central areas tend to retain an important residential function. Both of these factors result in a more compact central area and the transport factor in particular has restricted urban sprawl to levels below that of cities in MEDCs. The presence of extensive areas of informal settlement in the outer areas also results in higher suburban densities. However, in the more advanced LEDCs, where car ownership is rising rapidly, significant sprawl is now occurring.

Section 3.3 Activities

1 With reference to Figure 3.30, briefly explain the differences between the three models illustrated.

2 Identify the main features of Mann's land use model for a typical British city.

3 Briefly describe and explain the main elements of the model illustrated in Figure 3.34.

4 Comment on the main characteristics of the model of Latin American cities shown in Figure 3.35.

5 a Define the term *urban density gradient*.
   b How and why do urban density gradients differ between cities in MEDCs and LEDCs?

Factors affecting the location of urban activities

A range of factors affect the location of urban activities such as retailing, manufacturing, office functions, education, health, leisure and open space. Most if not all of these factors can be placed under two general headings:

- Market forces – the demand and supply of land in various locations dictates its price.
- Local or central government planning decisions – planners can overrule market forces where they consider it necessary for the public good. Government may be able to decide, within certain constraints, where the locations of public housing, open spaces, schools, hospitals and public buildings should be. Under extreme conditions government can issue compulsory purchase orders. This is most likely to happen when privately owned land is in the way of a planned new transport route.

Manufacturing industry

The relatively compact nature of towns and cities during the Industrial Revolution years of the nineteenth century resulted in a concentration of manufacturing industry in the inner cities of the twentieth century as the era of the motor vehicle allowed cities to sprawl far beyond their previous limits. However, as the decades evolved the disadvantages of inner city location became more and

more obvious. The first reaction to the constraints of inner city sites was to select new suburban locations, but increasingly, from the 1960s in particular, manufacturing industry has been attracted to rural areas. The process of **deindustrialisation**, involving the filter-down of manufacturing industry from MEDCs to newly industrialised countries, has resulted in many factory closures in more affluent countries. The term **post-industrial city** is now commonly used when referring to MEDCs.

The explanation for the inner city decline of manufacturing industry lies largely in **constrained location theory**. This identifies the problems encountered by manufacturing firms in congested cities, particularly in the inner areas:

- The industrial buildings of the nineteenth and early twentieth centuries, mostly multi-storey, are generally unsuitable for modern manufacturing, with a preference for single-storey layout.
- The intensive nature of land use usually results in manufacturing sites being hemmed in by other land users, thus preventing on-site expansion.
- The size of most sites is limited by historical choice and frequently deemed to be too small by modern standards, making change of use to housing, recreation or other uses likely. Old sites can rarely accommodate industrial estates, the preferred form of industrial location in most local authority areas.
- Where larger sites are available, the lack of environmental regulations in earlier times has often resulted in high levels of contamination. In such situations reclamation is very costly indeed.
- The high level of competition for land in urban areas has continuously pushed up prices to prohibitive levels for manufacturing industry in many towns and cities.

Other factors specific to inner cities which have contributed to manufacturing loss are:

- Urban planning policies in the form of the huge slum clearance schemes of the 1950s, 1960s and 1970s meant that factories located in slum housing areas were frequently demolished too.
- Regional economic planning also had an impact in some areas, with incentives to industry to relocate to another part of a country.
- Before the era of decline, important inter-firm linkages had been built up in inner city areas. As these links were steadily broken, the locational *raison d'être* of the remaining inner city firms gradually evaporated.

Although manufacturing employment has declined in cities as a whole in recent decades, job loss has been much more severe in inner cities than in suburban areas. Thus there has been a marked relative shift of manufacturing employment within urban areas in favour of the suburbs. And in a few instances manufacturing employment in the suburbs has shown an absolute increase.

The movement of people from inner to suburban areas increased the relative strength of the latter in terms of labour supply. For some industries population movement also meant a locational shift of their markets. Investment in new roads, particularly motorways, dual-carriageways and ring roads has given many suburban areas a very high level of accessibility. Industrial estates in suburban areas are usually much larger than those in inner areas because of contrasts in building density and competition for land. Land prices and rents are in general considerably lower in suburban locations. Also, the quality of life is perceived to be significantly higher in suburban locations.

Retailing

The location and characteristics of retailing have changed significantly in most cities in recent decades. Changes within the CBD itself is discussed in the next section. Outside the CBD large urban areas have witnessed the development of particular features:

- Suburban CBDs: as urban areas increase in population size and urban sprawl occurs, more people find themselves at a considerable distance from the central CBD. Suburban retail and business centres develop to satisfy this demand.
- Retail parks: these entities are characterised by retail units requiring very large floorspace and a large area for car parking. They are invariably located along key arterial and ring roads.
- Urban superstores: these single-owner retail units (very large supermarkets) are located at points of high accessibility and consumer demand.
- Out-of-town shopping centres: large indoor shopping centres are located at the edge of cities or in the rural areas beyond. Table 3.5 summarises the advantages and disadvantages of out-of-town shopping centres.
- Internet shopping and home delivery services: such services are rapidly increasing in popularity and threaten the future existence of certain types of shops.

Other services

The range of urban services that people use over a long time period can be extensive, often changing significantly during a person's lifetime. The location of some of these services may change more than others. For example:

- Health: there has been a tendency in many countries to invest in larger hospitals and health centres in order to achieve economies of scale, resulting in the closure of smaller local hospitals and clinics. Thus the average person has to travel further to reach their nearest hospital.
- Education: although primary schools have tended to remain local in character, secondary education is generally being provided in larger schools than in the past, increasing the distance between such schools, resulting in longer 'journey to school' times. This has considerable implications for traffic congestion in cities.
- Sport: the redevelopment of sports stadia (football, cricket, baseball etc.) often results in a move from an inner city to a suburban or edge-of-city location due to a shortage of space and congestion in inner city locations.

Over the years an increasing number of land uses which require large sites and are mainly used by urban residents have been located in the **rural–urban fringe**. This is the boundary zone where rural and urban land uses meet. It is an area of transition from agricultural and other rural land uses to urban use. The rural–urban fringe is characterised by a mixture of land uses, all of which require a great deal of space. Such uses include theme parks, horse-racing courses, golf courses, cemeteries, hospitals and colleges. It is logical for these land uses to locate where the space requirements can be met as close as possible to the continuous built-up area.

Table 3.5 Advantages and disadvantages of out-of-town shopping centres

Advantages
Plenty of free parking
Lots of space so shops are not cramped
New developments so usually quite attractive
Easily accessible by car
Being large means the shops can sell large volumes of goods and often at slightly lower prices
Having a large shop means that individual shops can offer a greater range of goods than smaller shops
Being on the edge of town means the land price is lower so the cost of development is kept down
Developments on the edge of town reduce the environmental pressures and problems in city centres
Many new jobs may be created both in the short term (construction industry) and in the long term (retail industry and linked industries such as transport, warehousing, storage, catering, etc.)

Disadvantages
They destroy large amounts of undeveloped greenfield sites
They destroy valuable habitats
They lead to pollution and environmental problems at the edge of town
An increase in impermeable surfaces (shops, car parks, roads, etc.) may lead to an increase in flooding and a decrease in water quality
They only help those with cars (or those lucky enough to live on the route of a courtesy bus) – people who do not benefit might include the elderly, those without a car, those who cannot drive
Successful out-of-town developments may take trade away from city centres and lead to a decline in sales in the CBD
Small businesses and family firms may not be able to compete with the vast multinational companies that dominate out-of-town developments – there may be a loss of the 'personal touch'
They cause congestion in out-of-town areas
Many of the jobs created are unskilled

Figure 3.39 Pedestrianised precinct: CBD of Reading, UK

Figure 3.40 Large indoor shopping centre: the Eaton Centre, Toronto, Canada

A major issue with regard to service provision is the role of **key workers** such as nurses, teachers and police officers. Such workers are absolutely vital for the efficient running of an urban area. However, many key workers on modest salaries struggle with high costs of housing in many cities. Some cities have developed schemes to help key workers with the cost of housing.

The changing central business district

The central business district is the commercial core of an urban area exhibiting the highest land values (Figures 3.39 and 3.40). It is the focus of public transport systems and in theory at least the most accessible area in a city. A high level of accessibility results in high land values and rents which in turn encourages vertical development. Most large CBDs exhibit a core and a frame (Figure 3.41).

Major retailing and office functions dominate the core alongside theatres, cinemas, restaurants, bars, hotels and key public buildings. Vertical zoning is often apparent with retailing occupying lower floors and offices above. Similar functions often locate together, for example department stores and theatres. The high land values of the CBD result in extremely low residential populations. This contrasts with the very high pedestrian flows recorded in CBDs – a combination of a large number of people attracted to the CBD to purchase goods and services and the very significant number of people who work there.

Traffic congestion is a universal problem in CBDs and thus it is not surprising that this is the urban zone with the greatest traffic restrictions. In London a congestion charge zone covers much of the CBD. At the time of writing motorists had to pay £8 a day to enter the zone.

CBDs change over time. Common changes in many MEDCs and an increasing number of LEDCs have been:

- pedestrianised zones
- indoor shopping centres
- environmental improvements
- greater public transport coordination
- ring roads around the CBD with multi-storey car parks.

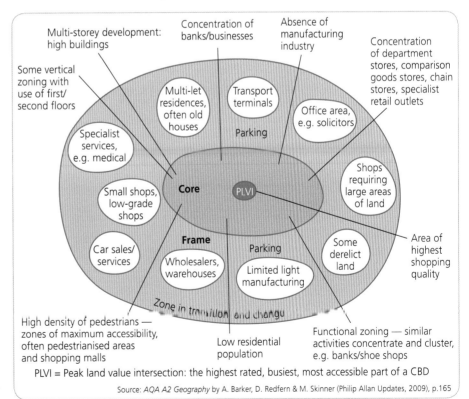

Figure 3.41 The key features of the CBD

Source: AQA A2 Geography by A. Barker, D. Redfern & M. Skinner (Philip Allan Updates, 2009), p.165

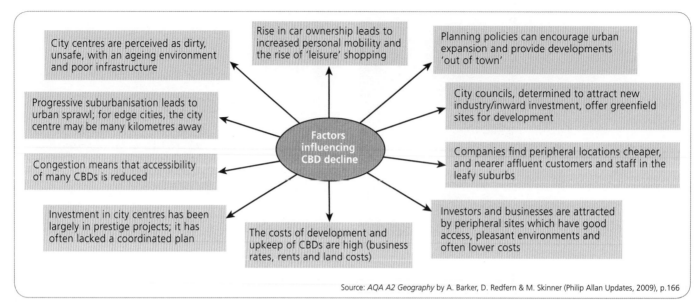

Source: *AQA A2 Geography* by A. Barker, D. Redfern & M. Skinner (Philip Allan Updates, 2009), p.166

Figure 3.42 Factors influencing CBD decline

Some parts of the CBD may expand into the adjoining inner city (a zone of assimilation) while other parts of the CBD may be in decline (a zone of discard). The CBD is a major factor in the economic health of any urban area. Its prosperity can be threatened by a number of factors (Figure 3.42). CBDs are often in competition with their nearest neighbours and are constantly having to upgrade their facilities to remain attractive to their catchment populations.

Urban redevelopment can be a major factor in CBD change. The redevelopment of London Docklands changed London's CBD from a bi-nuclear entity (the West End and the City) to its current tri-nuclear form (West End, City, Canary Wharf). In the West End retailing is the dominant function whereas in the City offices dominate – for example, the latter area contains the Bank of England, the Stock Exchange and Lloyd's of London (insurance). Canary Wharf was planned to have a good mixture of both offices and retailing. It has been an important development in maintaining London's position as a major global city (Figure 3.43).

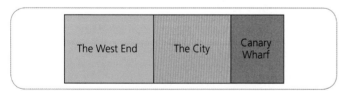

Figure 3.43 London's CBD

Residential segregation

Residential segregation is very apparent in cities in both MEDCs and LEDCs. London provides a prime example. On all socio-economic measures the contrast between the relative deprivation of inner London and the affluence of outer London is striking. London is made up of the City of London, and the 32 boroughs, of which 13 are in inner London and 19 in outer London (Figure 3.44).

The most intense deprivation in inner London is concentrated towards the east (the East End). However, significant contrasts exist within virtually all boroughs so that the better-off wards (subdivisions of boroughs) in some inner London boroughs often record a higher quality of life than the least affluent wards in outer London boroughs. The pattern found within boroughs is often quite intricate, forming the '**residential mosaic**' that social geographers frequently talk about. The process of gentrification (section 3.2) invariably increases residential segregation.

The urban mosaic model highlights three main features:
- Income: people on high incomes have a very wide choice of where to live. Because housing is a very important factor in people's lives most people tend to live in the best houses and locations they can afford. People on low incomes have very limited choice for houses and locations.
- Ethnicity: people from particular ethnic groups tend to cluster together in particular areas which are sometimes called 'ethnic villages' (see Topic 2 Migration, page 142).
- Age: most people move a number of times during their lives. The location and type of property they live in is often affected by their age and family size. For example, young people often rent small flats; families with children require more space and tend to buy the largest properties they can afford; older people, once their children have left home, often 'trade down' to a smaller property. As certain types of property tend to be in different areas, people often move from one area to another as their 'life cycle' progresses.

The following three indicators show the contrast between inner and outer London according to three key single indicators from the 2001 census.
- Households with no car or van 2001: the availability of a car or van is a significant factor in personal mobility which can have a significant impact on the quality of life. Figure 3.44 shows the contrast between inner and outer London. Eight London boroughs have at least 50 per cent of households with no car or van. The lowest figure in inner London is the 41 per cent recorded by Wandsworth. In contrast eight outer London boroughs have figures below 25 per cent, with the lowest being Hillingdon (22 per cent).

Figure 3.44 London: percentage of households without a car or van

- Households in owner-occupied accommodation 2001: most people will buy their own house or flat if they can afford to do so. The considerable increase in owner-occupation in the UK in recent decades is testament to this argument. The range of owner-occupation in inner London is from a low of 29 per cent in Tower Hamlets to 52 per cent in Wandsworth. The range in outer London is from 49 per cent in Greenwich to 79 per cent in Havering and Bexley.
- Rate of unemployment 2001: the range in inner London was from 5.7 per cent in Hackney to 3.4 per cent in Wandsworth. In outer London the range was from 4.4 per cent in Greenwich to 2 per cent in Havering and Sutton.

Urban renaissance

Urban renaissance is a common theme running through strategic planning in most MEDCs and in an increasing number of LEDCs. It is about:

- creating a high quality of life in urban areas
- more sustainable living – putting people close to services and facilities, reducing traffic and minimising the need to travel by car

- maintaining and creating attractive living environments
- social well-being, housing and jobs for all sectors of the community that need them
- having a good transport system, promoting good urban design, and meeting community needs.

Section 3.3 Activities

1 Discuss the factors that have changed the location of manufacturing industry in developed world cities.

2 Explain the reasons for the changing location of urban retailing.

3 Describe and explain the changes that have occurred in central business districts

4 a What is residential segregation?
  b Discuss the factors highlighted by the urban mosaic model.
  c Describe and explain the differences shown in Figure 3.44.

3.4 The management of urban settlements

Squatter settlements in São Paulo

About 32 per cent of the world's urban population live in **slums**. The problem of poor housing quality is overwhelmingly concentrated in LEDCs. São Paulo (Figure 3.45) has the largest slum population in South America. Here, urban poverty is concentrated in two types of housing:

- **favelas** (squatter settlements/shanty towns)
- **corticos** (decaying formal housing, mainly in the inner city).

Favelas in São Paulo, unlike Rio de Janeiro, have developed fairly recently. Their rapid growth dates back to 1980, with their share of the population having jumped from 5 per cent to almost 20 per cent since then. Although both natural change and rural–urban migration have fallen significantly in recent years, the housing problem remains immense. Figure 3.46 shows the location of favelas in São Paulo. Look at Figure 3.45 to see the boundary of the official city of São Paulo.

Regional Administration District

ᴥ Favelas (1892 registered)

Regional Divisions of HABI

- HABI-Center (36 Favelas)
- HABI-North (402 Favelas)
- HABI East (301 Favelas)
- HABI South-east (214 Favelas)
- HABI South (939 Favelas)

Figure 3.46 The location of favelas in São Paulo

The population of the metropolitan area (2000 census) is almost 18 million. In international terms São Paulo is a compact urban area. At approximately 8110 per km² the population density is more than twice that of Paris and almost three times that of Los Angeles.

The extreme inequality in São Paulo was highlighted in a report in August 2002 by the city administration. Measuring each district's quality of life using the United Nations **Human Development Index**, the report found that Moema, the city's richest district, has a higher standard of living than Portugal and was only slightly behind Spain. On the other hand, São Paulo's poorest district, Marsilac, where 8400 people just maintain a living in favelas scattered across a

Metropolitan area of São Paulo
Municipality of São Paulo
Urbanised area
■ CBD
1 Avenida Paulista
2 Jardins
3 Bom Retiro
4 Liberdade
5 Bras
6 New corporate nucleus
Other land uses
Wooded areas
Serra do Mar
Reservoirs
⊕ Airports
— Major roads

0 km 20

Source: *Advanced Geography: Concepts & Cases*, P. Guinness & G. Nagle (Hodder Education, 1999), p.132

Figure 3.45 Greater São Paulo

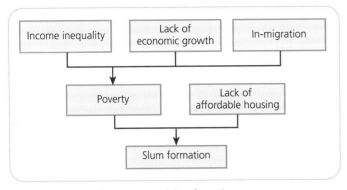

Figure 3.47 Inequality, poverty and slum formation

patch of surviving Atlantic rainforest, was worse off than even Sierra Leone, the world's poorest country. Figure 3.47 shows the relationship between inequality, poverty and slum formation.

The slum housing problem

It is estimated that substandard housing occupies 70 per cent of São Paulo's area – approximately 1500 km². Two million people – 20 per cent of the population – live in favelas while over half a million people live in converted older homes and even factories in São Paulo's inner core, known as corticos (see above). Often whole families share a single room which may lack electricity and plumbing. Rat and cockroach infestations are common. More than 60 per cent of the population growth in the 1980s is considered to have been absorbed by the favelas.

By the beginning of the twentieth century São Paulo was socially divided between the affluent who lived in the higher central districts and the poor who were concentrated on the floodplains and along the railways. The rapid acceleration of urbanisation between 1930 and 1980 built on the existing pattern of segregation. However, by the late 1970s this pattern was beginning to change, with growing numbers of poor migrants spreading into virtually all areas of the city. The 'lost decade' of the 1980s witnessed the rapid development of shanty towns (favelas) at the urban periphery, and inner-city slum tenements (corticos). Until the early 1980s, the cortico was the dominant form of slum housing when the favela broke out of its traditional urban periphery confines and spread throughout the city to become the new dominant type of slum. This happened as the newly arrived urban poor sought out every empty or unprotected urban space. It is estimated that favela residents now outnumber those living in corticos by 3:1. The rapid spread of the favelas in the 1980s mixed up the pattern of centre/periphery segregation in São Paulo. However, public authorities constantly removed favelas in the areas valued by the property market. The action of private property owners regaining possession of their land has driven favelas to the poorest, most peripheral and hazardous areas (floodplains, hill slopes etc.). Few favelas remain in well-served regions, although the largest two, Heliopolis and Paraisopolis, are located in these areas.

Heliopolis is São Paulo's largest slum. Established about 40 years ago heliopolis means 'city of the sun' in Greek. People first came to this location to play football but later they began

to build shacks and the favela was established. One hundred thousand people live here in a mix of absolute and semi-poverty. Access to facilities is very limited. For example, there is one library with about 300 books for the whole community. In Paraisopolis almost 43 000 people are crammed into an area of 150 ha near the CBD and elite residential areas.

The location of favelas

The location of squatter settlements is strongly linked to the city's physical and environmental situation. A large number are found in municipal and privately-owned areas:
- near gullies
- on floodplains
- on river banks
- along railways
- beside main roads
- adjacent to industrial areas.

These are areas that have often been avoided in the past by the formal building sector because of building difficulties and hazards. The nature of favela construction makes them vulnerable to fire, landslide and other hazards (Figure 3.48). In recent years local government has been particularly concerned with:
- uncontrolled occupation close to watersheds in the southern zone (concerns about flooding and water contamination)
- the rapid growth of favelas in another environmental preservation area, the Serra da Cantareira – the concerns here are the destruction of the original Atlantic forest and landslides.

Saturday, December 21, 2002

FIRE DEVASTATES SAO PAULO SHANTYTOWN 8:11:01PM

A fire destroyed great parts of a shantytown in São Paulo, Brazil today, authorities said, leaving one person dead and 1,115 people homeless.

The fire probably started after an explosion in one of the wooden shacks of the Favela Paraguai, a slum in the eastern São Paulo district of Vila Prudent, Lt Eduardo Fernandes from São Paulo's state civil defence told The Associated Press.

The blaze then quickly spread to nearby dwellings also made out of wood and destroyed about 900 slum houses.

Firemen found the body of Manoel Jose de Negeiros, 54, in a burned-down hut when they had managed to extinguish the flames after three hours, Fernandes said.

São Paulo Major Marta Suplicy, visiting the fire site today, said to avoid new fires in slum areas the cash-strapped city needed federal funds to finance housing programmes.

Fires in shantytowns in Brazilian cities are frequent as many of the illegal settlements are made out of makeshift wooden shacks that lack basic safety standards and are prone to gas explosions.

Figure 3.48 News report – fire devastates São Paulo shanty town

Figure 3.49 A favela in central São Paulo

The transformation of favelas

Initially favelas are densely packed informal settlements made of wood, cardboard, corrugated iron and other makeshift materials. Later they are replaced by concrete block constructions. Often only one wall at a time will be built as a family saves up enough money to buy materials for the next wall (Figure 3.49). Then, concrete tiles will replace corrugated iron or other makeshift materials on the roof. The large-scale improvement in favelas is due to residents' expectations of remaining where they are as a result of changes in public policy in the past 30 years, from one of slum removal to one of slum upgrading.

Attempts to tackle the slum housing problem

Over time, a range of attempts have been made to tackle the housing crisis in São Paulo. These include:

- a federal bank (BNH) which funded urban housing projects and low-interest loans to lower and middle-income home buyers
- a state-level cooperatives institute (INCOOP) which helped build housing for state workers such as teachers
- a state-level development company (CODESPAULO) for housing for low-income families and financing of slum upgrading projects
- a collaborative private sector/state company scheme (COHAB) to develop housing for limited-income families
- a municipally managed COHAB for public housing construction, which also funded self-help projects ('mutiroes') to upgrade substandard housing.

During the period 1965–82, over 150 000 housing units were built or upgraded, mostly through COHAB. Since the early 1980s, because of cutbacks at federal and state levels, the public housing burden has fallen more heavily on the municipality. Due to its own financial problems the number of housing units built by the municipality each year since the mid-1980s has averaged fewer than 6000 a year.

The administration of leftist mayor Luiza Erundina (1989–92) tried to speed up public house building. Here the emphasis was on **self-help housing initiatives**, known as 'mutiroes'. The city supplied funding directly to community groups. The latter engaged local families to build new or renovate existing housing. However, the annual house building total only increased to 8000 during this period.

The rise and fall of Projeto Cingapura (The Singapore Project)

This ambitious urban renewal plan, based on the experience of Singapore, is an example of south–south technology and information transfer. The Cingapura Project ran from its inception in 1995 to early in 2001. It was abandoned after it had provided only a modest increase in the available housing stock. At the outset, São Paulo's planners felt that the Singapore model was especially applicable because of the limited availability and high cost of urban land in both cities.

- Most housing blocks were built next to slum housing whose residents were to receive priority.
- Early buildings were low rise, with higher buildings preferred as the project advanced.
- When built, ownership passed to the municipal COHAB which collected rents (R$57.00 per month).
- Each new project was assigned a social worker to oversee the transfer of families from favela to temporary settlements to new housing unit.
- Landscaping and leisure areas were included in the layout of developments.
- A criticism has been that no provision was made for small-scale businesses within the projects.

While there was general encouragement for the initiative, a range of problems resulted in only 14 000 units being constructed as opposed to the 100 000 planned:

- Only a fraction of the proposed funding was made available.
- The unit cost escalated sharply.
- Once buildings were occupied, residents began to identify serious quality of life issues. Living space was widely seen as inadequate.
- Although rents were set modestly they proved beyond the means of many who fell behind with payments.

A new strategy

The election of socialist mayor Marta Suplicy in 2000 marked a change in strategy towards the housing issue:

- The new administration promised to spend R$3 billion on housing during its term in office.
- The 1000 unfinished Cingapura housing units were to be completed.

Santo André, with a current population of 650,000, is part of the São Paulo Metropolitan Area. Santo André has been undergoing a period of transformation, from its industrial past to an expanding tertiary sector. The economic gap between the rich and poor has grown, exacerbated by the slowdown of the Brazilian economy during the 1990s. As a result, living conditions have deteriorated and a number of favelas – areas of extreme poverty – have emerged.

The municipality is promoting an Integrated Programme of Social Inclusion as a strategy to alleviate poverty. The objective of the programme is to establish new ways of formulating and implementing local public policies on social inclusion. Fourteen principal partners, local, national and international, are actively involved in the programme. Four areas were chosen for the pilot phase, selected through a participatory budgeting process, resulting in a total amount of US$5.3 million, which has been invested in the provision of urban infrastructure and services.

The project has seen the improvement of basic services in some of the worst neighbourhoods. Micro-credit facilities have been made available to small-scale entrepreneurs, while health care has been made more accessible through community health agents. Other social programmes have been implemented including literacy campaigns for adults and programmes aimed at street children. Recreational facilities have been made available, serviced plots have been transferred to families and low income families rehoused in apartment buildings. An index has been developed to measure social inclusion and data collection is carried out on a regular basis. One of the most important results has been the engagement of a wide range of actors and the creation of effective communication channels. All activities have taken into account gender participation and mainstreaming. The administration intends to extend the pilot programme to all slum areas in the city, through differentiated slum upgrading projects while strengthening the approach towards regularization of land tenure. In addition, the programme will attend to all families facing situations of extreme economic exclusion through a revised minimum income policy and through the up scaling of existing programmes. Three initiatives from Santo André on Good Governance, Traffic Management and Administrative Reform are featured on the Best Practices database.

The effective reduction of urban poverty and social exclusion in Santo André is based on a number of key principles:

- Well targeted government interventions in the urban sector can foster citizenship and enable people to create more productive urban livelihoods.
- The active participation of the urban poor in decision-making promotes effective formulation and implementation of local action plans.
- The participatory budgeting process, an innovative approach to urban governance and decision-making, provides a real voice for the urban poor in both the allocation and use of municipal and other resources.
- The Municipality of Santo André has shown that while effective leadership needs to be ensured by the local administration it, in turn, needs to devolve decision-making and implementation powers to the community.
- Inter-agency collaboration and effective channels of communication between various actors and stakeholders is critical to successful slum improvement and reduction of poverty and social exclusion.
- Principles of equity, civic engagement and security are key to success.

Source: 'The Challenge of Slums' – global report on human settlement 2003, Earthscan

Figure 3.50 Social inclusion in Santo André

- The new strategy would be designed to obtain maximum impact for minimum cost. The concept of the mutirao (self-help scheme) was resurrected, assisting families in self-construction or upgrading of their own homes.
- The house unit cost of self-help schemes is between R$11 000 and R$15 000 compared with over R$20 000 for housing units in the Cingapura Project.
- A flagship scheme to alleviate poverty in favelas is under way in Santo André (Figure 3.50).

Section 3.4 Activities

1 What is the difference between favelas and corticos?

2 Describe the extent of inequality in São Paulo.

3 Describe the location of São Paulo's favelas shown in Figure 3.46.

4 Explain the links illustrated by Figure 3.47.

5 Describe and explain the types of urban locations where favelas develop.

6 Review the attempts made in São Paulo to tackle the slum housing problem.

Case Study

The provision of infrastructure for a city: Cairo

Cairo, the capital city of Egypt, is situated on the banks of the River Nile (Figure 3.51) about 200 km south of the Mediterranean Sea. It extends along the banks of the Nile for about 30 km. It is the largest city in Africa and one of the most densely populated metropolitan areas in the world. The population has risen rapidly over the last 50 years (Figure 3.52). The average population density is about 30 000 per km^2.

Much of the infrastructure of Cairo is designed for a population of about 2 million people and thus is under considerable strain from the tremendous demands being put on it by a much larger population. Housing is overcrowded and in short supply. Other elements of the urban infrastructure including transport, education, health, water and sewerage are under extreme pressure from the rapidly rising population (Figure 3.53). City planners have tried to improve the situation, but finding sufficient funds for new infrastructure has been a continuing challenge.

Planners generally recognise two types of infrastructure: hard infrastructure and soft infrastructure. The former refers

Figure 3.51 Cairo

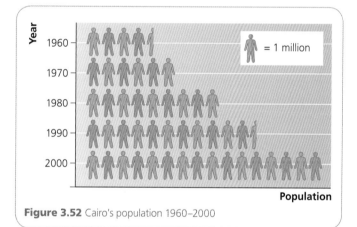

Figure 3.52 Cairo's population 1960–2000

to transportation, communication, sewerage, water and electric systems, while the term soft infrastructure covers housing, education, health, leisure and other associated facilities. Both are vital to a city's economy and the quality of life of its residents.

Transport

Transportation in Cairo comprises an extensive road network, rail system, subway system, and maritime services. Road transport is facilitated by personal vehicles, taxi cabs, privately owned public buses, and Cairo microbuses.

Road transport has required a high level of investment as the city has expanded in land area and population. Seven bridges now span the River Nile. Downtown expressways and lesser flyovers bypass congested areas and new roads knit outlying suburbs into the urban fabric. A 100 km ring-road expressway was completed in the 1990s. It surrounds the outskirts of the city, with exits that reach outer Cairo districts. Many argue that the new road system has been essential, but critics say that new roads simply generate more traffic. A 2007 survey of traffic congestion in Middle East cities placed Cairo as the second most congested city after Dubai, with a total daily commute time of 1 hour and 33 minutes on average.

Cairo's metro, currently the only one in Africa, ranks among the fifteen busiest in the world, with over 700 million passenger rides annually and an average of about 2 million passenger rides a day. The metro underground system (Figure 3.54) was developed in an attempt to decrease the number of vehicles on Cairo's roads. Line 1 was opened in 1987 and Line 2 in the late 1990s. Construction began on Line 3 in late 2000. Three further lines are planned to be constructed by 2022.

On all metro trains, the middle two cars of each train are reserved for women. These cars are used as an option for women who do not wish to ride with men in the same car; however, women can still ride other cars freely. Many informal settlements on the outskirts of Cairo are not adequately served by the public bus network or the metro.

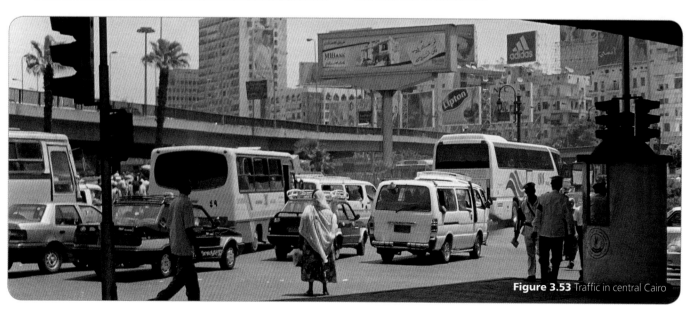

Figure 3.53 Traffic in central Cairo

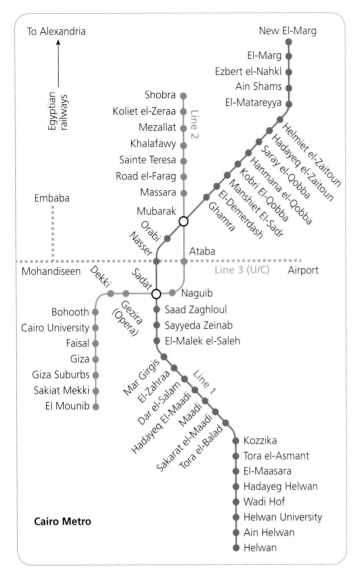

Figure 3.54 Cairo's metro underground system

Cairo's international airport is the second busiest airport in Africa. It has had to expand to keep pace with demand. The airport has three terminals with a third (and largest) opened on 27 April 2009. Terminal 2 was closed in April 2010 for major renovation works to the building's structure and facilities. A third parallel runway is currently under construction and will replace the current crossing runway once it goes into operation in 2010. A new cargo terminal is also under construction. The expansion of Cairo airport has been vital for Cairo's global city status. Cairo is at the Beta+ level according to the GaWC classification of world cities (Table 3.4).

Water supply and sanitation

Water supply and sanitation are arguably the most vital elements in the infrastructure of any city. The Greater Cairo Waste Water project provided a new sewerage system for Greater Cairo covering an urban area of some 700 km². It was designed with the main

objective of removing wastewater from the urban areas of the city and to treat sewage to permit its safe re-use for the irrigation and crop fertilisation of desert areas and the Nile delta. Most of the work was completed in the 1990s. Before the project was completed it was common to see sewage oozing from manholes in some parts of the city. The largest wastewater treatment plant in Egypt is located in Gabal el Asfar to the north-east of Cairo, serving more than 6 million people once its first stage had been completed in 2004. A planned expansion of the plant would increase its capacity to 2.5 million m³/day, serving 12 million people.

In spite of considerable improvements in recent decades, connections to the public sanitation network are missing from entire areas, such as Batn El Ba'ara and Establ Antar.

Water supply continues to be a problem in a 'water scarce' country. Surface waters from the Nile River are the major source of bulk water supply in Cairo. However, its distribution system is inadequate. According to the government's National Research Centre, 40 per cent of Cairo's inhabitants do not get water for more than three hours per day, and three large districts do not receive any piped water. The lowest-income groups in informal settlements on the periphery remain unserved by existing water and wastewater systems. Very significant new investment will be required to improve this situation.

Housing

Three of the world's 30 largest slums are in Cairo. In total there are about 8 million slum dwellers in Greater Cairo. The poor find shelter in old graveyard tombs, mushrooming multistorey informal settlements, subdivided tenements, crumbling grand houses, new government peri-urban apartment blocks, substandard inner city houses and boarding houses. Significant numbers of people live on the rubbish tips, eking out a living from what they can find. According to the Greater Cairo Slums Survey (2004), the majority of households (51 per cent) in slums rent their dwellings and electricity is available to 99 per cent of slum households.

With an estimated 1 million people, the huge Manshiet Nasser slum sits on the rocks where the Eastern Desert plateau meets the Nile valley. The Egyptian government has been reluctant to recognise this illegal squatter settlement since it sprang up about 30 years ago, by providing basic services.

The City of the Dead is located between the old city of Cairo and the eastern desert (Figure 3.55). This is a vast cemetery which has been the burial place of Cairo for more than a millennium. Many of the tombs of the more affluent were placed in buildings which homeless people have occupied due to the severe shortage of housing in Cairo. The City of the Dead is now home to a large population. It is lacking in services for obvious reasons, but people have even rigged up their own electrical supplies to many of the tombs for lighting.

New urban initiatives, such as the ten new cities on the periphery of Cairo, were designed to decentralise population and relieve the burden of in-migration, but the scheme has had only limited success. A UN report published in 2010 noted that although the new cities established near Cairo reduced the deficit in housing in Cairo, 'they did little to improve living conditions (and) access to

183

Figure 3.55 The City of the Dead

services, as these cities lack employment opportunities and public transport facilities available in the centre of the city'.

The housing problem remains immense. Many analysts point to poor management and lack of visionary planning as the central problem.

Pollution infrastructure

Cairo suffers from high levels of air, noise and land-based pollution. The city is attempting to set up infrastructural facilities with the aim of reducing the impact of the pollution problem:

- In 1998, 36 monitoring stations were established to measure concentrations of sulphur and nitrogen dioxides, carbon monoxide, ozone and particulate matter.
- In 2004, the city acquired 70 rice-straw presses in order to reduce pollution caused by straw burning.
- In an attempt to reduce harmful vehicle emissions more inspection stations have been opened, along with an on-road testing (ORT) programme.
- Older buses are gradually being replaced by newer models with low-emission natural gas engines.
- The Environmental Affairs Authority is mapping noise pollution. This will help plan the location of future infrastructure such as roads, bridges, hospitals, schools and residential areas.
- In 2002 the Greater Cairo clean-up campaign began.

Recent infrastructure developments

- The General Organization of Physical Planning (GOPP) has received a grant from the Japan Poverty and Human Resources Development Fund for the preparation of the Heliopolis–New Cairo Tram project. The first stage is the preparation of the Environmental and Social Impact Assessment (ESIA). The Heliopolis–New Cairo tram project intends to upgrade the link from the Stadium station to Nasr City station and extend it to reach and serve New Cairo, with a total length of around 29 km in the first phase of the project.
- Egypt's first public/private partnership was formed in 2009 to provide a wastewater treatment facility that will improve sanitation services in New Cairo, a satellite city on the outskirts of Cairo. New Cairo's current population is 550 000, but this is expected to increase to 3 million by 2029.

Section 3.4 Activities

1 With reference to an atlas and Figure 3.51, describe the location of Cairo.

2 Describe and explain the growth of Cairo's population since 1960.

3 Distinguish between *hard infrastructure* and *soft infrastructure*.

4 a Describe the main elements of Cairo's transport infrastructure.

   b Why is transportation so important to the successful development of a city?

5 Why is significant investment in water supply and sanitation vital in a large city?

6 Comment on the slum housing problem in Cairo.

Inner London: the inner city of an MEDC

You have learned something about London in general and inner London in particular in previous sections. This case study builds on that information. Although small parts of inner London have always been affluent and the process of gentrification has significantly upgraded many other areas, there remains a considerable gap in the **quality of life** between inner and outer London (Figure 3.58) with high levels of deprivation in the former. Recently the population of inner London has increased (reurbanisation) after a long period of decline (Figure 3.56). The population peaked at 5 million in 1900 but then steadily dropped to a low of 2.5 million in 1983. This substantial fall was due largely to declining employment opportunities as manufacturing industries closed (deindustrialisation) and a fall in the number of jobs in the service sector as population fell. The more recent change in the population of inner London has had a significant impact on population structure (Figure 3.57) with a considerable increase in the young adult age groups.

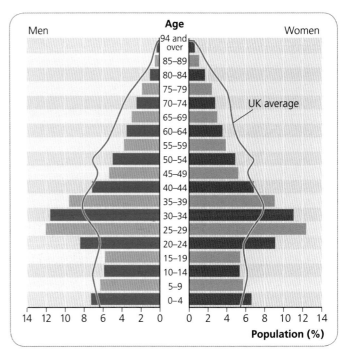

Figure 3.57 Population structure of inner London compared with the UK average

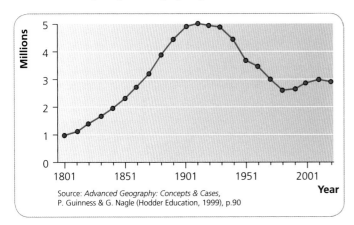

Figure 3.56 Population change in inner London

Source: *Advanced Geography: Concepts & Cases*, P. Guinness & G. Nagle (Hodder Education, 1999), p.90

Characteristics of inner London

- Half of all adults are single compared with 30 per cent across England as a whole.
- Fewer than one-third are married or remarried compared with 51 per cent in England.
- Forty-eight per cent of the population of inner London are aged between 20 and 44 compared with the national average of 35 per cent.
- Only 28 per cent of inner London's population are aged 45 years and over compared with 40 per cent for England.
- In inner London over half of workers travel to work by public transport and less than a quarter by motor vehicle.
- At 38 per cent, inner London has the lowest proportion of owner-occupiers in England. The national average is 68 per cent.

- In inner London 38 per cent of households are renting from a social landlord (local authority or housing association) and 22 per cent from a private landlord. The averages across England are 19 per cent and 12 per cent respectively.

The National Index of Multiple Deprivation 2004: the position of inner London

The 2004 Index of Multiple Deprivation (IMD 2004) measured **deprivation** for every local authority (council) area in England. There is a total of 354 local authorities in England.

The IMD 2004 includes six district measures of deprivation as follows:

- The average scores and average ranks measures are two ways of depicting the average level of deprivation across the entire district.
- The extent measure is the proportion of a district's population that lives in the most deprived SOAs in England (a Super Output Area is a geographical area designed for the collection and publication of small-area census statistics).
- The local concentration measure shows the severity of multiple deprivation in each local authority, measuring 'hot spots' of deprivation.
- The income scale and employment scale measures show the number of people experiencing income and employment deprivation respectively.

In the 50 most deprived districts (local authority areas), London boroughs were placed in the following positions (a rank of 1 equates to the most deprived borough in the country under each measure):

Figure 3.58 London: Index of Multiple Deprivation

- *Average score*: Tower Hamlets (4), Hackney (5), Newham (11), Camden (19), Lambeth (23), Westminster (39), Greenwich (41), Barking and Dagenham (42), Waltham Forest (47).
- *Average rank*: Hackney (1), Tower Hamlets (2), Newham (6), Lambeth (13), Westminster (33), Lewisham (38), Hammersmith (42).
- *Extent*: Hackney (1), Tower Hamlets (2), Newham (6), Haringey (10), Southwark (13), Camden (21), Lambeth (22), Greenwich (41).
- *Local concentration*: Westminster (19), Tower Hamlets (22), Haringey (46), Hackney (47).
- *Income scale*: Newham (7), Tower Hamlets (8), Hackney (9), Lambeth (15), Haringey (17), Southwark (18), Brent (22), Lewisham (23), Ealing (27), Enfield (28), Islington (30), Croydon (31), Greenwich (36), Waltham Forest (37), Camden (43), Barnet (47).
- *Employment scale*: Lambeth (21), Newham (24), Hackney (26), Haringey (32), Tower Hamlets (34), Islington (38), Brent (39), Ealing (42), Camden (47), Croydon (50).

Overall, inner London boroughs appear 41 times in the 50 most deprived districts list over the six measures. This contrasts with 13 times for the outer London boroughs. Figure 3.58 shows the extent of multiple deprivation in London.

Figure 3.59 Deteriorating terraced housing in inner London

The inner city problem: a sequence of explanations

The nature of and linkage between London's inner city problems is reasonably illustrated by the web of decline, deprivation and despair (Figure 3.60). Over the years a number of different explanations of the inner city problem in London and the UK in general have appeared (Table 3.6). For over two decades after the Second World War, inner city problems were attributed primarily to poor housing and other aspects of the run-down built environment. The solutions were clearance and redevelopment. Every London borough has local authority estates dating from this period.

From the late 1960s to the mid-1970s the focus of attention shifted to issues of social deprivation. Within this broad area three alternative explanations emerged:

- A culture of poverty – families of a certain kind pass on an antisocial lifestyle from one generation to the next. Social norms in certain areas encouraged vandalism, early school-leaving, early marriage, early child-rearing, crime and a general disrespect for authority.
- The cycle of deprivation (Figure 3.61), which was seen as preventing the poor from improving the quality of their lives.
- Institutional malfunctioning characterised by poor links between social and welfare services on the one hand and populations most in need on the other.

From the mid-1970s two additional explanations emerged which focused on the structural (economic) fabric of the inner city:

- Resource maldistribution as a result of the decentralisation of population, industry and commerce to the suburbs and beyond. The massive decline of inner city manufacturing was seen as the most important deprivation factor.

Figure 3.60 Inner city web of decline, deprivation and despair

Source: *British Inner Cities*, by H. Matthews, OUP, 1991

Table 3.6 Different explanations of the inner city problem

Perspective	Perceived problem	Goal	Means
Physical decay	Obsolescence	Better built environment	Physical planning
Culture of poverty	Pathology of deviant groups	Better social adjustment	Social education
Cycle of deprivation	Individual inadequacy	Better families	Social work
Institutional malfunction	Planning failure	Better planning	Coordinated planning
Resource maldistribution	Inequality	Reallocation of resources	Positive discrimination
Structural conflict	Underdevelopment	Redistribution of power	Political change

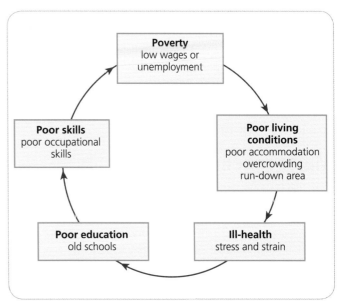

Figure 3.61 The cycle of deprivation

- Structural conflict whereby large companies benefit from keeping the inner city underdeveloped, viewing it as an area providing a pool of expendable, unskilled labour, and cheap land, which can be taken up or abandoned according to fluctuations in the economy. This explanation sees the need for capitalism to be replaced by a socialist system of production.

Although not all local authority housing estates are in inner cities, a significant proportion are (Figure 3.62). Recent studies have confirmed that such estates are increasingly becoming the focal points of deprivation with very high levels of unemployment. Half of all social housing tenants arc now in the poorest fifth of the population and those entering such housing are far poorer than those moving out. This is in effect the spatial marginalisation of those who are already socially marginalised. The processes of reurbanisation and gentrification are likely to accelerate this division. Where gentrification expands the 'international' city, the poor are further pushed out into the worst segment of the housing market.

Figure 3.62 Local authority housing estate in inner London, characterised by deck access

Government responses since the late 1990s have focused on trying to tackle the 'social exclusion' of the poor by targeting health, education, employment and child poverty in particular. The establishment of education, health and employment action zones brought improvements to a number of areas. One health action zone was set up in the Lambeth, Southwark and Lewisham health authority in south London, where the hospitals, social service departments, police and probation services discovered they were all dealing with problems from the same families. In spite of a concerted effort to tackle child poverty, the level in inner London remains particularly high – 48 per cent in 2007 after housing costs were taken into account.

Major regeneration projects

Two regeneration projects in particular merit special attention and they have already been mentioned earlier in this book – the redevelopment of London Docklands and the regeneration of the Lower Lea valley in association with the Olympic Games.

A significant number of redevelopment schemes have been completed along the banks of the River Thames in inner London, mainly involving the replacement of industry with housing. The riverside urban landscape has changed significantly in the last 50 years. Between the 1960s and 1980s there was a reasonable balance between social housing and private residential development, but in more recent decades private housing has dominated with a considerable fall in the amount of social housing being built.

Transport and pollution

London's air quality remains the worst in the UK. Particularly high pollution levels are recorded in large parts of central and inner London. High levels of congestion and pollution have been caused by increasingly high volumes of motor vehicles. Road traffic accounts for 60 per cent of nitrogen oxide emissions and 70 per cent of fine particulate emissions in London.

Many people complain about the inadequacy and relatively high cost of public transport. However, the pre-pay Oyster card scheme has proved very popular and free bus travel for children has benefited poor families in particular. The extension of the Docklands Light Railway and of the Jubilee Underground Line and other public transport improvements have generally been well received.

People on low incomes are much less likely to drive in London than people elsewhere. Among the poorest 10 per cent of Britain's households, car ownership is just 18 per cent in Greater London compared with 25 per cent nationally.

Section 3.4 Activities

1 Describe the changes in inner London's population shown in Figure 3.56.

2 Account for the differences in the population structure between inner London and the UK average.

3 With reference to Figure 3.58 and data supplied in the text, describe and comment on the variations in multiple deprivation in London.

4 Examine the evolution of explanation with regard to inner city problems.

Case Study

China: Strategies for reducing urbanisation

Strategies for reducing urbanisation and urban growth in LEDCs include:

- encouraging fertility decline
- promoting agricultural development in rural areas
- providing incentives to companies to relocate from urban to rural areas
- providing incentives to businesses to develop in rural areas
- developing the infrastructure of rural areas.

All these strategies require significant resources which are usually in short supply in LEDCs.

Restricting rural–urban migration: China's hukou system

For many years the Chinese government followed a relatively restrictive policy towards urbanisation, in part by means of policies that sought to limit rural–urban migration. One explanation for this centres on communist ideology. Another focuses on the interaction of China's development strategy with urbanisation. As the government sought to maximise the pace of industrialisation, limiting urbanisation was seen as having the advantage of reducing the need for large investments in urban housing infrastructure, thus allowing more investment to flow to industry. However, in more recent years, restrictions on migration to urban areas have been gradually eased to satisfy the growing demand for labour in China's rapidly expanding industries (Figures 3.63 and 3.64).

For some time China has had a fear of uncontrolled population movement. Since the Chinese Communist Party came to power in 1949, regulating and controlling migration has been one of China's most consistent development policies. From the 1950s the main instrument used to control rural–urban migration has been the population register system (the *hukou* system) which identified people as either 'urban' or 'rural'. Permission was required to leave the countryside and was only given if potential migrants could produce documentary evidence that they had an urban job to go to. Food rationing was also used to restrict movement from the countryside. Grain and oil rations in the cities were made available only to people in possession of urban household registration documents.

Alongside these measures, the authorities since the 1950s have periodically encouraged large numbers of people to leave the cities, some voluntarily, others very reluctantly. In the 1950s and 1960s significant numbers of people were sent from urban areas to develop oilfields in northern and north-eastern China, and to colonise new land for cereal cultivation. The government was also keen to increase population in the sparsely peopled western provinces in an effort to achieve more balanced regional development and for reasons of national security. In total the main migratory direction in China at this time was from the densely populated central and eastern provinces to the sparsely populated and remote border provincial regions in the northern and western parts of the country. Heilongjiang, Inner Mongolia, Xinjiang, Quinghai and Ningxia in particular received large numbers of migrants.

The 'back to the villages' movement in the early 1960s saw 20 million people leave large cities to return to their rural origins. Alongside this counterstream, large-scale deportations of urban youth to the countryside occurred from the mid-1950s onwards. Between 1969 and 1973 alone an estimated 10 to 15 million urban school-leavers were resettled in rural areas. The twin objectives were to relieve urban pressure and to improve rural productivity. The latter would be achieved by the higher level of education the young urbanites would bring to the countryside. Thus, in contrast to the situation in many LEDCs, in-migration accounted for only about 30 per cent of urban growth in China during the 1950s, 1960s and 1970s.

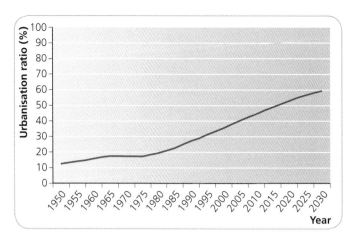

Figure 3.63 Urbanisation in China

Figure 3.64 Tian'anmen Square, Beijing

This unpopular process continued until the late 1970s, after which it was reversed in support of China's industrialisation strategy. Now the emphasis on regional development shifted to the coastal regions to speed up economic development. As a result many coastal regions such as Jiangsu, Zhejiang and Guangdang experienced rapid population and economic growth. The relaxation of controls on rural–urban migration in the 1980s resulted in rapid urbanisation. The huge increase in construction projects attracted many rural migrants but there was huge competition for every job in the formal sector, leaving many disappointed and forced to scratch a living in the informal sector.

Although considerable changes in migration restrictions were introduced in the early 1980s, the household registration system was not dismantled and it continues to provide the framework within which migration takes place. Local authorities in rural areas continue their efforts to limit out-migration while local governments in city destinations have erected barriers in terms of employment discrimination and the 'deportation' of migrants back to their areas of origin. Without urban household registration migrants cannot get access to schooling, healthcare and housing.

Figure 3.65 Expo 2010 Shanghai poster

Figure 3.66 Fujian Province: location, municipalities and principal cities

Source: XZhu, 2004 :217

Balanced development

China's urbanisation strategy emphasises balanced development. Large-scale urbanisation leads to an influx of rural population to the urban areas, putting immense pressure on the large cities. In order to reduce urbanisation's impact on the large cities, China's urbanisation strategy focuses on promoting the development of small and medium-sized cities, ensuring multi-faceted development of regional economies. The objective is that if rural dwellers decide to migrate to an urban area they will look closely at smaller urban areas within their own region as an alternative to longer migrations to the largest cities in China.

In situ urbanisation

The emergence and development of ***in situ* urbanisation** has been one of the major characteristics of urbanisation in China since the 1980s. This process occurs when rural settlements transform themselves into urban or quasi-urban entities with very little movement of population. Over 20 000 small towns in China have developed in this way. The advantages of this process are seen as:

- benefiting significant numbers of the rural population who are often neglected in the development process
- diverting many potential rural–urban migrants who would otherwise head for slum areas in established cities.

On the other hand critics have argued that the process lacks the benefits of agglomeration economies in large cities and has serious negative effects on the environment. However, in terms of the latter, this has to be balanced against the environmental implications of very large cities.

Quanzhou municipality in Fujian Province

In situ urbanisation is well developed in Quanzhou in Fujian Province (Figure 3.66). Significant economic development in recent decades has seen the proportion of workers employed in agriculture fall considerably, yet Quanzhou's urbanisation level measured by conventional criteria is still quite low. According to the 2000 census, Quanzhou's non-agricultural employment was 67.4 per cent, well above the provincial average of 52.2 per cent. In less than 20 years most of Quanzhou's rural residents had completed the transfer from the agricultural to non-agricultural sectors. However, census data also showed that only 38.9 per cent of Quanzhou's population lived in towns and cities, lower than the provincial average of 42.2 per cent. Rather than moving to existing cities, especially large ones, most of Quanzhou's rural dwellers have been absorbed by township and village enterprises (TVEs) located at the bottom level of the settlement hierarchy. TVEs have been the most important factor in Quanzhou's socio-economic development since the reform era, offering local rural dwellers many opportunities of *in situ* development instead of moving to existing cities, especially megacities, as is commonly the case in many other LEDCs.

Quanzhou is not the only place with well-developed TVEs absorbing considerable numbers of rural dwellers into local non-agricultural activities. There is clear evidence of this process elsewhere in Fujian Province and in other provinces in China.

Section 3.4 Activities

1 State three ways in which LEDCs have tried to limit urbanisation.

2 Explain China's *hukou* system.

3 Briefly describe China's policy of balanced development with regard to urbanisation.

4 Describe the process of *in situ* urbanisation.

1 Tropical environments

1.1 Tropical climates

The tropical environment is the area between 23.5°N and 23.5°S (Figure 1.1). This area covers about 50 million km² of land, almost half of it in Africa. According to the climatologist Köppen, there are three types of tropical climate (A). These include rainforest climates (Af), monsoon climates (Am) and savanna climates (Aw). These are shown on Figure 1.1.

Figure 1.1 Tropical climates

191

Air masses

The original concept of an air mass was that it was a body of air whose physical properties, especially temperature and humidity, were uniform over a large area. By contrast, it is now redefined as a large body of air in which the horizontal gradients (variation) of the main physical properties are fairly slack. It is generally applied only to the lower layers of the atmosphere, although air masses can cover areas tens of thousands of km² (Figure 1.2).

Air masses derive their temperature and humidity from the regions over which they lie. These regions are known as source regions. The principal ones are:

- areas of relative calm, such as semi-permanent high pressure areas
- where the surface is relatively uniform, including deserts, oceans and ice-fields.

Air masses can be modified when they leave their sources, as Figure 1.3 illustrates.

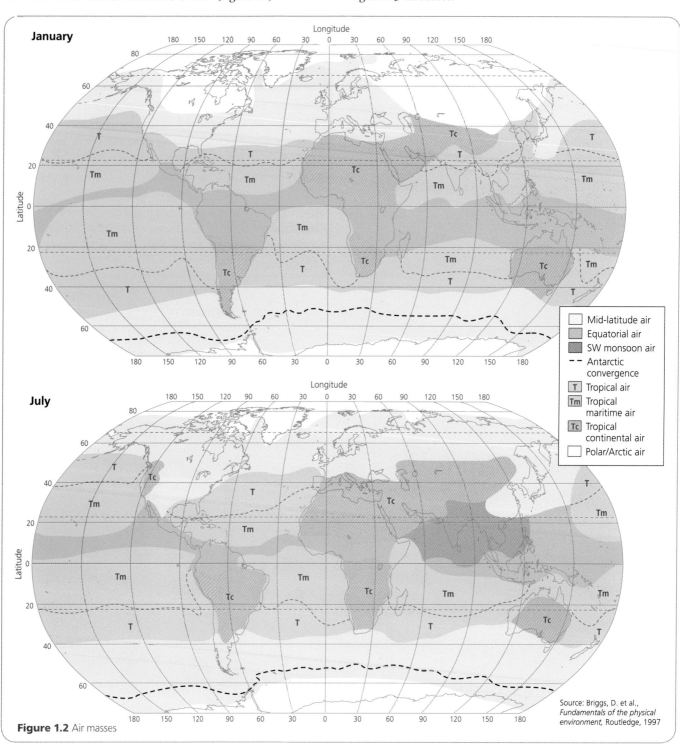

Figure 1.2 Air masses

Source: Briggs, D. et al., *Fundamentals of the physical environment*, Routledge, 1997

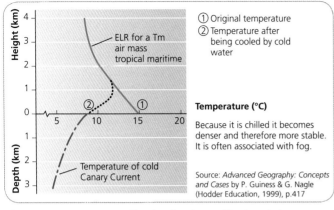

Figure 1.3 Temperature profiles showing the modification of air masses

The initial classification of air masses was made by Tor Bergeron in 1928. Primarily they are classified first by the latitude of the source area (which largely controls its temperature) and secondly by whether the source area is continental (dry) or maritime (moist) (Table 1.1). A maritime tropical (mT) air mass is one that is warm and moist. A third subdivision refers to the stability of the air mass – that is, whether it has cooled and become more stable, or whether it has become warmer and less stable (Figure 1.3).

As air masses move from their source regions they may be changed due to:
- internal changes and
- the effects of the surface over which they move.

These changes create **secondary air masses** (Table 1.1). For example, a warm air mass that travels over a cold surface is cooled and becomes more stable. Hence it may form low cloud or fog but is unlikely to produce much rain. By contrast, a cold air mass that passes over a warm surface is warmed and becomes less stable. The rising air is likely to produce more rain. Air masses that have been warmed are given the suffix 'w' and those that have been cooled are given the suffix 'k' (*kalt*).

Table 1.1 Dominant air masses in tropical environments

Approx. latitude of source	Label	Temp. (°C) winter/ summer	Stability winter/summer
Equatorial (0–10°)	cE (continental equatorial)	25/25	Moist/neutral
	mE (maritime equatorial)	25/25	Moist/neutral
Subtropical (30°)	cT (continental tropical)	15/25	Stable, dry/neutral
			Stable/stable
	mT (maritime tropical)	18/22	

Section 1.1 Activities

1 Define the term *air mass*.

2 Outline the main characteristics of mE and cT air masses.

3 Compare the seasonal distribution of tropical air masses as shown in Figure 1.2.

Intertropical convergence zone (ITCZ)

Winds between the tropics converge on a line known as the ITCZ or equatorial trough. It is actually a band a few hundred kilometres wide, enclosing places where wind flows are inwards and subsequently rise convectively (Figure 1.4).

| ITCZ | Intertropical Convergence Zone | ZAB | Zaïre Air Boundary | SPCZ | South Pacific Convergence Zone |
| H | Centre of high pressure | | | | |

Source: Linacre, E. and Geerts, B., *Climates and Weather Explained*, Routledge, 1997

Figure 1.4 ITCZ and surface winds

The ITCZ lies at about 5°N on average. This is known as the meteorological equator. It wanders seasonally, lagging about two months behind the change in the overhead Sun. The latitudinal variation is most pronounced over the Indian Ocean because of the large Asian continental land mass to the north. Over the eastern Atlantic and eastern Pacific Oceans the ITCZ move seasonally due to the cold Benguela and Peru ocean currents.

The movement of the ITCZ over South Africa, for example, is complicated by the land's shape, elevation and location. There is a southerly spur of the ITCZ known as the Zaire Air Boundary (ZAB) (Figure 1.4). The largest and most prominent spur in the South Pacific is the South Pacific Convergence Zone (SPCZ), which is related to the 'warm pool' near Papua New Guinea, and is most pronounced in summer. It lies mostly over water. There is a convergence of:
- moist northerlies from the semi-permanent high pressure in the south-east Pacific, and
- south-easterlies from mobile highs moving across the south-west Pacific in summer.

Winds at the ITCZ are commonly light or non-existent, creating calm conditions called the doldrums. There are, though, occasional bursts of strong westerlies, known as a westerly wind burst.

Subtropical high pressure

Centres or ridges of high pressure imply subsiding air and a relatively cold atmosphere. They tend to be found over continents, especially in winter. There is a high-pressure belt over south-east Australia in winter, whereas high pressure is located south of the continent in summer, when the sea is colder (Figure 1.5).

The subtropical high or warm anticyclone is caused by cold air descending at the tropopause. Two rings of high pressure lie

around 30–35° north and south. The position of the high pressure coincides with the subsiding part of the Hadley cell, so it alters in response to the seasonal drift of the ITCZ, but only over 5–10°. On average, highs cross the east coast of Australia south of Sydney in summer, whereas in winter they pass further north.

The subtropical high-pressure belt tends to lie over the ocean, especially in summer, when there are low pressures over the continents caused by heating. One subtropical high is anchored over the eastern Pacific by an anticyclonic swirl induced by the Andes. The high there shifts from 32° in January to 23° in July. The high is particularly strong due to the cold ocean surface, except during El Niño events. Another semi-permanent high lies over the Indian Ocean, moving nearer to Australia in summer and Africa in winter.

Highs tend to be larger than low pressure systems, reaching up to 4000 km in width and 2000 km north–south. Therefore smaller pressure gradients are involved and so winds are lighter.

The subtropical high-pressure belt is intersected by cold fronts. The subtropical high pressure areas generally move eastwards at speeds of 30–50 km/hr – hence a 4000 km system moving at an average of 40 km/hr would take about 4 days to pass over – if it keeps moving.

An anticyclone's movement may sometimes stall, and it may travel a distance equivalent to less than 20° latitude in a week. This is known as a blocking anticyclone, or blocking high. It is not so common in the southern hemisphere because there are fewer land masses and mountain ranges to disturb the air flow.

Effects

Highs at the surface are associated with subsidence. A temperature inversion may occur, especially where there is a cold high in winter over a continent. Where there is moisture at low level and air pollution, low-level stratus clouds may form causing an anticyclonic gloom, as found in Santiago and Melbourne in winter, for example.

Arid climates result from a prevalence of high pressure. North East Brazil is arid, even at a latitude of 8°S, because it protrudes far enough into the South Atlantic to be dominated by high pressure. The same is true for the Galapagos Islands, dominated by the South Pacific High, even though they are located at the equator.

January

July

The continuous lines and shaded areas show the number of hours in a month when high pressure is centred over an area. The dotted lines show the number of hours that a centre of low pressure is positioned over a location. The shaded areas have high pressure centred there for at least 24 hours per month

Figure 1.5 Seasonal high pressure over Australia

> ### Section 1.1 Activities
>
> **1** Outline the main cause of the subtropical high-pressure belt.
>
> **2** Explain why it varies seasonally.
>
> **3** Describe the seasonal changes that occur to the ITCZ and wind patterns, as shown in Figure 1.4.

Ocean currents

The oceanic gyre (swirl of currents) explains why east coasts are usually warm and wet, because warm currents carry water polewards and raise the air temperature of maritime areas. In contrast, cold currents carry water towards the equator and so lower the temperatures of coastal areas. West coasts tend to be cool and dry due to:

- the advection of cold water from the poles and
- cold upwelling currents.

For instance, in South Africa the east coast is 3–8 °C warmer than the west coast. An exception is Australia where the southward Leeuwin Current brings warmth to Perth. Continental east coasts in the subtropics are humid and west coasts arid – this is mainly due to the easterly winds around the tropics.

Table 1.2 shows the mean monthly temperatures and rainfall of some coastal cities on the west and east sides of three continents.

Table 1.2 A comparison of mean monthly temperatures (°C) and rainfall of some coastal cities

Continent	Coast	Place	Temperature (°C)		Rainfall (mm)	
			January	July	January	July
Around 23°S						
South America	West	Antofagasta	21	14	0	5
	East	Rio de Janeiro	26	21	125	41
South Africa	West	Walvis Bay	19	15	0	0
	East	Maputo	25	18	130	13
Australia	West	Carnarvon	27	17	20	46
	East	Brisbane	25	15	163	56
Around 34°S						
South America	West	Santiago	21	9	3	76
	East	Buenos Aires	23	10	79	56
South Africa	West	Cape Town	21	12	79	56
	East	Durban	24	17	127	85
Australia	West	Perth	23	13	8	170
	East	Sydney	22	12	89	117

Section 1.1 Activities

Using examples, compare the temperatures of west coast locations with those of east coast locations for the same latitude.

How do you explain this pattern?

Wind

The temperature of the wind is determined by the area where the wind originates and by the characteristics of the surface over which it subsequently blows. A wind blowing from the sea tends to be warmer in winter, but cooler in summer, than the corresponding wind blowing from the land.

Monsoon

The word *monsoon* is used to describe wind patterns that experience a pronounced seasonal reversal. The most well-known monsoon is that experienced in India, but there are also monsoons in East Africa, Arabia, Australia and China. The basic cause is the difference in heating of land and sea on a continental scale.

In India two main seasons can be observed:

- the north-east monsoon (Figure 1.6a) consisting of (a) the winter season (January and February) and (b) a hot dry season between March and May
- the south-west monsoon (Figure 1.6b), consisting of (a) the rainy season of June–September and (b) the post-monsoon season of October–December. Most of India's rain falls during the south-west monsoon.

During the winter season winds generally blow outwards since high pressure is centred over the land. Nevertheless, parts of southern India and Sri Lanka receive some rain, while parts of north-west India receive rainfall as a result of depressions. These winter rains are important as they allow the growth of cereals during the winter. Mean temperatures in winter range from 26 °C in Sri Lanka to about 10 °C in the Punjab (these differences are largely the result of latitude). Northern regions and interior areas have a much larger temperature range than in coastal areas. In the north, daytime temperatures may reach over 26 °C, while frosts at night are common.

The hot dry season occurs between March and May. It gradually spreads northwards throughout India. Daytime temperatures in the north may exceed 49 °C while coastal areas remain hot and humid. Vegetation growth is prevented by these conditions and many rivers dry up.

In spring, the high pressure system over India is gradually replaced by a low pressure system. As there is low pressure over the equator, there is little regional air circulation. However, there are many storms and dust storms. Increased humidity near the coast leads to rain. Parts of Sri Lanka, the southern part of India and the Bay of Bengal receive rain and this allows the growth of rice and tea. For most of India, however, there is continued drought.

The rainy season occurs as the low pressure system intensifies. Once pressure is low enough it allows for air from the equatorial low and the southern hemisphere to be sucked in, bringing moist air. As it passes over the ocean it picks up more moisture and causes heavy rain when it passes over India.

The south-west monsoon in southern India generally occurs in early June, and by the end of the month it affects most of the country, reaching its peak in July or early August (Figure 1.7). Rainfall is varied, especially between windward and leeward sites. Ironically, the low-pressure system over north west India is one of the driest parts of India, as the monsoon has shed its moisture en route. The monsoon weakens after mid-September but its retreat is slow and may take up to three months. Temperature and rainfall fall gradually, although the Bay of Bengal and Sri Lanka still receive some rainfall.

The most simple explanation for the monsoon is that it is a giant land–sea breeze. The great heating of the Asian continent

Figure 1.6 The Asian monsoon

Source: *Access to Geography: Climate and Society* by G. Nagle (Hodder Education, 2002), p.43

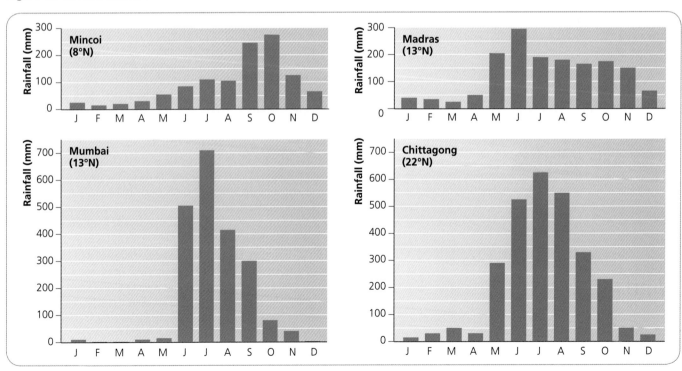

Figure 1.7 Rainfall in selected Indian stations

and the high mountain barrier of the Himalayas, barring winds from the north, allow the equatorial rain systems to move as far north as 30°N in summer. At this time central Asia becomes very hot, warm air rises and a centre of low pressure develops. The air over the Indian Ocean and Australia is colder, and therefore denser, and sets up an area of high pressure. As air moves from high pressure to low pressure, air is drawn into Asia from over the oceans. This moist air is responsible for the large amount of rainfall that occurs in the summer months. In the winter months the sun is overhead in the southern hemisphere. Australia is heated (forming an area of low pressure), whereas the intense cold over central Asia and Tibet causes high pressure. Thus in winter air flows outwards from Asia, bringing moist conditions to Australia. The mechanism described here, a giant land–sea breeze is, however, only part of the explanation.

Between December and February the north-east monsoon blows air outwards from Asia. The upper airflow is westerly, and this flow splits into two branches north and south of the Tibetan plateau. The Tibetan plateau – over 4000 m in height – is a major source of cold air in winter, especially when it is covered in snow. Air sinking down from the plateau, or sinking beneath the upper westerly winds, generally produces cold, dry winds. During March and April the upper airflows change and begin to push further north (in association with changes in the position of the overhead Sun). The more northerly jet stream (upper wind) intensifies and extends across India and China to Japan, while the southern branch of the jet stream remains south of Tibet and loses strength.

There are corresponding changes in the weather. Northern India is hot and dry with squally winds, while southern India may receive some rain from warm, humid air coming in over the ocean. The southern branch of the jet stream generally breaks down around the end of May, and then shifts north over the Tibetan plateau. It is only when the southern jet stream has reached its summer position, over the Tibetan plateau, that the south-west monsoon arrives. By mid-July the monsoon accounts for over three-quarters of India's rainfall. The temporal and spatial pattern is varied: parts of the north-west attract little rainfall, whereas the Bay of Bengal and the Ganges receive large amounts of summer rainfall. The monsoon rains are highly variable each year, and droughts are not uncommon in India. In autumn, the overhead Sun migrates southwards, as too does the zone of maximum insolation and convection. This leads to a withdrawal of the monsoon winds and rain from the region.

Section 1.1 Activities

1 Describe the seasonal variations in the monsoon, as shown in Figure 1.6.
2 Account for the variations in rainfall as shown in Figure 1.7.
3 Briefly explain the formation of the Asian monsoon.

Case Study

Pakistan's floods, August 2010

The heaviest monsoon rain to affect Pakistan for 80 years destroyed the homes of over 140 000 people, killing an estimated 1600, leaving 2 million homeless and affecting over 20 million people (Figure 1.8). Cases of the deadly disease cholera were reported following the flood.

Figure 1.8 Flooding in Pakistan, 2010. Image a was taken on 15 August 2010, while image b shows the same area a year previously. The blue patches show the extent of the flooding, which left 20 million people homeless.

The heavy rainfall, which was many times the usual expected during the monsoon and fell farther north and west than usual, exposed the lack of investment in water infrastructure, including big dams, much of which was built in the 1960s. Over 270 mm of rain fell in Peshawar in one 24-hour period. The removal of forest cover may also have allowed rainwater to drain faster into the rivers. Further flooding in mid-August prevented vital repairs of embankments, allowing water to reach previously unaffected areas. The floods were the worst since at least 1929. Water levels in the River Indus, which flows through the middle of Pakistan and has most of the population huddled around it, were said to be the highest in 110 years. For example, between 27 and 30 July, 373 mm of rain fell at Murree, 394 mm at Islamabad and 415 mm at Risalpur. Discharge at Guddu peaked at 1.18 million cusecs compared with a normal discharge of 327 000 cusecs.

One of the hardest-hit areas was the scenic Swat valley, further north, where the population was only just recovering from the Taliban takeover and a military operation in the previous year to drive out insurgents. One factor that may have contributed to the extreme flooding in Swat is the deforestation that accompanied the Taliban takeover. When the landowners fled after being targeted by the Taliban, the timber smugglers joined up with the insurgents to chop down as many trees as possible.

Agriculture was badly affected, causing spiralling food prices and shortages. Floods submerged 69 000 km² of Pakistan's most fertile crop area. The World Bank estimated that crops worth $1 billion (£640 million) were ruined and that the disaster would cut the country's growth in half. More than 200 000 animals also died.

Many roads, bridges and irrigation canals were destroyed, along with the electricity supply infrastructure. Also affected was Mohenjo-Daro, one of the largest settlements of the ancient Indus valley, built around 2500BC.

The government may have to spend $1.7 billion on reconstruction, and has said it will have to divert expenditure from other badly needed development programmes.

UN aid agencies and their partners requested almost $460 million (£295 million) to help Pakistan. Ten days after the start of the floods just $157 million had been pledged. Based on the estimate of 14 million people affected, the UN said this meant only $4.11 had been committed for each affected person. After the Kashmir earthquake in 2005, which left 2.8 million people needing shelter, $247 million was committed in the first ten days – $70 per person. Ten days after the Haiti earthquake, $495 had been committed for each person affected. Following criticism from the UN, Saudi Arabia pledged $100 million to the Pakistan flood appeal.

Section 1.1 Activities

Study Figure 1.8 showing the Indus valley before and during the 2010 floods. Compare the river during flood with that of normal flow.

World climates: a classification

The most widely used classification of climate is that of W. Köppen (Figure 1.9). His classification first appeared in 1900 and he made many modifications to it, before his death in 1936. Although it has been refined since, the current version bears many resemblances to its early patterns.

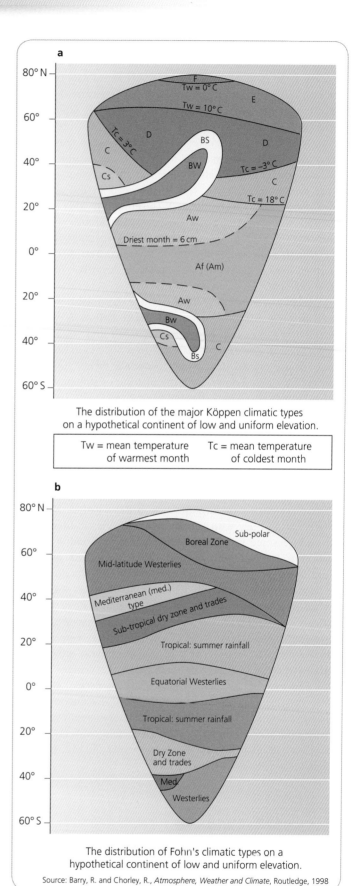

The distribution of the major Köppen climatic types on a hypothetical continent of low and uniform elevation.

Tw = mean temperature of warmest month	Tc = mean temperature of coldest month

The distribution of Fohn's climatic types on a hypothetical continent of low and uniform elevation.

Source: Barry, R. and Chorley, R., *Atmosphere, Weather and Climate*, Routledge, 1998

Figure 1.9 Köppen's climate classification

Köppen classified climate with respect to two main criteria: temperature and seasonality of rainfall. Indeed, five of the six main climatic types are based on mean monthly temperature:

A Tropical rainy climate – coldest month >18 °C

B Dry (desert)

C Warm temperate rainy climate – coldest month −3 °C to 18 °C; warmest month >10 °C

D Cold boreal forest climate – coldest month ≤−3 °C; warmest month ≥10 °C

E Tundra – warmest month 0–10 °C

F Perpetual forest climate – warmest month <0 °C.

The choice of the specific figures is as follows: 18 °C is the critical winter temperature for tropical forests; 10 °C is the poleward limit of forest growth; −3 °C is generally associated with 2–3 weeks of snow annually.

There are subdivisions that relate to rainfall:

f – no dry season

m – monsoonal (short dry season and heavy rains in the rest of the year)

s – summer dry season

w – winter dry season

Tropical humid climates and seasonally humid climates have a maximum temperature of >20 °C and a minimum monthly temperature of >13 °C. Tropical humid climates have a mean monthly rainfall of over 50 mm for between 8 and 12 months. In contrast, seasonally humid climates have a mean monthly rainfall of over 50 mm for between 1 and 7 months.

Tropical humid climates (Af) are generally located within 5–10° of the equator. Some higher latitudes may receive high levels of rainfall from unstable tropical easterlies. In Af climates the midday sun is always high in the sky – but high humidity and cloud cover keep temperatures from soaring. Some months such as April and October may be wetter due to movements of the ITCZ.

In contrast, seasonally humid climates (Aw) have a dry season, which generally increases with latitude. Rainfall varies from the moist low latitudes to semi-desert margins. As the midday Sun reaches its highest point (zenith), temperatures increase, air pressure falls, and strong convection causes thundery storms. However, as the angle of the noon Sun decreases, the rains gradually cease and drier air is re-established.

A variation of the Aw is the tropical wet monsoon (Am) climate. Winters are dry with high temperatures. They reach a maximum just before the monsoon, and then fall during the cloudy wet period when inflows of tropical maritime air bring high rainfall to windward slopes.

Section 1.1 Activities

1 Describe the main climate characteristics of Jakarta (Af) and Kolkata (Am), as shown on Figure 1.1.

2 How do you account for the differences between them?

Case Study

The climate of Brunei Darussalam

The climate of Brunei is influenced by its location on the north-west coast of Borneo within the equatorial tropics (Figure 1.10), and by the wind systems of South East Asia.

Brunei is located in an area of low pressure at the equator, sandwiched between two areas of high pressure over the subtropics. The low pressure 'trough' at the equator (the ITCZ) is the area where air masses from the northern and southern hemispheres converge. The annual movements of the ITCZ and the associated trade winds produce two main seasons in Brunei, separated by two transitional periods.

Between December and March, the north-east monsoon winds affect the South China Sea and Borneo. The average position of the ITCZ is between the latitudes of 5°S and 10°S, having moved southwards across Borneo and Brunei during late December. From June to September the ITCZ is situated at a latitude of around 15°N to the east of the Philippines but to the west the ITCZ becomes a monsoon trough. The first transitional period occurs in April and May and the second one in October and November.

On a longer time scale (three to seven years) the climate of Brunei is influenced by the El Niño Southern Oscillation (ENSO). The warm episode or El Niño is normally associated with prolonged dry conditions in Brunei Darussalam. In contrast, La Niña episodes are cold and wetter than normal.

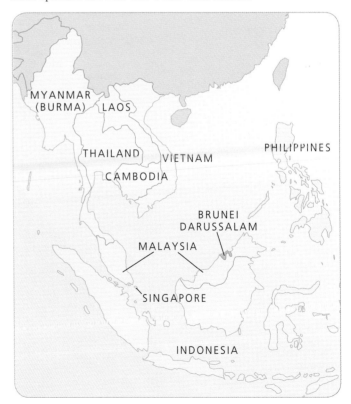

Figure 1.10 Location of Brunei Darussalam

The annual rainfall total exceeds 2300 mm. There are clear seasonal patterns, with two maxima and two minima. The first maximum is from late October to early January with December being the wettest month (Figure 1.11). The second minor maximum is from May to July with May being relatively wetter. This seasonality is a reflection of the two monsoon seasons in conjunction with the related movements of the ITCZ and the influence of the localised land–sea circulations. The lowest minimum occurs from late January to March and the next minor minimum is from June to August. The concept of a dry month or dry season in Brunei is relative!

The orographic effect on rainfall in Brunei is notable, particularly in Temburong District. The stations of Semabat and Selangan in Temburong have mean annual rainfall totals of over 4000 mm compared with stations nearer the coast such as Puni and Bangar with annual means of around 3600 mm. Rainfall in Brunei is characterised by high intensities (measured in mm per hour), with very large amounts falling over sharply delimited areas at short time intervals, in contrast to prolonged rainfalls associated with large-scale systems such as tropical cyclones (Figure 1.12).

The probability of thunderstorms shows that two peaks are evident: the higher peak in April and May from late afternoon to the early hours of the morning, and a secondary peak from September to November, mostly from late afternoon to just around midnight.

The temperature regime is notable for its uniformity, with only small variations both seasonally and in different parts of the country. Higher temperatures are generally recorded during the months of March to September with higher solar heating and less cloudiness and rainfall than in other months. Cold air surges originating from the Siberia/China area during the north-east monsoon season affect Brunei, resulting in lower minimum temperatures.

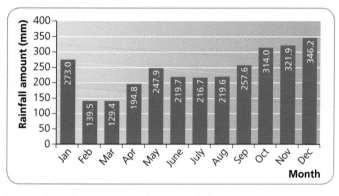

Figure 1.11 Mean monthly rainfall in Brunei, 1966–2006

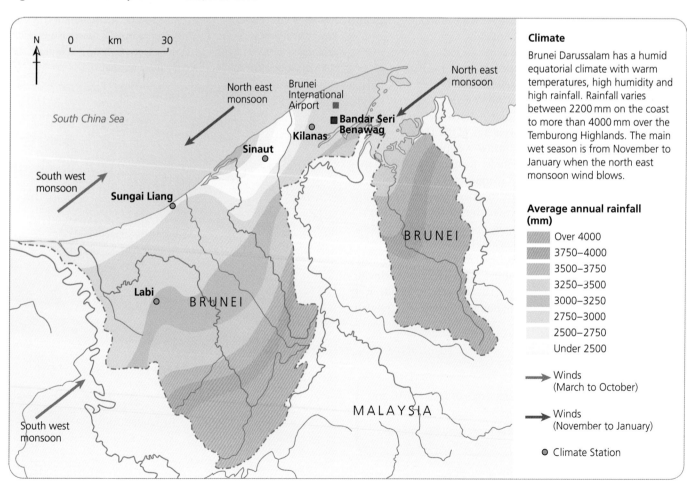

Figure 1.12 Variations of rainfall in Brunei

Section 1.1 Activities

1 Describe and explain the main climate characteristics for Brunei.

2 Describe and suggest reasons for spatial variations in Brunei's climate.

Case Study

The El Niño Southern Oscillation

This case study shows that there are major interruptions to the normal functioning of tropical climates. One such interruption is the El Niño Southern Oscillation (ENSO). El Niño, which means 'the Christ Child', is an irregular occurrence of warm surface water in the Pacific off the coast of South America that affects global wind and rainfall patterns (Figure 1.13). In July 1997 the sea surface temperature in the eastern tropical Pacific was 2.0–2.5 °C above normal, breaking all previous climate records. The El Niño's peak continued into early 1998 before weather conditions returned to normal.

During the 1920s Sir Gilbert Walker identified a characteristic of the Southern Oscillation that consisted of a sequence of surface pressure changes within a regular time period of three to seven years, and was most easily observed in the Pacific Ocean and around Indonesia. When eastern Pacific pressures are high and

Indonesian pressures are low relative to the long-term average, the situation is described as having a high Southern Oscillation Index (SOI). By contrast, when Pacific pressures are low and Indonesian pressures are high the SOI is described as low. In 1972 J.N. Walker identified a cell-like circulation in the tropics that operates from an east to west (interzonal) direction rather than a north–south (meridional) direction. The cell works by convection of air to high altitudes caused by intense heating followed by movement within the subtropical easterly jet stream and its subsequent descent.

El Niño is a phase of the Southern Oscillation when the trade winds are weak and the sea surface temperatures in the equatorial Pacific increase by between 1 and 4 °C. The impacts of the ENSO, which occurs every three to seven years and is the most prominent signal in year-to-year natural climate variability, are felt worldwide. During the 1982–83 ENSO, the most destructive event of the last century, damages amounted to about $13 billion. The event has been blamed for droughts (India, Australia), floods (Ecuador, New Zealand) and fires (West Africa, Brazil). Scientists are capable of forecasting the onset of El Niño up to one year in advance through sea surface temperature signals.

El Niño has been studied since the early 1900s. In 1904 Sir Gilbert Walker investigated annual variability of the monsoon. He discovered a correlation in the patterns of atmospheric pressure at sea level in the tropics, the ocean temperature, and rainfall fluctuations across the Pacific Ocean, which he named the Southern Oscillation. He showed that the primary characteristic of the Southern Oscillation is a seesaw in the atmospheric pressure at sea level between the south-eastern subtropical Pacific and the Indian Ocean. During normal conditions dry air sinks over the cold waters of the eastern tropical Pacific and flows westwards along

Source: Linacre, E. and Geerts, B., *Climates and Weather Explained*, Routledge, 1997

Figure 1.13 El Niño events

the equator as part of the trade winds. The air is moistened as it moves towards the warm waters of the western tropical Pacific. The sea surface temperature gradients between the cold waters along the Peruvian coast and the warm waters in the western tropical Pacific are necessary for the atmospheric gradients that drive circulation.

Climatic anomalies induced by El Niño have been responsible for severe damage worldwide. Among the effects of the 1997–98 El Niño were:

- a stormy winter in California (and the 1982–83 event took 160 lives and caused $2 billion damage in floods and mudslides)
- worsening drought in Australia, Indonesia, the Philippines, southern Africa and north-east Brazil
- drought and floods in China
- increased risk of malaria in South America
- lower rainfall in northern Europe
- higher rainfall in southern Europe.

Perception of the El Niño hazard has developed in a series of stages. Until the 1972–73 event it was perceived as affecting local communities and industries along the eastern Pacific coast near Peru, then between 1972/73 and 1982/83 El Niño was recognised as a cause of natural disasters worldwide. However, since 1982–83, countries have begun to realise that there is a need for national programmes that will use scientific information in policy planning and that an integrated approach from a number of countries is required to reduce the effects of El Niño.

Section 1.2 Activities

1 Describe the climatic processes that occur during El Niño events.

2 What were the possible effects of the 1997–98 El Niño season?

1.2 Tropical ecosystems

An **ecosystem** is the interrelationship between plants, animals, their biotic and abiotic environment. In contrast, **ecology** is the study of organisms in relation to the environment, and **biogeography** is the geographical distribution of ecosystems, where and why they are found.

A **community** is a group of populations (animals and plants) living and interacting with each other in a common habitat (such as a savanna or a tropical rainforest). This contrasts with the term **population**, which refers to just one species, such as a zebra.

The productivity of an ecosystem is how much organic matter is produced per annum. It is normal to refer to **net primary productivity** – that is, the amount of organic material produced

by plants and made available to the herbivores (Table 1.3). Net primary productivity varies widely, and is affected by water availability, heat, nutrient availability, age and health of plant species. In contrast, **biomass** is a measure of stored energy. Forest ecosystems normally have much higher rates of biomass than grassland ecosystems, since much of the energy is stored as woody tissue.

Table 1.3 A comparison of mean net primary productivity and biomass for the world's major biomes

Ecosystem	Mean NPP (kg/m²/yr)	Mean biomass (kg/m²)
Tropical rainforest	2.2	45
Tropical deciduous forest	1.6	35
Tropical scrub	0.37	3
Savanna	0.9	4
Mediterranean sclerophyll	0.5	6
Desert	0.003	0.002
Temperate grassland	0.6	1.6
Temperate forest	1.2	32.5
Boreal forest	0.8	20
Tundra and mountain	0.14	0.6
Open ocean	0.12	0.003
Continental shelf	0.36	0.001
Estuaries	1.5	1

Succession

Succession refers to the spatial and temporal changes in plant communities as they move towards a seral climax (Figure 1.14). Each **sere** or stage is an association or group of species, which alters the micro-environment and allows another group of species to dominate. At the start of succession (pioneer communities), there are few nutrients and limited organic matter. Organisms that can survive are small and biodiversity is low. In late succession, there is more organic matter, higher biodiversity and longer-living organisms (Figure 1.15). Nutrients may be held by organisms, especially trees, so nutrient availability may be low. A well-documented case of succession is that following the eruption of Krakatoa in 1883 (Table 1.4). The **climax community** is the group of species that are at a dynamic equilibrium with the prevailing environmental conditions. On a global scale, climate is the most important factor in determining large ecosystems or **biomes** such as tropical rainforest and temperate woodland (Figure 1.16). In some areas, however, vegetation distribution may be determined by soils rather than by climate. This is known as **edaphic** control. For example, in savanna areas, forests are found on clay soils, whereas grassland occupies sandy soils. On a local scale, within a climatic region, soils may affect plant groupings.

A **plagioclimax** refers to a plant community permanently influenced by human activity. It is prevented from reaching climatic climax by burning, grazing and so on. The maintenance of grasslands through burning is an example of plagioclimax.

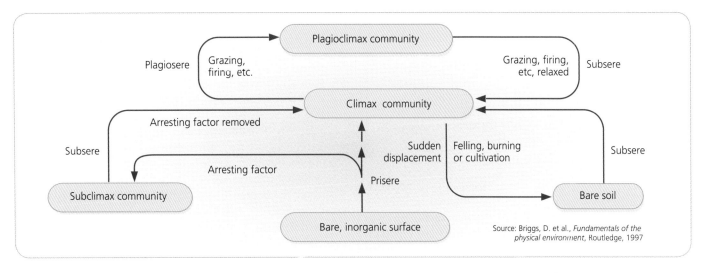

Figure 1.14 A model of succession

Source: Briggs, D. et al., *Fundamentals of the physical environment*, Routledge, 1997

Attribute	Early	Late
Organic matter	Small	Large
Nutrients	External	Internal
Nutrient cycles	Open	Closed
Role of detritus	Small	Large
Diversity	Low	High
Nutrient conservation	Poor	Good
Niches	Wide	Narrow
Size of organisms	Small	Large
life-cycles	Simple	Complex
Growth form	r species	k species
Stability	Poor	Good

Source: Briggs, D. et al., *Fundamentals of the physical environment*, Routledge, 1997

Figure 1.15 Community changes through succession

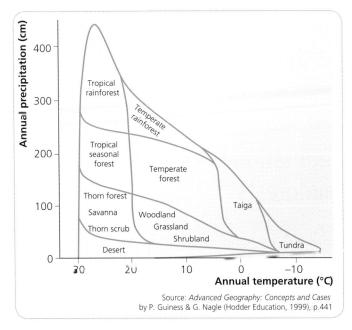

Source: *Advanced Geography: Concepts and Cases* by P. Guiness & G. Nagle (Hodder Education, 1999), p.441

Figure 1.16 The relationship between climate and vegetation

Table 1.4 Primary succession on Krakatoa after the 1883 volcanic eruption

Year	Total number of plant species	Vegetation on the coast	Vegetation on the lower slopes	Vegetation on the upper slopes
1883	Volcanic eruption kills all life on the island			
1884	No life survives			
1886	26	9 species of flowering plant	Ferns and scattered plants; blue-green algae beneath them on the ash surface	Ferns and scattered plants; blue-green algae beneath them on the ash surface
1897	64	Coastal woodland develops	Dense grass	Dense grasses with shrubs interspersed
1908	115	Wider belt of woodland with more species, shrubs and coconut palms	Dense grasses to 3 m high, woodland in the larger gullies	Dense grasses to 3 m high, woodland in the larger gullies
1919			Scattered trees in grassland, single or in groups with shade species beneath; thicket development in large gullies	Scattered trees in grassland, single or in groups with shade species beneath; thicket development in large gullies
1928	214			
1934	271		Mixed woodland largely taken over from savanna	Woodland with smaller trees, fewer species taking over
Early 1950s		Coastal woodland climax	Lowland rainforest climax	Submontane forest climax

Figure 1.17 shows a model of succession in a rainforest. A contemporary example of succession being affected by arresting factors is the rainforest of Chances Peak in Montserrat. In the early 1990s, Chances Peak had some of the finest tropical rainforest in the Caribbean region. It had a high biodiversity of plant life, insects, lizards, birds and bats. By January 1996, surveys indicated that vegetation loss from acid rain, gases, heat and dust on the top of Chances Peak and in the surrounding area was severe. The cloud forest had disappeared. Vegetation was gradually dying further down the mountain. On the east side, the lush forests of the Tar river valley were degraded from ash and gases, and were finally destroyed by lahars (mudflows) (Figure 1.18).

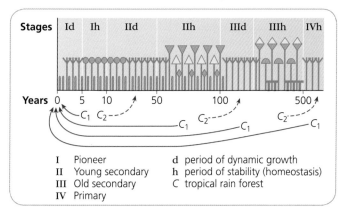

Figure 1.17 A model of succession in a rainforest from bare soil to primary forest

Figure 1.18 The effect of a volcanic eruption: Chances Peak, Montserrat

Volcanoes emit sulphurous gases. On a global scale the amount of sulphur from active volcanoes is minor compared with that from other sources. On a local scale the impacts from volcanic sulphur emissions have important consequences for plant and animal life. Acid rain increases leaching of some nutrients and renders other nutrients unavailable for uptake by plants.

By January 1996 the pH of the lake at the top of Chances Peak was 2.0 (1000 times more acidic than a pH of 5.0). Other lakes and streams measured about 1.5 at the same time.

Continued volcanic activity and erosion prevent reforestation. Sustained recovery will not take place until volcanic activity greatly reduces or stops. Recovery of the forest will start in two ways: seeds in the ground will start to germinate, and new seeds will blow in from surrounding areas. The rate of recovery will depend, in part, on the availability of seeds which in turn depends on the proximity of other forest species, and the availability of animals (for example birds) to disperse seeds. In Montserrat there is currently cloud forest in the Centre Hills and this may act as a source of new seeds for the southern Soufriere Hills close to the volcano. Pioneers will colonise the soil and make it suitable for other forest species. Early pioneer species must be able to tolerate high light intensities and high temperatures (because there is no longer any forest to provide shade). Species such as *Cecropia* are early pioneers: they are light tolerant, and their seeds are dispersed by a variety birds and bats (76 species of birds are known to feed on *Cecropia*). High light levels and high temperatures often stimulate the germination of these seeds. *Heliconia* and some palm species will colonise disturbed areas. Once these pioneer species have established, the shade they create often prevents other members of the same species from germinating and surviving. Thus new shade-tolerant species can now establish themselves. The forest therefore begins to increase in diversity. Studies in Puerto Rico have shown that some forests recover from hurricane destruction in about 40 years.

Vegetation in tropical rainforests

There is a wide variety of ecosystem types in the humid tropics (Figure 1.19). The tropical rainforest is the most diverse ecosystem or biome in the world, yet it is also the most fragile. This stems from the fact that conditions of temperature and humidity are so constant that species here specialise to a great extent. Their food sources are limited to only a few species. Thus when this biome is subjected to stress by human activity it often fails to return to its original state.

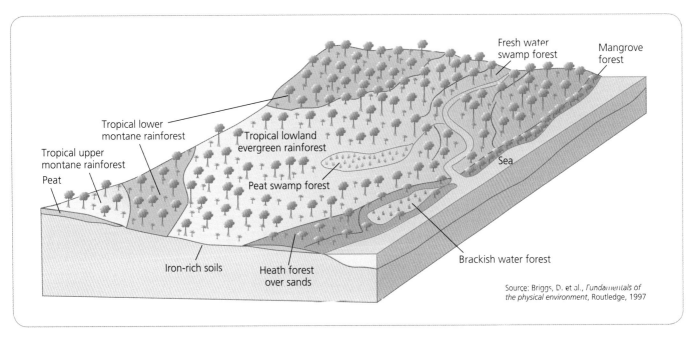

Figure 1.19 Tropical rainforest types

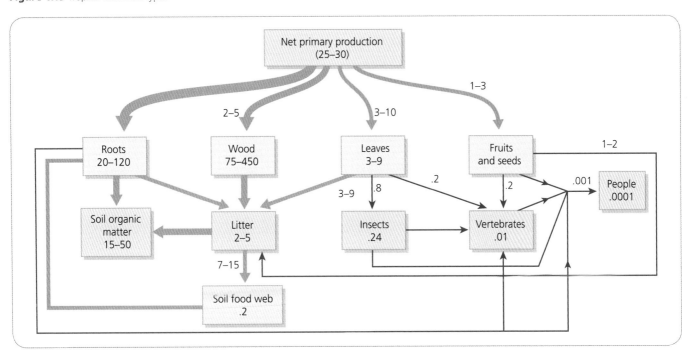

Figure 1.20 Energy flows in tropical rainforest

The net primary productivity (NPP) of this ecosystem is 2200 g/m²/yr. This means that the solar energy fixed by the green plants gives 2200 g of living matter per m² every year (Figure 1.20). This compares with the NPP for savanna of 900 g/m²/yr, temperate deciduous forests of 1200 g/m²/yr and agricultural land of 650 g/m²/yr. Figure 1.20 shows the pattern of production and consumption in a typical undisturbed area of tropical rainforest. Only a minute amount passes through animals (and even less through hunter-gatherers). Most of the plant material falls to the forest floor to become litter. Although the forest contains many animals it does not contain a large biomass of animals, in part because much of the plant material is inedible. The woody parts of plants are indigestible to animals. Leaves, fruits and seeds are digestible, but may contain chemicals that are poisonous to animals. Consequently, many animals specialise on particular plant species, upon which they feed successfully despite their toxicity. Many plants counter this with synchronised fruiting, sometimes as infrequent as once per decade, so that most of the time there is little food to support the animals that specialise in feeding on them.

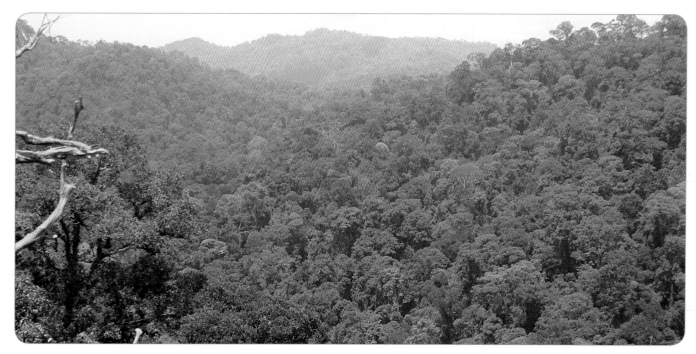

Figure 1.21 Tropical forest: Temburong National Park, Brunei

The hot, humid climate gives ideal conditions for plant growth and there are no real seasonal changes. The plants are therefore aseasonal and the trees shed their leaves throughout the year rather than in one season. There is a great variety of plant species – in some parts of Brazil there can be 300 tree species in 2 km² (Figure 1.21). The trees are tall and fast growing. The need for light means that only those trees that can grow rapidly and overshadow their competitors will succeed. Thus trees are notably tall and have long, thin trunks with a crown of leaves at the top; they also have buttress roots to support the tall trees.

There are broadly speaking three main layers of tiers of trees (Figure 1.22):

- **emergents** which extend up to 45–50 m
- a **closed canopy** 25–30 m high which cuts out most of the light from the rest of the vegetation and restricts its growth
- a limited **understorey** of trees, denser where the canopy is weaker; when the canopy is broken by trees falling, by clearance or at rivers, there is a much denser understory vegetation.

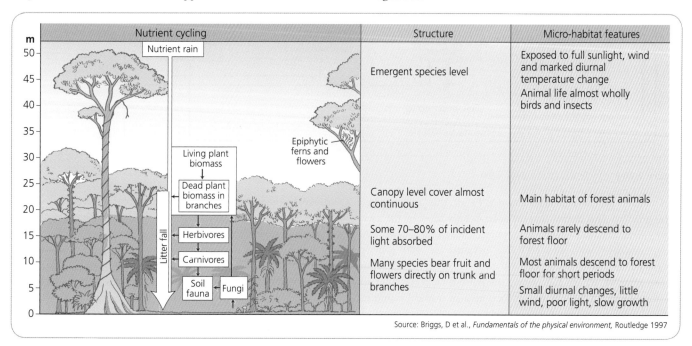

Source: Briggs, D et al., *Fundamentals of the physical environment*, Routledge 1997

Figure 1.22 Vegetation structure in a rainforest

Figure 1.23 A carnivorous pitcher plant, which takes its nutrients from insects and small mammals

Case Study

Civil war and the Rwandan rainforest

In 1925 the Albert National Park, an area of lush tropical rainforest, was established by Belgian colonial authorities. In 1979 UNESCO declared the park, renamed Virunga National Park, as Africa's first National Park Heritage Site, on account of its biodiversity. However, Virunga has been plagued by problems for decades and the park is being deprived of its ecological treasures:

- Political and economic breakdown in the Democratic Republic of Congo has starved the park of funds.
- In the 1960s much of the big game was killed by poachers, rebels and government soldiers during the civil war in the Congo.
- Tourism in the park no longer exists, thereby reducing the park's revenue.
- Poaching has halved the number of hippopotamuses and buffalo in the area.
- Villagers in the park have depleted the forest and overfished the lake.
- The crisis in Rwanda has intensified pressures on the land.

The park is being looted by Rwandan refugees and Hutu soldiers from around the town of Goma in eastern Congo. Up to 300 km² of forest was destroyed in less than six months in 1994. Nearly 900 000 refugees live within or near Virunga and up to 40 000 enter the park daily, notably for food and fuel. Soldiers, too, are cutting wood to sell to the refugees. The rivers are being polluted by human and animal waste and medical products, and the risk of disease transmission is very high. Once established it is almost impossible to move the refugee camps elsewhere and most of the refugees do not want to return to Rwanda as they fear for their safety.

Section 1.2 Activities

1 Explain why tropical rainforests have very high rates of productivity.

2 Suggest reasons why there are different types of rainforest as shown in Figure 1.19.

3 Describe and explain the vegetation structure of the tropical rainforest as shown in Figure 1.22.

Trees are shallow-rooted as they do not have problems getting water. Other layers include lianas and epiphytes, and the final layer is an incomplete field layer limited by the lack of light. The floor of the rainforest is littered with decaying vegetation, rapidly decomposing in the hot, humid conditions. Tree species include the rubber tree, wild banana and cocoa; pollination is not normally by wind due to the species diversity – insects, birds and bats which have restricted food sources.

Rainforest supports a large number of epiphytes, which are attached to the trees. Many of these are adapted to a system that requires only a small intake of nutrients. Some plants, such as the carnivorous pitcher plant (Figure 1.23), get their nutrients from insects and small mammals. There are also parasites taking nutrients from host plants, while those flora living on dead material are called saprophytes, an important part of the decomposing cycle. The fauna are as diverse as the flora.

Nutrient cycles

Nutrients are circulated and re-used frequently. All natural elements are capable of being absorbed by plants, either as gases or soluble salts. Only oxygen, carbon, hydrogen and nitrogen are needed in large quantities. These are known as **macronutrients**. The rest are **trace elements** or micronutrients, such as magnesium, sulphur, and phosphorus. These are needed only in small doses. Nutrients are taken in by plants and built into new organic matter. When animals eat the plants they take up the nutrients. These nutrients are eventually returned to the soil when the plants and animals die and are broken down by decomposers.

All nutrient cycles involve interaction between soil and the atmosphere and involve many food chains. Nevertheless, there is great variety between the cycles. Generally, gaseous cycles are more complete than sedimentary ones as the latter are more susceptible to disturbance, especially by human activity. Nutrient cycles can be sedimentary based, in which the source of the nutrient is from rocks, or they can be atmospheric based, as in the case of the nitrogen cycle.

Nutrient cycles can be shown by means of simplified diagrams (Gersmehl's nutrient cycles), which indicate the stores and transfers of nutrients (Figure 1.24). The most important factors that determine these are availability of moisture, heat, fire (in grasslands), density of vegetation, competition, and length of growing season.

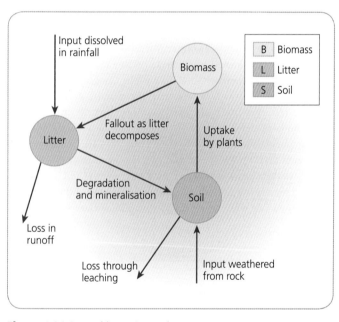

Figure 1.24 Gersmehl's nutrient cycle

The factors affecting the store of nutrients and their transfer are:
- the amount and type of weathering
- overland runoff and soil erosion
- eluviation
- the amount of rainfall
- rates of decomposition
- the nature of vegetation (woody species hold on to nutrients for much longer than annuals)
- the age and health of plants
- plant density
- fire.

Hence explaining the differences between nutrient cycles in different ecosystems involves a consideration of many processes.

In the tropical rainforest, the input of nutrients from weathering and precipitation is high (Figure 1.25) owing to the sustained warm wet conditions. Most of the nutrients are held in the biomass due to the continual growing season. Breakdown of nutrients is rapid and there is a relatively small store in the soil. Where vegetation has been removed, the loss of nutrients is high due to high rates of leaching and overland flow.

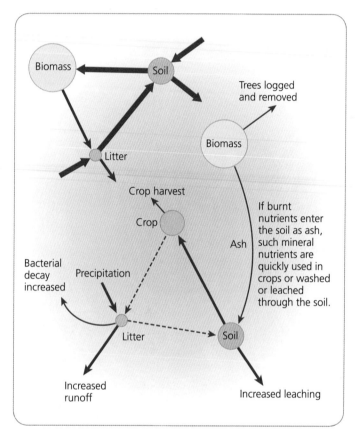

Figure 1.25 Nutrient cycle in a tropical rainforest

In contrast, in a savanna grassland ecosystem the biomass store is less than that of the tropical rainforest due to a shorter growing season. The litter store is also small due to fire. This means that the soil store is relatively large.

The savanna nutrient cycle differs from the tropical rainforest nutrient cycle because of the combined effects of a seasonal drought and the occurrence of fire. Consequently there is:
- a lower nutrient availability
- a reduced biomass store
- a small litter store
- a relatively large soil store.

Section 1.2 Activities

1 Describe and explain the main characteristics of the nutrient cycle associated with tropical rainforests.

2 Outline the changes that occur as a result of human activity. Suggest reasons for the changes you have identified.

Savanna ecosystems
Origin

Savannas are areas of tropical grassland that can occur with or without trees and shrubs. Savannas are widespread in low latitudes, covering approximately one-quarter of the world's land surface – 18 million km² (compared with 2.6 million km² covered by tropical rainforest). Their origin is partly related to natural conditions and partly to human activities, especially burning. They occur between the tropical rainforest and the hot deserts, but there is not a gradual transition from rainforest through savanna to desert – rather, the savanna is a mosaic of plant communities influenced by many factors: climate, soils, drainage, geomorphology, geology and human factors, such as burning and animal grazing (Figure 1.26). Savannas are under increasing pressure from human activities. Trying to protect them is not proving easy.

According to Hills (1965) the factors affecting the development of savannas can be divided into predisposing, causal, resulting and maintaining. For example, in South America, climate predisposes vegetation to grassland rather than forest because grass is better able to survive the dry period. Landscape may be a causal factor as it affects drainage; laterite may be a resulting factor (being caused by drainage but then in turning limiting the vegetation that can survive on impoverished soils), and fire a maintaining factor – human activity regulates the use of fire to produce grassland for grazing at the expense of forest.

Others suggest that edaphic (soil) characteristics may be important. Infertile soils with low water retention may only support grassland, whereas more fertile, moist soils may support forest. There is also a close relationship between soils and landscape – for example, soils at the base of slopes are often more moist and receive nutrients from further upslope.

Others suggest that savannas are the result of climate change in the Pleistocene period, when conditions were more arid. Many savanna trees are fire-resistant. Frequency of fire is important, as it allows fire-resistant species to invade. Woody species that take water from deeper may invade an area following over-grazing since the latter removes annual grasses and results in overland flow.

Climate

The climate that characterises savanna areas is a tropical wet/dry climate. However, there is great variation in the climate between savanna areas. The wet season occurs in summer: heavy convectional rain (monsoonal) replenishes the parched vegetation and soil. However, rainfall can range from as little as 500 mm to as much as 2000 mm (enough to support deciduous forest). However, all savanna areas have an annual drought: these can vary from as little as one month to as much as eight months. It is on account of the dry season that grasses predominate. Temperatures remain high throughout the year, ranging between 23 and 28 °C. The high temperatures, causing high evapotranspiration rates, and the seasonal nature of the rainfall cause a twofold division of the year into seasons of water surplus and water deficiency. This seasonal variation has a great effect on soil development.

Climate and soils

The link between climate and soil could hardly be closer (Figure 1.27). Soils in the savanna are often leached ferralitic soils. These are similar to soils of the rainforest but not as intensely weathered, less leached and exhibit a marked seasonal pattern in soil process. During the wet season the excess of precipitation (P) over potential evapotranspiration (E) means that leaching of soluble minerals and small particles will take place down through the soil. These are deposited at considerable depth. By contrast, in the dry season E > P. Silica and iron compounds are carried up through the soil and precipitated close to the surface. However, geomorphology plays an important role too. Some areas, notably at the base of slopes and in river valleys, are enriched by clay,

Source: Briggs, D. et al., *Fundamentals of the Physical Environment*, Routledge, 1997

Figure 1.26 Types of savanna

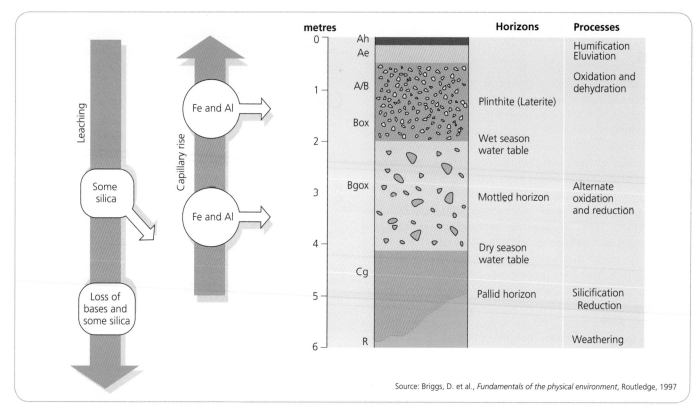

Source: Briggs, D. et al., *Fundamentals of the physical environment*, Routledge, 1997

Figure 1.27 Savanna soils

minerals and humus that is deposited there. By contrast plateaus, plains and the tops of slopes may be depleted of nutrients by erosion. The local variation in soil leads to variations in vegetation: this control by the soil is known as **edaphic** control. For example, on the thicker clay-based soils there is frequently woodland, whereas on the leached sandy soils, with poor water retention, grassland predominates. Savanna areas are frequently found on tectonically stable geological **shields**: these have therefore been weathered and are lacking in nutrients. Hence even some river valleys may not be as fertile as their temperate counterparts.

A soil catena (Figure 1.28) can be observed:

- thin, immature soils on the steep slopes close to the plateau top
- ferruginous soils on the freely drained slopes
- soils containing laterite where the lower part of the soil profile is affected by the water table
- vertisols (gleyed or waterlogged black soils) where the soil is largely beneath the water table.

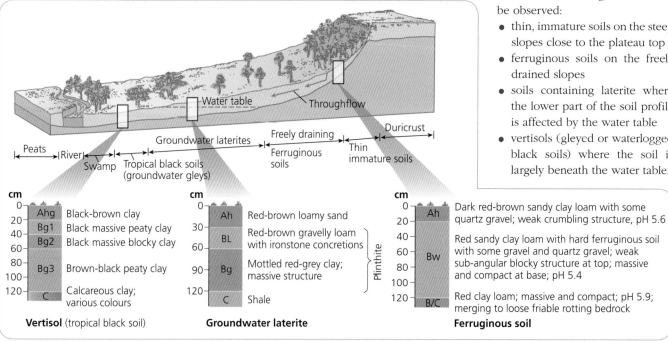

Figure 1.28 Soil catena in the savanna

Vegetation

Savanna vegetation is a mosaic including grasses, trees and scrub. All are **xerophytic** (adapted to drought) and therefore adapted to the savanna's dry season, and **pyrophytic** (adapted to fire). Adaptations to drought include deep tap roots to reach the water table, partial or total loss of leaves, and sunken stomata on the leaves to reduce moisture loss. Those relating to fire include a very thick bark and thick budding that can resist burning, the bulk of the biomass being below ground level, and rapid regeneration after fire. Unlike shrubs, where growth occurs from the tips, the growth tissue in grasses is located at the base of the shoot close to the soil surface, so burning, and even grazing, encourages the growth of grass relative to other plants.

The warm wet summers allow much photosynthesis and there is a large net primary productivity of 900 g/m²/year. This varies from about 1000 g/m²/year where it borders rainforest areas to only about 200 g/m²/year where it becomes savanna scrub. By contrast, the biomass varies considerably (depending on whether it is largely grass or wood) with an average of 4 kg/m. Typical species in Africa include the acacia, palm and baobab trees (Figure 1.29) and elephant grass, which can grow to a height of over 5 m. Trees grow to a height of about 12 m and are characterised by flattened crowns and strong roots.

Figure 1.29 A baobab tree, Kruger National Park, South Africa

The nutrient cycle also illustrates the relationship between climate, soils and vegetation (Figure 1.30). The store of nutrients in the biomass is less than that in the rainforest because of the shorter growing season. Similarly, the store in the litter is small because of fire. Owing to fire many of the nutrients are stored in the soil so that they are not burnt and leached out of the system. The role of fire, whether natural or caused by people, is very important (Figure 1.31). It helps to maintain the savanna as a grass community, it mineralises the litter layer, kills off weeds, competitors and diseases and prevents any trees from colonising relatively wet areas.

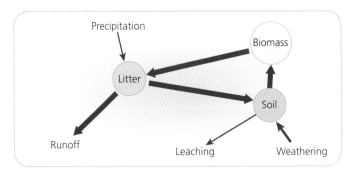

Figure 1.30 Savanna nutrient cycle

Figure 1.31 Fire is an important element of the savanna ecosystem

Other factors include the activities of animals. This includes locusts, for example, which can destroy large areas of grassland with devastating speed, and termites, which aerate the soil and break down up to 30 kg of cellulose per hectare each year. In some areas up to 600 termite hills per hectare can be found, thus having a significant effect on the upper horizons on the soil.

The fauna associated with savannas is diverse. The African savanna has the largest variety of grazers (over forty), including giraffe, zebra, gazelle, elephants and wildebeest (Figure 1.32). Selective grazing allows a great variety of herbivores: for example,

Figure 1.32 Savanna fauna: zebra

the giraffe feeds off the tops of the trees, the rhinoceros the lower twigs and gazelle the grass beneath the trees. These animals are largely migratory searching out water and fresh pastures as the dry season sets in. A variety of carnivores including lions, cheetahs and hyenas are also supported.

> ### Section 1.2 Activities
>
> **1** Outline the ways in which **a** savanna vegetation and **b** savanna fauna are adapted to seasonal drought.
>
> **2** Explain why fire is important in savanna ecosystems.

Tropical soils

The soils of these tropical areas are usually heavily leached and **ferralitic**, with accumulations of residual insoluble minerals containing iron, aluminium and manganese (Figure 1.33). A distinction can be made between leached ferralitic soils (of the rainforest) and weathered ferralitic soils that are found in savanna regions. The hot humid environment speeds up chemical weathering and decay of organic matter. This **biome** also covers ancient shield areas that have remained tectonically stable for a very long time and were unaffected by the Pleistocene glaciations. Not only are the soils well developed but they have been weathered for a long time and are therefore lacking in nutrients and so are inherently infertile. More than 80 per cent of the soils have severe limitations of acidity, low nutrient status, shallowness or poor drainage. This is unusual given the richness of the vegetation that it supports. However, the nutrients are mainly stored in the biomass due to the rapid leaching of nutrients from the A horizon (see Figure 1.27). There is only a small store of nutrients in the litter or the soil itself.

The rate of litter fall is high – 11 tonnes/ha/year – and there is humus turnover of 1 per cent a day. At 25–30 °C the breakdown and supply of litter is approximately equal. The rapid rates of decomposition and the rapid leaching of nutrients from the rooting area have led to an unusual adaptation in this ecosystem. The main agents of decay are fungi in **mycorrhizal** relationships with the tree roots. Nutrients are passed directly from the litter to the trees by the fungi (living on the tree roots). This bypasses the soil storage stage when there is a strong chance that the nutrients will be lost from the nutrient cycle completely.

The rapid decay of litter gives a plentiful supply of bases. Clay minerals break down rapidly and the silica element is carried into the lower layers. Iron and aluminium sesquioxides, which are relatively insoluble, remain in the upper layers, as they require acidic water to mobilise them. These leached red or red brown soils are termed **ferralitic** soils (Figure 1.27). Where it is wet the iron may be hydrated and yellow soils develop. Deep weathering is a feature of these areas and the depth of the regolith may be up to 150 m deep. Where a parent material allows free drainage and is poor in bases, such as a coarse sandstone, a tropical podsol will form.

A soil catena can be identified with ferralitic soils on the upper slopes, vertisols (tropical black clays) on the lower slopes and gleyed soils where drainage is impeded and alluvial soils close to rivers (Figure 1.28).

These soils are not easy to manage. If they are ploughed, severe soil erosion may occur. Vegetation interrupts the nutrient cycle. In the rainforest vegetation and soil are the major components in an almost closed nutrient cycle. The major store of plant nutrients is in the vegetation. The leaves and stems falling to the soil surface break down rapidly and nutrients are released during the processes of decomposition. These are almost immediately taken up by the plants. By contrast, the supply of nutrients from the underlying mineral soil is a small component. If the forest cover is removed, the bulk of the system's nutrient store is also removed. This leaves a well-weathered, heavily leached soil capable of supplying only low levels of nutrients.

Figure 1.33 Tropical red earth, Brunei

Even when the forest is burnt the nutrients held in the plant biomass store are often lost. During burning there may be gaseous losses and afterwards rainfall may leach nutrients from the ash on the surface. In addition the soils have a low cation exchange capacity. Unless a plant cover is rapidly established, most of the nutrients released from the plant biomass during burning will be lost within a short time. Thus shifting cultivation can only take place for a few years before the overall fertility of the soil is reduced to such an extent that it is not worthwhile continuing cropping the plot. Indeed farmers try to replicate the rainforest environment by intercropping. This provides shelter for the soil and protects it from the direct attack of intense rain (rainsplash erosion can otherwise be a serious problem). Compaction of the soil by heavy raindrops and the reduction of the infiltration capacity as a result will lead to overland flow and soil erosion even if there is only a slight slope.

Soils that are predominant in the region offer conditions only marginally suitable for most of these crops. They are often clayey textured, of low pH value, generally of less than medium fertility, and offer only restricted rooting depths.

Changes to rainforest soils

Tropical rainforests are disappearing at an alarming rate and 'green jungles' are being changed into to 'red deserts'. The loss of rainforest is up to 200 000 km²/year. By 2050 it is possible that there will be no extensive tracts of primary tropical rainforest, but simply isolated refuges of a few tens or hundreds of square kilometres. The tropical rainforest is a unique natural resource with a tremendous diversity of flora and fauna, much of which has still to be scientifically identified and studied.

To those who live within or close to the rainforest, the forest is a resource they are eager to exploit. To many economically marginal households, the land presently occupied by forest is seen as a way of improving their quality of their life, and to become self-sufficient in farming. Rainforests are areas of low population density, and in some areas are relatively unexploited. However, in some cases new farmers have little experience of the tropical environment. Some are the urban poor while others are farmers familiar with very different environments. Table 1.5 shows the distribution of the different types of soil in the humid tropics.

Table 1.5 Distribution of the main types of soil in the humid tropics

Soil type	Million hectares
Acid, infertile soils	938
Moderately fertile, well-drained soils	223
Poorly drained soils	119
Very infertile sandy soils	104
Shallow soils	75
Total	1459

Source: S. Nortcliff, 'The clearance of the tropical rainforest', *Teaching Geography*, April 1987

Table 1.6 shows the characteristics of an **oxisol** (leached ferruginous soil) under tropical rainforest in Amazonas State, Brazil. The oxisol is deep and acidic (low pH). It has a low cation exchange capacity (CEC) and a low base saturation. The cation exchange capacity is a measure of the soil's capacity to

Table 1.6 Characteristics of an oxisol under tropical rainforest in Amazonas, Brazil

Depth (cm)	% organic matter	% sand	% silt	% clay	pH1 (H_2O)	CEC2 meq/100 g	BS3 %
0–8	3.4	10	15	75	3.4	18	2
8–18	0.6	11	11	78	3.7	8	4
18–50	0.5	7	8	85	4.2	4	5
50–90	0.3	7	4	89	4.5	3	5
90–150	0.2	7	3	90	4.7	3	5
150–170	0.2	5	3	92	4.9	2	5

Notes:
1 pH determined in a 1:2.5 soil/water ratio
2 Cation exchange capacity expressed as milli-equivalents per 100 g of soil
3 Percentage base saturation (sum of base cations/CEC 100).

Source: S. Nortcliff, 'The clearance of tropical rainforest', *Teaching Geography*, April 1987

absorb and exchange positively charged ions (cations) such as potassium, calcium, magnesium, hydrogen and aluminium. The base saturation measures the proportion of the exchangeable cations that are bases (that is, not hydrogen and aluminium which are acidic). A low CEC and low base saturation mean that the soil has a poor reserve of nutrients readily available to plants and that it also has an undesirable balance between ions for plant growth. Thus it is infertile. In the oxisol the only horizon with a substantial CEC is the surface horizon, due to the presence of organic matter.

Research near Manaus in Brazil investigated changes in the soil's physical characteristics which resulted when rainforest was cleared, first using traditional slash and burn techniques and second using a bulldozer (Table 1.7). Several observations of soil characteristics were made, including changes in soil surface, dry bulk density, moisture content and infiltration rate.

Table 1.7 Soil moisture contents – comparisons between uncleared forest, burned and bulldozed sites, Amazonas, Brazil

Depth below final soil surface (cm)	Virgin forest	Burned	Bulldozed
	% soil moisture content		
0–10	52.1	40.8	40.8
10–20	44.4	40.4	39.4
20–40	41.4	40.4	38.6

On the site cleared by bulldozer the change in soil surface height ranged from 2 to 9 cm with an average of 5.7 cm. Thus much of the topsoil horizon was removed, leaving a denser subsurface horizon at or very close to the surface. The removal of the topsoil removes much of the soil organic matter, which is often the major store of plant nutrients within the soil.

There were increases in the soil dry bulk density resulting from the passage of heavy machinery over the surface, causing changes in the infiltration rate (the rate at which water can enter the soil) from over 200 cm/hour under uncleared forest to 192 cm/hour at the slash and burn site and to 39 cm/hour at the bulldozed site.

The moisture content of the 0–10 cm and 10–20 cm layers of both burned and bulldozed sites were similar, and were significantly lower than the uncleared forest site. These differences

Table 1.8 Crop response to forest clearance and different soil fertiliser applications, Vurimaguas in Peru

Fertility level	Slash and burn	Bulldozed	Bulldozed/ Burned
	Yield tonnes per hectare		
Maize (grain yield)	0	0.1	0
NPK	0.4	0.04	10
NPKL	3.1	2.4	76
Soyabeans (grain yield)	0	0.7	0.2
NPK	1.0	0.3	34
NPKL	2.7	1.8	67
Cassava (fresh root yield)	0	1 5.4	6.4
NPK	18.9	14.9	78
NPKL	25.6	24.9	97

Fertiliser applications:
N = 50 kg nitrogen per hectare
P = 172 kg phosphorus per hectare
K = 40 kg potassium per hectare
L = 4 tonnes lime per hectare

Sites labelled 0 received none of the above fertiliser applications.
Sites labelled NPK received applications of nitrogen, phosphorus and potassium.
Sites labelled NPKL received all applications.

reflect the removal of the organic matter during clearance. The organic matter acts both as a store of moisture and as a natural mulch restricting moisture loss.

Crop yields were higher in burned plots because of the nutrient content of the ash. The ash caused major changes in soil conditions. Soil acidity decreased and, compared with the bulldozed site, the organic matter was higher (although it was lower than that of the uncleared forest). The importance of ash to soil fertility and crop yield following clearance is substantial, especially in soils of low fertility.

Forest clearance in the tropics will continue in order to satisfy the demands of the growing population (see page 87ff). The priority therefore should be to slow down the rate of clearance. This can be done by making the most effective use of the cleared land and by limiting the need for forest clearance to replace land cleared at an earlier stage. These aims can be achieved by:

- increasing the productivity of land already cleared by selection of suitable crop and land management combinations
- minimising the damage that results from forest clearing methods by adopting methods of clearance and timing of clearance that produce the least detrimental effects
- restoring eroded or degraded land by the establishment of more appropriate land management systems.

Section 1.3 Activities

1 Study Table 1.5. Explain why tropical rainforests have some of the world's most luxuriant vegetation and yet some of the world's least fertile soils.

2 Using examples, examine the effects of human activities on tropical soils.

3 With the use of an example, describe and explain the formation of a soil catena.

1.3 Tropical landforms

Tropical landforms are diverse and complex. They are the result of many interrelated factors including climate, rock type, tectonics, scale, time, vegetation and, increasingly, human impact. In the early part of the twentieth century, the development of tropical landforms was thought to be largely the result of climate. Climatic geomorphology suggested that in a certain climate, a distinct set of processes and landforms would be produced. Critics of this idea showed that as the scale of the investigation became increasing small-scale and local, site-specific conditions, such as drainage and topography, become more important and the role of climate less important. In addition, many of the early studies of tropical landforms were in parts of tropical Africa, India and South America, regions that are tectonically stable.

Weathering

See also Paper 1: Core Geography, Physical Topic 3, page 63ff.
Mechanical and chemical weathering occur widely in the tropics. Much attention has been given to the processes of hydrolysis and exfoliation. **Hydrolysis** is a form of chemical weathering. Hydrolysis occurs on rocks with orthoclase feldspar, notably granite. Feldspar reacts with an acid water to produce kaolin (or kaolinite/china clay), silicic acid and potassium hydroxyl. The acid and hydroxyl are removed in solution, leaving kaolin as the end product. In the humid tropics, the availability of water and the consistently high temperatures maximise the efficiency of chemical reactions, and in the oldest part of the tropics these have been operating for a very long period. In contrast, in many savanna areas where there is less moisture, **exfoliation** or disintegration occurs. This is a form of mechanical weathering. Owing to large-scale diurnal (daytime/night-time) differences in the heating and cooling of rocks, rocks expand by day and contract by night. As rock is a poor conductor of heat, these stresses only occur in the outer layers of the rock, causing peeling or exfoliation.

In many regions, the depth of the weathering profile is very deep. As the depth increases, slopes may become less stable. Rapid mass movements are likely to take place in a cyclical pattern, once a certain amount of weathering has occurred (Figure 1.34).

Weathering profiles vary widely. The idealised weathering profile has three zones: residual soil, weathered rock, and relatively unweathered bedrock. The residual soil is a zone of eluviation caused by the infiltration of water. Weathering alters the structure and texture of the parent rock. Soluble components may be removed, leaving behind clay-sized materials, especially those containing iron, aluminium and silica. In the lower part of the residual horizon (the C horizon), features of the original rock such as structure, joints and faults may be recognisable. Weathered rock is also known as **saprolite**.

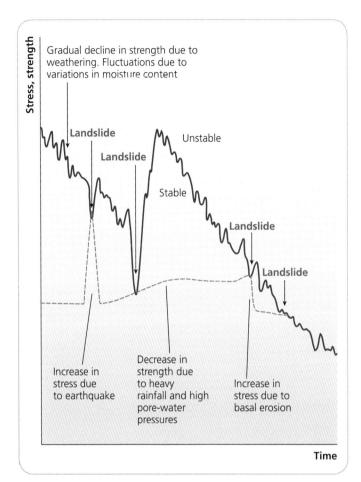

Figure 1.34 Cycles of weathering and landslides

In the weathered zone, at least 10 per cent of the rock is unweathered corestones. This zone is typically highly permeable, especially in the upper sections, and contains minerals in a wide range of weathering stages. In contrast, in the zone of unweathered bedrock, there is little alteration of feldspars and micas. The greatest depth at which unweathered rocks is reached occurs in areas where humid tropical conditions have existed for a prolonged time.

The 'weathering front' or 'basal surface of weathering' between solid rock and saprolite (weathered rock) may be very irregular. Typically, deep weathering occurs down to 30–60 m, but because of variations in jointing density and rock composition, the depth varies widely over short distances. Depth of weathering has been recorded at 90 m in Nigeria and Uganda, while in Australia a depth of 275 m has been measured in New South Wales, as well as 80 m in Victoria and 35 m in Western Australia.

Section 1.3 Activities

1 Describe the main types of weathering that occur in tropical environments.
2 Explain why 'deep weathering' may occur in some tropical environments.

Duricrusts

Duricrusts are concentrations of iron (ferricrete), aluminium (alcrete), silica (silcrete) and calcium carbonate (calcrete) found within the zone of weathering. It is also known as laterite. Calcrete tend to dominate drier regions (less than 840 mm) whereas ferricete, alcrete and silcrete are found in more humid regions. Many examples of bauxite (concentrations of aluminium) may be related to past climatic conditions.

Many different processes are involved in duricrust formation. True laterite is described as a **relict** feature that was formed in a previous period. It occurs when land has been uplifted and subsequently eroded by rivers. When the rivers expose the sub-surface laterite horizons it hardens irreversibly.

A laterite horizon is formed under the surface when iron and aluminium oxides are concentrated there by groundwater flow. This layer can be up to 1.5 m thick. When it is exposed to the air, the layer dries and hardens irreversibly. Laterite remains soft while it is moist and in a fresh state. It can even be cut into building materials. Deforestation and shifting cultivation may expose the laterite and cause a hardening of the horizon.

Duricrusts have an important role in geomorphology:
- they act as cap rocks to escarpments and terraces and protect otherwise weaker rocks (Figure 1.35)
- they cap mesa and other residual features
- they influence drainage patterns within soils.

Figure 1.35 Laterite acting as a cap rock

Section 1.3 Activities

1 Distinguish between the terms *calcrete* and *ferricrete*.
2 Explain how duricrusts may be formed.

Peneplanation, pediplanation and etchplains

Peneplanation begins with the rapid uplift of a region to produce an irregular surface (Figure 1.36). Weathering and river erosion reinforce the irregular surface. Along river valleys, river erosion is intense and cuts deep, steep valleys. Vertical erosion continues until base level is reached. Thereafter, river erosion ceases, and the interfluves (areas away from the rivers) reduced. Eventually, an area of low relief (peneplain) is produced separated by low erosional residuals (monadnocks) (Figure 1.37).

Pediplanation proposes the extension of plains at the expense of interfluves through the retreat of slopes though parallel retreat. Pediplanation begins with tectonic uplift, resulting in accelerating river erosion forming knick points, falls, rapids and gorges along river valleys. When base level is reached, lateral erosion begins. Hillslopes retreat through parallel retreat, leaving behind a low-angled pediment (Figure 1.38). Eventually they may produce a landscape of low-angle plains (pediments) separated by rocky hills known as kopjes (Figure 1.39).

Figure 1.36 The Three Rondavels – an early stage of peneplanation

Figure 1.37 Peneplanation

Figure 1.38 Pediplanation formed by parallel retreat

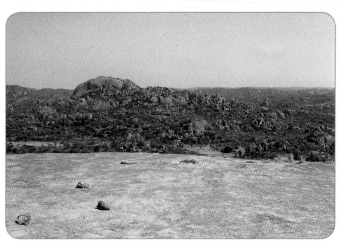

Figure 1.39 Castle Kopje near Bulawayo, Zimbabwe

An etchplain is an area of stripped and exposed unweathered bedrock. The development of etchplains occurs in ancient shield areas and is associated with deep weathering. Periods when weathering was more efficient resulted in the accumulation of great depths of weathered material. In contrast, there were periods when erosion was more rapid than weathering, leading to erosion of the weathered material.

The gradual lowering of the regolith surface by stripping may explain the extensive exposed rock plains called etchplains. These may be studded with inselbergs. According to Budel (1957) there are two levels of weathering – one at the surface and one at depth. Rivers at the surface flow over the regolith rather than cutting deep into them, and are constantly meandering and changing course. They erode fine particles and gradually lower the surface.

At depth, chemical weathering lowers the unweathered rock at the weathering front. The whole of the savanna is therefore being lowered by surface wash at the surface and chemical weathering at the weathering front. If the upper surface is lowered at a rate faster than the weathering front, then the latter will begin to

a The regolith surface is being lowered at a faster rate than the subterranean surface.

Smooth savanna plain

Shifting courses of shallow rivers

Marginal inselberg

Upper subaerial surface being lowered by 'wash'

Lower subterranean surface being lowered by chemical weathering

Deep, intensely weathered regolith

b The irregular subterranean surface is being exposed as inselbergs.

Savanna plain studded with inselbergs

Marginal inselberg

Figure 1.40 Etchplain formation (after Budel)

emerge as an etchplain (Figure 1.40). Etchplains can be seen at various stages of development. An alternative model to that shown in Figure 1.40 is shown in Figure 1.41. The stages are:

1 *Laterised etchplain*: low relief, extensive laterite deposits, little stream incision, few residual hills.

2 *Dissected etchplain*: swifter stream erosion; duricrust (laterite) breaking up, valley more deeply cut; mesas; some exposure of the weathering front as tors and domes.

3 *Partly stripped etchplain*: further dissection and waste removal; most laterite now removed, a few mesas, tors, castle kopjes and bornhardts.

4 *Stripped etchplain*: much rock exposed as convex hills; some basins still containing sediments.

5 *Incised etchplains*: the weathering surface is now exposed and is being eroded on a larger scale by rivers.

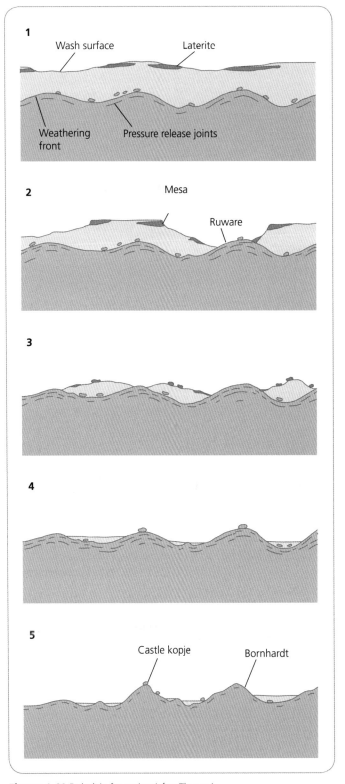

1

Wash surface

Laterite

Weathering front

Pressure release joints

2

Mesa

Ruware

3

4

5

Castle kopje

Bornhardt

Figure 1.41 Etchplain formation (after Thomas)

Section 1.3 Activities

With the use of annotated diagrams, distinguish between *pediplanation*, *peneplanation* and *etchplain* formation.

Figure 1.42 Spheroidal weathering

Figure 1.43 Tor formation

Residual hills (tors and inselbergs)

See also Paper 1: Core Geography, Physical Topic 3, pages 68–9.

The word *inselberg* describes any isolated hill or hills which stand prominently over a level surface. Inselbergs include:

- laterite-capped masses of saprolite
- hills of sedimentary rocks
- castle kopjes
- tors of residual core stones
- massive rock domes with near-vertical sides, called *bornhardts* or domed *inselbergs*.

Tors

Most tors and castle kopjes are found in strongly jointed rock. Tors are ridges or piles of spheroidally weathered boulders (Figure 1.42) that have their bases in the bedrock and are surrounded by weathered debris. They vary in height from 20 to 35 m and have core stones up to 8 m in diameter.

Tors are formed by chemical weathering of the rock along joints and bedding planes beneath the surface (Figure 1.43). If the joints are widely spaced the core stones are large whereas if the joints are close together the amount of weathering increases and the core stones are much smaller. If denudation of the surface exceeds the rate of chemical weathering at the weathering front, the blocks will eventually be exposed at ground level. Gradually the rocks below the surface will be chemically weathered and cause the collapse of the tor.

Good examples of tors are found on the Jos Plateau of Nigeria and in the Matopas region of Zimbabwe and around Harare.

Bornhardts

The monolithic domed inselberg or bornhardt is a characteristic landform of granite plateaus of the African savanna, but can also be found in tropical humid regions. They are characterised by steep slopes and a convex upper slope (Figure 1.44). Bornhardts are eventually broken down into residual castle kopjes.

Bornhardts occur in igneous and metamorphic rocks. Granite, an igneous rock, develops joints, up to 35 m below the surface, during the process of pressure release. Vertical jointing in granite is responsible for the formation of castle kopjes.

The two main theories for the formation of bornhardts include:

- the stripping or exhumation theory – increased

1 Laterite mesa landscape

Laterite mesa

Regolith

Unweathered granite

Vertical joints

2 Bornhardts begin to emerge

Surface lowering by wash

Dwala

Pressure release joints

Lowering by chemical weathering

3 Bornhardts dominate plains

Bornhardt

Vertical joints develop

4 Bornhardts fracture into castle kopjes

Castle kopje

Figure 1.44 Formation of bornhardts

a series of periods of deep weathering, changing climatic conditions and uplift, this evolutionary approach might be the most appropriate.

Classic examples of bornhardts include Mount Hora in the Mzimba District of Malawi, and Zuma Rock near Abuja in Nigeria.

Inselbergs

A striking feature of tropical plains is the rock hills known as inselbergs (Figure 1.45). Conditions especially favourable for residual hills occur in the seasonal tropics. Residual hills are best developed on volcanic materials, especially granite and gneiss, with widely spaced joints and a high potassium content. However, they can also be found on sedimentary rocks, such as sandstone.

Figure 1.45 Inselberg and low plains

Residual hills occur in a variety of sizes. The term *inselberg* usually describes an almost abrupt rise from the plains. Duricrust-topped hills are the major exception. The terms *tor* or *boulder inselberg* are used to describe spheroidally weathered boulders rooted in bedrock.

Residual hills are the result of stripping weathered regolith from a differentially weathered surface. The major debate is whether deep weathering is needed for hill formation. The two-stage model requires the development of a mass of weathered material beneath the ground and its subsequent removal. Alternatively, weathering and erosion could occur simultaneously. The diversity of residual hills suggests that both mechanisms operate simultaneously.

Section 1.3 Activities

1 Explain why tors may be described as 'joint-controlled'.

2 To what extent are inselbergs 'relict' features?

3 Describe the development of bornhardts and castle kopjes as shown in Figure 1.44.

removal of regolith occurs so that unweathered rocks beneath the surface are revealed

- Lester King's parallel retreat theory which states that the valley sides retreat until only remnant inselbergs are left. In the case of bornhardts, it seems that the major theory is that of etchplanation. There is a gradual evolution from the ruware through the bornhardt to an inselberg and then the residual castle kopje. As the theory invokes evolution through

Figure 1.46 Cockpit karst

Tropical karst

There are two major landform features associated with tropical karst. **Polygonal** or **cockpit karst** (Figure 1.46) is a landscape pitted with smooth-sided soil-covered depressions and cone-like hills. **Tower karst** is a landscape characterised by upstanding rounded blocks set in a region of low relief. Although water is less able to dissolve carbon dioxide in tropical areas, the higher temperatures and the presence of large amounts of organic matter produce high amounts of carbon dioxide in the soil water.

Some geographers believe that there is an evolution of limestone landscapes that eventually leads to cockpit karst and tower karst (Figure 1.47). However, according to Marjorie Sweeting (1989), the distinction between cockpit karst and tower karst is fundamental, as the hydrological and tectonic conditions associated with each are quite different.

Polygonal or **cockpit** karst is characterised by groups of hills, fairly uniform in height (Figure 1.48). These can be up to 160 m high in Jamaica, with a base of up to 300 m. They develop mainly as a result of solution. They are as common to some tropical areas as dry valleys and dolines are to temperate areas. Polygonal karst tends to occur in areas:

Solution holes
The surface is broken up by many small solution holes but the overall surface remains generally level.

Cockpit karst
Cockpit karst is usually a hilly area in which many deep solution holes have developed to give it an 'eggbox' appearance.

Tower karst
The widening and deepening of the cockpits has destroyed much of the limestone above the water table. Only a few limestone towers remain, sticking up from a flat plain of sediments that have filled in the cockpits at a level just above the water table. Eventually the towers will be entirely eroded, and disappear.

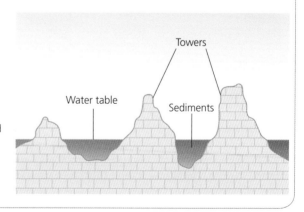

Figure 1.47 Cockpit karst and tower karst

Figure 1.48 Cockpit karst in northern Puerto Rico, from US Geological Survey map

0   Metres   500   Contour interval 10 metres

- that have been subjected to high rates of tectonic uplift and
- where vertical erosion by rivers is intense.

The spacing of the cones may be related to the original stream network. Concentrated solution along preferred routes, such as wider joints, leads to accelerated weathering of certain sections of the limestone, especially during times of high flow, such as during a storm. Water will continue to weather the limestone as far down as the water table. This creates closed depressions and dolines. Once the water table is reached water will flow laterally rather than vertically, so developing a flat plain.

An alternative theory suggests that the formation and subsequent collapse of cave systems is the main mechanism for cockpit karst formation. Caves in limestone migrate upwards through the hillside. Collapse of the ceiling is due to the solution by water percolating downwards. Every time the ceiling collapses, the ceiling gets higher and the floor is raised by the debris, so the whole chamber gets higher. Eventually the cave roof collapses.

By contrast, **tower karst** is much more variable in size than the conical hills of cockpit karst, and ranges from just a few metres to over 150 m in height in Sarawak. Other areas of tower karst include southern China, Malaysia, Indonesia and the Caribbean. They are characterised by steep sides, with cliffs and overhangs,

and with caves and solution notches at their base. The steepest towers are found on massive, gently tilted limestone. According to Sweeting, tower karst develops in areas where:

- tectonic uplift is absent or limited
- limestone lies close to other rocks
- the water table is close to the surface.

In wet monsoonal areas rivers will be able to maintain their flow over limestone, erode the surface and leave residual blocks set in a river plain. It is likely that there are other important processes. These include:

- differential erosion of rock with varying resistance
- differential solution along lines of weakness
- the retreat of cockpit karst slopes to produce isolated tower karst
- lateral erosion.

Why is China so important for tropical karst?

Southern China is one of the best areas in the world for the development of cockpit and tower karst (Figure 1.49). A number of conditions help explain this:

- large amounts of rainfall – over 2000 mm per annum (in the north of China where rainfall is low, limestone features include escarpments and dry valleys)
- long periods of slow uplift exposing broad, gently dipping plateaus
- thick beds of limestone, up to 3000 m deep, allowing spectacular landforms to develop.

Figure 1.49 Tropical karst, China

Underground features

Underground features include caves and tunnels formed by carbonation-solution and erosion by rivers. Carbonation is a reversible process. When calcium-rich water drips from the ceiling it leaves behind calcium in the form of **stalactites** and **stalagmites**. These are cave deposits formed by the precipitation of dissolved calcium carbonate. **Stalactites** develop from the top of the cave whereas **stalagmites** are formed on the base of the cave. Rates of deposition are slow; about 1 mm (the thickness of a coat of paint) per 100 years. The speed with which water drips from the cave ceiling appears to have some influence on whether stalactites (slow drip) or stalagmites (fast drip) are formed.

Blue Holes in the Bahamas

Sea-level changes in the Caribbean have caused some limestone caves to be submerged, forming **blue holes** (Figure 1.50). These are a major tourist attraction in The Bahamas, for example. The Bahamas has a variety of blue holes (Figure 1.51). The islands' limestone has been carved out by carbonation-solution over millennia, during periods when the sea level fluctuated – the seas were some 130 m lower 10 000 years ago, for example. As the sea level rose over the last 10 000 years it submerged many of the limestone sinks, caves and tunnels. These drowned sinks became the blue holes. The classic form of a blue hole is circular, extending in a bell shape beneath the surface. However, some open into the edge of an oceanic wall or are simply openings in a shallow reef. Not all blue holes are oceanic – many are found inland. The deepest known blue hole in The Bahamas reaches down to over 200 m, and many systems drop to around 100 m and then extend into a network of caverns and caves at the bottom.

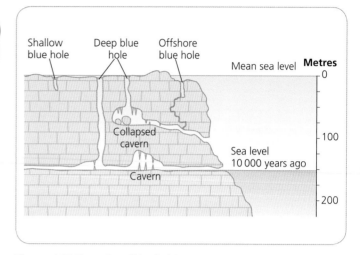

Figure 1.50 Formation of blue holes

Section 1.3 Activities

1 How are blue holes formed?

2 What is the difference between cockpit karst and tower karst?

3 Why is there so much carbonation in tropical areas?

Figure 1.51 Blue hole in The Bahamas

1.4 Sustainable management of tropical areas

Case Study

Sustainable agroforestry, Santa Rosa rainforest, Mexico

The Popoluca Indians of Santa Rosa in the Mexican rainforest practise a form of agriculture that resembles shifting cultivation, known as the **milpa system** (Table 1.9). This is a labour-intensive form of agriculture, using **fallow**. It is a diverse form of **polyculture** with over 200 species cultivated, including maize, beans, cucurbits, papaya, squash, water melon, tomatoes, oregano, coffee and chilli. The Popolucas have developed this system that mimics the natural rainforest. The variety of a natural rainforest is replicated in the form of shifting cultivation. For example, lemon trees, peppervine and spearmint are **heliophytes** (light-seeking plants), and prefer open conditions, not shade. By contrast, coffee is a **sciophyte** (shade-tolerant plant), while the mango tree requires damp conditions.

The close associations that are found in natural conditions are also seen in the Popolucas' farming system. For example, maize and beans go well together, as maize extracts nutrients from the soil whereas beans return them to the soil. Tree trunks and small trees are left because they are useful for many purposes, such as returning nutrients to the soil and preventing soil erosion. They are also used as a source of material for housing, hunting spears, and for medicines.

As in a rainforest the crops are multi-layered, with tree, shrub and herb layers. This increases NPP per unit area, because photosynthesis is taking place on at least three levels, and soil erosion is reduced, as no soil is left bare. Most plants are self-seeded and this reduces the cost of inputs. The Popolucas show a huge amount of ecological knowledge and management. In all, 244 species of plant are used in their farming system. Animals include chickens, pigs and turkeys. These are used as a source of food, for barter and in exchange for money, and their waste is used as manure. Rivers and lakes are used for fishing and catching turtles. Thus it is not entirely a subsistence lifestyle, since wood, fruit, turtles and other animals are traded for some seeds, mainly maize.

Pressures on the Popolucas

About 90 per cent of Mexico's rainforest has been cut down in recent decades, largely for new forms of agriculture. This is partly a response to Mexico's huge international debt and attempts by the government to increase its agricultural exports and reduce its imports. The main new forms of farming are:

- cattle ranching for export
- plantations of cash crops, such as tobacco.

However, these new methods are not necessarily suited to the physical and economic environment. Tobacco needs protection from too much sunlight and excess moisture, and the soil needs to be very fertile. The cleared rainforest is frequently left bare and this leads to soil erosion. Unlike the milpa system, these new forms of agriculture are very labour intensive. Pineapple, sugar cane and tobacco plantations require large inputs of fertiliser and pesticides. Inputs are expensive and the costs are rising rapidly.

Ranching prevents the natural succession of vegetation, because there is a lack of seed from nearby forests and the cattle graze off young seedlings. Grasses and a few legumes become dominant. One hectare of rainforest supports about 200 species of trees and up to 10 000 individual plants. By contrast, one hectare of rangeland supports just one cow and one or two types of grass. However, it is profitable in the short term because land is available, and it is supported by the Mexican government.

Extensive **monoculture** is increasingly mechanised, and uses large inputs of fertiliser, pesticides and insecticides. However, it is very costly and there are problems of soil deterioration and microclimatic change. Yet there is little pressure to improve efficiency because it is easy to clear new forest.

The Mexican rainforest can be described as a '**desert covered by trees**'. Under natural conditions it is very dynamic, but its **resilience** depends on the level of disturbance. Sustainable development of the rainforest requires the management and use of the natural structure and diversity – namely local species, local knowledge and skills – rather than a type of farming that has been developed elsewhere and then imported.

Table 1.9 A comparison between the milpa system and new forms of agriculture

	Milpa system	Tobacco plantation or ranching
NPP	High, stable	Declining
Work (labour)	High	Higher and increasing
Inputs (clearing and seeding)	Few	Very high 2.5–3 tonnes fertiliser/ha/yr
Crops	Polyculture (244 species used)	Monoculture (risk of disease, poor yield, loss of demand and/or overproduction)
Yield (compared with inputs)	200%	140% (at best)
Reliability of farming system	Quite stable	High-risk operation
Economic organisation	Mainly subsistence	Commercial
Money	None/little	More
Carrying capacity (livestock)	Several families/4 ha	1 family on a plantation (200 ha)
Ranching	1 ha of good land = 1 cow	20 ha of poor land = 1 cow

Section 1.4 Activities

1 Compare the Popolucas' methods of farming and the natural tropical rainforest ecosystem. What lessons can be learnt from this?

2 The tropical rainforest is described as a 'desert covered by trees'. What does this mean?

3 'Sustainable development of the rainforest is impossible without massive injections of technology and scientific know-how.' Evaluate this statement.

4 Despite the limitations of the rainforest for development, countries continue to exploit them. Why?

Case Study

Social forestry in the Congo

According to the Congolese Timber Industries Association, up to 80 per cent of the logging in the Congo is illegal. Over 20 million hectares of tropical rainforest have been given over to logging firms.

Lamoko on the Maringa River is on the edge of a massive stretch of rainforest in central Democratic Republic of Congo (DRC). In 2005, representatives of a major timber firm arrived to negotiate a contract with the traditional landowners. The company promised to build three simple village schools and pharmacies in the area for Lamoko and other communities. This is the kind of 'social responsibility' agreement that is encouraged by the World Bank.

Since February 2005, logging roads have been driven deep into the forests near Lamoko (Figure 1.52) and the company has started extracting and exporting teak and sapele trees – but the villages have yet to see their schools and pharmacies. The Lamoko agreement is just one of many contracts, or concessions, that European companies have signed with tribal chiefs in the DRC as the country begins to recover from a decade of civil wars and dictatorship. As many as 40 million of the poorest people in Africa depend on the Congolese forests. All the concessions handed out by the transition government are in inhabited areas. More than a third are home to indigenous pygmy communities.

It is believed that 20 foreign-owned forestry companies are active in the DRC, and that Chinese and other logging groups are also seeking to gain concessions. Most of the major logging companies, including Danzer, Trans-M, TB, NST, Olan, and Sicobois, have concession contracts signed after the World Bank moratorium.

The companies, which export both logs and sawn timber, supply wood all over Europe, mostly as finished products such as flooring, windows, furniture and doors. African teak wood is protected by global agreement and cannot be exported from some tropical countries such as Cameroon, which have few trees left, but there are still no restrictions on its export from the DRC.

Greenpeace and other international forestry groups say the fate of the Congo forests depends on the World Bank and other donors rejecting industrial logging. They are demanding a comprehensive land use plan for a country that is effectively lawless. The Bank accepts that logging could destroy the forests in a short time, leading to immense social problems.

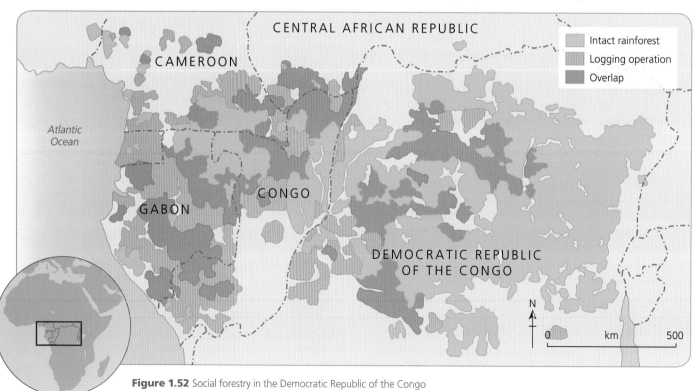

Figure 1.52 Social forestry in the Democratic Republic of the Congo

Case Study

CAMPFIRE, Zimbabwe – sustainable management in savanna areas

Almost 5 million people live in communal lands covering almost half of Zimbabwe. Most of this land can be described as savanna land. CAMPFIRE (Communal Areas Management Programme for Indigenous Resources) is a programme designed to assist rural development and conservation. It works with the people who live in communal lands, supporting the use of wildlife as an important natural resource. CAMPFIRE is helping people in these areas manage the environment in ways that are both sustainable and appropriate.

National Parks

Approximately 12 per cent of Zimbabwe is protected as National Parks or conservation areas, such as Hwange National Park and the Matopas. Many local people were evicted from their homes when the Parks were created. Most now live in the surrounding communal lands. They are no longer permitted to hunt the animals and harvest the plants now found inside protected areas. However, animals frequently roam outside Park boundaries, destroying crops and killing livestock and sometimes people. This has created much conflict between local people and National Park staff, often resulting in illegal hunting.

Raising awareness and raising money

The CAMPFIRE movement began in the mid-1980s. It encourages local communities to make their own decisions about wildlife management and control. It aims to help people manage natural resources so that plants, animals and people – the whole ecosystem – all benefit. It helps provide legal ways for such communities to raise money by using local, natural resources in a sustainable way. As a result, many communities now actively protect local wildlife, seeing it as a valuable asset. In some areas local people have even provided animals with emergency food and water in times of shortage.

Five particular activities help provide extra income to local communities:

- **Trophy hunting:** about 90 per cent of CAMPFIRE's income comes from selling hunting concessions to professional hunters and safari operators working to set government quotas. Individual hunters pay high fees to shoot elephant (US$12 000) and buffalo and are strictly monitored, accompanied by local, licensed professionals. Trophy hunting is considered to be the ultimate form of ecotourism as hunters usually travel in small groups, demand few amenities and cause minimal damage to the local ecosystem, yet provide considerable income.
- **Selling live animals:** this is a fairly recent development. Some areas with large wildlife populations sell live animals to National Parks or game reserves. For example, Guruve district raised US$50 000 by selling 10 roan antelope.
- **Harvesting natural resources:** a number of natural resources, for example crocodile eggs, caterpillars, river-sand and timber are harvested and sold by local communities. Skins and ivory can be sold from 'problem animals' (individual animals that persistently cause damage or are a threat can legally be killed).
- **Tourism:** in the past most revenue from tourists has not gone to local communities. During the 1990s pilot projects were set up and five districts now benefit from tourism. There has been development of specialist tourist areas, such as culture tourism, bird watching and visits to hot springs. Some local people are employed directly as guides, or run local facilities for tourists.
- **Selling wildlife meat:** where species are plentiful, for example impala, the National Parks Department supervises killing and selling of skins and meat. However, this raises relatively small sums of money.

Organisation

Each village taking part in the CAMPFIRE project has a wildlife committee responsible for counting animals, anti-poaching activities, conflicts that arise through 'problem animals', and environmental education. Game scouts are trained to help stop poaching and manage wildlife.

Quotas

For hunting concessions to be granted and wildlife managed sustainably, local communities need to monitor their wildlife populations and manage their habitats, protecting them from poaching or alternative forms of land use, for example farming. Every year the Department of National Parks helps to estimate the wildlife population totals so that sustainable quotas can be set.

Tour operators must, by law, keep detailed records of animals killed – their size, weight, length of certain animals and/or horns and tusks. This helps check that young animals are not being taken, which would put future numbers at risk. New quotas are not issued until operators produce these records for analysis by the Department for National Parks.

Up to 80 per cent of the money raised is given directly to local communities, which collectively decide how it should be spent. Money is used for the community, for example for building and equipping clinics and schools, constructing fences, drilling wells and building roads. In bad years, usually drought years, money may be used to buy maize and other foodstuffs. Since 1989 over 250 000 Zimbabweans have been involved in CAMPFIRE projects.

In 1980 Binga District in north-west Zimbabwe had just 13 primary schools, with most of its people living in poverty. Money from hunting concessions, fishing and tourism was used by Sinkatenge village (near Matusadona National Park) to build a 12 km length of electric fencing to enclose their fields, preventing animals from trampling their crops and providing full-time work for two local people to maintain it. Today, as a result of income from CAMPFIRE projects, the District has 56 primary and 9 secondary schools, and several health clinics and wells.

Masoka in the north-east was one of the first to join CAMPFIRE. Local people now receive more than four times their previous income via hunting concessions, using it to buy maize and other food in drought years, building a clinic, buying a tractor and funding their football team. For the first time here, local rural women were employed, working on CAMPFIRE projects. CAMPFIRE is also actively encouraging women to participate in community decision-making, something that has been traditionally dominated by men. Women have also been encouraged to attend workshops and take part in training schemes.

Nyaminyama District, on the southern edge of Lake Kariba, is introducing land use zoning, with specific areas for wildlife conservation, tourism, crocodile breeding and hunting. A recent WWF report estimated that CAMPFIRE has increased incomes in communal areas by up to 25 per cent.

The future

There are many advantages of CAMPFIRE's activities in Zimbabwe:

- It creates jobs – local people are trained and become involved as environmental educators, game scouts etc.
- It prompts environmental education and promotes the benefits of wildlife conservation to communities.
- It provides an incentive for people to conserve wild species.
- It generates funds, which are used for community projects or to supplement household incomes.
- Communal lands can act as game corridors between existing National Parks, protecting the genetic diversity of wild species.

Rural communities benefit from secure land tenure and rights over their wildlife. The ability of CAMPFIRE to assist wildlife conservation in Zimbabwe depends on two broader factors:

- the acceptance of hunting as a wildlife management tool by the international community
- placing economic value on wild species.

Section 1.4 Activities

1 Briefly explain the difficulties in developing tropical environments.

2 With the use of examples, outline opportunities for sustainable development in tropical environments.

2 Coastal environments

Introduction

Coastal environments are influenced by many factors, including physical and human processes. As a result there is a great variety in coastal landscapes. For example, landscapes vary on account of:

- **Lithology (rock type)** – hard rocks such as granite and basalt give rugged landscapes for example the Giant's Causeway in Northern Ireland, whereas soft rocks such as sands and gravels produce low, flat landscapes, as around the Nile delta, for example.
- **Geological structure** – concordant (Atlantic) or accordant (Pacific) coastlines occur where the geological strata lie parallel to the coastline, for example the south coast of Ireland, whereas discordant (Atlantic-type) coastlines occur where the geological strata are at right-angles to the shoreline, for example the south-west coastline of Ireland.
- **Processes** – erosional landscapes e.g. the east coast of England, contain many rapidly retreating cliffs, whereas areas of rapid deposition, e.g. the Netherlands, contain many sand dunes and coastal flats
- **Sea-level changes** – they interact with erosional and depositional processes to produce advancing coasts (those growing, either due to deposition and/or a relative fall in sea level) or retreating coasts (those being eroded and/or drowned by a relative rise in sea level).
- **Human impacts** are increasingly common – some coasts, for example in Florida, are extensively modified whereas others are more natural, for example Norway and Iceland.
- **Ecosystem types** – such as mangrove, coral, sand dune, saltmarsh and rocky shore – add further variety to the coastline.

Coastal zones

The coastal zone includes all areas from the deep ocean, which may lie beyond political jurisdiction (up to 320 km offshore), to 60 km inland. The inland areas may affect coastal areas through sediment supply and pollution sources, as well as being affected by coastal processes such as land–sea breezes. At the coast there is the **upper beach** or **backshore** (backed by cliffs or sand dunes), the **foreshore** (periodically exposed by the tides) and the **offshore** area (covered by water).

The coastal zone is a dynamic area with inputs and processes from land, sea and the atmosphere so is, geologically speaking, an area of very rapid change.

2.1 Wave, marine and sub-aerial processes

Waves result from friction between wind and the sea surface. Waves in the deep, open sea (waves of oscillation) are different from those breaking on shore. Waves of oscillation are forward surges of energy. Although the surface wave shape appears to move, the water particles actually move in a roughly circular orbit within the wave (Figure 2.1).

The **wave orbit** is the shape of the wave. It varies between circular and elliptical. The orbit diameter decreases with depth, to a depth roughly equal to wavelength (the distance between neighbouring crests or troughs), at which point there is no further movement related to wind energy – this point is called the **wave base**.

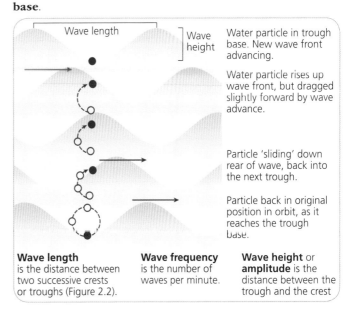

Wave length	Wave frequency	Wave height or
is the distance between two successive crests or troughs (Figure 2.2).	is the number of waves per minute.	**amplitude** is the distance between the trough and the crest

Figure 2.1 Water movement

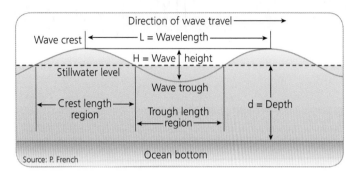

Figure 2.2 Wave terminology

Wave height is an indication of wave energy. It is controlled by wind strength, fetch (the distance of open water a wave travels over), and the depth of the sea. Waves of up to 12–15 m are formed in open sea and can travel vast distances away from the generation area, reaching distant shores as **swell waves**, characterised by a lower height and a longer wavelength. In contrast, storm waves are characterised by a short wavelength, greater height and high frequency.

Waves reaching the shore are known as **waves of translation**. As waves move further onshore, the wave base comes into contact with the seabed. Friction slows down the wave advance, causing the wave fronts to crowd together. Wavelengths are reduced and the wave height increases. The shortening of the wave causes an increase in wave height – this process is known as **wave shoaling**. Thus a **breaker** is formed.

There are three main types of breaker (Figure 2.3):
- **Spilling breakers** are associated with gentle beach gradients and steep waves (wave height relative to wave length). They are characterised by a gradual peaking of the wave until the crest becomes unstable; resulting in a gentle spilling forward of the crest.
- **Plunging breakers** tend to occur on steeper beaches than spilling breakers, with waves of intermediate steepness.

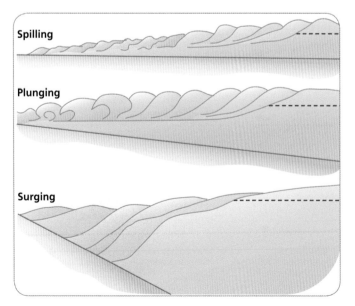

Figure 2.3 Types of breaker

They are distinguished by the shore-ward face of the wave becoming vertical, curling over, and plunging forward and downward as an intact mass of water.
- **Surging breakers** are found on steep beaches with low steepness waves. In surging breakers the front face and crest of the wave remain relatively smooth and the wave slides directly up the beach without breaking. In surging breakers a large proportion of the wave energy is reflected at the beach.

Once the breaker has collapsed, the wave energy is transmitted onshore as a 'wave of translation'. The swash will surge up the beach, with its speed gradually lessened by friction and the uphill gradient. Gravity will draw the water back as the backwash. There are two basic types of wave translation – constructive and destructive waves.

Constructive waves tend to occur when wave frequency is low (6–8 arriving onshore per minute), particularly when these waves advance over a gently shelving sea floor (formed, for example of fine material, such as sand) (Figure 2.4). These waves have been generated far offshore. The gentle offshore slope creates a gradual increase in friction, which will cause a gradual steepening of the wave front. Thus a **spilling** breaker is formed, where water movement is elliptical. As this breaker collapses, the powerful constructive swash surges up the gentle gradient. Because of its low frequency, the backwash of each wave has time to return to the sea before the next wave breaks – the swash of each wave is not impeded and retains maximum energy.

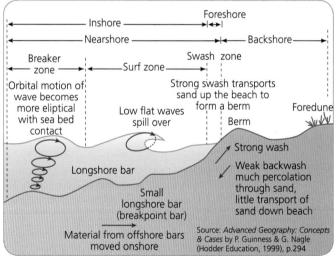

Figure 2.4 Constructive waves

Destructive waves are the result of locally generated winds, which create waves of high frequency (12–14 per minute) (Figure 2.5). This rapid approach of the waves, particularly if they are moving onshore up a steeply shelving coastline (formed from coarse material such as gravel or shingle), creates a rapid increase in friction and thus a very steep, **plunging** breaker where water movement is circular. Due to the rapid steepening and curling of the wave breaker, the energy of the wave is transmitted down the beach (on breaker collapse), accelerated by the steeper gradient, and so the wave becomes destructive, breaking down the beach material.

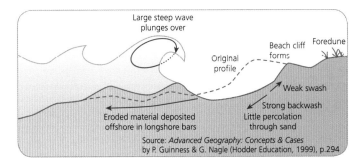

Figure 2.5 Destructive waves

Waves are dominant in some coastal environments whereas in others it is the tide or winds. This has an important impact on the landforms that are found there (Table 2.1).

Table 2.1 Processes and landforms in coastal environments

Wave dominated	Tide dominated	Wind dominated
Shore platforms	Mudflats	Sand dunes
Cliffs	Sandflats	
Beaches	Saltmarshes	
Spits, tombolos	Mangroves	
Deltas	Deltas	
High energy	Low energy	High energy

Section 2.1 Activities

1 Using annotated diagrams, outline the main differences between constructive and destructive waves.

2 Explain the meaning of the terms *swash*, *backwash* and *fetch*.

Tides and the tidal cycle

Tides are regular movements in the sea's surface, caused by the gravitational pull of the moon and Sun on the oceans. The moon accounts for the larger share of the pull. **Low spring tides** occur just after a new moon whereas **high spring tides** occur after a full moon. They occur when the Sun and the moon are aligned. **Neap tides** occur when the Sun and moon are at right-angles to the Earth. Tides are influenced by the size and shape of ocean basins, the characteristics of the shoreline, the Coriolis force, and meteorological conditions. In general:

- tides are greatest in bays and along funnel-shaped coastlines
- in the northern hemisphere water is deflected to the right of its path
- during low pressure systems water levels are raised 10 cm for every decrease of 10 mb.

The difference between high and low tide is called the **tidal range**. This varies from almost nothing in enclosed seas such as the Mediterranean to almost 15 m in the Bay of Fundy, Canada. Tidal range varies with distance from the **amphidromic point** (place where there is no tidal range) and according to the shape of the coast; the strength of tidal currents varies enormously. If the coast is funnelled, as the tide advances it is concentrated in an ever narrowing space. Therefore its height rises rapidly, producing a **tidal bore**. A good example is the Severn Bore, which occurs in the Severn Estuary between Wales and England as a wave of up to 1 m in height travelling at a speed of up to 30 km/hr.

Coastal areas can be classified into **microtidal**, which have a very low tidal range (less than 2 m), **mesotidal** (2–4 m) and **macrotidal** (over 4 m) (Figure 2.6). The tidal range has important influences on coastal processes:

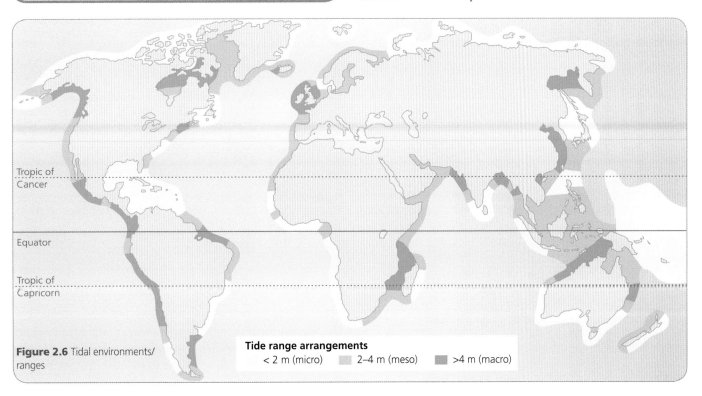

Figure 2.6 Tidal environments/ranges

Tide range arrangements
  < 2 m (micro)   2–4 m (meso)   >4 m (macro)

- it controls the vertical range of erosion and deposition
- weathering and biological activity is affected by the time between tides
- velocity is influenced by the tidal range and has an important scouring effect.

Rip currents are important for transporting sediment. They can be caused by tidal motion or by waves breaking along a shore. A cellular circulation is caused by differences in wave height parallel to the shore. Water from the higher sections of the breaker travels further up the shore and returns back through the points where lower sections have broken. Once rip currents are formed they modify the beach by creating cusps, which perpetuate the currents.

Storm surges

Storm surges are changes in the sea level caused by intense low pressure systems and high wind speeds. For every drop in air pressure of 10 mb, sea water is raised 10 cm. During tropical cyclones, low pressure may be 100 mb less than normal, raising sea level by 1 m. In areas where the coastline is funnel-shaped, this rise in level is intensified. During high tides the results can be devastating. Surges are common in the Bay of Bengal, on the south-east coast of the USA and in Japan. They are particularly hazardous in low-lying areas.

The Ganges delta experiences many storm surges. These may exceed 4 m and the accompanying storm waves can add a further 4 m to the wave height. The funnel shape of the Bay of Bengal forces water to build up. Seven of the nine worst storms this century have affected Pakistan. In 1970 over 300 000 people were killed in a surge. A further 225 000 people were killed in 1989, and in 1991 another 140 000 were killed in surges. In addition, millions were killed by the diseases and famines that followed, even more were made homeless and vast numbers of cattle were killed.

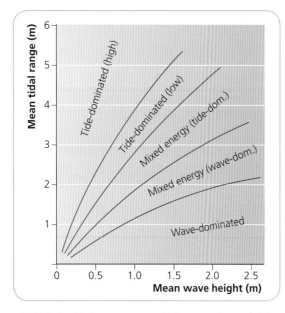

Figure 2.7 Relationship between mean tidal range and wave height

1 Define the terms *tidal range*, *tidal bore*, *amphidromic point* and *storm surge*.

2 Explain why tides are important.

3 Study Figure 2.7 carefully. Outline the relationship between mean wave height, mean tidal range, and dominant processes. Suggest reasons to explain your answer.

Wave refraction

As wave fronts approach the shore, their speed of approach is reduced as the waves 'feel bottom'. Usually, due to the interaction between onshore wind direction (and therefore direction of wave advance) and the trend of the coast, the wave fronts approach the shore obliquely. This causes the wave fronts to bend and swing around in an attempt to break parallel to the shore. The change in speed and distortion of the wave front is called wave refraction (Figure 2.8). If refraction is completed, the fronts break parallel to the shore. However, due primarily to the complexities of coastline shape, refraction is not always totally achieved – this causes longshore drift, which is a major force in the transport of material along the coast.

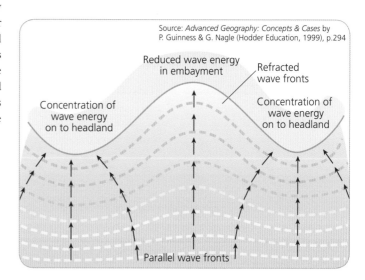

Source: *Advanced Geography: Concepts & Cases* by P. Guinness & G. Nagle (Hodder Education, 1999), p.294

Figure 2.8 Wave refraction

Wave refraction also distributes wave energy along a stretch of coast. Along a complex transverse coast with alternating headlands and bays, wave refraction concentrates wave energy and therefore erosional activity on the headlands, while wave energy is dispersed in the bays – hence deposition tends to occur in the bays.

If refraction is not complete, longshore drift occurs (Figure 2.9). This leads to a gradual movement of sediment along the shore, as the swash moves in the direction of the prevailing wind whereas the swash moves straight down the beach following the steepest gradient.

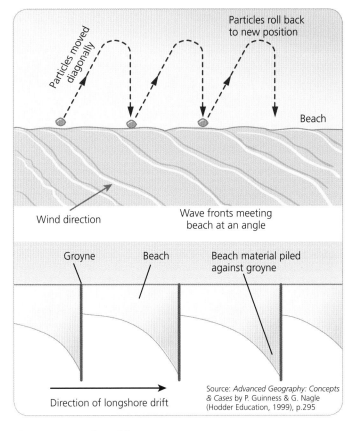

Figure 2.9 Longshore drift

Text within figure 2.9:
Particles moved diagonally
Particles roll back to new position
Beach
Wind direction
Wave fronts meeting beach at an angle
Groyne
Beach
Beach material piled against groyne
Direction of longshore drift
Source: *Advanced Geography: Concepts & Cases* by P. Guinness & G. Nagle (Hodder Education, 1999), p.295

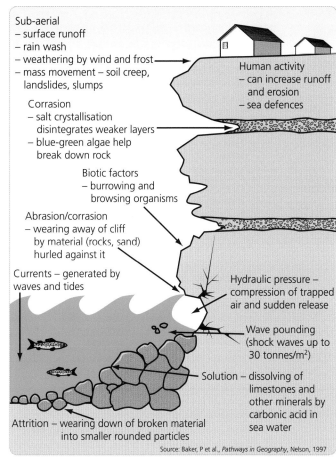

Figure 2.10 Types of erosion

Erosion

Waves perform a number of complex and interacting processes of erosion (Figure 2.10 and Table 2.2). **Hydraulic action** is an important process as waves break onto cliffs. As the waves break against the cliff face, any air trapped in cracks, joints and bedding planes is momentarily placed under very great pressure. As the wave retreats, this pressure is released with explosive force. Stresses weaken the coherence of the rock, aiding erosion (comparable to cavitation in rivers). This is particularly obvious in well-bedded and well-jointed rocks such as limestones, sandstones, granite and chalk, as well as in rocks that are poorly consolidated such as clays and glacial deposits. Hydraulic action is also notable during times of storm wave activity – for example, the average pressure of Atlantic storm waves is $11\,000\,kg/m^2$. Another term used for this process is **wave pounding**.

Corrasion is the process whereby a breaking wave can hurl pebbles and shingle against a coast, thereby abrading it. **Attrition** takes place as other forms of erosion continue. The eroded material is itself worn down by attrition, which partly explains the variety of sizes of beach material. **Solution** is a form of chemical erosion. In areas of calcareous (lime-rich) rock, waves remove material by acidic water. The source of the acidity is from organisms such as barnacles and limpets. These secrete organic acids which may make the water more acidic, especially in rock pools at low tide.

As wave action is constantly at work between high water mark (HWM) and low water mark (LWM) it causes undercutting of a cliff face, forming a notch and overhang. Breaking waves, especially during storms and spring tides, can erode the coast above HWM. As the undercutting continues, the notch becomes deeper and the overhang more pronounced. Ultimately the overhang will collapse, causing the cliff line to retreat. The base of the cliff will be left behind as a broadening **platform**, often covered with deposited material, with the coarsest near the cliff base, gradually becoming smaller towards the open sea.

In addition, sub-aerial, or cliff-face, processes include:

- **salt weathering** – the process by which sodium and magnesium compounds expand in joints and cracks thereby weakening rock structures
- **freeze–thaw weathering** – the process whereby water freezes, expands and degrades jointed rocks
- **biological weathering** – carried out by molluscs, sponges and sea urchins (very important on low-energy coasts)
- **solution weathering** – the chemical weathering of calcium by acidic water, which tends to occur in rock pools due to the presence of organisms secreting organic acids
- **slaking** – materials disintegrate when exposed to water; this can be caused by hydration cycles.

Mass movements are also important in coastal areas, especially slumping and rockfalls (see pages 71–6).

Table 2.2 Factors affecting the rate of erosion

Energy factors	
Waves	• Wave steepness – steep destructive waves formed locally have more erosive power than less steep constructive waves. • Wave breaking point – waves breaking at cliff base cause maximum erosion, whereas waves breaking off shore lose energy.
Tides	• Neap and spring tides vary the zone of wave attack. • Strong tidal currents can scour estuary channels.
Currents	• Longshore and rip currents can move large quantities of material.
Winds	• Onshore winds erode fine beach sand to form dunes. • Offshore winds may erode dunes and nourish the beach. • The longer the fetch the greater the wave energy potential.
Material factors	
Sediment supply	• Continual supply is necessary for abrasion, whereas an oversupply can protect the coast.
Beach/rock platform width	• Beaches/rock platforms influence wave energy by absorbing waves before they can attack cliffs.
Rock resistance	• Rock type influences the rate of erosion, e.g. granites are very resistant whereas unconsolidated volcanic ash has little resistance to wave attack. • Erosion is rapid where rocks of different resistance overlie one another.
Rock structure and dip	• Well-jointed or faulted rocks are very susceptible to erosion. • Horizontal or vertical structures produce steep cliffs. • Rocks dipping away from the sea produce gentle cliffs.
Shore geometry	
Offshore topography (bathymetry)	• A steep seabed creates higher and steeper waves than one with a gentle gradient. • Longshore bars cause waves to break off shore and lose energy.
Orientation of coast	• Headlands with vertical cliffs tend to concentrate wave energy by refraction. • Degree of exposure to waves influences erosion rates.
Direction of fetch	• The longer the fetch, the greater the potential for erosion by waves.

Case Study

Erosion in southern Nigeria

Lagos is located at a break in the coast, and the city developed rapidly in the nineteenth century and early twentieth century (Figure 2.11). Dredging started in 1907 and the harbour was begun in 1908. Breakwaters and a jetty provide a deepwater channel for large ships.

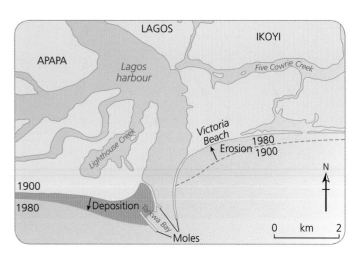

Figure 2.11 Erosion at Lagos, Nigeria

These developments interrupted the west–east longshore drift along the coast of West Africa. As a result, there has been an increase of deposition on Lighthouse Beach on the western updrift side of the jetty at Tarkwa Bay, which traps sediment, and an increase in erosion on the eastern downdrift side of the jetty and shipping channel. Victoria Beach has been eroded by almost 70 m/yr, and over 2 km of beach has been lost since then (Table 2.3). This beach is much used as a recreational area for the people of Lagos. Hence beach replenishment has been used here since 1976, but it continues to be eroded.

From time to time marine currents change direction, material is deposited in the channel leading to the harbour, and this has to be dredged to keep the channel clear. Continued deposition on Lighthouse Beach will eventually lead to deposition beyond the jetties of Tarkwa Bay, potentially cutting off the deep channel of Lagos Harbour.

Table 2.3 Erosion of the Niger delta

	m/year
Western delta	18–24
Central delta	15–20
Eastern delta	10–24

Wave transportation and deposition

Sediment transport is generally categorised into two modes:
• **Bedload** – grains transported by bedload are moved through continuous contact (**traction** or dragging) or discontinuous contact (**saltation**) with the sea floor. In traction, grains slide or roll along – a slow form of transport. Weak currents may transport sand or strong currents may transport pebbles and boulders. In saltation, the grains hop along the seabed. Moderate currents may transport sand whereas strong currents transport pebbles and gravel.

- **Suspended load** – grains are carried by turbulent flow and generally are held up by the water. Suspension occurs when moderate currents are transporting silts or strong currents are transporting sands. Grains transported as **wash loads** are permanently in suspension, and typically consist of clays and dissolved material.

Deposition is governed by sediment size (mass) and shape. In some cases sediments will flocculate (stick together), become heavier and fall out in deposition.

Sediment cells

The coastal sediment system, or **littoral cell system**, is a simplified model that examines coastal processes and patterns in a given area (Figure 2.12). It operates at a variety of scales from a single bay, for example Turtle Bay in North Queensland, Australia, to a regional scale, for example the south California coast. Each littoral cell is a self-contained cell, in which inputs and outputs are balanced.

Figure 2.12 Sediment cells

Dynamic equilibrium

The concept of dynamic equilibrium is important to littoral cells. This concept states that any system (or in this case littoral cell) is the result of the inputs and processes that operate within it. Change to one of the inputs (for example an increase in sediment to the shoreline following cliff collapse) causes a knock-on effect on the processers (such as longshore drift, transport or beach protection) and a resulting change in the landforms (such as stabilisation of cliffs or downdrift beach enlargement). The balance changes – hence **dynamic equilibrium**.

Case Study

Southern California: Oceanside littoral cell

Inputs into the Californian sediment cell (Figure 2.13) include:
- river deposits

- sediments from cliffs
- materials for beach replenishment
- north–south longshore drift.

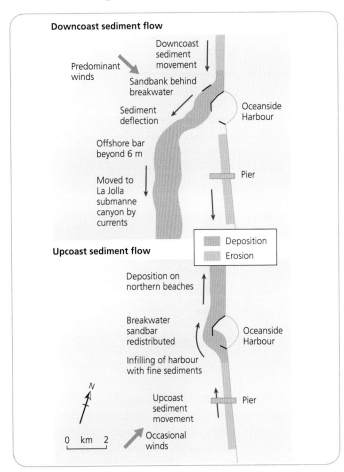

Figure 2.13 Sediment cells in southern California

Irregular and variable river supplies have been further reduced by 33 per cent due to dam construction. Most of the material supplied for beach replenishment is fine-grained silt and sand.

The region is very active. Each year rip currents and offshore currents move 100 000 m³ of sediment into the La Jolla submarine canyon and over 200 000 m³ of material drifts southwards. In addition, seasonal variations in constructive and destructive waves redistribute coastal sediments and sea levels are rising 6–15 mm each year.

Human impacts

- Dams have reduced the supply of sediment to the beaches by 33 per cent.
- Buildings, houses, swimming pools, boats, private protection schemes and roads are destabilising the cliffs.
- Oceanside Harbour in the north is blocking the southward movement of sediment and most is now diverted to offshore currents and to the La Jolla submarine canyon.

Human activity and longshore drift in West Africa

Ocean currents along the coast of West Africa have removed huge amounts of beach material along the coast between Ghana and Nigeria. This has affected settlements, tourism and industry. The increase in coastal retreat has been blamed on the construction of the Akosombo Dam on the Volta River in Ghana. The Guinea Current is among the strongest in the world, and is removing approximately 1.5 million m^3 of sand each year between the Ivory Coast and Nigeria (Figure 2.14). The effect on Ghana, Benin and Togo is potentially catastrophic.

Figure 2.14 Human activity and longshore drift along the coast of West Africa

The cause of the coastal retreat is traced to the building of the Akosombo Dam in 1961. It is just 110 km from the coast and disrupts the flow of sediment from the River Volta, preventing it from reaching the coast. Thus there is less sand to replace that which has already been washed away, so the coastline retreats due to erosion by the Guinea Current. Towns such as Keta, 30 km east of the Volta estuary, have been destroyed as their protective beach has been removed. Other towns in neighbouring Togo, Kpeme and Tropicana, are now threatened with destruction.

In Togo the problem has been intensified by the use of artificial breakwaters. In the mid-1960s a deepwater port was opened at Lomé, the country's capital, to improve trade with landlocked neighbouring countries such as Mali, Niger and Burkina Faso. Lomé is protected by a 1300 m breakwater, which obstructs the natural flow of the Guinea Current from west to east. Sand carried by the current collects on the westward (updrift) side of the breakwater. Thus the east side (downdrift) is open to erosion. The result has been the erosion of the beach and local infrastructure. In 1984 a 100 m stretch of the main Ghana–Benin highway was destroyed in just 24 hours. Erosion near the holiday resort of Tropicana caused the sea to advance 100 m towards the holiday complex. Ironically, the erosion uncovered a bed of resistant sandstone, which now protects the resort, but is not as attractive for the tourist trade as the sandy beach that previously existed. Kpeme, 18 km to the east of Tropicana, is a port from which most of Togo's processed phosphate is exported, accounting for more than half of Togo's foreign exchange. The jetty at Kpeme was threatened with erosion. To manage the risk, engineers have reinforced the foundations of the jetty with boulders. The boulders now trap sand and stop it from moving down the coastline. As a result, towns further east, such as Aneho, are now even more at risk from erosion. At a cost of between £1 million and £2 million to protect every kilometre of coastline, it is hard to imagine how the coast can be protected. If Togo were to protect its coastline by preventing the movement of sand eastwards, it might lead to an increase in erosion in Benin, where the foundations of oil wells may be threatened.

Section 2.1 Activities

1 Explain what is meant by the term *littoral cell* (sediment cell).

2 Why is there more erosion on some coasts than others? Use examples to support your answer.

3 Outline the ways in which human activities can disrupt the operation of sediment cells.

4 With the use of an annotated diagram, explain what happens when wave refraction takes place.

2.2 Coastal landforms of cliffed and constructive coasts

Cliffs and erosion

Cliff profiles are very variable and depend on a number of controlling factors. One major factor is the influence of bedding and jointing. The well-developed jointing and bedding of certain harder limestones creates a geometric cliff profile with a steep, angular cliff face and a flat top (bedding plane). Wave erosion opens up these lines of weakness, causing complete blocks to fall away and the creation of angular overhangs and cave shapes. In other well-jointed and bedded rocks, a whole variety of features is created by wave erosion, such as caves, geos, arches, stacks and stumps (Figure 2.15). Wave refraction concentrates wave energy on the flanks of headlands. If there are lines of weakness these may be eroded to form a **geo** (a widened crack or inlet). Geos may be eroded and enlarged to form caves, and if the caves on either side of a headland merge, an arch is formed. Further erosion and weathering of the arch may cause the roof of the arch to collapse, leaving an upstanding stack. The eventual erosion of the stack produces a stump. Good examples of arches and stacks are to be found at Etretat in northern France and at Dyrhooley, southern Iceland (Figure 2.16).

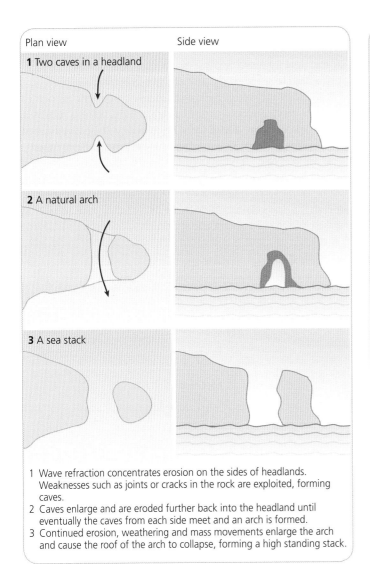

Plan view   Side view

1 Two caves in a headland

2 A natural arch

3 A sea stack

1 Wave refraction concentrates erosion on the sides of headlands. Weaknesses such as joints or cracks in the rock are exploited, forming caves.
2 Caves enlarge and are eroded further back into the headland until eventually the caves from each side meet and an arch is formed.
3 Continued erosion, weathering and mass movements enlarge the arch and cause the roof of the arch to collapse, forming a high standing stack.

Figure 2.15 Caves, arches, stacks and stumps

Figure 2.16 Cliffs and arches at Dyrhoolay, southern Iceland

Rocky shores can be divided into three main types (Figure 2.17): sloping shore platforms, sub-horizontal shore platforms, and plunging cliffs. As with all classifications, it is an over-simplification but it is useful in illustrating the range of features associated with rocky shores (Table 2.4).

Sloping shore platform

Cave, Shore platform, HWL, LWL, Debris, Pothole, Stack, Arch, Notch

Sub-horizontal shore platform

Cave, Ramp, Shore platform, HWL, LWL, Pool, Stack, Seaward drop, Furrow, Rampart, Pothole, Notch

Punging cliff

HWL, LWL, Plunging cliff

Figure 2.17 Types of rocky shoreline

Table 2.4 Summary of the main erosional processes on rocky shores

Process	Description	Conditions conducive to the process
Mechanical wave erosion		
Erosion	Loose material is removed by waves.	Energetic wave conditions and microtidal range
Abrasion	Rock surfaces are scoured by wave-induced flow with mixture of water and sediment.	'Soft' rocks, energetic wave conditions, a thin layer of sediment and microtidal range
Hydraulic action	Wave-induced pressure variations within the rock cause and widen rock cracks.	'Weak' rocks, energetic wave conditions and microtidal range

Continued overleaf

Table 2.4 Continued from previous page

Process	Description	Conditions conducive to the process
Weathering		
Physical weathering	Frost action and cycles of wetting/drying cause and widen rock cracks.	Sedimentary rocks in cool regions
Salt weathering	Volumetric growth of salt crystals in rocks widens cracks.	Sedimentary rocks in hot and dry regions
Chemical weathering	A number of chemical processes remove rock materials. These processes include hydrolysis, oxidation, hydration and solution.	Sedimentary rocks in hot and wet regions
Water-layer levelling	Physical, salt and chemical weathering working together along the edges of rock pools.	Sedimentary rocks in areas with high evaporation
Bio-erosion		
Biochemical	Chemical weathering by products of metabolism.	Limestone in tropical regions
Biophysical	Physical removal of rock by grazing and boring animals.	Limestone in tropical regions
Mass movements		
Rockfalls and toppling	Rocks fall straight down the face of the cliff.	Well-jointed rocks, undercutting of cliff by waves
Slides	Deep-seated failures.	Deeply weathered rock, undercutting of cliff by rock
Flows	Flow of loose material down a slope.	Unconsolidated material, undercutting of cliffs by waves

The dip of the bedding alone will create varying cliff profiles. For example, if the beds dip vertically, then a sheer cliff face is formed. By contrast, if the beds dip steeply seaward, then steep, shelving cliffs with landslips are the result.

Each cliff profile is, to some extent, unique, but a model of cliff evolution or modification (Figure 2.18) takes into account not only wave activity but also sub-aerial weathering processes.

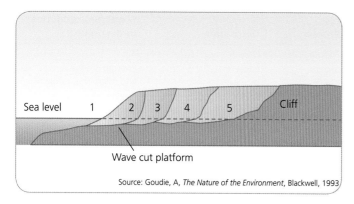

Source: Goudie, A, *The Nature of the Environment*, Blackwell, 1993

Figure 2.18 Evolution of wave-cut platforms

Many cliffs are composed of more than one rock type. These are known as **composite cliffs**. The exact shape and form of the cliff will depend on such factors as strength and structure of rock, relative hardness and the nature of the waves involved.

Figure 2.19 illustrates cliffs with rocks of different properties as well as varying wave energy. In Figure 2.19a there is relatively strong rock uniform resistance. Cliff retreat will be determined by rock strength – for granites this will be slow while for glacial tills it will be rapid (Table 2.5). In Figure 2.19b the rock strength is weaker (than in Figure 2.19a) and cliff retreat is faster. In addition, rock properties vary. Figure 2.19b shows that the form of the cliff depends on the relative position of the weaker rock: if it is at the base of the cliff, undercutting and collapse may occur; if it is near the top, the cliff is subject to sub-aerial processes and wave undercutting.

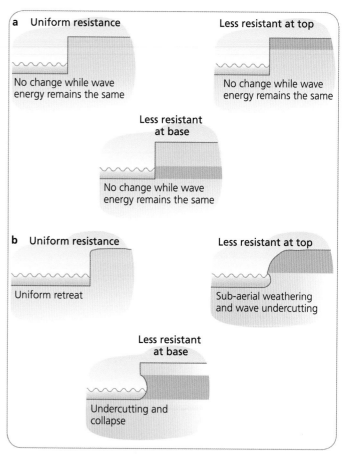

Figure 2.19 Effect of relationships between resistant and less resistant rocks in cliff morphology

Table 2.5 Mean cliff erosion rates

Rate	Rock type
< 0.001 m/yr	Granitic
0.01–0.01 m/yr	Limestone
0.01–0.1 m/yr	Shale
0.1–1 m/yr	Chalk
0.1–10 m yr	Quaternary deposits (glacial till)
10 m/yr	Volcanic ash

Figures 2.20a and b deal with horizontally bedded rock. In Figure 2.20a the beds are dipping landwards. Sliding is unlikely as the movement is landwards. However, in Figure 2.20b the movement is seawards, and the potential for sliding is great. Seaward-dipping rocks consequently pose greater management challenges than landward-dipping rocks.

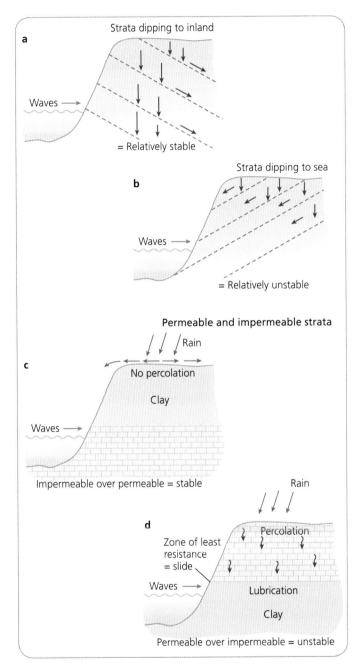

Figure 2.20 The controlling factors in cliff stability

Figures 2.20c and d show the impact of rock permeability on cliff development. If impermeable rock overlies permeable rock (Figure 2.20c) there is limited percolation and so the cliff is more stable. If permeable rock overlies impermeable rock, water may soak into the cliff, and slope failure is more likely where water builds up at the junction of the two rock types.

Another type of composite cliff is a **bevelled cliff** (Figure 2.21). This was formed in a number of stages:

1 A vertical cliff was formed due to marine processes in the last interglacial (warm period) when sea levels were higher than they are today.
2 During the subsequent glacial (cold) phase, sea levels dropped, and periglacial processes such as solifluction and freeze–thaw affected the former sea cliff, forming a bevelled edge.
3 When the sea levels rose again during the following interglacial, there was renewed wave erosion, which removes the debris and steepens the base of the cliff, leaving the upper part at a lower angle.

Figure 2.21 Bevelled cliffs

Cliff form can also be related to latitude. In the tropics, low wave energy levels and high rates of chemical weathering generally produce low-gradient coasts. Coastal cliffs in high latitudes are also characterised by relatively low gradients since the periglacial processes produce large amounts of cliff base materials. Temperate regions tend to have the steepest cliffs. The rapid removal of debris by high-energy waves prevents the build-up of material on the base, while active cliff development occurs as a result of undercutting.

Coastal platforms

As a result of cliff retreat, a platform along the coast is normally created (Figure 2.22). Traditionally, up to very recent times, this feature was described as a **wave-cut platform** (or abrasion platform), because it was believed that it was created entirely by wave action (Figure 2.18). However, there is some controversy over the importance of other agents of weathering and erosion in the production of the coastal platform, especially the larger ones.

Figure 2.22 A shore platform

In post-glacial times, sea level has not remained sufficiently constant to erode such platforms. However, some marine geomorphologists believe that these platforms could be **relict** or ancient features, originally cut long ago at a period when sea level was constant, and that the contemporary sea level is at about the same height and is just modifying slightly the ancient platform.

Secondly, in high latitudes, **frost action** could be important in supporting wave activity, particularly as these areas are now rising as a result of isostatic recovery (after intense glaciation). In other areas, **solution weathering**, **salt crystallisation** and **slaking** could also support wave activity, particularly in the tidal and splash zones. **Marine organisms**, especially algae, can accelerate weathering at low tide and in the area just above HWM. At night carbon dioxide is released by algae because photosynthesis does not occur. This carbon dioxide combines with the cool sea water to create an acidic environment, causing 'rotting'.

Other organisms, such as limpets, secrete organic acids which can slowly rot the rock. Certain marine worms (polychaetes and annelids), molluscs and sea urchins can actually 'bore' into rock surfaces, particularly of chalk and limestone.

Shore platform at Kaikoura peninsula, New Zealand

Well-developed shore platforms can be found at Kaikoura on South Island, New Zealand (Figure 2.23). These platforms are periodically exposed to high-energy waves (>1.5 m), but generally experience calm conditions (0.5 m). The average rate of platform lowering is 1.4 mm yr^{-1}. Despite the high-energy waves, the amount of wave energy delivered to the platform is low. This is because most of the offshore waves break before they hit the platform. Sub-aerial weathering appears to be the dominant process here, in particular the number of cycles of wetting and drying.

Figure 2.23 Kaikoura peninsula, New Zealand

1 Outline the main processes of coastal erosion.

2 Briefly explain the factors that affect the rate of erosion.

3 With the use of annotated diagrams, explain how stacks and stumps may be formed.

4 How are shore platforms formed?

Deposition

It is important to distinguish between two types of coastline:

- **Swash-aligned coasts** are oriented parallel to the crests of the prevailing waves (Figure 2.24a). They are closed systems in terms of longshore drift transport and the net littoral drift rates are zero.

- **Drift-aligned coasts** are oriented obliquely to the crest of the prevailing waves (Figure 2.24b). The shoreline of a drift-aligned coast is primarily controlled by longshore sediment transport processes. Drift-aligned coasts are open systems in terms of longshore transport. Spits, bars, tombolos and cuspate forelands are all features of drift-aligned coasts.

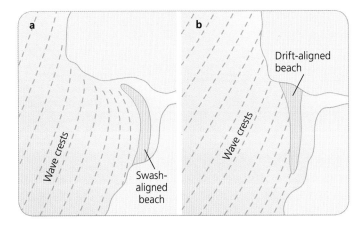

Figure 2.24 Swash-aligned and drift-aligned coasts

Beaches

A whole variety of materials can be moved along the coast by waves, fed by longshore drift. The coarse material is found deposited (and fallen from the backing cliffs) in the **backshore** and **foreshore** zones as **littoral deposits**. The finer material, worn down largely by attrition, is usually found in the **offshore** zone as **neritic** deposits.

The term **beach** refers to the accumulation of material deposited between low water mark (LWM) spring tides and the highest point reached by storm waves at high water mark (HWM) spring tides. A typical beach will have three zones: backshore,

foreshore and offshore (Figure 2.25). The backshore is a cliff or is marked by a line of dunes. Above and at HWM there may be a **berm** or **shingle ridge**. This is coarse material pushed up the beach by spring tides and aided by storm waves which fling material well above the level of the waves themselves. These are often referred to as storm beaches. The seaward edge of the berm is often scalloped and irregular due to the creation of beach **cusps** (Figure 2.26). Their origin is still controversial – they could be due to the edge of the swash itself which is often scalloped, or to the action of two sets of wave fronts approaching the shore obliquely from opposite directions. Once initiated, the cusps are self-perpetuating: the swash is broken up by the cusp projection, concentrating energy onto the cusp (compare with refraction onto headlands) which excavates material. Cusps develop best in areas of high tidal range where waves approach the coast at right-angles. The spacing of cusps is related to wave height and swash strength.

Figure 2.26 Cusps

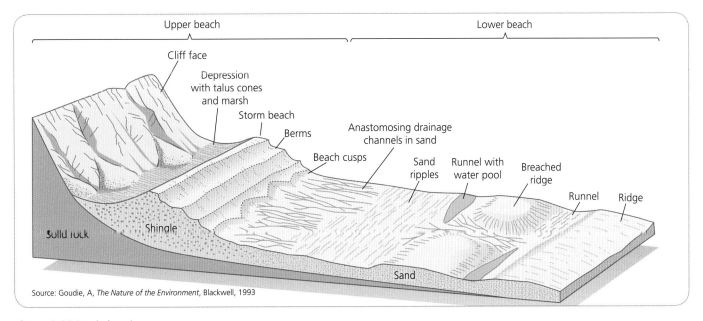

Source: Goudie, A, *The Nature of the Environment*, Blackwell, 1993

Figure 2.25 Beach deposits

239

The foreshore is exposed at low tide. The beach material may be undulating due to the creation of ridges, called **fulls**, running parallel to the water line, pushed up by constructive waves at varying heights of the tide. These are separated by troughs, called **swales**. Great stretches of sand, too, may comprise the foreshore. In areas of complex coast, sand beaches may only be exposed as small **bayhead beaches** in bays.

Offshore, the first material is deposited. In this zone, the waves touch the seabed and so the material is usually disturbed, sometimes being pushed up as **offshore bars**, when the offshore gradient is very shallow.

Excellent beach development occurs on a lowland coast (constructive waves), with a sheltered aspect/trend, composed of 'soft' rocks, which provide a good supply of material, or where longshore drift supplies abundant material.

Beach form is affected by the size, shape and composition of materials, the tidal range, and wave characteristics. As storm waves are more frequent in winter and swell waves more important in summer, many beaches differ in their winter and summer profile (Figure 2.27). Thus the same beach may produce two very different profiles at different times of the year. For example, constructive waves in summer may build up the beach but destructive waves in winter may change the size and shape of the beach. The relationship between wave steepness and beach angle is a two-way affair. Steep destructive waves reduce beach angle whereas gentle constructive waves increase it. In turn, a low gradient produces shallow water which in turn increases wave steepness. Hence plunging waves are associated with gentle beaches whereas surging waves are associated with steeper beaches.

Sediment size affects the beach profile through its percolation rate (Figure 2.27). Shingle/pebbles allow rapid infiltration and percolation, so the impact of swash and backwash are reduced. As the backwash is reduced it will not impede the next swash.

Seasonal beach profile

Beach profiles and particle size		
Material	*Diameter (mm)*	*Beach angle*
Cobbles	32	24°
Pebbles	4	17°
Coarse sand	2	7°
Medium sand	0.2	5°
Fine sand	0.02	3°
Very fine sand	0.002	1°

Upper sweep profile (summer)

High tide (spring)
High neap
Main sea level
Low neap
Low tide (spring)

Sweep zone

Lower sweep profile (winter)

Figure 2.27 Seasonal changes on a beach

If the swash is stronger than the backwash then deposition may occur. By contrast, sand produces a lower angle and allows less percolation. Backwash is likely to be greater than on a gravel beach. The pattern is made more complex because sediment size varies up a beach. The largest particles, the products of cliff recession, are found at the rear of a beach. Large, rounded material on the upper beach is probably supplied only during the highest spring tides and is unaffected by 'average' conditions. On the lower beach wave action is more frequent, attrition is common, and consequently particle size is smaller.

Section 2.2 Activities

1 Describe the distinction between drift-aligned and swash-aligned coastlines.

2 Explain the origin of **a** beaches and **b** cusps.

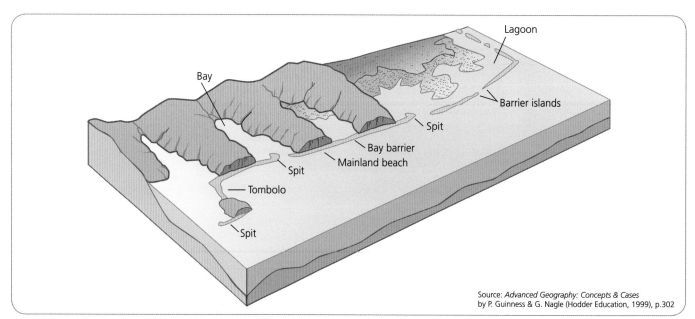

Lagoon

Bay

Barrier islands

Spit

Spit

Bay barrier

Mainland beach

Spit

Tombolo

Spit

Source: *Advanced Geography: Concepts & Cases* by P. Guinness & G. Nagle (Hodder Education, 1999), p.302

Figure 2.28 Localised depositional features

Localised depositional features

Bars, spits and other localised features develop where:
- abundant material is available, particularly shingle and sand
- the coastline is irregular due, for example, to local geological variety (transverse coast)
- deposition is increased by the presence of vegetation (reducing wave velocity and energy)
- there are estuaries and major rivers (Figure 2.28).

Offshore bars are usually composed of coarse sand or shingle. They develop as bars offshore on a gently shelving seabed. Waves feel bottom far offshore. This causes disturbance in the water which leads to deposition, forming an offshore bar below sea level. Between the bar and shore, lagoons (often called **sounds**) develop. If the water in the lagoon is calm, and fed by rivers, marshes and mudflats can develop. Bars can be driven onshore by storm winds and waves. A classic area for this is off the coast of the Carolinas in south-east USA.

Spits are common along an indented coast. For example, along a transverse coast where bays are common, or near river mouths (estuaries and rias), wave energy is reduced. The long, narrow ridges of sand and shingle that form spits are always joined at one end to the mainland. The simplest spit is a linear spit, but it may be curved at its distal (unattached) end.

Spits often become curved as waves undergo refraction. Cross-currents or occasional storm waves may assist this hooked formation. If the curved end is very pronounced it is known as a **recurved spit**. Many spits have developed over long periods of time and have a complex morphology. For example, a **compound recurved spit** has a narrow proximal (joined) end and a wide, recurved distal end that often encloses a lagoon – for example Presque Isle, Lake Erie (Figure 2.29) and Sandy Hook in New Jersey. The wide distal end usually consists of several dune/beach ridges associated with older shorelines demonstrating seaward migration of the shoreline.

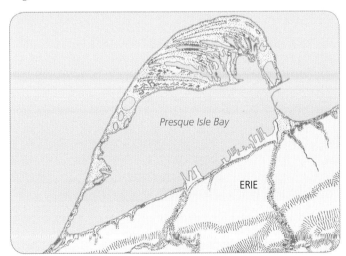

Figure 2.29 Compound recurved spit with lagoon: Presque Isle, Lake Erie

Spits grow in the direction of the predominant longshore drift, and are a classic example of a drift-aligned feature that can only exist through the continued supply of sediment.

Within the curve of the spit, the water is shallow and a considerable area of mudflat and saltmarsh (**salting**) is exposed at low water. These saltmarshes continue to grow as mud is trapped by the marsh vegetation. The whole area of saltmarsh is intersected by a complex network of channels, or **creeks**, which contain water even at low tide.

Section 2.2 Activities

Draw a labelled diagram to show the formation of a spit.

Bars

A bar is a ridge of material that is connected at both ends to the mainland. It is located above sea level. If a spit continues to grow lengthwise, it may ultimately link two headlands to form a **bay bar**. These are composed either of shingle, as in the case of the Low Bar in Cornwall, UK, or of sand, such as the *nehrung* of the Baltic coast, which pond back lagoons called *haff*.

Barrier islands

Barrier islands are natural sandy breakwaters that form parallel to a flat coastline. By far the world's longest series is that of roughly 300 islands along the east and southern coasts of the USA (Figure 2.30). The distance between barrier islands and the shore is variable. The islands are generally 200–400 m wide but some are wider. Some Florida islands are so close to the shore that residents do not even realise they are on an island. By contrast, parts of Hatteras Island in North Carolina are 20 km offshore.

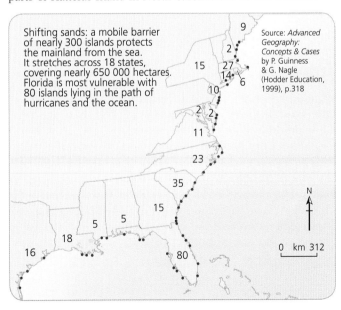

Figure 2.30 Barrier islands along the east coast of the USA

Barrier islands form only under certain conditions and America's eastern seaboard provides the ideal conditions for barrier islands (Figure 2.31). First, a gently sloping and low-lying coast unprotected by cliffs faces an ocean. Over the last 15 000 years, the sea level has risen by 120 m as glaciers and icecaps have melted. Wind and waves have formed sand dunes at the edge of the continental shelf. As the rising sea breaks over the dunes, this forms lagoons behind the sandy ridge, which divides into islands. Waves wash sand from the islands, depositing it further inland and forming new islands. Currents, flowing parallel to the coast, scour sand from barrier islands and deposit it further up or down the coast to form new islands. The island in Chatham Harbour appears to have migrated south over a period of 140 years.

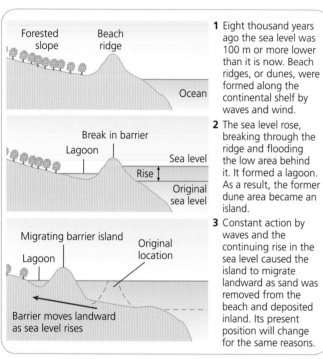

1 Eight thousand years ago the sea level was 100 m or more lower than it is now. Beach ridges, or dunes, were formed along the continental shelf by waves and wind.

2 The sea level rose, breaking through the ridge and flooding the low area behind it. It formed a lagoon. As a result, the former dune area became an island.

3 Constant action by waves and the continuing rise in the sea level caused the island to migrate landward as sand was removed from the beach and deposited inland. Its present position will change for the same reasons.

Figure 2.31 The formation of a barrier island

Tombolo

If a ridge of material links an island with the mainland, this ridge is called a **tombolo**. A typical example is Chesil Beach on the south coast of England (Figure 2.32). Chesil Beach is 25 km long, connecting the Isle of Portland with the mainland Dorset coast at Burton Bradstock, near Abbotsbury. At its eastern end, at Portland, the ridge is 13 m above sea level and composed of flinty pebbles about the size of a potato. At its western end, near Abbotsbury, the ridge is lower, only 7 m above sea level, and built of smaller flinty material about the size of a pea.

Figure 2.32 Chesil Beach tombolo

The height of the ridge and the sizing of material would suggest that dominant wave action occurred from east to west – the largest material is piled up at the eastern end, being the heaviest and most difficult to transport. Smaller, lighter material is carried further west before being deposited. However, the dominant wave action comes from the south-west, up the Channel from the Atlantic Ocean. In other words, the morphology of the ridge should be completely opposite to what it is.

The origin of Chesil Beach remains a problem. One theory to explain this situation is that Chesil is a very youthful feature and so is unstable in the present environment. Around 18 000–20 000 years ago, in the Pleistocene period, sea level fell to a level at least 100 m below its present position. As a result, much of what is now the English Channel was dry. During the Ice Age, vast amounts of debris were produced on the nearby land surface by glacial and periglacial action. This debris could have been carried into the dry Channel area by meltwater at the close of the Ice Age. As the sea level rose in early post-glacial times, this material could have been pushed onshore and trapped by the Isle of Portland and Lyme Bay. Present-day wave action is gradually sorting this material.

Cuspate forelands

Cuspate forelands consist of shingle ridges deposited in a triangular shape, and are the result of two separate spits joining, or the combined effects of two distinct sets of regular storm waves (Figure 2.33). A fine example is at Dungeness near Dover in the UK, where the foreland forms the seaward edge of Romney Marsh. As recently as AD900 this marsh was a bay. Within the last 1000 years it has silted up with mudflats and marshes as a direct result of the growth of the cuspate foreland. The shingle was deposited by longshore drift curling west from the North Sea and by the longshore drift flowing eastwards up the English Channel.

Figure 2.33 Dungeness, a cuspate foreland

Section 2.2 Activities

1 Distinguish between tombolos and cuspate forelands.

2 For either tombolos or cuspate forelands, explain how they are formed.

Sand dunes

Sand dunes form where there is a reliable supply of sand, strong onshore winds, a large tidal range and vegetation to trap the sand. Extensive sandy beaches are almost always backed by sand dunes because strong onshore winds can easily transport inland the sand that has dried out and is exposed at low water. The sand grains are trapped and deposited against any obstacle on land, to form dunes. Vegetation causes the wind velocity to drop, especially in the lowest few centimetres above the ground, and the reduction in velocity reduces energy and increases the deposition of sand. Dunes can be blown inland and can therefore threaten coastal farmland and even villages. Special methods are used to slow down the migration of dunes:

- planting of special grasses, such as marram, which has a long and complex tap root system that binds the soil
- erecting brushwood fences to reduce sand movement
- planting of conifers which can stand the saline environment and poor soils, such as Scots and Corsican pines.

Sand dune succession

Initially, sand is moved by the wind. However, wind speed varies with height above a surface. The belt of no wind is only 1 mm above the surface. As most grains protrude above this height they are moved by saltation. The strength of the wind and the nature of the surface are important. Irregularities cause increased wind speed and eddying, and more material is moved. On the leeward side of irregularities, wind speed is lower, transport decreases and deposition increases.

For dunes to become stable, vegetation is required. Plant succession and vegetation succession can be interpreted by the fact that the oldest dunes are furthest from the sea and the youngest ones are closest to the shore. On the shore, conditions are windy, arid and salty. The soil contains few nutrients and is mostly sand – hence the fore dunes are referred to as yellow dunes. Few plants can survive, although sea couch and marram can tolerate these conditions. Once the vegetation is established it reduces wind speed close to ground level. The belt of no wind may increase to a height of 10 mm. As grasses such as sea couch and marram need to be buried by fresh sand in order to grow, they keep pace with deposition. As the marram grows it traps more sand. As it is covered it grows more, and so on. Once established the dunes should continue to grow, as long as there is a supply of sand. However, once another younger dune, a fore dune, becomes established the supply of sand – and so the growth of the dune – is reduced.

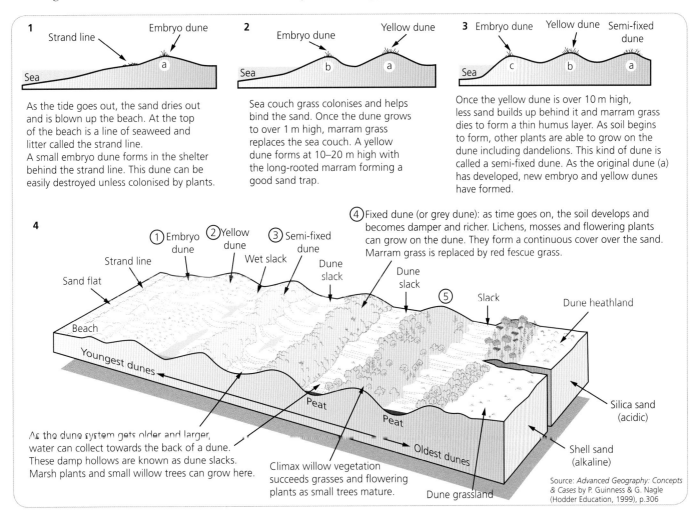

1 Strand line — Embryo dune

Sea — a

As the tide goes out, the sand dries out and is blown up the beach. At the top of the beach is a line of seaweed and litter called the strand line.
A small embryo dune forms in the shelter behind the strand line. This dune can be easily destroyed unless colonised by plants.

2 Embryo dune — Yellow dune

Sea — b — a

Sea couch grass colonises and helps bind the sand. Once the dune grows to over 1 m high, marram grass replaces the sea couch. A yellow dune forms at 10–20 m high with the long-rooted marram forming a good sand trap.

3 Embryo dune — Yellow dune — Semi-fixed dune

Sea — c — b — a

Once the yellow dune is over 10 m high, less sand builds up behind it and marram grass dies to form a thin humus layer. As soil begins to form, other plants are able to grow on the dune including dandelions. This kind of dune is called a semi-fixed dune. As the original dune (a) has developed, new embryo and yellow dunes have formed.

4
Sand flat — Strand line — ① Embryo dune — ② Yellow dune — ③ Semi-fixed dune — Wet slack — Dune slack — Dune slack — ⑤ Slack — Dune heathland

Beach
Youngest dunes

④ Fixed dune (or grey dune): as time goes on, the soil develops and becomes damper and richer. Lichens, mosses and flowering plants can grow on the dune. They form a continuous cover over the sand. Marram grass is replaced by red fescue grass.

As the dune system gets older and larger, water can collect towards the back of a dune. These damp hollows are known as dune slacks. Marsh plants and small willow trees can grow here.

Peat — Peat

Climax willow vegetation succeeds grasses and flowering plants as small trees mature.

Oldest dunes — Dune grassland

Silica sand (acidic)
Shell sand (alkaline)

Source: *Advanced Geography: Concepts & Cases* by P. Guinness & G. Nagle (Hodder Education, 1999), p.306

Figure 2.34 Sand dune succession

As the dune gets higher the supply of fresh sand is reduced to dunes further back. Thus marram dies out. In addition, as wind speeds are reduced, evapotranspiration losses are less, and the soil is moister. The decaying marram adds some nutrients to the soil, which in turn becomes more acidic. In the slacks, the low points between the dunes, conditions are noticeably moister, and marsh vegetation may occur.

Towards the rear of the dune system 'grey' dunes are formed – grey due to the presence of humus in the soil. The climax vegetation found here depends largely upon the nature of the sand. If there is a high proportion of shells (providing calcium), grasslands are found. By contrast, acid dunes are found on old dunes where the calcium has been leached out, and on dunes based upon outwash sands and gravels. Here acid-loving plants such as heather and ling dominate. Pine trees favour acid soils, whereas oak can be found on more neutral soils. Thus the vegetation at the rear of the sand dune complex is quite variable (Figure 2.34).

Section 2.2 Activities

1 Under what conditions do sand dunes form?

2 Describe and explain the typical succession that is found on sand dunes.

Mudflats and saltmarshes

Figure 2.35 Saltmarsh vegetation

The intertidal zone – the zone between high tide and low tide – experiences severe environmental changes in salinity, tidal inundation and sediment composition. Halophytic (salt-tolerant) plants have adapted to the unstable, rapidly changing conditions (Figure 2.35).

Saltmarshes are typically found in three locations: on low-energy coastlines, behind spits and barrier islands, and in estuaries and harbours.

Silt accumulates in these situations and on reaching sea level forms mudbanks. With the appearance of vegetation, saltmarsh is formed. The mudbanks are often intersected by creeks.

A thin layer of mud forms over sand which is covered at each tide. The only plants are algae growing on the mud.

More mud deposited and the first plants appear. The plants trap more mud and silt. The marsh is covered at each high tide and channels are cut as the water recedes.

Salicornia herbacea   Spartina townsendii

Glyceria maritima   Halimione portulacoides

Armeria maritima   Limonium vulare

Further plants appear higher up the marsh. This accelerates mud accretion. Channels deepen as the marsh surface rises.

More plants move into the higher zones and the mud deepens. High tides still flood the marsh but low tides are confined to the creeks, which are further eroded as the water runs off.

The marsh is now growing slowly and the mud is very deep. Further plants colonise the higher zones. Erosion undercuts the creek banks and some collapse leaving bare salt pans above the collapse. Apart from creeks and pans, the marsh is covered with vegetation and only the highest tides fully cover it with water.

Juncus maritimus   Festuca rubra

Figure 2.36 Saltmarsh formation at Scolt Head Island

Saltmarsh succession

Scolt Head Island is located on the north Norfolk coast of England, and is exposed to cold winds from the east (Figure 2.36). At high tide it is cut off by the sea, while at low tide it is joined to the mainland. The island developed from an extensive sand and shingle foreshore. Wave action during storms seas, sorted the shingle from the sand, forming shingle ridges near the high water mark. The early ridges were unstable and mobile. However, as they became more stable, dunes developed and gradually moved the island westwards, in a series of stages. Most of the shingle came from offshore glacial deposits, while other shingle was drifted along the shore. Each of the former ends of the island are marked by curving lateral ridges of shingle, some with high and well developed dunes.

The marshes change in age, and height, from east to west. The older marshes are higher, with more developed creek patterns. However, in some cases human activity has disrupted the pattern. Drainage may lead to settling and subsidence, so the oldest marshes may not always be the highest.

The marshes include small basins called pans. These can result from creeks being dammed by bank collapse. This impedes drainage, and the water in the pan slowly evaporates, leaving very salty water in the pan. High salinity will inhibit vegetation growth, and so the floor of the pan remains bare.

On Scolt Head Island the vegetation is varied and natural. By contrast, many other marshes in southern England are dominated by the recently introduced cord grass (*Spartina anglica*). Once the bare marshflat is formed, the first plants, such as green algae (*Enteromorpha*), colonise the mudflat. The algae trap sediment from the sea and provide ideal conditions for the seeds of the salt-tolerant marsh samphire (*Salicornia*), and eel grass (*Zostera*) which then colonise the marsh. These plants increase the rate of deposition by slowing down the water as it passes over the vegetation. This is known as **bioconstruction**. Gradually, the clumps of vegetation become larger and the flow of tidal waters is restricted to specific channels, namely the creeks. The slightly increased height of the surface around plants leads to more favourable conditions. Here plants are covered by sea water for shorter periods of time and this encourages other plants to colonise, such as sea aster, sea pea, and seablite. These are even more efficient at trapping sediment and the height of the saltmarsh increases. New plants colonise as the marsh grows, including sea lavender, sea pink, and sea purslane. As the height increases, tidal inundation of the marsh become less frequent, and the rate of growth slows down. Sea rush (*Juncus*) and saltwort (*Salsola kali*) become the most common plants. It takes about 200 years on Scolt Head to progress from the marsh samphire stage to the sea rush stage.

Section 2.2 Activities

1 Outline the environmental conditions in which mudflats and saltmarshes occur.

2 Describe the typical succession associated with saltmarshes.

2.3 Coral reefs

Coral reefs are calcium carbonate structures, made up of reef-building stony corals. Coral is limited to the depth of light penetration and so reefs occur in shallow water, ranging to depths of 60 m. This dependence on light also means that reefs are only found where the surrounding waters contain relatively small amounts of suspended material. Although corals are found quite widely, reef-building corals live only in tropical seas, where temperature, salinity and a lack of turbid water are conducive to their existence.

Coral reefs occupy less than 0.25 per cent of the marine environment, yet they shelter more than 25 per cent of all known marine life, including polyps, fish, mammals, turtles, crustaceans and molluscs. There are as many as 800 different types of rock-forming corals. Some estimates put the total diversity of life found in, on and around all coral reefs at up to 2 million species.

The development of coral

All tropical reefs begin life as polyps – tiny, soft animals, like sea anemones – which attach themselves to a hard surface in shallow seas where there is sufficient light for growth. As they grow, many of these polyps exude calcium carbonate, which forms their skeleton. Then as they grow and die these 'rock'-forming corals create the reefs.

Polyps have small algae, *zooxanthellae*, growing inside them. There is a symbiotic relationship between the polyps and the algae – that is, both benefit from the relationship. The algae get shelter and food from the polyp, while the polyp also gets some food via photosynthesis. This photosynthesis (turning light energy from the Sun into food) means that algae need sunlight to live, so corals only grow where the sea is shallow and clear.

Rate of growth

Tropical reefs grow at rates ranging from less than 2.5 cm to 60 cm per year, forming huge structures over incredibly long periods of time – which makes them the largest and oldest living systems on Earth. The 2600 km Great Barrier Reef off eastern Australia, for example, was formed over 5 million years.

Distribution

The distribution of coral (Figure 2.37) is controlled by seven main factors:

- **Temperature** – no reefs develop where the mean annual temperature is below 20 °C. Optimal conditions for growth are between 23 °C and 25 °C.
- **Depth of water** – most reefs grow in depths of water less than 25 m, and so they are generally found on the margins of continents and islands.

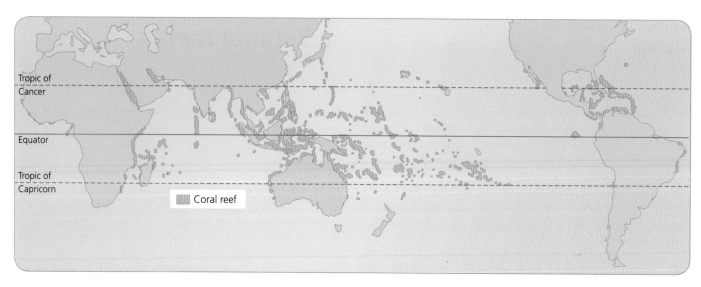

Figure 2.37 World distribution of coral reefs

- **Light** – corals prefer shallow water because the tiny photosynthetic algae that live in the coral need light – in return they supply the coral polyps with as much as 98 per cent of their food requirements.
- **Salinity** – corals are marine organisms and are intolerant of water with salinity levels below 32 psu although they can tolerate high salinity levels (> 42 psu) as found in the Red Sea or the Persian Gulf.
- **Sediment** – sediment has a negative effect on coral – it clogs up their feeding structures and cleansing systems and sediment-rich water reduces the light available for photosynthesis.
- **Wave action** – coral reefs generally prefer strong wave action which ensures oxygenated water and where there is a stronger cleansing action. This helps remove any trapped sediment and also supplies microscopic plankton to the coral. However, in storm conditions, such as the South Asian tsunami, the waves may be too destructive for the coral to survive.
- **Exposure to the air** – coral die if they are exposed to the air for too long. They are therefore mostly found below the low tide mark.

Types of coral

- **Fringing reefs** are those that fringe the coast of a landmass (Figure 2.38). They are usually characterised by an outer reef edge capped by an algal ridge, a broad reef flat, and a sand-floored 'boat channel' close to the shore. Many fringing reefs grow along shores that are protected by barrier reefs and are thus characterised by organisms which are best adapted to low wave-energy conditions.
- **Barrier reefs** occur at greater distances from the shore than fringing reefs and are commonly separated from it by a wide, deep lagoon. Barrier reefs tend to be broader, older, and more continuous than fringing reefs; the Beqa barrier reef off Fiji stretches unbroken for more than 37 km; that off Mayotte in the Indian Ocean for around 18 km. The largest barrier-reef system in the world is the Great Barrier Reef, which extends 2600 km along the east Australian coast, usually tens of kilometres offshore. Another long barrier reef is located in the Caribbean off the coast of Belize between Mexico and Guatemala.

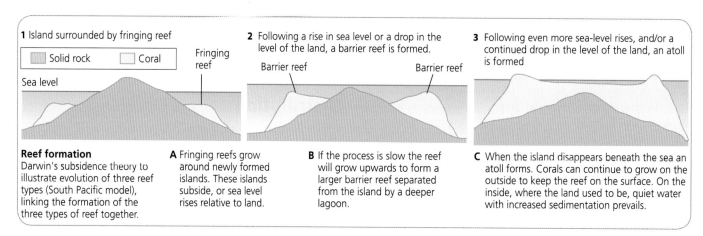

Figure 2.38 Formation of fringing reefs, barrier reefs and atolls

- **Atoll reefs** rise from submerged volcanic foundations and often support small islands of wave-borne detritus. Atoll reefs are essentially indistinguishable in form and species composition from barrier reefs except that they are confined to the flanks of submerged oceanic islands, whereas barrier reefs may also flank continents. There are over 300 atolls in the Indian and Pacific Oceans but only 10 are found in the western Atlantic.
- **Patch reef** describes small circular or irregular reefs that rise from the sea floor of lagoons behind barrier reefs or within atolls.

Section 2.3 Activities

1 Outline the main factors that limit the distribution of coral reefs.

2 Describe the main types of coral reef.

Origin

The origin of fringing reefs is quite clear – they simply grow seaward from the land. Barrier reefs and atolls, however, seem to rise from considerable depth, far below the level at which coral can grow, and many atolls are isolated in deep water. The lagoons between the barrier and the coast are usually 45–100 m in depth, and often many kilometres in width – and this requires some explanation.

In 1842 Charles Darwin, supported by Dana and others, explained the growth of barrier reefs and atolls as a gradual process, the main reason being subsidence. In his classic book *The Structure and Distribution of Coral Reefs*, Darwin outlined the way in which coral reefs could grow upwards from submerging foundations. From this, it became clear that fringing reefs might be succeeded by barrier reefs and then by atoll reefs. A fringing reef grows around an island, for example, and as the island slowly subsides, the coral continues to grow, keeping pace with the subsidence. Coral growth is more vigorous on the outer side of the reef, so it forms a higher rim, whereas the inner part forms an increasingly wide and deep lagoon (Figure 2.39). Eventually the inner island is submerged, forming a ring of coral that is the atoll. Supporters of Darwin have shown that submergence has taken place, as in the case of drowned valleys along parts of Indonesia and along the Queensland coast of Australia. However, in other areas, such as the Caribbean, there is little evidence of submergence.

An alternative theory was that of Sir John Murray, who in 1872 suggested that the base of the reef consisted of a submarine hill or plateau rising from the ocean floor. These reached within 60 m of the sea surface and consisted of either sub-surface volcanic peaks or wave-worn stumps. According to Murray, as a fringing reef grows, pounded by breaking waves, masses of coral fragments gradually accumulate on the seaward side, washed there by waves, and are cemented into a solid bank.

Yet another theory was that of Daly. He suggested that a rise in sea level might be responsible. A rise did take place in post-glacial

times as ice sheets melted. He discovered traces of glaciation on the sides of Mauna Kea in Hawaii. The water there must have been much colder and much lower (about 100 m) during glacial times. All coral would have died, and any coral surfaces would have been eroded by the sea. Once conditions started to warm, and sea level was rising, the previous coral reefs provided a base for the upward growth of coral. This theory helps account for the narrow, steep-sided reefs that comprise most atolls, some of which have 75° slopes.

Figure 2.39 Theories of coral formation

Darwin's theory still receives considerable support. While Daly was correct in principle, it is now believed that erosion of the old reefs was much less rapid than was previously believed, and that the time available during the glacial low sea-level stages was inadequate for the formation of these bevelled platforms. Much of the erosional modification is now believed to be due to sub-aerial karstic (limestone) processes such as carbonation-solution.

Section 2.3 Activities

Outline the main theories of atoll formation.

The value of coral

Biodiversity

Coral reefs are among the most biologically rich ecosystems on Earth. About 4000 species of fish and 800 species of reef-building corals have been described. Coral reefs have often been described as 'the rainforests of the sea'. They resemble tropical rainforests in two ways: both thrive under nutrient-poor conditions (where nutrients are largely tied up in living matter), yet support rich communities through incredibly efficient recycling processes. Additionally, both exhibit very high levels of species diversity. However, coral reefs and other marine ecosystems contain a greater variety of life forms than do land habitats.

The NPP (net primary productivity) of coral reefs is 2500 g/m^{-2}/year and its biomass is 2 kg/m^{-2}.

Coral reefs are not only important for their biodiversity, they are important to people, too:

- **Seafood** – in LEDCs, coral reefs contribute about one-quarter of the total fish catch, providing food for up to a billion people in Asia alone. If properly managed, reefs can yield, on average, 15 tonnes of fish and other seafood per km^2 per year.
- **New medicines** – coral reef species offer particular hope because of the array of chemicals produced by many of these organisms for self-protection. Corals are already being used for bone grafts, and chemicals found within several species appear useful for treating viruses, leukaemia, skin cancer, and other tumours.
- **Other products** – reef ecosystems yield a host of other economic goods, ranging from corals and shells made into jewellery and tourism curios to live fish and corals used in aquariums, and sand and limestone used by the construction industry.

Coral reefs also offer a wide range of environmental services, some of which are difficult to quantify but are of enormous importance to nearby inhabitants. These services include:

- **Recreational value** – the tourism industry is one of the fastest-growing sectors of the global economy. Coral reefs are a major draw for snorkellers, scuba divers and recreational fishers (Figure 2.40).

Figure 2.40 Coral reef, Antigua

- **Coastal protection** – coral reefs buffer adjacent shorelines through wave action and the impact of storms (Figure 2.41). The benefits of this protection are widespread, and range from maintenance of highly productive mangrove fisheries and wetlands to supporting local economies that are built around ports and harbours, which in the tropics are often sheltered by nearby reefs.

Figure 2.41 Storm waves batter a coral platform

Coral reefs are therefore of major biological and economic importance. Countries such as Barbados, the Seychelles and the Maldives rely on tourism. Tourists attracted to Florida's reefs bring in US$1.6 billion annually, and the global value of coral reefs in terms of fisheries, tourism and coastal protection is estimated to be US$375 billion!

Section 2.3 Activities

Outline the main value of coral reefs.

Human impact

Overfishing, destruction of the coastal habitat and pollution from industry, farms and households are endangering not only fish – the leading individual source of animal protein in the human diet – but also marine biodiversity and even the global climate. There are natural threats, too. Dust storms from the Sahara have introduced bacteria into Caribbean coral, while global warming may cause coral bleaching (see below). Many areas of coral in the Indian Ocean were destroyed by the 2004 tsunami.

According to the World Resources Institute, 58 per cent of the world's coral reefs are at high or medium risk of degradation, with more than 80 per cent of South East Asia's extensive reef systems under threat.

Coral bleaching

Reef-building corals need warm, clear water. Unfortunately, pollution, sedimentation, global climate change and several other natural and anthropogenic pressures threaten this fundamental, biological need, effectively halting photosynthesis of the zooxanthellae and resulting in the death of the living part of the coral reef.

As noted above, coral lives in a symbiotic relationship with algae called zooxanthellae. Zooxanthellae live within the coral animal tissue and carry out photosynthesis, providing energy not only for themselves but for the coral too. Zooxanthellae give the coral its colour. However, when environmental conditions become stressful, zooxanthellae may leave the coral, leaving the coral in an energy deficit and without colour – a process that is referred to as **coral bleaching**. If the coral is re-colonised by zooxanthellae within a certain time, the coral may recover, but if not the coral will die. Coral bleaching can be caused by increases in water temperature of as little as 1–2 °C above the average annual maxima. The shallower the water the greater the potential for bleaching. As well as being caused by unusually warm waters – particularly if the water temperature exceeds 29 °C – bleaching may also be the result of changes in salinity, excessive exposure to ultraviolet radiation, and climate change.

1998 coral bleaching

The 1998 episode of coral bleaching and mortality was the largest ever recorded on coral reefs globally, with major effects in the Arabian/Persian Gulf, East Africa, throughout the Indian Ocean, in South East Asia, parts of the western Pacific, and the Caribbean and Atlantic region. Overall, it was estimated that 16 per cent of the world's area of coral reefs was severely damaged.

In 1998 there was extensive and intensive bleaching affecting the majority of coral reefs around Puerto Rico and the northern Caribbean. In the south-west region a large number of coral colonies bleached completely (100 per cent of the living surface area) down to 40 m deep. Maximum temperatures measured during 1998 in several reef localities ranged from 30.15 °C (20 m deep) to 31.78 °C at the surface.

Like other parts of the wider Caribbean region, there was moderate to severe coral bleaching in 1998, but generally there were low levels of mortality. At one site in Barbados, approximately 20 per cent of bleached corals did not survive, but most reefs are showing signs of recovery from hurricanes, and sediment and bleaching damage from the previous 10 years.

Global assessment 2004

A 2004 report estimated that about one-fifth of the world's coral reefs are so damaged they are beyond repair. While the percentage of reefs recovering from past damage has risen, 70 per cent of the world's reefs are threatened or have already been destroyed, which is an increase from 59 per cent in 2000. Almost half of the reefs severely damaged by coral bleaching in 1998 are recovering, but other reefs are so badly damaged that they are unrecognisable as coral reefs.

The destruction of reefs is cause for economic, as well as ecological, concern, especially for the communities that depend on coral reefs for the fish they provide and the revenue they draw as tourist attractions.

The report states that the main causes of reef decline are climate change which causes bleaching, poor land management practices which damage the reefs with sediments, nutrients and other pollutants, overfishing and destructive fishing practices, and coastal development. Other threats loom, especially climate change. Increased water temperatures have already been blamed for the single most destructive event for corals, the 1998 bleaching.

The most damaged reefs are in the Persian Gulf where 65 per cent have been destroyed, followed by reefs in South and South East Asia where 45 and 38 per cent, respectively, are considered destroyed. There are also more recent reports that many reefs in the wider Caribbean have lost 80 per cent of their corals.

The report also provides some good news: the percentage of recovering reefs has increased when compared with the last global assessment. Most of the recovered reefs are in the Indian Ocean, part of the Great Barrier Reef off the coast of Australia and in the western Pacific, especially in Palau. In 2004, Australia increased protection of the Great Barrier Reef from 4 per cent to 33 per cent, and 34 per cent of Ningaloo Reef Marine Park was made off-limits from fishing.

Initiative in Climate Change and Coral Reefs, 2010

According to the Global Coral Reef Monitoring Network and the International Coral Reef *Initiative in Climate Change and Coral Reefs* published in 2010, the world's coral reefs were probably the first ecosystem to show major damage as a result of climate change. Reefs will suffer catastrophic collapse from climate change within the next few decades unless there are major and immediate reductions in greenhouse gas emissions. Global climate change will cause irreparable damage to coral reefs in our lifetime for several reasons:

- Increasing sea surface temperatures will cause more coral bleaching and mortality during summer. The abundance of many coral species will be reduced and some species may become extinct.
- Ocean temperatures will increase beyond the current maximum of natural variability, making bleaching a frequent, or eventually an annual, event.
- Increasing ocean acidification will reduce calcification in corals and other calcifying organisms, resulting in slower growth, weaker skeletons and eventual dissolution.
- A predicted increase in severe tropical storms will result in the destruction of corals and the erosion of coastlines.

Already 19 per cent of the world's coral reefs have effectively been lost, and 35 per cent more are seriously threatened with destruction, mostly due to direct human threats. Climate change will cause even more dramatic losses, not just to tropical but also to coldwater corals

Climate change, coral and people

About 500 million people depend on coral reefs for some food, coastal protection, building materials and income from tourism. Among these, about 30 million people are dependent on coral reefs to provide their livelihoods, build up their land and support their cultures. Global climate change threatens these predominantly poor people, with many living in 80 small developing countries. Human wellbeing will be reduced for many people in rapidly growing tropical countries; 50 per cent of the world's population are predicted to live on coasts by 2015. This growth is putting unsustainable pressures on coastal resources. In 2009, the United Nations Environment Programme estimated that the coral reef area of 284 000 km² provides the world with more than US$100 billion per annum in goods and services. Even moderate climate change will seriously deplete that value.

Evidence of climate change damage to coral reefs

Mass coral bleaching was unknown in the long oral history of many countries such as the Maldives and Palau, before their reefs were devastated in 1998. About 16 per cent of the world's corals bleached and died in 1998. In that year, 500–1000-year-old corals died in Vietnam, in the Indian Ocean and the western Pacific.

Coral bleaching was only recorded as minor local incidents before the first large-scale bleaching was observed in 1983. The hottest years on record in the tropical oceans were in 1997/98, 2003, 2004 and 2005; the major bleaching years for Caribbean corals were in 1998 and 2005. Records for hurricanes in the wider Caribbean were broken in 2005. The bottom cover of corals on Caribbean reefs has dropped by more than 80 per cent since 1977, with much of this decline due to disease, coral bleaching or coral disease following bleaching. Any coral recovery was often reversed by other human pressures or by more bleaching and disease.

Between 50 and 90 per cent of corals died from bleaching on many reefs in the Indian Ocean in 1998. This caused major losses in tourism incomes and reduction in fish habitats. The first major bleaching event on the Great Barrier Reef was in 1998; since then there has been major bleaching in 2002 and 2006. The growth rate of some corals species has declined by 14 per cent on the Great Barrier Reef since 1990, either due to temperature stress or ocean acidification or both. Other reef areas report similar results.

Ocean temperatures have risen in all oceans in the last 40 years, as seen from satellite images and other measures over 135 years from the National Oceanic and Atmospheric Administration of the USA.

Coral bleaching and death has reduced tourism incomes in countries like the Maldives, Palau and throughout the Caribbean. Sea-level rise has already threatened some coral island countries, such as Kiribati, Tuvalu, Marshall Islands and Maldives, with inundation, erosion, loss of agriculture and displacement of people and cultures.

Sustaining coral

Global climate change seriously threatens the future of coral reefs. Current scientific thought is that coral reefs may become one of the first ecosystem casualties of climate change and could become functionally extinct if carbon dioxide levels rise to above 450 ppm – which could happen by 2030. It could affect the livelihoods of up to 500 million people whose lives depend on coral, and reduce the $100 billion that coral provides to the human economy. Global climate change and other human activities have affected about 19 per cent of the world's coral. Global temperatures are expected to rise by at least 2 °C, leading to widespread coral bleaching, extinction of coral species, more fragile skeletons, and greater risk of storm damage. This will make low-lying coastal communities more vulnerable to coastal hazards. This damage and the probable sea-level rise of 0.8–1.2 m will seriously affect communities on Kiribati, the Marshall Islands, the Maldives and Tuvalu, and many communities will cease to exist. More than 3000 scientists at the 2008 International Coral Reef Symposium urged that greenhouse gases be reduced by 2018 in order to preserve coral reefs.

To avoid permanent damage and support people in the tropics it is recommended that:
- the world community reduces the emissions of greenhouse gases and develops plans to sequester carbon dioxide
- damaging human activities (sedimentation, overfishing, blasting coral) are limited, to allow coral to recover from climate change threats
- assistance is provided to LEDCs
- alternative livelihoods are developed that reduce the pressure on coral reefs
- local coastal management practices are introduced
- strategies are developed to cope with climate change damage
- the management, monitoring and enforcement of regulations are improved
- more coral reefs are designated as Marine Protected Areas (MPAs) to act as reservoirs of biodiversity, including many remote and uninhabited reefs that are still in good condition.

Section 2.3 Activities

1 Outline the main human impacts on coral reefs.
2 Examine the effects of sea-level change on coral reefs and describe the consequences.
3 To what extent is it possible to manage coral reefs?

2.4 Sustainable management of coasts

Human pressures on coastal environments create the need for a variety of coastal management strategies. These may be long-term or short-term, sustainable or non-sustainable. Successful management strategies require a detailed knowledge of coastal processes. Rising sea levels, more frequent storm activity and continuing coastal development are likely to increase the need for coastal management.

Shoreline management plans (SMPs)

SMPs are plans in England and Wales designed to develop sustainable coastal defence schemes. Sections of the coast are divided up into littoral cells and plans are drawn up for the use and protection of each zone. Defence options include:

- do nothing
- maintain existing levels of coastal defence
- improve the coastal defence
- allow retreat of the coast in selected areas.

Coastal management involves a wide range of issues:

- planning
- coastal protection
- cliff stabilisation and ground movement studies
- coastal infrastructure including seawalls, esplanades, car parks, paths
- control of beaches and public safety
- recreational activities and sport
- beach cleaning
- pollution and oil spills
- offshore dredging
- management of coastal land and property.

Coastal defence

Coastal defence covers protection against coastal erosion (coast protection) and flooding by the sea.

The coastal zone is a dynamic system that extends seawards and landwards from the shoreline. Its limits are defined by the extent of natural processes and human activities. Coastal zone management is concerned with the whole range of activities that take place in the coastal zone and promotes integrated planning to manage them. Conflicting activities in coastal areas include housing, recreation, fishing, industry, mineral extraction, waste disposal and farming.

Hard engineering structures

The effectiveness of seawalls depends on their cost and their performance. Their function is to prevent erosion and flooding (Figure 2.42) but much depends on whether they are:

- sloping or vertical
- permeable or impermeable
- rough or smooth
- what material they are made from (clay, steel or rock for example).

In general, flatter, permeable, rougher walls perform better than vertical, impermeable smooth walls.

Cross-shore structures such as groynes, breakwaters, piers, and strongpoints have been used for many decades. Their main function is to stop the drifting of material. Traditionally, groynes were constructed from timber, brushwood and wattle. However, modern cross-shore structures are often made from

rock (Figure 2.43). They are part of a more complex form of management that includes beach nourishment and offshore structures.

Figure 2.42 A seawall and esplanade

Figure 2.43 A rock strongpoint

Managed natural retreat

'Managed retreat' allows nature to take its course – erosion in some areas, deposition in others. Benefits include less money spent, and the creation of natural environments. In parts of East Anglia in the UK, hard engineering structures are being replaced by bush defences, and some farmland is being sacrificed to erosion and being allowed to develop into saltmarsh.

Issues of coastal management

Tables 2.6, 2.7 and 2.8 present some of the issues involved with coastal management: different methods that can be put in place (hard and soft engineering), their costs, advantages and disadvantages. Figure 2.44 shows some of these methods of protection.

Table 2.6 Cost-benefit analysis of coastal defence

Costs	Benefits
Cost of building Maintenance/repair Increased erosion downdrift due to beach starvation or reduced longshore drift Reduced access to beach during works Reduced recreational value Reduced accessibility Smaller beach due to scour Disruption of ecosystems and habitats Visually unattractive Works disrupt natural processes	Protected buildings, roads and infrastructure (gas, water, sewerage, electricity services) Land prices rise Peace of mind for residents Employment on coastal defence works

Table 2.7 Conflicts and management strategies – relationships between human activities and coastal zone problems

Human activity	Agents/consequences	Coastal zone problems
Urbanisation and transport	Land use changes (e.g. for ports, airports); road, rail, and air congestion; dredging and disposal of harbour sediments; water abstraction; wastewater and waste disposal	Loss of habitats and species diversity; visual intrusion; lowering of groundwater table; salt water intrusion; water pollution; human health risks; eutrophication; introduction of alien species
Agriculture	Land reclamation; fertiliser and pesticide use; livestock densities; water abstraction	Loss of habitats and species diversity; water pollution; eutrophication; river channelisation
Tourism, recreation and hunting	Development and land use changes (e.g. golf courses); road, rail and air congestion; ports and marinas; water abstraction; wastewater and waste disposal	Loss of habitats and species diversity; disturbance; visual intrusion; lowering of groundwater table; salt water intrusion in aquifers; water pollution; eutrophication; human health risks
Fisheries and aquaculture	Port construction; fish processing facilities; fishing gear; fish farm effluents	Overfishing; impacts on non-target species; litter and oil on beaches; water pollution; eutrophication; introduction of alien species; habitat damage and change in marine communities
Industry (including energy production)	Land use changes; power stations; extraction of natural resources; process effluents; cooling water; windmills; river impoundment; tidal barrages	Loss of habitats and species diversity; water pollution; eutrophication; thermal pollution; visual intrusion; decreased input of fresh water and sediment to coastal zones; coastal erosion

Table 2.8 Coastal management

Type of management	Aims/methods	Strengths	Weaknesses
Hard engineering	To control natural processes		
Cliff base management	*To stop cliff or beach erosion*		
Seawalls	Large-scale concrete curved walls designed to reflect wave energy	Easily made; good in areas of high density	Expensive. Lifespan about 30–40 years. Foundations may be undermined
Revetments	Porous design to absorb wave energy	Easily made; cheaper than seawalls	Lifespan limited
Gabions	Rocks held in wire cages absorbs wave energy	Cheaper than seawalls and revetments	Small scale
Groynes	To prevent longshore drift	Relatively low costs; easily repaired	Cause erosion on downdrift side; interrupt sediment flow
Rock armour	Large rocks at base of cliff to absorb wave energy	Cheap	Unattractive; small-scale; may be removed in heavy storms
Offshore breakwaters	Reduce wave power offshore	Cheap to build	Disrupt local ecology
Rock strongpoints	To reduce longshore drift	Relatively low cost; easily repaired	Disrupt longshore drift; erosion downdrift
Cliff face strategies	*To reduce the impacts of sub-aerial processes*		
Cliff drainage	Removal of water from rocks in the cliff	Cost-effective	Drains may become new lines of weakness; dry cliffs may produce rockfalls
Cliff grading	Lowering of slope angle to make cliff safer	Useful on clay (most other measures are not)	Uses large amounts of land – impractical in heavily populated areas
Soft engineering	Working with nature		
Offshore reefs	Waste materials, e.g. old tyres weighted down, to reduce speed of incoming wave	Low technology and relatively cost effective	Long-term impacts unknown
Beach nourishment	Sand pumped from seabed to replace eroded sand	Looks natural	Expensive; short-term solution
Managed retreat	Coastline allowed to retreat in certain places	Cost-effective; maintains a natural coastline	Unpopular; political implications
'Do nothing'	Accept that nature will win	Cost-effective!	Unpopular; political implications
Red-lining	Planning permission withdrawn; new line of defences set back from existing coastline	Cost-effective	Unpopular; political implications

a Gabions
b Groynes
c Gabion mattress
d Revetment
e Cliff drains

Figure 2.44 Some methods of coastal protection

Case Study

The USA's eastern seaboard

Along many parts of the USA's eastern seaboard, seawalls have protected buildings, but not beaches. Many beaches along the east coast have disappeared in the last one hundred years or so, such as Marshfield, Massachusetts, and Monmouth Beach, New Jersey. As sea level rises, the beaches and barrier islands (barrier beaches) that line the coasts of the Atlantic Ocean and the Gulf of Mexico from New York to the Mexican border, are in retreat. This natural retreat does not destroy the beaches or barrier islands, it just moves them inland.

The problem is that much of the shore cannot retreat naturally because there are industries and properties worth billions of dollars on them. Many important cities and tourist centres, such as Miami, Atlantic City and Galveston (Texas) are sited on barrier islands. Consequently, many shoreline communities have built

seawalls and other protective structures to protect them from the power of destructive waves. Such fortifications, which can cost millions of dollars for a single kilometre, protect structures, at least for the short term, but they accelerate erosion elsewhere. The first great seawall was built at Galveston after a hurricane in 1900 devastated the city and killed more than 6000 people. The city survived a later hurricane, but lost its beach. Now, the rising sea level is making protection by the seawalls less effective. Much of the city is less than 3 m above sea level.

Three factors put the east coast of the USA at particularly high risk from changing sea levels. First, the flat topography of the coastal plains from New Jersey southward means that a small rise in sea level can make the ocean advance a long way inland. A rise of just a few millimetres each year in sea level could push the ocean a metre inland, while a rise of a few metres could threaten large areas such as southern Florida. Miami, in particular, faces severe problems as it is the lowest-lying US city facing the open ocean. Few places in metropolitan Miami are more than 3 m above sea level.

Second, much of the North American coast is sinking relative to the ocean, so local sea levels are rising faster than global averages. The level of tides along the coasts shows that subsidence varies between 0.5 and 19.5 mm a year. By contrast, the west coast, in particular Alaska, is rising (Figure 2.45).

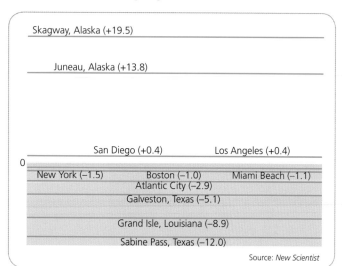

Skagway, Alaska (+19.5)

Juneau, Alaska (+13.8)

San Diego (+0.4)   Los Angeles (+0.4)

0

New York (−1.5)   Boston (−1.0)   Miami Beach (−1.1)
                    Atlantic City (−2.9)
                    Galveston, Texas (−5.1)

                    Grand Isle, Louisiana (−8.9)
                    Sabine Pass, Texas (−12.0)

Source: *New Scientist*

Figure 2.45 Relative sea-level change in the USA

Third, extensive coastal development has accelerated erosion. While sea level rises, apartment blocks, resorts and second homes have developed rapidly along the shoreline. By 1990, 75 per cent of Americans lived within 100 km of a coast (including the Great Lakes shores).

Until the late 1970s, most Americans assumed they could successfully protect their coastline against the rising sea. Now they are considering an alternative: strategic retreat. The term *retreat* does not mean abandoning the shore, but moving back from it. Instead of protecting the coast with seawalls, buildings are moved away from the rising sea, and new buildings are not allowed to be too close to the sea. Engineers have stopped challenging nature and have begun to work with natural coastal processes.

In the long term this makes the most economic sense. While it is impossible and impractical to abandon coastal cities such as Boston and New York (Figure 2.46), state and federal governments are discouraging some new coastal development, especially in areas presently undeveloped.

The nature of erosion further complicates the issue. It is far from a uniform process. Most erosion occurs during coastal storms, especially at high tide. Wind-driven waves create storm surges that flood low-lying areas, causing severe damage. In addition, annual storm intensities are very variable, so coastal geologists try to plan for '100-year' storms – that is, an intensity likely to be experienced only once every century. This can make their plans seem excessively cautious to coastal residents, especially in areas that have not experienced a severe storm for many years.

Erosion is a dynamic process that varies from storm to storm and from point to point along the shore. Nevertheless, in many places there are observable cycles of erosion and deposition. During calm conditions, moderate currents often redeposit large

Figure 2.46 Coastal protection in New York

quantities of sediment removed during a severe storm. This natural compensation reduces total erosion, but it can also disguise the real hazards of storms.

For example, storm damage at Chatham, a town on Cape Cod in Massachusetts, illustrates the dynamics of erosion. In 1987, winter storms broke through a barrier beach separating Chatham Harbour from the Atlantic. This dramatically increased erosion in areas exposed to the full strength of ocean waves. By 1988, more than 20 m had been eroded from the shore.

The events at Chatham are part of a 140-year cycle of erosion and deposition. The ocean moves sand along the eastern shore of Cape Cod, forming and then eroding a barrier island that protects Chatham Harbour. Once the ocean breaks through, currents deposit sand on the north side of the inlet, building the island southward. The inlet moves south, as the ocean erodes the southern island. Eventually, the northern island builds far enough south that the ocean again breaks through during a storm.

Some ocean currents passing through the inlet erode the mainland. As the inlet moves south, currents in the harbour deposit sand in areas eroded earlier. Many homes now threatened were built over 50 years ago on sand dunes that were deposited during the last cycle of erosion and beach building.

In other parts of Cape Cod, and elsewhere along the American coast, erosion is changing the shoreline permanently. The sea is eroding about a metre a year from the glacial banks (which now form sandy cliffs) on the east side of Cape Cod. These cliffs and Cape Cod were formed 15 000 years ago at the end of the Ice Age. The Cape is less than 2 km wide at its narrowest point: if nature takes its course, the northern end will be left an island within a few thousand years. Human interference, such as building seawalls, could accelerate this.

Further south, erosion has isolated the Cape Hatteras lighthouse, located on a barrier island off the coast of North Carolina. The lighthouse was built in 1870 about 460 m from the ocean, but by the 1930s the ocean had eroded all but about 30 m. Except for a small promontory around the lighthouse itself, the shore has receded nearly 500 m since 1870.

Erosion is evident at many other places along the coast of the Atlantic and the Gulf of Mexico. Major resorts such as

Miami Beach and Atlantic City have pumped in dredged sand to replenish eroded beaches. Erosion threatens islands to the north and south of Cape Canaveral, although the cape itself appears safe. Resorts built on barrier beaches in Virginia, Maryland, and New Jersey have also suffered major erosion.

Overall losses are not well known. Massachusetts loses about 26 ha a year to rising seas. Nearly 10 per cent of that loss is from the island of Nantucket, south of Cape Cod. However, these losses pale into insignificance when compared with Louisiana, which is losing 40 ha of wetlands a day – about 15 500 ha a year.

Florida's extreme measures to combat erosion are well known. Intense development of Miami Beach in the 1920s started the widespread exploitation of coastal areas exposed to major storms and erosion. At the same time coastal towns in New Jersey, such as Sea Bright and Monmouth Beach, began building seawalls and groynes to prevent erosion. Since 1945 there have been many developments in coastal areas near large cities, especially for holiday homes and retirement communities.

Hard defences can cost millions of dollars a kilometre, and they require maintenance. Despite their cost, seawalls have failed at several places, including in Texas, South Carolina and California. This is usually due to flaws in construction or poor maintenance.

Many US coastal geologists believe that the best compromise between building defences and leaving the shore to be eroded is pumping sand from other locations, usually offshore, to replace eroded sand. The main limitations include the cost and the possible loss of the new sand. For example, between 1976 and 1980 the US Army Corps of Engineers spent $64 million on beach replenishment and flood prevention at Miami Beach. Erosion quickly removed 30 m of the new sand, but then the beach stabilised at 60 m wide. Other coastal resorts, including Atlantic City and Virginia Beach, Virginia, have chosen to add sand rather than build structures to keep out the sea.

Elsewhere, land use management has been introduced. Regulations vary widely. North Carolina, Maine and Massachusetts are in the forefront of restricting development. In Massachusetts, for example, there are restrictions on new developments of natural areas, although it is neither practical nor possible to abandon Boston's city centre or the international airport, both of which are built on low-lying land facing the harbour. The Massachusetts Wetlands Protection Act limits building on coastal land. The regulations ban seawalls or permanent structures to control erosion on coastal dunes, as these are dynamic areas that supply the sand to beaches. Similarly, North Carolina was one of the first coastal states to legislate that land be left between the shore and new buildings to allow for erosion. Since 1979, small new buildings must be located inland of a line that marks 30 times the annual rate of erosion from the shore. In 1983, the state doubled the distance from the sea for large buildings. In addition, in 1986 the state banned the construction of hard defences, such as rock strongpoints and groynes. Although this was a controversial decision, people and developers have adjusted, in part because the state's beaches are a major economic asset. Moreover, few people want huge seawalls and tiny beaches.

Other states, such as South Carolina and Texas, impose few limitations, or even encourage coastal development. For example, developers have built high-rise condominiums close to the shore line at Myrtle Beach, South Carolina. Similarly, at Galveston, Texas, a new beach-front apartment block was built at the west end of the Galveston seawall, where the rate of erosion is 5 m a year.

Rising sea levels and retreating coasts could pose continuing tough economic and environmental issues for Americans in the future. Some forms of protective hard engineering are certainly justified for major coastal cities such as New York, but it might not be justified for less developed areas such as Carolina Beach, North Carolina.

Section 2.4 Activities

1 Suggest why the US eastern seaboard needs coastal protection.

2 Identify the forms of coastal management that have been used. To what extent have they been effective?

Case Study

Sea sand mining at Mangawhai–Pakiri, New Zealand

A proposal by Kaipara Excavators is to mine designated areas of the continental shelf close to Auckland for 2 million m³ of sand at depths of 25–60 m, over an area of 500 km², in the course of 35 years. If such sand were taken from the entire area, it would amount to no more than a fraction of a millimetre per year. But it is feared that the operation will affect nearby beaches. From an environmental viewpoint, disturbing such a large area, even once in 30 years, would disturb the bottom communities that together form the sea soil. Before 1970, sand was mined from the Omaha Beach, off the Whangateau Harbour. This has been blamed for the Omaha sand spit changing shape and eroding badly in the early 1970s, before remedial groynes were built.

Sand has become a very important mineral for the expansion of society. It is used in the making of glass and concrete, for roads, reclamation, on building sites, and for the replenishment of beaches. Clean sand is a rare commodity on land, but common in sand dunes and beaches. On average, people 'use' over 200 kg of sand per person each year. This sand is taken from what are essentially non-renewable resources. In New Zealand the cost of 1 m³ of replenishment sand is about NZ$40.

Central to the need for using any resource is the question of how long one can do so before it runs out – its *sustainability*. Although sand is one of the world's most plentiful resources (perhaps as much as 20 per cent of the Earth's crust is sand), clean sand is becoming rare, particularly since muddy deposits from soil erosion worldwide are now filling the coastal shelves and basins.

In 1994, the Minister of Conservation granted commercial sand extractors five resource consents (coastal permits) to dredge sand from the nearshore seabed at Mangawhai and Pakiri (Figure 2.47). The permits allowed a total of up to 165 000 m³ of sand to be won annually for 10 years. The permits ended in 2004.

Figure 2.47 Pakiri Beach, New Zealand

A working party, chaired by the Auckland Regional Council (ARC), was set up to oversee the study. This was required to investigate:

- the overall extent and volume of the sand
- the long-term sustainable level of near-shore extraction (less than 25 m deep)
- adverse effects on the environment.

Their specific objectives were to:

- establish a sediment budget and quantify sediment transport
- determine the long-term shoreline trend and short-term fluctuations
- determine the broad sediment characteristics and composition of the sand resource
- determine the relationship (if any) between extraction and the long-term shoreline trend.

The study concluded that there were very large amounts of 'modern' sand in dunes, beach, near shore and offshore. There were also extremely large amounts of Pleistocene sands underlying the modern sand. However, the amount of sand is static, with extraction exceeding inputs. Since the end of the last Ice Age, the shoreline has widened by 150–200 m although since 1920 the shoreline has varied by 40 m but without a long-term trend. Moreover, where extraction occurred, the retreat of shoreline could not be related to extraction. It was found that in the embayment no effects due to extraction could be proven.

The study offered the following options:

1 Sand extraction should be continued at its present rate.
2 Sand extraction in the near-shore area should be phased out since it will eventually cause the gradual retreat of the embayment shoreline.

The Pakiri–Mangawhai sand system is bounded by rocky promontories in the north and south. Deep waves arrive from the north-east through the gap between Great Barrier Island and the Hen and Chicken Islands. Sea winds are predominantly easterly (westerly winds are land winds). These two forces move the sand around in the area, but little escapes. The easterly winds, generated locally, cause short waves breaking on the beach and moving the beach sand north-west along the beach in the littoral zone (estimated at 0.78 million m³/yr). By the headlands, the sand moves into deeper water where it is moved back towards the beach in a south-westerly direction by large storm waves arriving from the north-east. The sand store here is thus essentially static.

The main concern was that the mining company would operate near existing shores, where there are known quantities of quality sand. Such sand is essentially a non-renewable resource. It also belongs to the beach/dune system. The beach and dunes have high amenity value, sought after by holidaymakers and day trippers from Auckland and further afield. They are used for swimming, walking, surfing, fishing, shellfish gathering, and horse-riding. They are already under threat from sedimentation (Pakiri and Mangawhai rivers) and inappropriate coastal uses (forests, dune planting and housing). However, by dredging in water deeper than 25 m there should not be a problem.

How other countries protect their beaches

Other countries share similar issues in protecting their beaches (Table 2.9).

Table 2.9 National regulations on beach protect

Country	Regulation
France	Dredging must take place beyond 3 nautical miles (5.5 km) offshore of beaches and in depths greater than 20 m.
UK	Dredging is prohibited landward of the 19–22 m isobath (contour) and within 600 m of the coast.
Japan	Dredging is prohibited within 1 km of the coast. All operations must be in water depths greater than 20 m.
Malaysia	Coastal Engineering Technical Centre criteria are that mining is permitted seaward of the 10 m isobath, or 2 km offshore for the east coast of Peninsular Malaysia.
Netherlands	Mining is permitted seaward of the 20 m isobath.
USA (New York)	Mining is permitted seaward of the 18 m isobath.

Section 2.4 Activities

1 What is meant by sand mining?

2 To what extent is sand mining sustainable?

One of the main attractions for tourists in Australia is the Great Barrier Reef. The Reef extends for over 2000 km and covers an area of 343 800 km² (Figure 2.48). It consists of over 2900 reefs and is the world's largest living structure. It is also the most used marine park in the world.

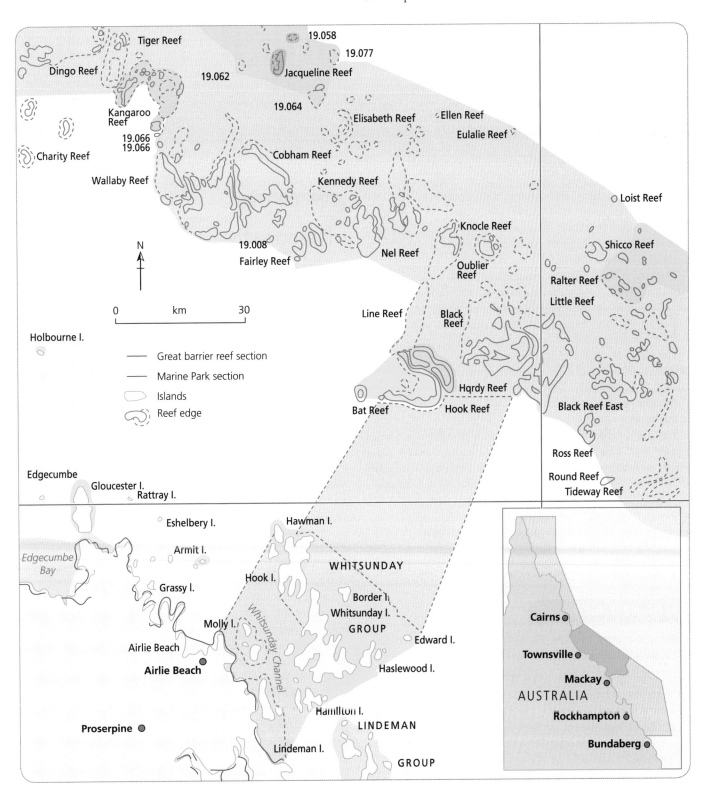

Figure 2.48 Part of the Great Barrier Reef, Australia

	Bait netting and gathering	Camping	Collecting (recreational – not coral)	Collecting – (commercial)	Commercial netting (see also bait netting)	Crabbing and oyster gathering	Diving, boating, photography	Line fishing (bottom fishing, trolling etc.)	Research (non-manipulative)	Research (manipulative)	Spear fishing	Tourist and education facilities and programme	Traditional hunting, fishing and gathering	Trawling
General Use 'A'	Yes	Permit	Limited	Permit	Yes	Yes	Yes	Yes	Yes	Permit	Yes	Permit	Permit	Yes
General Use 'B'	Yes	Permit	Limited	Permit	Yes	Yes	Yes	Yes	Yes	Permit	Yes	Permit	Permit	No
Marine National Park 'A'	Yes	Permit	No	No	No	Limited	Yes	Limited	Permit	Permit	Yes	Permit	Permit	Yes
Marine National Park 'B'	No	Permit	No	No	No	No	Yes	No	Permit	Permit	No	Permit	No	No
Scientific Research	No	No	No	No	No	No	No	No	Permit	Permit	No	No	No	No
Preservation Zone	No	No	No	No	No	No	No	No	Permit	Permit	No	No	No	No

Figure 2.49 Land use zoning along the Barrier Reef

The Great Barrier Reef supports 1500 species of fish, 400 species of coral, and 4000 species of molluscs. It is a major feeding ground for many endangered species and is a nesting ground for many species of turtle. It was placed on the World Heritage List in 1981.

The reef is now carefully managed but previously it suffered from the effects of tourism, agriculture, and recreational and commercial fishing. Each year 77 000 tonnes of nitrogen, 11 000 tonnes of phosphorus and 15 million tonnes of sediment are washed into the coastal waters from Queensland.

The Great Barrier Reef Marine Park Authority is responsible for the management and development of the reef. It follows the Agenda 21 philosophy, namely that resources must be used and managed in such a way that they are not destroyed or devalued for future generations.

The main type of management is that of land use zoning (Figure 2.49). This means that some areas can be used for some things, such as recreation or fishing, while other areas are used for other activities such as scientific research and conservation. The main aims of zoning are to:

- ensure permanent conservation of the area
- provide protection for selected species and ecosystems
- separate conflicting activities
- preserve some untouched areas
- allow human use of the reef as well as protecting the reef.

Section 2.4 Activities

1 Using examples, describe the variety of pressures that affect coral reefs.

2 Why is the Great Barrier Reef a World Heritage Site?

3 Study Figure 2.49.
  a What is meant by the term *land use zoning*?
  b How do the types of activities that are allowed in the Preservation Zone compare with the activities that are allowed in General Use 'A'?

Case Study

Balancing the needs of tourism and the environment: lessons from the Giant's Causeway

The Giant's Causeway in Northern Ireland is famous for its geology and geomorphology, its cliffs and its rare plant environments. As a result it attracts over 370 000 visitors each year. This puts a great strain on the attractions that the visitors come to see – the cliffs, the headlands and, especially, the paths that get them to the sites. The public footpath network (Figure 2.50) provides easy access to the Causeway, bays and headlands, providing some dramatic views of the area. These paths have been developed over a period of about 150 years, and now comprise three main routes.

The area has been designated a World Heritage Site by UNESCO, largely as a result of its unique geological formations – the hexagonal columns of basalt formed by the rapid cooling of lava when it reached the sea (Figure 2.51). It is also classified as a National Nature Reserve and an Area of Outstanding Natural Beauty. These titles recognise the importance of the Causeway coast and confirm that management is essential to maintain its character. However, the designations also reflect the pressure on the area as a result of its many visitors.

One of the main problems is that of footpath erosion as a result of both natural processes and human pressure. Erosion from natural causes, such as wave action, freeze–thaw weathering and landslides occurs mostly in winter. Landslides are common in much of the area but are especially common on the headlands. This is largely due to the high rates of wave erosion on the flanks of the headland destabilising the slopes above. The Chimney Tops headland is particularly subject to mass movements. In some parts the paths have become so unsafe they have been closed off. The lower section between Port na Spaniagh and Hamilton's Seat has been closed to the public since 1994. This was due to landslides removing part of the path and covering other parts of the path with debris.

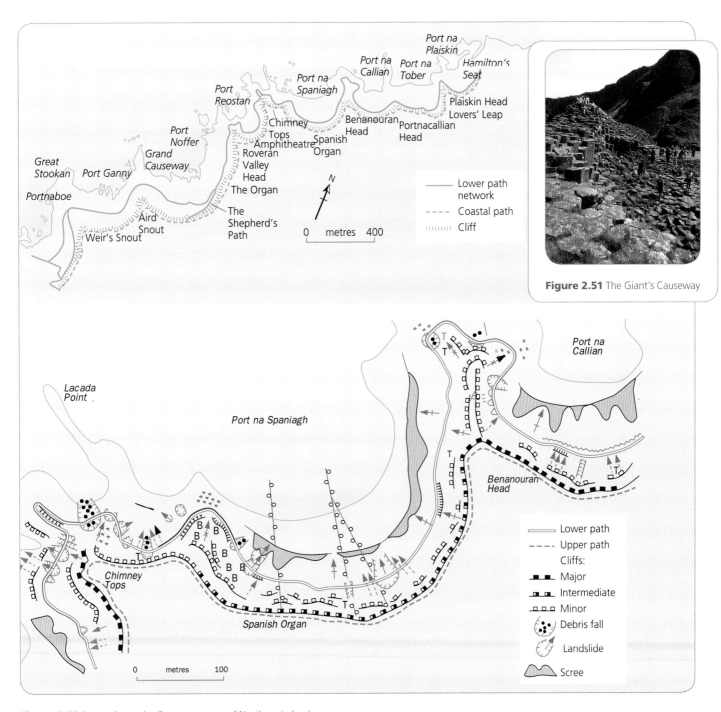

Figure 2.51 The Giant's Causeway

Figure 2.50 Footpaths on the Causeway coast of Northern Ireland

The hazards related to footpaths can be divided into two categories:

1 the nature of the footpath itself, including whether it is even, deeply rutted, safe to walk on and so on

2 the position of the footpath in the landscape, for example at the top of a cliff, at the base of a cliff.

The lower footpath, for example, covers areas that are actively being weathered and eroded, especially in winter months.

As a result the Causeway authorities have developed a four-fold classification of risk:

1 Least hazardous areas – including places where the path runs along a flat surface with no cliff or scree slope on the seaward side; the landward side is overlooked by small cliffs and/or debris slopes.

2 Hazardous – seaward edges are close to steep cliffs (>40°) but landward they are overlooked by minor slopes.

3 Very hazardous – seaward edges are close to steep cliffs (>40°) and landward they are overlooked by steep slopes (>40°).

4 Extremely hazardous – seaward edges are close to steep cliffs (>40°) and landward they are overlooked by steep slopes

(>40°) which continuously shed debris and are subject to major slope failures.

The area from the Organ to Port na Spaniagh is important for visitors. It gives some of the best views of the coastline and provides a limited experience of walking the cliffs. However, the path is subject to rockfalls and landslides. The path from Port na Spaniagh to Hamilton's Seat is very hazardous and subject to active slope failure. It too is subject to rockfalls, landslides and complete collapse of parts of the cliff.

There are techniques available to protect the paths, such as pinning the slope, spraying with concrete (to 'glue' the slope) or providing wire meshes to catch the falling rocks. However, these are visually disruptive and are not compatible with the status of a heritage coast. The Causeway coast has a wide variety of habitats in need of protection. The decision was therefore taken to close the footpath, and this has proved quite successful. There was little opposition to the plan since only about 8 per cent of visitors used the path before it was closed, and closure of that part of the path network has been balanced by investment and upgrading of other areas. There is now more information provided, more signposts, and more viewing areas. There is a clear policy of educating the visitors to appreciate the nature of the Causeway coastline.

Section 2.4 Activities

1 Briefly outline the attractions of the Causeway coast.

2 a Identify the types of mass movement on Figure 2.50.
  b Why are mass movements such a hazard on the Chimney Tops headland?

3 Hazardous environments

3.1 Hazardous environments resulting from crustal (tectonic) movement

Global distribution of tectonic hazards

Tectonic hazards include seismic activity (earthquakes), volcanoes and tsunami. Most of the world's earthquakes occur in clearly defined linear patterns (Figure 3.1). These linear chains generally follow plate boundaries. For example, there is a clear line of earthquakes along the centre of the Atlantic Ocean in association with the Mid-Atlantic Ridge (a constructive plate boundary). Similarly, there are distinct lines of earthquakes around the Pacific Ocean. In some cases these linear chains are quite broad – for example the line of earthquakes along the west coast of South America, and around the eastern Pacific associated with the subduction of the Nazca Plate beneath the South American Plate – a destructive plate boundary. Broad belts of earthquakes are associated with subduction zones (where a dense ocean plate plunges beneath a less dense continental plate) whereas narrower belts of earthquakes are associated with constructive plate margins, where new material is formed and plates are moving apart. Collision boundaries, such as in the Himalayas, are also associated with broad belts of earthquakes, whereas conservative plate boundaries, such as California's San Andreas fault line, give a relatively narrow belt of earthquakes (this can still be over 100 km wide). In addition, there appear to be isolated occurrences of earthquakes. These may be due to human activities, or to isolated plumes of rising magma, known as hotspots.

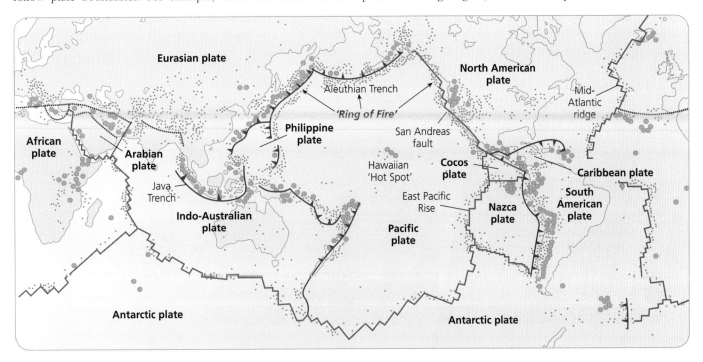

Figure 3.1 Distribution of plates, plate boundaries, volcanoes and earthquakes

Volcanoes

Most volcanoes are found at plate boundaries (Figure 3.1) although there are some exceptions, such as the volcanoes of Hawaii, which occur over hotspots. About three-quarters of the Earth's 550 historically active volcanoes lie along the Pacific Ring of Fire. This includes many of the world's most recent volcanoes, such as Mt Pinatubo in the Philippines, Mt Unzen (Japan), Mt Agung (Java), Mt Chichon (Mexico), Mt St Helens (USA) and Nevado del Ruiz (Colombia). Other areas of active vulcanicity include Iceland, Montserrat in the Caribbean, and Mt Nyiragongo in Democratic Republic of Congo. Most volcanoes that are studied are above land, but some submarine volcanoes, such as Kick 'em Jenny off Grenada in the Caribbean, are also monitored closely.

Volcanoes are found along the boundaries of the Earth's major plates. Although the deeper levels of the Earth are much hotter than the surface, the rocks are usually not molten because the pressure is so high. However, along the plate boundaries there is molten rock, magma, which supplies the volcanoes.

Most of the world's volcanoes are found in the Pacific Rim or Ring of Fire (see Figure 3.1). These are related to the subduction beneath either oceanic or continental crust. Subduction in the oceans provides chains of volcanic islands known as island arcs, such as the Aleutian Islands formed by the Pacific Plate subducting beneath the North American Plate. Where the subduction of an oceanic crust occurs beneath the continental crust, young fold mountains are formed. The Andes, for example, have been formed where the Nazca Plate subducts beneath the South American Plate.

Not all volcanoes are formed at plate boundaries. Those in Hawaii, for example, are found in the middle of the ocean (see Figure 3.2). The Hawaiian Islands are a line of increasingly older volcanic islands which stretch north-west across the Pacific Ocean. These volcanoes can be related to the movement of plates above a hot part of the fluid mantle. A mantle **plume** or **hotspot** – a jet of hot material rising from the deep within the mantle – is

responsible for the volcanoes. Hotspots can also be found beneath continents, as in the case of the East African Rift Valley, and can produce isolated volcanoes. These hotspots can play a part in the break-up of continents and the formation of new oceans.

At subduction zones volcanoes produce more viscous lava, tend to erupt explosively and produce much ash. By contrast volcanoes that are found at mid-ocean ridges or hotspots tend to produce relatively fluid basaltic lava, as in the case of Iceland and Hawaii. At mid-ocean ridges hot fluid rocks from deep in the mantle rise up due to convection currents. The upper parts of the mantle begin to melt and basaltic lava erupts, forming new oceanic crust. By contrast at subduction zones a slab of cold ocean floor slides down the subduction zone, warming up slowly. Volatile compounds such as water and carbon dioxide leave the slab and move upwards into the mantle so that it melts. The hot magma is then able to rise.

Huge explosions occur wherever water meets hot rock. Water vaporises, increasing the pressure until the rock explodes. Gases from within the molten rock can also build up high pressures. However, the likelihood of a big, explosive eruption depends largely on the viscosity of the magma and hence its composition. Gases dissolve quite easily in molten rock deep underground due to the very high pressures there. As magma rises to the surface the pressure drops and some of the gas may become insoluble and form bubbles. In relatively fluid magma the bubbles rise to the surface. By contrast, viscous magma can trap gas so that it builds up enough pressure to create a volcanic eruption.

The style of eruption is greatly influenced by the processes operating at different plate boundaries, which produce magma of different, but predictable, composition. Some minerals melt before others in a process called **partial melting**. This alters the composition of molten rock produced. Partial melting of the Earth's mantle produces basalt. At subduction zones the older and deeper slabs experience greater partial melting and this produces a silica-rich magma.

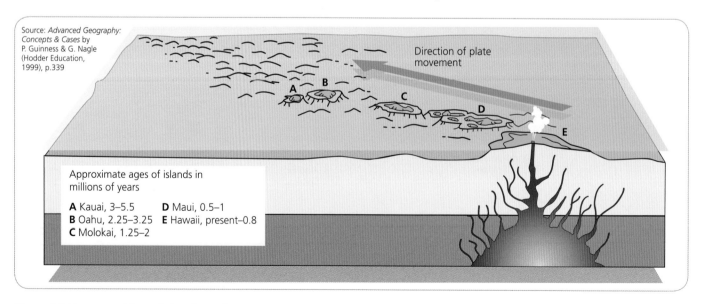

Figure 3.2 Hotspots and the evolution of Hawaii

Tsunamis

Up to 90 per cent of the world's tsunamis occur in the Pacific Ocean. This is because they are associated with subduction zones and as Figure 3.1 shows, most subduction zones are found in the Pacific Ocean.

Earthquakes
What is an earthquake?

An earthquake is a series of vibrations or seismic (shock) waves which originate from the focus – the point at which the plates release their tension or compression suddenly (Figure 3.3). The **epicentre** marks the point on the surface of the Earth immediately above the focus of the earthquake. A large earthquake can be preceded by smaller tremors known as **foreshocks** and followed by numerous **aftershocks**. Aftershocks can be particularly devastating because they damage buildings that have already been damaged by the first main shock. Seismic waves are able to travel along the surface of the Earth and also through the body of the Earth.

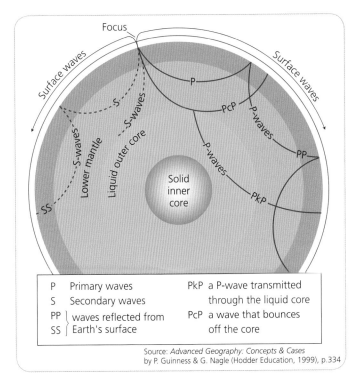

P	Primary waves	PkP	a P-wave transmitted through the liquid core
S	Secondary waves		
PP	waves reflected from	PcP	a wave that bounces off the core
SS	Earth's surface		

Source: *Advanced Geography: Concepts & Cases* by P. Guinness & G. Nagle (Hodder Education, 1999), p.334

Figure 3.3 Seismic waves

Following an earthquake two types of **body waves** (waves within the Earth's interior) occur. The first are P-waves (primary waves or pressure waves) and the second are the transverse S-waves. These are a series of oscillations at right-angles to the direction of movement.

P-waves travel by compression and expansion, and are able to pass through rocks, gases and liquids. S-waves travel with a side-to-side motion, and are able to pass through solids but not liquids

and gases, since they have no rigidity to support sideways motion. In 1909 Andrija Mohorovičić, a Yugoslavian geophysicist who was studying earthquakes in Croatia, detected four kinds of seismic wave, two of them pressure waves and two of them sheer waves. Seismographs close to the earthquake epicentre showed slow-travelling P-waves and S-waves. By contrast those further away from the shock showed faster-moving S-waves and P-waves. These shock waves are reflected or refracted when they meet rock with different densities. If the shock waves pass through denser rocks they speed up. If they pass through less dense rocks they slow down. Mohorovičić deduced that the slower waves had travelled from the focus of the earthquake through the upper layer of the crust. By contrast the faster waves must have passed through the denser material in the Earth's core, this denser material speeded up the waves and deflected them. He suggested that a change in density from 2.9 g/cm^3 to 3.3 g/cm^3 marks the boundary between the Earth's crust and the mantle below. This boundary is known as the Mohorovičić Discontinuity or quite simply the Moho.

Later geologists found a shadow zone, an area between 105° and 142° from the source of the earthquake, within which they could not detect shock waves. The explanation was that the shock waves had passed from a solid to a liquid. Thus S-waves would stop and P-waves would be refracted. The geologists concluded that there was a change in density from 5.5 g/cm^3 at 2900 km to a density of 10 g/cm^3. This was effectively the boundary between the mantle and the core. Within the Earth there is an inner core of very dense solid material – the density of the inner core goes up to as much as 13.6 /cm^3 at the centre of the Earth.

The nature of rock and sediment beneath the ground influences the pattern of shocks and vibrations during an earthquake. Unconsolidated sediments such as sand shake in a less predictable way than solid rock. Hence the damage is far greater to foundations of buildings. P-waves from earthquakes can turn solid sediments into fluids like quicksand by disrupting sub-surface water conditions. This is known as **liquefaction** or **fluidisation** and can wreck foundations of large buildings and other structures.

Earthquakes and plate boundaries

The movement of oceanic crust into the subduction zone creates some of the deepest earthquakes recorded, from 700 km below the ground. When the oceanic crust slides into the hotter fluid mantle it takes time to warm up. As the slab descends it distorts and cracks and eventually creates earthquakes. However, subduction is relatively fast so by the time the crust has cracked it has slid several hundred kilometres down into the mantle.

In areas of active earthquake activity the chances of an earthquake increase with increasing time since the last earthquake. Plates move at a rate of between 1.5 and 7.5 cm a year (the rate fingernails grow at). However, a large earthquake can involve a movement of a few metres which could occur every couple of hundred years rather than movements of a few centimetres each year. Many earthquakes are caused by the pressure created by moving plates. This increases the stress on rocks, the rocks deform and eventually give way and snap. The snapping is the release of energy, namely the earthquake. The size of the earthquake depends upon the thickness of the descending slab and the rate of movement. Along mid-ocean ridges earthquakes are small because the crust is very hot, and brittle faults cannot extend more than a few kilometres. The strength of an earthquake is measured by the Richter Scale and the Mercalli Scale.

The Richter and Mercalli Scales

In 1935 Charles Richter of the California Institute of Technology developed the Richter Scale to measure the magnitude of earthquakes. The scale is logarithmic, so an earthquake of 5.0 on the Richter Scale is 10 times more powerful than one of 4.0 and 100 times more powerful than one of 3.0. Scientists are increasingly using the **Moment Magnitude Scale** which measures the amount of energy released and produces figures that are similar to the Richter Scale. For every increase on the scale of 0.1 the amount of energy released increases by over 30. Every increase of 0.2 represents a doubling of the energy released.

By contrast the Modified Mercalli Intensity Scale relates ground movement to commonplace observations around light bulbs and bookcases (Table 3.1). It has the advantage that it allows ordinary eyewitnesses to provide information on how strong the earthquake was. It is important to remember that these scales are only used to measure the 'strength' of an earthquake, not to predict earthquakes. Table 3.2 gives some idea of the number and magnitude of earthquakes experienced around the world each year.

Table 3.1 The Modified Mercalli Scale

1	Rarely felt.
2	Felt by people who were not moving, especially on upper floors of buildings; hanging objects may swing.
3	The effects are notable indoors, especially upstairs. The vibration is like that experienced when a truck passes.
4	Many people feel it indoors, a few outside. Some are awakened at night. Crockery and doors are disturbed and standing cars rock.
5	Felt by nearly everyone; most people are awakened. Some windows are broken, plaster becomes cracked and unstable objects topple. Trees may sway and pendulum clocks stop.
6	Felt by everyone; many are frightened. Some heavy furniture moves, plaster falls. Structural damage is usually quite slight.
7	Everyone runs outdoors. Noticed by people driving cars. Poorly designed buildings are appreciably damaged.
8	Considerable amount of damage to ordinary buildings, many collapse. Well-designed ones survive but with slight damage. Heavy furniture is overturned and chimneys fall. Some sand is fluidised.
9	Considerable damage occurs even to buildings that have been well designed. Many are moved from their foundations. Ground cracks and pipes break.
10	Most masonry structures are destroyed, sub-wooden ones survive. Railway tracks bend and water slops over river banks. Landslides and sand movements occur.
11	No masonry structure remains standing, bridges are destroyed. Broad fissures occur in the ground.
12	Total damage. Waves are seen on the surface of the ground, objects are thrown into the air.

Table 3.2 Annual frequency of occurrence of earthquakes of different magnitude based on observations since 1900

Descriptor	Magnitude	Annual average	Hazard potential
Great	≥ 8	1	Total destruction, high loss of life
Major	7–7.9	18	Serious building damage, major loss of life
Strong	6–6.9	120	Large losses, especially in urban areas
Moderate	5–5.9	800	Significant losses in populated areas
Light	4–4.9	6200	Usually felt, some structural damage
Minor	3–3.9	49 000	Typically felt but usually little damage
Very minor	Less than 3	9000 per day	Not felt, but recorded

Factors affecting earthquake damage

The extent of earthquake damage is influenced by a variety of factors:

- **Strength and depth of earthquake** and **number of aftershocks** – the stronger the earthquake the more damage it can do. For example, an earthquake of 6.0 on the Richter Scale is 100 times more powerful than one of 4.0; the more aftershocks there are the greater the damage that is done. Earthquakes that occur close to the surface (shallow-focus earthquakes) potentially should do more damage than earthquakes deep underground (deep-focus earthquakes) as more of the energy of the latter is absorbed by overlying rocks.
- **Population density** – an earthquake that hits an area of high population density such as the Tokyo region of Japan, could inflict far more damage than one that hits an area of low population and building density
- The **type of buildings** – MEDCs generally have better-quality buildings, more emergency services and the funds to recover from disasters. People in MEDCs are more likely to have insurance cover than those in LEDCs.
- The **time of day** – an earthquake during a busy time, such as rush hour, may cause more deaths than one at a quiet time. Industrial and commercial areas have fewer people in them on Sundays, homes have more people in them at night.
- The **distance from the centre (epicentre)** of the earthquake – the closer a place is to the centre (epicentre) of the earthquake, the greater the damage that is done.
- The **type of rocks and sediments** – loose materials may act like liquid when shaken, a process known as **liquefaction**; solid rock is much safer and buildings should be built on flat areas formed of solid rock.
- **Secondary hazards** – an earthquake may cause mudslides and tsunamis (high sea waves) and fires; also contaminated water, disease, hunger and hypothermia.
- **Economic development** – this affects the level of preparedness and effectiveness of emergency response services, access to technology, and quality of health services.

Deaths following an earthquake can be substantial, as Table 3.3 shows quite clearly.

Table 3.3 The world's worst earthquakes by death toll in the twenty-first century

Country	Year	Death toll (est.)	Richter Scale
Haiti	2010	300 000	7.0
South East Asia	2004	248 000	9.1
Kashmir, Pakistan	2005	86 000	7.6
Chengdu, China	2008	78 000	7.9
Bam, Iran	2003	30 000	6.6

Resultant hazards of earthquakes

Most earthquakes occur with little if any advance warning. Some places, such as California and Tokyo which have considerable experience of earthquakes, and have developed 'earthquake action plans' and information programmes to increase public awareness about what to do in an earthquake.

Most problems are associated with damage to buildings, structures and transport systems (Table 3.4). The collapse of building structures is the direct cause of many injuries and deaths, but it also reduces the effect of the emergency services. In some cases more damage is caused by the aftershocks that follow the main earthquake, as they shake the already weakened structures. Aftershocks are more subdued but longer lasting and more frequent than the main tremor. Buildings partly damaged during the earthquake may be completely destroyed by the aftershocks.

Table 3.4 Earthquake hazards and impacts

Primary hazard	Impacts
Ground shaking	Loss of life
Surface faulting	Loss of livelihood
	Total or partial destruction of building structure
Secondary hazard	Interruption of water supplies
Ground failure and soil liquefaction	Breakage of sewage disposal systems
	Loss of public utilities such as electricity and gas
Landslides and rockfalls	Floods from collapsed dams
	Release of hazardous material
Debris flow and mudflow	Fires
	Spread of chronic illness
Tsunamis	

Some earthquakes involve surface displacement, generally along fault lines. This may lead to the fracture of gas pipes, as well as causing damage to lines of communication. The cost of repairing such fractures is considerable.

Earthquakes may cause other geomorphological hazards such as landslides, liquefaction (the conversion of unconsolidated sediments into materials that act like liquids) and tsunamis. For example, the Good Friday earthquake (magnitude 8.5), which shook Anchorage (Alaska) in March 1964, released twice as much energy as the 1906 San Francisco earthquake, and was felt over an area of nearly 1.3 million km². More than 130 people were killed, and over $500 million of damage was caused. It triggered large avalanches and landslides which caused much damage. It

also caused a series of tsunamis through the Pacific as far as California, Hawaii and Japan.

The relative importance of factors affecting earthquakes varies a great deal. For example, the Kobe earthquake of January 1995 had a magnitude 7.2 and caused over 5000 deaths. By contrast, the Northridge earthquake which affected parts of Los Angeles in January 1994 was 6.6 on the Richter Scale but caused only 57 deaths. On the other hand, an earthquake of force 6.6 at Maharashtra in India, in September 1993, killed over 22 000 people.

So why did these three earthquakes have such differing effects? Kobe and Los Angeles are on known earthquake zones and buildings are built to withstand earthquakes. In addition, local people have been prepared for earthquake events. By contrast Maharashtra has little experience of earthquakes. Houses were unstable and quickly destroyed, and people had little idea of how to manage the situation.

Another earthquake in an area not noted for seismic activity shows that damage is often most serious where buildings are not designed to withstand shaking or ground movement. In the 1992 Cairo earthquake many poor people in villages and the inner city slums of Cairo were killed or injured when their old, mud-walled homes collapsed. At the same time many wealthy people were killed or injured when modern high-rise concrete blocks collapsed – some of these had actually been built without planning permission.

Case Study

Earthquake in Haiti: 12 January 2010, 16.53 local time, 7.0 magnitude

The country of Haiti occupies the western part of Hispaniola, a Caribbean island that it shares with the Dominican Republic. Haiti is characterised by poverty, environmental degradation, corruption and violence. On 12 January 2010 an earthquake recorded as 7.0 on the Richter Scale occurred 25 km south-west of Port-au-Prince at a depth of just 13 km (Figure 3.4). Aftershocks were as strong as 5.9, occurring just 9 km below the surface and 56 km south-west of the city. A third of the population were affected. About 300 000 people were killed in the earthquake, 250 000 more were injured and some 1 million made homeless.

Hispaniola sits on the Gonave microplate, a small strip of the Earth's crust squeezed between the North American and Caribbean tectonic plates. This makes it vulnerable to rare but violent earthquakes. The Dominican Republic suffered a serious 'quake in 1946, but the Enriquillo-Plantain Garden fault which separates the plates on the Haitian side of the border had been accumulating stress during more than a century of inactivity. Two things magnified its destructive power: its epicentre was just 25 km south-west of Port-au-Prince and its focus was only 13 km below ground.

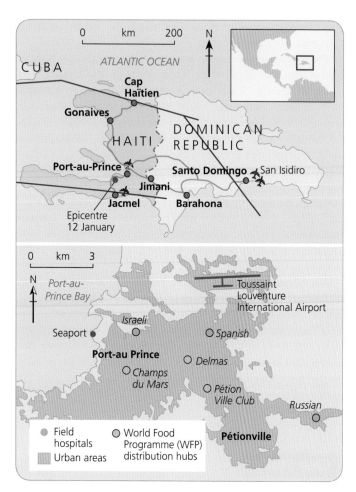

Figure 3.4 Haiti earthquake

The region is hopelessly ill-suited to withstand a shaking. Most of Port-au-Prince's 2 million residents live in tin-roofed shacks perched on unstable, steep ravines. After a school collapsed in the suburb of Pétionville in 2008, the capital's mayor said that 60 per cent of its buildings were shoddily constructed and unsafe even under normal conditions.

The Red Cross estimated that 3 million people – a third of Haiti's population – might need emergency aid. Seven days after the earthquake, the UN had managed to get food to only 200 000 people. Help – including doctors, trained sniffer dogs, and tents, blankets and food – was pledged from other countries, including Mexico, Venezuela, China, UK, France, Germany, Canada and Cuba.

Financial assistance also poured in. The UN released $10 million from its emergency fund and European countries pledged $13.7 million. Haiti's institutions were weak even before the disaster. Because the 'quake devastated the capital, both the government and the UN, which has been trying to build a state in Haiti since 2004, were seriously affected, losing buildings and essential staff.

Following the Haiti earthquake, plans were discussed for the rescue, rehabilitation and reconstruction of the country. Reconstructing Haiti is a challenge to an international community that has failed over decades to lift the island state out of poverty,

corruption and violence. Since 2000 more than $4 billion has been given to Haiti to rebuild communities and infrastructure devastated by tropical storms, floods and landslides, but mismanagement, a lack of co-ordination and attempts by global institutions to use Haiti as an economic test-bed are believed to have frustrated all efforts. A foreign debt of $1.5 billion has weighed down the economy.

Earthquake in Maule, Chile: 27 February 2010, 3.34 local time, 8.8 magnitude

The 2010 Chilean earthquake occurred off the coast of the Maule region of Chile on 27 February 2010, lasting 90 seconds. The cities of Arauco and Coronel experienced the strongest tremors. The earthquake triggered a tsunami which devastated several coastal towns in south-central Chile and damaged the port at Talcahuano. However, the death toll was just 521 victims. This has been put down to Chile's building standards, emergency preparations, and higher standard of living.

Earthquakes and human activity

Human activities can trigger earthquakes, or alter the magnitude and frequency of earthquakes, in three main ways:
- through underground disposal of liquid wastes
- by underground nuclear testing and explosions
- by increasing crustal loading.

Disposal of liquid waste

In the Rocky Mountain Arsenal in Denver, Colorado, wastewater was injected into underlying rocks during the 1960s (Figure 3.5). Water was contaminated by chemical warfare agents, and the toxic wastes were too costly to transport off-site for disposal. Thus it was decided to dispose of it down a well over 3500 m deep. Disposal began in March 1962 and was followed soon afterwards by a series of minor earthquakes, in an area previously free of earthquake activity. None of the earthquakes caused any real damage, but they did cause alarm. Between 1962 and 1965 over 700 minor earthquakes were monitored in the area.

The injection of the liquid waste into the bedrock lubricated and reactivated a series of deep underground faults which had been inactive for a long time. The more wastewater was put down the well, the larger the number of minor earthquakes. When the link was established, disposal stopped. In 1966 the well was filled in and the number of minor earthquake events detected in the area fell sharply.

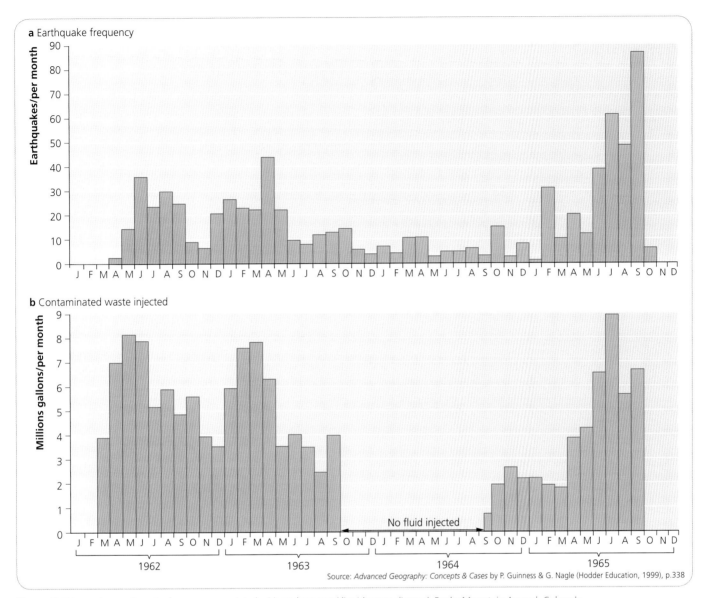

Figure 3.5 Increasing earthquake frequency associated with underground liquid waste disposal, Rocky Mountain Arsenal, Colorado

Source: *Advanced Geography: Concepts & Cases* by P. Guinness & G. Nagle (Hodder Education, 1999), p.338

Underground nuclear testing

Underground nuclear testing has triggered earthquakes in a number of places. In 1968 testing of a series of 1200 tonne bombs in Nevada set off over 30 minor earthquakes in the area over the following three days. Since 1966 the Polynesian island of Moruroa has been the site of over 80 underground nuclear explosion tests by France. More than 120 000 people live on the island. In 1966 a 120 000 tonne nuclear device was detonated, producing radioactive fallout that was measured over 3000 km downwind.

Increased crustal loading

Earthquakes can be caused by adding increased loads on previously stable land surfaces. For example, the weight of water behind large reservoirs can trigger earthquakes. In 1935 the Colorado River was dammed by the Hoover Dam to form Lake Mead. As the lake filled, over a period of ten years, and the underlying rocks adjusted to the new increased load of

over 40 km³ of water, long dormant faults in the area were reactivated, causing over 6000 minor earthquakes. Over 10 000 events were recorded up to 1973, about 10 per cent of which were strong enough to be felt by residents. None caused damage.

Section 3.1 Activities

1 Comment on the relationship between earthquake frequency and magnitude as shown in Table 3.2.

2 Account for the location of **a** shallow-focus earthquakes and **b** deep-focus earthquakes.

3 Study Figure 3.5, which shows the relationship between earthquake frequency and underground liquid waste disposal. Describe the relationship between the two variables. Suggest reasons to explain the relationship.

What should people do about earthquakes?

People deal with earthquakes in a number of ways. These include:

- do nothing and accept the hazard
- adjust to living in a hazardous environment – strengthen your home
- leave the area.

The main ways of preparing for earthquakes include:

- better forecasting and warning
- improve building design, building location
- establish emergency procedures.

There are a number of ways of predicting and monitoring earthquakes, which involve the measurement of:

- small-scale ground surface changes
- small-scale uplift or subsidence
- ground tilt
- changes in rock stress
- micro-earthquake activity (clusters of small 'quakes)
- anomalies in the Earth's magnetic field
- changes in radon gas concentration
- changes in electrical resistivity of rocks.

One particularly intensively studied site is Parkfield in California, on the San Andreas fault. Parkfield, with a population of fewer than 50 people, claims to be the earthquake capital of the world. It is heavily monitored by instruments:

- strain meters measure deformation at a single point
- two-colour laser geodimeters measure the slightest movement between tectonic plates
- magnetometers detect alterations in the Earth's magnetic field, caused by stress changes in the crust.

Nevertheless, the 1994 Northridge earthquake was not predicted and it occurred on a fault that scientists did not know existed. Technology helps, but not all of the time.

Volcanoes

Types of volcano

The shape of a volcano depends on the type of lava it contains. Very hot, runny lava produces gently sloping **shield volcanoes (Hawaiian type)**, while thick material produces **cone-shaped volcanoes (Plinian type)**. These may be the result of many volcanic eruptions over a long period of time. Part of the volcano may be blasted away during eruption. The shape of the volcano also depends on the amount of change there has been since the volcanic eruption. Cone volcanoes are associated with destructive plate boundaries, whereas shield volcanoes are characteristic of constructive boundaries and hotspots.

Volcanoes are classified in a number of ways. These include the type of flow, the type of eruption (Figure 3.6) and the level of activity.

Aa flow is a few metres thick. It consists of two distinct zones – an upper rubbly part, and a lower part of solid lava which cools slowly. Aa surfaces are a loose jumble of irregularly shaped cindery blocks with sharp sides. By contrast, **pahoehoe** flow is the least viscous of all lavas; rates of advance can be slow. It has a cool surface, with flow underneath the surface. Pahoehoe surfaces can be smooth and glossy but may also have cavities; surfaces may also be crumpled with channels.

The amount of silica makes the difference between volcanoes that erupt continuously, such as those on Iceland and Hawaii, and those where eruptions are infrequent but violent, such as in Japan and the Philippines. Lava released where the oceans meet the continents absorbs silica-rich sediments; this causes the lava to become less viscous and block the vents until enough pressure has built up to break them open.

Each year about 20 km² of land is covered by lava flows. These may initially reach temperatures of over 1000 °C, resulting

Magma rises through open fissure

Vent — Cone

Icelandic lava eruptions are characterised by persistent fissure eruption. Large quantities of basaltic lava build up vast horizontal plains. On a large scale they have formed the Deccan Plateau and the Columbia Plateau.

Hawaiian eruptions involve more noticeable central activity than the Icelandic type. Runny, basaltic lava travels down the sides of the volcano in lava flows. Gases escape easily. Occasional pyroclastic activity occurs but this is less important than the lava eruption.

Strombolian eruptions are characterised by frequent gas explosions which blast fragments of runny lava into the air to form cones. They are very explosive eruptions with large quantities of pyroclastic rock thrown out. Eruptions are commonly marked by a white cloud of steam emitted from the crater.

In **Vulcanian eruptions**, violent gas explosions blast out plugs of sticky or cooled lava. Fragments build up into cones of ash and pumice. Vulcanian eruptions occur when there is very viscous lava which solidifies rapidly after an explosion. Often the eruption clears a blocked vent and spews large quantities of volcanic ash into the atmosphere.

Vesuvian eruptions are characterised by very powerful blasts of gas pushing ash clouds high into the sky. They are more violent than vulcanian eruptions. Lava flows also occur. Ash falls to cover surrounding areas.

In a **Plinian eruption**, gas rushes up through sticky lava and blasts ash and fragments into the sky in a huge explosion. The violent eruptions create immense clouds of gas and volcanic debris several kilometres thick. Gas clouds and lava can also rush down the slopes. Part of the volcano may be blasted away during the eruption.

Figure 3.6 Types of volcanic eruption

Figure 3.7 Lava flow, Mt Etna

Table 3.5 Hazards associated with volcanic activity

Direct hazards (primary hazards)	Indirect hazards (secondary hazards)	Socio-economic impacts
Pyroclastic flows	Atmospheric ash fallout	Destruction of settlements
Volcanic bombs (projectiles)	Landslides	Loss of life
Lava flows	Tsunamis	Loss of farmland and forests
Ash fallout	Acid rainfall	Destruction of infrastructure – roads, airstrips and port facilities
Volcanic gases	Lahars (mudflows)	
Earthquakes		Disruption of communications

Ash and debris falls steadily from the volcanic cloud, blanketing the ground with a deposit known as a pyroclastic fall. These can be very dangerous, especially as the fine ash particles can damage people's lungs. Also ash is fairly heavy – a small layer only a few centimetres thick can be enough to cause a building to collapse. Dust and fine particles also cause havoc with global climate patterns. Pyroclastic falls are powerful enough to knock down trees and to leave a trail of destruction. Some of them are extremely hot – up to 700 °C. Figure 3.8 shows the pyroclastic flows associated with the eruption of Soufrière volcano on Montserrat.

Figure 3.8 Pyroclastic flows and lahars, Montserrat

in severe social and economic disruption. However, cooled lava flows are very fertile and therefore attract dense population settlement and intense agricultural production.

There are a number of ways of reducing lava flows. These include spraying them with water, bombing them, and seeding the lava with foreign nuclei. For example, in 1973 a lava flow which threatened the town of Vestmannaeyar in Iceland was sprayed with water for months, thereby slowing down its advance.

Active volcanoes are volcanoes that continue to erupt or at risk of erupting. **Extinct** volcanoes have stopped erupting, and **dormant** volcanoes are ones that have not erupted for a very long time but could still erupt. It is an arbitrary classification, and the distinction between dormant and extinct is difficult to define.

Volcanic hazards

Volcanic hazards (Table 3.5) can be divided into six main categories.

- lava flows (Figure 3.7)
- ballistics and tephra clouds
- pyroclastic flows (Figure 3.8)
- gases and acid rain
- lahars (mudflows) (Figure 3.8)
- glacier bursts (jökulhlaups).

Lahars, or volcanic mudflows, are another hazard associated with volcanoes. A combination of heavy rain and unstable ash increase the hazard of lahars. The hazards associated with volcanic eruption also vary spatially. Close to the volcano people are at risk of large fragments of debris, ash falls and poisonous gases. Further away pyroclastic flows may prove hazardous, and mudflows and debris flows may have an impact on more distant settlements. In addition, volcanoes can lead to tsunamis and to famine. Although there is good evidence for the spatial distribution of volcanoes, there is little discernible pattern in their distribution in terms of when they occur.

The ash fallout from the Eyjafjallajökull glacier in Iceland (April 2010) caused widespread disruption to European air travel. No-one was killed in the eruption but the economic cost was great. It was a truly global impact as countries that traded with the EU were badly affected.

Volcanic strength

The strength of a volcano is measured by the Volcanic Explosive Index (VEI). This is based on the amount of material ejected in the explosion, the height of the cloud it creates, and the amount of damage caused. Any explosion above level 5 is considered to be very large and violent. A VEI 8 refers to a supervolcano.

Table 3.6 The biggest volcanic eruptions

Eruption	Date	Volume of material ejected (km³)
Mt St Helens, USA	1980	1
Mt Vesuvius, Italy	AD 79	3
Mt Katmai, USA	1912	12
Mt Krakatoa, Indonesia	1883	18
Mt Tambora, Indonesia	1815	80

Section 3.1 Activities

1 What are the main hazards associated with volcanoes?

2 Study Table 3.6, which shows volcanic disasters since 1800.
  a Describe the location of these disasters.
  b How do you account for this pattern?

Predicting volcanoes

Scientists are increasingly successful in predicting volcanoes. Since 1980 they have correctly predicted 19 of Mt St Helens' 22 eruptions, and Alaska's Redoubt volcano in 1989. There have been false alarms: in 1976, 72 000 residents of Guadeloupe were forced to leave their homes, and in 1980 Mammoth Lake in California suffered from a reduction in tourist numbers owing to mounting concern regarding volcanic activity.

Volcanoes are easier to predict than earthquakes since there are certain signs. The main ways of predicting volcanoes include monitoring using:

- seismometers to record swarms of tiny earthquakes that occur as the magma rises (Figure 3.9)
- chemical sensors to measure increased sulphur levels
- lasers to detect the physical swelling of the volcano
- ultrasound to monitor low-frequency waves in the magma, resulting from the surge of gas and molten rock, as happened at Pinatubo, El Chichon and Mt St Helens
- observations, such as of Gunung Agung (Java, Indonesia).

However, it is not always possible to state exactly when a volcanic eruption will happen. The US Geological Survey predicted the eruption of Mt Pinatubo in 1991, and successfully evacuated the area. However, it was unsuccessful in predicting a volcanic eruption at Mammoth Mountain Ski Area in California, USA – the false prediction reduced visitor numbers to the resort and caused economic distress to local business people.

In Montserrat, volcanic activity has made over 60 per cent of the southern and central parts of the island uninhabitable. Plymouth was evacuated three times in 1995 and 1996. The volcano was responsible for 19 deaths – all of them farmers – caught out by an eruption during their return to the Exclusion Zone. Volcanic dust is another hazard, as it is a potential cause of silicosis and aggravates asthma. There are many hazards around Plymouth (Figure 3.10).

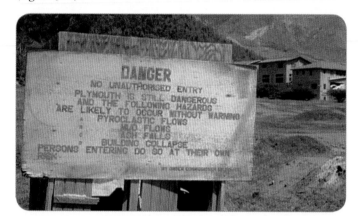

Figure 3.10 Hazard sign in Plymouth, Montserrat

Volcanic management includes monitoring and prediction (Figure 3.11). GPS is used to monitor changes in the surface of the volcano – volcanoes typically bulge and swell before an eruption. The development of 'risk maps' can be used to good effect, as in the case of Montserrat. There are risks on other Caribbean islands too. St Vincent and St Kitts are high-risk islands whereas St Lucia, Grenada and Nevis are lower risk.

Figure 3.9 A seismograph reading (Montserrat)

Figure 3.11 Montserrat Volcanic Observatory

Living with a volcano

People often choose to live in volcanic areas because they are useful in a variety of ways:

- Some countries, such as Iceland and the Philippines, were created by volcanic activity.
- Some volcanic soils are rich, deep and fertile, and allow intensive agriculture, for example in Java. However, in other areas, for example Sumatra and Iceland, the soils are poor. In Iceland this is because the climate is too cool to allow chemical weathering of the lava flows, while in Sumatra the soils are highly leached.
- Volcanic areas are important for tourism, for example St Lucia and Iceland.
- Some volcanoes are culturally symbolic and are part of the national identity, such as Mt Fuji in Japan.

Secondary hazards of tectonic events
Lahars and mudflows

Case Study

Nevado del Ruiz, Colombia

One hazard that is closely associated with volcanic activity is the lahar, or mudflow:

- Rain brings soot and ash back to ground and this becomes a heavily saturated mudflow.
- Heat from volcanoes melts snow and ice – the resulting flow picks up sediment and turns it into a destructive lahar.

Nevado del Ruiz is a volcano in Colombia which rises to an altitude of 5400 m and is covered with an icecap 30 m thick, covering an area of about 20 km^2. In 1984, small-scale volcanic activity resumed, and large-scale activity returned in November 1985. Scientists monitoring the mountain recorded earthquakes and soon after a volcanic eruption threw hot, pyroclastic material onto the icecap, causing it to melt. Condensing volcanic steam, icemelt and pyroclastic flows combined to form lahars which moved down the mountain, engulfing the village of Chinchina, killing over 1800 people and destroying the village (Figure 3.12).

Conditions worsened as further eruptions melted more ice, creating larger lahars which were capable of travelling further down the mountain into the floodplain of the Rio Magdalena. Within an hour it had reached the city of Armero, 45 km away. Most of Armero, including 22 000 of its 28 000 residents, were crushed and suffocated beneath lahars up to 8 m thick. Those who were saved were those who just happened to be further up the slope. Images of people trapped in the mud were relayed across the world.

The volcanic eruption was relatively small but the presence of the icecap made the area especially hazardous.

Section 3.1 Activities

1 Why do volcanoes and icecaps sometimes occur in the same place?
2 Study Figure 3.12, which shows the location of Armero. Why do you think so many people lived there?

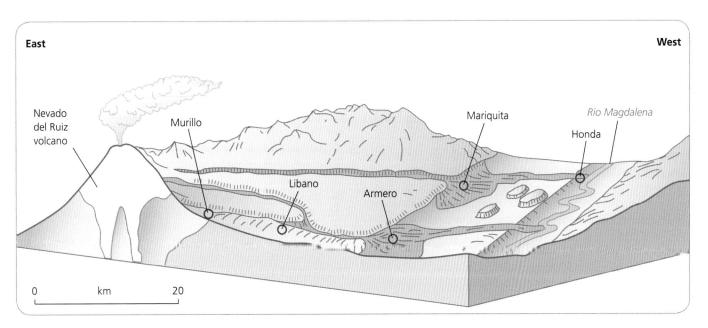

Figure 3.12 Nevado del Ruiz lahar

Volcanic gases

Lake Nyos, Cameroon

Cameroon lies just north of the equator in West Africa. It contains a large number of deep crater lakes, such as Lake Nyos, formed as a result of tectonic activity. Lake Nyos is nearly 2 km wide and over 200 m deep. In August 1986 a huge volume of gas escaped from the lake and swept down into neighbouring valleys for a distance of up to 25 km (Figure 3.13). The ground-hugging clouds of gas were up to 50 m thick and travelling at speeds of over 70 km per hour. Some 1700 people were suffocated, 3000 cattle died and all other animal life in the area was killed. Plants, however, were unaffected.

The gas was carbon dioxide. Because it is heavier and denser than oxygen, the 50 m cloud deprived people and animals of oxygen, so they were asphyxiated. The source of carbon dioxide was a basaltic chamber of magma, deep beneath Cameroon. It had been leaking into and accumulating in Lake Nyos for some time. Due to its depth, water in the lake became stratified into layers of warmer water near the surface, and colder denser water near the bottom of the lake. The cold dense water absorbed the carbon dioxide, which was then held down by the weight of the overlying waters.

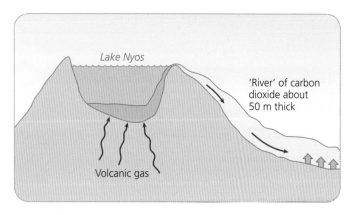

Figure 3.13 Lake Nyos, Cameroon

The disaster occurred after the water at the bottom of the lake was disturbed. The cause of the disturbance is unclear. It could have been a deep volcanic eruption, an earthquake, a change in water temperature, or a climatic event. Whatever the cause, the effect was like an erupting champagne bottle. Once the overlying pressure was reduced, carbon dioxide escaped into the surrounding area causing rapid death among people and animals.

It is likely that such a tragedy will happen again. It is believed that only about 66 per cent of the carbon dioxide escaped from the lake, and that it has begun to build up again. It may take several decades for the gas cloud to occur again, or maybe even centuries, but the potential for a disaster is there.

1 Explain why the disaster at Lake Nyos affected animals but not plants.

2 Cameroon is not close to a tectonic boundary. How do you explain the tectonic hazard in an area that is not close to a known boundary?

Tsunamis

The term *tsunami* is the Japanese for 'harbour wave'. Ninety per cent of tsunamis occur in the Pacific basin. They are generally caused by earthquakes (usually in subduction zones) but can be caused by volcanoes (for example Krakatoa in 1883) and landslides (for example Alaska in 1964).

Tsunamis have the potential to cause widespread disaster, as in the case of the South Asian tsunami on 26 December 2004 (Figure 3.14). Owing to the loss of life among tourists, it came to be seen as a global disaster, killing people from nearly 30 countries. Between 180 000 and 280 000 people were killed in this tsunami.

Figure 3.14 Tsunami damage in Phuket, Thailand

The cause of the tsunami was a giant earthquake and landslide caused by the sinking of the Indian Plate under the Eurasian Plate. Pressure had built up over many years and was released in the earthquake which reached 9.0 on the Richter Scale.

The main impact of the Boxing Day tsunami, as it came to be known, was on the Indonesian island of Sumatra, the closest inhabited area to the epicentre of the earthquake. More than 70 per cent of the inhabitants of some coastal villages died. Apart from Indonesia, Sri Lanka suffered more from the tsunami than anywhere else. At least 31 000 people are known to have died there, when the southern and eastern coastlines were devastated.

Potential tsunamis due to earthquakes and landslides

A lake formed by a landslide in northern Pakistan could burst its banks at any time, possibly triggering a giant wave that could sweep down the Himalayan valley and swamp dozens of villages (Figure 3.15). The level of the Attabad lake, which was formed by a landslide in early January 2010, rose alarmingly fast to within a few metres of its limit.

Figure 3.15 Area of potential tsunamis in the Himalayas

Pakistani authorities are concerned that immense water pressure could cause the lake wall to suddenly collapse, sending a tidal wave up to 60 m high into the valley below and affecting up to 25 000 people.

The Attabad lake started to form after a landslide blocked the Karakoram highway, which links Pakistan and China. The water level rose rapidly, swelled by meltwater from nearby glaciers, swamping 120 houses and displacing about 1300 people. Another 12 000 people were evacuated from the potential flood zone downstream.

The world's largest landslide dam was formed in 1911 on the Murghab River in Tajikistan. The 550 m dam has never breached because lake outflows are greater than inflows.

Geomorphologists estimate that 35 natural dams have formed over 500 years in the Pakistani section of the Himalayas. The latest was the Hattian dam, formed by the 2005 earthquake.

Case Study

Peruvian tsunami, 2010

Tsunamis can be caused by forces that are not tectonic. For example, in 2010 a massive ice block, measuring 500 m by 200 m, broke from a glacier and crashed into a lake in the Peruvian Andes, causing a 23 m tsunami and sending muddy torrents through nearby towns, killing at least one person.

The chunk of ice detached from the Hualcan glacier about 320 km north of the capital, Lima. It plunged into a lagoon known

as lake 513, triggering a tsunami that breached 23 m-high levees and damaged Carhuaz and other villages.

Around 50 homes and a water-processing plant serving 60 000 residents were wrecked. Due to global warming there has been an increase in the number of glaciers melting, breaking and falling on overflowing lakes.

Tsunami warning systems

At present it is impossible to predict precisely where and when a tsunami will happen. In most cases it is only possible to raise the alarm once a tsunami has started. In the cases of submarine volcanoes it is possible to monitor these to predict the risk of tsunami. For example, Kick 'em Jenny, north of Grenada, has erupted 10 times since the late 1970s and grown by 50 m. Volcanologists believe it could cause a tsunami and threaten Venezuela.

The first effective tsunami warning system was developed in 1948 in the Pacific, following the 1946 tsunami. The system consisted of over 50 tidal stations and 31 seismographic stations, spread between Alaska, Hong Kong and Cape Horn.

When water passes a critical threshold a warning is automatically sent to Honolulu (Hawaii). In addition, the earthquake epicentre is plotted and magnitude investigated. Its effectiveness has been improved by the use of satellites, and it is now operated by the US National Oceanic and Atmospheric Administration (NOAA).

In theory there is time to issue warnings. A tsunami off the coast of Ecuador will take 12 hours to reach Hawaii, 20 hours to reach Japan. A tsunami from the Aleutians will take 5 hours to reach Hawaii. However, the impacts will vary with shoreline morphology.

Other tsunami early warning systems include those in Japan and Kamchatka (Russia). However, many LEDCs lack early warning systems, as was so tragically exposed in the 2004 Boxing Day tsunami. Following the 2010 Chile earthquake a tsunami warning was issued. Fortunately, there was little evidence of any large-sized waves affecting areas other than part of the Chilean coast.

During the 2010 Indonesian tsunami, in which over 400 people died, the tsunami early warning system that had been put in place failed to work. The system had been vandalised in the Mentawai Islands, which were worst affected by the tsunami.

Factors affecting the perception of risk

At an individual level there are three important influences upon an individual's response to any hazardous event:

1 Experience – the more experience a person has of environmental hazards the greater the adjustment to the hazard.
2 Material well-being – those who are better off have more choices.
3 Personality – is the person a leader or a follower, a risk-taker or risk-minimiser?

Ultimately there are just three choices:
1   Do nothing and accept the hazard.
2   Adjust to the situation of living in a hazardous environment.
3   Leave the area.
It is the adjustment to the hazard that we are interested in.

The level of adjustment will depend, in part, upon the risks caused by the hazard. This includes:
*   identification of the hazards
*   estimation of the risk (probability) of the environmental hazard
*   evaluation of the cost (loss) caused by the environmental hazard.

Section 3.1 Activities

1 Outline the causes of tsunamis.

2 To what extent is it possible to manage the impacts of tsunamis?

3.2 Hazardous environments resulting from mass movements

Classification of mass movements

Mass movements can be classified in a number of ways. The main ones include speed of movement (see *Paper 1: Core Geography, Physical Topic 3*, Figure 3.22, page 71) and the amount of water present (see *Paper 1: Core Geography, Physical Topic 3*, Figure 3.21, page 71). In addition, it is possible to distinguish between different types of movement, such as falls, flows, slides and slumps (see *Paper 1: Core Geography, Physical Topic 3*, pages 74–76).

Impacts of mass movements

The likelihood of a slope failing can be expressed by its safety factor. This is the relative strength or resistance of the slope, compared with the force that is trying to move it. The most important factors that determine movement are gravity, slope angle and pore pressure (Figures 3.16 and 3.17).

Gravity has two effects. First it acts to move the material downslope (a slide component). Second it acts to stick the particle to the slope (a stick component). The downslope movement is proportional to the weight of the particle and slope angle. Water lubricates particles and in some cases fills the spaces between the

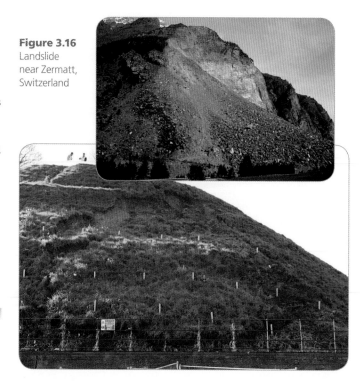

Figure 3.16 Landslide near Zermatt, Switzerland

Figure 3.17 Landslip on a slope in Oxford, UK

particles. This forces them apart under pressure. Pore pressure will greatly increase the ability of the material to move. This factor is of particular importance in movements of wet material on low-angle slopes (Table 3.7).

Table 3.7 Increasing stress and decreasing resistance

Factor	Examples
Factors contributing to increased shear stress	
Removal of lateral support through undercutting or slope steepening	Erosion by rivers and glaciers, wave action, faulting, previous rockfalls or slides
Removal of underlying support	Undercutting by rivers and waves, subsurface solution, loss of strength by exposure of sediments
Loading of slope	Weight of water, vegetation, accumulation of debris
Lateral pressure	Water in cracks, freezing in cracks, swelling, pressure release
Transient stresses	Earthquakes, movement of trees in wind
Factors contributing to reduced shear strength	
Weathering effects	Disintegration of granular rocks, hydration of clay minerals, solution of cementing minerals in rock or soil
Changes in pore-water	Saturation, softening of material pressure
Changes of structure	Creation of fissures in clays, remoulding of sands and clays
Organic effects	Burrowing of animals, decay of roots

Landslides are a common natural event in unstable, steep areas (Figure 3.18). Landslides may lead to loss of life, disruption of transport and communications, and damage to property and infrastructure. The annual repair cost for roads in the Caribbean is estimated to be US$15 million.

Figure 3.18 Mam Tor landslide, Derbyshire, UK

Tropical storm activity may trigger landslides. In Jamaica in 2001, tropical storm Michelle triggered a number of debris flows, many 2–3 km in length. Similarly, tropical storm Mitch (1998) caused a mudflow 20 km long and 2–3 km wide, which killed more than 1500 people in the town of Posoltega in Nicaragua and surrounding villages.

The two main forces that trigger landslides in the Caribbean are:
- seismic activity
- heavy rainfall.

Jamaica is subject to frequent landslides. In the Blue Mountains, over 80 per cent of the slopes are greater than 2°. The area is also geologically young, heavily fractured, and the bedrock is deeply weathered, making it unstable. The largest historic landslide in the region occurred on Judgement Cliff, eastern Jamaica, where an estimated 80 million m³ of material was moved.

Human activities can increase the risk of landslides, for example by:
- increasing the slope angle, for instance cutting through high ground – slope instability increases with increased slope angle
- placing extra weight on a slope, for instance new buildings – this adds to the stress on a slope
- removing vegetation – roots may bind the soil together and interception by leaves may reduce rainfall compaction
- exposing rock joints and bedding planes which may increase the speed of weathering.

There have been various attempts to manage the landslide risk. A number of landslide hazard maps have been produced for the region. Methods to combat the landslide hazard are largely labour intensive and include:
- building restraining structures such as walls, piles, buttresses and gabions – these may hold back minor landslides
- excavating and filling steep slopes to produce gentler slopes – this can reduce the impact of gravity on a slope
- draining slopes to reduce the build-up of water – this decreases water pressure in the soil
- watershed management, for example afforestation and agroforestry ('farming the forest') – this increases interception and reduces overland flow.

However, many settlements are located on unsuitable land because no-one else wants that land. Relocation following a disaster can also occur. For example, at Mayeyes near Ponce in Puerto Rico the site was cleared following a landslide. Similarly, the Preston Lands landslide in 1986 in Jamaica resulted in the local community being relocated.

Section 3.2 Activities

1 Suggest why hazards due to mass movement are common throughout many parts of the Caribbean.

2 How can human activity increase the risk of landslides?

Case Study

Landslides in Puerto Rico

Approximately 70–80 per cent of Puerto Rico is hilly or mountainous (Figure 3.19). Average annual precipitation in Puerto Rico ranges from less than 1000 mm along the southern coast, to more than 4000 mm in the rainforest of the Sierra de Luquillo in the north-eastern part of the island. Rain in Puerto Rico falls throughout the year, but about twice as much rain falls each month from May to October – the tropical storm season – as falls from November to April. In October 1985, a tropical wave, which later developed into tropical storm Isabel, struck the south-central coast of Puerto Rico, and produced extreme rainfall.

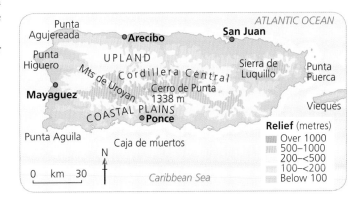

Figure 3.19 Puerto Rico: relief

Puerto Rico can be divided into three distinct physiographic provinces: Upland, Northern Karst and Coastal Plains. The Upland province includes three major mountain ranges and is covered by dense tropical vegetation. Slopes as steep as 45° are common. The Northern Karst province includes most of north-central and north-western Puerto Rico north of the Upland province. The Coastal Plains province is a discontinuous, gently sloping area. Puerto Rico's major cities are built primarily in the Coastal Plain province, although population growth has pushed development onto adjacent slopes of the Upland and Northern Karst provinces. Some 60 per cent of the 3.35 million population lives in the four largest cities – San Juan, Ponce, Mayaguez, and Arecibo – which are located primarily on flat or gently sloping coastal areas. However, continuing growth of these urban centres, is pushing development onto surrounding steep slopes.

All major types of landslide occur in Puerto Rico. Most of the Upland province and the Northern Karst province, on account of their high relief, steep slopes and abundant rainfall, have continuing landslide problems. The drier south-western part normally experiences landslides only during exceptionally heavy rainfall.

Debris slides and debris flows – rapid downslope sliding or flowing of disrupted surface rock and soil – are particularly hazardous because they happen with little or no warning. Rock falls are common on very steep natural slopes and especially on the numerous steep road cuttings on the island.

A major tropical storm in October 1985 triggered thousands of debris flows as well as a disastrous rock slide that destroyed the Mameyes district of Ponce, killing at least 129 people. The Mameyes landslide was the worst ever landslide experienced in Puerto Rico. More than 100 homes were destroyed, and about as many were later condemned and removed because of continuing risk from landslides.

The greatest cost to public works in Puerto Rico is road maintenance. The frequency of serious storms suggests that a long-term average of perhaps five fatalities per year could occur, tens of houses be destroyed or made unfit to live in, and hundreds be damaged by landslides each year.

Section 3.2 Activities

1 Suggest why Puerto Rico is so vulnerable to landslides.

2 How could the threat of landslides be reduced?

Case Study

China's landslides, 2010

China experienced its deadliest landslide in decades in 2010. At least 700 people died in north-western Gansu province when an avalanche of mud and rock engulfed the small town of Zhouqu. Zhouqu town is in a valley. Heavy rain quickly ran off the steep, barren hills, triggering mudslides and swelling the river. Landslides levelled an area about 5 km long and 500 m wide, and more than 300 houses collapsed.

Officials have warned for years that heavy tree-felling and rapid hydro development were making the mountain area around Zhouqu vulnerable to landslips. One government report in 2009 called the Bailong river a 'high-occurrence disaster zone for landslides'.

The landslide created a loose earth dam. Water levels behind the barrier fell slightly after controlled explosions created a channel to funnel off some of the water.

The landslide was the worst to hit China in 60 years, and was the most deadly single incident in a year of heavy flooding that killed nearly 1500 people.

Mudslides

Case Study

Human causes: the Italian mudslides, 1998

In May 1998 mudslides swept through towns and villages in Campania, killing nearly 300 people. Hardest hit was Sarno, a town of 35 000 people (Figure 3.20). In the two weeks before the mudslide, up to a year's rainfall had fallen. Geologically the area is unstable – it has active volcanoes, such as Etna and Vesuvius, many mountains and scores of fast-flowing rivers. Following the mudslide a state of emergency was declared in the Campania region, and up to £18 million was allocated for repairing the damage. Campania is one of Italy's most vulnerable regions – since 1892 scientists have recorded at least 1173 serious landslides in Campania and Calabria. Since 1945, landslides and floods have caused an average of seven deaths every month (Table 3.8).

Figure 3.20 Sarno, Italy

However, the disaster was only partially natural – much of it was down to human error. The River Sarno had dwindled to a trickle of water and part of the river bed had been cemented over. The clay soils of the surrounding mountains had been rendered dangerously loose by forest fires and deforestation. Houses had been built up hillsides identified as landslide zones, while

Table 3.8 Floods and landslides in Italy since 1950

Year	Region	Event	Deaths
1951	Calabria	Floods	100
1951	Polesine, Veneto	Floods	89
1954	Salerno, Campania	Floods	297
1963	Longarone, Veneto	Landslide, floods	1800
1966	Florence, Tuscany	Floods	35
1985	Val di Stava, Trentino	Landslide, floods	269
1987	Valtelina, Lombardy	Floods, landslide	53
1994	Alessandria, Piedmont	Floods	68
1996	Versilia, Tuscany	Floods, landslide	14
1998	Sarno and Siano, Campania	Mudslide, floods	285

Italy's sudden entry into the industrial age in the 1960s led to the uncontrolled building of houses and roads, and deforestation. Nowhere was this more evident than in Campania. Over 20 per cent of the houses in Sarno were built without permission. Most are shoddily built over a 2 m thick layer of lava formed by the eruption of Vesuvius in AD 79. Heavy rain can make this lava liquid and up to 900 million tonnes of material are washed down in this way every year. Much of the region's fragility is, therefore, due to mass construction, poor infrastructure and poor planning.

It is likely that similar landslides will be experienced in Spain, Portugal, Greece and Turkey as these countries are developed. All across southern Europe the natural means by which excess rainfall can be absorbed harmlessly are being destroyed. First the land is cleared for development (even land that may have been designated as green belt land). The easiest way to clear the vegetation is to set it on fire. The growing incidence of forest fires around the Mediterranean is not coincidental. Many are started deliberately by developers to ensure that the area loses its natural beauty. One of the side-effects of fire is to loosen the underlying soil.

Throughout southern Europe the easiest way for an individual to add on an extension or build a house is not to submit plans for approval but just to go ahead. In Sicily up to 20 000 holiday homes have been built on beaches, cliffs and wetlands, in defiance of planning regulations. In Italy 217 000 houses have been built without permission, and without proper drainage or foundations. Many stand close to an apparently dry river bed that can become a torrent during a storm. One Campanian town, Villaggio Coppola Di Castelvolturno, with a population of 15 000 inhabitants, was created entirely without authorisation.

Section 3.2 Activities

1 What are the natural reasons why Italy is at risk from mudslides?

2 What human factors have increased the risk of mudslides in the region?

3 Why is the threat of mudslides increasing throughout the Mediterranean region?

Case Study

The Venezuelan mudslides

The Venezuelan mudslides of 1999 were the worst disaster to hit the country for almost 200 years (Figure 3.21). The first two weeks of December saw an unusually high amount of rainfall in Venezuela. Precipitation was 40–50 per cent above normal in most of the eastern Caribbean during 1999. On 15 and 16 December the slopes of the 2000 m Mt Avila began to pour forth avalanches of rock and mud, burying large parts of a 300 km stretch of the central coast. The rains triggered a series of mudslides, landslides and flash floods which claimed the lives of between 10 000 and 50 000 people in the narrow strip of land between the mountains and the Caribbean Sea. Over 150 000 people were left homeless by landslides and floods in the states of Vargas and Miranda.

Figure 3.21 Venezuela

Hardest hit was the state of Vargas. Countless mountainside slum dwellings were either buried in the mudslide or swept out to sea. Most of the dead were buried in mudslides that were 8–10 m deep. The true number of casualties may never be known. The mudslides also destroyed roads, bridges and factories, buried crops in the fields, destroyed telecommunications, and also ruined Venezuela's tourist industry for the immediate future. The international airport of Caracas was temporarily closed and the coastal highway was destroyed or closed in many places. Flash floods damaged hundreds of containers at the seaport in Maiquetía. Hazardous materials in some containers were leaked into the ground and into the sea. Flash flood damage halted operations at the Maiquetía seaport and hampered efforts to bring in emergency supplies immediately after the disaster. Economic damage was estimated at over US$3 billion.

The disaster was not just related to heavy rainfall. The government blamed corrupt politicians from previous governments and planners who had allowed shanty towns to grow up in steep valleys surrounding the coast and the capital, Caracas.

The immediate response was a search-and-rescue operation to find any survivors in the mudflows, landslides and buildings that had been damaged or destroyed. Few survivors were found after the first few days. The other short-term response was to provide emergency relief – accommodation, water purification tablets, food and medicines to those in need. The relief operation was severely hindered by the poor state of the infrastructure which made operations difficult.

Ironically, the government had already been planning to redistribute part of Venezuela's population away from the overcrowded coast to the interior. Up to 70 per cent of Venezuela's population live in this small area. This plan is now likely to be put in place much more quickly.

Government plans for rebuilding

The Venezuela government announced a plan to restore Venezuela's northern coastal region by rebuilding thousands of homes there, expanding the country's main airport and constructing canals that can direct rivers away from communities.

The plan includes building 40 000 new homes in the hard-hit state of Vargas. The resort towns of Macuto and Camuri Chico will be restored as tourist destinations, and $100 million will be spent to expand Venezuela's main international airport. The country's main seaport, also in Vargas, will also be 'modernised'.

The towns that were utterly devastated by the disaster, where most structures were swept out to sea, will not be rebuilt. Instead, these towns, including the coastal community of Carmen de Uria (Figure 3.22), will be turned into parks, bathing resorts or other outdoor facilities.

Figure 3.22 Landslide at Carmen de Uria

2005 hazards

In 2005 floods and mudslides brought on by heavy rains in the northern and central coast of Venezuela caused fourteen deaths. Some 18 000 people were affected, while 2840 houses were damaged and a further 363 destroyed. In many cases those that were affected in the 1999 mudslides were also affected in 2005.

Section 3.2 Activities

1 What were the causes of the Venezuelan mudslides?

2 Why were the impacts so great?

Table 3.9 summarises some of the hazards that are experienced in mountainous areas around the world.

Table 3.9 Examples of hazards in mountainous areas

Hazards	Disaster event
Rockslides	Elm, Swiss Alps, 1881
	Vaiont Dam, Italian Alps, 1963
Mud and debris flows	European Alps, 1987
	Huanuco Province, Peru, 1989
Debris torrents	Coast Range, British Colombia
	Rio Colorado, Chile, 1987
Avalanches	Hakkari, Turkey, 1989
	Western Iran, 1990
Earthquake-triggered mass movements	Campagna, Italy, 1980
	Mt Ontake, Japan, 1984
Vulcanism-triggered mass movements	Mt St Helens, USA, 1980
	Nevado del Ruiz, Colombia, 1985
Weather-triggered mass movements from volcanoes	Mt Kelut, Indonesia, 1966
	Mt Semeru, Java, 1981
Natural dams and dam-break floods	
• Landslide dams	Indus Gorge, Western Himalayas, 1841
	Ecuadorean Andes, 1987
	Sichuan earthquake, 2008
• Glacier dams	'Ape Lake', British Colombia, 1984
• Moraine dams	Khumbu, Nepal, Himalaya,1985
• Avalanche dams	Santa River, Peruvian Andes, 1962
• Vegetation dams	New Guinea Highlands, 1970
• Artificial dam failures	Buffalo Creek, Appalachians, USA, 1972
	Shanxi Province, China, 1989

Avalanches

Avalanches are mass movements of snow and ice. Newly fallen snow may fall off older snow, especially in winter, while in spring partially thawed snow moves, often triggered by skiing. Avalanches occur frequently on steep slopes over 22°, especially on north-facing slopes where the lack of sun inhibits the stabilisation of the snow. They are also very fast. Average speeds in an avalanche are 40–60 km per hour, but speeds of up to 200 km per hour have been recorded in Japan.

Avalanches are classified in a number of ways (Figure 3.23). At first, a distinction was made between airborne powder-snow avalanches and ground-hugging avalanches. Later classifications have included:

- the type of breakaway – from a point formed with loose snow, or from an area formed of a slab
- position of the sliding surface – the whole snow cover or just the surface
- water content – dry or wet avalanches
- the form of the avalanche – whether it is channelled in cross-section or open.

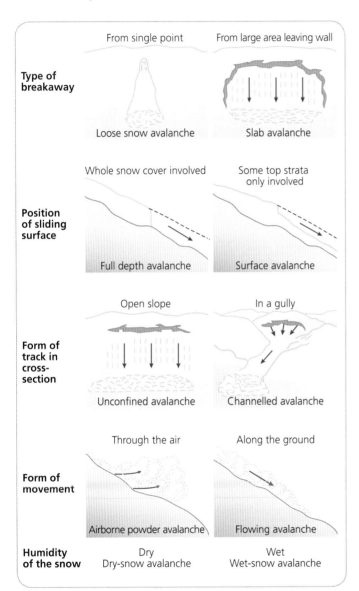

Figure 3.23 A classification of avalanches

Although avalanches cannot be prevented, it is possible to reduce their impact (Figures 3.24 and 3.25). So why do avalanches occur? The underlying processes in an avalanche are similar to those in a landslide. Snow gets its strength from the interlocking of snow crystals and cohesion caused by electrostatic bonding of snow crystals. The snow remains in place as long as its strength is greater than the stress exerted by its weight and the slope angle.

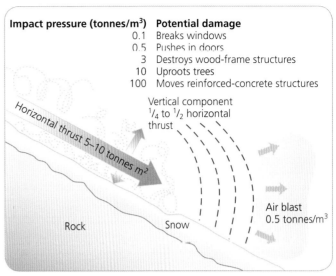

Impact pressure (tonnes/m³)	Potential damage
0.1	Breaks windows
0.5	Pushes in doors
3	Destroys wood-frame structures
10	Uproots trees
100	Moves reinforced-concrete structures

Figure 3.24 Avalanche impact

Figure 3.25 Measures to reduce the impact of avalanches

The process is complicated by the way in which snow crystals constantly change. Changes in overlying pressure, compaction by freshly fallen snow, temperature changes and the movement of meltwater through the snow cause the crystal structure of the snow to change. It may become unstable and move downslope as an avalanche.

Loose avalanches, comprising fresh snow, usually occur soon after a snowfall. By contrast, slab avalanches occur at a later date, when the snow has developed some cohesion. The latter are usually much larger than loose avalanches and cause more destruction. They are often started by a sudden rise in temperature which causes melting. The meltwater lubricates the slab, and makes it unstable. Many of the avalanches occur in spring (Table 3.10) when the snowpack is large and temperatures are rising. There is also a relationship between the number of avalanches and altitude (Table 3.11).

Table 3.10
Occurrence of avalanches in the French Alps

December	10%
January	22%
February	32%
March	23%
April	13%

Table 3.11 Avalanches and altitude in the Swiss Alps

Altitude (m)	No. of avalanches	% of total
Above 3000	326	3
2500–3000	2210	24
2000–2499	3806	41
1500–1999	2632	28
Below 1500	394	4

Section 3.2 Activities

1 Suggest reasons why avalanches are clustered in the months January to March. Give details on at least **two** reasons.

2 Table 3.11 shows the distribution of avalanches with altitude in Switzerland. The tree-line is at about 1500 m and the snow line is at 3000 m. Describe the distribution of avalanches with altitude. How do you explain this pattern?

Case Study

The European avalanches of 1999

The avalanches that killed 75 people in the Alps in February 1999 were the worst in the area for nearly a hundred years. Moreover, they occurred in an area that was thought to be fairly safe. In addition, precautionary measures had been taken, such as an enormous avalanche wall to defend the village of Taconnaz, and a second wall to stop the Taconnaz glacier advancing onto the motorway that runs into the mouth of the Mt Blanc tunnel. However, the villages of Montroc and Le Tour, located at the head of the Chamonix Valley, had no such defences.

The avalanche that swept through the Chamonix Valley killed 11 people and destroyed 18 chalets (Figure 3.26). Rescue work was hampered by the low temperatures (–7 °C), which caused

the snow to compact and made digging almost impossible. The avalanche was about 150 m wide, 6 m high and travelled at a speed of up to 90 km/hr. It crossed a stream and even travelled uphill for some 40 m. Residents were shocked, since they had not experienced an avalanche so powerful, so low in the mountains and certainly not one capable of moving uphill.

Nothing could have been done to prevent the avalanche. Avalanche warnings had been given the day before, as the region had experienced up to 2 m of snow in just three days. However, buildings in Montroc were not considered to be at risk. In fact, they were classified as being in the 'white zone', almost completely free of danger. By contrast, in the avalanche danger zones no new buildings have been developed for many decades. Avalanche monitoring is so well established and elaborate that it had caused villagers and tourists in the 'safe' zone to think that they really were safe. In Montroc the experience was the equivalent of the eruption of an extinct volcano – the last time the snow above Montroc had caused an avalanche was in 1908.

Meteorologists have suggested that disruption of weather patterns resulting from global warming will lead to increased snowfalls in the Alps that are heavier and later in the season. This would mean that the conventional wisdom regarding avalanche 'safe' zones would need to be re-evaluated.

Snowslides 2009/10

In December 2009 and January 2010 dozens of people were caught in the path of avalanches. The increase in snowslide activity sent ominous rumblings through the communities of Europe's Alpine resorts. Residents live in fear of seeing a repeat of early 1999 when 75 people were killed over a period of three weeks, or even of 1950/51, when more than 265 people died in three months.

Heavy snowfall combined with rain and an easing of the extreme cold prompted Météo France, the national meteorological service, to raise the avalanche warning to level 4 (out of five) meaning 'high risk'.

In 2009 scientists in London warned that global warming, in the form of rising temperatures and melting permafrost, could make avalanches more frequent.

Section 3.2 Activities

1 What is an *avalanche*?

2 What are the factors that increase the risk of an avalanche?

3 What were the conditions in Europe in February 1999 that led to widespread avalanches?

4 How and why may the threat of avalanches change in the next decades?

5 Study Figure 3.26.
  a Describe the site of Montroc and Le Tour.
  b What are the attractions for tourists shown on Figure 3.27? Use the grid provided to give grid references.
  c What is the map evidence to suggest that the area is at risk of hazardous events?

Avalanches are more likely when:
• slopes are steeper than 30°
• a lot of new snow falls over a short period
• winds lead to drifts
• old snow melts and refreezes, encouraging new snow to slide off.
At Montroc, heavy snow fell on Monday and Tuesday, but melting and refreezing of old snow was thought not to be responsible.

2 Sheer weight of new snow causes massive avalanche

3 Tuesday 9 February, 2.35pm (1.35pm GMT): a tidal wave of snow 150 m wide and 6 m high crashes down into the valley at 60 mph and buries much of the village of Montroc

4 10 people killed, 11 rescued unhurt, five with minor injuries, one seriously injured. Two believed missing

6 Snow storms on Tuesday night prevent rescues by helicopter during the first vital hours. The snow is packed so high that only mechanical diggers can hack their way through to the chalets

1 Over six feet of snow falls in a few days on the Chamonix valley

5 The force of the avalanche is so great that it sweeps through Montroc and travels 40 m uphill to smash into the village of Le Tour. The avalanche carries some of the chalets as far as 400 m (a quarter of a mile)

Mont Blanc

Les Houches

Chamonix

La Flégerè

Le Praz

Les Grandes Montets

Bec Rouge

Mgne de Peclerey

Les Chosalets

Argentière

Le Tour

Montroc

SWITZERLAND
Le Tour
Argentière ⚫ ⚫ Montroc
FRANCE
⚫ Chamonix
⚫ Taconnaz
Mt Blanc ▲
ITALY
0 km 3

Figure 3.26 Causes and consequences of the Montroc–Le Tour avalanche

Figure 3.27 Survey map of the Alps: area affected by 1999 avalanches

3.3 Hazards resulting from atmospheric disturbances

Tropical storms (cyclones)

Tropical storms bring intense rainfall and very high winds, which may in turn cause storm surges and coastal flooding, and other hazards such as flooding and mudslides. Tropical storms are also characterised by enormous quantities of water. This is due to their origin over tropical seas. High-intensity rainfall, as well as large totals – up to 500 mm in 24 hours – invariably cause flooding. Their path is erratic, so it is not always possible to give more than 12 hours' notice of their position. This is insufficient for proper evacuation measures. In North America and the Caribbean, tropical storms are referred to as hurricanes.

Tropical storms develop as intense low pressure systems over tropical oceans. Winds spiral rapidly around a calm central area known as the eye. The diameter of the whole tropical storm may be as much as 800 km although the very strong winds that cause most of the damage are found in a narrower belt up to 300 km wide. In a mature tropical storm pressure may fall to as low as 880 millibars (mb). This, and the strong contrast in pressure between the eye and outer part of the tropical storm, leads to very strong winds.

Tropical storms move excess heat from low latitudes to higher latitudes. They normally develop in the westward-flowing air just north of the equator (known as an easterly wave). They begin life as a small-scale tropical depression, a localised area of low pressure that causes warm air to rise. This causes thunderstorms which persist for at least 24 hours, and may develop into tropical storms, which have greater wind speeds of up to 117 km/hr (73 mph). However, only about 10 per cent of tropical disturbances ever become tropical storms, with wind speeds above 118 km/hr (74 mph).

For tropical storms to form a number of conditions are needed (Figure 3.28):

- Sea temperatures must be over 27 °C to a depth of 60 m (warm water gives off large quantities of heat when it is condensed – this is the heat that drives the tropical storm).
- The low pressure area has to be far enough away from the equator so that the Coriolis force (the force caused by the rotation of the Earth) creates rotation in the rising air mass – if it is too close to the equator there is insufficient rotation and a tropical storm would not develop.
- Conditions must be unstable – some tropical low pressure systems develop into tropical storms (not all of them) but scientists are unsure why some do and others do not.

Tropical storms are the most violent, damaging and frequent hazard to affect many tropical regions (Figure 3.29). They are measured on the Saffir-Simpson Scale, which is a 1–5 rating based on the tropical storm's intensity (Table 3.12). It is used to give an estimate of the potential property damage and flooding expected along the coast from a tropical storm landfall. Wind speed is the determining factor in the scale, as storm surge values are highly dependent on the slope of the continental shelf and the shape of the coastline in the landfall region. Tropical storms can also cause considerable loss of life. Hurricane Georges (1998) killed more than 460 people, mainly in Dominican Republic and Haiti.

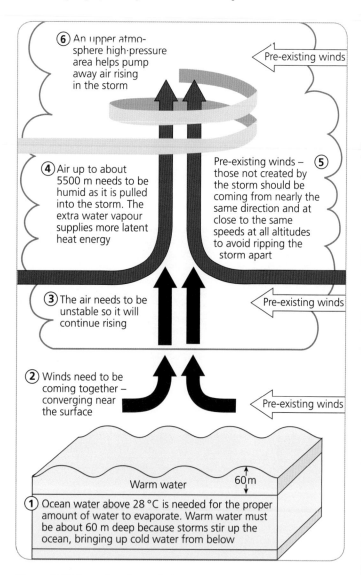

Figure 3.28 Formation of a tropical storm

There are a number of significant factors affecting the impact of tropical storms:

- Tropical storm paths are unpredictable, which makes effective management of the threat difficult. It was fortunate for Jamaica that Hurricane Ivan (2004) (Figure 3.30) suddenly changed course away from the most densely populated parts of the island where it had been expected to hit. In contrast it was unfortunate for Florida's Punta Gorda when Hurricane Charley (2004) moved away from its predicted path.

Figure 3.29 Distribution of tropical storms

Table 3.12 Saffir-Simpson Scale of tropical storm strength

Category 1	Category 4
Winds 119–153 km/hr; storm surge generally 1.2–1.5 m above normal	***Winds 210–249 km/hr; storm surge generally 3.9–5.5 m above normal***
No real damage to building structures. Damage primarily to unanchored mobile homes. Also, some coastal road flooding and minor pier damage.	Some complete roof structure failures on small residences. Complete destruction of mobile homes. Extensive damage to doors and windows. Land below 3 m above sea level may be flooded, requiring massive evacuation of residential areas as far inland as 10 km.
Category 2	
Winds 154–177 km/hr; storm surge generally 1.8–2.4 m above normal	**Category 5**
Some damage to roofing materials, doors and windows. Considerable damage to vegetation, mobile homes and piers. Coastal and low-lying escape routes flood 2–4 hours before arrival of the tropical storm eye. Small craft in unprotected anchorages break moorings.	***Winds greater than 249 km/hr; storm surge generally greater than 5.5 m above normal***
Category 3	Complete roof failure on many residences and industrial buildings. Some complete building failures with small utility buildings blown over or blown away. Complete destruction of mobile homes. Severe and extensive window and door damage. Low-lying escape routes are cut by rising water 3–5 hours before arrival of the centre of the tropical storm. Major damage to lower floors of all structures located less than 4.5 m above sea level and within 500 m of the shoreline. Massive evacuation of residential areas on low ground within 8–16 km of the shoreline may be required.
Winds 178–209 km/hr; storm surge generally 2.7–3.6 m above normal	
Some structural damage to small residences and utility buildings. Mobile homes are destroyed. Flooding near the coast destroys smaller structures with larger structures damaged by floating debris. Land below 1.5 m above mean sea level may be flooded inland 13 km or more. Evacuation of low-lying residences close to the shoreline may be necessary.	

- The strongest storms do not always cause the greatest damage. Only six lives were lost to Hurricane Frances in 2004, but 2000 were taken by Jeanne when it was still categorised as just a 'tropical storm' and had not yet reached full tropical storm strength.
- The distribution of the population throughout the Caribbean islands increases the risk associated with tropical storms. Much of the population lives in coastal settlements and is exposed to increased sea levels and the risk of flooding.

- Hazard mitigation depends upon the effectiveness of the human response to natural events. This includes urban planning laws, emergency planning, evacuation measures and relief operations such as re-housing schemes and the distribution of food aid and clean water.
- LEDCs continue to lose more lives to natural hazards, due to inadequate planning and preparation. By way of contrast, insurance costs continue to be greatest in American states such as Florida, where multi-million-pound waterfront homes proliferate.

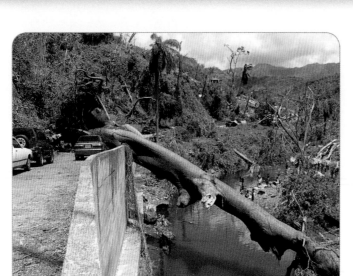

Figure 3.30 Damage in Grenada after Hurricane Ivan

Tropical storm management

Information regarding tropical storms is received from a number of sources including:

- satellite images
- aircraft that fly into the eye of the tropical storm to record weather information
- weather stations at ground levels
- radars that monitor areas of intense rainfall.

Preparing for tropical storms

Housing is particularly vulnerable to tropical storms. Hurricane Luis (1995) caused damage to 90 per cent of Antigua's houses, while Hurricane Gilbert (1988) made 800 000 people temporarily homeless in Jamaica. To limit damage to houses, owners are now encouraged to fix tropical storm straps to roofs and put storm shutters over windows. Houses built on stilts allow flood waters to pass away safely.

There are a number of ways in which national governments and agencies can help prepare for a tropical storm. These include risk assessment, land use zoning, floodplain management and reducing the vulnerability of structures and organisations.

Risk assessment

The evaluation of risks of tropical cyclones can be shown in a hazard map. Particular information may be used to estimate the probability of cyclones striking a country:

- analysis of climatological records to determine how often cyclones have struck, their intensity and locations
- history of winds speeds, frequencies of flooding, height, location and storm surges over a period of about 50–100 years.

Land use zoning

The aim is to control land use so that the most important facilities are placed in the least vulnerable areas. Policies regarding future development may regulate land use and enforce building codes for areas vulnerable to the effects of tropical cyclones.

Floodplain management

A plan for floodplain management should be developed to protect critical assets from flash, riverine and coastal flooding.

Reducing vulnerability of structures and infrastructures

- New buildings should be designed to be wind and water resistant. Design standards are usually incorporated into building codes.

Before a tropical storm
- Know where your emergency shelters are.
- Have disaster supplies on hand:
  - Flashlight and extra batteries
  - First aid kit
  - Non-perishable (canned food) and water
  - Essential medicines
  - Cash and credit cards.
- Protect your windows.
- Permanent shutters are the best protection. A lower-cost approach is to put up plywood panels.
- Trim back branches from trees.
- Trim branches away from your home and cut out all dead or weak branches on any trees on your property.
- Check your home and car insurance.
- Make arrangements for pets and livestock.
- Develop an emergency communication plan.

During a tropical storm
- Listen to the radio or television for tropical storm progress reports.
- Check emergency supplies.
- Make sure your car is full of fuel.
- Bring in outdoor objects such as lawn furniture, toys and garden tools, and anchor objects that cannot be brought inside.
- Secure buildings by closing and boarding up windows.
- Remove outside antennas and satellite dishes.

After a tropical storm
- Assist in search and rescue.
- Seek medical attention for persons injured.
- Clean up debris and effect temporary repairs.
- Report damage to utilities.
- Watch out for secondary hazards: fire, flooding, etc.

Figure 3.31 What to do before, during and after a tropical storm

- Communication and utility lines should be located away from the coastal area or installed underground.
- Areas of building should be improved by raising the ground level to protect against flood and storm surges.
- Protective river embankments, levees and coastal dikes should be regularly inspected for breaches due to erosion and opportunities should be taken to plant mangrove trees to reduce breaking wave energy.
- Vegetation cover should be increased to help reduce the impact of soil erosion and landslides, and facilitate the absorption of rainfall to reduce flooding.

There are many other things that individuals can do to prepare for a tropical storm, and to learn how to act during and after a storm (Figure 3.31).

A tropical storm watch is issued when there is a threat of tropical storm conditions within 24–36 hours. A tropical storm warning is issued when tropical storm conditions (winds of 120 km/hr or greater, or dangerously high water and rough seas) are expected in 24 hours or less. A tropical storm warning is issued when there are risks of tropical storm winds within 24 hours. A tropical storm watch is issued when tropical storm winds are expected within 36 hours.

The emergency relief offered after a tropical storm can take many forms – food supplies, clean water, blankets and medicines. Much of this is provided in tropical storm shelters. In some communities emergency electricity generators may be needed. The community normally becomes involved in the clean-up operation, and electricity and phone companies work to restore power lines and communications.

Long-term redevelopment may include construction of new buildings in areas away from the coastline and on high ground. Long-term reconstruction in Grenada following Hurricane Ivan concentrated on housing and community projects, water supply and sanitation, transport and communications, agriculture, fisheries and small businesses, schools and government expenses.

Case Study

Cyclone Nargis, 2 May 2008

Cyclone Nargis was a strong tropical cyclone (Figure 3.32). It formed on 27 April 2008, made landfall by 2 May and died out by 3 May. It involved winds of up to 165 km/hr (sustained for 3 minutes) and winds of over 215 km/hr (sustained for over 1 minute). At its peak, air pressure dropped to 962 mb. Around 146 000 people were killed and it caused damage estimated at $10 million. As well as Burma (Myanmar) parts of Bangladesh, India and Sri Lanka were affected. However, it was the Burmese government's actions – or rather their lack of them – that caused widespread anger and disbelief.

The Burmese government identified 15 townships in the Irrawaddy delta that had suffered the worst. Seven of them had lost 90–95 per cent of housing, with 70 per cent of their population dead or missing. The land in the Irrawaddy delta is very low-lying. It is home to an estimated 7 million of Burma's 53 million people. Nearly 2 million of the densely packed area's inhabitants live on land that is less than 5 m above sea level, leaving them extremely vulnerable. As well as the cost in lives and homes, there is the agricultural loss to the fertile delta, which is seen as Burma's 'rice bowl'.

Figure 3.32 Cyclone Nargis

It was the worst-ever natural disaster in Burma. There were over 80 000 deaths in Labutta and a further 10 000 in Bogale. The UN estimated that 1.5 million people were severely affected by Cyclone Nargis. Thousands of buildings were destroyed; 75 per cent of the buildings in the town of Labutta collapsed and a further 20 per cent had their roofs ripped off. Up to 95 per cent of buildings in the Irrawaddy delta were destroyed.

According to aid agencies trying to get into Burma, up to 1 million people could have died from the cyclone due to lack of relief. Relief efforts were delayed for political reasons. Burma's political leaders declined international aid; the World Food Programme said the delays were 'unprecedented in modern humanitarian relief efforts'. Within two weeks, an earthquake in China had deflected aid and sympathy away from Burma.

On 6 May the Burmese junta (military government) finally asked the UN for aid, but accepted it only from India. Many nations and organisations hoping to deliver relief were unable to do so – the Burmese government refused to issue visas to many of them. On 9 May the junta officially declared that its acceptance of international aid would be limited to food, medicines and some other specified supplies as well as financial aid, but would allow additional foreign aid workers to operate in the country.

India is one of the few countries to maintain close relations with Burma. It launched Operation Sahayata under which it supplied two ships and two aircraft. However, the Burmese government denied Indian search and rescue teams and media access to critical cyclone-hit areas. On 16 May India's offer to send a team of 50 medical personnel was accepted. Cyclone survivors needed everything – emergency shelter to keep them dry, all basic food, and medicines.

Many Burmese people were displeased with their government, which had provided no warning of the cyclone. According to some reports, Indian meteorologists had warned Burma of Cyclone Nargis 48 hours before it hit the country's coast. People also believed the mayhem caused by the cyclone and associated flooding was further exacerbated by the government's uncooperative response.

The delays attracted international condemnation. More than a week after the disaster, only 1 out of 10 people who were homeless, injured or threatened by disease and hunger had received any kind of aid. More than two weeks later, relief had only reached 25 per cent of people in need. Some news stories stated that foreign aid provided to disaster victims was modified to make it look as if it came from the military regime, and state-run television continuously ran images of General Than Shwe ceremonially handing out disaster relief.

Uninterrupted referendum

Despite objections raised by the Burmese opposition parties and foreign nations in the wake of the natural disaster, the junta proceeded with a previously scheduled constitutional referendum. However, voting was postponed from 10 to 24 May in Yangon and other areas hardest hit by the storm.

Tornadoes

Tornadoes are small and short-lived but highly destructive storms. Because of their severe nature and small size, comparatively little is known about them. Measurement and observation within them are difficult. A few low-lying, armoured probes called 'turtles' have been placed successfully in tornadoes. Tornadoes consist of elongated funnels of cloud which descend from the base of a well-developed cumulonimbus cloud, eventually making contact with the ground beneath. In order for a vortex to be classified as a tornado, it must be in contact with the ground *and* the cloud base. Within tornadoes are rotating violent winds, perhaps exceeding 100 m per second. Pressure gradients in a tornado can reach an estimated 25 mb per 100 m (this compares with the most extreme pressure gradients of about 20 mb per 100 km in a larger-scale cyclone).

How tornadoes form

Moisture, instability, lift and wind shear are the four key ingredients in tornado formation (Figure 3.33). Most tornadoes, but not all, rotate *cyclonically* – that is, anticlockwise in the northern hemisphere and clockwise south of the equator. The standard explanation is that warm moist air meets cold dry air to form a tornado. Many thunderstorms form under these conditions (near warm fronts and cold fronts), which never even come close to producing tornadoes. Even when the large-scale environment is extremely favourable for tornado-type thunderstorms, not every thunderstorm spawns a tornado. The most destructive and deadly tornadoes develop from supercells, which are rotating thunderstorms with a well-defined low pressure system called a *mesocyclone*.

Figure 3.33 Formation of tornadoes in the USA

Tornadoes can last from several seconds to more than an hour. The convectional activity which creates the source cloud is itself highly variable, and a single cloud can spawn a number of different tornado vortices, either simultaneously or in sequence, beneath different areas of the cloud, as parts of it develop and decay. Movement is generally with the parent cloud, perhaps with the funnel twisting sinuously across the ground beneath. Once contact with the ground is made, the track of a tornado at ground level may frequently extend for only a few kilometres, though there are examples of sustained tracks extending over hundreds of kilometres. The diameter of the funnel is rarely more than 200 m; track length and width are therefore limited.

Tornadoes, being associated with extreme atmospheric instability, show both seasonal and locational preference in their incidence. 'Favoured' areas are temperate continental interiors in spring and early summer, when insolation is strong and the air may be unstable, although many parts of the world can be affected by tornado outbreaks at some time or another. The Great Plains of the USA, including Oklahoma, Texas and Kansas, have a high global frequency (Figure 3.34), and tornadoes are particularly likely to be experienced here at times when cool, dry air from the Rockies overlies warm, moist 'Gulf' air. Some areas of the USA experience tornadoes from a specific direction, such as north-west in Minnesota or south-east in coastal south Texas. This is because of an increased frequency of certain tornado-producing weather patterns, for example tropical storms in south Texas, or north-west-flow weather systems in the upper Mid West.

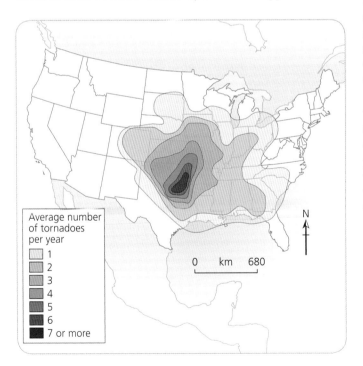

Figure 3.34 Tornado Alley, USA

Some tropical storms in the USA fail to produce any tornadoes, while others cause major outbreaks. The same tropical storm may produce none for a while, and then erupt with tornadoes – or vice versa. Hurricane Andrew (1992), for example, spawned several tornadoes across the Deep South after crossing the Gulf, but produced none during its rampage across southern Florida. Katrina (2005) spawned numerous tornadoes after its devastating landfall.

The size and strength of tropical cyclones is not related to the birth of tornadoes. Relatively weak tropical storms like Danny (1985) have spawned significant supercell tornadoes well inland, as have larger, more intense storms like Beulah (1967) and Ivan (2004). In general, the bigger and stronger the wind fields are with a tropical cyclone, the bigger the area of favourable wind shear for supercells and tornadoes. But supercell tornadoes (whether or not in tropical cyclones) also depend on instability, lift and moisture. Surface moisture isn't lacking in a tropical cyclone, but sometimes instability and lift are too weak. This is why tropical systems tend to produce more tornadoes in the daytime, and near any fronts that may become involved in the cyclone circulation.

Tornado damage

About a thousand tornadoes hit the USA each year. On average, tornadoes kill about 60 people per year – most from flying or falling (crushing) debris. A tornado's impact as a hazard is extreme. There are three damaging factors at work. First, the winds are often so strong that objects in the tornado's path are simply removed or very severely damaged. Second, strong rotational movement tends to twist objects from their fixings, and strong uplift can carry some debris upwards into the cloud. Third, the very low atmospheric pressure near the vortex centre is a major source of damage. When a tornado approaches a building, external pressure is rapidly reduced, and unless there is a nearly simultaneous and equivalent decrease in internal pressure, the walls and roof may explode outwards in the process of equalising the pressure differences.

Most tornado damage is due to multiple-vortex tornadoes or very small, intense single-vortex tornadoes. The winds in most multiple-vortex tornadoes may only be strong enough to do minor damage to a particular house. But one of the smaller subvortices, perhaps only a few metres across, may strike the house next door with winds over 300 km/hr, causing complete destruction. Also, there are great differences in construction from one building to the next, so that even in the same wind speed, one may be flattened while the other is barely touched.

Although winds in the strongest tornadoes may far exceed those in the strongest tropical storms, tropical storms typically cause much more damage individually and over a season, and over far bigger areas. Economically, tornadoes cause about a tenth as much damage per year, on average, as tropical storms. Tropical storms tend to cause much more overall destruction than tornadoes because of their much larger size, longer duration and the variety of ways they damage property. The destructive core in tropical storms can be tens or hundreds of kilometres across, last many hours and damage structures through storm surge and flooding caused by heavy rain, as well as from wind. Tornadoes, in contrast, tend to be a few hundred yards in diameter, last for minutes and primarily cause damage from their extreme winds.

Tornado damage scale

Dr T. Theodore Fujita developed a damage scale for winds, including tornadoes, which is supposed to relate the degree of damage to the intensity of the wind (Table 3.13). The F-scale should be used with caution as it does not take into account differences in building structure and materials.

Work on a new Enhanced F-Scale was started in 2006. The Enhanced F-scale will be a much more precise way to rank tornado damage than the original, because it will classify damage F0–F5 calibrated by engineers across more than 20 different types of buildings. A team of meteorologists and engineers has worked on this for several years. The idea is that a 'one size fits all' approach does not work in rating tornado damage, and a tornado scale needs to take into account the typical strengths and weaknesses of different types of construction. This is because the same wind does different things to different kinds of buildings. In the Enhanced F-scale there will be different, customised standards for assigning any given F rating to a well-built, well-anchored wood-frame house compared with a garage, school, skyscraper, unanchored house, barn, factory, utility pole or other type of structure. In a real-life tornado track, these ratings can be mapped together more smoothly to produce an accurate damage analysis.

Table 3.13 Fujita tornado damage

Category F0	Light damage (<73 mph); some damage to chimneys; branches broken off trees; shallow-rooted trees pushed over; signboards damaged.
Category F1	Moderate damage (73–112 mph); peels surface off roofs; mobile homes pushed off foundations or overturned; moving vehicles blown off road.
Category F2	Considerable damage (113–157 mph); roofs torn off frame houses; mobile homes demolished; railway trucks overturned; large trees snapped or uprooted; light-object missiles generated; cars lifted off ground.
Category F3	Severe damage (158–206 mph); roofs and some walls torn off well-constructed houses, trains overturned; most trees in forest uprooted; heavy cars lifted off ground and thrown.
Category F4	Devastating damage (207–260 mph); well-constructed houses levelled; structures with weak foundations blown some distance; cars thrown and large missiles generated.
Category F5	Incredible damage (261–318 mph); strong frame houses lifted off foundations and swept away; automobile-sized missiles fly through the air in excess of 109 yards; trees debarked; incredible phenomena will occur.

Note: this scale was created in the USA, so measurements are imperial.

Managing tornadoes

The main problem with anything that could realistically stand a chance of affecting a tornado (for example an atomic bomb) is that it would be even more deadly and destructive than the tornado itself. Lesser things (like huge piles of dry ice) would be too hard to deploy in the right place fast enough, and would probably not have a significant effect on the tornado.

Nor is there any proof that seeding can or cannot change tornado potential in a thunderstorm. This is because there is no way of knowing that the things a thunderstorm does after it has been seeded would not have happened *anyway*. This includes any presence or lack of rain, hail, wind gusts or tornadoes. Because the effects of seeding are impossible to prove or disprove, there is a great deal of controversy among meteorologists about whether it works, and if so, under what conditions and to what extent.

Case Study

Tornadoes in Indiana

Indiana is in what is considered to be 'Tornado Alley' (see Figure 3.34 and Table 3.14), a swathe of states extending from the south-east USA to the interior plains. Although the state lacks the high frequency of tornadoes seen in places like Kansas and Oklahoma, it makes up for it in the intensity of its tornadoes.

Tornadoes can occur in any month, but March–June is considered tornado season in Indiana. Historically, the most destructive tornadoes strike in March and April. June holds the record for the most tornadoes in Indiana on any given day (37), and for the most in a single month (44). Both records were set in 1990, which is also the year when the state experienced the most tornadoes (49).

From 1950 to November 2001, 1024 tornadoes caused more than $1.7 billion in damage in Indiana, and killed 223 people.

Indiana was one of three mid-western states in the path of the deadliest tornado in American history. On 18 March 1925, the Tri-State Tornado travelled a record 352 km on the ground from Missouri through Illinois and into Indiana where it struck Posey, Gibson and Pike counties. The town of Griffin lost 150 homes, and 85 farms near Griffin and Princeton were devastated. About half of Princeton was destroyed with losses totalling nearly $2 million. The funnel finally dissipated just outside Princeton, 3½ hours after it had begun. Nearly 700 people died, 74 of them in Indiana. Murphysboro in Illinois lost 234 people, a record for a single community.

In April 1965, 11 tornadoes struck 20 counties in central and northern Indiana, killing 137 people. More than 1700 people were injured and property damage exceeded $30 million. It was Indiana's worst tornado disaster. The tornadoes that devastated Indiana were part of an outbreak in which nearly 50 tornadoes struck the Great Lakes region on 11–12 April, causing 271 deaths and more than 3400 injuries.

The most destructive tornado outbreak of the twentieth century was the 'Super Outbreak' of 3–4 April 1974. During a 16-hour period, 148 tornadoes hit 13 states, including Indiana. The path of destruction stretched over 4000 km. More than 300 people died and more than 5000 were injured. The most notable tornado in this group destroyed much of Xenia, Ohio. In Indiana, 21 tornadoes struck 39 counties, killing 47 people. Seven produced damage rated F5, the maximum possible, and 23 more were rated F4. This was one of only two outbreaks with over 100 confirmed tornadoes, the other being during tropical storm Beulah in 1967 (115 tornadoes).

Table 3.14 Indiana tornado disasters

Date	Place	Damage
13 April 1852	New Harmony	16 killed
14 May 1886	Anderson	43 killed
23 March 1913	Terre Haute	21 killed
11 March 1917	New Castle	21 killed
23 March 1917	New Albany	45 killed
28 March 1920	Allen through Wayne counties	39 killed by three tornadoes
17 April 1922	Warren through Delaware counties	14 killed
18 March 1925	'Tri-State Tornado': Posey, Gibson and Pike counties	74 killed
26 March 1948	Coatesville destroyed	20 killed
21 May 1949	Sullivan and Clay counties	14 killed
11 April 1965	'Palm Sunday Outbreak': 11 tornadoes, 20 counties	137 killed
3 April 1974	'Super Outbreak': 21 tornadoes hit 39 counties	47 killed
2 June 1990	37 tornadoes hit 31 counties	8 killed

Section 3.3 Activities

1 Briefly explain how tornadoes are formed.

2 Using examples, outline the factors that affect tornado damage.

3 To what extent is it possible to manage the risk of tornado damage?

3.4 Sustainable management of hazardous environments

Assessing and mitigating damaging effects of mass movement

Landslides and other forms of mass movement are widespread and cause extensive damage and loss of life each year. With careful analysis and planning, together with appropriate stabilisation techniques, the impacts of mass movement can be reduced or eliminated.

Assessment of the hazards posed by potential mass movement events are based partly on past events, to evaluate their magnitude and frequency. In addition mapping and testing of soil and rock properties determines their susceptibility to destabilising processes. Maps showing areas that could be affected by mass movement processes are important tools for land use planners.

For example, valleys in the Cascade Range of Washington and Oregon, USA have experienced extensive mudflows from volcanic activity over the last 10 000 years. Hazard maps prepared before the eruption of Mt St Helens and Mt Pinatubo proved extremely useful, as the mudflows generated by these eruptions had very similar distributions to those produced in earlier times (Figure 3.35).

Figure 3.35 Hazard map of Mt Pinatubo

a Rock bolts and retaining wall

Gravel pack

Original slope

Weephole

Building pad

Foundation

Blocks with enforcing rods

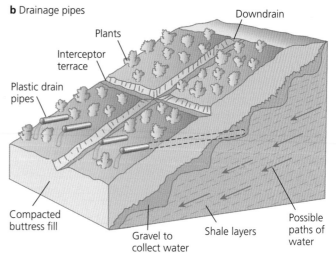

b Drainage pipes

Downdrain

Plants

Interceptor terrace

Plastic drain pipes

Compacted buttress fill

Gravel to collect water

Shale layers

Possible paths of water

c Slope regrading

Bulldozer

Slope oversteepened by slide or waves undercutting

Material moved from top to bottom of slope

Figure 3.36 Engineering techniques for slope stabilisation

Figure 3.37 Engineering techniques, Brunei

Eliminating or restricting human activities in areas where slides are likely may be the best way to reduce damage and loss of life. Land that is susceptible to mild failures may be suitable for some forms of development (for example, recreation or parkland) but not others (for example, residential or industrial). Early warning systems can provide forecasts of intense rain. High-risk areas can then be monitored and remedial action taken.

In addition to assessment, prediction and early warning, some engineering schemes can be applied to reduce the damage of mass wasting (Figure 3.36). These include retaining devices, drainage pipes, grading of slope and diversion walls (Figure 3.37). Concrete blocks or gabions may be used to strengthen slopes. Slopes subject to creep can be stabilised by draining or pumping water from saturated sediment. Oversteepened slopes can be made gentler by regrading. However, not all communities can afford such measures and so may opt for low-cost sustainable forms of management.

Case Study

The use of geo-materials for erosion and sediment control

In Malaysia, early research on bio-engineering involved studies on plant selection for the re-vegetation of cut slopes along highways. More recent research (2000/01) involved gully erosion control and vegetation establishment on degraded slopes. These techniques have incorporated the coppicing abilities of cut stems and the soil-binding properties of roots into civil designs, to strengthen the ground and to control erosion. Bio-engineering designs have great potential and application in Malaysia because in deforested upland sites, landslides are common, particularly during the wetter months between November and January. Post-landslide restoration works involving conventional civil designs are costly and sometimes not practical at remote sites. Due to cost constraints, the remoteness of the sites and low risk to lives and property, bio-engineering was the option taken for erosion control, slope stabilisation and vegetation establishment.

The study took place at Fraser's Hill, in the state of Pahang, Malaysia. The area receives 20–410 mm of rainfall each month. The temperature is moderate, ranging from 18 to 22 °C annually, with high humidity, ranging from 85 to 95 per cent every month. The surrounding vegetation is lower montane forest.

Two study plots were chosen, and a control plot. Initial works involved soil nailing, using 300 live stakes of *angsana* tree branches and 200 cut stems of *ubi kayu*. Subsequently major groundworks involved the installation of geo-structures (structures constructed from geo-materials such as bamboo and brush bundles, coir rolls and straw wattles). The volume of sediment trapped by the geo-structures was measured every two weeks, while plant species that were established on the retained sediments and on geo-materials were identified. The number of live stakes that produced shoots and roots were also recorded. Ten 1 m tall saplings of *Toona sinensis*, a fast-growing tree species, were planted at the toe of the slope for long-term stability.

The first slope failure was caused by seepage of drainage water into the cut slope of the access road. The total area affected by the landslide was about 0.25 ha. Two large trees, 4–5 m tall, were uprooted and ground vegetation and debris were washed downhill, preventing road access. The second and more extensive failure was located uphill and was a rotational failure. It covered an area of about 0.75 ha. The landslide was probably triggered by seepage of water from a badly damaged toe drain beside the road.

Bio-engineering design

After six months

The bio-engineering designs involved the installation of 11 bamboo bundles (faschines), and 16 brush bundles along rills and gullies. At suitable sites along contours, 10 coir rolls and 5 straw wattles were installed, using live stakes and steel wiring. Lighter geo-materials such as straw wattles and brush faschines were positioned on the upper slope face, while heavier geo-materials such as coir rolls were positioned lower down.

At the end of six months the situation at each study site was assessed (Table 3.15).

Table 3.15 Selected geo-materials and total volume of sediment retained over six months at the two study sites

Geo-materials	Total sediment retained m³	Total number of migrant species
Bamboo faschine	1.7	14
Brush faschine	1.0	17
Coir roll	2.2	20
Straw wattle	0.2	26
Total sediment retained by different geo-materials	5.1	–
Total number of migrant species	–	77

Live stakes and Toona sinensis saplings

At the end of six months, the live stakes had become living trees. A high percentage of *angsana* stakes (93 per cent) sprouted shoots and roots after a month, and 75 per cent of *ubi kayu* stems sprouted leaves within a week. Thus live stakes were effective in stabilising unstable slopes.

Vegetation cover on slopes helped reduce soil erosion because shoots helped reduce the intensity of raindrops falling on the exposed soil. Furthermore root-reinforced soils functioned like micro-soil nails to increase the shear strength of surface soils.

Slope stability

The indicator poles at both study sites moved less than 8°, unlike the indicator poles from the control plot, which moved about 20°. Without erosion control measures, there was aggressive soil erosion during heavy pours, which caused scouring of the steep slope below the tarred road and resulted in an overhang of the road shoulder.

Trapped sediments and vegetation establishment

A total of 57 geo-structures retained 5.1 m³ of sediment after six months. The retained sediments and decomposing geo-materials also trapped moisture and provided ideal conditions for the germination of incoming seeds. After six months it was found that 77 plant species were established.

After one year

A year after the study was first implemented, about 75 per cent of one study site was covered by vegetation, while 90 per cent of the second plot was re-vegetated. There was no more incidence of landslide at these two plots. However, at the control plot there was further soil erosion, which resulted in further undercutting of the slope face.

At the control plot, after one year, only seven plant species were present. These were weeds. The poor vegetation cover was probably due to unstable soil conditions caused by frequent soil erosion and minor landslides. It is believed that vegetation cover can provide a layer of roots beneath the soil layer and this contributes additional shear strength to the soil and slope stability.

The geo-structures were installed at a cost of about US$3078, which was cheaper than restoration works using conventional civil structures such as rock gabions, which cost about US$20 000. As the site is quite remote, higher transportation and labour costs would have contributed to the higher cost of constructing a rock gabion at this site. On the other hand, the geo-materials that are abundantly available locally are relatively cheap to make or purchase, and this contributed to the low project cost. The geo-structures were non-polluting, required minimal post-installation maintenance, were visually attractive and could support greater biodiversity within the restored habitats. The geo-materials used in this project, such as faschines, coir rolls and straw wattles, biodegrade after about a year and become organic fertilisers for the newly established vegetation.

After 18 months the restored cut slopes were almost covered by vegetation, and there was no further incident of landslides. The geo-structures installed on site were cost-effective and visually attractive. The restored cut slopes were more stable and supported higher biological diversity.

Assessment of costs

The geo-structures cost approximately $3000 to install. In contrast, a rock gabion would have cost about $20 000 to install (as the area is remote, transport costs would increase, and there would be increased emissions of greenhouse gases). Moreover, the geo-structures were visually attractive, could support biodiversity, were locally available, and took just two weeks to install. In terms of a cost-benefit analysis, therefore, the geo-structure has a great deal to offer.

Hazard management, risk assessment and perception

Hazard management includes a body of theory which includes risk, prediction, prevention, event, and recovery. For example, **vulnerability** refers to the geographic conditions that increase the susceptibility of a community to a hazard or to the impacts of a hazard event. **Risk** is the probability of a hazard event causing harmful consequences (expected losses in terms of death, injuries, property damage, economy and environment).

A **hazard** is a threat (whether natural or human) that has the potential to cause loss of life, injury, property damage, socio-economic disruption or environmental degradation. In contrast, a **disaster** is a major hazard event that causes widespread disruption to a community or region, with significant demographic, economic and/or environmental losses.

A number of stages can be observed in the build up to a disaster and in its aftermath (Table 3.16).

Rehabilitation refers to people being able to make safe their homes and be able to live in them again. This can be a very long drawn-out process, taking up to a decade for major construction projects.

As well as dealing with the aftermath of a disaster, governments try to plan to reduce impacts in future events. This was seen after the South Asian tsunami of 2004. Before the event a tsunami early-warning system was not in place in the Indian Ocean. Following the event, as well as emergency rescue, rehabilitation and reconstruction, governments and aid agencies in the region developed a system to reduce the impacts of future tsunamis. It is just part of the progress needed to reduce the impact of hazards and to improve safety in the region.

Learning to live with earthquakes

Most places with a history of earthquakes have developed plans that enable people to deal with them. The aim is to reduce

Table 3.16 Aspects of the temporal sequences or phases of disasters, with reported durations and selected features of each phase

Stage	Duration	Features
I Preconditions		
Phase 1	Everyday life (years, decades, centuries)	'Lifestyle' risks, routine safety measures, social construction of vulnerability, planned developments and emergency preparedness.
Phase 2	Premonitory developments (weeks, months, years)	'Incubation period' – erosion of safety measures, heightened vulnerability, signs and problems misread or ignored.
II The disaster		
Phase 3	Triggering event or threshold (seconds, hours, days)	Beginning of crisis; 'threat' period: impending or arriving flood, fire, explosion; danger seen clearly; may allow warnings, flight or evacuation and other pre-impact measures. May merge with…
Phase 4	Impact and collapse (instant, seconds, days, months)	… the disaster proper: concentrated death, injury, devastation. Impaired or destroyed security arrangements. Individual and small groups cope as isolated survivors. Followed by or merging with …
Phase 5	Secondary and tertiary damages (days, weeks)	… exposure of survivors, post-impact hazards, delayed deaths.
Phase 6	Outside emergency aid (weeks, months)	Rescue, relief, evacuation, shelter provision, clearing dangerous wreckage, 'organised response'. National and international humanitarian efforts.
III Recovery and reconstruction		
Phase 7	Clean-up and 'emergency communities' (weeks, years)	Relief camps, emergency housing. Residents and outsiders clear wreckage, salvage items. Blame and reconstruction debates begin. Disaster reports, evaluations, commissions of enquiry.
Phase 8	Reconstruction and restoration (months, years)	Reintegration of damaged community with larger society. Re-establishment of 'everyday life', possibly similar to, possibly different from pre-disaster. Continuing private and recurring communal grief. Disaster-related development and hazard-reducing measures.

the effect of the earthquakes and thus save lives, buildings and money. The ways of reducing earthquake impact include earthquake prediction, building design, flood prevention and public information.

Preparation

Earthquakes killed about 1.5 million people in the twentieth century and the number of earthquakes appears to be rising. Most of the deaths were caused by the collapse of unsuitable and poorly designed buildings. More than a third of the world's largest and fastest-growing cities are located in regions of high earthquake risk, so the problems are likely to intensify.

Figure 3.38 Aseismic design

It is difficult to stop an earthquake from happening, so prevention normally involves minimising the prospect of death, injury or damage by controlling building in high-risk areas, and using aseismic designs (Figure 3.38). In addition, warning systems can be used to warn people of an imminent earthquake and inform them of what to do when it does happen. Insurance schemes are another form of preparation, by sharing the costs between a wide group of people.

The seismic gap theory states that over a prolonged period of time all parts of a plate boundary must move by almost the same amount. Thus if one part of the plate boundary has not moved and others have, then the part that has not moved is most likely to move next. This theory has been used successfully to suggest that an earthquake was likely in the Loma Prieta segment of the San Andreas fault. The Loma Prieta earthquake occurred in 1989. Following the 2004 South Asian tsunami geologists identified a seismic gap in the Central Kuril segment of the Kuril-Kamchatka trench. Two earthquakes measuring 8.3 and 8.2 on the Richter Scale occurred in November 2006 and January 2007 within the Central Kuril segment.

Building design

Increasingly, as the availability of building land is reduced, more and more people are living in seismic areas. This increases the potential impact of an earthquake. However, buildings can be designed to withstand the ground-shaking that occurs in an earthquake (Figure 3.39). Single-storey buildings are more suitable than multi-storey structures, because this reduces the number of people at risk, and the threat of collapse over roads and evacuation routes. Some tall buildings are built with a 'soft storey' at the bottom, such as a car park raised on pillars. This collapses in an earthquake, so that the upper floors sink down onto it and this cushions the impact. Basement isolation – mounting the

Figure 3.39 Building design

foundations of a building on rubber mounts which allow the ground to move under the building – is widely used. This isolates the building from the tremors.

Building reinforcement strategies include building on foundations built deep into underlying bedrock, and the use of steel-constructed frames that can withstand shaking. Land use planning is another important way of reducing earthquake risk (Figure 3.40).

Safe houses

The earthquake in Haiti was a reminder that billions of people live in houses that cannot withstand shaking. Yet safer ones can be built cheaply – using straw, adobe and old tyres, for example – by applying a few general principles (Figure 3.41).

In wealthy cities in fault zones, the added expense of making buildings earthquake-resistant has become a fact of life. Concrete walls are reinforced with steel, for instance, and a few buildings even rest on elaborate shock absorbers. Strict building codes were credited with saving thousands of lives when a magnitude 8.8 'quake hit Chile in February 2010. But in less developed countries, like Haiti, conventional earthquake engineering is often unaffordable. However, cheap solutions do exist.

In Peru in 1970 an earthquake killed 70 000 or more people, many of whom died when their houses crumbled around them. Heavy, brittle walls of traditional adobe – cheap, sun-dried brick – cracked instantly when the ground started buckling. Subsequent shakes brought roofs thundering down. Existing adobe walls can be reinforced with a strong plastic mesh installed under plaster; in a 'quake these walls crack but do not collapse, allowing occupants to escape. Plastic mesh could also work as a reinforcement for concrete walls in Haiti and elsewhere.

Other engineers are working on methods that use local materials. Researchers in India have successfully tested a concrete house reinforced with bamboo. A model house for Indonesia rests on ground-motion dampers – old tyres filled with bags of sand. Such a house might be only a third as strong as one built on more sophisticated shock absorbers, but it would also cost much less – and so be more likely to be adopted in Indonesia. In northern Pakistan, straw is available. Traditional houses are built of stone and mud, but straw is far more resilient, and warmer in winter. However, cheap ideas aren't always cheap enough.

Since 2007 some 2500 houses in Peru have been strengthened with plastic mesh or other reinforcements, with another 700 scheduled for 2010.

Controlling earthquakes

In theory, by altering the fluid pressure deep underground at the point of greatest stress in the fault line, a series of small and less damaging earthquake events may be triggered. This could release the energy that would otherwise build up to create a major event. Additionally, a series of controlled underground nuclear explosions might relieve stress before it reached critical levels.

Prediction and risk assessment

There are a number of methods of detecting earthquakes – distortion of fences, roads and buildings are some examples, changing levels of water in boreholes is another. As strain can change the water-holding capacity or porosity of rocks by closing

Source: *Advanced Geography: Concepts & Cases* by P. Guinness & G. Nagle (Hodder Education, 1999), p.348

Figure 3.40 Land use planning

	Pakistan	Haiti	Peru	Indonesia
Most destructive quake	8 October 2005	12 January 2010	31 May 1970	26 December 2004
Location	Northern Pakistan/Kashmir	Port-au-Prince area	Chimbote	Sumatra
Magnitude	7.6	7.0	7.9	9.1
Fatalities	75 000	222 500	70 000	227 900 (including the global tsunami deaths)

Light walls and gables
Lightweight structures are subject to smaller forces and are less likely to fall when the ground shakes

Quake-resistant houses are being built in Pakistan – of straw. The compressed bales are held together by nylon netting and sandwiched between layers of plaster

Light roofs
In Haiti heavy concrete roofs collapsed on many homes; sheet-metal roofs on wooden trusses are more resistant

Small windows
Small, regularly spaced openings create fewer weak spots in walls. But the bigger problem in Haiti was that walls were not properly reinforced.

Bamboo

Reinforced walls
The reinforcing rods need not be made of metal. Natural materials such as eucalyptus or bamboo work well too

In Peru the walls of some adobe houses have been reinforced with a plastic mesh to prevent collapse

Mesh

Crown beam

Corner column

Confined masonry
In Indonesia and elsewhere, brick walls can be framed and connected to the roof by corner columns and a crown beam of reinforced concrete. In a quake the structure moves as a unit

Shock absorbers
Tyres filled with stones or sand and fastened between floor and foundation can serve as cheap ground-motion absorbers for many types of building

Figure 3.41 A safe house

and opening their tiny cracks then water levels in boreholes will fluctuate with increased earthquake activity. Satellites can also be used to measure the position of points on the surface of the Earth to within a few centimetres. However, predicting earthquakes is not simple. Some earthquakes are very irregular in time and may only occur less than once every one hundred years. By contrast other parts of the Earth's surface may continually slip and produce a large number of very small earthquakes. In addition different parts of a fault line may behave differently. Areas that do not move are referred to as seismic gaps; areas that move and have lots of mini earthquakes may be far less hazardous.

Earthquake prediction is only partly successful although it offers a potentially valuable way of reducing the impact of earthquakes. Some aspects are relatively easy to understand. For example, the location of earthquakes is closely linked with the distribution of fault lines. However, the timing of earthquakes is difficult to predict. Previous patterns and frequencies of earthquake events offer some clues as to what is likely to happen in the future but the size of an earthquake event is difficult to predict.

The most reliable predictions focus on:
- measurement of small-scale ground surface changes
- small-scale uplift or subsidence
- ground tilt

- changes in rock stress
- micro-earthquake activity (clusters of small 'quakes)
- anomalies in the Earth's magnetic field
- changes in radon gas concentration
- changes in electrical resistivity of rocks.

Measurements of these are made using a variety of instruments (Table 3.17).

Table 3.17 Monitoring for earthquake prediction

Instrument	Purpose
Seismometers	To record micro-earthquakes
Magnetometer	To record changes in the Earth's magnetic field
Near-surface seismometer	To record larger shocks
Vibreosis truck	To create shear waves to probe the earthquake zone
Strain meters	To monitor surface deformation
Sensors in wells	To monitor changes in groundwater levels
Satellite relays	To relay data to the US Geological Survey
Laser survey equipment	To measure surface movement

Source: C. Park, *The Environment*, Routledge 1997

One particularly intensively studied site is Parkfield in California, on the San Andreas fault – see page 268.

The sustainable livelihoods approach for volcano-related opportunities

In an article entitled 'Living with Volcanoes: The sustainable livelihoods approach for volcano-related opportunities', Ilan Kelman and Tamsin Mather outlined ways in which people could have a sustainable livelihood in volcanic areas.

The destructive forces of volcanoes are well known, for example Mt Pelée in Martinique killed approximately 30 000 people in St Pierre, while in 1985 lahars from Nevado del Ruiz, Colombia killed approximately 25 000 people. National/regional impacts are represented by the 1783/84 eruptions of Laki on Iceland which killed 24 per cent of Iceland's population and caused thousands of deaths elsewhere in Europe. Global volcano-related impacts have been noticeable through weather alteration, as was the case following the 1991 Mt Pinatubo eruption in the Philippines.

However, human fatalities linked to volcanoes have been relatively few. The death toll attributed to volcanoes since AD 1 is approximately 275 000. As with many disasters, volcano-related disasters also have psychological impacts.

Literature dealing with the volcanic risk perception tends to focus on threats and dangers from volcanoes, along with possible preparation measures, whereas information regarding perceptions of volcano-related benefits or opportunities are more limited.

The contributions of volcanoes to society are widespread. For example, the Mt Etna region represents just under 7 per cent of the land area of Sicily, yet is home to over 20 per cent of the population. Reasons for this intense human activity on the lower slopes of the volcano are not difficult to find, including fertile soils and a reliable freshwater supply. The Soufrière volcano on St Vincent brings agricultural, mining, quarrying and tourism benefits to St Vincent and the Grenadines. There are also geothermal resources, and the use of volcanic materials for making items such as basalt hammers and pumice, along with the archaeological and artistic gains from volcanism.

Dealing with environmental hazards

As exemplified by Mt Etna in Italy and Mt Mayon in the Philippines, people have good reasons for living near or on volcanoes, including good farmland and reliable water supplies. This sometimes yields dangers, despite the rewards. To balance the dangers or potential dangers with the gains or potential gains from environmental hazards, including volcanoes, a four-option framework has been developed (Table 3.18).

The first option is to do nothing, accepting that volcanic disasters will happen. Depending on the volcano, this option might be more viable or less viable. Mt Etna in Italy frequently erupts, so doing nothing could lead to a disaster depending on the extent and characteristics of an eruption. In contrast, Mt Jefferson in the USA has not erupted in several centuries and doing nothing could be an option there.

The second option is to try to protect society from volcanic hazards, such as by strengthening roofs against tephra fall,

Table 3.18 Options and consequences for dealing with environmental hazards

Option for dealing with environmental hazards	Main implications
1 Do nothing	Disasters occur.
2 Protect society from hazards	Not always feasible and leads to risk transference which augments vulnerability.
3 Avoid hazards	Not always feasible and can exacerbate other problems, augmenting vulnerability.
4 Live with the hazards and risks	Livelihoods are integrated with environmental threats and opportunities.

building structural defences against lahars, pumping sea water onto lava (Heinaey, Iceland 1973), diverting lava (Mt Etna), or slowly degassing Lake Nyos, Cameroon. However, this protection option is not always feasible. For example, not all gas releases could be averted through degassing. Large pyroclastic flows and lava flows are challenging to stop or even to redirect, although structures could be designed to afford some level of protection against these hazards. Moreover, reliance on protective measures could lead to a false sense of security without tackling the root causes of vulnerability.

The third option is to avoid volcanic hazards, but that is not always feasible. Volcanic impacts are often not local and are sometimes even global, so all places on Earth have the potential for being severely affected by volcanic activity. Additionally, with global population increasing, constraints on land and resources frequently leave little option other than to inhabit areas that are potentially affected by volcanic hazards.

Moreover, avoiding volcanic hazards could cause further problems. Volcanic activity can yield advantages which might outweigh the problems. Moving away from volcanoes could yield other concerns, perhaps exposure to other environmental hazards or perhaps social challenges. After Montserrat's volcano started erupting in 1995, some families moved to England, only to be disappointed at the low standard of education in English schools. Many Montserratians were shocked, too, at the level of crime risk to which they were exposed on neighbouring Caribbean islands.

The fourth option, living with risk, means accepting that environmental hazards are a part of life and of a productive livelihood. A component of living with risk is localising disaster risk reduction. Disaster risk reduction, including pre-disaster activities such as preparedness and mitigation and post-disaster activities such as response and recovery, is best achieved at the local level with community involvement. The most successful outcomes are seen with broad support and action from local residents, rather than relying on external specialists or interventions. Although the long dormancy periods of volcanoes and significant uncertainties about eruptive pathways might make community interest in disaster risk reduction wane, few communities are vulnerable only to volcanic hazards.

The sustainable livelihoods approach

Sustainable livelihoods can be defined as creating and maintaining means of individual and community living that are flexible, safe and healthy from one generation to the next. The sustainable livelihoods approach is important in its application to volcanic scenarios in four ways:

1 Understanding, communicating, and managing vulnerability and risk and local perceptions of vulnerability and risk beyond the immediate threats to life.
2 Maximising the benefits to communities of their volcanic environment, especially during quiescent periods, without increasing vulnerability.
3 Managing crises.
4 Managing reconstruction and resettlement after a crisis.

Applying the sustainable livelihoods approach

Managing vulnerability and risk

The first application of the sustainable livelihoods approach to volcanoes is understanding, communicating and managing vulnerability and risk along with local perceptions of vulnerability and risk beyond immediate threats to life.

Thinking ahead of the event ensures that:
- local livelihoods are preserved, meaning that the population has an easier post-disaster recovery except for cases of extreme destruction
- the affected population is confident that their livelihoods will remain, so they will be more willing to shelter and evacuate without putting their lives at risk for the sake of livelihoods.

Examples include attempts to prevent lava blocking Heimaey's harbour and balancing ski access to Ruapehu during active episodes, especially in light of the continuing lahar threat. In these instances, it was decided that saving only lives without considering livelihoods was unacceptable. Risk and vulnerability have been managed to achieve a balance between lives and livelihoods: living with volcanic risk.

Maximising community benefits sustainably

The second application is maximising the benefits to communities of their volcanic environment, especially during quiescent periods, while decreasing vulnerability. The livelihood benefits of volcanoes can be placed into three main categories: physical resources (e.g. mining), energy resources (e.g. heat), and social resources (e.g. tourism).

Volcanoes play an important role in the formation of precious metal ores. However, if the volcano's activity increases, the mining resources, equipment and expected income could be jeopardised. The 2006 eruption of a 'mud volcano' in eastern Java, which was highly destructive to local livelihoods, resulted from borehole drilling.

Managing crises

The third application is managing crises. Emergency response and humanitarian relief are adopting the sustainable livelihoods approach, such as for the sectors of transitional settlement and shelter and food security.

Managing reconstruction and resettlement

The fourth application is managing reconstruction and/or resettlement after a volcanic crisis. Montserrat provides a good example. Resettlement in the island's north (Figures 3.46 and 3.47), away from the most dangerous zones due to volcanic activity, included housing construction which was completed without sufficient attention to local culture, other hazards, or livelihoods. The resettlement saved lives, but did not adopt a local approach to living with risk. Long-term problems emerged which the sustainable livelihoods approach might have prevented.

Disadvantages

Volcano-related evacuations have sometimes forced people to choose between staying in poorly managed shelters with no livelihood prospects and returning home to their livelihoods despite a high risk of injury or death from the volcano. This issue was witnessed in Montserrat, exacerbated by economic structures that encouraged farming in the exclusion zone (Figure 3.42).

Figure 3.42 Cattle in the exclusion zone, Montserrat

Towards reducing volcanic impacts

Considering livelihoods is important in successful volcanic disaster risk reduction because they contribute to living with volcanic risk based on a localised approach. Living with volcanoes at the local level requires changes of perception and action resulting in advantages for volcanic disaster risk reduction, although there can also be potential disadvantages (Figure 3.43). With the local population involved in monitoring, understanding, communicating, making decisions, and taking responsibility for aspects of volcanic disaster risk reduction – with external guidance and assistance where requested – disadvantages can be minimised.

Figure 3.43 It is not always possible to see volcanic impacts as positive

Three points emerge from applying the sustainable livelihoods approach to localised living with volcanic risk:

- First, not all livelihoods near volcanoes are volcano-related. Productive agriculture could be due to floodwaters rather than volcanic deposits.
- Second, not all volcanic activity necessarily yields livelihoods, or livelihoods that should be encouraged. Tourism and research activities in active craters (Figure 3.44), for example, tend to be discouraged in vulcanology. That level of risk-taking could also make the livelihood vulnerable. For example, if tourists were killed by a volcano, the area's tourism could suffer.
- Third, resource availability does not always imply resource use. Mining could be deemed too externally dependent or too environmentally and socially destructive to be worthwhile pursuing.

Volcanic risk perception and communication studies show that not everyone living by a volcano understands or accepts the actual or potential implications of the volcano. Risk and disasters

Figure 3.44 The world's only drive-in volcanic crater, St Lucia

emerge from volcanoes, but livelihood opportunities emerge from volcanoes too. Those opportunities form an integral part of volcanic disaster risk reduction.

Despite volcanic benefits, living with volcanic risk is not always feasible and volcanoes should not be relied on for livelihoods without careful consideration of potential drawbacks. Other approaches – do nothing, protect, and avoid – should be considered, as well as appropriate combinations of the approaches for different combinations of volcanic risks, volcanic benefits and societal desires.

Case Study

Montserrat

The Soufrière volcano on Montserrat is a well-used example of the effects of a volcano in an LEDC. It is over ten years since the main eruption in 1997 in which 19 people died. The capital city, Plymouth, was abandoned, and became a modern-day Pompeii. Much of the southern third of the island became an exclusion zone (Figure 3.45). So how have things changed since 1997?

By 2002 Montserrat was experiencing something of a boom. The population, which had dropped in size from over 11 000 before the eruption to less than 4000 in 1999, had risen to over 8000. The reason was very clear. There were many jobs available on the island. There were many new buildings, including new government buildings, a renovated theatre, new primary schools, and lots of new housing in the north of the island. There was even a new football pitch and stadium (Figure 3.46) – which has not been used for the last five years! There were plans to build a new medical school and a school for hazard studies. These have not been built.

Figure 3.45 Plymouth and Soufrière, Montserrat

However, by the summer of 2009 it was very clear that conditions on Montserrat had changed. The population had fallen to a little over 5000. There are two main reasons for this. The first is the relative lack of jobs. Although there was an economic boom in the early 2000s, once the new buildings were built many of the jobs disappeared. There are still plans to redevelop the island – a new urban centre is being built at Little Bay but that will not be complete until 2020. The museum has been built but not much else (Figure 3.47). Thus there are some jobs available but not so many as there were previously. Second, one of the new developments on Montserrat was a new airstrip. Once this was built, the UK and US governments stopped subsidising the ferry that operated between Antigua and Montserrat. This made it more difficult to get to Montserrat, both for visitors or for people importing basic goods. Thus the number of tourists to the island fell and the price of goods on the island rose. Many Montserratians were against the airstrip and campaigned unsuccessfully for the port to be kept open. It is possible to charter a boat and sail to Montserrat but it is far more expensive than taking a ferry.

Thus with fewer jobs in construction, a declining tourist sector, and rising prices, many Montserratians left the island for a second time. Many went to Antigua and others went to locations such as Canada, the USA and the UK. Much of the aid that was given to Montserrat following the eruptions of 1997 has dried up. The UK provided over $120 million of aid but announced in 2002 that it was phasing out aid to the island. Nevertheless, in 2004 it announced a £40 million aid deal over three years.

The volcano has been relatively quiet for the last few years. However, there was an event in May 2006 which was relatively unreported. The Soufrière dome collapsed, causing a tsunami which affected some coastal areas of Guadeloupe and English Harbour and Jolly Harbour in Antigua. The Guadeloupe tsunami was 1 m high and the one in Antigua between 20 and 30 cm. No-one was injured in the tsunami but flights were cancelled between Venezuela and Miami, and to and from Aruba, due to the large amount of ash in the atmosphere.

Figure 3.46 Montserrat football pitch

Figure 3.47 Montserrat museum

So while volcanic activity in Montserrat is currently quiet, the volcano continues to have a major impact on all those who remain on the island. The economic outlook for the island does not look good – and that is largely related to the lack of aid, the difficulty and cost of reaching Montserrat, and the small size of the island and its population.

Section 3.4 Activities

1 To what extent is the management of the Soufrière Volcano on Montserrat an example of sustainable development? Give reasons for your answer.

2 Briefly explain the main methods of dealing with earthquakes.

3 In what ways is it possible to manage the risk of volcanoes?

4 Outline the advantages of geo-engineering over hard engineering structures for slope stabilisation.

4 Arid and semi-arid environments

4.1 The distribution and climatic characteristics of hot arid and semi-arid environments

Figure 4.1 and Tables 4.1 and 4.2 show the distribution of arid environments. While Africa has the greatest proportion of these, Australia is the most arid continent with about 75 per cent of the land being classified as arid or semi-arid. Most arid areas are located in the tropics, associated with the subtropical high pressure belt. However, some are located alongside cold ocean currents (such as the Namib and Atacama deserts), some are located in the lee of mountain ranges (such as the Gobi and Patagonian deserts), while others are located in continental interiors (such as the Sahara and the Australian deserts).

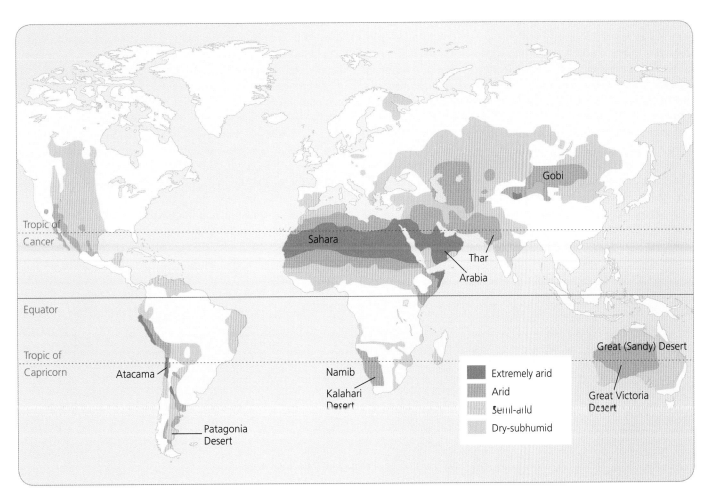

Figure 4.1 The global distribution of arid areas

Table 4.1 The extent of global arid areas (as a percentage of the global land area)

Classification	Semi-arid	Arid	Extremely arid	Total
Koppen (1931)	14.3	12.0	–	26.3
Thornthwaite (1948)	15.3	15.3	–	30.6
Meigs (1953)	15.8	16.2	4.3	36.3
Shantz (1956)	5.2	24.8	4.7	34.7
UN (1977)	13.3	13.7	5.8	32.8

Table 4.2 Distribution of arid lands by continent (as a percentage of the global total)

Africa	37
Asia	34
Australasia	13
North America	8
South America	6
Europe	2

There are many definitions of the term 'arid'. Literary definitions use such terms as 'inhospitable', 'barren', 'useless', 'unvegetated' and 'devoid of water'. Scientific definitions have been based on a number of criteria including climate, vegetation, drainage patterns, and erosion processes. What they share is a consideration of moisture availability, through the relationship between precipitation and evapotranspiration.

Most modern systems for defining aridity are based on the concept of water balance – that is, the relationship that exists between inputs in the form of precipitation (P) and the losses arising from evaporation and transpiration (E). The actual amount of evapotranspiration that will occur depends on the amount of water available, hence geographers use the concept of potential evapotranspiration (PE) which is a measure of how much evapotranspiration would take place if there was an unlimited supply of water.

Meigs' (1953) classification is probably the most widely used today. It was produced for UNESCO and was concerned with food production. Arid areas that are too cold for food production (such as polar and mountainous regions) were omitted. Meigs based his classification scheme on Thornthwaite's (1948) indices of moisture availability (Im):

Im = (100 S – 60D)/PE

where PE is potential evapotranspiration, S is moisture surplus and D is moisture deficit, aggregated on an annual basis and taking soil moisture storage into account.

When P = PE throughout the year the index is 0.

When P = 0 throughout the year, the index is –60.

When P greatly exceeds PE throughout the year, the index is 100 (see Figure 4.2).

Meigs identified three types of arid area:

- semi-arid: –40 < Im <20
- arid: –56 < Im < –40
- hyper-arid (extremely arid): < –56 Im.

Grove (1977) attached mean annual precipitation to the first two categories – 200–500 mm for arid, and 25–200 mm for semi-arid – but these are only approximate. Hyper-arid areas have no seasonal precipitation and occur where twelve consecutive months without precipitation have been recorded. According to these definitions, arid areas cover about 36 per cent of the global land area.

Aridity is a permanent water deficit whereas drought is an unexpected short-term shortage of available moisture.

Rainfall effectiveness (P–E) is influenced by a number of factors:

- rates of evaporation – this is affected by temperature and wind speed, and in hot, dry areas evaporation losses are high
- seasonality – winter rainfall is more effective than summer rainfall since evaporation losses are lower
- rainfall intensity – heavy intense rain produces rapid runoff with little infiltration
- soil type – impermeable clay soils have little capacity to absorb water whereas porous sandy soils may be susceptible to drought.

Another classification is based on rainfall totals. This states that semi-arid areas are commonly defined as having a rainfall of less than 500 mm per annum, while arid areas have less than 250 mm and extremely arid areas less than 125 mm per annum. In addition to low rainfall, dry areas have variable rainfall. For example, annual rainfall variability in a rainforest area might be 10 per cent. If the annual rainfall is about 2000 mm this means that in any one year the rainfall would be somewhere between 1800 mm and 2200 mm. As rainfall total decreases, variability increases. For example, areas with a rainfall of 500 mm have

Figure 4.2 The index of aridity

an annual variability of about 33 per cent. This means that in such areas rainfall could range between 330 mm and 670 mm. This variability has important consequences for vegetation cover, farming and the risk of flooding.

All three areas are considered as part of the arid zone. This is because:

- the division between the three is arbitrary and varies depending on the classification used
- annual precipitation is highly variable and in any one year could be extremely low
- these areas share the same processes and landforms
- in the twentieth century, climate change and human activities have caused the expansion of some arid areas into semi-arid areas
- semi-arid areas are often termed deserts by their inhabitants.

It is important to remember that there are other factors that influence arid areas. There are hot deserts (tropical and subtropical) and cold deserts (high latitude and high altitude). Coastal deserts, such as the Atacama and the Namib, have very different temperature and humidity characteristics from deserts of continental interiors, such as central areas of the Sahara. There are also shield deserts, as in India and Australia, which are tectonically inactive, and mountain and basin deserts, such as south-west USA, which are undergoing mountain building.

Causes of aridity

Arid conditions are caused by a number of factors. The main cause is the global atmospheric circulation. Dry, descending air associated with the **subtropical high pressure** belt is the main cause of aridity around 20°–30°N (Figure 4.3a). Here, the stable, adiabatically warmed, subsiding body of air prevents rising air from reaching any great height. Convection currents are rarely able to reach sufficient height for condensation and precipitation. After the air has subsided it spreads out from the centre of high pressure (Figure 4.3a). It thereby prevents the incursion of warm maritime air into the region, reinforcing its aridity. The distribution of land and sea prevents the formation of a single zone of high

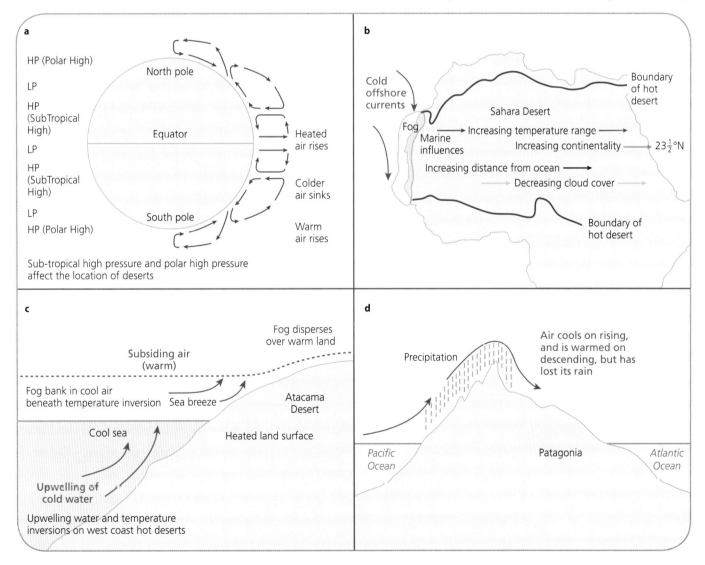

Figure 4.3 The causes of aridity

303

pressure – rather it is divided into discrete cells such as those over South America and Africa. Tropical and subtropical deserts cover about 20 per cent of the global land area. These are large arid zones composed of central arid areas surrounded by relatively small, marginal semi-arid belts. Rainfall is very unreliable and largely associated with seasonal movements of the inter-tropical convergence zone.

In addition, distance from sea, **continentality**, limits the amount of water carried by winds (Figure 4.3b). Precipitation and evapotranspiration are usually lower than in arid areas resulting from subtropical high pressure belts. Cold winters are common. These areas are characterised by a relatively small area of aridity surrounded by an extensive area of semi-aridity. The three major northern hemisphere deserts (Gobi and Turkestan in Asia and the Great Basins in North America) are mid-continental and receive little rain. The major central deserts of Australia and Africa also receive little rain as the precipitation is lost when air masses pass over the land. Rainshadow effects further increase the aridity of continental interiors.

In other areas, such as the Atacama and Namib deserts, **cold offshore currents** limit the amount of condensation into the overlying air (Figure 4.3c). Cold currents reinforce climatic conditions, causing low sea-surface evaporation, high atmospheric humidity, low precipitation (very low rainfall, with precipitation mainly in the form of fog and dew) and a small temperature range.

Others are caused by intense **rainshadow effects**, as air passes over mountains. This is certainly true of the Patagonian desert (Figure 4.3d). This can reinforce aridity that has been caused primarily by atmospheric stability or continentality. The prevailing winds in the subtropics are trade winds, which blow from the north-east in the northern hemisphere and the south-east in the southern hemisphere. Where the trade winds meet mountain barriers, such as the Andes or the Rockies, the air is forced to rise. Orographic or relief rainfall is formed on the windward side but on the lee side dehydrated air descends, creating a rainshadow effect. If the mountain ranges are on the east side of the continent then the rainshadow effect creates a much larger extent of arid land. For example, in Australia the Great Dividing Range intercepts rain on the east coast, creating a rainshadow effect to the west.

A final cause, or range of causes, is human activities. Many of these have given rise to the spread of desert conditions into areas previously fit for agriculture. This is known as desertification, and is an increasing problem.

Section 4.1 Activities

1 Explain the term *rainfall effectiveness*.

2 Describe the location of the world's dry areas as shown on Figure 4.1.

3 Briefly explain why there are deserts on the west coast of southern Africa and the west coast of South America.

4 Explain the main causes of aridity.

Desert rainfall

The main characteristic of deserts is their very low rainfall totals. Some coastal areas have extremely low rainfall: Lima in Peru receives just 45 mm of rain and Swakopmund in Namibia just 15 mm. Very often they may receive no rain in a year. Desert rain is also highly variable. The inter-annual variability (V) is expressed:

$$V\ (\%) = \frac{\text{mean deviation from the average}}{\text{the average rainfall}} \times 100\%.$$

Variability in the Sahara is commonly 50–80 per cent compared with just 20 per cent in temperate humid areas. Moreover, individual storms can be substantial. In Chicama, Peru, 394 mm fell in a single storm in 1925, compared with the annual average of just 4 mm! Similarly, at El Djem in Tunisia 319 mm of rain fell in three days in September 1969, compared with the annual average of 275 mm.

However, many desert areas receive low-intensity rainfall. Analysis of figures for the Jordan desert and for Death Valley in south-west USA show that most rainfall events produce 3–4 mm, similar to temperate areas. In coastal areas with cold offshore currents, the formation of fog can provide significant amounts of moisture. In the coastal regions of Namibia fog can occur up to 200 times a year, and extend 100 km inland. Fog provides between 35 and 45 mm of precipitation per annum. Similarly, in Peru, fog and low cloud provide sufficient moisture to support vegetation growth.

Temperature

Deserts exhibit a wide variation in temperature. Continental interiors show extremes of temperature, both seasonally and diurnally. In contrast, coastal areas have low seasonal and diurnal ranges. The temperature in coastal areas is moderated by the presence of cold, upwelling currents. Temperature ranges are low – in Callao in Peru it is just 5°C, but typically it is around 10°C. In contrast, in the Sahara the annual range can be up to 20°C. Mean annual temperatures are also lower in coastal areas – 17°C in the Namib and 19°C in the Atacama.

Continental interiors have extremes of temperature, often exceeding 50°C. Daily ranges may exceed 20°C. In winter, frost may occur in a high altitude interior desert.

Classification of desert climates
Semi-arid outer tropical climate (BShw)

Bordering the deserts, these areas have long dry winters dominated by subsiding air. Brief, erratic rains occur, associated with the ITCZ at its poleward limit. However, owing to the hot temperatures and rapid evaporation, this climate zone is less effective for plant growth. Years of average rainfall may be

Table 4.3 Climate data for some arid cities

Cairo

	J	F	M	A	M	J	J	A	S	O	N	D	Yr
Temperature													
Daily max. (°C)	19	21	24	28	32	35	35	35	33	30	26	21	28
Daily min. (°C)	9	9	12	14	18	20	22	22	20	18	14	10	16
Average monthly (°C)	14	15	18	21	25	28	29	28	26	24	20	16	22
Rainfall													
Monthly total (mm)	4	4	3	1	2	1	0	0	1	1	3	7	27
Sunshine													
Daily average	6.9	8.4	8.7	9.7	10.5	11.9	11.7	11.3	10.4	9.4	8.3	6.4	9.5

Lima

	J	F	M	A	M	J	J	A	S	O	N	D	Yr
Temperature													
Daily max (°C)	28	29	29	27	24	20	20	19	20	22	24	26	24
Daily min (°C)	19	20	19	17	16	15	14	14	14	15	16	17	16
Average monthly (°C)	24	24	24	22	20	17	17	16	17	18	20	21	20
Rainfall													
Monthly total (mm)	14	1	1	1	5	5	8	8	8	3	3	1	45
Sunshine													
Daily average	6.3	6.8	6.9	6.7	4	1.4	1.1	1	1.1	2.5	4.1	5	3.9

Timbuktu, Mali

	J	F	M	A	M	J	J	A	S	O	N	D	Yr
Temperature													
Daily max (°C)	31	35	38	41	43	42	38	35	38	40	37	31	37
Daily min (°C)	13	16	18	22	26	27	25	24	24	23	18	14	21
Average monthly (°C)	22	25	28	31	34	34	32	30	31	31	28	23	29
Rainfall													
Monthly total (mm)	0	0	0	1	4	20	54	93	31	3	0	0	206
Sunshine													
Daily average	9.1	9.5	9.6	9.7	9.8	9.4	9.6	9	9.3	9.5	9.5	8.9	9.4

followed by many years of drought, as in the case of the Sahel region south of the Sahara.

Semi-arid: poleward of hot deserts (BShs)

Summer months are dry and very hot. During winter occasional rain is associated with mid-latitude depressions. These areas are very variable in terms of rainfall – years of drought may be followed by storms, bringing hundreds of millimetres of rain. Winter rain generally supports coarse grass and drought-tolerant plants.

Hot desert climates (BWh)

In the subtropics descending air affects the very dry western parts of landmasses between 20° and 25° and strongly influences adjacent areas. Even if the air contains a considerable amount of water vapour, relative humidity is low. Stable, subsiding air prevents convective updraughts, which rarely reach sufficient height for cumulonimbus clouds to develop. Occasionally they may develop and result in sheetwash and flash flooding.

During the day temperatures may reach 50°–55°C, and at night, due to the clear skies, they may fall to 20°–25°C. During winter, daytime temperatures may reach 15°–20°C whereas at night it may be cold enough to allow dew to form.

Section 4.1 Activities

1 Explain the term *rainfall variability*.

2 Compare and contrast the seasonal and monthly temperature ranges for Lima and Timbuktu.

3 Using an atlas, locate Lima and Timbuktu. Using their geographical location, suggest reasons for the differences you have noted in their seasonal and monthly temperature ranges.

4 Compare and contrast the precipitation totals for Cairo, Lima and Timbuktu. Suggest reasons for the differences you have identified.

Climate change in deserts

During the Pleistocene Ice Age, high latitudes contained more ice (30 per cent of the world surface) than today (10 per cent of the world surface), while low-latitude areas experienced increased rainfall – episodes known as pluvials. Some deserts, however, received less rainfall – these dry phases are known as interpluvials.

There is widespread evidence for pluvial periods in deserts (Figure 4.4):

- shorelines marking higher lake levels around dry, salty basins
- fossil soils of more humid types, including horizons containing laterite
- spring deposits of lime, called tufa, indicating higher groundwater levels
- river systems now blocked by sand dunes
- animal and plant remains in areas that are now too arid to support such species
- evidence of human habitation, including cave paintings.

Wetter conditions existed in the tropics, causing lakes to reach much higher levels and rivers to flow into areas that are now dry. On the margins of the Sahara, Lake Chad may have been 120 m deeper than it currently is, and may have extended hundreds of kilometres north of its present position.

The evidence for drier conditions includes sand dune systems in areas that are now too wet for sand movement to occur. Dunes cannot develop to any great degree in continental interiors unless the vegetation cover is sparse enough to allow sand movement. If the rainfall is much over 150 mm this is generally not possible. Satellite imagery and aerial photographs have shown that some areas of forest and savanna, with 750–1500mm of rain, contain areas of ancient degraded dunes. Today, about 10 per cent of the land area between 30°N and 30°S is covered by active sand deserts but about 18 000 years ago this area was about 30 per cent sand desert.

Case Study

Climate change in Australia

Glacial periods triggered decreased rainfall and increased windiness. At least eight episodes of dune building have occurred over the last 370 000 years. The largest sand dune system in the world is the Simpson desert which was formed only 18 000 years ago. The Simpson desert covers 159 000 km² and consists of linear dunes 10–35 m high and up to 200 km long (Figure 4.5). They run parallel to each other with an average spacing over 510 m. The dunes are fixed (vegetated) except for their crests which are mobile. The Simpson desert dunes form part of a continental anticlockwise swirl which relates to the dominant winds of the subtropical anticyclone system.

Figure 4.5 Dunes in Australia

Figure 4.4 The evidence for climate change in the Sahara

4.2 Processes producing desert landforms

Weathering

Weathering in deserts is superficial and highly selective. The traditional view was that all weathering in deserts was mechanical due to the relative absence of water. However, it is increasingly realised that chemical weathering is important, and that water is important for mechanical weathering, especially exfoliation. Weathering is greatest in shady sites and in areas within reach of soil moisture. Chemical weathering is enhanced in areas that experience dew or coastal fog. As rainfall increases, weathering increases and soils tend to have more clay, less salt and more distinct horizons. Salt weathering is frequent in arid areas because desert rocks often have soluble salts, and these salts can disintegrate rocks through salt crystal growth and hydration.

Salt crystallisation causes the decomposition of rock by solutions of salt (Figure 4.6). There are two main types of **salt crystal growth**. First, in areas where temperatures fluctuate around 26–28 °C sodium sulphate (Na_2SO_4) and sodium carbonate (Na_2CO_3) expand by about 300 per cent. This creates pressure on joints, forcing them to crack. Second, when water evaporates, salt crystals may be left behind. As the temperature rises, the salts expand and exert pressure on rock. Both mechanisms are frequent in hot desert regions where low rainfall and high temperatures cause salts to accumulate just below the surface.

Figure 4.6 Salt crystallisation

Experiments investigating the effectiveness of saturated salt solutions have shown a number of results:

- The most effective salts are sodium sulphate, magnesium sulphate and calcium chloride.
- The rate of disintegration of rocks is closely related to porosity and permeability.
- Surface texture and grain size control the rate of rock breakdown. This diminishes with time for fine materials and increases over time for coarse materials.
- Salt crystallisation is more effective than insolation weathering, hydration, or freeze–thaw. However, a combination of freeze–thaw and salt crystallisation produces the highest rates of breakdown.

Thermal fracture refers to the break-up of rock as a result of repeated changes in temperature over a prolonged period of time. **Disintegration** or **insolation weathering** is found in hot desert areas where there is a large diurnal temperature range. In many desert areas daytime temperatures exceed 40 °C whereas night-time temperatures are little above freezing. Rocks heat up by day and contract by night. As rock is a poor conductor of heat, stresses occur only in the outer layers. This causes peeling or **exfoliation** to occur. Griggs (1936) showed that moisture is essential for this to happen. In the absence of moisture, temperature change alone did not cause the rocks to break down. The role of salt in insolation weathering has also been studied. The expansion of many salts such as sodium, calcium, potassium and magnesium has been linked with exfoliation. However, some geographers find little evidence to support this view.

In some instances rocks may be split in two. **Block disintegration** is most likely to result from repeated heating and cooling. Such rocks are known as *kernsprung*. A more localised effect is **granular disintegration**. This occurs due to certain grains being more prone to expansion and contraction than others – this exerts great pressure on the grains surrounding them and forces them to break off.

The most effective salts are, in descending order, sodium sulphate (Na_2SO_4), magnesium sulphate ($MgSO_4$) and calcium chloride ($CaCl_3$). Sodium sulphate caused a 100 g block of stone to break down to about 30 g – a loss of 70 per cent (Figure 4.7). Similarly, magnesium sulphate reduced a 95 g block to just over 40 g, a loss of over 50 per cent. The least effective salts were common salt (NaCl) and sodium carbonate (Na_2CO_3).

Hydration is the process whereby certain minerals absorb water, expand and change. For example gypsum is changed to anhydrate. Although it is often classified as a type of chemical weathering, mechanical stresses occur as well. When anhydrite ($CaSO_4$) absorbs water to become gypsum ($CaSO_4.2H_2O$) it expands by about 0.5 per cent. More extreme is the increase in volume of up to 1600 per cent by shales and mudstones when clay minerals absorb water.

Freeze–thaw occurs when water in joints and cracks freezes at 0 °C. It expands by about 10 per cent and exerts pressure up to a maximum of 2100 kg/cm^2 at −22 °C. This greatly exceeds most rocks' resistance. However, the average pressure reached in freeze–thaw is only 14 kg/cm^2.

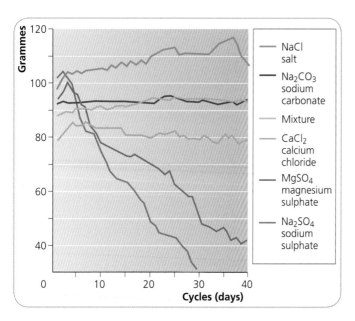

Figure 4.7 Chemical solution

Freeze–thaw is most effective in environments where moisture is plentiful and there are frequent fluctuations above and below freezing point. It can occur in deserts at high altitude and in continental interiors in winter.

Section 4.2 Activities

Briefly explain the processes of salt crystallisation and insolation weathering.

Wind action

The importance of wind in deserts has been hotly debated by geographers. At the end of the nineteenth century, it was considered to be a very effective agent in the formation of desert landforms. By contrast, in the twentieth century the role of wind was played down, in part because much of the research into deserts took place in high-relief, tectonically active areas such as the south-west USA. It was argued that:

- wind-eroded landscaped were only superficially eroded
- some features, such as playas, were formed by other processes, especially tectonic ones
- desert surfaces were protected from the wind by crusts, salts and gravel
- wind erosion depends on the availability of abrasive sands and only operates over a limited height range
- water is still very active.

However, in the middle of the twentieth century the use of aerial photography and satellites showed major features aligned with prevailing wind systems, such as yardangs in the Sahara, Iran, Peru and Arabia. In addition, examination of desert playas, which are large and frequent, showed that some are tectonic but others are aeolian. Dunes on the lee side of playas suggest that the dunes were deposited by excavating winds. In the Qattara Depression in the Sahara, 3335 km^3 of material has been removed by the wind. Moreover, meteorological observations of dust storms have illustrated the importance of winds. The Great American Dust Storm of 12 November 1933, which marked the beginning of the Dust Bowl, stretched from Canada to western Ohio and the Missouri Valley, an area larger than France, Italy and Hungary! The increased frequency of dust storms in the USA was due to severe drought and poor agricultural techniques. Although the land was not desert, it took on desert characteristics. In the 1970s, there was an increase in the number of dust storms in the Sahel region of Africa. Some of these storms travelled across the Atlantic to reach the Caribbean and were also associated with an increase in asthma there, partly as a result of increased dust, and partly as a result in the transfer of bacteria by winds across the Atlantic Ocean. Finally, as already noted, during the last glaciations some areas in the tropics were wetter and some were drier. It is estimated that the rate of dust removal and deposition was one hundred times greater then it is at present.

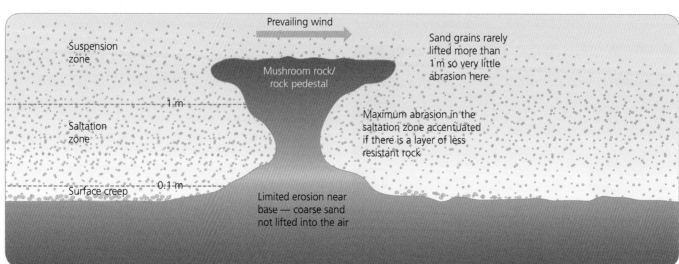

Figure 4.8 Wind erosion

Erosion

By itself, wind can only blow away loose, unconsolidated material so gradually lowering the surface by **deflation**. At wind speeds of 40 km/hr, sand grains will move by surface creep and saltation. Much transport of sand will therefore be limited to a metre or so above the surface (Figure 4.8). Higher wind speeds will cause dust storms. Extremely rare gusts of over 150 km/hr are need to roll pebbles along the ground. Fine dust is moved easily by light winds.

As well as blowing away layers of unconsolidated material over wide areas, deflation can be localised to produce deflation basins. It is not fully understood why localised deflation occurs – faulting may produce the initial depression that is enlarged by the eddying nature of the wind; differential erosion could also cause the initial trigger, as could solution weathering in a past pluvial period. Many such basins are found in the Sahara west of Cairo. Some basins have become so deflated that their bases reach the water table and so form an oasis, for example the Baharia and Farafra oases and the massive Qattara Depression which lies 120 m below sea level.

Selective deflation causes various different types of desert landscape:

- hammada desert – all loose material is blown away leaving large areas of bare rock, often strewn with large, immovable weathered rocks
- desert pavement – pebbles are concentrated, for example by a flash flood, and packed together into a mosaic; the tops are then worn flat by wind erosion and perhaps become shiny as a coat of desert varnish develops
- reg desert – here the finest material has been deflated, leaving a gravelly or stony desert
- erg desert – this is the classic sandy desert.

Wind erosion only takes place when the wind is loaded with loose materials, especially sand grains. Dust particles are ineffective. The wind throws the particles of sand against rock faces, creating abrasion or corrosion (a sand-blast effect). Large rock fragments, too heavy to be transported by the wind, are worn down on the windward side – these worn fragments are called ventifacts.

In areas of homogeneous rock, the wind will smooth and polish the surface. However, if the rocks are heterogeneous; for example, weakened by joints or faults, some dramatic landforms will result from wind erosion, with rock faces etched, grooved, fluted and honeycombed, forming towers, pinnacles and natural arches. Undercutting (abrasion occurring at about 1 m above the ground) is common, and produces distinctive landforms, including:

- **gours** – mushroom pinnacles where the base has been undercut, and bands of hard and soft rock have been differentially sand-blasted
- **zeugens** – develop where differing rock strata lie horizontally; after being eroded by the wind, the rocks form small plateau-like blocks which are isolated residuals of the original plateau – called mesas (if quite large) and buttes (if relatively small) in parts of Colorado, USA
- **yardangs** – occur where hard and soft rocks lie side by side; the softer rocks are worn down to form troughs while the harder rocks stand up as wind-worn ridges or yardangs.

Wind-borne material is in constant motion and consequently attrition of this material occurs, the particles becoming rounder and smaller. Wind rounds material more effectively than running water because:

- wind speeds are greater
- distances over which the attrition takes place are often much greater
- the grains are not protected by a film of water.

Section 4.2 Activities

Outline the ways in which wind can erode desert surfaces.

Transport

Sand-sized particles are well suited to transport by the wind. Sand movement occurs when wind speeds exceed 20 km/hr. Grains initially begin to roll, and then follow a bouncing action, known as saltation. The saltating grains are typically 0.15–0.25 mm in diameter. In contrast larger grains (0.26–2 mm) move by surface creep and smaller grains (0.05–0.14 mm) move through suspension.

Deposition

Deposition occurs when the wind speed is reduced. The form taken by the deposited material is influenced by:

- the nature of any surface irregularity
- the amount and type of material carried by the wind, itself controlled by velocity
- the flow pattern of the dominant wind (shaping the material being deposited)
- the presence or absence of vegetation and groundwater.

Deserts occupy about 20 per cent of the world and their area is expanding – for example the arid belt of the southern Sahara, known as the Sahel, has extended considerably into the savanna lands of Ethiopia, causing widespread famine there.

Sand drifts (temporary pockets of sand found in 'wind shadow' areas) and sand sheets (wide areas of flat or undulating sandscape) are common in desert areas. However, the formation of different types of sand dune seems to typify desert deposition.

Sand dunes

Only about 25–33 per cent of the world's deserts are covered by dunes and in North America only 1–2 per cent of the deserts are ergs (sandy deserts) (Table 4.4). Large ergs are found in the Sahara and Arabia. The sand that forms the deserts comes from a variety of sources: alluvial plains, lake shores, sea shores and from weathered sandstone and granite.

The geometry of dunes is varied and depends on the supply of sand, the wind regime, vegetation cover and the shape of the ground surface.

Some dunes are formed in the lee of an obstacle. A nebkha is a small dune formed behind a tree or shrub whereas a lunette dune is formed in the lee of a depression (Figure 4.9). Lunettes may reach a height of about 10 m. They are asymmetric in cross-section, with the steeper side facing the wind. However, most dunes do not require an obstacle for their formation.

Table 4.4 The relative importance (percentage figures) of major dune types in the world's deserts

Desert	Thar	Takla Makan	Namib	Kalahari	Saudi Arabia	Ala Shan	South Sahara	North Sahara	North–east Sahara	West Sahara	Average
Linear dunes	13.96	22.12	32.84	85.85	49.81	1.44	24.08	22.84	17.01	35.49	30.54
Crescent dunes	54.29	36.91	11.80	0.59	14.91	27.01	28.37	33.34	14.53	19.17	24.09
Star dunes	–	–	9.92	–	5.34	2.87	–	7.92	23.92	–	5.00
Dome dunes	–	7.40	–	–	–	0.86	–	–	0.8	–	0.90
Sheets and streaks	31.75	33.56	45.44	13.56	23.24	67.82	47.54	35.92	39.25	45.34	38.34
Undifferentiated	–	–	–	–	6.71	–	–	–	4.50	–	1.12

Barchan dunes are crescent-shaped and are found in areas where sand is limited but there is a constant wind supply. They have a gentle windward slope and a steep leeward slope up to 33°. Variations include barchan ridges and tranverse ridges, the latter forming where sand is abundant, and where the wind flow is checked by a topographic barrier, or increased vegetation cover. Barchans can be as wide as 30 m.

Parabolic dunes have the opposite shape to barchans – they are also crescent-shaped but point downwind. They occur in areas of limited vegetation or soil moisture.

Linear dunes, or seifs, are commonly 5–30 m high, and occur as ridges 200–500 m apart. They may extend for tens, if not hundreds, of kilometres. They are found in areas where there is a seasonal change in wind direction. It is believed that

| **a** Dune formation | **b** Linear dunes or seifs | **c** Star dunes | **d** Dome dunes |
| **e** Reversing dunes | **f** Parabolic dunes | **g** Barchan dunes | **h** Barchanoid ridge |

Figure 4.9 Some sand dune types

some regularity of turbulence is responsible for their formation (Figure 4.10).

Where the winds come from many directions, star dunes may be formed. Limbs may extend from a central peak. Star dunes can be up to 150 m high and 2 km wide.

Dune types can merge. Crescent barchans can be transformed into longitudinal seif dunes, depending on the wind regime. The over-emphasis on barchans and seif dunes is somewhat misleading. Less than 1 per cent of sand dunes are of these types. Dunes are not necessarily longitudinal or transverse – many are oblique. Grain size is also important – coarse sand is associated with rounded dunes, of subdued size and long wavelength. Fine sand produces stronger relief with smaller wavelengths.

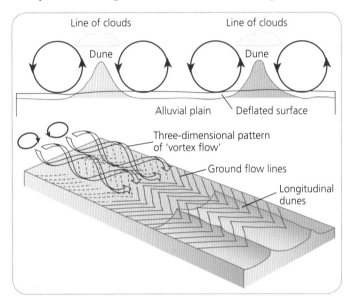

Figure 4.10 Turbulence and the formation of seif dunes

Section 4.2 Activities

Comment on the regional distribution, and relative importance, of linear dunes as shown in Table 4.4.

The role of water

Despite the low rainfall in arid regions, rivers play an important part in the development of many arid landforms. Rainfall may be irregular and sporadic but some desert areas experience occasional heavy downpours.

Rivers in arid lands can be divided into three types:
- **Exogenous** rivers have their origin in humid areas – they are exotic rivers. The Nile flows through the Sahara but rises in the monsoonal Ethiopian Highlands and in equatorial Lake Victoria.
- **Endoreic** rivers flow into inland lakes. The Jordan River flows into the Dead Sea and the Bear River flows into the Great Salt Lake.
- **Ephemeral** rivers flow only after rainstorms. They can generate high amounts of discharge because torrential

downpours exceed the infiltration capacity of the soils.

Most ephemeral streams consist of many braided channels separated by islands of sediment.

Even areas of low-intensity rain can generate much overland flow. This is because of the lack of vegetation and the limited soil development. The presence of duricrusts also reduces the ability of water to infiltrate the soil.

Surface runoff is typically in the form of sheet flow, where water flows evenly over the land. The runoff may become concentrated into deep, steep-sided valleys known as wadis or arroyos.

Stream flow in dry areas is seasonal, and in some cases erratic. This increases the potential for flooding due to a combination of:
- high velocities
- variable sediment concentrations
- rapid changes in the location of channels.

According to some geographers, erosion is most effective in dry areas. This is because of the relative lack of vegetation. When it rains a large proportion of rain will hit bare ground, compact it, and lead to high rates of overland runoff. By contrast, in much wetter areas, such as rainforests, the vegetation intercepts much of the rainfall and reduces the impact of rainsplash. At the other extreme, areas that are completely dry do not receive enough rain to produce much runoff. Hence it is the areas which have variable rainfall (and a variable vegetation cover) that experience the highest rates of erosion and runoff (Figure 4.11). Moreover, as the type of agriculture changes, the rate of erosion and overland runoff change (Figure 4.12). Under intense conditions this creates gullies.

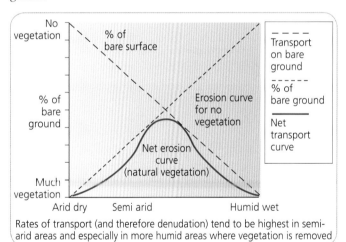

Rates of transport (and therefore denudation) tend to be highest in semi-arid areas and especially in more humid areas where vegetation is removed

Figure 4.11 Rainfall, vegetation cover and soil erosion

There is a paradox that in deserts most runoff occurs on low-angle slopes. This is due to particle size. Coarse debris makes up the steeper slopes while fine material makes up the low-angle slopes. Coarse debris allows more infiltration, so there is less overland flow on steeper slopes.

High concentrations of sediment in runoff from desert uplands illustrate (a) the erodibility of unvegetated areas, and (b) the contemporary nature of the work of water in deserts. Desert streams are cloudy and muddy – up to 75 per cent of the flow may be solid matter. This solid matter is important for the formation of

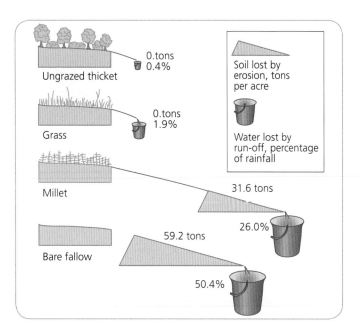

Figure 4.12 The impact of vegetation type on runoff and soil erosion

alluvial fans (and for silt building up behind dams). An **alluvial fan** is a cone of sediment occurring between a mountain and a lowland plain (Figure 4.13). They can be up to 20 km wide and up to 300 m at the apex. They generally form when a heavily sediment-laden river emerges from a canyon. The river, no longer confined to the narrow canyon, spreads out laterally, losing height, energy and velocity, so that deposition occurs; larger particles are deposited first and finer materials are carried further away from the mountain.

On a larger scale **pediments** are gently sloping areas (< 7°) of bare rock where there is a distinct break with the mountain

Figure 4.13 An alluvial fan

region (Figure 4.14). One idea is that pediments are the result of river deposition, similar to an alluvial fan. Another idea is that they are the result of lateral planation (see pages 216–17). A third hypothesis involves sub-surface weathering. This is likely to be accentuated at the junction of the mountain and the plain because of the concentration of water there through percolation. The weathering will produce fine-grained material that can be removed, in the absence of vegetation cover, by sheetfloods, wind and other processes. If a number of alluvial fans merge, the feature is known as a **bajada** (**bahada**).

Salt lakes (**chottes/playas**) are found in the lowest part of the desert surface, where ephemeral streams flow into inland depressions, for example the Chott el Djerid of Tunisia. After flowing into the depression, water evaporates, leaving behind a thick crust. Sodium chloride is the most common salt found in such locations, but there could also be gypsum (calcium sulphate), sodium sulphate, magnesium sulphate, and potassium and magnesium chlorides.

In some semi-arid areas water action creates a landscape known as badlands. These are areas where soft and relatively impermeable rocks are moulded by rapid runoff which results from heavy but irregular rainfall. There is insufficient vegetation to hold the regolith and bedrock together, and rainfall and runoff are powerful enough to create dramatic landforms. Badlands generally have the following features:

- wadis of various sizes with debris-covered bottoms
- gullies that erode headwards, leading to their collapse
- slope failure and slumping
- alluvial fans at the base of slopes
- natural arches formed by the erosion of a cave over time.

An excellent example of badland topography is in southern Tunisia around Matmata.

Wadis are river channels that vary in size from a few metres in length to over 100 km. They are generally steep-sided and flat-bottomed. They may be formed by intermittent flash floods or they may have been formed during wetter pluvial periods in the Pleistocene. The relative infrequency of flash floods in some areas where wadis are found could suggest that they were formed at a time when storms were more frequent and more intense. In contrast, **arroyos** are channels that have enlarged by repeated flooding. They are common in semi-arid areas on alluvium and solid rock.

Mesas are plateau-like features with steep sides at their edges. **Buttes** are similar but much smaller. Water has eroded most of the rock leaving a thin pillar. **Inselbergs** (see page 219) may be the result of deep chemical weathering during wetter pluvial periods. Overlying sediments were subsequently removed by river activity. They are isolated steep-sided hills. A good example is Uluru (Ayers Rock) in Australia.

High runoff and sediment yields cause much dissection and high drainage densities (total length of water channel per km^2). In the Badlands of the USA, drainage densities can be as high as $350 km/km^2$, whereas in a typical temperate region it is $2–8 km/km^2$. In contrast, in sandy deserts (high infiltration) drainage densities can be as low as $0–1 km/km^2$.

Features in the arid landscape

Plateaux
large, flat areas at high a ltitude

Canyons
Very deep gorges, usually dry. If there is a river, it is usually exotic. The Fish River Canyon in Namibia is an excellent example

Butte
An isolated peak, often the remnant of a former mesa or plateau

Wadis
Dry gullies that have been eroded by flash floods. Heavy rainstorms (1 0~250 mm) create rushing torrents on steep slopes

Mesa
A relatively large area of plateau that has become isolated from the main plateau either by erosion or through slope retreat

Pediments
Shallow slopes formed at the base of a cliff or steep hill

Wind

Inselbergs
Also known as kopjes or bomhardts, are isolated domes of resistant rock. They can be formed by parallel retreat of slopes (pediplanation) or by exhumation where the basal surface is exposed a result of surface stripping

Hard rock
Soft rock

Yardangs

Zeugens

Salt pans (playas)
Sites of former or occasional lakes

Alluvial fans
Cones of sediment that are deposited by rivers owing to anabrupt loss of energy as they leavetheir mountain channels and enter onto a plain

Oasis
Formed when the waterbearing rocks are exposed at the surface. This is commonly done by deflation

Barchan or crescent dunes
Sand dunes are formed where wind speed is high and constant and where there is a large supply of sand

Figure 4.14 Desert landforms

Section 4.2 Activities

1 Define the terms *exogeneous*, *endoreic* and *ephemeral*.

2 Explain how **a** alluvial fans and **b** pediments are formed.

Equifinality: different processes, same end product

A question frequently asked is whether desert landforms are the result of wind action or water action. This is a simplification because there are other processes than wind and water acting in desert regions. For example, stone pavements are surfaces of coarse debris lying above finer material. They could be caused by:

- deflation of fine material, leaving coarse material behind
- removal of fine material by rainsplash or sheetwash
- vertical sorting by frost action or hydration.

It may even be a combination of processes.

Similarly, depressions can be caused by a variety of processes:

- deflation removing finer material, as in the Qattara Depression, Sahara
- tectonic – for example block faulting in the basin and range region of the USA
- solution of limestone during a pluvial period, as for example in Morocco
- animal activity, as for example in Zimbabwe where herds are concentrated near water holes and accentuate the initial depression.

Gully development is normally associated with river activity. However, there are different reasons for their development:

- Some are related to increased discharge due to climate change.
- Others are caused by the removal of vegetation by people exposing the surface to accelerated rates of erosion.
- Some develop where concrete structures have been built to improve runoff.
- Tectonic disturbances can initiate gully development, especially uplift.
- Catastrophic flooding may be responsible for some gully development.

4.3 Soils and vegetation

An ecosystem is the interrelationship between plants and animals and their living and non-living environments. A biome is a global ecosystem, such as the tropical rainforest, savanna or hot desert ecosystem.

Deserts have low rates of biomass productivity – on average net primary productivity of 90 g/m²/yr. This is due to the limited amount of organic matter caused by extremes of heat and lack of moisture. Productivity can generally be positively correlated with water availability. Despite the diversity of life forms found in deserts, desert flora and fauna are relatively species poor. At the continental scale, species diversity of lizards and rodents has been correlated with increasing precipitation. Desert vegetation is simple in that its structure is poorly developed and its cover becomes increasingly open and discontinuous with increasing aridity.

Energy flow in deserts is controlled by water, which can be very irregular. The impact of herbivores in deserts is similar to that in other ecosystems, with about 2–10 per cent of the primary production being directly consumed. Some studies have indicated that 90 per cent or more of seed production may be eaten by seed-eaters such as ants and rodents.

Owing to the low and irregular rainfall, inputs to the nutrient cycle (dissolved in rain and as a result of chemical weathering) are low (Figure 4.15). Most of the nutrients are stored in the soil, and there are very limited stores in the biomass and litter. This is due to the limited amount of biomass and litter in the desert environment. In some deserts nutrient deficiency (especially of nitrogen and/or phosphorus) may become critical. The rapid growth of annuals following a rain event rapidly depletes the store of available nutrients, while their return in decomposition is relatively slow.

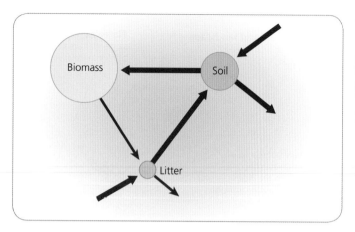

Figure 4.15 Nutrient cycle in a desert

Decomposition, like growth, is slow. Microbial decomposers are limited. Two important processes are involved in nutrient cycling:

- the fragmentation, erosion and transport of dead organic matter (DOM) by wind and runoff
- consumption of DOM by detritivores such as termites, ants and mites, which are relatively abundant in deserts.

In the absence of leaching, nutrients may accumulate in the upper layers of the soil. A large proportion of the nutrients is held either in young tissue, or in the fertile islands surrounding large plants where, as a result of slightly lower temperatures and higher humidity, decomposition is lower and DOM accumulates.

Despite the extreme short-term variability of the desert environment, the desert ecosystem is considered, in the long term, to be both stable and resilient. This is due to the adaptations of desert organisms to survive water stress – in some cases for years.

Plant and animal adaptations

Desert plants and animals have acquired similar morphological, physiological and behavioural strategies which, although not unique to desert organisms, are often more highly developed and effectively utilised than their moist counterparts.

The two main strategies are avoidance and tolerance of heat and water stress (Table 4.5). The *evaders* comprise the majority of the flora of most deserts. They can survive periods of stress in an inactive state or by living permanently or temporarily in cooler and/or moister environments such as below shrubs or stone, in rock fissures or below ground. Of desert animals about 75 per cent are subterranean, nocturnal or active when the surface is wet. In such ways plants and animals can control their temperature and water loss.

Table 4.5 Adaptations of plants and animals to hot desert environments

	Plants	Animals
Stress-evading strategies		
	• Inactivity of whole plants • Cryptobiosis* of whole plant • Dormancy of seeds	• Dormancy/inactivity of seeds in time (diurnal and seasonal) and space (take refuge in burrows) • Cryptobiosis of mature animals (aestivation of snails, hibernation) • Cryptobiosis of eggs, shelled embryos, larvae: permanent habitation or temporary use of stress-protected microhabitats
Structural and physiological stress-controlling strategies		
Strategies reducing water expenditure	• Small surface : volume ratio • Regulation of water loss by stomatal movements • Xeromorphic features • Postural adjustments	• Small surface : volume ratio • Regulation and restriction of water loss by concentrated urine, dry faeces, reduction of urine flow rate • Structures reducing water • Postural adjustment
Strategies to prevent death by overheating	• Transpiration cooling • High heat tolerance • Mechanisms decreasing and/or dissipating heat load	• Evaporative cooling • High heat tolerance • Mechanisms decreasing and/or dissipating heat load
Strategies optimising water uptake	• Direct uptake of dew, condensed fog and water vapour • Fast formation of water roots after first rain • Halophytes: uptake of saline water, high salt tolerance, salt-excreting glands	• Direct and indirect uptake of dew, condensed fog and water vapour (e.g. arthropods, water enrichment of stored food) • Fast drinking of large quantities of water (large mammals), uptake of water from wet soil (e.g. snails) • Uptake of highly saline water, high salt tolerance, salt-excreting glands
Strategies to control reproduction in relation to environmental conditions	• 'Water clocks' of seed dispersal and germination • Suppression of flowering and sprouting in extreme years	• Sexual maturity, mating and birth synchronised with favourable conditions • Sterility in extreme drought years

* Cryptobiosis – an ametabolic state of life in response to adverse environmental stress. When the environment becomes hospitable again, the organism returns to its metabolic state.

Temperature adaptations

Desert plants and animals are able to function at higher temperatures than their mesis (moist environment) counterparts. Some cacti such as the prickly pear can survive up to 65 °C, while crustose lichens can survive up to 70 °C. The upper lethal levels for animals are lower, although arthropods, particularly beetles and scorpions, can tolerate 50 °C. Plants and animals are able to modify the heat of the desert environment in a number of ways:

- Changing the orientation of the whole body enables the organism to minimise the areas and/or time they are exposed to maximum heat – many gazelle, for example, are long and thin.
- Light colours maximise reflection of solar radiation.
- Surface growth (spines and hairs) can absorb or reflect heat, which (a) keeps the undersurface cooler and (b) creates an effective boundary layer of air, which insulates the underlying surface.
- Body size is especially important in controlling the amount of heat loss – evaporation and metabolism are proportional to the surface area of the plant or animal. The smaller the organism the larger the surface area : volume ratio and the greater the heat loss.
- Large desert animals such as the camel and the oryx can control heating by means of evaporative cooling. Cooling by transpiration is also thought to be most effective in cacti and small-leaved desert shrubs because of their surface area to volume ratio.

Water loss

Physical droughts refer to water shortages over an extended period of time. Physiological drought occurs when drought conditions are experienced by plants despite there being sufficient soil moisture. In hot arid areas this is associated with high rates of evapotranspiration. To reduce water loss, desert plants and animals have many adaptations. Again a small surface area to volume ratio is an advantage (Figure 4.16b). Water regulation by plants can be controlled by diurnal closure of stomata, and xerophytic plants have a mix of thick, waxy cuticles, sunken stomata and leaf hairs (Figure 4.16e). The most drought resistant plants are the succulents, including cacti, which possess well-

Figure 4.16 Plant adaptations to drought

developed storage tissues (Figure 4.16a), small surface to volume ratios, and rapid stomatal closure especially during the daytime, and deep tap roots (Figure 4.16b and 4.16c).

Some plants and many arthropods are drought-resistant. The creosote bush can survive up to a year without rain. Rapid uptake of water is also a characteristic of many desert organisms, including lichen, algae and camels. Animals can rapidly imbibe, and salt-tolerant plants have a high cell osmotic pressure that allows the efficient uptake of alkaline water. The roots of many desert plants can exert a greater suction pressure so they can extract water from fine water-retentive soils.

Reproduction

Desert survival is also dependent on an organism's ability to reproduce itself. Desert fauna and flora have developed several different strategies. High seed production and efficient dispersal are more essential than in humid environments. Some seeds have built-in 'water clocks' and will not germinate until a certain amount of water becomes available. Some arid-zone shrubs, such as the ironwood and the smokewood, have seeds with coats so tough that germination can only take place after severe mechanical abrasion during torrential flash floods. In both plants and animals reproduction is suppressed during periods of drought.

Desert soils

Desert soils, called aridisols, have a low organic content and are only affected by limited amounts of leaching. Soluble salts tend to accumulate in the soil either near the water table or around the depth of moisture percolation. As precipitation declines, this horizon occurs nearer to the surface. Desert soils also have a limited clay content.

The accumulation of salt in desert soils is important. Salt concentrations may be toxic to plants. This is more likely in areas where there is a high water table or in the vicinity of salt lakes. Soils with a saline horizon of NaCl (sodium chloride) are called solonchaks and those with a horizon of Na_2CO_3 (sodium carbonate) are termed solonetz. Solonchaks are white alkali soils whereas solonetz are black alkali soils. A high concentration of salt can cause the breakdown of soil structure, increase water stress, and affect the health of plants.

Sometimes the concentration of salts becomes so great that crusts are formed on the surface or sub-surface. There are different types of hard crust (duricrusts). Calcrete or caliche is formed of calcium carbonate and is the most common crust in warm desert environments. It can be up to 40 m comprising boulders, gravels, silt and calcareous materials. It predominates in areas of between 200 mm and 500 mm.

Silcrete is a crust cemented by silica. It may produce an impermeable hard pan in a soil. Silcretes are found in areas that have more than 50 mm but less than 200 mm of rain, such as southern Africa and Australia. Gypcrete (gypsum crusts) and sodium chloride crusts pose great difficulties for agriculture. They are generally located in areas of less than 50 mm of rain. They are formed mainly by the evaporation of salts.

Case Study

Salinisation in Pakistan

Irrigation has been practised in Pakistan since at least the eighth century AD. Much of the irrigation takes place along the Indus and Punjab rivers. The irrigation system here is among one of the most complex in the world, and provides Pakistan with most of its food and commercial crops, such as wheat, cotton, rice, oil seed, sugar cane and tobacco. Hence the health of the irrigated area is essential to the health of the national economy.

Many of the drainage canals are in a poor state. Many are unlined and seepage is a major problem. Consequently, there has been a steady rise in the water table which has caused widespread waterlogging and salinisation. Up to 40 000 ha of irrigated land are lost annually.

There have been attempts to rectify the problem. Two main methods are used: pumping water from aquifers (to reduce the water table), and vertical and horizontal drainage of saline water. These have met with some success. In parts of the lower Indus plain, water tables have been reduced by as much as 7 m, and up to 45 per cent of saline soils have been reclaimed. However, the use of reclaimed land for agriculture only results in salinisation again.

Desertification

Desertification is defined as land degradation in humid and semi-arid areas – that is, not including non-desert (arid) areas. It involves the loss of biological and economic productivity and it occurs where climatic variability (especially rainfall) coincides with unsustainable human activities (Figure 4.17). For example, if the surface cover is removed and the surface colour becomes lighter, its reflectivity (albedo) changes. It reflects more heat, absorbs less, and so there will be less convectional heating, less rain and possibly more drought. Desertification occurs in discontinuous and isolated patches – it is not the general extension of deserts as a consequence of natural events like prolonged droughts, as in China in the 2000s.

Desertification leads to a reduction in vegetation cover and accelerated soil erosion by wind and water, lowering the carrying capacity of the area affected. Desertification is one of the major environmental issues in the world today. At present, 25 per cent of the global land territory and nearly 16 per cent of the world's population are threatened by desertification.

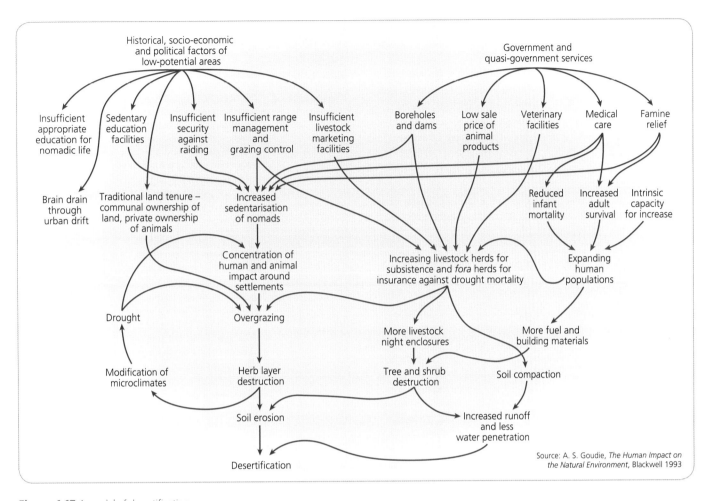

Figure 4.17 A model of desertification

Causes of desertification

Desertification can be a natural process intensified by human activities. All the areas affected by desertification are marginal and characterised by highly variable rainfall. An exception to this are the parts of the rainforest desertified following inappropriate farming techniques.

Natural causes of desertification include temporary drought periods of high magnitude and long-term climate change towards aridity. Many people believe that it is a combination of increasing animal and human population numbers, which causes the effects of drought to become more severe. Desertification occurs when already fragile land in arid and semi-arid areas is over-exploited. This overuse can be caused by overgrazing, when pastoralists allow too many animals to graze on a fixed area of land; overcultivation, where the growing of crops exhausts soil nutrients; and deforestation, when too few trees are left standing after use as firewood, to act as windbreaks or to prevent soil erosion.

- **Overgrazing** is the major cause of desertification worldwide. Vegetation is lost both in the grazing itself and in being trampled by large numbers of livestock. Overgrazed lands then become more vulnerable to erosion as compaction of the soils reduces infiltration, leading to greater runoff, while

trampling increases wind erosion. Fencing, which confines animals to specific locations, and the provision of water points and wells, have led to severe localised overgrazing. Boreholes and wells also lower the water table, causing soil salinisation.

- **Overcultivation** leads to diminishing returns, where the yield decreases season by season, requiring an expansion of the areas to be cultivated simply to maintain the same return on the agricultural investment. Reducing fallow periods and introducing irrigation are also used to maintain output, but all these contribute to further soil degradation and erosion by lowering soil fertility and promoting salinisation.

- **Deforestation** is most obvious where land has been cleared to extend the area under cultivation and in the surrounds of urban areas where trees are stripped for firewood. The loss of vegetation cover increases rainsplash erosion and the absence of root systems allows easy removal of the soil by wind and water.

Other factors are involved, including the following:

- The mobility of some people has been limited by governments, especially where their migratory routes crossed international boundaries. Attempts to provide permanent settlements have led to the concentration of population and animals, with undesirable consequences.

- Weak or non-existent laws have failed to provide environmental protection for marginal land by preventing or controlling its use.
- Irrational use of water resources has caused water shortages or salinisation of soil.
- International trade has promoted short-term exploitation of land by encouraging cash crops for export. This has disrupted local markets and created a shortage of staple foods.
- Civil strife and war diverts resources away from environmental issues.
- Ignorance of the consequences of some human actions, and the use of inappropriate techniques and equipment, have contributed to the problem.

Consequences of desertification

There are some serious consequences of desertification (Table 4.6).

Table 4.6 Consequences of desertification

Environmental	Economic	Social and cultural
• Loss of soil nutrients through wind and water erosion • Changes in composition of vegetation and loss of biodiversity as vegetation is removed • Reduction in land available for cropping and pasture • Increased sedimentation of streams because of soil erosion and sediment accumulations in reservoirs • Expansion of area under sand dunes	• Reduced income from traditional economy (pastoralism and cultivation of food crops) • Decreased availability of fuelwood, necessitating purchase of oil/kerosene • Increased dependence on food aid • Increased rural poverty	• Loss of traditional knowledge and skills • Forced migration due to food scarcity • Social tensions in reception areas for migrants

Combating desertification

There are many ways of combating desertification, which depend on the perceived causes (Table 4.7).

Section 4.3 Activities

1 Suggest a definition for the term *desertification*.
2 Outline the main natural causes of desertification.
3 Briefly explain two examples of desertification caused by people.
4 Comment on the effects of desertification.
5 To what extent is it possible to manage desertification?

Table 4.7 The strategies for preventing desertification, and their disadvantages

Cause of desertification	Strategies for prevention	Problems and drawbacks
Overgrazing	Improved stock quality: through vaccination programmes and the introduction of better breeds, yields of meat, wool, and milk can be increased without increasing the herd size. Better management: reducing herd sizes and grazing over wider areas would both reduce soil damage.	Vaccination programmes improve survival rates, leading to bigger herds. Population pressure often prevents these measures.
Overcultivation	Use of fertilisers: these can double yields of grain crops, reducing the need to open up new land for farming. New or improved crops: many new crops or new varieties of traditional crops with high-yielding and drought-resistant qualities could be introduced. Improved farming methods: use of crop rotation, irrigation and grain storage can all increase and reduce pressure on land.	Cost to farmers. Artificial fertilisers may damage the soil. Some crops need expensive fertiliser. Risk of crop failure. Some methods require expensive technology and special skills.
Deforestation	Agroforestry: combines agriculture with forestry, allowing the farmer to continue cropping while using trees for fodder, fuel and building timber. Trees, protect, shade and fertilise the soil. Social forestry: village-based tree-planting schemes involve all members of a community. Alternative fuels: oil, gas, and kerosene can be substituted for wood as sources of fuel.	Long growth time before benefits of trees are realised. Expensive irrigation and maintenance may be needed. Expensive. Special equipment may be needed.

Case Study

Desertification in China

Parts of China are among the most seriously desertified areas in the world. More than 27 per cent, or 2.5 million km², of the country comprises desert (whereas just 7 per cent of Chinese land feeds about a quarter of the world's population). China's phenomenal economic growth over the last ten years has been at a serious environmental cost. According to the China State Forestry Administration, the desert areas are still expanding by between 2460 and 10 400 km² per year. Up to 400 million people are at risk of desertification in China – the affected area could cover as much as 3.317 million km² or 34.6 per cent of the total land area. Much of it is happening on the edge of the settled area – which suggests that human activities are largely to blame.

Causes of desertification

Desertification is widely distributed in the arid, semi-arid and dry sub-humid areas of north-west China, northern China and western parts of north-east China (Figure 4.18). Much of the country is affected by a semi-permanent high-pressure belt, which causes aridity. In addition, continental areas experience intensive thunderstorms, which can cause accelerated soil erosion. Drought plagues large parts of northern China. In addition to dry weather, human activities such as livestock overgrazing, cultivation of steep slopes, rampant logging and excessive cutting of branches for firewood were at the root of the crisis.

Figure 4.18 Desertification in China

- In the Inner Mongolia Autonomous Region over 133 000 ha of rangeland has been seriously degraded by overgrazing. The density of animals now exceeds the carrying capacity of the land.
- On the loess plateau, cultivation of steep slopes is the main cause of desertification. On slopes of less than 5° the loss of topsoil per annum is about 15 tonnes/ha. In contrast, on slopes of over 25° it rises to 120–150 tonnes/ha. However, there is very little loss of soil on terraced slopes.
- Illegal collection of fuelwood and herbal medicines has removed more than one-third of vegetation in the Qaibam basin since the 1980s.

Rates and types of desertification

In China the main types of desertification include sandy desertification caused by wind erosion, land degradation by water erosion, soil salinisation, and other land degradation caused by engineering construction of residential areas, communications, and industrial activities such as coal mining and oil extraction, for example (Tables 4.8 and 4.9).

Table 4.8 Areas of land in China desertified by different processes

Types of desertification	Area (km²)	% of total
Wind erosion	379 600	44.1
Water erosion	394 000	45.7
Salinisation	69 000	8.3
Engineering construction	19 000	1.9
Total	861 600	100.0

Table 4.9 Soil degradation in China (million ha)

		Negligible	Light	Moderate	Strong	Extreme
Water erosion	Loss of topsoil	15.8	105.9	44.9	3.8	0.2
	Terrain deformation	0.5	7.9	5.9	24.0	–
	Off-site effects	0.2	0.2	0.2	–	–
Wind erosion	Loss of topsoil	1.7	65.9	2.5	+	+
	Terrain deformation	+	7.2	5.5	57.9	–
	Off-site effects	+	2.0	6.5	0.2	–
Chemical deterioration	Fertility decline	32.4	31.7	4.8	–	–
	Salinisation	0.5	6.8	2.6	–	–
	Desertification	–	+	–	–	–
Physical deterioration	Aridification	–	23.7	–	–	–
	Compaction and crusting	–	0.5	–	–	–
	Waterlogging	3.8	–	–	–	–
Total degradation	All types	55.0	251.9	72.9	86.0	0.25

Note: (–) no significant occurrence; (+) less than 0.1 but more than 0.01 million ha; for calculation of the totals (+) is equivalent to 0.05 million ha.

Sandy desertification through wind erosion

In northern China the main land degradation is sandy desertification caused by wind erosion, an area that covers about 379 600 km² and is mainly distributed in the arid and semi-arid zones where the annual rainfall is below 500 mm.

Sandy desertification in northern China has been caused mainly by irrational human economic activities, and the growth rate of desertified land increased from 1560 km²/yr during the 1950s to 2100 km²/yr between the mid-1970s to the late 1980s, and since the late 1980s has increased to 2460 km²/yr.

Desertification through water erosion

Soil loss through water erosion is the most serious land degradation in China. By a rough estimate, annual soil loss caused by water erosion has reached about 5 billion tonnes, of which about two-fifths pours into the seas.

Salinisation

About 69 000 km² of China's farmland has been salinised, mainly in the arid and semi-arid regions of north-west China and the sub-humid regions of the North China Plain.

Desertification caused by engineering construction

A new type of desertification has spread very quickly with some large-scale projects such as the development of oilfields and mining, construction of residential areas, and communications. These developments have led to increased wind and water erosion.

Some consequences of desertification

Desertification brings many adverse impacts. It causes a decrease in farmland availability, declining crop productivity, falling incomes, disruptions to communications, and may eventually cause out-migration. Desertification also causes an increase in sand storms, silting of rivers and reservoirs, and increased soil erosion.

- Desertification causes annual direct economic losses valued at US$6.5 billion.
- In the north-west, where there are the biggest problems, desertification has escalated rapidly (see above).
- Each year another 180 000 ha of farmland in China is salinised, causing productivity to fall by 25–75 per cent, and about 200 000 ha turns into desert; about 2 million ha of pasturage are degraded each year.
- Erosion claims about 5 billion tonnes of China's topsoil each year, washing away nutrients equivalent to 54 million tonnes of chemical fertiliser – twice the amount China produces in a year.
- In the 1950s dust storms affected Beijing once every seven or eight years, and only every two or three years in the 1970s. By the early 1990s, dust storms were an annual problem.
- Desertification has led to a heavy loss of land in pastoral, dry farming areas in northern China and in hilly areas in southern China.
- The government fears that encroaching sands will reach Beijing by the year 2035 as any serious drought turns farmlands into dunes in northern parts of the country, just 100 km away. These dunes are advancing at a rate of 3.5 km a year.

Possible solutions

The China National Research and Development Centre on Combating Desertification (RDCCD) was established to assist the government in implementing the UN Convention to Combat Desertification, which was established to enable China and other countries to combat desertification by developing profitable techniques and environmentally improved practices, and to meet the needs of poverty alleviation.

There are a number of effective measures that can be taken to combat desertification (Table 4.10).

Table 4.10 Methods of combating desertification

Method	Description
Fixing sand by planting	Effective; economic – source of additional fuel and forage
Fixing sand by engineering	Cover sand with straw, clay, pebbles, branches – used successfully along railways, motorways and near cities
Fixing sand using chemical methods	Create a protective layer over the sand – used in areas of high economic value such as airports and railways
Water-saving techniques	Spray irrigation, drip irrigation, prevention of seepage in channels, water transport in pipes
Integrated water management	Terraces, check dams, silt arresters

In 1978 China implemented a forest shelterbelt development programme in its northern, north-western and north-eastern regions. Sixteen million ha of plantations were established, which increased the forest cover from 5 per cent to 9 per cent. It also brought 10 per cent of the desertified land under control and protected 11 million ha of farmland. In 1991 this was extended as a nationwide campaign.

To protect Beijing the government issued a ban on the foraging and distribution of three wild plants – facai, liquorice and ephydra – grown in the country's dry western regions. It also plans to build a green belt of forest around Beijing.

Major problems in combating desertification

China is a developing country, and as economic growth exerts great pressure on its funds, the state input to combat desertification is limited. In addition:
- Public awareness needs to be raised, and education regarding desertification improved.
- Legislation is incomplete and the legal enforcement system is imperfect.
- The speed at which desertification is being tackled lags behind the rate of development.
- There is a shortage of funds to combat desertification.

Conclusions

China suffers as a result of desertification. This is the result of a combination of natural reasons and human ones. Economic growth and population pressure are placing a great strain on China's environment. Nevertheless, there have been a number of strategies to tackle desertification, and some of these have had impressive results. However, despite these successes, the rate of desertification appears to be exceeding the rate of environmental restoration. Unless China can tackle its desertification problem, there will be an increase in problems related to its overall development and standards of living.

Section 4.3 Activities

1 Outline **a** the causes and **b** the impacts of desertification in China.
2 To what extent is it possible to manage desertification in China?

Soil degradation

Soil degradation is the decline in quantity and quality of soil. It includes erosion by wind and water, biological degradation (for example the loss of humus and plant/animal life), physical degradation (loss of structure, changes in permeability), and chemical degradation (acidification, declining fertility, changes in pH), salinisation and chemical toxicity.

Causes of degradation

The universal soil loss equation (USLE) A = RKLSCP is an attempt to predict the amount of erosion that will take place in an area on the basis of certain factors that increase susceptibility to erosion (Table 4.11).

Table 4.11 Factors relating to the universal soil loss equation

Factor	Description
Ecological conditions	
Erosivity of soil R	Rainfall totals, intensity and seasonal distribution. Maximum erosivity occurs when the rain falls as high-intensity storms. If such rain is received when the land has just been ploughed or full crop cover is not yet established, erosion will be greater than when falling on a full canopy. Minimal erosion occurs when rains are gentle, and fall onto frozen soil or land with natural vegetation or a full crop cover.
Erodibility K	The susceptibility of a soil to erosion. Depends upon infiltration capacity and the structural stability of soil. Soil with a high infiltration capacity and high structural stability that allow the soil to resist the impact of rainsplash have the lowest erodibility values.
Length–slope factor LS	Slope length and steepness influence the movement and speed of water down the slope, and thus its ability to transport particles. The greater the slope, the greater the erosivity; the longer the slope, the more water is received on the surface.
Land use type	
Crop management C	Most control can be exerted over the cover and management of the soil, and this factor relates to the type of crop and cultivation practices. Established grass and forest provide the best protection against erosion, and of agricultural crops, those with the greatest foliage and thus greatest ground cover are optimal. Fallow land or crops that expose the soil for long periods after planting or harvesting offer little protection.
Soil conservation P	Soil conservation measures can reduce erosion or slow the runoff of water, such as contour ploughing and use of bunds, strips and terraces.

Source: adapted from Hugget et al., *Physical Geography – a Human Perspective*, Arnold 2004

The complexity of soil degradation means that it is hard to make a single statement about its underlying causes. Soil degradation encompasses several issues at various spatial and time scales (Figure 4.19):

- Water erosion – water erosion accounts for about 60 per cent of soil degradation. There are many types of erosion including surface-, gully-, rill- and tunnel-erosion.
- Wind erosion, especially of fine-grained loess and silt-sized materials or smaller.
- Acidification is the change in the chemical composition of the soil, which may trigger the circulation of toxic metals.
- Eutrophication (nutrient enrichment) may degrade the quality of groundwater. Over-abstraction of groundwater may lead to dry soils.
- Salt-affected soils are typically found in marine-derived sediments, coastal locations and hot arid areas where capillary action brings salts to the upper part of the soil. Soil salinity has been a major problem in Australia following the removal of vegetation for dryland farming.

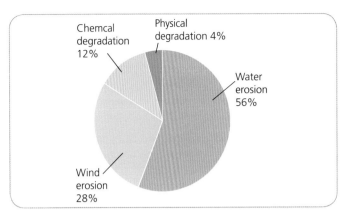

Figure 4.19 Types of soil degradation

- Atmospheric deposition of heavy metals and persistent organic pollutants may change soils so that they become less suitable to sustain the original land cover and land use.
- Climate change will probably intensify the problem. It is likely to affect hydrology and hence land use.

Climate change, higher average temperature and changing precipitation patterns may have three direct impacts on soil conditions. The higher temperatures cause higher decomposition rates of organic matter. Organic matter in soil is important as a source of nutrients and it improves moisture storage. More floods will cause more water erosion, while more droughts will cause more wind erosion.

Besides these direct effects, climate change may:
- create a need for more agricultural land to compensate for the loss of degraded land
- lead to higher yields for the major European grain crops due to the carbon dioxide fertilisation – the increase in carbon dioxide in the atmosphere leads to increased plant growth by allowing increased levels of photosynthesis.

These two indirect effects appear to balance out.

Human activities

Human activities have often led to degradation of the world's land resources (Figure 4.20 and Table 4.12). A global assessment of human-induced soil degradation has shown that damage has occurred on 15 per cent of the world's total land area (13 per cent

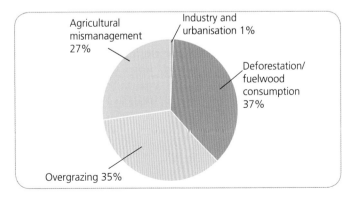

Figure 4.20 Causes of soil degradation

light and moderate, 2 per cent severe and very severe). These impacts frequently lead to a reduction in yields. Land conservation and rehabilitation are essential parts of sustainable agricultural development. While severely degraded soil is found in most regions of the world, the negative economic impact of degraded soil may be most severe in countries that are most dependent on agriculture for their income.

Table 4.12 Human activities and their impact on soil erosion

Action	Effect
Removal of woodland or ploughing established pasture	The vegetation cover is removed, roots binding the soil die and the soil is exposed to wind and water. Particularly susceptible to erosion if on slopes.
Cultivation	Exposure of bare soil surface before planting and after harvesting. Cultivation on slopes can generate large amounts of runoff and create rills and gullies.
Grazing	Overgrazing can severely reduce the vegetation cover and leave the surface vulnerable to erosion. Grouping of animals can lead to overtrampling and creation of bare patches. Dry regions are particularly susceptible to wind erosion.
Roads or tracks	They collect water due to reduced infiltration that can cause rills and gullies to form.
Mining	Exposure of the bare soil.

Managing soil degradation

Abatement strategies, such as afforestation, for combating accelerated soil erosion are lacking in many areas. To reduce the risk of soil erosion, farmers are encouraged towards more extensive management practices such as organic farming, afforestation, pasture extension, and benign crop production. Nevertheless, there is a need for policy makers and the public to intensify efforts to combat the pressures on and risks to the soil resource.

Methods to reduce or prevent erosion can be mechanical, for example physical barriers such as embankments and windbreaks, or they may focus on vegetation cover and soil husbandry. Overland flow of water can be reduced by increasing infiltration.

Mechanical methods include building bunds, terracing and contour ploughing, and planting shelterbelts (trees or hedgerows). The key is to prevent or slow the movement of rainwater downslope. Contour ploughing takes advantage of the ridges formed at right-angles to the slope which act to prevent or slow the downward accretion of soil and water. On steep slopes and those with heavy rainfall, such as areas in South East Asia that experience the monsoon, contour ploughing is insufficient so terracing is practised. The slope is broken up into a series of level steps, with bunds (raised levees) at the edge. The use of terracing allows areas to be cultivated that would not otherwise be suitable. In areas where wind erosion is a problem, shelterbelts of trees or hedgerows are used. The trees act as a barrier to the wind and disturb its flow. Wind speed is reduced which therefore reduces its ability to disturb the topsoil and erode particles.

Preventing erosion by different cropping techniques largely focuses on:

- maintaining a crop cover for as long as possible
- keeping in place the stubble and root structure of the crop after harvesting
- planting a grass crop.

A grass crop maintains the action of the roots in binding the soil, minimising the action of wind and rain on a bare soil surface. Increased organic content allows the soil to hold more water, thus preventing aerial erosion, and stabilising the soil structure. In addition, care is taken over the use of heavy machinery on wet soils and ploughing on soils sensitive to erosion, to prevent damage to the soil structure.

There are three main approaches in the management of salt- and chemical-affected soils:

- flush the soil and leach the salt away
- apply chemicals, for example gypsum (calcium sulphate), to replace the sodium ions on the clay and colloids with calcium ones
- reduce evaporation losses in order to limit the upward movement of water in the soil.

Soil degradation is a complex issue. It is caused by the interaction of physical forces and human activities. Its impact is increasing and it is having a negative effect on food production. Some areas are more badly affected than others but in a globalised world the impacts are felt worldwide. The methods of dealing with soil degradation depend on the cause of the problem, but also on the resources available to the host country. Degradation is a problem that is not going to go away and is likely to increase over the next decades as population continues to grow, and people use increasingly marginal areas.

Section 4.3 Activities

1 Explain the meaning of the term *soil degradation*.

2 Outline the natural causes of soil degradation.

3 a Comment on the human causes of soil degradation.
   b To what extent is it possible to manage soil degradation?

4 Study Table 4.13, which shows annual soil losses from a small catchment in the Lake Victoria basin.
   a Describe how the range of soil loss varies with the type of land cover.
   b Suggest reasons for the patterns you have identified in a.

Table 4.13 Annual soil losses from a small catchment in the Lake Victoria basin

Land use	Land cover (%)	Range of soil loss (tonnes/ha/yr)
Annual cropland	6	65–93
Rangeland	15	42–68
Bananas/Coffee	63	36–47
Bananas	6	22–32
Forest	1	0
Papyrus marsh	9	0

4.4 Sustainable management of arid and semi-arid environments

Sustainable management is management that meets the needs of the present generation without compromising the ability of future generations to meet their own needs. It is a process by which human potential (quality of life) is improved and the environment (resource base) is used and managed to supply humanity on a long-term basis.

Nearly three-quarters of the world's drylands are degraded and it has been estimated that desertification costs an estimated $42 million each year. Are there sustainable options for the world's drylands?

Changing land use trends

Case Study

Game farming in the Eastern Cape province of South Africa

A shift from pastoralism to game farming has been identified in the Eastern Cape province of South Africa since the 1980s (Figure 4.21). Examples include Bushbuck Ridge Game Farm, AddoAfrique Estate, and Kichaka Lodge. In some cases this change has been made by private landowners to diversify their operations. In other cases, private landowners have removed all stock and replaced it with game. In a survey of the Eastern Cape region of South Africa, it was found that 2.5 per cent of the study area had converted entirely from stock to game farming. A total of 41 game species was recorded on the 63 game farms surveyed. Most farmers expressed a positive attitude towards game farming and are trying to implement conservation measures. The main activity for which game is utilised is hunting, both recreational and trophy hunting. The foreign ecotourist and the hunting market have been strong driving forces behind the introduction of **extra-limital** (non-native) species to the region.

This change in land use has drawn the attention of scientists worldwide, and specifically with reference to desertification of rangelands. Desertification currently affects about one-sixth of the world's population and 70 per cent of all drylands, which amounts to 3.6 billion ha. Widespread poverty is one of the key impacts of desertification.

In South Africa, the thicket vegetation of the Eastern Cape has been recognised as being particularly vulnerable to degradation, due mainly to years of overgrazing. Over 95 per cent of this

Figure 4.21 Location of the Eastern Cape province of South Africa

vegetation is under threat from overgrazing by domestic stock, bush clearing for agriculture and urban development, coastal resort development and invasion by alien vegetation.

The average game farm size is 4496 ha. Most of the game farms are concentrated in the south and central regions of the Eastern Cape. Land use changes first started to occur in the 1970s, and were characterised by two basic trends that included either the landowners themselves changing from being stock farmers to game farmers, or investors purchasing stock farms and financing their conversion to game farms.

Utilising game has provided an important secondary income to most mixed farmers. The impetus behind the growing game industry can be attributed to a number of socio-political, economic and ecological motivations. For example:

- Recently changed labour legislation stipulates increased wages for workers on farms. This has made landowners regard game farming as an alternative to stock farming, as it is considered to be potentially less labour-intensive than traditional stock farming;
- Increased stock theft, especially of small domestic stock, has rendered stock farming economically less viable.
- Vermin such as the jackal and caracal sometimes come from adjacent game farms' statutory reserves and this has resulted in increased stock losses.
- Decades of overgrazing have led to rangeland degradation, thereby reducing livestock production. By (re)introducing (indigenous) game species that are better adapted to their natural environment, periodic droughts can be survived both economically and demographically.
- Game is considered to contribute, in the long term, to veld restoration (rather than its degradation).
- There is good potential for foreign exchange earnings from trophy hunting and tourism.

A total of 41 game species were recorded on the 63 farms surveyed. The high diversity that was recorded was not, however, found on any single farm. Rather, 11–15 species occurred on a third of the game farms, with only five game farmers maintaining more than 20 species.

Game farming has been described as a potential ecologically sustainable form of land use, but the introduction of extra-limital species may threaten this state. In order to guarantee tourist satisfaction, farmers have found it necessary to erect game-proof fences around their farms with the purpose of introducing 'hunting' or 'tourist' species, whether indigenous or extra-limital. Kudu and bushbuck, both indigenous to thicket vegetation, are among the most desired hunting species in the Eastern Cape. Promotion of these animals as hunting species may promote ecologically sound farming practices, without the introduction of extra-limital species.

There is also the ecological risk of allowing certain species to hybridise by keeping such species in the same fenced area. Some farmers in the survey had both blue and black wildebeest species on their property, and some had both Blesbok and Bontebok antelope; both pairs of species have the ability to hybridise.

Figure 4.22 Gully erosion due to overgrazing

Figure 4.23 Concentration of sheep at a waterhole – note the irrigation scheme in the background

Section 4.4 Activities

1 Define sustainable development.

2 To what extent is game farming a form of sustainable development? Justify your views.

Case Study

The establishment of drought-resistant fodder in the Eastern Cape

Pastureland in the Eastern Cape is especially fragile due to drought and overgrazing (Figures 4.22 and 4.23). In the former homelands, Ciskei and Transkei, there are additional problems of population pressure and, sometimes, the absence of secure land ownership policies. During periods of prolonged drought, levels of cattle, sheep and goats decrease significantly. However, trying to decrease herd size has proved unpopular and unsuccessful. An alternative is to produce drought-resistant fodder crops such as the American aloe and the prickly pear, saltbrush and the indigenous gwanish.

The American aloe (Figure 4.24) has traditionally been used for fencing, for kraals (animal compounds) and for soil conservation, but has also been used as a fodder in times of drought. It has a number of advantages:

- it requires little moisture
- it is not attacked by any insects
- although low in protein, it raises milk production in cows
- it can be used for soil conservation

Figure 4.24 American aloe

- after 10 years it produces a pole that can be used for fencing or building
- it can act as a windbreak
- the juice of the aloe is used in the production of tequila.

Saltbrush provides protein-rich fodder which is eaten by sheep and goats. Goats, in particular, thrive on saltbrush. It requires less than half the water need by other crops such as lucerne, and once established it requires no irrigation. It remains green throughout the year and therefore can provide all-year fodder. However, it is difficult to propagate and needs high-quality management.

The spineless cactus or prickly pear (Figure 4.25) features prominently in the agriculture of many countries, such as Mexico, Peru and Tunisia, where it is used as fodder and as a fruit crop for 2–3 months each year. This plant is becoming more widespread in the Eastern Cape. Two varieties are common: one, insect-resistant, is used as fodder in times of drought, while the other, which needs to be sprayed to reduce insect damage, yields high-quality fruit. The fruit is sold at prices comparable with apples and oranges. Pruning is needed annually. This provides up to 100 tonnes of fodder/ha/yr.

Figure 4.25 Prickly pear

In the former Ciskei region of the Eastern Cape, drought in the 1980s prompted the government to embark on a series of trials with prickly pear, saltbrush and American aloe in order to create more fodder. One of the main advantages of the prickly pear is its low water requirements. This makes it very suitable to the region where rainfall is low and unreliable. Although there are intensive irrigation schemes in the region, such as at Keiskammahoek, these are expensive and are inappropriate to the area and to the local people.

Although prickly pear is mainly used as a fodder and fruit crop, it is also used for the production of carminic acid for the cochineal dye industry and as a means of soil conservation. Nevertheless, prickly pear has been described by some development planners as a 'weed, the plant of the poor, a flag of misery … inconsistent with progress'.

Section 4.4 Activities

1 Outline the advantages of the American aloe plant.

2 Comment on the advantages and disadvantages of using the prickly pear.

Case Study

Essential oils in the Eastern Cape

About 65 per cent of the world production of essential oils is from LEDCs such as India, China, Brazil, Indonesia, Mexico, Egypt and Morocco. However the USA is also a major producer of essential oils such as peppermint and other mints. The South African essential oils industry has only recently emerged in this area. Currently the South African essential oils industry exports mainly to MEDCs in Europe (49 per cent), the USA (24 per cent) and Japan (4.5 per cent). The most significant essential oils produced by South Africa are eucalyptus, citrus, geranium and buchu.

Globally, the essential oils industry – valued at around $10 billion – is enjoying huge expansion. Opportunities include increasing production of existing products, and extending the range of crops grown. Developing the essential oils industry in South Africa would achieve much-needed agricultural and agri-processing diversification in the province.

Currently, the South African essential oils industry comprises about 100 small commercial producers, of which fewer than 20 per cent are regular producers.

Several factors make South Africa an attractive essential oils market:

- Much of the demand is in the northern hemisphere and seasonal effects make southern hemisphere suppliers globally attractive.
- South Africa traditionally has strong trade links with Europe, as a major importer of fragrance materials.
- South Africa is being established as a world-class agricultural producer in a wide range of products.

The Eastern Cape is set to become one of the main contributors to South Africa's burgeoning essential oils industry, with 10 government-sponsored trial sites currently in development throughout the province. Six of these form part of the Essential Oil Project of Hogsback, where approximately 8 ha of communal land are being used. A project at Keiskammahoek has been operational since 2006. These trials form part of a strategy to develop a number of essential oil clusters in the Eastern Cape.

The production of essential oils holds considerable potential as a form of sustainable agricultural development in the former Ciskei region of the Eastern Cape. Not only are the raw materials already here but it is a labour-intensive industry and would employ a large number of currently unemployed and underemployed people.

The essential oils industry has a number of advantages:

- It is a new or additional source of income for many people.
- It is labour-intensive and local in nature.
- Many plants are already known and used by local people as medicines, and they are therefore culturally acceptable (Figure 4.26).
- In their natural state the plants are not very palatable nor of great value and will not therefore be stolen.
- Many species are looked upon as weeds. Removing these regularly improves grazing potential as well as supplying raw materials for the essential oils industry.

Figure 4.26 A herbalist's preparation table

Some species such as geranium, peppermint and sage require too much land, labour and water to be very successful. Wild als (*Artemesia afra*) is an indigenous mountainous shrub, used for the treatment of colds. Its oil has a strong medicinal fragrance and is used in deodorants and soaps. Double cropping in summer when the plant is still growing and in autumn at the end of the growing season yields the best results. Demand for *Artemisia* has not outstripped the supply of naturally growing material but it is increasingly being cultivated as a second crop. It requires minimal input in terms of planting, tillage and pest control, and it is relatively easy to establish and manage. Moreover, it can stabilise many of the maize fields and slopes where soil erosion is a problem. The local people are very enthusiastic about growing it, especially when they are given appropriate economic incentives.

Khakibush or *Tagetes* is an aromatic. In the former Ciskei area it is a common weed in most maize fields. Oil of tagetes is an established essential oil, although its market is limited. Local people are again quite enthusiastic about collecting khakibush if the incentives are there. Harvesting takes place over a period of up to three months and provides a great deal of extra employment, as well as eradicating a weed. At present the supply of khakibush and those in the maize fields is sufficient to meet demand. An increase in demand might lead to the establishment of *Tagetes* as secondary crop in maize fields – not just as a 'weed'.

Section 4.4 Activities

1 Suggest why the essential oils industry has developed in the Eastern Cape province.

2 To what extent could the essential oils industry be considered a form of sustainable development?

1 Production, location and change

1.1 Agricultural systems and food production

Factors affecting agricultural land use

A wide range of factors combine to influence agricultural land use and practices on farms. These can be placed under the general headings of physical, economic, political and social/cultural factors.

Physical factors

North America, for example, has many different physical environments. This allows a wide variety of crops to be grown and livestock kept. New technology and high levels of investment have steadily extended farming into more difficult environments. Irrigation has enabled farming to flourish in the arid west, while new varieties of wheat have pushed production northward in Canada. However, the physical environment remains a big influence on farming. There are certain things that technology and investment can do little to alter. So relief, climate and soils set broad limits as to what can be produced. This leaves the farmer with some choices, even in difficult environments. The farmer's decisions are then influenced by economic, political and social/cultural factors.

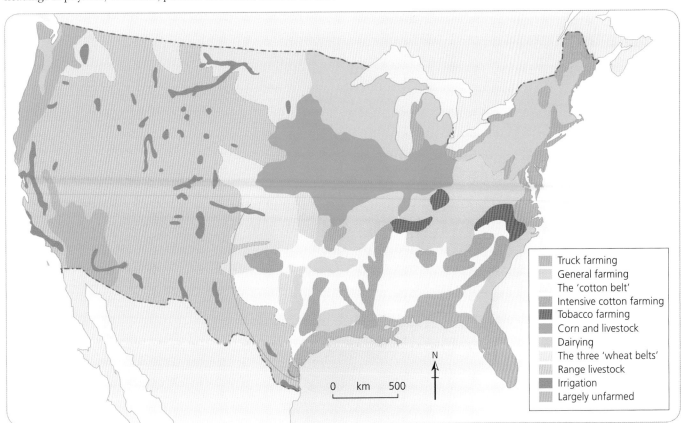

Legend:
- Truck farming
- General farming
- The 'cotton belt'
- Intensive cotton farming
- Tobacco farming
- Corn and livestock
- Dairying
- The three 'wheat belts'
- Range livestock
- Irrigation
- Largely unfarmed

0   km   500

N

Figure 1.1 Agricultural regions of the USA

Figure 1.1 shows the agricultural regions of the USA. Look at relief and climate maps of the USA in an atlas and see how the agricultural regions vary according to different physical conditions. Temperature is a critical factor in crop growth as each type of crop requires a minimum growing temperature and a minimum length of growing season. Latitude, altitude and distance from the sea are the major influences on temperature. Precipitation is equally important – not just the annual total but also the way it is distributed throughout the year. Long, steady periods of rainfall to infiltrate into the soil are best, making water available for crop growth. In contrast, short heavy downpours can result in rapid surface runoff, leaving less water available for crop growth and soil erosion.

Soil type and fertility have a huge impact on agricultural productivity. Often, areas that have never been cleared for farming were ignored because soil fertility was poor or was perceived to be poor. In some regions wind can have a serious impact on farming, for example causing bush fires in some states such as California. Locally, aspect and the angle of slope may also be important factors in deciding how the land is used.

Cotton, for example, needs a frost-free period of at least 200 days. Rainfall should be over 625 mm a year with not more than 250 mm in the autumn harvest season. Cotton production is now highly mechanised. Irrigation has allowed cotton to flourish in the drier western states of California, New Mexico and Texas. In contrast, the area under cotton has fallen considerably in the south. A crop pest called the cotton boll weevil, which caused great destruction to cotton crops in the past, has been a big factor in the diversification of agriculture in the southern states.

In contrast, corn is grown further north than cotton. Corn needs a growing season of at least 130 days. For the crop to ripen properly, summer temperatures of 21 °C are needed, with warm nights. Precipitation should be over 500 mm with at least 200 mm in the three summer months.

In Canada, the USA's northern neighbour, farming is severely restricted by climate. Less than 8 per cent of the total area of the country is farmed. Seventy per cent of Canada lies north of the thermal limit for crop growth and most farms are within 500 km of the main border (apart from Alaska) with the USA. Other high-latitude countries such as Russia also suffer considerable climatic restrictions on agriculture.

Water is vital for agriculture. **Irrigation** is an important factor in farming not just in North America, but in many other parts of the world as well. Figure 1.2 shows the divide by world region between **rainfed water** for crop use and irrigation water. The figures in the circles refer to the total amount of rainfed water used. Here the highest totals are for East Asia, South Asia, and Sub-Saharan Africa. The highest proportion of irrigation water use is in the Middle East and North Africa, and South Asia. Irrigated farming accounts for 70 per cent of global annual water consumption. This rises to over 90 per cent in some countries such as India. Table 1.1 compares the main types of irrigation. This is an example of the ladder of agricultural technology, with surface irrigation being the most traditional method and sub-surface (drip) irrigation the most advanced technique.

More than half of production from rainfed areas

More than 75% of production from rainfed areas

More than half of production from irrigated areas

More than 75% of production from irrigated areas

Note: Production refers to gross natural production. The pie charts show total crop water evapotranspiration in km³ by region

Global total: 7130 km³
(80% from green water, 20% from blue water)

Blue water

Green water

Figure 1.2 World distribution of rainfed and irrigation water for crop use

Figure 1.3 Goats feeding from a bowl because the ground is frozen, in cold central Asia

Table 1.1 Main types of irrigation

	Efficiency (%)
Surface – used in over 80% of irrigated fields worldwide	
Furrow Traditional method; cheap to install; labour-intensive; high water losses; susceptible to erosion and salinisation	20–60
Basin Cheap to install and run; needs a lot of water; susceptible to salinisation and waterlogging	50–75
Aerial (using sprinklers) – used in 10–15% of irrigation worldwide	
Costly to install and run; low-pressure sprinklers preferable	60–80
Sub-surface ('drip') – used in 1% of irrigation worldwide	
High capital costs; sophisticated monitoring; very efficient	75–95

Source: 'The Water Crisis: A Matter of Life and Death', *Understanding Global Issues*, p7

Figure 1.4 A food market in Morocco

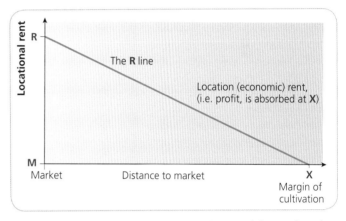

Figure 1.5 The relationship between economic rent and distance from the market

Economic factors and agricultural technology

Economic factors include transport, markets, capital and technology. The role of government is a factor here too, but this is considered in the next section, 'Political factors'.

The costs of growing different crops and keeping different livestock vary. The market prices for agricultural products also vary and can change from year to year. The necessary investment in buildings and machinery can mean that some changes in farming activities are very expensive. These will be more difficult to achieve than other, cheaper changes. Thus it is not always easy for farmers to react quickly to changes in consumer demand.

In most countries there has been a trend towards fewer but larger farms. Large farms allow **economies of scale** to operate, which reduce the unit costs of production. As more large farms are created, small farms find it increasingly difficult to compete and make a profit. Selling to a larger neighbouring farm may be the only economic solution. The EU is an example of a region where average farm size varies significantly. Those countries with

a large average farm size have more efficient agricultural sectors than countries with a small average farm size.

Distance from markets has always been an important influence on agricultural practices. Heinrich von Thünen published a major theoretical work on this topic in 1826. He was mainly concerned with the relationships between three variables:

- distance of farms from the market
- the price received by farmers for their products
- **economic rent** (the profit from a unit of land).

Von Thünen argued that the price a farmer obtained for a unit of his product was equal to its price at market less the cost of transporting it to the market. Thus the nearer a farmer was to the market the greater his returns from the sale of his produce (Figure 1.4). The logic of this is that land closest to the market would be the most intensively farmed land with farming intensity decreasing with increasing distance from the market. At a certain distance from the market, transport costs would be so high that they would equal the profit from farming and therefore make cultivation illogical (Figure 1.5). Farmers setting out to maximise their profits would choose that activity or combination of farming activities that would give the best economic rent (profit). Although this theory is almost two centuries old, it still holds a basic logic.

Agricultural technology is the application of techniques to control the growth and harvesting of animal and vegetable products. The development and application of agricultural technology requires investment and thus it is an economic factor. Advances in agricultural technology can be traced back to the Neolithic Revolution. Table 1.2 shows the last two sections of a timeline of agricultural advance published in Wikipedia (the table only shows major and selected advances and thus omits a whole range of smaller improvements).

Table 1.2 Timeline of agricultural technology

British Agricultural Revolution
1700 – British Agricultural Revolution begins in the UK
1809 – French confectioner Nicolas Appert invents canning
1837 – John Deere invents steel plough
1863 – International 'Corn Show' in Paris with corn varieties from different countries
1866 – George Mendel publishes his paper describing Mendelian inheritance
1871 – Louis Pasteur invents pasteurisation
1895 – Refrigeration introduced in the USA for domestic food preservation, and in the UK for commercial food preservation 1930 – First use of aerial photos in earth sciences and agriculture
Green Revolution
1944 – Green Revolution begins in Mexico
2000 – Genetically modified plants cultivated around the world
2005 – Lasers used to replace stickers by writing on food to 'track and trace' and identify individual pieces of fresh fruit

Source: Wikipedia

The status of a country's agricultural technology is vital for its food security and other aspects of quality of life. An important form of aid is the transfer of agricultural technology from more advanced to less advanced nations (Figure 1.6). China is now playing a major role in this process. Eighty per cent of the population in rural Sub-Saharan Africa is reliant on agriculture as a source of income and employment. Yet agricultural productivity has stagnated. The agricultural sector is mostly made up of small-scale farms. But small farmers face serious barriers to their development:

- They have limited access to new technologies, such as new crop varieties and better methods of storage.
- They have difficulty accessing finance and suffer from a lack of investment in areas such as roads, agricultural equipment and silos.
- They lack support from areas such as market boards and advisory services.
- They contend with market constraints such as an inability to produce the right amount or quality for customers, price variations, and inadequate storage systems.

TECA is an FAO (Food and Agriculture Organization of the United Nations) initiative which aims at improving access to information and knowledge sharing about proven technologies in order to enhance their adoption in agriculture, livestock, fisheries and forestry thus addressing food security, climate change, poverty alleviation and sustainable development.

Agro-industrialisation, or industrial agriculture, is the form of modern farming that refers to the industrialised production of livestock, poultry, fish and crops. This type of large-scale, **capital intensive farming** originally developed in Europe and North America and then spread to other MEDCs. It has been spreading rapidly in many LEDCs since the beginning of the **Green Revolution**. Industrial agriculture is heavily dependent on oil for every stage of its operation. The most obvious examples are fuelling farm machinery, transporting produce, and producing fertilisers and other farm inputs. Table 1.3 shows the general characteristics of agro-industrialisation. Not all farms and

CHINA AGREES TO HELP IMPROVE AFRICAN FOOD PRODUCTION – KENYA

First published Thursday 12 August 2010, 03:10pm ©2010 Dow Jones

Nairobi – (Dow Jones) – China has agreed to transfer agricultural technology to Africa to enable the continent to boost production and thereby guarantee world food security, the Kenyan vice president press office said in a statement Thursday. The Beijing declaration for the massive agricultural technology transfer came as the China-Africa Agricultural Forum, in which vice president Kalonzo Musyoka represented Kenya, drew to a close Thursday.

Reading the declaration, the Chinese deputy Prime Minister Hui Liangyu said global food security should be the number one priority of governments, given that acute food shortages were bound to lead to food crises and hence social and political instability. 'China is the largest developing economy able to feed 20% of the world's population on the proceeds of 9% of the planet's arable land. If we partner with Africa with a much higher percentage of arable land yet contains most

of the developing countries we should be able to guarantee international food security,' the statement quoted Hui as saying.

The declaration called for a leap in Africa's agricultural output by transforming its rural agriculture through an infusion of Chinese agricultural characteristics, the statement said.

This will involve educating rural farmers, setting up modern farming demonstration centers, using better quality seeds, and new technology in appropriate faming machinery as well as soil improvement techniques, said the statement.

– By George Mwangi, contributing to Dow Jones Newswires; +254 735 781853; gmwangio@gmail.com
Copyright © Automated Trader Ltd. 2010
Fig: Agricultural Technology

Figure 1.6 China agrees to help improve African food production regions involved in agro-industrialisation will display all these characteristics – for example, intensive market gardening units may be relatively small but the capital inputs are extremely high.

Table 1.3 The characteristics of agro-industrialisation

- Very large farms
- Concentration on one (monoculture) or a small number of farm products
- A high level of mechanisation
- Low labour input per unit of production
- Heavy usage of fertilisers, pesticides and herbicides
- Sophisticated ICT management systems
- Highly qualified managers
- Often owned by large agribusiness companies
- Often vertically integrated with food processing and retailing

Regions where agro-industrialisation is clearly evident on a large scale include:

- the Canadian Prairies
- the corn and wheat belts in the USA
- the Paris basin (Figure 1.7)
- East Anglia in the UK
- the Russian steppes
- the Pampas in Argentina
- Mato Grosso in Brazil
- the Murray-Darling basin in Australia.

Figure 1.7 Large-scale maize cultivation in the Paris basin, France

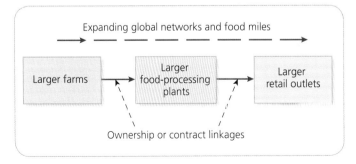

Figure 1.8 Agro-industrialisation – increasing vertical integration

Agro-industrialisation is a consequence of the globalisation of agriculture, the profit ambitions of large agribusiness companies and the drive for cheaper food production. Over the last half-century every stage in the food industry has changed in the attempt to make it more efficient (in an economic sense). Vertical integration has become an increasingly important process with extended linkages between the different stages of the food industry (Figure 1.8).

Political factors

The influence of government on farming has steadily increased in many countries. For example, in the USA the main sectors of federal farm policy over the past half-century have been the following:

- **Price support loans:** loans that tide farmers over until they sell their produce. The government sets a price for each farm product it is willing to support. If the farmer cannot sell the product for at least this price, they can keep the loan and let the government keep the crop that secured it.
- **Production controls:** these limit how much a farmer can produce of surplus crops. Farmers lose price-support loans and other benefits if they don't comply.
- **Income supplements:** these are cash payments to farmers for major crops in years when market prices fail to reach certain levels.

The decisions made by individual farmers are therefore heavily influenced by government policies such as those listed above. However, in centrally planned economies the state has far more control. This was the case for many years in the former Soviet Union and China. Although much has changed in both of these countries in recent decades, the influence of government on farming still remains stronger than in most other parts of the world.

An agricultural policy can cover more than one country, as evidenced by the EU's Common Agricultural Policy. The CAP is a set of rules and regulations governing agricultural activities in the EU. The need for Europe to ensure a reliable and adequate supply of food in the post-Second World War period was one of the main reasons for its introduction in 1960. It is expensive to run: each year every EU taxpayer contributes about £80 to the CAP.

Social/cultural factors

What a particular farm and neighbouring farms have produced in the past can be a significant influence on current farming practices. There is a tendency for farmers to stay with what they know best, and often a sense of responsibility from one generation to the next to maintain a family farming tradition. Tradition matters more in some farming regions than others.

A traditional rainforest system

Shifting cultivation is a traditional farming system that developed a long time ago in tropical rainforests. An area of forest is cleared to create a small plot of land which is cultivated until the soil became exhausted. The plot is then abandoned and a new area cleared. Frequently the cultivators work in a circular pattern, returning to previously used land once the natural fertility of the soil has been renewed. Shifting cultivation is also known as 'slash and burn' and by various local names such as *chitimene* in Central Africa.

In the Amazon rainforest shifting cultivation has been practised for thousands of years by groups of Amerindians who initially had no contact with the outside world. It is likely that there are some isolated groups where this situation still exists, but for most Amerindians there are now varying degrees of contact with mainstream Brazilian society. As a result there has been a gradual blending of modern ideas with traditional practices.

Legal rights and land tenure

Land tenure means the way in which land is or can be owned. In the past, inheritance laws had a huge impact on the average size of farms. In some countries it has been the custom on the death of a farmer to divide the land equally between all his sons, but rarely between daughters. Also dowry customs may include the giving of land with a daughter on marriage. The reduction in the size of farms by these processes often reduced them to operating at only a subsistence level.

Women face widespread discrimination around the world with regard to land and property. The agrarian reforms implemented in many countries from the 1950s and through the 1970s were 'gender blind'. They were often based on the assumption that all household members would benefit equally, when this was simply not the case. For example, many women in LEDCs lose their homes, inheritance and possessions and sometimes even their children when their partners die. This may force women to adopt employment practices that increase their chances of contracting HIV.

In most societies women have very unequal access to, and control over, rural land and associated resources. The UN's Food and Agriculture Organization has stated that 'denying large segments of rural society equitable access to land and to the benefits of land tenure regularisation creates unanticipated costs and is a major contributing factor to extreme poverty, dependence and rural migration leading to land abandonment, social instability and many other negative conditions because of the unforeseen externalities that arise.' It is now generally accepted that societies with well-recognised property rights are also the ones that thrive best economically and socially.

Section 1.1 Activities

1 List the main physical factors that can influence farming.

2 Look at Figure 1.1. Suggest why almost all of the USA's range livestock and irrigated farming is in the west.

3 Describe and attempt to explain the variations by world region shown in Figure 1.2.

4 Summarise the information presented in Table 1.1.

5 Describe and explain the relationship shown in Figure 1.5.

6 Discuss the characteristics of agro-industrialisation.

7 Briefly state the importance of advances in agricultural technology.

8 Give an example of how one social/cultural factor can affect farming.

Agricultural systems

Individual farms and general types of farming can be seen to operate as a **system**. A farm requires a range of inputs such as labour and energy so that the processes (throughputs) that take place on the farm can be carried out. The aim is to produce the best possible outputs, such as milk, eggs, meat and crops. A profit will only be made if the income from selling the outputs is greater than expenditure on the inputs and processes. Figure 1.9 illustrates the agricultural system. It shows how physical, cultural, economic and behavioural factors form the inputs. Decision-making at different scales from the individual farmer to governments and

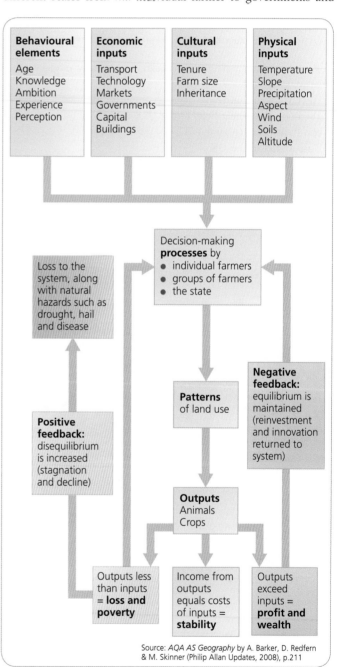

Source: *AQA AS Geography* by A. Barker, D. Redfern & M. Skinner (Philip Allan Updates, 2008), p.211

Figure 1.9 The agricultural system

international organisations such as the EU influence the processes. The nature and efficiency of the processes dictates the range, scale and quality of the outputs. Agricultural systems are dynamic human systems which change as farmers attempt to react to a range of physical and human factors.

Different types of agricultural system can be found within individual countries and around the world. The most basic distinctions are between:

- arable, pastoral and mixed farming
- subsistence and commercial farming
- extensive and intensive farming
- organic and non-organic farming.

Arable farms cultivate crops and are not involved with livestock. An arable farm may concentrate on one crop such as wheat or may grow a range of different crops. The crops grown on an arable farm may change over time. For example, if the market price of potatoes increases, more farmers will be attracted to grow this crop. **Pastoral farming** involves keeping livestock such as dairy cattle, beef cattle, sheep and pigs. **Mixed farming** involves cultivating crops and keeping livestock together on a farm.

Subsistence and commercial farming

Subsistence farming is the most basic form of agriculture where the produce is consumed entirely or mainly by the family who work the land or tend the livestock. If a small surplus is produced it may be sold or traded. Examples of subsistence farming are shifting cultivation and nomadic pastoralism. Subsistence farming is generally small-scale and labour-intensive with little or no technological input.

In contrast, the objective of **commercial farming** is to sell everything that the farm produces. The aim is to maximise yields in order to achieve the highest profits possible. Commercial farming can vary from small-scale to very large-scale (Figure 1.10).

Figure 1.10 Maize farming in Brazil

Extensive and intensive farming

Extensive farming is where a relatively small amount of agricultural produce is obtained per hectare of land, so such farms tend to cover large areas. Inputs per unit of land are low. Extensive farming can be both arable and pastoral in nature. In contrast, **intensive farming** is characterised by high inputs per unit of land to achieve high yields per hectare. Examples of intensive farming include market gardening, dairy farming and horticulture. Intensive farms tend to be relatively small in terms of land area.

Organic farming

Organic farmers do not use manufactured chemicals and so this type of farming is practised without chemical fertilisers, pesticides, insecticides or herbicides. Instead, animal and green manures are used, along with mineral fertilisers such as fish and bone meal. Organic farming therefore requires a higher input of labour than mainstream farming. Weeding is a major task with this type of farming. Organic farming is less likely to result in soil erosion and is less harmful to the environment in general. For example, there will be no nitrate runoff into streams and much less harm to wildlife.

Organic farming tends not to produce the 'perfect' potato, tomato or carrot. However, because of the increasing popularity of organic produce it commands a substantially higher price than mainstream farm produce.

Section 1.1 Activities

1 Describe the inputs, processes and outputs for the agricultural system shown in Figure 1.9.

2 a Explain the difference between arable and pastoral farming.
  b What is mixed farming?

3 Examine the differences between **a** commercial and subsistence farming and **b** intensive and extensive farming.

4 Describe the characteristics of organic farming.

Case Study

A pastoral system: sheep farming in Australia

Characteristics and location

Sheep farming in Australia occupies an area of about 85 million hectares, making it one of Australia's major land uses. It is a classic example of extensive farming which can be seen to operate clearly as a system. The main physical input is the extensive use of natural open ranges, which are often fragile in nature. Australia's sheep farms are located predominantly in inland and semi-arid areas. Human inputs are low compared with most other types of agriculture, with very low use of labour and capital per hectare. The main processes are grazing, lambing, dipping and shearing. The outputs are lambs, sheep, wool and sheep skins.

Australia is the world's leading sheep-producing country with a total of about 120 million sheep. As well as being the largest wool producer and exporter, Australia is also the largest exporter of live sheep and a major exporter of lamb and mutton. The sheep and wool industry is an important sector of Australia's economy.

Sheep are raised throughout southern Australia in areas of moderate to high rainfall and in the drier areas of New South Wales and Queensland. Seventy-five per cent of the country's sheep are Merinos which produce very high quality wool for clothing. Merino sheep are able to survive in harsh environments and yet produce heavy fleeces. Sixteen per cent of Australia's sheep are bred for meat production and are a mixture of breeds such as Border Leicester and Dorset. The remaining 9 per cent are a mixture of Merino and cross-bred sheep used for wool and meat production. There are about 60 000 sheep farms in Australia overall, carrying from a few hundred sheep to over 100 000 animals.

Sheep and wool production occurs in three geographical zones (Figure 1.11):
- high rainfall coastal zone
- wheat/sheep intermediate zone
- pastoral interior zone.

About a quarter of all sheep are farmed in the pastoral zone (Figure 1.12). Sheep farming in Australia in general is extensive in nature but this type of agriculture is at its most extensive in the pastoral zone, which is the arid and semi-arid inland area. Here, summer temperatures are high, rainfall is low and the area is prone to drought. Because of the lack of grass in this inhospitable environment, sheep are often left to eat saltbush and bluebush. In the pastoral zone the density of sheep per hectare is extremely low due to the poor quality of forage. The overall farming input in terms of labour, capital, energy and other inputs is also very low – it is in fact the lowest input per hectare of farmland in the country. Not surprisingly, farms can be extremely large.

In the coastal and intermediate zones the best land is reserved for arable farming, dairy and beef cattle and market gardening. Sheep are frequently kept on the more marginal areas, for example on higher and colder land in the New South Wales highlands where more profitable types of farming are not viable.

About two-thirds of Australia's sheep are on farms that support more than 2000 animals. The smallest sheep farms are generally those on the better-quality land, where it is possible to keep many more animals per hectare than in the pastoral zone.

Farming issues

The main issues in Australian sheep farming areas are:
- weed infestation, which is difficult to control on very large extensive farms that yield relatively small profits per hectare
- destruction of wildlife habitats due to sheep grazing, particularly in marginal areas
- the occurrence of periodic droughts which make farming even more difficult in low-rainfall areas
- soil loss from wind erosion and loss of soil structure – in some areas this is transforming traditional 'mainstream' farming areas into marginal lands
- animal welfare, particularly in the most inhospitable environments where the low human input means that individual animals may not be seen for long periods
- increasing concern about the shortage of experienced sheep shearers.

Regarding the last point, many shearers have left the industry because of poor working conditions and the attraction of better-paid jobs in the mining industry and elsewhere. The number of experienced shearers fell by about a quarter between 2003 and 2006. A good shearer can shear up to 200 sheep in one day.

Sheep farming in Australia is a major user of land resources in a generally fragile landscape. Changes in farming systems are required in some locations to address the issues facing the industry. Failure to do so will result in the progressive decline in utility of the resource base for the sheep and wool industry.

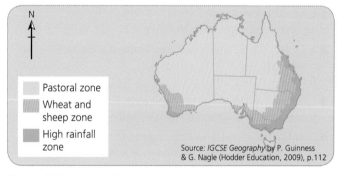

Pastoral zone

Wheat and sheep zone

High rainfall zone

Source: *IGCSE Geography* by P. Guinness & G. Nagle (Hodder Education, 2009), p.112

Figure 1.11 Australia's three geographical zones

Figure 1.12 Sheep farm in Australia's pastoral zone

Section 1.1 Activities

1 Why is sheep farming in Australia considered to be 'extensive farming'?

2 Describe the three geographical zones in which sheep are kept.

3 Briefly discuss the main issues affecting sheep farming in Australia today.

Case Study

An arable system: intensive rice production in the Lower Ganges valley

Location

An important area of intensive subsistence rice cultivation is the Lower Ganges valley (Figures 1.13 and 1.14) in India and Bangladesh. The Ganges basin is India's most extensive and productive agricultural area and its most densely populated. The delta region of the Ganges occupies a large part of Bangladesh, one of the most densely populated countries in the world. Rice contributes over 75 per cent of the diet in many parts of the region. The physical conditions in the Lower Ganges valley and delta are very suitable for rice cultivation:

- Temperatures of 21 °C and over throughout the year allow two crops to be grown annually. Rice needs a growing season of only 100 days.
- Monsoon rainfall over 2000 mm provides sufficient water for the fields to flood, which is necessary for wet rice cultivation.

- Rich alluvial soils have built up through regular flooding over a long time period during the monsoon season.
- There is a seasonal dry period which is important for harvesting the rice.

A water-intensive staple crop

Rice is the staple or main food crop in many parts of Asia. This is not surprising considering its high nutritional value. Current rice production systems are extremely water-intensive. Ninety per cent of agricultural water in Asia is used for rice production. The International Rice Research Institute estimates that it takes 5000 litres of water to produce 1 kg of rice. Much of Asia's rice production can be classed as intensive subsistence cultivation where the crop is grown on very small plots of land using a very high input of labour. Rice cultivation by small farmers is sometimes referred to as 'pre-modern intensive farming' because of the traditional techniques used, in contrast to intensive farming systems in MEDCs such as market gardening which are very capital intensive.

'Wet' rice is grown in the fertile silt and flooded areas of the lowlands while 'dry' rice is cultivated on terraces on the hillsides. A **terrace** is a levelled section of a hilly cultivated area. Terracing is a method of soil conservation. It also prevents the rapid runoff of irrigated water. Dry rice is easier to grow but provides lower yields than wet rice.

The farming system

Paddy fields (flooded parcels of land) characterise lowland rice production (Figure 1.15). Water for irrigation is provided either when the Ganges floods or by means of gravity canals. At first, rice is grown in nurseries. It is then transplanted when the **monsoon rains** flood the paddy fields. The flooded paddy fields may be stocked with fish for an additional source of food. The main rice crop is harvested when the drier season begins in late October. The rice crop gives high yields per hectare. A second rice crop can then be planted in November but water supply can be a problem in some areas for the second crop.

Figure 1.13 The Lower Ganges valley

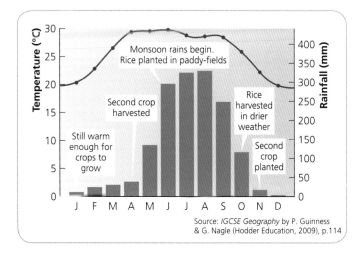

Figure 1.14 Climate graph for Kolkata

Figure 1.15 Rice paddy field scene in the Lower Ganges valley

335

Water buffalo are used for work. This is the only draft animal adapted for life in wetlands. The water buffalo provide an important source of manure in the fields. However, the manure is also used as domestic fuel. The labour-intensive nature of rice cultivation provides work for large numbers of people. This is important in areas of very dense population where there are limited alternative employment opportunities. The low incomes and lack of capital of these subsistence farmers mean that hand labour still dominates in the region. It takes an average of 2000 hours a year to farm 1 ha of land. A high labour input is needed to:

● build the embankments (bunds) that surround the fields – these are stabilised by tree crops such as coconut and banana

● construct irrigation canals where they are required for adequate water supply to the fields

● plant nursery rice, plough the paddy field, transplant the rice from the nursery to the paddy field, weed and harvest the mature rice crop

● cultivate other crops in the dry season and possibly tend a few chickens or other livestock.

Rice seeds are stored from one year to provide the next year's crop. During the dry season when there may be insufficient water for rice cultivation, other crops such as cereals and vegetables are grown. Farms are generally small, often no more than 1 ha. Many farmers are tenants and pay for use of the land by giving a share of their crop to the landlord.

Section 1.1 Activities

1 Describe the location of the Lower Ganges valley.

2 Why is rice cultivation in the area considered to be an intensive form of agriculture?

3 Explain why the physical environment provides good conditions for rice cultivation.

4 Describe the inputs, processes and outputs of this type of agriculture.

Issues in the intensification of agriculture and the extension of cultivation

Agricultural production can be achieved in two ways, by:

● increasing the land under cultivation through, for example, irrigation, or extending farming onto marginal land

● increasing the yield per hectare when scientific advance allows such changes to occur.

The intensification of agriculture has occurred through the use of high-yielding crop varieties, fertilisers, herbicides and pesticides, and irrigation. The result has been a substantial increase in global food production over the last 60 years. However, increasing agricultural production has not just been achieved by the more intensive farming of long-established agricultural land but also by the extension of cultivation into previously unfarmed areas. This has occurred with varying degrees of success.

The industrialised farmlands of today all too frequently lack the wildflowers, birds and insects that lived there in the past. These sterilised landscapes provide relatively cheap food, but at high environmental cost. These costs are typically borne by the citizens of the countries concerned rather than by the producers. Land conversion and intensification can alter ecosystems to such an extent that serious local, regional and global consequences result:

● *local*: increased soil erosion, lower soil fertility, reduced biodiversity

● *regional*: pollution of groundwater, eutrophication of rivers and lakes

● *global*: impacts on global atmospheric conditions.

The intensification of agriculture can result in soil degradation. **Soil degradation** is a global process. It involves both the physical loss (erosion) and the reduction in quality of topsoil associated with nutrient decline and contamination. It has a significant impact on agriculture and also has implications for the urban environment, pollution and flooding. The loss of the upper soil horizons containing organic matter and nutrients and the thinning of **soil profiles** reduces crop yields on degraded soils. Soil degradation can cancel out gains from improved crop yields. The statistics on soil degradation make worrying reading:

● Globally it is estimated that 2 billion ha of soil resources have been degraded. This is equivalent to about 15 per cent of the Earth's land area. Such a scale of soil degradation has resulted in the loss of 15 per cent of world agricultural supply in the last 50 years.

● For three centuries ending in 2000, topsoil had been lost at the rate of 300 million tonnes a year. Between 1950 and 2000 topsoil was lost at the much higher rate of 760 million tonnes a year.

● During the past 40 years nearly one-third of the world's cropland has been abandoned because of soil erosion and degradation.

● In Sub-Saharan Africa, nearly 2.6 million km² of cropland has shown a 'consistent significant decline' according to a March 2008 report by a consortium of agricultural institutions. Some scientists consider this to be a 'slow-motion disaster'.

● In the UK, 2.2 million tonnes of topsoil is eroded annually and over 17 per cent of arable land shows signs of erosion.

● It takes natural processes about 500 years to replace 25 mm of topsoil lost to erosion. The minimum soil depth for agricultural production is 150 mm. From this perspective, therefore, productive fertile soil can be considered a non-renewable, endangered ecosystem.

The Global Assessment of Human-induced Soil Degradation (GLASOD) is the only global survey of soil degradation to have been undertaken. Figure 1.16 is a generalised map of the findings of this survey. It shows that substantial parts of all continents have

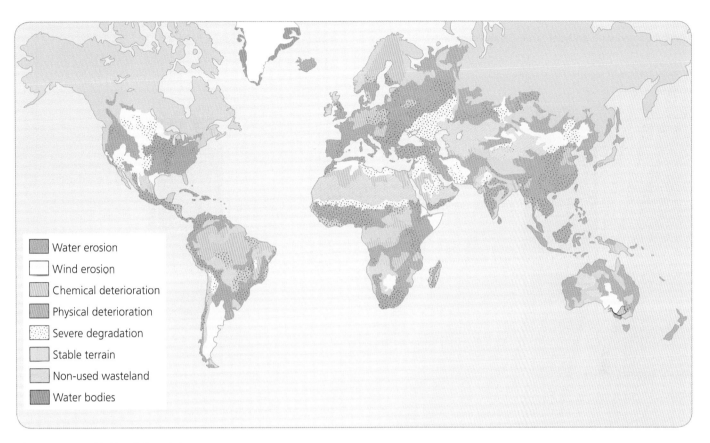

Figure 1.16 Worldwide soil degradation types

been affected by various types of soil degradation. The GLASOD calculation is that damage has occurred on 15 per cent of the world's total land area – 13 per cent light and moderate with 2 per cent severe and very severe (Figure 1.17).

The International Forum of Soils, Society and Global Change in September 2007 referred to 'the massive degradation of land and soil around the world which is contributing to climate change and threatening food security'. The Forum noted that:

- At least a quarter of the excess carbon dioxide in the atmosphere has come from changes in land use, such as deforestation, in the last century.
- Without the cover of vegetation, land becomes more reflective. It also loses fertility and the capacity to support vegetation and agricultural crops.
- The Intergovernmental Panel on Climate Change should develop a special report on the link between land degradation and climate change. By addressing soils and protecting the land cover and vegetation it is possible to obtain high value in terms of mitigating climate change.
- A better understanding of the capacity for carbon sequestration in soil is needed.
- Degradation of soil and land in already marginally productive land is a significant issue for many LEDCs, particularly in northern Africa, the Sahara region and parts of Asia, including China. Many of these regions have fragile ecosystems where any human interventions can lead to serious degradation.

Figure 1.17 Infertile saline soil in the south of France

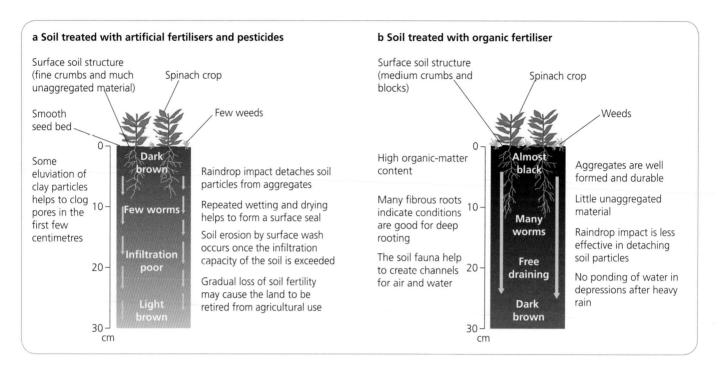

a Soil treated with artificial fertilisers and pesticides

Surface soil structure (fine crumbs and much unaggregated material)

Spinach crop

Smooth seed bed

Few weeds

Some eluviation of clay particles helps to clog pores in the first few centimetres

Dark brown

Raindrop impact detaches soil particles from aggregates

Few worms

Repeated wetting and drying helps to form a surface seal

Infiltration poor

Soil erosion by surface wash occurs once the infiltration capacity of the soil is exceeded

Light brown

Gradual loss of soil fertility may cause the land to be retired from agricultural use

cm

b Soil treated with organic fertiliser

Surface soil structure (medium crumbs and blocks)

Spinach crop

Weeds

High organic-matter content

Almost black

Aggregates are well formed and durable

Many fibrous roots indicate conditions are good for deep rooting

Little unaggregated material

Many worms

Raindrop impact is less effective in detaching soil particles

The soil fauna help to create channels for air and water

Free draining

No ponding of water in depressions after heavy rain

Dark brown

cm

Figure 1.18 Two soil profiles

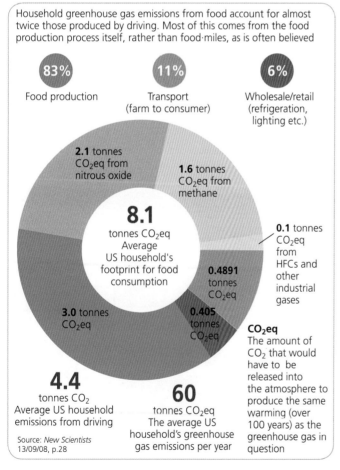

Household greenhouse gas emissions from food account for almost twice those produced by driving. Most of this comes from the food production process itself, rather than food-miles, as is often believed

83% Food production

11% Transport (farm to consumer)

6% Wholesale/retail (refrigeration, lighting etc.)

2.1 tonnes CO_2eq from nitrous oxide

1.6 tonnes CO_2eq from methane

8.1 tonnes CO_2eq Average US household's footprint for food consumption

0.1 tonnes CO_2eq from HFCs and other industrial gases

0.4891 tonnes CO_2eq

0.405 tonnes CO_2eq

3.0 tonnes CO_2eq

CO_2eq The amount of CO_2 that would have to be released into the atmosphere to produce the same warming (over 100 years) as the greenhouse gas in question

4.4 tonnes CO_2 Average US household emissions from driving

60 tonnes CO_2eq The average US household's greenhouse gas emissions per year

Source: *New Scientists* 13/09/08, p.28

Figure 1.19 Comparison of household greenhouse gas emissions from food and driving

Research has shown that the heavy and sustained use of artificial fertiliser can result in serious soil degradation. In Figure 1.18, soil profile a illustrates the problems that can result. In contrast, soil profile b shows a much healthier soil treated with organic fertiliser. In the artificially fertilised soil the ability of the soil to infiltrate water has been compromised by the breakdown of **soil aggregates** to fine particles which have sealed the surface. Pore spaces have been filled up by the fine soil material from the broken crumbs. This can result in ponding in surface depressions followed by soil erosion.

It has been estimated that food production and consumption accounts for up to twice as many greenhouse emissions as driving vehicles. Figure 1.19 shows US data published in the *New Scientist*. The average US household's footprint for food consumption is 8.1 tonnes of carbon dioxide equivalent, compared with 4.4 tonnes from driving.

The environmental impact of the Green Revolution

Much of the global increase in food production in the last 50 years can be attributed to the Green Revolution which took agro-industrialisation to LEDCs on a large scale. India was one of the first countries to benefit when a high-yielding variety seed programme (HVP) commenced in 1966–67. In terms of production it was a turning point for Indian agriculture, which had virtually reached stagnation. The HVP introduced new hybrid varieties of five cereals: wheat, rice, maize, sorghum and millet. All were drought-resistant with the exception of rice, were very responsive to the application of fertilisers, and had a shorter growing season than the traditional varieties they replaced. Although the benefits of the Green Revolution are clear, serious criticisms have also been made, many linked to the impact on the environment:

- High inputs of fertiliser and pesticide have been required to optimise production – this is costly in both economic and environmental terms.
- The problems of salinisation and waterlogged soils have increased, along with the expansion of the irrigated area leading to the abandonment of significant areas of land.
- High chemical inputs have had a considerable negative effect on biodiversity.
- People have suffered ill-health due to contaminated water and other forms of agricultural pollution.

In the early 1990s nutritionists noticed that even in countries where average food intake had risen, incapacitating diseases associated with mineral and vitamin deficiencies remained commonplace and in some instances had actually increased. The problem is that the high-yielding varieties introduced during the Green Revolution are usually low in minerals and vitamins. Because the new crops have displaced the local fruits, vegetables and legumes that traditionally supplied important vitamins and minerals, the diet of many people in LEDCs is now extremely low in zinc, iron, vitamin A and some other micronutrients.

In India's Punjab, yield growth has flattened since the mid-1990s. Over-irrigation has resulted in a steep fall in the water table, now tapped by 1.3 million tube wells. Since the beginning of the Green Revolution in Asia, the amount of land under irrigation has tripled.

The Green Revolution has been a major factor enabling global food supply to keep pace with population growth, but with growing concerns about a new food crisis, new technological advances may well be required to improve the global food security situation.

Section 1.1 Activities

1 Describe the distribution of soil degradation types shown in Figure 1.16. Refer to all elements of the key and make reference to all continental areas.

2 Describe and explain the differences shown in the soil profiles illustrated in Figure 1.18.

3 Summarise the data presented in Figure 1.19.

4 Discuss the environmental impact of the Green Revolution.

1.2 The management of agricultural change

Agriculture remains vital to the lives of many individual people and communities, and to the economies of many countries, particularly in LEDCs. Jamaica is an example of a country where the management of agricultural change can be observed at both the level of the individual farm and the country a whole (Figure 1.20).

Figure 1.20 Large plantation of bananas in Jamaica

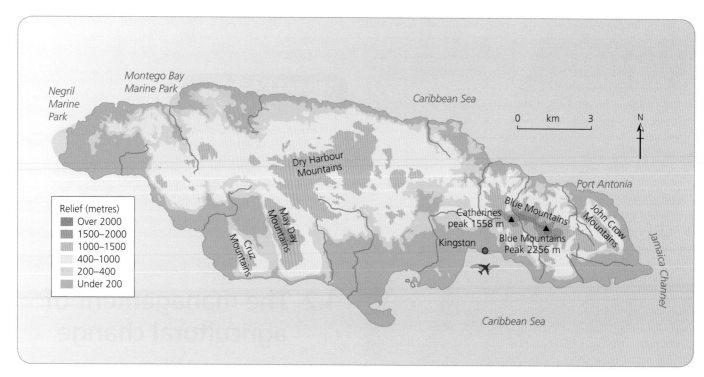

Figure 1.21 Jamaica: relief and drainage

Physical background

Jamaica has considerable variety of topography and geology (Figure 1.21). Approximately half of the island lies above 1000 m, which has a significant influence on its various microclimates. The country has a highland interior formed by a series of mountain ranges along the major west-north-west to east-south-east axis of the island. The central mountain ranges form the main watershed for rivers which drain either to the north or the south, except for the Plantain Garden River which drains to the east. Flat coastal plains surround the central mountain ridge. The climate of Jamaica is mainly subtropical or tropical maritime.

The importance of agriculture

Agriculture in Jamaica is dominated by the production of **traditional crops** such as sugar, bananas, coffee, cocoa and spices. In addition a number of **non-traditional crops** including sweet potatoes, yams and hot peppers are cultivated for both domestic and international markets. In terms of livestock, Jamaica has well-developed beef, dairy and poultry sectors. The products of these, together with those of the pork and small ruminant industries, are mainly for domestic consumption. The maritime and inland fish sectors serve both domestic and export markets. Over the past two decades the major export earner, sugar, has experienced a considerable decline. Both sugar and bananas in particular have had to contend with price and market insecurity as a result of preference erosion in the EU market. Additional problems for Jamaican agriculture have arisen in relation to non-traditional products such as milk, food aid, and the dumping of surpluses on the local markets.

Although it has faced significant challenges, the agricultural sector continues to play an important role in terms of:
- food security
- employment
- income
- rural livelihoods (Figure 1.22).

Agriculture contributes 7 per cent to Jamaica's GDP and employs about 20 per cent of the workforce.

Figure 1.22 Jamaican farming scene – a smallholding

Recent changes in Jamaican farming

Table 1.4 shows that the total amount of land in farming fell by almost 23 per cent between 1996 and 2007 as significant areas of **marginal land** were abandoned. Land devoted to crops declined by 13 per cent during this period, while land given over to pasture fell by a massive 49.6 per cent. The difficulties of making a living on marginal land were the main reason, as people sought other means of employment, particularly in urban areas.

A significant problem has been the removal of **preferential treatment** for bananas on the European market, which is creating greater competition and lowering prices. Some farmers no longer consider bananas a profitable venture and have stopped farming. This is particularly true of small farmers who are unable to achieve the economies of scale of their larger competitors. However, farmers have had to face other problems such as 'praedial larceny', by which farmers are robbed of their produce, in some cases even before the crops are mature. For small farmers such theft can turn a modest profit into a loss, with resultant rural–urban migration. Disease is another problem. For example, Moko disease, which affects bananas and similar species, for example plantains, has infected some farms and resulted in losses to farmers.

Table 1.4 Area in farming in Jamaica, 1996 and 2007

Items	2007		1996		Change 1996–2007	
	Area in ha	% of total	Area in ha	% of total	Absolute change	% change
Total land in farming	**325 810**	**100.0**	**421 550**	**100.0**	**–95 740**	**–22.7**
Active farmland	202 727	62.2	273 229	64.8	–70 502	–25.8
Crops	154 524	47.4	177 580	42.1	–23 056	–13.0
Pasture	48 203	13.8	95 649	22.7	–47 446	–49.6
Inactive farmland	114 048	35.0	134 204	31.8	–20 157	–15.0
Ruinate and fallow	80 560	24.7	87 300	20.7	–6 740	–7.7
Woodland and other land on farm	33 488	10.3	46 905	11.1	–13 417	–28.6
Land identified to be in farming but no information reported	9 035	2.8	14 116	3.2		

Source: www.statinja.gov.jm

Climatic hazards often have a substantial impact on farming in Jamaica. In 2005, for example, agricultural GDP fell by 7.3 per cent. The reasons for this decline included:

- the long-term effects of Hurricane Ivan
- the drought that occurred between January and April 2005

- the impacts of Hurricanes Dennis and Emily and tropical storm Wilma in 2005, which caused combined losses of $994 million.

In addition, there have been economic and political difficulties. The European Commission proposed a 36 per cent cut in the price paid for raw sugar exports from African, Caribbean and Pacific countries, starting in 2006. In the 1950s, Jamaica had 20 working sugar factories, but by 2005 this number had fallen to eight.

Policy responses

In response the Jamaican government announced a new policy for a sustainable local sugar industry. The main elements of the policy were:

- to centre the industry around three products – raw sugar for export and domestic markets, molasses for the manufacture of rum, and ethanol for fuel
- to set a production target of 200 000 tonnes of raw sugar per year.

Commodity-specific policies for bananas included rationalisation of areas under production, provision of technical support for irrigation and extension, and the restructuring of the banana insurance scheme. For the cocoa industry, expansion in production, increased efficiencies and identification of more lucrative markets were the main strategies.

Jamaica has also produced a New Agricultural Development Plan which aims to transform the farming sector by 2020. The main objectives of the plan are to halt the decline of the agricultural sector, to restore productivity to agricultural resources, and to ensure that farming communities provide meaningful livelihoods and living environments for those who depend on the agricultural sector. The New Agricultural Development Plan aims to increase production in eight key areas, through:

- The Small Ruminant Industry Development Project
- The National Organic Agriculture Project
- Protected Cultivation (Hydroponics)
- The Beekeeping Enhancement Project
- Marketing (Agribusiness Enhancement Project)
- The Fruit Tree Crop Development Project
- Ornamental Horticulture
- The Fisheries Development Project.

As exports of some traditional farm products have declined, the Jamaican government has tried to encourage **agricultural diversification**. This is exemplified by Table 1.5, which divides exports into 'traditional' and 'non-traditional'. Look at the agricultural products under these headings. Also take note of the manufacture of agricultural products.

Poultry is an example of a farming sector in which significant benefits have accrued through:

- internal structural changes
- reorganisation of the production system
- the introduction of higher levels of technology.

The spice industry is another example. This traditionally operated at the cottage level, but with government encouragement the industry has been restructured and modernised to increase its share

Table 1.5 Exports of traditional and non-traditional commodities, January–December 2009

Commodities	Jan–Dec 2009
Total traditional exports	**55 026 594**
Agriculture	**3 440 439**
Banana	559
Citrus	149 080
Coffee	2 978 540
Cocoa	157 750
Pimento	154 509
Mining and quarrying	**40 645 392**
Bauxite	8 326 228
Alumina	32 302 855
Gypsum	16 309
Manufacture	**10 940 763**
Sugar	6 405 019
Rum	4 296 721
Citrus products	46 208
Coffee products	133 061
Cocoa products	59 753
Total non-traditional exports	**55 465 717**
Food	**10 538 829**
Pumpkins	31 319
Other vegetables and preparations thereof	210 663
Dasheen	122 669
Yams	1 650 806
Papayas	253 032
Ackee	1 199 038
Other fruits and fruit preparations	553 278
Meat and meat preparations	249 329

Commodities	Jan–Dec 2009
Dairy products and birds' eggs	568 153
Fish, crustaceans and molluscs	418 816
Baked products	951 342
Juices excluding citrus	604 530
Animal feed	459 184
Sauces	935 614
Malt extract and preparations thereof	333 266
Other food exports	1 776 465
Beverages and tobacco (excl. rum)	**4 672 930**
Non-alcoholic beverages	755 157
Alcoholic beverages (excl. rum)	3 912 774
Tobacco	4 999
Crude materials	**1 476 079**
Limestone	95 439
Waste and scrap metals	1 115 360
Other	265 280
Other	**38 777 879**
Mineral fuels, etc.	18 887 511
Animal and vegetable oils & fats	16 432
Chemicals (excl. ethanol)	2 546 690
Ethanol	15 151 290
Manufactured goods	1 401 815
Machinery and transport equipment	155 332
Wearing apparel	129 250
Furniture	63 388
Other domestic exports	421 261

Source: Statistical Institute of Jamaica

of international markets. The exploitation of **niche markets** has been a major aspect of the modernisation of Jamaican agriculture.

In March 2010, Jamaica's Minister of Agriculture the Honourable Dr Christopher Tufton, announced that the government was working to prepare a new agriculture land use policy for the island, with the aim of getting fallow fields back into production. Dr Tufton made this statement at a meeting held to discuss the Arable Lands Irrigated and Growing for the Nation (ALIGN) project. The ALIGN programme is intended to boost agricultural production in Jamaica by providing irrigation on arable land.

Land degradation

Jamaica is having to address the issue of land degradation. A report published in the early 2000s stated: 'While land degradation in Jamaica is not as serious as in some parts of Africa or even like that in its Caribbean neighbour Haiti, it is a problem that must be confronted.' Some of the most seriously degraded areas of the island are in the southern coastal sections of the parishes of Clarendon, Manchester and St Catherine and particularly on the southern coastal border areas of Manchester and St Elizabeth.

ICT and agriculture

The government has recognised the contribution ICT can make to enhancing the sector's efficiency and productivity. Current initiatives include:

- **Agri-Business Information System (ABIS):** Currently under development, this computer-based information system will collect and disseminate to interested parties information on crops, marketing, agricultural stakeholders, and agricultural production.
- **Geographical Information Systems (GIS):** The Forest Department and the Rural Physical Planning Division are currently using GIS as a tool in the mapping and management of Jamaica's forest and land resources. The private sector, in turn, is using GIS for the purpose of advertising and marketing agricultural products via the internet.

Evaluation

The range of policies introduced by the government in recent years has undoubtedly helped to bring about beneficial changes in Jamaican agriculture. More efficient management and new agricultural technology have been introduced into both the traditional and non-traditional farming sectors. The product range has been broadened and more attention has been placed on marketing. ICT systems have played an increasing role in this push for modernisation. However, limited funding has meant that progress has not always been as rapid as hoped and climatic hazards have at times proved costly. The erosion of preferential treatment in EU markets has been a significant setback although Jamaica did have advance warning this was going to happen. There is little that small countries like Jamaica can do in terms of world trade agreements and fluctuating international demand and prices. Nevertheless this should not deter governments from making the best policy provisions they can.

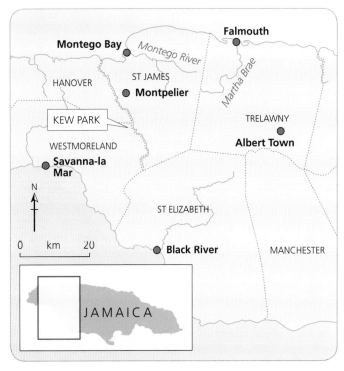

Figure 1.23 The location of Kew Park farm

Section 1.2 Activities

1 With reference to Figure 1.21, describe the relief and drainage of Jamaica.

2 In what ways is the agricultural sector important to Jamaica?

3 Discuss the differences between Jamaica's traditional and non-traditional farm products.

4 How has the government tried to improve the fortunes of the country's agricultural sector?

Case Study

Kew Park farm, Jamaica

Kew Park farm is a mixed commercial farm in the west of Jamaica. It is located high in the hills of the parish of Westmoreland, overlooking the Great River valley that forms the border between Westmoreland and St James (Figures 1.23 and 1.24). Kew Park covers an area of about 385 ha and is run along with Copse Mountain Farm (about 425 ha). The two farms together form one unit, Kew Park. This is a very hilly part of Jamaica. About 30 per cent of Kew Park can only be accessed on foot and about 15 per cent of the total area is not farmed at all. Good management has been essential for the farm's survival as an economic entity because of the physical hazards and economic obstacles the farm has had to face.

Most of the farmed area is allocated to beef cattle; much of the breeding research for the Jamaican Red Poll was conducted here. At present there are five pedigree Jamaica Red Poll herds and two commercial herds on the farm – a total of about 700 animals. The cattle are raised extensively, but are confined in grass pastures by either barbed-wire fences or dry-stone walls. Other parts of the farm support a variety of agricultural activities:

- Above about 400 m, an area of 16 ha is planted with arabica coffee, producing the 'Estate' brand. Much of the primary processing of the coffee is done on the farm, but it is then sent to Kingston to be graded, roasted and packed. Kew Park has a licence to export the processed coffee, although much

Figure 1.24 Kew Park farm

of it is sold locally. Kew Park has worked hard for 20 years to develop the quality of its coffee and its reputation. Decisions such as this can take many years to really pay off. The high quality of Kew Park coffee has resulted in the farm being one of a relatively small number being granted a licence to export. The farm's website states: 'Kew Park Estate Coffee

343

has been carefully expanded over the past 20 years to fit the coffee in to the land; working always for the long term sustainability of the farm, the people who work here, and the environment on which it depends.'

- Two hectares are given over to citrus fruits (ortaniques). However, the fruit are not of prime quality as the climate is too wet and the trees are not well maintained.
- There are 2 ha of lychees, which is a difficult crop to grow, but there is a good local market for the fruit.
- The farm supports some 2000 free-range chickens. The eggs are washed and packed on the farm and sold locally.
- Five pig units comprise a total of 120 sow units (breeding animals) and 2500 fatteners. Kew Park has a contract to provide a local processor with 120–150 pigs a week.

Life in rural Jamaica is not easy and Kew Park provides the only full-time employment in the area. Wages are low. Some staff live in houses owned by the estate but most travel from their own homes nearby.

Farm managers have had to be constantly aware of the costs of all their inputs, such as labour, animal stock, seeds and machinery. The costs of the processing that is carried out on the farm also have to be calculated. Knowledge of local and more distant markets in terms of both access and price are important. Because Kew Park produces a number of farm products, the allocation of resources for different purposes must be done carefully. A more favourable price for one particular farm product may justify a larger share of farm resources if it is felt that the increase in price is not just a temporary upturn.

The farm also has to be aware of government agricultural policies and incentives. Often the balance between costs and revenue is marginal, which makes correct decision-making crucial.

The damage caused by a pest known as the coffee berry borer can eliminate the profit expected from a coffee crop in Jamaica. The female borer, which is a tiny beetle just 1.5 mm long, drills into coffee berries and lays its eggs inside. There can be up to fifty per berry. Once hatched, the young borers eat the beans from within, leaving them worthless. Combating the borer is an expensive task. Existing methods include traps, parasitic insects and insecticides. The most effective insecticide is endosulfan which is highly toxic. Jamaica's Coffee Industry Board will phase out its use by 2010.

However, a more natural solution may be at hand. Migratory warblers (birds) spend winter in Jamaica and like to feast on the coffee berry borers. Research has estimated that growers who enlist these birds to control berry borers could save as much as $96/ha every year. This should create an economic incentive for coffee producers to manage their farms in ways that aid bird conservation. In particular this means planting or maintaining pockets of trees instead of clear cutting which has been the traditional method. Peter Williams at Kew Park thinks this is a good idea, but the farm has yet to make a final decision about going along this route.

Figure 1.25 shows the section of the farm's website devoted to 'Kew Park Essentials'. Many of the traditional herbal remedies,

spicy foods and refreshers date back to the indigenous Tainos (Arawaks); others were introduced by African slaves, indentured labourers from China and India, and other migrants to the island. Even though conventional medicine is well established in Jamaica, folk medicine is still widely practised, particularly in the rural areas. Popular remedies include some of the herbs and spices grown at Kew Park. Although production of these products is not new, the marketing of them has changed considerably in recent years, reaching an international audience through the farm's website and other channels. This aspect of the farm's production has accounted for an increasing proportion of its income in recent years.

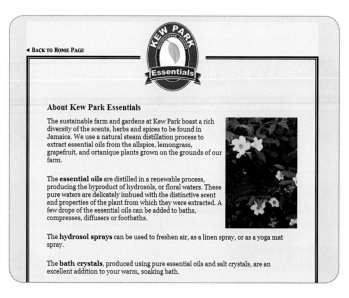

Figure 1.25 Website advert for 'Kew Park Essentials'

Evaluation

The relief and location of the farm have always presented certain challenges to Kew Park. The farm is in a hilly part of the country, some distance from Kingston, the capital city. However, careful locational choices within the farm and management of the farm's product range, along with incisive marketing, have built a good reputation for the farm. The farm has responded to international markets by extending the range of its non-traditional products in particular. Its use of ICT has been an important part of this process. However, individual farms have no influence on national and international policies and thus they must be able to react to policy changes at both these levels, as well as dealing with the challenges presented by the physical environment.

Section 1.2 Activities

1 Describe the location of Kew Park farm.

2 Discuss the farm's product range.

3 What are the main problems the farm has had to contend with?

1.3 Manufacturing and related service industry

Industrial location: influential factors

Every day, decisions are made about where to locate industrial premises, ranging from small workshops to huge industrial complexes. In general, the larger the company the greater the number of real alternative locations available. For each possible location a wide range of factors can affect total costs and thus influence the decision-making process. The factors involved in industrial location differ from industry to industry and their relative importance is subject to change over time. These factors can be broadly subdivided into physical and human. Table 1.6 provides a brief summary and introduction to this topic.

Raw materials

Industries that use raw materials directly, such as oil refining and metal smelting, are known as **processing industries**. Once the dominant type of manufacturing, processing industries are in a minority today as most industries now use components and parts made by other firms.

The processes involved in turning a raw material into a manufactured product usually result in **weight loss** so that the transport costs incurred in bringing the raw materials to the factory will be greater than the cost of transporting the finished product to market. If weight loss is substantial the location of the factory will be drawn towards its most costly-to-transport raw material(s). Figure 1.26 shows a simple example of weight loss where two tonnes each of two raw materials are required to manufacture one tonne of the finished product.

The clearest examples of this influence are where one raw material only is used. In the UK, sugar beet refineries are centrally located in crop-growing areas because there is a 90 per cent weight loss in manufacture (Figure 1.27). Frozen pea factories are

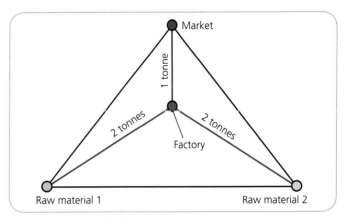

Figure 1.26 Weight loss diagram

Figure 1.27 Sugar refinery in France

Table 1.6 Factors of industrial location

Physical factors	Human factors
Site: the availability and cost of land: large factories in particular need flat, well-drained land on solid bedrock. An adjacent water supply may be essential.	**Capital (money):** business people, banks and governments are more likely to invest money in some areas than others.
Raw materials: industries requiring heavy and bulky raw materials which are expensive to transport generally locate as close to these raw materials as possible.	**Labour:** increasingly it is the quality and cost of labour rather than the quantity that are the key factors. The reputation, turnover and mobility of labour can also be important.
Energy: at times in the past, industry needed to be located near fast-flowing rivers or coal mines. Today, electricity can be transmitted to most locations. However, energy-hungry industries, such as metal smelting, may be drawn to countries with relatively cheap hydro-electricity.	**Transport and communications:** transport costs are lower in real terms than ever before but remain important for heavy, bulky items. Accessibility to airports, ports, motorways and key railway terminals may be crucial factors for some industries.
Natural routeways and harbours: these were essential in the past and are still important today as many modern roads and railways still follow natural routeways. Natural harbours provide good locations for ports and industrial complexes are often found at ports.	**Markets:** the location and size of markets is a major influence for some industries.
Climate: some industries such as the aerospace and film industries benefit directly from a sunny climate. Indirect benefits, such as lower heating bills and a more favourable quality of life, may also be apparent.	**Government influence:** government policies and decisions can have a big direct and indirect impact. Governments can encourage industries to locate in certain areas and deny them planning permission in others.
	Quality of life: highly skilled personnel who have a choice about where they work will favour areas where the quality of life is high.

also strategically located in the growing areas. Here the weight loss is much less, but to achieve prime quality the peas must be processed very quickly after picking.

In many processing industries technological advance has reduced the amount of raw material required per finished product and in some cases less bulky and cheaper substitutes have been found. Thus, across the industrial board as a whole, the raw material requirement per unit of finished product has been reduced.

Tidewater locations are particularly popular with industries that use significant quantities of imported raw materials. Examples include flour milling, food processing, chemicals and oil refining. Tidewater locations are **break-of-bulk** points where cargo is unloaded from bulk carriers and transferred to smaller units of transport for further movement. However, if raw materials are processed at the break-of-bulk point, significant savings in transport costs can be made.

Markets

Where a firm sells its products may well have a considerable influence on where the factory is located. Where the cost of distributing the finished product is a significant part of total cost and the greater part of total transport costs, a market location is logical. A small number of industries, including soft drinks and brewing, are 'weight gaining' and are thus market-oriented in terms of location. The heavy weight gain for both of these industries comes from the addition of water, a ubiquitous resource. The baking industry is also cited frequently as an example of weight gain but here it is largely a case of increase in volume rather than weight, although the impact on transport costs is similar.

However, there are other reasons for market location. Industries where fashion and taste are variable need to be able to react quickly to changes demanded by their customers. Clear examples of this can be seen on both the national and international scales. In terms of the latter, one of the reasons why the global car giants spread themselves around the world is to ensure that they can produce vehicles that customers will buy in the different world regions. Ford, for example, recognised a long time ago that Europeans prefer smaller cars than Americans do.

Energy

The **Industrial Revolution** in Britain and many other countries was based on the use of coal as a fuel, which was usually much more costly to transport than the raw materials required for processing. It is therefore not surprising that outside of London most of Britain's industrial towns and cities developed on coalfields or at ports nearby. The coalfields became focal points for the developing transport networks – first canals, then rail, and finally road. The investment in both **hard and soft infrastructure** was massive, so even when new forms of energy were substituted for coal, many industries remained at their coalfield locations, a phenomenon known as **industrial inertia**. Apart from the advantages of the infrastructure being in place, the cost of relocating might be prohibitive. Also, a certain number of new industries have been attracted to urban areas on coalfields

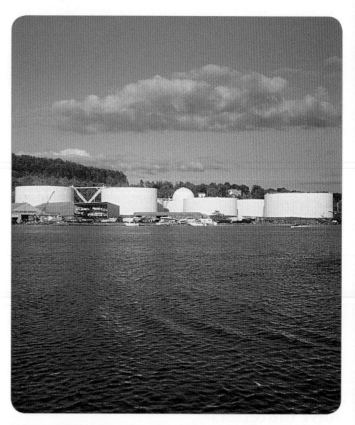

Figure 1.28 Oil storage at Parry Sound, Ontario, Canada

because of the acquired advantages available, such as a pool of skilled labour and the existing network of linkages between firms. However, overall the coalfields have suffered considerable economic distress due to the decline of coal and the traditional industries associated with it. In many MEDCs these areas are now the main 'problem' regions.

During the twentieth century the construction of national electricity grids and gas pipeline systems made energy virtually a ubiquitous resource in MEDCs (Figure 1.28). As a result most modern industry is described as **footloose**, meaning that it is not tied to certain areas because of its energy requirement or other factors. However, there are some industries that are constrained in terms of location because of an extremely high energy requirement. For example, the lure of low-cost hydro-electric power has resulted in a huge concentration of electro-metallurgical and electro-chemical industries in southern Norway.

Section 1.3 Activities

1 a What are *raw materials*?
   b How can raw materials influence industrial location?

2 For what reasons are companies likely to chose a market location?

3 Explain the importance of break-of-bulk points.

4 Discuss industrial inertia as a factor in industrial location.

5 What are footloose industries?

Transport

Although it was once a major locational factor, the share of industry's total costs accounted for by transportation has fallen steadily over time. For example, for most manufacturing firms in the UK, transportation now accounts for less than 4 per cent of total costs. The main reasons for this reduction are:

- major advances in all modes of transport
- great improvements in the efficiency of transport networks
- technological developments moving industry to the increasing production of higher value/lower bulk goods.

The cost of transport has two components: fixed costs and line-haul costs. **Fixed (terminal) costs** are accrued by the equipment used to handle and store goods, and the costs of providing the transport system. **Line-haul costs** refer to the cost of actually moving the goods and are largely composed of fuel costs and wages. In Figure 1.29 the costs of the main methods of freight transport are compared. While water and pipeline transport have higher fixed costs than rail (Figure 1.30) and road, their line-haul costs are significantly lower. Air transport, which suffers from both high fixed and line-haul costs, is only used for high-

Figure 1.30 Timber being transported on the Trans-Siberian railway, Russia

value freight or for goods such as flowers which are extremely perishable. Other factors affecting the cost of transport are:

- the type of load carried – perishable and breakable commodities which require careful handling are more costly to move than robust goods such as iron ore and coal
- the type of journey – those that involve transferring cargo from one mode of transport to another are more costly than those using the same mode of transport throughout
- the degree of competition within and between the competing modes of transport.

Land

The space requirements of different industries, and also of firms within the same industry, vary enormously. Technological advance has made modern industry much more space-efficient than in the past. However, modern industry is horizontally structured (on one floor) as opposed to, for example, the textile mills of the nineteenth century which had four or five floors. In the modern factory, transportation takes up much more space than it used to – for example, consider the area required to park cars for a firm employing 300 people.

During the Industrial Revolution entrepreneurs had a relatively free choice of where to locate in terms of planning restrictions, providing of course that they could afford to purchase the site they wanted. However, with the passage of time more and more areas have become unavailable to industry, mainly in an effort to conserve the environment. Areas such as National Parks, Country Parks and Areas of Special Scientific Interest now occupy a significant part of most countries. In urban areas, land use zoning places a considerable restriction on where industry may locate, and green belts often prohibit location at the edge of urban areas.

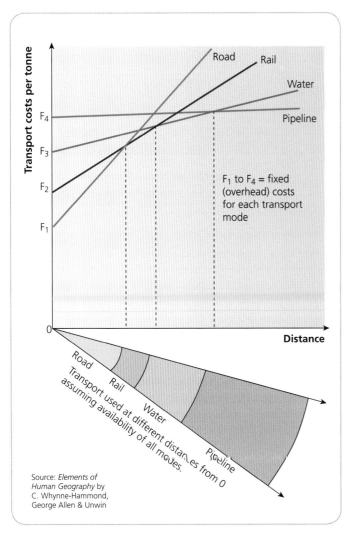

F_1 to F_4 = fixed (overhead) costs for each transport mode

Source: *Elements of Human Geography* by C. Whynne-Hammond, George Allen & Unwin

Figure 1.29 Transport costs and distance

Capital

Capital represents the finance invested to start up a business and to keep it in production. That part of capital invested in plant and machinery is known as fixed capital as it is not mobile compared with working capital (money). Capital is obtained either from shareholders (share capital) or from banks or other lenders (loan capital). Some geographers also use the term 'social capital' which is the investment in housing, schools, hospitals and other amenities valued by the community, which may attract a firm to a particular location.

In the early days of the Industrial Revolution in present-day MEDCs, the availability of capital was geographically constrained by the location of the major capital-raising centres and by limited knowledge – and thus confidence – about untested locations. It was thus one of the factors that led to the clustering of industry. In the modern world the rapid diffusion of information and the ability to raise and move capital quickly within and across international borders means that this factor has a minimal constraining influence in MEDCs today. However, in less developed economies the constraints of capital are usually greater, depending on the level of economic development. It is the perceived risk that is the vital factor. The political unrest that has affected so many African countries in recent decades has made it very difficult for these nations to raise the amount of capital desired.

Virtually all industries have over time substituted capital for labour in an attempt to reduce costs and improve quality. Thus, in a competitive environment, capital has become a more important factor in industry. In some industries the level of capital required to enter the market with a reasonable chance of success is so high that just a few companies monopolise the market. This has a major influence on the geography of manufacturing. The aircraft industry, for instance, has a massive barrier to entry in terms of the capital required to compete successfully.

The issue of foreign direct investment (FDI) is considered in detail on pages 446–47.

Section 1.3 Activities

1 Why has the relative cost of transport declined significantly over time for most industries?

2 Distinguish between fixed transport costs and line-haul costs.

3 Discuss 'land' as a factor in industrial location.

4 How does capital influence industrial location?

Labour

The interlinked attributes of labour that influence locational decision-making are cost, quality, availability and reputation.

Although all industries have become more capital-intensive over time, labour still accounts for over 20 per cent of total costs in manufacturing industry. The cost of labour can be measured in two ways: as wage rates, and as unit costs (Figure 1.31). The former is simply the hourly or weekly amount paid to employees,

while the latter is a measure of productivity, relating wage rates to output. Industrialists are mainly influenced by unit costs, which explains why industry often clusters where wages are higher rather than in areas where wage rates are low. It is frequently, although not always, the high quality and productivity of labour that pushes up wages in an area. In such an area unit costs may well be considerably lower than in an economically depressed area with poor-quality labour and lower wage rates. Certain skills sometimes become concentrated in particular areas, a phenomenon known as the **sectoral spatial division of labour**. As the reputation of a region for a particular skill or set of skills grows, more firms in that particular economic sector will be attracted to the area.

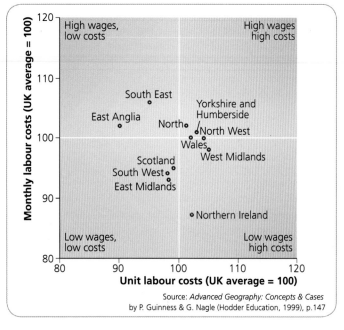

Source: *Advanced Geography: Concepts & Cases* by P. Guinness & G. Nagle (Hodder Education, 1999), p.147

Figure 1.31 Regional variations in labour costs in the UK

Variation in wage rates can be identified at different scales. By far the greatest disparity is at the global scale. The low wages of LEDCs with reasonable enough levels of skill to interest foreign companies has been a major reason for transnational investment in regions such as South East Asia and Latin America. A filter-down of industry to lower and lower wage economies can be recognised in particular in Asia – this topic is examined in more detail on pages 452–53.

Recent analyses of labour costs in manufacturing have highlighted the wide variations in non-wage labour costs, which include employer social security contributions, payroll taxes, holiday pay, sick leave and other benefits.

The availability of labour as measured by high rates of unemployment is not an important location factor for most industries. The regions of the UK that have struggled most to attract new industry are the traditional industrial areas which have consistently recorded the highest unemployment rates in the country. In such regions, although there are many people available for work, they frequently lack the skills required by modern industry. The physical dereliction and the social problems generated by unemployment also act to deter new investment. Where availability really has an impact is in sparsely populated areas because large prospective employers know that they will struggle to assemble enough workers with the skills demanded. Such regions are therefore often ruled out at the beginning of the locational search.

The fact that there have always been considerable regional differences in unemployment in the UK, a relatively small country, indicates that the **geographical mobility of labour** is limited. A major factor impeding the movement of labour from region to region is the huge differential in the cost of housing between the South East and the traditional industrial areas. In general the degree of geographical mobility increases with skill levels and qualifications. It is the most able and financially secure that can best overcome the obstacles to mobility.

People can of course move from one type of job to another within the same town or region. Such movement is referred to as **occupational mobility**. However, like geographical mobility it is limited in extent. People who have been employed in heavy industry in particular often find it very difficult to adjust to a working environment that is less physically demanding but requires much more in terms of concentration.

The reputation of a region's labour force can influence inward investment. Regions with militant trade unions and a record of work stoppages are frequently avoided in the locational search. In the USA, manufacturing firms often avoid states in the north-east where trade union membership is high, favouring instead the south and the west where union influence is minimal. Trade union membership in the UK and most other countries has weakened in recent decades for two main reasons:

- many governments have passed legislation to restrict the power of unions
- the decline in employment in manufacturing, the historic nucleus of trade unionism, has had severe implications for membership; unions are particularly unpopular in Asia.

Economies of scale: internal and external

Both internal and external economies of scale can be recognised. Internal economies of scale occur when an increase in production results in a lowering of unit costs. This is a major reason why firms want to increase in size. The reduced costs of production can be passed on to customers and in this way a company can increase its market share. Alternatively it can increase its profits. Economists recognise five types of **internal economies of scale**:

- **Bulk-buying economies:** as businesses grow their bargaining power with suppliers increases.
- **Technical economies:** businesses with large-scale production can use more advanced machinery or use existing machinery more efficiently. A larger firm can also afford to invest more in research and development.
- **Financial economies:** larger firms find it easier to find potential lenders and to raise money at lower interest rates.

- **Marketing economies:** as a business gets larger, it is able to spread the cost of marketing over a wider range of products and sales, thus cutting the average marketing cost per unit.
- **Managerial economies:** as a company grows, there is more potential for managers to specialise in particular tasks and thus become more efficient.

However, it is possible that an increase in production at some stage might lead to rising unit costs. If this happens **diseconomies of scale** are said to exist. In Figure 1.32 the average cost of production at output Q is C_2. Increasing output beyond this point reduces unit costs and thus economies of scale are achieved. This continues until output Q_2 is reached when the lowest unit costs of production are achieved (C). Beyond this point, unit costs rise and diseconomies of scale are occurring.

External economies of scale (agglomeration economies) are the benefits that accrue to a firm by locating in an established industrial area. External economies of scale can be subdivided into:

- urbanisation economies, which are the cost savings resulting from urban location due to factors such as the range of producer services available and the investment in infrastructure already in place, and
- localisation economies which occur when a firm locates close to suppliers (backward linkages) or to firms that it supplies (forward linkages) – this reduces transport costs, allows for faster delivery, and facilitates a high level of personal communication between firms.

However, when an urban-industrial area reaches a certain size, urbanisation diseconomies may come into play. High levels of traffic congestion may push up transport costs. Intense competition for land will increase land prices and rents. If the demand for labour exceeds the supply, wages will rise. So locating in such a region may no longer be advantageous, with fewer new firms arriving and some existing firms relocating elsewhere. In the USA

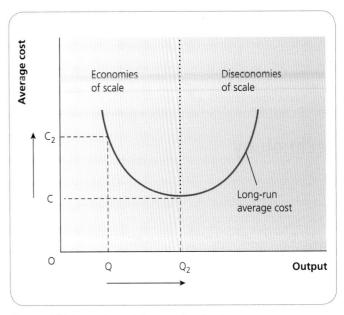

Figure 1.32 Economies and diseconomies of scale

Figure 1.33 Model illustrating the problems of rapid growth in the Santa Clara valley (Silicon Valley)

such a process has occurred in the Santa Clara valley (Silicon Valley) with entrepreneurs looking in particular at the less crowded mountain states such as Arizona and Colorado (Figure 1.33).

Government policies

In the old-style centrally planned economies of the communist countries or former communist countries, the influence of government on industry was absolute. In other countries the significance of government intervention has depended on:

- the degree of public ownership
- the strength of regional policy in terms of restrictions and incentives.

Governments influence industrial location for economic, social and political reasons. Regional economic policy largely developed after the Second World War, although examples of legislation with a regional element can be found before this time. There is a high level of competition both between countries and between regions in the same country to attract foreign direct investment.

Technology

Technology can influence industrial location in two main ways:

- The level of technological development in a country or region in terms of infrastructure and human skills has a major impact on the type of industry that can be attracted.
- Technological advance may induce a company or industry to move to alternative locations that have now become more suitable due to the new developments in technology.

Figure 1.34 is a useful summary of the different stages of technological development. Advances in technology can stimulate new industrial clusters, as has happened with biotechnology in a number of countries.

Figure 1.34 Stages of technology development by innovation effort

Frontier innovation
Create new technologies: as leader or follower

Technology improvement & monitoring
Improve products, processes and skills to raise productivity and competitiveness, based on own R&D, licensing, interactions with other firms or institutions

Significant adaptation
Change products and processes, plant layout, productivity management and quality systems, procurement methods and logistics to adapt technology to local or export-market needs. This is based on in-house experimentation and R&D as well as on search and interactions with other firms and institutions

Basic production
Train workers in essential production and technical skills; reach plant design capacity and performance levels; configure products and processes; set up essential quality management systems; institute supervisory, procurement and inventory management systems; establish in-bound and out-bound logistics

---

Section 1.3 Activities

1 Distinguish between *wage rates* and *unit costs*.

2 Define the *sectoral spatial division of labour*.

3 With regard to labour, briefly discuss the impact on industrial location of cost, quality, availability and reputation.

4 Explain internal economies of scale.

5 How can diseconomies of scale occur?

5 What are external economies of scale?

6 Briefly review the impact of **a** government policies and **b** technology on industrial location.

Slovakia: the changing location of EU car manufacturing

Car manufacturing is one of the world's largest industries. Within the EU, investment in car manufacturing has shifted from western to eastern Europe in recent years as countries like Slovakia have joined the EU (Figure 1.35). This is because eastern EU countries like Slovakia can manufacture cars at a lower cost than western EU countries.

The location factors that have attracted the car industry to Slovakia are:

- relatively low labour costs
- low company taxation rates
- a highly skilled workforce, particularly in areas that were once important for heavy industry
- a strong work ethic resulting in high levels of productivity
- low transport costs because of proximity to western European markets
- very low political risk because of the stable nature of the country
- attractive government incentives due to competition between Slovakia and other potential receiving countries
- good infrastructure in and around Bratislava and other selected locations
- an expanding regional market for cars as per capita incomes increase.

Volkswagen expands

Prior to EU membership, Slovakia already boasted a Volkswagen (VW) plant with an output of 250 000 cars a year. The Bratislava plant is one of the top three Volkswagen factories in the world producing the Polo, the Touareg and the SEAT Ibiza.

In addition to its car manufacturing plant in Bratislava, which was founded in 1991, VW also has a plant manufacturing components in Martin, which opened in 2000. Between the two plants, VW employs 8700 workers. A number of companies supplying parts to VW have also opened up in Slovakia.

Other recent investment

In 2006, Hyundai opened a major car factory in Slovakia. The location of the factory is near Zilina, 200 km north-east of Bratislava. As with other large car plants, it is attracting some of its main suppliers to locate nearby. With its seven suppliers, the total investment is estimated to be $1.4 billion.

In 2006, Peugeot opened a large new car plant in Trnava, 50 km from Bratislava. When it reaches maximum production this state-of-the-art plant will export 300 000 cars a year to western Europe and to other parts of the world.

Section 1.3 Activities

1 Why have Slovakia and other eastern EU countries been so keen to attract foreign car manufacturers?

2 Discuss the reasons for such a high level of investment in car manufacturing in Slovakia by foreign TNCs.

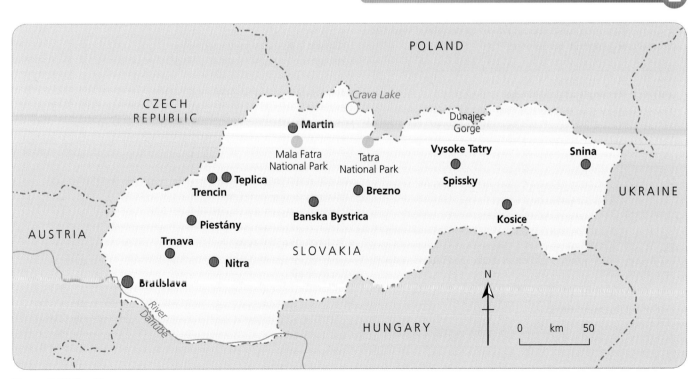

Figure 1.35 Slovakia

Industrial agglomeration and functional (industrial) linkages

Industrial agglomeration is the clustering together and association of economic activities in close proximity to one another. Agglomeration can result in companies enjoying the benefits of external economies of scale (Figure 1.37). This means the lowering of a firm's costs due to external factors. For example, the grouping together of a number of companies may encourage local government to upgrade the transport infrastructure and attract bus companies to run new services. Companies may be able to share certain costs, such as security and catering. Such benefits are greatly increased if they actually do business together.

Alfred Weber published his *Theory of the Location of Industries* in 1909. At that turn of the century, transportation was a much greater element of total industrial costs than it is today, and for many industries it was the major cost. Thus it is not surprising that Weber developed his theory around the cost of transportation. However, he did recognise that other elements of total cost could also vary, particularly labour and the savings associated with agglomeration.

Weber referred to the savings that could be made when firms located together as 'agglomeration economies'. In Figure 1.37 the least transport cost location and the critical isodapanes for agglomeration for three factories are shown. Only in area 5 will all three factories benefit from agglomerating there.

The success of one company may attract other companies from the same or industry groups. Alternatively, a number of smaller firms may combine to produce components for a larger product.

Industrial (functional) linkages are the contacts and flows of information between companies that can happen more cheaply and easily when companies locate in close proximity. Three types of linkage are generally recognised:

Figure 1.36 A container ship, Seattle dockside

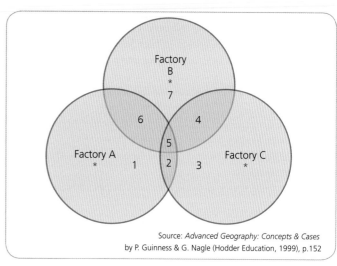

Source: *Advanced Geography: Concepts & Cases* by P. Guinness & G. Nagle (Hodder Education, 1999), p.152

Figure 1.37 Agglomeration economies

a Vertical (or simple chain) linkages

The raw material goes through several successive processes:

b Horizontal (or simple origin) linkages

An industry relies on several other industries to provide its component parts:

c Diagonal linkages

An industry makes a component which can be used subsequently in several industries :

d Technological linkages

A product from one industy is used subsequently as a raw material by other industries:

Figure 1.38 Types of industrial linkage

- backward linkages: to firms providing raw materials, components and services needed in its production processes and activities
- forward linkages: to firms further processing the product or using it as a component part
- horizontal linkages: with other companies involved in the same processes or production, for example collaboration in research or marketing.

Figure 1.38 shows examples of the linkages that can induce companies to locate together.

Industrial estates

An **industrial estate** is an area zoned and planned for the purpose of industrial development. Industrial estates are also known as industrial parks and trading estates. A more 'lightweight' version is the business park or office park, which has offices and light industry, rather than larger-scale industry.

Industrial estates can be found in a range of locations, from inner cities to rural areas. In inner cities they tend to be relatively small, but nevertheless important to local employment. Industrial estates are usually located close to transport infrastructure, especially where more than one transport mode meet. The logic behind industrial estates includes:

- concentrating dedicated infrastructure in a delimited area to reduce the per-business expense of that infrastructure
- attracting new business by providing an integrated infrastructure in one location
- separating industrial uses from residential areas to try to reduce the environmental and social impact of the industrial uses
- providing for localised environmental controls that are specific to the needs of an industrial area
- eligibility of industrial estates for grants and loans under regional economic development policies.

Export processing zones

There are a number of different types of **export processing zones** (EPZs), including free trade zones, special economic

Table 1.7 Export processing zones – types of zones

	Trade	Manufacturing			Services		
	Free port	Special economic zone	Industrial free zone/EPZ	Enterprise zone	Information processing zone	Financial services zone	Commercial free zone
Physical characteristics	Entire city or jurisdiction	Entire province, region or municipality	Enclave or industrial park	Part of city or entire city	Part of city or 'zone within zone'	Entire city or 'zone within zone'	Warehouse area, often adjacent to port or airport
Economic objectives	Development of trading centre and diversified economic base	Deregulation; private sector investment in restricted area	Development of export industry	Development of SMEs in depressed areas	Development of information processing centre	Development of offshore banking, insurance, securities hub	Facilitation of trade and imports
Duty-free goods allowed	All goods for use in trade, industry, consumption	Selective basis	Capital equipment and production inputs	No	Capital equipment	Varies	All goods for storage and re-export of imports
Typical activities	Trade, service, industry, banking, etc.	All types of industry and services	Light industry and manufacturing	All	Data processing, software development, computer graphics	Financial services	Warehousing, packaging, distribution, trans-shipment
Incentives: • taxation • customs duties • labour laws • other	Simple business start-up; minimal tax and regulatory restraints. Waivers with regard to termination of employment and overtime. Free repatriation of capital, profits and dividends, preferential interest rates.	Reduced business taxes; liberalised labour codes; reduced foreign exchange controls. No specific advantages; trade unions are discouraged within the SEZ.	Profits tax abatement and regulatory relief; exemption from foreign exchange controls. Free repatriation of profits. Trade union freedom restricted despite the fact that EPZs are required to respect national employment regulations. 15 years' exemptions on all taxes (maximum).	Zoning relief; simplifed business registration; local tax abatement; reduction of licensing requirements. Trade unions are prohibited. Government mandated liberal policies on hiring and firing of workers.	De-monopolisation and deregulation of telcoms; access to market-priced INTELSAT services. A specific authority manages labour relations. Trade union freedom restricted.	Tax relief, strict confidentiality; deregulation of currency exchange and capital movements. Free repatriation of profits.	Exemption from import quotas. Reinvested profits wholly tax-free.

continued overleaf

	Trade	Manufacturing			Services		
	Free port	**Special economic zone**	**Industrial free zone/EPZ**	**Enterprise zone**	**Information processing zone**	**Financial services zone**	**Commercial free zone**
Domestic sales	Unrestricted within free port; outside free port, upon payment of full duty	Highly restricted	Limited to small portion of production			Limited to small portion of production	Unlimited, upon payment of full duty
Other features	Additional incentives and streamlined procedures	Developed by socialist countries	May be extended to single-factory sites				
Typical examples	Hong Kong (China), Singapore, Bahamas free port, Batam Labuan, Macao	China (southern provinces incl. Hainan and Shenzhen)	Ireland, Taiwan (China), Malaysia, Dominican Republic, Mauritius, Kenya, Hungary	Indonesia, Senegal	India (Bangalore), Caribbean	Bahrein, Dubai, Caribbean, Turkey, Cayman Islands	Jebel Ali, Colon Miami (US FTZ), Mauritius, Iran

Source: www.ilo.org

zones, bonded warehouses, and free ports. The International Labour Organisation (ILO) has defined EPZs as 'industrial zones with special incentives set up to attract foreign investors, in which imported materials undergo some degree of processing before being re-exported'. This can also include electronic data. EPZs have evolved from initial assembly and simple processing activities to include high-tech and science parks, finance zones, logistics centres and even tourist resorts. Table 1.7 summarises the different types of EPZ.

Table 1.8 shows the considerable global increase in number of EPZs, rising from 79 in 1975 to 3500 in 2006. Asia and Central America have the largest share of employment in EPZs. Apart from China, which has 40 million people working in EPZs, the rest of Asia has 15 million people employed in EPZs. In Central America, 5 million workers come into this category.

Table 1.8 The development of export processing zones

Years	1975	1986	1997	2002	2006
Number of countries with EPZs	25	47	93	116	130
Number of EPZs or similar types of zone	79	176	845	3000	3500
Employment (millions)	n.a.	n.a.	22.5	43	66
– of which China	n.a.	n.a.	18	30	40
– of which other countries with figures available	0.8	1.9	4.5	13	26

The formal and informal sectors of employment

The concept of the informal sector was introduced into international usage in 1972 by the ILO. Jobs in the **formal sector** will be known to the government department responsible for taxation and to other government offices. Such jobs generally provide better pay and much greater security than jobs in the **informal sector**. Fringe benefits such as holiday and sick pay may also be available. Formal sector employment includes health and education service workers, government workers, and people working in established manufacturing and retail companies.

In contrast, the informal sector is that part of the economy operating outside official government recognition. Employment is generally low-paid and often temporary and/or part-time in nature. While such employment is outside the tax system, job security will be poor with an absence of fringe benefits. About three-quarters of those working in the informal sector are employed in services. Typical jobs are shoe-shiners, street food stalls, messengers, repair shops and market traders (Figure 1.39). Informal manufacturing tends to include both the workshop sector, making for example cheap furniture, and the traditional craft sector. Many of these goods are sold in bazaars and street markets.

The government estimates that about 5 per cent of all employment in the UK is in the informal sector. This usually occurs when people insist on being paid in cash and do not declare this to the Inland Revenue. Examples may be window cleaners, part-time bar staff, cleaners and builders. In LEDCs the informal sector may account for up to 40 per cent of the total economy.

A World Bank report recognises two types of informal sector activities:

- coping strategies (survival activities): casual jobs, temporary jobs, unpaid jobs, subsistence agriculture, multiple job holding
- unofficial earning strategies (illegality in business):
  - unofficial business activities: tax evasion, avoidance of labour regulation and other government or institutional regulations, no registration of the company
  - underground activities: crime, corruption (activities not registered by statistical offices).

The advantages of the informal sector are that it:

- provides jobs and reduces unemployment and underemployment
- alleviates poverty
- bolsters entrepreneurial activity
- facilitates community cohesion and solidarity.

Activities in the informal sector have to contend with a significant number of obstacles. For example:

- There is little access to credit for workers in the informal sector to finance their activities, although in some countries microcredit is being used to fill this gap.
- The World Bank estimates that the size of the informal labour market varies from the estimated 4–6 per cent in the high-income countries to over 50 per cent in the low-income countries. Its size and role in the economy increases during economic downturns and periods of economic adjustment and transition.
- Women in Informal Employment: Globalising and Organising (WIEGO) is a global research-policy network that seeks to improve the status of the working poor, especially women, in the informal economy. It does so by highlighting the size, composition, characteristics and contribution of the informal economy through improved statistics and research.

Informal sector employment can be found in all parts of urban areas but is particularly concentrated in and around the CBD where potential demand for such services is at its highest. It is also often concentrated at key tourism locations where the informal crafts sector is in clear evidence. Informal sector employment is also attracted to industrial areas offering food and other services to industrial workers.

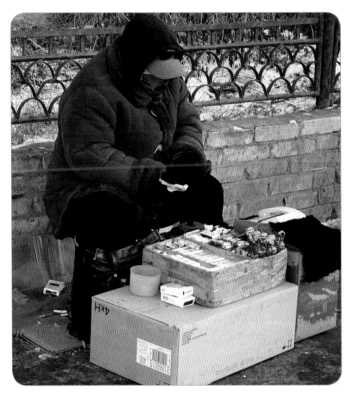

Figure 1.39 Informal sector – selling cigarettes on the street in Ulaanbaatar

1.4 The management of industrial change: India

Case Study

India

With in excess of 1 billion people, India has the second largest population in the world. India is the 'I' in **BRIC**, the new buzzword for the economies tipped for rapid growth: Brazil, Russia, India and China. Because of its recent rapid economic growth (Figure 1.40), India is classed as a newly industrialised country (NIC). However, unlike other Asian economies such as South Korea, Taiwan, Thailand and Malaysia, which all became NICs at an earlier date, the recent transformation of the Indian economy has been based more on the service sector than on manufacturing. This has been at least partly due to a low level of **foreign direct investment** in manufacturing, a situation that began to change in the early 1990s with the introduction of a number of important economic reforms.

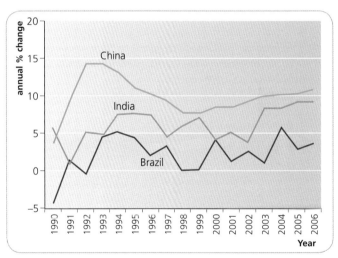

Figure 1.40 Annual percentage change of GDP in India, China and Brazil

The service sector accounts for 52 per cent of India's GDP, with industry responsible for 28 per cent and agriculture for 17 per cent (Figure 1.41). The situation with regard to employment is very different. Agriculture leads with 52 per cent of the workforce. Services account for 34 per cent and industry 14 per cent.

Textiles is the largest industry in the country, employing about 20 million people and accounting for one-third of India's exports. The car industry has expanded significantly in recent times and is now the seventh largest in the world, with a production of 2.6 million vehicles in 2009. However, it is in the field of software and ICT in general that India has built a global reputation. Figure 1.42 shows the major manufacturing hubs in India for automobiles (Figure 1.43), machine tools, textiles and pharmaceuticals.

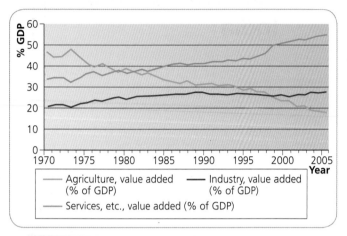

Figure 1.41 Main economic sectors' share of Indian GDP

Traditional industrial policy

In 1950, India was arguably the first non-communist LEDC to institute a fully-fledged industrial policy. The objective of India's policy was to co-ordinate investment decisions in both the public and private sectors and to bring certain strategic industries and companies under public ownership. Following the example of the former Soviet Union, five-year plans were set up and this state-directed industrialisation model was followed from 1950 to 1980. The five-year plans were designed to bring about economic and social development within a 'socialist' framework. The main objectives of the plans were to:

- industrialise
- raise per capita incomes

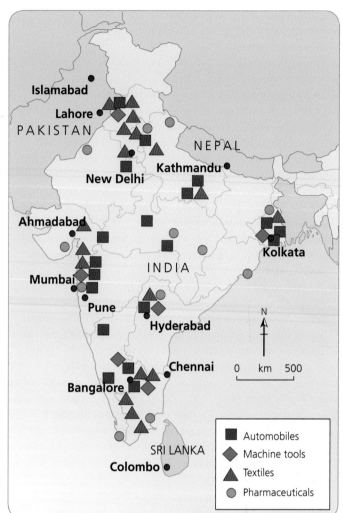

Figure 1.42 Major manufacturing hubs in India

Figure 1.43 Car manufacturing in India

- achieve equity in the distribution of gains from economic development
- reduce the existing concentration of economic power
- achieve a more even regional distribution of industrial development.

The role of **heavy industry**, particularly of iron and steel, was emphasised, with the public sector playing a major role in the structural transformation of the economy from what was primarily an agricultural society. Investment in the private sector would be based not on the issue of profitability, but according to the requirements of the overall national plan. Technological self-reliance became an important element of industrial policy. Here, the objective was to produce as much as possible inside India itself and keep imports to a minimum. This would be important for India's trade balance and also advance technical knowledge in the country.

Industrial policy measures under the five-year plans included:
- industrial licensing – a firm that wanted to manufacture a new product or sought a substantial expansion of its existing capacity had to obtain a government licence
- strict import controls
- subsidising exports
- strict controls on investment by transnational corporations.

The range of controls made India one of the most protected economies in the world. High tariffs made imports very expensive and thus controlled their volume. The Indian model was not just influenced by the Soviet Union but also by Fabian socialism and UK labour party thinkers like Harold Laski. In the 1980s the model began to erode (as some liberalisation measures were introduced) and it was virtually abandoned after a serious external liquidity crisis in 1991.

The Planning Commission has taken the major role in formulating industrial policy and in guiding India's ongoing industrial revolution. It is still widely accepted by the country's mainstream political parties.

Many economists argue that India made a serious error from 1950 in taking on so many aspects of socialist central planning. The main criticisms were that there were far too many rules and regulations which proved to be a major hindrance in the successful development of private sector industry. There was widespread corruption and massive inefficiency. Considerable aid from the West seemed to have very little impact on the industrial sector. However, opinion does differ widely on this subject.

Economic reform

The currency crisis of 1991 proved to be a major turning point, instigating bold economic reforms that resulted in rapid economic growth that is likely to double average productivity levels and living standards in India every 16 years. The economic reforms were based on:
- liberalisation – fewer government regulations and restrictions in the economy
- deregulation – changing regulatory policies and laws to increase competition among suppliers of commodities and services

- market orientation – more careful analysis of demand in domestic and global markets.

Tariffs on imports were significantly reduced along with other non-tariff trade barriers as a result of India's membership of the World Trade Organisation (WTO). The essence was greater freedom from government control. This 'unshackling' of the economy is credited with increasing the growth rate of GDP from 3 to 3.5 per cent during the period 1950–80 and to 6 to 7 per cent in recent decades. The international financial institutions (IFIs) regard India as a major beneficiary of globalisation and are urging India to undertake even more reforms to open up its economy even further.

Instead of planning inputs and outputs for each company and each industry, the government adopted indicative planning. However, it maintained high tariffs by international standards and restrictions on portfolio and foreign direct investment. India has been determined to be master of its own policies and not to blindly copy the 'Western model'.

India's technological success has not been confined to the ICT industry. The country's corporations have achieved significant growth in a number of industries including in particular pharmaceuticals and auto components. It is one of only three countries in the world to build super-computers on its own, and one of only six countries in the world to launch satellites.

The relationship between growth of manufacturing and that of services is an issue of considerable significance for the economic development of the country.

Regional policy

Like many other countries, India adopted regional economic planning and tried to encourage a better spread of industry around the country. In the early 1970s, backward states and districts were identified and a scheme of incentives for industry to locate in these regions was introduced. This included:
- a grant of 15 per cent of fixed capital investment
- transport subsidies
- income tax concessions.

In 1977 central government decided that no more industrial licences would be granted in and around metropolitan cities and urban areas with a population of 500 000 and more. In 1980 new initiatives confirmed the government's commitment to correcting regional imbalance. The number of industrial concentrations has risen from about half a dozen in 1965 to more than 40 today, indicating a significant spatial expansion. In terms of international comparison, India has achieved a reasonable degree of success in its attempts to narrow regional imbalance.

Industrial policy and ICT

In the last two decades India has spawned a modern, highly export-oriented ICT industry. The export intensity of Indian software is more than 70 per cent, compared with an overall export intensity of 10 per cent for the economy as a whole. The country's comparative advantage lies largely in the availability of low-cost skilled labour. In 2000 the comparative salaries of software professionals in India were less than a tenth of those of similar professionals in the USA. The background to this success was established in the era of traditional industrial policy, which more recent reforms have magnified. In the pre-1980 era:

- A large number of engineering colleges were established, particularly in the south of India under entrepreneurial state governments. These colleges were subsidised to a considerable degree by state and central government.
- The government's philosophy in this period was to create a broad science and technology base to transform the Indian economy by stimulating domestic innovation. The benefits of this process were particularly felt by the ICT, biotechnology and pharmaceutical industries.
- The government's role in the establishment of Bangalore as a hub attracting the bulk of the country's technological and scientific activity was fundamental to the development of the

city as a global centre of ICT. Bangalore was favoured partly because of its distance from Pakistan and China, countries with which India has had difficult relations in the past. NASSCOM, the Indian software association, has stated: 'The software and services industry has received immense support from the government both at the central and state level. This support in the form of tax incentives and other benefits has been instrumental in the growth of software and services exports.'

With the background set in the traditional industrial policy era, the age of reform has seen the ICT industry flourish, attracting high levels of foreign direct investment.

Future industrial policy

The direction taken by the Planning Commission in the future will have a major impact on India's economic performance (Figure 1.44). Many Indian economists stress the importance of

By Niranjan Rajadhyaksha

Some Japanese scholars have used a picturesque analogy to describe the gradual spread of development in Asia, with countries escaping mass poverty in a V-shaped formation that resembles a flock of flying geese.

Japan led the way after World War II, till rising wage costs in the 1960s led to the shift of low-value manufacturing to other regional economies in decadal waves that pulled millions off the farm and into the factory.

Most Asian countries that prospered used explicit industrial policies – and a rigged exchange rate – to build manufacturing prowess. Such policies went out of fashion in recent decades, but seem to have made a comeback in the entire ideological churn in the wake of the Western financial crisis.

World Bank chief economist Justin Lin says it is time to rethink development policy, with the state playing an important role even though 'the market is the basic mechanism for effective resource allocation'. There are clear signs that there has been a change in the attitude of the Indian government as well: industrial policy is making a quiet comeback in India.

The contours of the new industrial policy seem quite different from the sort of policies followed by Nehruvian India and other Asian countries in their early stages of development. 'The needs of building competitive enterprises and meeting WTO requirements need to be taken into account,' Planning Commission member Arun Maira told me during a telephonic chat. This means the new industrial policy that is emerging will not have much of the old statist and protectionist policy mix: protection through high import tariffs, preferential access to bank funds, promotion of national champions and resource allocation by a government agency.

Yet, there is a clear belief that the country needs an explicit industrial strategy. The government will choose which industries need encouragement and design suitable policies. Physical and social infrastructure will also be developed, a process that should lower transaction costs and raise the rates of return on investment.

Maira gave me three key policy parameters that will be kept in mind in designing the new economic strategy – there should be a growth in quality jobs, the Indian economy should get strategic depth in capital goods such as power and telecom equipment, and defence and security issues should be kept in mind.

There will be both technical and political economy challenges here. The technical challenge is to identify industries that need a helping hand, and one assumes that government agencies have an understanding of India's factor endowments and comparative advantages. The political economy challenge is perhaps even more complex. Comparative advantage rapidly changes in the modern economy and technology cycles are getting shorter. Policy will have to be flexible if India is not to stagnate.

A market economy has immense flexibility. Japan was a pioneer of successful industrial policy, but it lost the flexibility that it needed to fight its long economic stagnation. South Korea provides another lesson. Industrial policy there led to the formation of industrial conglomerates – the chaebol – and the gradual decline into crony capitalism.

What the Planning Commission has now set out to do is thus interesting but fraught with risks of regulatory capture and rent-seeking by favoured industrial groups. Maira says it is important that the focus of industrial policy remains on sectors rather than companies, in the attempts to forge closer collaboration between 'productive sectors and policymakers'.

Figure 1.44 India's new industrial policy

achieving the best possible balance between the manufacturing and the service sectors. The general feeling is that India should take advantage of its strength in ICT and use it extensively in all areas of the economy to upgrade agriculture, industry and services in order to compete more effectively in the global economy. A major issue is the distribution of the gains and losses from globalisation. It seems that most gains have accrued to the Indian urban middle-class of around 100 million people, which amounts to less than 10 per cent of the country's population.

The state of India's infrastructure is also an important issue. Infrastructure in India is at a lower level than that in China and other newly industrialised countries in the region. Current spending on the elements of infrastructure such as railways, roads, seaports and airports is about 6 per cent of GDP. This is about 50 per cent below what the government itself thinks needs to be spent. Because of the huge sums of money involved, the Planning Commission suggests that it can only be done by creating a partnership with the private sector.

Bangalore: India's high-tech city

Bangalore, Hyderabad and Chennai, in the south, along with the western city of Pune and the capital city Delhi, have emerged as the centres of India's high-technology industry.

Bangalore is the most important individual centre in India for high-tech industry. The city's pleasant climate, moderated by its location on the Deccan Plateau over 900 m above sea level, is a significant attraction to foreign and domestic companies alike (Figures 1.45 and 1.46). Known as 'the Garden City', Bangalore claims to have the highest quality of life in the country. Because of its dust-free environment, large public-sector undertakings such as Hindustan Aeronautics Ltd and the Indian Space Research Organisation were established in Bangalore by the Indian government. The state government also has a long history of support for science and technology. The city prides itself on

a 'culture of learning' which gives it an innovative leadership within India.

In the 1980s Bangalore became the location for the first large-scale foreign investment in high-technology in India when Texas Instruments selected the city above a number of other contenders.

Figure 1.45 Location of Bangalore

BANGALORE

- Bangalore is the location of 925 software companies employing more than 80 000 IT workers. Bangalore accounts for nearly 40 per cent of India's software exports.
- The city has 46 integrated circuit design companies, 166 systems software companies and 108 communications software companies. Over 40 per cent of Bangalore's software exports are in these high-technology areas.
- Major companies include Tata Consulting Services (TCS), Infosys Technologies, Wipro and Kshema Technologies.
- The 170 000 m² International Tech Park was set up as a joint venture between the government of Karnataka state, the government of Singapore, and the House of TATA. The Electronic City is an industrial area with over 100 electronics companies including Infosys, Wipro, Siemens, Motorola and TI.
- The city has attracted outsourcing right across the IT spectrum from software development to IT enabled services.
- The city boasts 21 engineering colleges.
- NASDAQ, the world's biggest stock exchange, with a turnover of over $20 trillion, opened its third international office in Bangalore in 2001.

Figure 1.46 Bangalore Factfile

Other multinationals soon followed as the reputation of the city grew. Important backward and forward linkages were steadily established over time. Apart from ICT industries, Bangalore is also India's most important centre for aerospace and biotechnology.

India's ICT sector has benefited from the filter-down of business from MEDCS. Many European and North American companies which previously outsourced their ICT requirements to local companies are now using Indian companies because:

- labour costs are considerably lower
- a number of MEDCs have significant ICT skills shortages

- India has a large and able English-speaking workforce (there are about 50 million English-speakers in India).

Since 1981, the city's population has more than doubled from 2.4 million to over 5 million, while the number of vehicles has grown even faster, from fewer than 200 000 cars and scooters to over 1.6 million. The city's landscape has changed dramatically, with many new glass-and-steel skyscrapers and numerous cybercafés.

Section 1.4 Activities

1 Why is India described as a *newly industrialised country*?

2 Describe the trends shown in Figure 1.40.

3 Describe and explain the changing share of India's GDP by the three main economic sectors.

4 With reference to an atlas map of India and Figure 1.42, comment on the spatial distribution of India's major manufacturing hubs.

5 Discuss the development of traditional industrial policy in India.

6 Comment on the changes in industrial policy that began in the early 1990s.

7 How has the Indian government tried to narrow regional industrial imbalance?

8 In terms of future industrial policy, produce a 100-word summary of Figure 1.44.

9 How has government policy helped to build India's ICT industry into one of global prominence?

2 Environmental management

2.1 Sustainable energy supplies

Non-renewable and renewable energy

Non-renewable sources of energy are the **fossil fuels** and nuclear fuel. These are finite, so as they are used up the supply that remains is reduced. Eventually these non-renewable resources could become completely exhausted. **Renewable energy** can be used over and over again. The sources of renewable energy are mainly forces of nature that are sustainable and which usually cause little or no environmental pollution. Renewable energy includes hydro-electric (HEP), biomass, wind, solar, geothermal, tidal and wave power.

At present, non-renewable resources dominate global energy. The challenge is to transform the global **energy mix** to achieve a better balance between renewables and non-renewables. The key energy issues for individual countries are the three S's: Sustainability, Security and Strategy.

Energy shortages have occurred on a number of occasions in the past. Figure 2.1 predicts what could happen in the USA as a result of significant energy shortages.

Factors affecting the demand for and supply of energy

At the national scale there are huge variations in energy demand and supply. Demand is primarily governed by the size of a country's population and its level of economic development. The gap between the world's richest and poorest countries in terms of energy demand is huge. Growth in energy demand is particularly rapid in newly industrialised countries such as China and India. A country's energy policy can have a significant impact on demand if it focuses on efficiency and sustainability as opposed to concentrating solely on building more power stations and refining facilities. High levels of pollution due to energy consumption can be a strong stimulus to developing a cleaner energy policy.

As might be expected, global variations in energy supply occur for a number of reasons. These can be broadly subdivided into physical, economic and political factors. Table 2.1 shows examples for each of these groupings. The combination of factors operating in each country can vary significantly.

ENERGY CRISIS AMERICA: A PREVIEW

As the energy crisis deepens people will make fewer trips, plan trips better, drive less and carpool. High-mileage cars will be in demand and the SUV market will die. With less and slower driving due to high petrol prices the number of accidents will go down. Park and Ride schemes will become more prevalent and the government will encourage energy savings with tax breaks.

Businesses will turn off advertising lights and more people will wash their clothes in cold water. In poor areas there will be more deaths from heat in the summer and more deaths from cold in the winter due to energy costs. Fuel riots may occur.

The energy crisis will increase illegal immigration from Mexico where there is increasing unemployment. This will add to social tensions. Chronic heating oil shortages may cause a greater migration to the Sun Belt. The middle class may shrink with more people sinking into poverty. There will be more homelessness. Eventually energy efficiency measures unthinkable today will become the law of the land. Extreme right wing politicians will call for military control of all Middle East oil for the good of the world.

Source: Gasprices-usa.com/EnergyCrisisUSA

Figure 2.1 Prediction of the future with energy shortages

The key factor in supply is energy resource endowment. Some countries are relatively rich in domestic energy resources while others are lacking in such resources and heavily reliant on imports. However, resources by themselves do not constitute supply. Capital and technology are required to exploit resources.

Table 2.1 Factors affecting the supply of energy

Physical
• Deposits of fossil fuels are only found in a limited number of locations.
• Large-scale HEP development requires high precipitation, major steep-sided valleys and impermeable rock.
• Large power stations require flat land and geologically stable foundations.
• Solar power needs a large number of days a year with strong sunlight.
• Wind power needs high average wind speeds throughout the year.
• Tidal power stations require a very large tidal range.
• The availability of biomass varies widely according to climatic conditions.

Economic
• The most accessible, and lowest-cost, deposits of fossil fuels are invariably developed first.
• Onshore deposits of oil and gas are usually cheaper to develop than offshore deposits.
• Potential HEP sites close to major transport routes and existing electricity transmission corridors are more economical to build than those in very inaccessible locations.
• In poor countries foreign direct investment is often essential for the development of energy resources.
• When energy prices rise significantly, companies increase spending on exploration and development.

Political
• Countries wanting to develop nuclear electricity require permission from the International Atomic Energy Agency.
• International agreements such as the Kyoto Protocol can have a considerable influence on the energy decisions of individual countries.
• Potential HEP schemes on 'international rivers' may require the agreement of other countries that share the river.
• Governments may insist on energy companies producing a certain proportion of their energy from renewable sources.
• Legislation regarding emissions from power stations will favour the use of, for example, low-sulphur coal, as opposed to coal with a high sulphur content.

The use of energy in all countries has changed over time due to a number of factors:

• Technological development – for example: (a) Nuclear electricity has only been available since 1954. (b) Oil and gas can now be extracted from much deeper waters than in the past. (c) Renewable energy technology is advancing steadily.

• Increasing national wealth: as average incomes increase, living standards improve which involves the increasing use of energy and the use of a greater variety of energy sources.

• Changes in demand: at one time all of Britain's trains were powered by coal and most people also used coal for heating in their homes. Before natural gas was discovered in the North Sea, Britain's gas was produced from coal (coal gas).

• Changes in price: the relative prices of the different types of energy can influence demand. Electricity production in the UK has been switching from coal to gas over the past 20 years mainly because power stations are cheaper to run on natural gas.

• Environmental factors/public opinion: public opinion can influence decisions made by governments. People today are much better informed about the environmental impact of energy sources than they were in the past.

Section 2.1 Activities

1 Look at Table 2.1. Select two bullet points from each of the three categories to investigate further. Present your findings to others in your class.

2 For the UK, find out when:
  a the last steam trains (burning coal) stopped being used on Britain's general railway network
  b nuclear electricity first came on line
  c North Sea gas first came on line.

Trends in consumption of conventional energy resources

The fossil fuels dominate the global energy situation. Their relative contributions are (2008): oil 34.8 per cent, coal 29.3 per cent, natural gas 24.1 per cent. In contrast, HEP accounted for 6.4 per cent and nuclear energy 5.5 per cent of global energy. The main data source used in this topic is the *BP Statistical Review of World Energy*. It includes commercially traded fuels only. It excludes fuels such as wood, peat and animal waste which, though important in many countries, are unreliably documented in terms of production and consumption statistics.

Figure 2.2 shows the regional pattern of energy consumption for 2008. Consumption by type of fuel varies widely by world region:

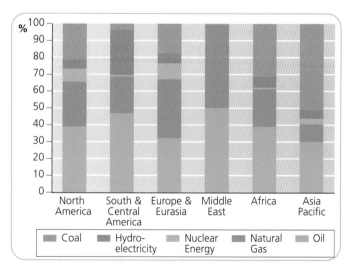

Figure 2.2 The regional pattern of energy consumption, 2008

- **Oil:** nowhere is the contribution of oil less than 30 per cent and it is the main source of energy in four of the six regions shown in Figure 2.2. In the Middle East it accounts for approximately 50 per cent of consumption.
- **Coal:** only in the Asia Pacific region is coal the main source of energy. In contrast it accounts for only 4 per cent in South and Central America and 1.5 per cent in the Middle East.
- **Natural gas:** natural gas is the main source of energy in Europe and Eurasia and it is a close second to oil in the Middle East. Its lowest share of the energy mix is 11 per cent in the Asia Pacific region.
- **Hydro-electricity:** the relative importance of hydro-electricity is greatest in South and Central America (26.3 per cent). Elsewhere its contribution varies from 6.2 per cent in Africa to less than 1 per cent in the Middle East.
- **Nuclear energy:** nuclear energy is not presently available in the Middle East and it makes the smallest contribution of the five energy sources in Asia Pacific, Africa and South and Central America. It is most important in Europe and Eurasia and North America.

Figure 2.3 shows how global consumption of the five major traditional sources of energy changed between 1983 and 2008. Figure 2.4 shows the change in daily oil consumption by world region from 1983 to 2008. From less than 60 million barrels daily global in the early 1980s, demand rose steeply to 84.5 million barrels a day in 2008. The largest increase has been in the Asia Pacific region which now accounts for 30.1 per cent of consumption. This region now uses more oil than North America, which accounts for 27.4 per cent of the world total. In contrast, Africa consumed only 3.4 per cent of global oil, behind South and Central America with 6.9 per cent.

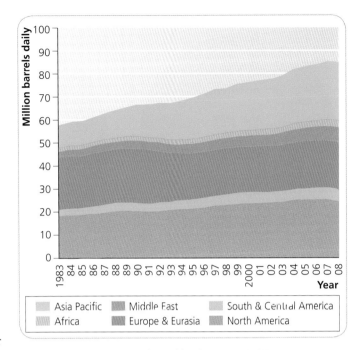

Figure 2.4 Oil consumption by world region, 1983–2008

Oil: global patterns and trends

The pattern of regional production is markedly different from that of consumption. In 2008, the Middle East accounted for 31.9 per cent of production, followed by Europe and Eurasia (21.7 per cent), North America (15.8 per cent), and Africa (12.4 per cent). Within the Middle East, Saudi Arabia dominates production, alone accounting for 13.1 per cent of the world total. The Russian Federation accounts for over half the total production of Europe and Eurasia.

Figure 2.5 illustrates the spatial distribution of **proved oil reserves**. In the period 1988–2008, proved reserves rose considerably but much more so in the latter part of the period than in the earlier part. However, the problem is that demand is increasing at a faster rate than proved reserves. In 2008, the Middle East accounted for almost 60 per cent of global proved reserves. The main countries contributing to this figure are: Saudi Arabia 21 per cent; Iran 10.9 per cent; Iraq 9.1 per cent; Kuwait 8.1 per cent; and the United Arab Emirates 7.8 per cent. Europe and Eurasia held the second largest proved reserves with 11.3 per cent of the world total; the Russian Federation accounted for over half of this last figure.

Table 2.2 shows the **reserves-to-production (R/P) ratio** for the world in 2008. While the R/P ratio is almost 79 years in the Middle East it is only 14.8 years in North America and 14.5 years in Asia Pacific.

The US government's Energy Information Agency predicts that the demand for oil will rise by 54 per cent in the first quarter of the twenty-first century. This amounts to an extra 44 million barrels of oil each day by 2025. Much of this extra demand will come from Asia. All estimates indicate that the Persian Gulf's share of the oil trade will rise steadily over the next two decades and along with it the risk of terrorist attack and embargo by the key producing countries.

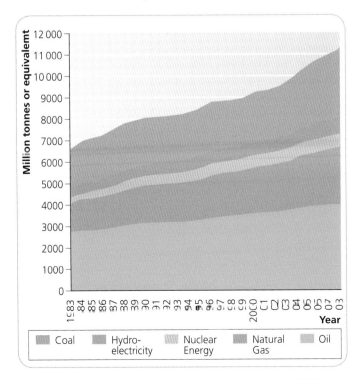

Figure 2.3 Global consumption of major energy sources, 1983–2008

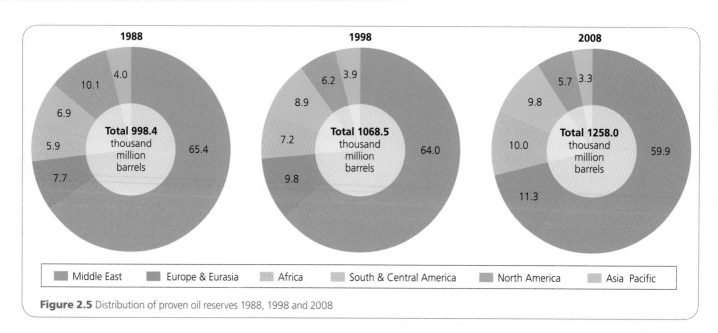

Figure 2.5 Distribution of proven oil reserves 1988, 1998 and 2008

Table 2.2 Oil reserves to production ratio 2009

Region	Reserves/Production ratio (years)
North America	15.0
South and Central America	80.6
Europe and Eurasia	21.2
Middle East	84.8
Africa	36.0
Asia Pacific	14.4
World	45.7

Source: *BP Statistical Review of World Energy 2010*

When will global peak oil production occur?

There has been growing concern about when global oil production will peak and how fast it will decline thereafter. For example, in the USA oil production peaked in 1970. There are concerns that there are not enough large-scale projects underway to offset declining production in well-established oil production areas. The rate of major new oilfield discoveries has fallen sharply in recent years. It takes six years on average from first discovery for a very large-scale project to start producing oil. The International Energy

Agency expects **peak oil production** somewhere between 2013 and 2037, with a fall by 3 per cent a year after the peak. The US Geological Survey predicts that the peak is 50 years or more away.

In a report published by **OPEC (Organisation of Petroleum Exporting Countries)** in 2009, this major energy organisation stated that 'the global reserve/resource base can easily meet forecast demand growth for decades to come' (Figure 2.7). OPEC highlights improved recovery techniques in existing oilfields, the number of new discoveries and the increasing use of non-conventional oil resources. The organisation argues that technological advance continues to blur the distinction between conventional and non-conventional oil.

However, in total contrast, the Association for the Study of Peak Oil and Gas (ASPO) predicts that the peak of global oil production would come as early as 2011 (Figure 2.8), stating: 'Fifty years ago the world was consuming 4 billion barrels of oil per year and the average discovery was around 30 billion. Today we consume 30 billion barrels per year and the discovery rate is now approaching 4 billion barrels of crude oil per year'. If ASPO is correct and the oil peak is imminent, there is not enough time to shift energy use to alternative sources.

Figure 2.6 Supply of and demand for oil **a** An oil well in Dorset, UK **b** Marine petrol station on the Amazon River near Manaus, Brazil

Figure 2.7 The headquarters of OPEC in Vienna

ASPO has been criticised because it has changed its prediction of the year when peak oil will occur a number of times. ASPO argues that this is understandable as new data becomes available. It also points out that hard information is often jealously guarded, making the true nature of the supply/demand balance difficult to judge.

Between 1998 and 2008 global oil production increased by 11 per cent. This compares, over the same period, with the following changes in the other four traditional sources of traded energy:

- a rise of 35 per cent in natural gas production
- a 49 per cent increase in coal production
- a 13 per cent increase in nuclear energy
- a 22 per cent rise in HEP.

A number of renewable energy sources showed more spectacular percentage gains, but from a much lower base.

Section 2.1 Activities

1 Explain why the locations of global oil production and consumption vary so widely.

2 Define the *reserves-to-production ratio*. Describe how this varies around the world.

3 a Why is the prediction of peak oil production so important?
   b Suggest why the predictions of when peak oil production will occur vary so widely.

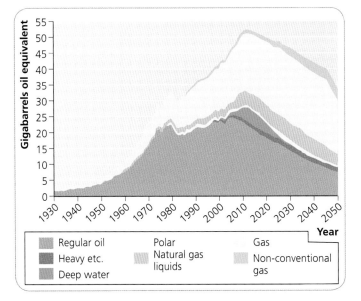

Figure 2.8 Peak oil production – according to ASPO

Natural gas

Global production of natural gas increased from 2273 billion m^3 in 1998 to 3066 billion m^3 in 2008 (Table 2.3). All eight world regions showed an increase in production. However, the largest producing world regions, Europe/Eurasia and North America, recorded the lowest percentage increases between 1998 and 2008. The highest relative changes were in the Middle East and Africa (Figure 2.9).

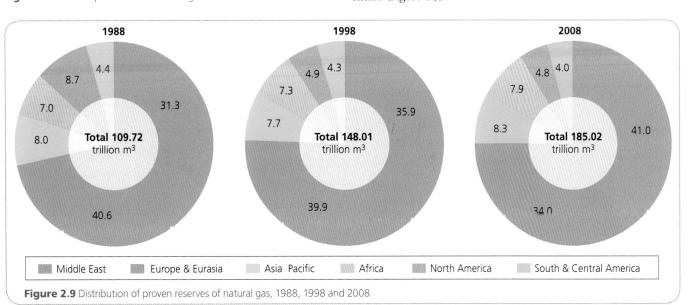

Figure 2.9 Distribution of proven reserves of natural gas, 1988, 1998 and 2008

On an individual country basis, natural gas production is dominated by the Russian Federation (19.6 per cent of the global total) and the USA (19.35 per cent). There is a very substantial gap between these two natural gas giants and the next largest producers, which are Canada (5.7 per cent), Iran (3.8 per cent) and Norway (3.2 per cent).

Table 2.3 Natural gas production by world region, 1999–2009

Region	1999	2009	% change
North America	747.2	813.0	9
South & Central America	92.0	151.6	65
Europe & Eurasia	915.8	973.0	6
Middle East	194.7	407.2	109
Africa	119.7	203.8	70
Asia Pacific	262.6	438.4	67
Total world	2332.0	2987.0	28

Source: *BP Statistical Review of World Energy* 2010

There is a much stronger correlation between consumption and production of natural gas than for oil, due mainly to the different ways these two energy products are transported. Global consumption of natural gas in 2008 was led by Europe and Eurasia (37.8 per cent), North America (27.6 per cent) and Asia Pacific (16.0 per cent).

During the period 1988–2008, proved reserves of natural gas increased substantially (Figure 2.9). The global share of proved reserves in the Middle East has risen considerably while the share held in Europe and Eurasia has declined significantly. On an individual country basis, the largest reserves in 2008 were in the Russian Federation (23.4 per cent), Iran (16 per cent) and Qatar (13.8 per cent). In 2008 the global reserves-to-production ratio stood at 60.4 years.

Coal

Figure 2.10 shows the production and consumption of coal by world region for 1998 and 2008. Coal production is dominated by the Asia Pacific region, accounting for 61.1 per cent of the global total in 2008. Much of this coal is produced in China which alone mines 42.5 per cent of the world total. The next largest producing countries were the USA (18.0 per cent), Australia (6.6 per cent), India (5.8 per cent) and the Russian Federation (4.6 per cent). Like natural gas, there is a strong relationship between the production and consumption of coal by world region. Consumption is led by Asia Pacific (61.5 per cent), North America (18.4 per cent) and Europe and Eurasia (15.8 per cent). China alone consumed 42.6 per cent of world coal in 2008.

Table 2.4 shows proved reserves of coal at the end of 2008. There is a fairly even spread between three regions: Europe/ Eurasia, Asia Pacific and North America. However, in terms of the reserves-to-production ratio then the figure for Asia Pacific at 64 years is significantly below that for other world regions. Coal reserves can become exhausted within a relatively short time period. In the nineteenth and early twentieth centuries countries such as Germany, the UK and France were significant producers. Today there are very few operational coal mines in these three countries (Figure 2.11).

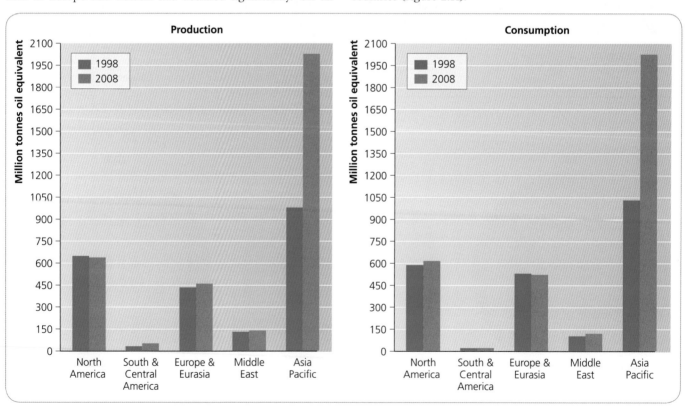

Figure 2.10 Coal production and consumption

Table 2.4 Proved coal reserves 2009

Region	Reserves/Production ratio (years)
North America	235
South & Central America	181
Europe & Eurasia	236
Middle East & Africa	131
Asia Pacific	59
Total world	119

Source: *BP Statistical Review of World Energy 2010*

Figure 2.11 A former coal mine in the Massif Central region of France, which was closed in the early 1990s – it is now a museum to the coal industry

Extending the 'life' of fossil fuels

There are a number of technologies that can improve the use and prolong the life of fossil fuels. These include coal gasification, clean coal technologies and the extraction of unconventional natural gas. Such techniques may be very important in buying time for more renewable energy to come on-line.

Coal gasification is the technology that could transform the situation. At present electricity from coal gasification is more expensive than that from traditional power plants but if more stringent pollution laws are passed in the future, this situation could change significantly.

The coal industry in a number of areas may be on the point of a limited comeback with the development of **clean coal technology**. This new technology has developed forms of coal that burn with greater efficiency and capture coal's pollutants before they are emitted into the atmosphere. The latest 'supercritical' coal-fired power stations, operating at higher pressures and temperatures than their predecessors, can operate at efficiency levels 20 per cent above those of coal-fired power stations constructed in the 1960s. Existing power stations can be upgraded to use clean coal technology.

Conventional natural gas, which is generally found within a few thousand metres or so of the surface, has accounted for

most of the global supply to date. However, in recent years 'unconventional' deposits have begun to contribute more to supply. The main categories of **unconventional natural gas** are:

- deep gas
- tight gas
- gas-containing shales
- coalbed methane
- geopressurised zones
- arctic and sub-sea hydrates.

Unconventional deposits are clearly more costly to extract but as energy prices rise and technology advances, more and more of these deposits are attracting the interest of governments and energy companies.

Nuclear power: a global renaissance?

No other source of energy creates such heated discussion as nuclear power. The main concerns about nuclear power are:

- power plant accidents, which could release radiation into air, land and sea
- radioactive waste storage/disposal
- rogue state or terrorist use of nuclear fuel for weapons
- high construction costs
- the possible increase in certain types of cancer near nuclear plants.

With 103 operating reactors, the USA leads the world in the use of nuclear electricity. This amounts to 31 per cent of the world's total (Figure 2.12), producing 20 per cent of the USA's electricity. At one time the rise of nuclear power looked unstoppable. However, a serious incident at the Three Mile Island nuclear power plant in Pennsylvania in 1979, and the much more serious Chernobyl disaster in the Ukraine in 1986, brought any growth in the industry

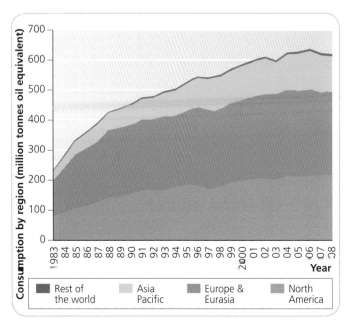

Figure 2.12 Nuclear energy consumption by world region

to a virtual halt. No new nuclear power plants have been ordered in the USA since then, although public opinion has become more favourable in recent years, as memories of the Three Mile Island and Chernobyl incidents recede into the past, and as worries about polluting fossil fuels increase.

The big advantages of nuclear power are:
- there are zero emissions of greenhouse gases
- it means reduced reliance on imported fossil fuels.

The next major consumers of nuclear energy after the USA are France (16.1 per cent of the 2008 world total) and Japan (9.2 per cent). France obtains 78 per cent of its electricity from nuclear power and is thinking about replacing its older plants with new ones. But it has yet to decide on this course. Other countries, deeply concerned about their ability to satisfy demand, are going ahead with plans for new nuclear power plants. China currently produces 6600 megawatts (MW) of power from nine reactors. It aims to increase this to 40 000 MW. India already has 15 operating nuclear power plants, with eight more under construction.

A few countries have developed **fast breeder reactor** technology. These reactors are very efficient at manufacturing plutonium fuel from their original uranium fuel load. This greatly increases energy production – but it could prove disastrous should the plutonium get into the wrong hands, as plutonium is the key ingredient for nuclear weapons.

Section 2.1 Activities

1 Compare the changes in production of the five traditional forms of energy between 1998 and 2008.

2 Using Table 2.3, describe how the global production of natural gas changed between 1999 and 2009.

3 Draw up a table to present the information illustrated in Figure 2.9.

4 Discuss recent changes in the production and consumption of coal.

5 Describe the trends shown in Figure 2.12.

Renewable energy resources

Hydro-electricity dominates renewable energy production. The newer sources of renewable energy making the largest contribution to global energy supply are wind power and biofuels.

Hydro-electric power

Of the traditional five major sources of energy, HEP is the only one that is renewable. It is by far the most important source of renewable energy. The 'big four' HEP nations of China (see pages 377–78), Canada, Brazil and the USA account for almost 50 per cent of the global total. However, most of the best HEP locations are already in use, so the scope for more large-scale development is limited. In many countries, though, there is scope for small-scale HEP plants to supply local communities.

Figure 2.13 shows the pattern of consumption by world region from 1983. In 2008 the countries with the largest share of the world total were: China (18.5 per cent), Canada (11.7 per cent), Brazil (11.5 per cent) (Figure 2.14), and the USA (7.9 per cent).

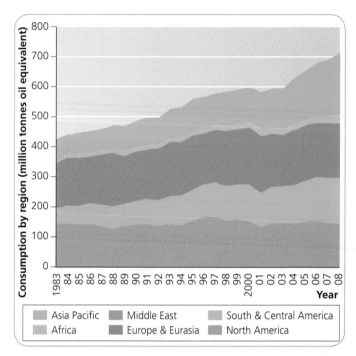

Figure 2.13 Hydro-electricity consumption by world region, 1983–2008

Figure 2.14 Inside the Itaipù hydro-electric power plant, Brazil

Although HEP is generally seen as a clean form of energy, it is not without its problems, which include:
- Large dams and power plants can have a huge negative visual impact on the environment.
- They may obstruct the river for aquatic life.
- There may be a deterioration in water quality.
- Large areas of land may need to be flooded to form the reservoir behind the dam.
- Submerging large forests without prior clearance can release significant quantities of methane, a greenhouse gas.

Wind power

The worldwide capacity of wind energy is approaching 100 000 MW. Global wind energy is dominated by a relatively small number of countries. Germany is currently the world leader with 23.6 per cent of global capacity. Germany, the USA and Spain together account for almost 58 per cent of the world total (Figure 2.15).

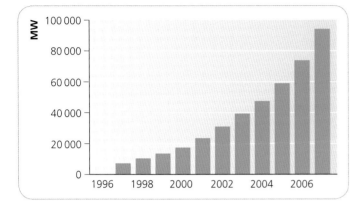

Figure 2.15 Wind energy – global cumulative installed capacity, 1996–2007

Wind energy has reached the 'take-off' stage both as a source of energy and a manufacturing industry. As the cost of wind energy improves further against conventional energy sources, more and more countries will expand into this sector. However, projections regarding the industry still vary considerably because of the number of variables involved.

Costs of generating electricity from wind today are only about 10 per cent of what they were 20 years ago, due mainly to advances in turbine technology. Thus at well-chosen locations wind power can now compete with conventional sources of energy. Wind energy operators argue that costs should fall further due to (a) further technological advances and (b) increasing economies of scale. One large turbine manufacturer has stated that it expects turbine costs to be reduced by 3.5 per cent a year for the foreseeable future.

Apart from establishing new wind energy sites, **repowering** is also beginning to play an important role. This means replacing first-generation wind turbines with modern multi-megawatt turbines, which give a much better performance. The advantages of this are:

- more wind power from the same area of land
- fewer wind turbines
- higher efficiency, lower costs
- enhanced appearance as modern turbines rotate at a lower speed and are usually more visually pleasing due to enhanced design
- better grid integration as modern turbines use a connection method similar to conventional power plants.

As wind turbines have been erected in more areas of more countries (Figure 2.16), the opposition to this form of renewable energy has increased:

- People are concerned that huge turbines located nearby could blight their homes and have a significant impact on property values.

- There are concerns about the hum of turbines disturbing both people and wildlife.
- Skylines in scenically beautiful areas might be spoiled for ever.
- Turbines can kill birds. Migratory flocks tend to follow strong winds, although wind companies argue that they avoid siting wind turbines near migratory routes.
- Suitable areas for wind farms are often near the coast where land is expensive.
- Turbines can affect TV reception nearby.
- There is an opportunity cost of heavy investment in wind compared with the alternatives.

The development of large offshore wind farms, for example in UK waters, has become an increasingly debatable issue, mainly due to the visual environmental impact of such large installations. In September 2010, the Thanet Offshore Wind Project in the UK was the largest in the world at 300 MW.

The recent rapid increase in demand for turbines has resulted in a shortage of supply. New projects now have to make orders for turbines in large blocks up to several years in advance in order to ensure firm delivery dates from manufacturers. Similarly the investment from manufacturers is having to rise significantly to keep pace with such buoyant demand.

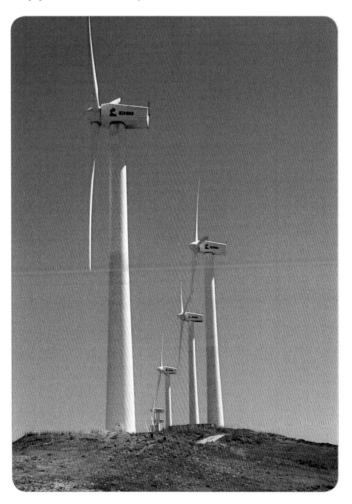

Figure 2.16 Wind farm, northern Spain

Biofuels

Biofuels are fossil fuel substitutes that can be made from a range of agri-crop materials including oilseeds, wheat, corn and sugar. They can be blended with petrol and diesel. In recent years, increasing amounts of cropland have been used to produce biofuels. Initially, environmental groups such as Friends of the Earth and Greenpeace were very much in favour of biofuels, but as the damaging environmental consequences became clear, such environmental organisations were the first to demand a rethink of this energy strategy.

The main methods of producing biofuels are:

- Crops that are high in sugar (sugar cane, sugar beet, sweet sorghum) or starch (corn/maize) are grown and then yeast fermentation is used to produce ethanol.
- Plants containing high amounts of vegetable oil (such as oil palm, soybean and jatropha) are grown, and the oils derived from them are heated to reduce their viscosity. They can then be burned directly in a diesel engine, or chemically processed to produce fuels such as biodiesel.
- Wood can be converted into biofuels such as woodgas, methanol or ethanol fuel.
- Cellulosic ethanol can be produced from non-edible plant parts, but costs are not economical at present. This method is seen as the potential second generation of biofuels.

Ethanol is the most common biofuel globally, particularly in Brazil and the USA (Figure 2.17). It accounts for over 90 per cent of total biofuel production. Ethanol can be used in petrol engines when mixed with gasoline. Most existing petrol engines can run on blends of up to 15 per cent ethanol. Global production of ethanol has risen rapidly in recent decades. For example, in the USA the amount of maize turned into ethanol increased from 15 million tonnes in 2000 to 85 million tonnes in 2007 – this amounts to about one-third of US maize production. The USA and Brazil are by far the largest producers of ethanol in the world. Together, these two countries produce 87.9 per cent of the world total. However, production in the European Union and China is growing significantly.

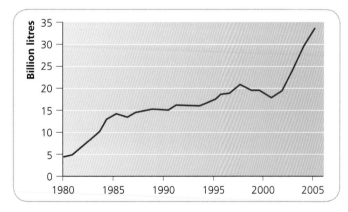

Figure 2.17 World ethanol production, 1980–2005

In contrast to the USA, Brazil uses sugar cane to produce ethanol. More than half of Brazil's sugar cane crop is now used for this purpose. Sugar cane-based ethanol can be produced in

Brazil at about half the cost of maize-based ethanol in the USA. This difference is due to:

- climatic factors
- land availability
- the greater efficiency of sugar in converting the Sun's energy into ethanol.

The USA has set a target of increasing the use of biofuels to 160 billion litres by 2017. This is about five times the current level. The objective is to replace approximately 15 per cent of imported oil with domestically produced ethanol. Subsidies are an important element in encouraging biofuel production. In 2006, US tax credits for maize-based ethanol production amounted to around $2.5 billion. This sum is expected to increase with rising production.

Global biodiesel production and capacity have risen significantly in recent years. Biodiesel is the most common biofuel produced in Europe, with the continent accounting for over 63 per cent of global production. Germany and France are the leading producers within Europe. Biodiesel can be used in any diesel engine when mixed with mineral diesel, usually up to a limit of 15 per cent biodiesel. Rapeseed oil is the major source of Europe's biodiesel. After the EU, the USA is the second most important producer of biodiesel. In the latter, soybean oil is the main source for production.

Increasing investment is taking place in research and development of the so-called 'second generation' biodiesel projects including algae and cellulosic diesel. Other important trends in the industry are a transition to larger plants and consolidation among smaller producers.

Geothermal electricity

Geothermal energy is the natural heat found in the Earth's crust in the form of steam, hot water and hot rock. Rainwater may percolate several kilometres below the surface in permeable rocks, where it is heated due to the Earth's **geothermal gradient**. This is the rate at which temperature rises as depth below the surface increases. The average rise in temperature is about 30°C per km, but the gradient can reach 80°C near plate boundaries.

This source of energy can be used to produce electricity, or its hot water can be used directly for industry, agriculture, bathing and cleansing (Figure 2.18). For example, in Iceland hot springs supply water at 86°C to 95 per cent of the buildings in and around Reykjavik. At present virtually all the geothermal power plants in the world operate on steam resources, and they have an extremely low environmental impact.

First begun in Larderello, Italy, in 1904, electricity generation using geothermal energy is now taking place in 24 countries, 5 of which use it to produce 15 per cent or more of their total electricity. In the first half of 2008, total world installed geothermal power capacity passed 10 000 MW. This is enough electricity to meet the needs of 60 million people. In 2010, capacity was estimated to increase to 13 500 MW across 46 countries, equivalent to 27 coal-fired power plants. The USA is the world leader in geothermal electricity with plants in Alaska, California, Hawaii, Nevada and Utah. Total production accounts for 0.37 per cent of the electricity used in the USA. Other leading geothermal electricity using countries are the Philippines, Italy, Mexico, Indonesia, Japan, New Zealand and Iceland.

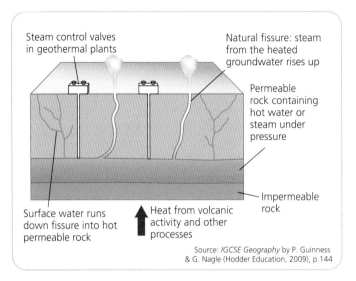

Steam control valves in geothermal plants

Natural fissure: steam from the heated groundwater rises up

Permeable rock containing hot water or steam under pressure

Impermeable rock

Surface water runs down fissure into hot permeable rock

Heat from volcanic activity and other processes

Source: *IGCSE Geography* by P. Guinness & G. Nagle (Hodder Education, 2009), p.144

Figure 2.18 Geothermal power

Solar power

From a relatively small base the installed capacity of solar electricity is growing rapidly. Experts say that solar power has huge potential for technological improvement, which could make it a major source of global electricity in years to come (Figure 2.19). According to some estimates, over $30 billion was invested in the solar sector in 2007. A recent study has predicted that the global solar market could develop into a $100 billion industry by 2013, reaching 23GW installed capacity from 4.9GW in 2008. Spain, Germany, Japan and the USA currently lead the global market for solar power.

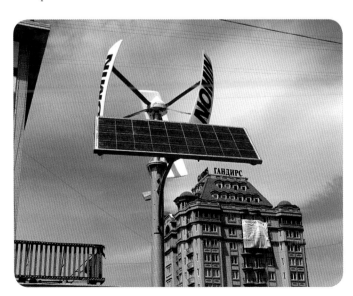

Figure 2.19 Solar panels and mini wind turbines powering street lights in Ulaanbaatar, Mongolia

Solar electricity is currently produced in two ways:

- **Photovoltaic (PV) systems** – these are solar panels that convert sunlight directly into electricity. Germany has the largest installed PV capacity, which has risen from 100 MW in 2000 to 4150 MW at the end of 2007. Much of this increase is due to the revised 'feed-in tariff system' which is part of the Renewable Energy Sources Act. This has made solar power a more attractive proposition for electricity utilities. Spain has moved into third place in PV capacity after introducing a similar feed-in tariff structure in 2004. Rapid growth in other countries such as France, Italy, South Korea and the USA has been due to various incentive packages and local market conditions (Table 2.5).
- **Concentrating Solar Power (CSP)** systems use mirrors or lenses and tracking systems to focus a large area of sunlight into a small beam. This concentrated light is then used as a heat source for a conventional thermal power plant. The most developed CSP systems are the solar trough, parabolic dish and solar power tower. Each method varies in the way it tracks the Sun and focuses light. In each system a fluid is heated by the concentrated sunlight, and is then used for power generation or energy storage.

Table 2.5 Installed photovoltaic peak power capacity (MW), 2007

World	7841
Germany	3862
Japan	1919
USA	830.5
Spain	655
Italy	120.2
Australia	82.5
South Korea	77.6
France	75.2
Netherlands	53.3

Source: Wikipedia

Another idea being considered is to build solar towers. Here a large glassed-in area would be constructed with a very tall tower in the middle. The hot air in this 'greenhouse' would rise rapidly up the tower, driving turbines along the way.

Traditional solar panels comprise arrays of photovoltaic cells made from silicon. These cells absorb photons in light and transfer their energy to electrons, which form an electrical circuit. However, standard solar panels:

- are costly to install
- have to be tilted and carefully positioned so as not to shade neighbouring panels.

A number of companies are now developing a new technique to manufacture solar panels. This involves using different materials and building them in very thin layers or films, almost like printing on paper, to produce the photovoltaic effect. The cost of production is reduced because the layers or films use less material, and they can be deposited on bases such as plastic, glass or metal.

Tidal power

Although currently in its infancy, a study by the Electric Power Research Institute has estimated that as much as 10 per cent of US electricity could eventually be supplied by tidal energy. This potential could be equalled in the UK and surpassed in Canada.

Tidal power plants act like underwater windmills, transforming sea currents into electrical current. Tidal power is more predictable than solar or wind power, and the infrastructure is less obtrusive, but start-up costs are high. The 240 MW Rance facility in north-western France is the only utility-scale tidal power system in the world. However, the greatest potential is Canada's Bay of Fundy in Nova Scotia. A pilot plant was opened at Annapolis Royal in 1984, which at peak output can generate 20 MW. More ambitious projects at other sites along the Bay of Fundy are under consideration, but there are environmental concerns. The main concerns are potential effects on fish populations, levels of sedimentation building up behind facilities, and the possible impact on tides along the coast.

Section 2.1 Activities

1 Suggest reasons for the variations and trends in the consumption of hydro-electricity by world region.

2 Discuss recent changes in the installed capacity of wind energy.

3 a What are biofuels?
   b Why has biofuel production expanded so rapidly?
   c Examine the advantages and disadvantages of biofuels.

4 a What is geothermal energy?
   b Explain the geographical locations of the main producing countries.

5 Explain the difference between photovoltaic and concentrated solar power systems.

Fuelwood in LEDCs

In LEDCs about 2.5 billion people rely on fuelwood, charcoal and animal dung for cooking. Fuelwood and charcoal are collectively called fuelwood, which accounts for just over half of global wood production. Fuelwood provides much of the energy needs for Sub-Saharan Africa. It is also the most important use of wood in Asia. Table 2.6 shows the number of people in the world living without electricity.

Table 2.6 Number of people living without electricity, 2004

South Asia	706 million
Sub-Saharan Africa	547 million
East Asia	224 million
Other regions	101 million

In LEDCs the concept of the 'energy ladder' is important. Here, a transition from fuelwood and animal dung to 'higher-level' sources of energy occurs as part of the process of economic development. Income, regional electrification and household size are the main factors affecting the demand for fuelwood. Forest

depletion is therefore initially heavy near urban areas but slows down as cities become wealthier and change to other forms of energy. It is the more isolated rural areas that are most likely to lack connection to an electricity grid. It is in such areas that the reliance on fuelwood is greatest. Wood is likely to remain the main source of fuel for the global poor in the foreseeable future.

The collection of fuelwood does not cause deforestation on the same scale as the clearance of land for agriculture, but it can seriously deplete wooded areas. The use of fuelwood is the main cause of indoor air pollution in LEDCs. Indoor air pollution is responsible for 1.5 million deaths every year. More than half of these deaths are of children below the age of 5.

Some notable trends
Trends in MEDCs

The USA consumes almost one-quarter of global oil output but has only 2.5 per cent of its proven reserves. Although petrol prices have risen significantly in the USA in recent years, they remain less than half the price in the UK. Of the 20 million barrels a day consumed in the USA, 25 per cent is used for transportation. However, the oil efficiency of US vehicles is at a 20-year low – a result of complacency in the period of low energy prices. The USA's high dependence on oil leaves it vulnerable to supply shocks and also pushes prices higher for the rest of the world. The only realistic way to limit the demand for oil in the USA is to increase the tax on petrol substantially. However, it is unlikely that any American President would take such a big political risk.

Deindustrialisation and increasing energy efficiency in MEDCs in general has resulted in a relatively modest increase in demand compared with NICs (Table 2.7). In fact, Germany and the UK actually show a decrease in Table 2.7. This is partly due to higher efficiency rates, but also due to the fact that the data only includes the five traditional sources of energy and this excludes renewable energy such as wind power. The other MEDCs illustrated in the table are the USA and Japan.

Table 2.7 Primary energy consumption, 1997–2007 (million tonnes oil equivalent)

	Country	1997	2007
MEDCs	USA	2204.8	2361.4
	Japan	506.6	517.5
	Germany	337.8	311.0
	UK	220.4	215.9
NICs	South Korea	179.6	234.0
	Malaysia	37.8	57.4
	China	961.4	1863.4
	India	260.6	404.4
LEDCs	Bangladesh	10.6	20.3
	Pakistan	41.2	58.3
	Peru	10.9	13.8
	Algeria	26.5	34.7

Trends in NICs

It is the newly industrialised countries that are increasing their energy demand at the fastest rate. China alone has accounted for one-third of the growth in global oil demand since 2000. China passed Japan as the world's second largest user of oil in 2004. Its average daily consumption of 6.63 million barrels is about twice its domestic production. Because of this situation its oil imports doubled between 1999 and 2004. However, oil consumption per person is still only one-fifteenth of that in the USA. As this gap narrows it will have a considerable impact on global demand. The demand for oil in China is expected to increase by 5–7 per cent a year. If this occurs, China will take over from the USA as the world's largest consumer of oil by 2025. Rising demand is concentrated in the large industrial cities which are located mainly in the eastern coastal zone.

China is by far the largest consumer of coal and the gap between China and the rest of the world will steadily increase in the future. China is expected to need 3242 million tonnes of coal a year by 2025. It is likely that China will build several hundred new coal-fired power stations to satisfy its demand for energy. This will have a huge impact on greenhouse gas emissions. Industry accounts for 71 per cent of total energy demand, which is very high indeed. China accounts for half of world cement production and a third of world steel production. Other newly industrialised countries such as India, Malaysia and South Korea (Table 2.7) are also recording high increases in energy demand.

Trends in LEDCs

Most LEDCs struggle to fund their energy requirements. In Table 2.7 data is presented for Bangladesh, Pakistan, Peru and Algeria. As might be expected, there is considerable variation in the rate of growth. Energy demand is influenced by a number of factors, two of which are the rate of economic development and the rate of population growth.

There is a strong positive correlation between GNP per capita and energy use. In poor countries it is the high and middle income groups who generally have enough money to purchase sufficient energy and they also tend to live in locations where electricity is available. Around the world 2 billion people lack access to household electricity. It has been estimated that connecting these people to electricity services would add only 1 per cent extra to emissions of greenhouse gases. In the poorest countries of the world, traditional biomass often accounts for 90 per cent or more of total energy consumption.

The environmental impact of energy

Increasing energy insecurity has stimulated exploration of technically difficult and environmentally sensitive areas. Such exploration and development is economically feasible when energy prices are high, but becomes less so when prices fall.

No energy production location has suffered more environmental damage than the Niger delta in West Africa.

Case Study

The Niger delta

The Niger delta covers an area of 70 000 km², making up 7.5 per cent of Nigeria's land area. It contains over 75 per cent of Africa's remaining mangroves. A report published in 2006 estimated that up to 1.5 million tonnes of oil has been spilt in the delta over the past 50 years. The report, compiled by WWF, says that the delta is one of the five most polluted spots on Earth. Pollution is destroying the livelihoods of many of the 20 million people who live in the delta. The pollution damages crops and fishing grounds, and is a major contributor to the upsurge in violence in the region. People in the region are dissatisfied with bearing the considerable costs of the oil industry but seeing very little in terms of the benefits. The report accused the oil companies of not using the advanced technologies available to them to combat pollution. However, Shell claims that 95 per cent of oil discharges in the last five years have been caused by sabotage.

The flaring (burning) of unwanted natural gas found with the oil is a major regional and global environmental problem. The gas found here is not useful because there is no gas pipeline infrastructure to take it to consumer markets. It is estimated that 70 million m³ are flared off each day. This is equivalent to 40 per cent of Africa's natural gas consumption. Gas flaring in the Niger delta is the world's single largest source of greenhouse gas emissions.

One of the world's largest wetlands, and Africa's largest remaining mangrove forest, have suffered an environmental disaster:

- Oil spills, acid rain from gas flares and the stripping away of mangroves for pipeline routes have killed off fish.
- Between 1986 and 2003, more than 20 000 ha of mangroves disappeared from the coast, mainly due to land clearing and canal dredging for oil and gas exploration.
- The oilfields contain large amounts of natural gas. This is generally burnt off as flares rather than being stored or reinjected into the ground. Hundreds of flares have burned continuously for decades. This causes acid rain and releases greenhouse gases.
- The government has recognised 6817 oil spills in the region since the beginning of oil production. Critics say the number is much higher.
- Construction and increased shipping have changed local wave patterns causing shore erosion and the migration of fish into deeper water.
- Various types of construction have taken place without adequate environmental impact studies.

The federal environmental protection agency has only existed since 1988 and **environmental impact assessments** were not compulsory until 1992.

Case Study

Oil sands in Canada and Venezuela

Huge tar sand deposits in Alberta, Canada and Venezuela could be critical over the next 50 years as the world's production of conventional oil falls. Such synthetic oil, which can also be made from coal and natural gas, could provide a vital bridge to an era of new technologies.

The estimates of economically recoverable oil sand reserves in Canada vary considerably: *Oil & Gas Journal* estimates close to 180 billion barrels, while the *BP Statistical Review of World Energy* puts the figure at about 17 billion barrels, based on oil sands under active development. (The Canadian oil sands are not included on the International Energy Agency's industry lists of the ten countries with the largest proven oil reserves.) Even the higher industry estimate is only about a six-year world supply, as the world now consumes close to 30 billion barrels of oil a year. At present about 33 000 employees work the Alberta oil sands. Tar sands production reached 1 million barrels a day in 2005 and is projected to increase fivefold by 2030 – still about half of Saudi Arabia's current output and less than 5 per cent of world production in 2030.

However, there are serious environmental concerns about the development of tar sands:

- It takes 2 tonnes of mined sand to produce 1 barrel of synthetic crude, leaving lots of waste sand.
- It takes about three times as much energy to produce a barrel of Alberta oil-sands crude as it does a conventional barrel of oil. Thus oil sands are large sources of greenhouse gas emissions.

Venezuela's heavy-oil production has not kept pace with that of Canada, but is now about 500 000 barrels of synthetic crude a day, with plans to expand production to 1 million barrels a day by 2010 in the Orinoco tar belt.

Pathways crossing difficult environments

As energy companies have had to search further afield for new sources of oil, new energy pathways have had to be constructed. Some major oil and gas pipelines cross some of the world's most inhospitable terrain. The Trans-Alaskan Pipeline (TAP) crosses three mountain ranges and several large rivers. Much of the pipeline is above ground to avoid the permafrost problem. Here, the ground is permanently frozen down to about 300 m, apart from the top metre which melts during the summer. Building foundations and the uprights that hold the pipeline above ground have to extend well below the melting zone (called the active layer). The oil takes about six days to make the 1270 km journey. Engineers fly over the pipeline every day by helicopter to check for leaks and other problems. Problems such as subsidence have closed the pipeline for short periods.

Section 2.1 Activities

1 Why is fuelwood a vital source of energy in many poor countries?
2 With reference to Table 2.7, describe and explain contrasting trends in energy consumption between MEDCs, NICs and LEDCs.
3 The Niger delta has been described as an 'environmental disaster area'. Briefly discuss this assertion.
4 Outline the advantages and disadvantages of exploiting oil-sand deposits.
5 What are energy pathways and why are they so important?

2.2 The management of energy supply

Case Study

China

'The fact that China overtook the US as the world's largest energy consumer symbolises the start of a new age in the history of energy'.
Faith Birol, International Energy Agency chief economist, 2010

China overtakes the USA as the world's top energy user

The International Energy Agency published new data in mid-2010 showing that China overtook the USA in total energy usage in 2009. The USA had held the top position in the energy usage league for more than a century. In 2009, China consumed 2.2 billion tonnes of oil equivalent compared with 2.17 billion tonnes in the USA. Only a decade before, China's total energy consumption was about half that of the USA. The demand for energy in China continues to increase significantly as the country expands its industrial base. However, energy usage per person in the USA is much higher, with the average American using five times more than the Chinese average.

In 2008, China's energy consumption breakdown by traditional energy sources was:

- coal 70.2 per cent
- oil 18.7 per cent
- hydro-electricity 6.6 per cent
- natural gas 3.6 per cent
- nuclear energy 0.75 per cent.

China's energy strategy

China's energy policy has evolved over time. As the economy expanded rapidly in the 1980s and 1990s, much emphasis was placed on China's main energy resource, coal, in terms of both increasing production and building more coal-fired power stations. However, this was at the expense of an alarmingly high casualty rate among coal miners (Figure 2.20). Stung by both internal and external criticism the Chinese central government and local governments have acted to improve mine safety. Figure 2.20 shows that coalmining deaths have fallen considerably in recent years, although the mining death rate still remains very high by international standards.

China was also an exporter of oil until the early 1990s although it is now a very significant importer (Figure 2.21). This transformation has had a major impact on Chinese energy policy as the country has sought to secure overseas sources of supply. Chinese investment in energy resources in Africa has risen rapidly but the country has also negotiated a range of long-term contracts in Latin America, the Middle East and Asia. This has included deals with Iran which have drawn international criticism. Long-term energy security is viewed as essential if the country is to maintain the pace of its industrial revolution.

Coal is the dirtiest of the fossil fuels and thus the environmental consequences of such a heavy reliance on coal were all too

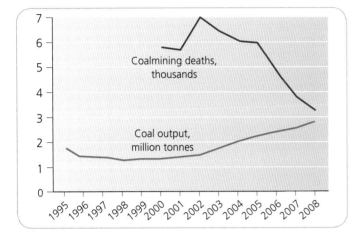

Figure 2.20 China's coal output, 1995–2008

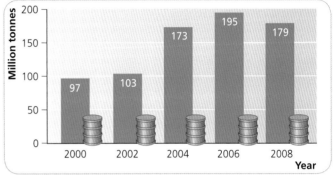

Figure 2.21 Oil imports to China, 2000–08

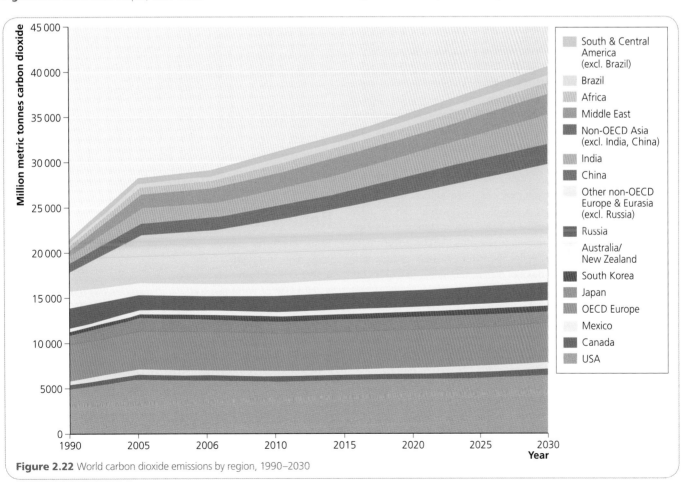

Figure 2.22 World carbon dioxide emissions by region, 1990–2030

predictable. According to Greenpeace, 80 per cent of China's carbon dioxide emissions and 85 per cent of its sulphur dioxide pollution come from burning coal. Greenpeace also noted in 2009 that a new coal-fired power station is built in China every 7–10 days. This is a startling figure. Figure 2.22 shows carbon dioxide emissions for China and other world regions from 1990, and predictions to 2030. China is not only facing pressure to reduce emissions from inside the country itself but also from the international community.

In recent years China has tried to take a more balanced approach to energy supply and at the same time reduce its environmental impact. The main policy objectives set out in recent years are:

- energy conservation
- placing a strong emphasis on domestic resources
- diversified energy development
- environmental protection
- mutually beneficial international cooperation.

The 11th Five Year Plan (2006–10) focused on two major energy-related objectives:

- to reduce energy use per unit GDP by 20 per cent
- to ensure a more secure supply of energy.

China intends to reach its energy conservation target by:

- structural adjustment – accelerating the development of the service sector and low-energy intensive industries
- technical improvement – increasing research and development on advanced conservation techniques
- improving energy-efficiency legal regulations and standards systems
- strengthening energy pricing reform and giving the market correct price signals.

Because of the dominant position of coal in China's energy mix, the development of clean coal technology is central to China's energy policy with regard to fossil fuels. China has emerged in the past two years as the world's leading builder of more efficient, less polluting coal power plants. It has begun constructing such clean coal plants at a rate of one a month. The government has begun requiring power companies to retire an older, more polluting power plant for each new one they build.

China has recently built a small, experimental facility near Beijing to remove carbon dioxide from power station emissions and use it to provide carbonation for beverages. The government also has a short list of possible locations for a large experiment to capture and store carbon dioxide. So far, though, it has no plans to make this a national policy.

The further development of nuclear and hydro power is another important strand of Chinese policy. The country also aims to stabilise and increase the production of oil while augmenting that of natural gas and improving the national oil and gas network. Nuclear power reached a capacity of 9.1 GW by the end of 2008, with a target capacity of 40 GW by 2020. By the end of 2009 China had 11 operational nuclear reactors with a further 17 under construction. The World Nuclear Association (WNA) says that China has a further 124 nuclear reactors planned. This will lead to a dramatic increase in China's demand for uranium, the raw material of nuclear reactors.

China's strategic petroleum reserve

Priority was also given to building up the national oil reserve (Figure 2.23). In 2007 China announced an expansion of its crude reserves into a two-part system. Chinese reserves would consist of a government-controlled strategic reserve complemented by mandated commercial reserves. The government-controlled reserves are being completed in three phases. Phase one consisted of a 101.9 million barrel reserve, mostly completed by the end of 2008. The second phase of the government-controlled reserves, with an additional 170 million barrels, will be completed by 2011. A third phase will expand reserves by 204 million barrels, with the goal of increasing China's strategic reserve to 90 days of supply by 2020.

Figure 2.23 China's special petroleum reserve (SPR)

China is following the USA and other countries in building up a petroleum reserve. This will protect China to a certain extent from fluctuations in the global oil price which can arise for a variety of reasons.

Renewable energy policy

Total renewable energy capacity in China reached 226 GW in 2009. This included:

- 197 GW of hydro-electricity
- 25.8 GW of wind energy
- 3.2 GW of biomass
- 0.4 GW of grid-connected solar photovoltaic (PV) power
- 34 MW of geothermal power
- 4 MW of marine energy.

Renewable energy contributed more than one-quarter of China's total installed energy capacity, with hydro-electricity by far the largest contributor. China's wind power capacity grew 30-fold between 2005 and 2009 to become the second largest in the world behind the USA. The year 2008 saw the initial development of China's offshore wind farm policy. China's wind turbine manufacturing industry is now the largest in the world. Chinese

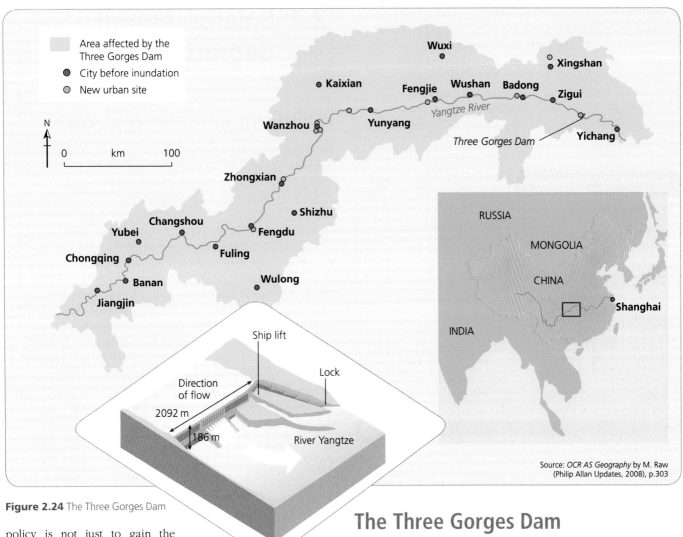

Figure 2.24 The Three Gorges Dam

Source: *OCR AS Geography* by M. Raw
(Philip Allan Updates, 2008), p.303

policy is not just to gain the energy advantages of wind energy but also to develop it as a significant industrial sector. China is now also the largest manufacturer of solar PV power, supplying almost 40 per cent of all solar PV worldwide in 2009. The solar hot water market in China has also continued to boom, partly as a result of a new rural energy subsidy programme for home appliances, for which solar hot water qualifies.

China's current draft energy plan for 2020 sets targets of:

- 300 GW of hydro-electricity
- 150 GW of wind energy
- 30 GW of biomass
- 20 GW of solar PV power.

This would amount to almost one-third of China's planned power capacity of 1600 GW by 2020. Much of China's progress in the renewable energy sector has been due to the landmark 2005 Renewable Energy Law. Major elements of this legislation included:

- renewable portfolio standards (mandated market share)
- feed-in tariffs for biomass
- 'government guided' prices for wind power
- an obligation for utilities to purchase all renewable power generated.

The Three Gorges Dam

The Three Gorges Dam across the Yangtze River in China is the world's largest electricity generating plant of any kind (Figure 2.24). The dam is over 2 km long and 100 m high. The lake impounded behind it is over 600 km long. All of the originally planned components were completed in late 2008. Currently there are 32 main generators with a capacity of 700 MW each. Six additional generators in the underground power plant are being installed and should become fully operational in 2011. When totally complete the generating capacity of the dam will be a massive 22 500 MW.

One objective of such a large capacity is to reduce China's dependence on coal. The dam supplies Shanghai and Chongqing in particular with electricity. This is a multipurpose scheme that also increases the river's navigation capacity and reduces the potential for floods downstream. The dam has raised water levels by 90 m upstream, transforming the rapids in the gorge into a lake, allowing shipping to function in this stretch of the river. The dam will protect an estimated 10 million people from flooding.

However, there was considerable opposition to the dam because:

- over one million people had to be moved to make way for the dam and the lake

- much of the resettlement has been on land above 800 m above sea level which is colder and has less fertile soils
- the area is seismically active and landslides are frequent
- there are concerns that silting will quickly reduce the efficiency of the project
- significant archaeological treasures were drowned
- the dam interferes with aquatic life
- the total cost is estimated at $70 billion; many people argue that this money could have been better spent.

Section 2.2 Activities

1 Describe and explain the trends shown in Figure 2.20.

2 Discuss the changes in carbon dioxide emissions shown in Figure 2.22.

3 Comment on the 'mix' of China's energy consumption in 2008.

4 Why is China building up a strategic petroleum reserve?

5 Discuss China's renewable energy policy.

6 a Explain the objectives of the Three Gorges Dam.
  b For what reasons was the construction of the Three Gorges Dam opposed?

2.3 Environmental degradation

Pollution: land, air and water

Pollution is the dominant factor in the **environmental degradation** of land, air and water and impacts significantly on human health. Figure 2.25 shows the considerable global variations in deaths from urban air pollution. Compare the relatively low incidence in western Europe with the very high level in China and a number of other Asian countries (Figure 2.26). According to the World Health Organisation, diseases causes by air pollution kill 650 000 Chinese every year. This is the highest incidence in the world. Two of the world's most polluted places on Earth are in China – Linfen and Tianying. A recent study in China revealed that children exposed to highly polluted air while in the womb had more changes in their DNA, and a higher risk of developmental problems, than did those whose mothers breathed cleaner air during pregnancy. Apart from the direct effects on health of pollution, there are considerable indirect economic effects which include the cost of healthcare for pollution-related illnesses, interruptions to the education of children which may cause them to leave school with lower qualifications than expected, and lost labour productivity. Pollution also has a considerable negative

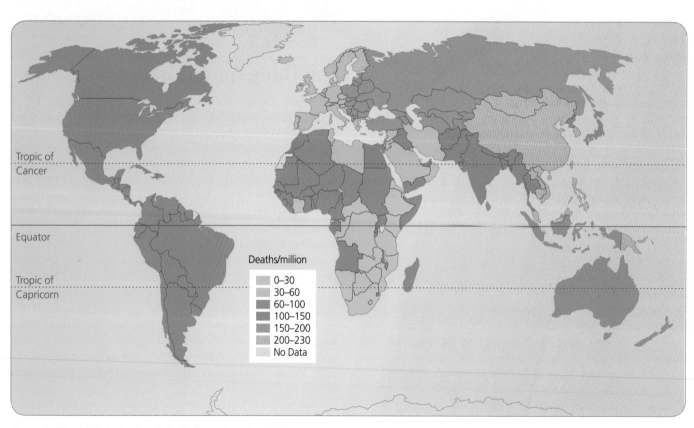

Figure 2.25 Global distribution of deaths from urban air pollution

Figure 2.26 Air pollution over Ulaanbaatar, Mongolia

impact on ecosystems all over the world. In some regions the changes brought about by pollution have been little short of catastrophic.

Virtually every substance is **toxic** at a certain dosage. The most serious polluters are the large-scale processing industries which tend to form agglomerations as they have similar locational requirements (Table 2.8). The impact of a large industrial agglomeration may spread well beyond the locality and region to cross international borders. For example, prevailing winds in Europe generally carry pollution from west to east. Thus the problems caused by acid rain in Scandinavia have been due partly to industrial activity in the UK. Dry and wet deposition can be carried for considerable distances. For example, pollution found in Alaska in the 1970s was traced back to the Ruhr industrial area in Germany.

Table 2.8 China's most polluting industries

Industrial sector	Examples
Fuel and power	Power stations, oil refineries
Mineral industries	Cement, glass, ceramics
Waste disposal	Incineration, chemical recovery
Chemicals	Pesticides, pharmaceuticals, organic and inorganic compounds
Metal industries	Iron and steel, smelting, non-ferrous metals
Others	Paper manufacture, timber preparation, uranium processing

Pollution is the major **externality** of industrial and urban areas. It is at its most intense at the focus of pollution-causing activities, declining with distance from such concentrations. For some sources of pollution it is possible to map the **externality gradient and field** (Figure 2.27). In general, health risk and environmental impact is greatest immediately around the source of pollution and the risk decreases with distance from the

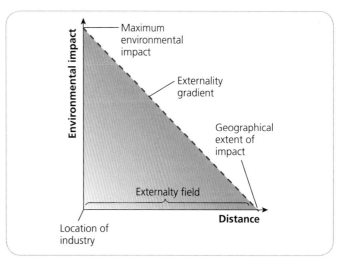

Figure 2.27 Externality gradient and field

Table 2.9 Major sources and health and environmental effects of air pollutants

	Major sources	Health effects	Environmental effects
Sulphur dioxide (SO_2)	Industry	Respiratory and cardiovascular illnesses	Precursor to acid rain, which damages lakes, rivers and trees; damage to cultural relics
Nitrous oxide (NO_x)	Vehicles, industry	Respiratory and cardiovascular illnesses	Nitrogen deposition leading to over-fertilisation and eutrophication
Particulate matter	Vehicles, industry	Particles penetrate deep into lungs and can enter bloodstream	Visibility
Carbon monoxide (CO)	Vehicles	Headaches and fatigue, especially in people with weak cardiovascular health	
Lead (Pb)	Vehicles (burning leaded gasoline)	Accumulates in bloodstream over time; damages nervous system	Kills fish/animals
Ozone (O_3)	Formed from reaction of nitrous oxides and VOCs	Respiratory illnesses	Reduced crop production and forest growth; smog precursor
Volatile organic compounds (VOCs)	Vehicles, industrial processes	Eye and skin irritation; nausea, headaches, carcinogenic	Smog precursor

source. However, atmospheric conditions and other factors can complicate this pattern. Exposure to pollution can result in health and environmental effects (Table 2.9) that range from fairly minor to severe.

Pollution control in MEDCs

Considering the intense use of energy and materials, levels of pollution have generally declined in MEDCs:

- In recent decades increasingly strict environmental legislation has been passed in these countries. This is the beginning of a process to make polluters pay for the cost of their actions themselves, rather than expecting society as a whole to pay the costs.
- Industry has spent increasing amounts on research and development to reduce pollution – the so-called 'greening of industry'.
- The most polluting activities, such as commodity processing and heavy manufacturing, have been relocated to the emerging market economies.

The expectation is that after a certain stage of economic development in a country, the level of pollution and the degradation it causes will decline (Figure 2.28).

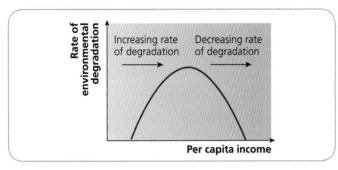

Figure 2.28 The environmental Kuznets curve

Types and amounts of pollution change with economic development. In low-income economies where primary industries frequently dominate, pollution related to agriculture and mining often predominates. As countries industrialise, manufacturing industries, energy production and transport become major polluters. The focal points of pollution will be the large urban-industrial complexes. The newly industrialised countries of the world are in this stage. In contrast, the MEDCs have experienced deindustrialisation as many of their major polluting industries

have filtered down to NICs. This has resulted in improved environmental conditions in many MEDCs in general, although pollution from transportation has often increased.

It is important to consider the different levels of impact between one-off pollution incidents (**incidental pollution**) and longer-term pollution (**sustained pollution**). The former is mainly linked to major accidents caused by technological failures and human error. Causes of the latter include ozone depletion and global warming. Some of the worst examples of incidental pollution are shown in Table 2.10.

Major examples of incidental pollution, such as Chernobyl and Bhopal, can have extremely long-lasting consequences which are often difficult to determine in the earlier stages. The effects of both accidents are still being felt more than two decades after they occurred.

It is usually the poorest people in a society who are exposed to the risks from both incidental and sustained pollution. In the USA the geographic distribution of both minorities and the poor has been found to be highly correlated to the distribution of air pollution, municipal landfills and incinerators, abandoned toxic waste dumps, and lead poisoning in children. The race correlation is even stronger than the class correlation. Unequal environmental protection undermines three basic types of equity:

- procedural equity, which refers to the extent that planning procedures, rules and regulations are applied in a non-discriminatory way
- geographic equity, which refers to the proximity of communities to environmental hazards and locally unwanted land uses such as smelters, refineries, sewage treatment plants and incinerators
- social equity, which refers to the role of race and class in environmental decision making.

Ironically some government actions have created and exacerbated environmental inequity. More stringent environmental regulations have driven noxious facilities to follow the path of least resistance towards poor, overburdened communities where protesters lack the financial support and professional skills of more affluent areas, or where the prospect of bringing in much needed jobs justifies the risks in the eyes of some residents.

Table 2.10 Major examples of incidental pollution

Location	Causes and consequences
Seveso, Italy	In July 1976 a reactor at a chemical factory near Seveso in northern Italy exploded, sending a toxic cloud into the atmosphere. An area of land 18 km² was contaminated with the dioxin TCDD. The immediate after-effects, seen in a small number of people with skin inflammation, were relatively mild. However, the long-term impact has been much worse. The population is suffering increased numbers of premature deaths from cancer, cardiovascular disease and diabetes.
Bhopal, India	A chemical factory owned by Union Carbide leaked deadly methyl isocyanate gas during the night of 3 December 1984. The plant was operated by a separate Indian subsidiary which worked to much lower safety standards than those required in the USA. It has been estimated that 8000 people died within two weeks, and a further 8000 have since died from gas-related diseases. The NGO Greenpeace puts the total fatality figure at over 20 000. Bhopal is recognised as the world's worst industrial disaster.
Chernobyl, Ukraine	The world's worst nuclear power plant accident occurred at Chernobyl, Ukraine in April 1986. Reactor number four exploded, sending a plume of highly radioactive fallout into the atmosphere which drifted over extensive parts of Europe and eastern North America. Two people died in the initial explosion and over 336 000 people were evacuated and resettled. In total 56 direct deaths and an estimated 4000 extra cancer deaths have been attributed to Chernobyl. The estimated cost of $200 billion makes Chernobyl the most expensive disaster in modern history.
Harbin, China	An explosion at a large petrochemical plant in the north-east Chinese city of Harbin released toxic pollutants into a major river. Benzene levels were 108 times above national safety levels. Benzene is a highly poisonous toxin which is also carcinogenic. Water supplies to the city were suspended. Five people were killed in the blast and more than 60 injured. Ten thousand residents were temporarily evacuated.

Sustained pollution: ozone depletion and skin cancer

The ozone layer in the stratosphere prevents most harmful ultraviolet (UV) radiation from passing through the atmosphere. However, chlorofluorocarbons (CFCs) and other ozone-depleting substances have caused an estimated decline of about 4 per cent a decade in the ozone layer of the stratosphere since the late 1970s. Depletion of the ozone layer allows more UV radiation to reach the ground, leading to more cases of skin cancer, cataracts and other health and environmental problems. Widespread global concern resulted in the Montreal Protocol banning the production of CFCs and related ozone-depleting chemicals.

Skin cancer is the fastest-growing type of cancer in the USA. In the UK it is the second most common cancer in young people aged 20–39. Overexposure to UV radiation is the major cause. Skin cancer generally has a 20 to 30-year latency period. There is a significant relationship between skin cancer and latitude in the USA and Canada. However, the use of tanning salons has also been criticised, with a number of studies linking the use of artificial tanning to cases of skin cancer.

Sustained pollution, such as that caused by ozone-depleting substances, usually takes much longer to have a substantial impact on human populations than incidental pollution, but it is likely to affect many more people in the long term. Likewise, tackling the causes of sustained pollution will invariably be a much more difficult task, as the sources of incidental pollution are much more localised compared with the more ubiquitous nature of sustained pollution.

Case Study

China's 'cancer rivers'

China's rapid economic growth has led to widespread environmental problems. Pollution problems are so severe in some areas that the term 'cancer village' has become commonplace. In the village of Xiditou, south-east of Beijing, the cancer rate is 30 times the national average. This has been blamed on water and air contaminated by chemical factories. Tests on tap water have found traces of highly carcinogenic benzene that were 50 per cent above national safe limits. In the rush for economic growth, local governments eagerly built factories, but they had very limited experience of environmental controls. Some facts support this:

- The Chinese government admits that 300 million people drink polluted water.
- This water comes from polluted rivers and groundwater.
- 30 000 children in China die of diarrhoea or other water-borne illnesses each year.
- The River Liao is the most polluted, followed by waterways around Tianjin and the River Huai.

Case Study

The BP oil spill in the Gulf of Mexico

On 20 April 2010 a large explosion occurred on the BP-licensed drilling rig *Deepwater Horizon* sited in the Gulf of Mexico. Eleven oil workers died and a blowout preventer, intended to prevent the release of crude oil, failed to activate. The rig sank in 1500 m of water, with reports of an oil slick 8 km long on the surface. Oil leaked from the well until 15 July when BP sealed it with a capping stack.

Estimates of the amount of oil gushing from the well reached up to 40 000 barrels a day. The US government estimated that 4.9 million barrels of oil were spilled in total, making it the largest accidental oil spill in history. It was surpassed only by the 1991 Persian Gulf spill in which Iraq intentionally spilled twice this amount.

The environmental impact occurred in four ecosystems: the offshore waters, inshore coastal waters, the sea bed, and shoreline wetlands and beaches. The spill also inflicted serious economic and psychological damage on communities along the Gulf Coast that depend on tourism, fishing and drilling. Although President Obama has called the BP oil spill 'the worst environmental disaster America has ever faced', it seems that at the time of writing (late 2010) the worst environmental fears have not been realised.

Section 2.3 Activities

1. Define **a** *pollution* and **b** *environmental degradation*.
2. **a** With reference to Figure 2.25, describe the global distribution of deaths from urban air pollution.
   b Suggest reasons for the spatial variations you have identified.
3. Which industries are the largest polluters?
4. Write a brief explanation of Figure 2.27.
5. Explain the relationship illustrated by Figure 2.28.

Water: demand, supply and quality
The global water crisis

The longest a person can survive without water is about ten days. All life and virtually every human activity needs water. It is the world's most essential resource and a pivotal element in poverty reduction. But for about 80 countries, with 40 per cent of the world's population, lack of water is a constant threat (Figure 2.29). And the situation is getting worse, with demand for water doubling every 20 years. In those parts of the world where there is enough

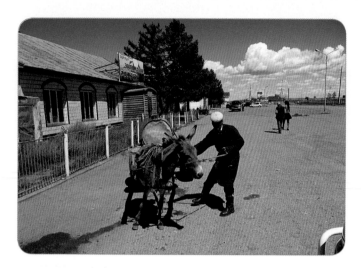

Figure 2.29 Water collection/distribution in central Asia

water, it is being wasted, mismanaged and polluted on a grand scale. In the poorest nations it is not just a question of lack of water; the paltry supplies available are often polluted.

Securing access to clean water is a vital aspect of development. The lack of clean, safe drinking water is estimated to kill almost 4500 children per day. Out of the 2.2 million unsafe drinking water deaths in 2004, 90 per cent were children under the age of 5. While deaths associated with dirty water have been virtually eliminated from MEDCs, in LEDCs most deaths still result from water-borne disease.

Water scarcity has been presented as the 'sleeping tiger' of the world's environmental problems, threatening to put world food supplies in jeopardy, limit economic and social development, and create serious conflicts between neighbouring drainage basin countries. In the twentieth century, global water consumption grew six-fold – twice the rate of population growth. Much of this increased consumption was made possible by significant investment in water infrastructure, particularly dams and reservoirs, affecting nearly 60 per cent of the world's major river basins.

The UN estimates that two-thirds of world population will be affected by 'severe water stress' by 2025. The situation will be particularly severe in Africa, the Middle East and South Asia. The UN notes that already a number of the world's great rivers, such as the Colorado in the USA, are running dry, and that **groundwater** is also being drained faster than it can be replenished. Many major **aquifers** have been seriously depleted which will present serious consequences in the future.

The Middle East and North Africa face the most serious problems. Since 1972 the Middle East has withdrawn more water from its rivers and aquifers each year than is being replenished. Yemen and Jordan are withdrawing 30 per cent more from groundwater resources annually than is being naturally replenished. Israel's annual demand exceeds its renewable supply by 15 per cent. In Africa, 206 million people live in water-stressed or water-scarce areas.

The Pilot Analysis of Global Ecosystems (PAGE), undertaken by the World Resources Institute, calculated water availability and demand by river basin. This analysis estimated that at present

2.3 billion people live in **water-stressed areas** with 1.7 billion resident in **water-scarce areas**. The PAGE analysis forecasts that these figures will rise to 3.5 billion and 2.4 billion people respectively by 2025.

The Water Project, a leading non-governmental organisation (NGO), has recently stated the following with regard to water:
- At any one time, half of the world's hospital beds are occupied by patients suffering from water-borne diseases.
- Over one-third of the world's population has no access to sanitation facilities.
- In LEDCs, about 80 per cent of illnesses are linked to poor water and sanitation conditions.
- One out of every four deaths of children under the age of 5 worldwide is due to a water-related disease.
- In LEDCs, it is common for water collectors, usually women and girls, to have to walk several kilometres every day to fetch water. Once filled, pots and cans can weigh as much as 20 kg.

Millennium Development Goal 7, target 10 states: 'Halve, by 2015, the proportion of people without sustainable access to safe water and basic sanitation'. A World Health Organisation report in 2004 estimated that to meet the target, an additional 260 000 people per day up to 2015 should gain access to improved water sources, and an extra 370 000 people per day should gain access to improved sanitation. This is a rate of improvement that may prove much too difficult to achieve in a number of countries, given the current resources available. In an effort to add impetus to global water advancement the UN proclaimed the period 2005–15 as the International Decade for Action, 'Water for Life'.

The link between poverty and water resources is very clear, with those living on less than $1.25 a day roughly equal to the number without access to safe drinking water. Access to safe water is vital in the prevention of diarrhoeal diseases which result in 1.5 million deaths a year, mostly among children under 5. Improving access to safe water can be among the most cost-effective means of reducing illness and mortality (Figure 2.30). The UN World Water Development Report stated: 'The real tragedy is the effect it has on the everyday lives of poor people, who are blighted by the burden of water-related disease, living in degraded and often dangerous environments, struggling to get an education for their children and to earn a living, and to get enough to eat. The brutal truth is that the really poor suffer a combination of most, and sometimes all, of the problems in the water sector.'

Figure 2.30 The narrow irrigation zone along the banks of the River Nile, Egypt

Water utilisation at the regional scale

Every year 110 000 km³ of precipitation falls onto the Earth's land surface. This would be more than adequate for the global population's needs, but much of it cannot be captured and the rest is very unevenly distributed. For example:

- Over 60 per cent of the world's population live in areas receiving only 25 per cent of global annual precipitation.
- The arid regions of the world cover 40 per cent of the world's land area, but receive only 2 per cent of global precipitation.
- The Congo River and its tributaries account for 30 per cent of Africa's annual runoff in an area containing 10 per cent of Africa's population.

Figure 2.31 shows what happens to the precipitation reaching land surfaces. '**Green water**' is that part of total precipitation that is absorbed by soil and plants, then released back into the air. As such it is unavailable for human use. However, green water scarcity is the classic cause of famine. Green water accounts for 61.1 per cent of total precipitation. The remaining precipitation, known as '**blue water**', collects in rivers, lakes, wetlands and groundwater. It is available for human use before it evaporates or reaches the ocean. As Figure 2.31 shows, only 1.5 per cent of total precipitation is directly used by people.

Total world blue water withdrawals are estimated at 3390 km³, with 74 per cent for agriculture, mostly irrigation (Figure 2.32). About 20 per cent of this total comes from groundwater. Although agriculture is the dominant water user, industrial and domestic uses are growing at faster rates. Demand for industrial use has expanded particularly rapidly.

The amount of water used by a population depends not only on water availability but also on levels of urbanisation and economic development. As global urbanisation continues, the demand for

potable water in cities and towns will rise rapidly. In many cases demand will outstrip supply.

In terms of agriculture, more than 80 per cent of crop **evapotranspiration** comes directly from rainfall, with the remainder from irrigation water diverted from rivers and groundwater. However, this varies considerably by region. In the Middle East and North Africa, where rainfall is low and unreliable, more than 60 per cent of crop evapotranspiration originates from irrigation.

Figure 2.33 contrasts water use in MEDCs and LEDCs. In the latter, agriculture accounts for over 80 per cent of total water use, with industry using more of the remainder than domestic allocation. In the MEDCs agriculture accounts for slightly more than 40 per cent of total water use. This is lower than the amount allocated to industry. As in LEDCs, domestic use is in third place.

As LEDCs industrialise and urban-industrial complexes expand, the demand for water grows rapidly in the industrial and domestic sectors. As a result the competition with agriculture for

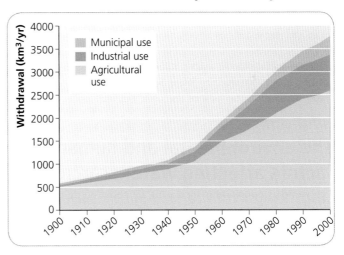

Figure 2.32 Global water use (agriculture, industry, domestic), 1900–2000

Figure 2.31 Where does the rain go?

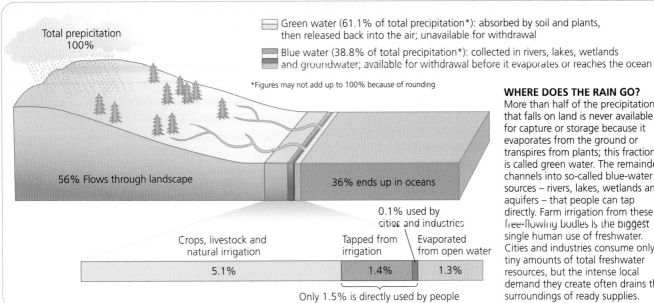

Green water (61.1% of total precipitation*): absorbed by soil and plants, then released back into the air; unavailable for withdrawal

Blue water (38.8% of total precipitation*): collected in rivers, lakes, wetlands and groundwater; available for withdrawal before it evaporates or reaches the ocean

Total precipitation 100%

*Figures may not add up to 100% because of rounding

56% Flows through landscape

36% ends up in oceans

0.1% used by cities and industries

Crops, livestock and natural irrigation	Tapped from irrigation	Evaporated from open water
5.1%	1.4%	1.3%

Only 1.5% is directly used by people

WHERE DOES THE RAIN GO?
More than half of the precipitation that falls on land is never available for capture or storage because it evaporates from the ground or transpires from plants; this fraction is called green water. The remainder channels into so-called blue-water sources – rivers, lakes, wetlands and aquifers – that people can tap directly. Farm irrigation from these free-flowing bodies is the biggest single human use of freshwater. Cities and industries consume only tiny amounts of total freshwater resources, but the intense local demand they create often drains the surroundings of ready supplies.

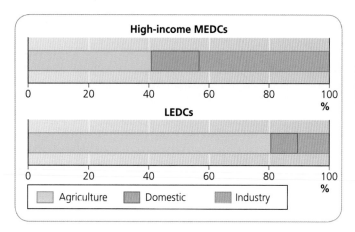

Figure 2.33 Water for agricultural, industrial and domestic uses in MEDCs and LEDCs

Figure 2.34 The dried-up bed of the Rio Oja, northern Spain

water has intensified in many countries and regions. This is a scenario that has already played itself out in many MEDCs where more and more difficult decisions are having to be made on how to allocate water.

Large variations in water allocation can also exist within countries. For example, irrigation accounts for over 80 per cent of water demand in the west of the USA, but only about 6 per cent in the east.

The environmental and human factors affecting water scarcity

The world's population is increasing by about 80 million a year. This converts to an increased demand for freshwater of around 64 billion m³ per year, which equates to the total annual flow rate of the River Rhine.

A country is judged to experience water stress when water supply is below 1700 m³ per person per year. When water supply falls below 1000 m³ per person a year, a country faces water scarcity for all or part of the year. These concepts were developed by the Swedish hydrologist Malin Falkenmark.

Water scarcity is to do with the availability of potable water. **Physical water scarcity** is when physical access to water is limited. This is when demand outstrips a region's ability to provide the water needed by the population. It is the arid and semi-arid regions of the world that are most associated with physical water scarcity. Here temperatures and evapotranspiration rates are very high and precipitation low. In the worst-affected areas, points of access to safe drinking water are few and far between

However, annual precipitation figures fail to tell the whole story. Much of the freshwater supply comes in the form of seasonal rainfall (Figure 2.34), as exemplified by the monsoon rains of Asia. India gets 90 per cent of its annual rainfall during the summer monsoon season from June to September. National figures can also mask significant regional differences. Analysis of the supply and demand situation by river basin can reveal the true extent of such variations. For example, the USA has a relatively high average water-sufficiency figure of 8838 m³ per person a year. However, the Colorado river basin has a much lower figure

of 2000, while the Rio Grande river basin is lower still at 621 m³ per person a year.

However, in increasing areas of the world, physical water scarcity is the result of human activity, largely overuse. Examples of physical water scarcity include:

- Egypt has to import more than half of its food because it does not have enough water to grow it domestically.
- The Murray-Darling basin in Australia has diverted large quantities of water to agriculture.
- The Colorado river basin in the USA once had an abundant supply of water, but resources have been heavily overused leading to very serious physical water scarcity downstream.

Figure 2.35 shows these regions and other parts of the world that suffer from physical water scarcity.

Economic water scarcity exists when a population does not have the necessary monetary means to utilise an adequate supply of water. The unequal distribution of resources is central to economic water scarcity, where the crux of the problem is lack of investment. This occurs for a number of reasons, including political and ethnic conflict. Figure 2.35 shows that much of Sub-Saharan Africa is affected by this type of water scarcity.

Scientists expect water scarcity to become more severe, largely because:

- the world's population continues to increase significantly
- increasing affluence is inflating the per capita demand for water
- there is an increasing demand for production of biofuels – biofuel crops are heavy users of water
- climate change is increasing aridity and reducing supply in many regions
- many water sources are threatened by various forms of pollution.

The Stockholm International Water Institute has estimated that each person on Earth needs a minimum of 1000 m³ of water per year for drinking, hygiene and growing food for sustenance. Whether this water is available depends largely on where people live on the planet, as water supply is extremely inequitable. For example, major rivers such as the Yangtze, Ganges and Nile are severely overused and the levels of underground aquifers beneath major cities such as Beijing and New Delhi are falling.

In many parts of the world the allocation of water depends largely on the ability to pay. A recent article in *Scientific American*, entitled 'Facing the freshwater crisis', quotes an old

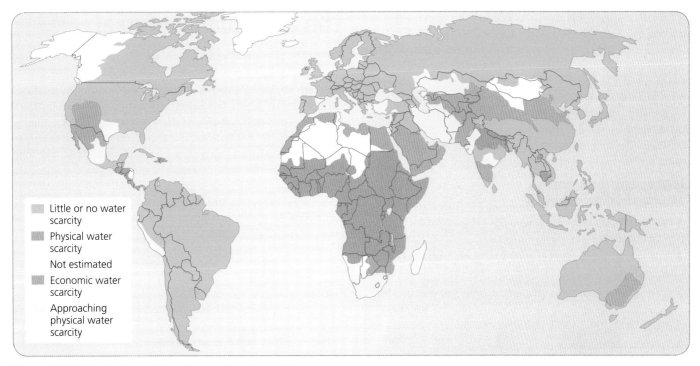

Figure 2.35 Physical water scarcity and economic water scarcity

saying from the American West: 'Water usually runs downhill, but it always runs uphill to money' – meaning that poorer people and non-human consumers of water, the fauna and flora of nearby ecosystems, usually lose out when water is scarce.

Figure 2.36 illustrates the huge extent of the global water gap between selected groups of MEDCs and LEDCs. The daily usage figures for the USA and Australia are particularly high. Many of the LEDCs illustrated have water use figures below the water poverty threshold. Water scarcity is playing a significant role in putting the break on economic development in a number of countries (Table 2.11).

Virtual water

The importance of the concept of **virtual water** is being increasingly recognised. Virtual water is the amount of water that is used to produce food or any other product and is thus essentially embedded in the item. One kilogram of wheat takes around 1000 litres of water to produce, so the import of this amount of

Table 2.11 The countries with the least access to an improved water source have among the world's fastest-growing populations

	Population with improved drinking water source (%)	Population (millions)	
	2006	**mid-2008**	**mid-2025**
Afghanistan	22	32.7	50.3
Somalia	29	9.0	14.3
Papua New Guinea	40	6.5	8.6
Ethiopia	42	79.1	110.5
Mozambique	42	20.4	27.5
Niger	42	14.7	26.3
Equatorial Guinea	43	0.6	0.9
Congo, Dem. Rep.	46	66.5	109.7
Fiji	47	0.9	0.9
Madagascar	47	18.9	28.0
Nigeria	47	148.1	205.4

Source: C Haub and M.M. Kent, 2008 World Population Data Sheet

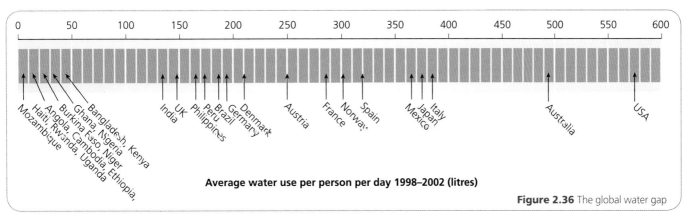

Average water use per person per day 1998–2002 (litres)

Figure 2.36 The global water gap

wheat into a dry country saves that country this amount of water. According to *Scientific American* (August 2008, p34), 'The virtual water concept and expanded trade have also led to the resolution of many international disputes caused by water scarcity. Imports of virtual water in products by Jordan have reduced the chance of water-based conflict with its neighbour Israel, for example.'

The size of global trade in virtual water is more than 800 billion m³ of water a year. This is equivalent to the flow of ten Nile Rivers. Greater liberalisation of trade in agricultural products would further increase virtual water flows.

Section 2.3 Activities

1 How far do you think you could walk carrying water weighing 20 kg?

2 Write a brief explanation of the information presented in Figure 2.31.

3 Draw up a table to show how global water use changed for municipal, industrial and agricultural uses for the following years: 1900, 1940, 1980, 2000 (Figure 2.32).

4 Describe and explain the different ways in which water is used in **a** high-income countries and **b** LEDCs.

5 a Explain the difference between *physical water scarcity* and *economic water scarcity*.

   b Describe and attempt to explain the spatial variations shown in Figure 2.35.

6 Briefly summarise the information shown in Figure 2.36.

Figure 2.37 Public drinking water point in Vienna, Austria

The degradation of rural environments

Rural environments supply humankind with most of its food and gene pool and contain the vast majority of the world's forested land. However, rural areas all around the world have been degraded at a rapid rate over the past century. This has been due primarily to population growth and increasing pressures on the land, although urban activities through processes such as climate change can also have profound consequences for rural environments. The UN's Food and Agriculture Organisation lists five root causes of unsustainable agricultural practices and degradation of the rural environment (Figure 2.38).

- **Policy failure**
Leading among the causes of unsustainable agriculture are inadequate or inappropriate policies which include pricing, subsidy and tax policies which have encouraged the excessive, and often uneconomic, use of inputs such as fertilisers and pesticides, and the overexploitation of land. They may also include policies that favour farming systems which are inappropriate both to the circumstances of the farming community and to available resources.

- **Rural inequalities**
Rural people often know best how to conserve their environment, but they may need to overexploit resources in order to survive. Meanwhile commercial exploitation by large landowners and companies often causes environmental degradation in pursuit of higher profits.

- **Resource imbalances**
Almost all of the future growth in the world's population will be in LEDCs, and the biggest increases will be in the poorest countries of all, those least equipped to meet their own needs or invest in the future.

- **Unsustainable technologies**
New technologies have boosted agricultural production worldwide, but some have had harmful side-effects which must be contained and reversed, such as resistance of insects to pesticides, land degradation through wind or water erosion, nutrient depletion, or poor irrigation management and the loss of biological diversity.

- **Trade relations**
As the value of raw materials exported by LEDCs has fallen, their governments have sought to boost income by expansion of crop production and timber sales that have damaged the environment.

Source: www. fao.org

Figure 2.38 Five root causes of unsustainable practices

Agro-industrialisation (industrial agriculture) has had a massive impact on rural ecosystems. This is the form of modern farming that refers to the industrialised production of livestock, poultry, fish and crops. This type of large-scale, capital-intensive farming originally developed in Europe and North America and then spread to other parts of the developed world. It has been spreading rapidly in many LEDCs since the beginning of the **Green Revolution**. Industrial agriculture is heavily dependent on oil for every stage of its operation. The most obvious examples are fuelling farm machinery, transporting produce, and producing fertilisers and other farm inputs. Figure 2.39 shows the general characteristics of agro-industrialisation. Not all farms and regions involved in agro-industrialisation will display all these characteristics, for example, intensive market gardening where farms may be relatively small although the capital inputs are extremely high.

- Very large farms
- Concentration on one (monoculture) or a small number of farm products
- A high level of mechanisation
- Low labour input per unit of production
- Heavy use of fertilisers, pesticides and herbicides
- Sophisticated ICT management systems
- Highly qualified managers
- Often owned by large agribusiness companies
- Often vertically integrated with food processing and retailing

Figure 2.39 The characteristics of agro-industrialisation

Regions where agro-industrialisation is clearly evident on a large scale include:
- the Canadian Prairies
- the corn and wheat belts in the USA
- the Paris basin
- East Anglia in the UK
- the Russian steppes
- the Pampas in Argentina
- Mato Grosso in Brazil
- the Murray-Darling basin in Australia.

Agro-industrialisation is a consequence of the globalisation of agriculture, the profit ambitions of large agribusiness companies, and the drive for cheaper food production. Over the last half-century every stage in the food industry has changed in the attempt to make it more efficient (in an economic sense). Vertical integration has become an increasingly important process with increasing linkages between the different stages of the food industry.

Farming and food production around the world is becoming increasingly dominated by large biotechnology companies, food brokers and huge industrial farms. The result is a complex movement of food products around the world. The food products, both fresh and processed, available in a typical supermarket have a much wider global reach than they did 20 years ago.

Large agricultural companies are continually seeking to produce new products, increase market share and reduce costs in order to increase their competitiveness. An increasing percentage of agricultural land in LEDCs has come under the control of outside influences, either directly or indirectly. Direct ownership by TNCs invariably means the cultivation of crops for export at the expense of food production for the domestic population. But even when farms are not foreign owned, International Monetary Fund policies may dictate that land is used to produce for the export market. This may not always be a bad thing, but if a country is undergoing food shortages at the same time it is an ironic situation.

However, there has been an increasing reaction to high-input farming as more and more people have become concerned about the use of fertilisers, pesticides, herbicides and other high-investment farming practices which are having a significant impact on the environment. The main evidence of this concern is the growth of the organic food market and the increasing sale of food resulting from more 'gentle' farming practices.

The environmental impact of capital-intensive farming

There is a growing realisation that the modes of production, processing, distribution and consumption that prevail, because in the short to medium term they are the most profitable, are not necessarily the most healthy or the most environmentally sustainable (Figure 2.40). In many parts of the world agro-industrialisation is having a devastating impact on the environment, causing:
- deforestation
- land degradation and desertification
- salinisation and contamination of water supplies
- air pollution
- increasing concerns about the health of long-term farm workers
- landscape change
- declines in biodiversity.

About a third of the world's farmland is already affected by salinisation, erosion or other forms of degradation.

Figure 2.40 Gobi desert – climate change has resulted in further land degradation

The global cattle population is currently around 1.5 billion. The pasture required amounts to about a third of all the world's agricultural land. A further third of this land is taken up by animal feedcrops. An estimated 1.3 billion people are employed in the livestock industry. The balance between livestock and grass is sustainable at present, but as the demand for meat increases, the pressures that cattle make on the land may well soon exceed supply. More cattle means more manure. Manure is often used to restore depleted soil, but can lead to pollution by heavy metals such as cadmium, nickel, chromium and copper.

In 2000, annual global meat consumption was 230 million tonnes. The forecast for 2050 is 465 million tonnes. There is a strong relationship between meat consumption and rising per capita incomes (Figure 2.41) although anomalies do occur due to cultural traditions. It is no coincidence that many committed environmentalists are vegetarian. A study at the University of Chicago calculated that changing from the average American diet to a vegetarian one could cut annual emissions by almost 1.5 tonnes of carbon dioxide.

Large-scale farming has been expanding geographically into a number of fragile environments, particularly into areas of rainforest. *The State of the World's Forests 2007*, published by the FAO, reported that between 1990 and 2005, the world's total forest area was reduced by 3 per cent. This is a rate of 7.3 million ha per year.

Mainly because of the uniformity required by large food companies, important breeds of livestock are becoming extinct. The FAO's *State of the World's Animal Genetic Resources* report stated that at least one livestock breed a month had been lost over the previous seven years. Food scientists are concerned about this trend as genetic resources are the basis of food security.

Agro-industrialisation is characterised by large areas of monoculture which, among other things, leaves crops more vulnerable to disease due to the depletion of natural systems of pest control. Monoculture results in reliance on pesticides which in turn causes a downward environmental cycle (Figure 2.42).

Poverty and rural degradation

The interactions shown in Figure 2.43 illustrate certain poverty-environment processes where poor households are 'compelled' to degrade environmental resources. However, this should not hide the fact that much environmental degradation is caused by large-scale commercial operations and government policy. There are also an increasing number of sustainable schemes being practised in poor rural areas.

Poor households can suffer significantly from the actions of large-scale rural operations. They may be pushed onto more marginal lands by logging, ranching or mining operations. Government policy can also have a significant negative effect on the poor, for example if land or tree tenure rights are insecure.

Urban/rural impact

Urban areas can affect the environmental degradation of their rural surroundings in a number of ways. For example, untreated wastewater is a major pollutant of rivers, which can contaminate estuaries and coastal fishing areas, and can pollute the drinking-water supplies of rural communities downstream. Urban use of groundwater can result in a depletion of the aquifer to the detriment of small farmers who rely on shallow wells. In arid areas, cities many kilometres inland can cause saltwater intrusion under coastal areas as a result of groundwater pumping. On a larger scale the huge urban-industrial complexes of the world are the main cause of climate change, which is having an adverse impact on the entire planet.

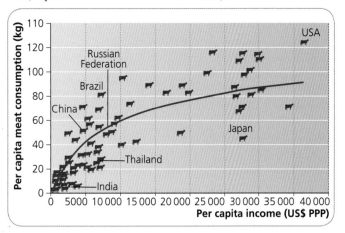

Figure 2.41 Meat consumption and income

Figure 2.42 Land degradation in southern Italy

Section 2.3 Activities

1 Discuss the five root causes of unsustainable practices set out in Figure 2.38.

2 Describe and explain the relationship between per capita income and per capita meat consumption illustrated in Figure 2.41. Suggest reasons for significant anomalies. What statistical technique could you use to assess the relationship between these two variables?

3 Produce a 100-word summary of the relationships illustrated in Figure 2.43.

Figure 2.43 Poverty–environment links

The degradation of urban environments

The environmental quality of urban areas has a huge impact on their populations. The degradation of urban environments occurs mainly through urbanisation, industrial development and inadequate infrastructure. Few urban residents can escape the effects of poor air and water quality, inadequate sanitation, a lack of proper solid waste management, and the improper storage and emission of hazardous substances. Figure 2.44 shows how urban environmental problems can act at different scales, affecting households, communities and cities.

The relationship between the urban poor and the environment is different to that between the rural poor and the environment. The urban poor are particularly affected by poor environmental services such as sub-standard housing, a lack of sanitation, and other aspects of urban poverty.

Case Study

Urban degradation in China

The rapid industrialisation of China as it has moved from being an LEDC to a **newly industrialised country (NIC)** has significantly increased the range and scale of environmental issues. A recent study concluded that 16 of the world's 20 most polluted cities are in China. Three-quarters of urban residents breathe in polluted air and 750 000 die prematurely each year from air pollution-related respiratory diseases. As urban environmental problems have mounted, national and city governments have been forced to act. In this way China has followed the countries that have industrialised before it.

In 1998 the World Resources Institute declared Lanzhou the world's most polluted city. It is a major industrial centre, burning large quantities of coal every day. The city is surrounded by hills,

Amenity loss	Traffic congestion	**City**	Loss of heritage and historical buildings	Reduced property and building values
Accidents and disasters	Polluted land	**Community**	Inappropriate and inadequate technology use	Inadequate tax/financial revenues
Flooding and surface drainage	Garbage dumping	**Household** Household health, garbage generation, air/water/noise pollution, spread of diseases	Lack of understanding of environmental problems	Lack of, and inappropriate, laws and legislation
Toxic and hazardous wastes/dumps	Flooding	Noise pollution	Natural disasters	High living densities
Loss of agricultural land and desertification	Air pollution	Water pollution	Inadequate supply and transmission loss of electricity	Misguided urban, government and management practices

Figure 2.44 The scales of urban environmental problems

which limit the dispersal of pollution. The city has addressed its environmental problems by:

- attempting to close some heavy industries
- relocating some industries from inner-city to edge-of-city locations
- restricting emissions based on air quality warnings with yellow and red level alerts to reduce factory pollution
- investment in the supply of natural gas and cleaner coal
- restricting traffic
- planting trees on surrounding hillsides to reduce dust storms.

The 2008 Olympic Games brought Beijing's air pollution problems to the world's attention. Emergency measures brought the clearest skies Beijing had seen for ten years. The city government is now looking to the long term. From 1 October 2009, motor vehicles registered outside Beijing failing to meet exhaust emission standards have been banned from entering the city. The Ministry for Environmental Protection is insisting that all vehicles now comply with certain standards. In addition new investment is planned for public transport and improvements to cycleways.

In July 2009, the Beijing municipal government launched a strategy for the improved disposal of the 18 410 tonnes of domestic refuse generated by the city every day. These measures include building more environmentally friendly disposal sites, improving incineration technologies, and enforcing household waste separation and recycling. The last Saturday of every month has been designated as a 'recyclable resources collecting day'. However, people in China are not yet as 'recycling aware' as populations in richer countries. Much needs to be done in terms of environmental education to improve this situation.

Beijing will run out of space for landfills in just four years. More than a third of Chinese cities are facing a similar crisis. At present, only 10 per cent of waste is incinerated. However, significantly increasing **incineration** requires substantial investment and there is always considerable opposition from people living close to the sites selected for new incinerators. The main concern is the significant amounts of heavy metals and dioxins released into the atmosphere by incinerators. The city government has

promised to improve incineration standards to reach the level currently required in the EU. China lags far behind countries like Japan and the USA where 90 per cent and 30 per cent respectively of all refuse is burned. Bio-treatment, in which refuse is turned into fertiliser, is another method Beijing is keen to develop. Planned new facilities will see the proportions of incineration, bio-treatment and landfill reach 2:3:5 in 2012 and 4:3:3 in 2015.

In Shenzhen, about three-quarters of complaints from residents about pollution concern noise – far higher than complaints about water, air and solid waste pollution. Methods being discussed to curb noise levels include limiting the number of vehicles, reducing speed limits, adopting better materials for road construction, and implementing methods such as green belts and sound barriers which will help to reduce noise.

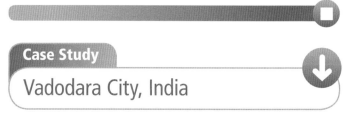

Case Study

Vadodara City, India

As India has progressed from being an LEDC to an NIC, the country has witnessed considerable economic and social progress. However, there have been negative aspects to development, such as environmental degradation and an increase in the incidence of degenerative and respiratory diseases, particularly in urban areas.

Vadodara is the largest city in the state of Gujarat. A high rate of population increase has led to considerable shortfalls in supplies of drinking water and in the sanitation system. This has had an impact on water-borne disease in particular, although there are very large variations within the urban area (Figure 2.45). There is a very strong relationship between the prevalence rates of gastroenteritis and infective hepatitis, and socio-economic grouping. For example, Fatepura, Gajrawadi and Panigate, the wards with the highest rates for both diseases, all have large slum populations. Disease rates are also high in Shiyabaug and

a

b

Ward number	Name of ward	Prevalence rate per 10 000 population (2003)	
		Gastroenteritis	Infective hepatitis
1	City	16.79	15.95
2	Fatepura	18.22	20.22
3	Gajrawadi	24.42	25.90
4	Sindvaimata Road	2.99	9.47
5	Shiyabaug	8.31	10.49
6	Sayajigunj	0.47	1.00
7	Belbaug	1.14	4.01
8	Raopura	8.64	13.44
9	Panigate	17.84	14.63
10	Subhanpura	0.45	3.25
	Total	8.19	10.99

Figure 2.45 Spatial distribution of water-borne diseases in Vadodara City

the City, where population densities are very high alongside environmental degradation, inadequate water supply and poor sewerage infrastructure. Elsewhere both population density and slum populations are lower.

An article entitled 'Development, Environment and Urban Health in India' (*Geography*, 2007, pages 158–9) concluded that 'The poorer sections of society can either not afford to take care of their physical and other needs or are unaware of the need to do so, the result being unclean living areas.'

The impact of rural areas

Runoff from fertilisers and pesticides can contaminate downstream urban water supplies. Deforestation, watershed degradation and soil eroding practices can exacerbate flood–drought cycles. Deteriorating conditions in rural areas can give added impetus to rural–urban migration, placing additional pressures on the urban environment. This is part of a process known as the 'urbanisation of poverty'.

Section 2.3 Activities

1 Discuss the scales of urban environmental problems illustrated by Figure 2.44.

2 With reference to Figure 2.45, describe and explain the spatial distribution of water-borne diseases in Vadodara City.

3 How can the activities of rural areas have an impact on urban environmental degradation?

Constraints on improving degraded environments

There are numerous constraints on improving the quality of degraded environments:

- In many LEDCs, population growth continues at a high rate, putting increasing pressure on already fragile environments.
- High rates of rural–urban migration can lead to rapidly deteriorating environmental conditions in large urban areas, at least in the short term.
- Environmental hazards, often made worse by climate change, present an increasing challenge in some world regions. In many regions natural hazards have increased in scale and unpredictability.
- Poor knowledge about the environmental impact of human actions is a significant factor in many locations where perhaps moderate adaptation of human behaviour could bring about beneficial changes.
- Poor management at both central and local government levels may result in problems that can at least be partially rectified, not being addressed. The quality of governance has been recognised as a key factor in the general development process.
- Many degraded environments require substantial investment to bring in realistic solutions. Such finance is beyond the means of many poor countries. However, there may be a choice between low-cost and high-cost schemes as Table 2.12 illustrates.
- Civil war has put back development by decades in some countries. Land mines which have yet to be cleared have put large areas off limits in some countries.

Corruption and crime can also reduce the effectiveness of schemes to reduce environmental degradation. An article in *The Guardian* newspaper in October 2009 stated that a revolutionary

Table 2.12 Technical and institutional costs in resource management by and for poor people

	High institutional costs	Low institutional costs
Relatively high technical costs	Large-scale irrigation Arid or semi-arid land reforestation or pasture improvement Sodic or saline land reclamation Mangrove reforestation Integrated river basin management Many transboundary resources, e.g. international rivers, air quality Resettlement schemes Water pollution reduction programmes Rural road maintenance Ocean fisheries management	Small-scale hill irrigation Food crop systems on difficult soils Localised water harvesting structures Centralised provision of energy services Solar energy for individual households Pipe sewer systems Emissions reduction devices Improved public transport
Relatively low technical costs	Aquifer management Protection of critical areas Coastal fisheries management Coral reef management Pasture management Land reform programmes Integrated pest management Wild game management	Treadle pump irrigation Humid tropics reforestation Small water harvesting systems Joint forest management regimes Improved cooking stoves and cooking energy for poor families Sloping agricultural land technology (SALT) Small-scale quarrying Household-based sanitation systems

Source: UNDP

UN scheme to cut carbon emissions by paying poorer countries to preserve their forests was a recipe for corruption and without strong safeguards could be hijacked by organised crime. Many countries and organisations have strongly backed the UN plans to expand the global carbon market to allow countries to trade the carbon stored in forests.

The protection of environments at risk

Environments at risk can be protected in various ways. At the most extreme, human activity and access can be totally banned, such as in Wilderness Areas; or extremely limited, as is usually the case in National Parks. However, in many areas it is usually necessary to sustain significant populations and rates of economic activity, particularly in LEDCs. In these cases various types of sustainable development policies need to be implemented. Individual environments can be assessed in terms of:

- Needs – what needs to be done to reduce environmental degradation as far as possible without destroying the livelihoods of the resident population?
- Measures – what are the policies and practices that can be implemented to achieve these aims at various time scales?
- Outcomes – how successful have these policies been at different stages of their implementation? Have policies been modified to cope with initially unforeseen circumstances?

Sometimes degraded environments cross international borders and effective action requires close co-operation between countries. Degradation in one country, for example the large-scale removal of forest cover in Nepal, can have severe implications for a country downstream of a river system, in this case India.

Section 2.3 Activities

1 Discuss the constraints on improving the quality of degraded environments.

2 Write a brief summary of the framework presented in Table 2.12.

2.4 The management of a degraded environment

Case Study

Namibia: community development

Namibia, in south-west Africa, is a very sparsely populated country with a generally dry climate. Approximately half its 2.1 million people live below the international poverty line of $1.25 a day. Environmental degradation and sustainability are significant issues in its marginal landscapes, with the government attempting to tackle these issues and reduce poverty at the same time. The causes of degradation have been mainly uncontrolled exploitation by a low-income population forced to think only in the short term in order to survive, and lack of management at all levels of government in earlier years. As the degradation process intensified, the government, assisted by international agencies, indentified the problems and put in place a significant strategy.

Namibia's Communal Conservancy Program is regarded as a successful model of community-based natural resource management, with an improving record for wildlife numbers and poverty reduction. The programme gives rural communities unprecedented management and use rights over wildlife which have created new incentives for communities to protect this valuable resource and develop economic opportunities in tourism.

The conservancy programme began in 1996. By 2007 it had expanded to 50 registered conservancies which now cover nearly 11.9 million ha (Figure 2.46). This encompasses over 14 per cent of the area of the country, benefiting more than 230 000 rural dwellers. Many more communities are in the process of formally establishing conservancies. **Communal conservancies** are legally recognised common property resource management organisations in Namibia's communal lands. The use rights given to conservancies include the rights to hunt, capture, cull and sell 'huntable game'. However, the government determines the overall culling rate and establishes quotas for protecting game used for trophy hunting.

An obvious sign of success is the significant increase in the numbers of wildlife in the conservancies after decades of decline. In the north-west conservancies, elephant numbers more than doubled between 1982 and 2000, and populations of oryx,

Figure 2.46 Namibia's community conservancies

Figure 2.47 Namibian Association of CBNRM Support Organisations (NACSO)

Organisation	Support activities
Legal Assistance Centre	Supplies legal advice and advocacy on issues related to community-based natural resource management (CBNRM)
Namibia Community-Based Tourism Association	Serves as an umbrella organisation and support provider for community-based tourism initiatives
Namibia Non-Governmental Organisation Forum	Represents a broad range of NGOs and community-based organisations
Namibia Nature Foundation Rössing Foundation	Provides assistance through grants, financial administration, technical support, fundraising, and monitoring and evaluation
Multi-disciplinary Research Centre	Provides training and materials for CBNRM partners
Namibia Development Trust	Centre of the University of Namibia provides research-related support
Centre for Research Information	Provides assistance to established and emerging conservancies in southern Namibia
Action in Africa – Southern Africa Development and Consulting	Provides research, developmental assistance, and market linkages for natural plant products
!NARA	Conducts capacity training in participatory, democratic management for conservancy communities and institutions supporting communities
Desert Research Foundation of Namibia	Researches arid land management, conducts participatory learning projects with communities about sustainable management, and engages policymakers to improve regulatory framework for sustainable development
Rural People's Institute for Social Empowerment	Provides assistance to established and emerging conservancies in southern Kunene and Erongo regions
Integrated Rural Development and Nature Conservation	A field-based organisation working to support conservancy development in Kunene and Caprivi regions
Nyae Nyae Development Foundation	Supports San communities in the Otjozondjupa region in the Nyae Nyae Conservancy
Ministry of Environment and Tourism	MET is not a formal member, but attends meetings and participates in NACSO working groups. Provides a broad spectrum of support in terms of policy, wildlife monitoring and management, and publicity.

Sources: MET 2005; NEEN 2004 a, b, c; Weaver 2007; Jones 2008 in Update 'Scaling up Namibia's community conservancies', p.32

springbok and mountain zebra rose tenfold. This improvement results from a decline in illegal hunting and poaching due to the economic value that conservancy communities now place on healthy wildlife populations.

The conservancies benefit from a number of 'new' economic activities including:

- contracts with tourism companies
- selling hunting concessions
- managing campsites
- selling wildlife to game ranchers
- selling crafts.

These activities are in addition to traditional farming practices which were usually at the subsistence level. The diversification of economic activity made possible by the conservancy programme has increased employment opportunities where few existed beforehand, and also raised incomes.

The significant participation of conservancy populations has been central to the design of the programme. Conservancies are built around the willingness of communities to work collectively. Often, they form when neighbouring villages and tribal authorities agree to trace a boundary around their shared borders and manage the wildlife within this area. The conservancy programme has inbuilt flexibility which allows communities to choose diverse strategies for wildlife management and distributing benefits.

Support from and co-operation between a number of different institutions has been important to the development of the programme (Figure 2.47). Such institutions bring substantial experience and skills in helping conservancies to develop. Running skills training programmes has been an important aspect of such support. For example, communal conservancies are able to call on the experience of various NGOs for help and advice. This enables good practice in one area to be applied in other areas. The Namibian Community-based Tourism Association has been instrumental in helping communities negotiate levies and income-sharing agreements with tourism companies.

Figure 2.48 shows the rapid expansion of the total land area under management of conservancies from 1998 to 2005. From less

than 20 000 km² in 1998, by 2005 the total land area went beyond 100 000 km². The rate of increase was particularly impressive between 2002 and 2005. The population living in conservancy areas also rose rapidly in the latter period and now exceeds 200 000 (Figure 2.49). This is about one-tenth of the country's population.

Although rural poverty remains significant in Namibia, the conservancy programme has resulted in substantial progress, with income rising year on year. Figure 2.50 shows the development

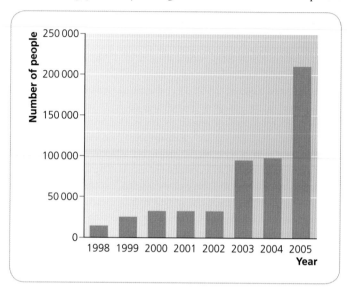

Figure 2.49 Communal conservancies – population living in conservancy areas, 1998–2005

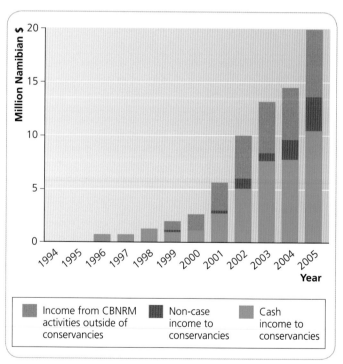

Figure 2.50 Income from conservancies and other community-based natural resource management in Namibia, 1994–2005

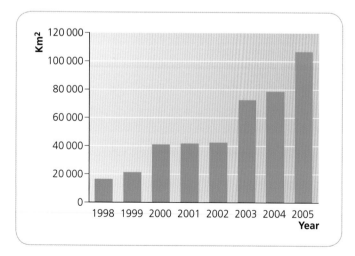

Figure 2.48 Communal conservancies – total land under management, 1998–2005

of conservancy income between 1994 and 2005, while Table 2.13 shows the detailed breakdown of conservancy-related income in 2006. In 2006, conservancy income reached nearly N$19 million. Income from small businesses associated with the conservancies but not directly owned by them brought in another N$8 million.

An important aspect of development has been the involvement of women in the employment benefits. Such jobs have included being game guards and natural resource monitors, as well as serving tourists in campgrounds and lodges.

Rising income from conservancies has made possible increasing investment in social development projects. Expenditure on such projects more than doubled from 2003 to 2005. This has made conservancies an increasingly important element in rural development.

Table 2.13 Conservancy-related income, 2006

Source of income	Value in N$	% of total conservancy income
Miscellaneous	34 788	0.1
Premium hunting	43 600	0.2
Veld products	39 000	0.1
Thatching grass	2 450 481	9.1
Shoot and sell hunting	504 883	1.9
Interest earned	161 807	0.6
Craft sales	474 343	1.8
Campsites and community-based tourism enterprises	3 746 481	14.0
Trophy meat distribution	870 219	3.2
Game donation	860 950	3.2
Use of own game	739 629	2.8
Trophy hunting	6 113 923	22.8
Joint venture tourism	10 794 668	40.2
Total	26 834 772	100.0

Source: WWF et al. 2007: 113

Scaling-up resource management

Following the perceived success of community conservancies, the Namibian government has extended the concept to **community forests** (Figure 2.51). Establishing a community forest is similar to the process of forming a conservancy. This is a good example of the '**scaling-up' process** from one natural resource system to another. Based on the Forest Act of 2001, the project helps local communities to establish their own community forests, to manage and utilise them in a sustainable manner. Because many rural Namibians are poor, it is important that they have a greater say in how forest resources are managed and share the benefits of properly managed forest resources.

Forest fires and uncontrolled cutting have been two of the main problems facing forest-protection efforts in Namibia for some time. About 4 million ha of forest and veld are burnt annually,

Based in large part on the success of CBNRM in the conservancies, the Namibian government enacted legislation in 2001 allowing the formation of community forests – areas within the country's communal lands for which a community has obtained management rights over forest resources such as timber, firewood, wild fruits, thatch grass, honey, and even some wildlife (MET 2003). The establishment of the community forest program shows how the scaling-up process can reach across natural resource systems, affecting natural resource policy at the broadest level. Although the community forest program and the conservancy program are now administered separately by different ministries, some groups have expressed interest in merging the programs to allow a more integrated approach to managing natural resources at the community level (Tjaronda 2008).

Establishing a community forest is similar to the process of forming a conservancy. Communities must:
• Submit a formal application to the government;
• Elect a forest management committee from the community;
• Develop a constitution;
• Select, map, and demark a community forest area;
• Submit a forest management plan describing how the community will harvest forest resources sustainably and manage other activities such as grazing and farming within the forest area;
• Specify use rights and bylaws necessary to act on their management plan;
• Craft a plan to ensure the equitable distribution of revenues to all community members; and
• Obtain permission from the area's traditional authority (MET 2003).

As of April 2008, a total of 45 community forests had been formed (although only 13 were officially gazetted), encompassing 2.2. million ha and benefiting some 150,000 Namibians. In the north-eastern region alone, 16 registered forests have generated more than N$300,000 (US$38,000) since 2005 (The Namibian 2008; Tjaronda 2008).

Figure 2.51 Extending the conservancy concept: community forests in Namibia

mostly as a result of fires started deliberately to improve grazing and to clear hunting grounds.

The advent of community forests has led to improved forest resource management. It has also improved the livelihoods of local people based on the empowerment of local communities with forest use rights. Villagers in community forests derive an income by marketing forestry products such as timber and firewood, poles, wild fruits, devil's claw, thatching grass, tourism, honey from beekeeping, wildlife, woven baskets and other crafts.

Country Pilot Partnership for Integrated Sustainable Land Management

The Government of Namibia has identified land degradation as a serious problem which demands remedial intervention. Five government departments together with international agencies have established a Country Pilot Partnership for Integrated Sustainable Land Management. The activities will be funded through the Global Environment Facility (GEF) in partnership with the United Nations Development Programme (UNDP) as implementing lead agency. Other organisations including the European Union are also involved.

The pilot project began in early 2008 and will run until late 2011. The project objective is to develop and pilot a range of coping mechanisms for reducing the vulnerability of farmers and pastoralists to climate change, including variability. It is taking place both within and outside communal conservancies. Its organisation is at least partly based on what Namibia has learned from the establishment of communal and forest conservancies.

3 Global interdependence

3.1 Trade flows and trading patterns

Visible and invisible trade

Trade refers to the exchange of goods and services for money. The origin and continuing basis of global interdependence is trade. The global trading system developed at the time of European colonial expansion. Here, a 'colonial division of labour' emerged in which LEDCs exported primary products, agriculture and minerals, while Europe and North America exported manufactured goods. This remained the general pattern of world trade until the post-Second World War period when a more complex pattern of international trade emerged. Trade is the most vital element in the growth of the global economy. World trade now accounts for 25 per cent of GDP – double its share in 1970 (Figure 3.1).

Trade results from the uneven distribution of resources over the Earth's surface. Even countries with an abundance of resources and a wide industrial base cannot produce all of the goods and services that their populations desire. So they buy goods and services from other countries, providing they have the money to pay for them. Goods and services purchased from other countries are termed '**imports**'. In contrast, goods and services sold to other countries are called '**exports**'. Imports along with exports form the basis of international trade. The difference between the value of a country's imports and exports is known as the **balance of trade**.

Figure 3.1 Vancouver, Canada – much of Canada's trade with Asia passes through Vancouver

A trade deficit occurs when the value of a country's imports exceeds the value of its exports, A country can make up this difference by using its savings or by borrowing, but clearly such a situation cannot continue indefinitely. In contrast, a positive or favourable balance of trade is known as a **trade surplus**.

Visible trade involves items that have a physical existence and can actually be seen. Thus raw materials (primary products) such as oil and food, and manufactured goods (secondary products) such as cars and furniture, are items of visible trade. **Invisible trade** is trade in services, which include travel and tourism, and business and financial services.

Global inequalities in trade flows

Merchandise trade growth in real terms slowed significantly in 2008 to 2 per cent, compared with 6 per cent in 2007 (Figure 3.2). But trade still managed to grow faster than global output, as is usually the case when production growth is positive. Growth for the year was below the average 5.7 per cent registered during the 1998–2008 period. The share of developing economies in world merchandise trade set new records in 2008, with exports rising to 38 per cent of the world total and imports increasing to 34 per cent. The emergence of different generations of newly industrialised countries since the 1960s has radically altered the trade pattern that existed in the previous period.

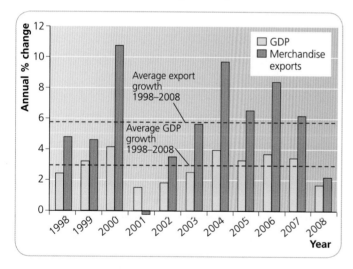

Figure 3.2 Growth in the volume of world merchandise trade and GDP, 1998–2008

Table 3.1 shows the spatial distribution of world trade in merchandise trade (visible trade) for the top 20 countries. Germany was the largest exporter of merchandise in 2008 with 9.1 per cent of the global share. Both China and the USA accounted for over 8 per cent of global exports each. It is interesting to note the presence of two relatively small European countries in the top ten, the Netherlands and Belgium. The top ten countries accounted for 50.7 per cent of world exports in 2008 and the top twenty countries were responsible for 70.2 per cent of the global total.

However, the USA dominates imports by a huge margin, taking over 13 per cent of the world total. The USA's trade deficit is something that worries many economists, as it is a situation that cannot be maintained indefinitely. In terms of the value of

Table 3.1 Merchandise trade: leading exporters and importers, 2008

Rank	Exporters	Value ($ billion)	Share (%)
1	Germany	1465	9.1
2	China	1428	8.9
3	USA	1301	8.1
4	Japan	782	4.9
5	Netherlands	634	3.9
6	France	609	3.8
7	Italy	540	3.3
8	Belgium	477	3.0
9	Russian Federation	472	2.9
10	UK	458	2.8
11	Canada	456	2.8
12	Korea, Republic of	422	2.6
13	Hong Kong, China:	370	2.3
	– domestic exports	17	0.1
	– re-exports	353	2.2
14	Singapore	338	2.1
	– domestic exports	176	1.1
	– re-exports	162	1.0
15	Saudi Arabia	329	2.0
16	Mexico	292	1.8
17	Spain	268	1.7
18	Taipei, Chinese	256	1.6
19	United Arab Emirates	232	1.4
20	Switzerland	200	1.2
Rank	Importers	Value ($ billion)	Share (%)
1	USA	2166	13.2
2	Germany	1206	7.3
3	China	1133	6.9
4	Japan	762	4.6
5	France	708	4.3
6	UK	632	3.8
7	Netherlands	547	3.5
8	Italy	556	3.4
9	Belgium	470	2.9
10	Korea, Republic of	435	2.7
11	Canada	418	2.5
12	Spain	402	2.5
13	Hong Kong, China	393	2.4
	– retained exports	98	0.6
14	Mexico	323	2.0
15	Singapore	320	1.9
	– retained exports	157	1.0
16	Russian Federation	292	1.8
17	India	292	1.8
18	Taipei, Chinese	240	1.5
19	Poland	204	1.2
20	Turkey	202	1.2

Source: www.wto.org Press/554 23/3/09

Table 3.2 World merchandise trade by region, 2008

Region	Exports ($ billion)	Imports ($ billion)
World	15 775	16 120
North America	2 049	2 909
South and Central America	602	595
Europe	6 456	6 833
Commonwealth of Independent States	703	493
Africa	561	466
Middle East	1 047	575
Asia	4 355	4 247

Source: WTO

Table 3.3 Leading exporters and importers in commercial services, 2008

Rank	Exporters	Value ($ billion)	Share (%)
1	USA	522	14.0
2	UK	283	7.6
3	Germany	235	6.3
4	France	153	4.1
5	Japan	144	3.9
6	Spain	143	3.8
7	China	137	3.7
8	Italy	123	3.3
9	India	106	2.8
10	Netherlands	102	2.7
11	Ireland	96	2.6
12	Hong Kong, China	91	2.4
13	Belgium	89	2.4
14	Switzerland	74	2.0
15	Korea, Republic of	74	2.0
16	Denmark	72	1.9
17	Singapore	72	1.9
18	Sweden	71	1.9
19	Luxembourg	68	1.8
20	Canada	62	1.7

Rank	Importers	Value ($ billion)	Share (%)
1	USA	364	10.5
2	Germany	285	8.2
3	UK	199	5.7
4	Japan	166	4.8
5	China	152	4.4
6	France	137	3.9
7	Italy	132	3.8
8	Spain	108	3.1
9	Ireland	103	3.0
10	Korea, Republic of	93	2.7
11	Netherlands	92	2.6
12	India	91	2.6
13	Canada	84	2.4
14	Belgium	84	2.4
15	Singapore	76	2.2
16	Russian Federation	75	2.2
17	Denmark	62	1.8
18	Sweden	54	1.6
19	Thailand	46	1.3
20	Australia	45	1.3

Source: www.wto.org Press/554 23/3/09

imports, the USA is followed by Germany with 7.3 per cent of the global total and China with 6.9 per cent. Table 3.2 shows world merchandise trade by region, illustrating the extent to which Europe, Asia and North America dominate global trade, accounting for 81.5 per cent of the world total between them. Africa accounted for only 3.6 per cent of world merchandise exports in 2008, and South and Central America 3.8 per cent.

In recent decades trade in commercial services has increased considerably. However, in terms of total value it is still less than a quarter of that of merchandise trade. The USA is the largest importer and exporter, with a particularly large lead in exports (Table 3.3). The USA accounts for 14 per cent of world exports in commercial services. The UK (7.6 per cent) ranks second in the export of services, ahead of Germany (6.3 per cent), France (4.1 per cent) and Japan (3.9 per cent).

The USA imported 10.5 per cent of trade in commercial services in 2008, followed by Germany (8.2 per cent) and the UK (5.7 per cent). China's global influence in trade in commercial services is significantly less than for merchandise trade. China is ranked seventh for exports of commercial services and fifth for imports. However, this will undoubtedly change over the next decade as the service sector in China expands. India too is rapidly moving up the world league table in trade in commercial services.

Table 3.4 shows world commercial services trade by region. Again, Europe, Asia and North America (Figure 3.3) dominate the global situation, with 90 per cent of the world total. Africa accounts for only 2.4 per cent of global trade in services and South and Central America 2.9 per cent.

Table 3.4 World commercial services trade by region, 2008

Region	Exports ($ billion)	Imports ($ billion)
World	3730	3470
North America	603	473
South and Central America	109	117
Europe	1919	1628
Commonwealth of Independent States	83	114
Africa	88	121
Middle East	94	158
Asia	837	858

Source: WTO

Figure 3.3 The Great Lakes waterway system is an important trade route in North America

399

Factors affecting global trade

A range of factors influence the volume, nature and direction of global trade, including:

- resource endowment
- comparative advantage
- locational advantage
- investment
- historical factors
- terms of trade
- changes in the global market
- trade agreements.

Resource endowment

Resource endowment is a significant factor in world trade. For example, the Middle East countries dominate the export of oil. Along with a few other countries elsewhere in the world, such as Venezuela and Nigeria, they form OPEC, the Organisation of Petroleum Exporting Countries.

OPEC is an intergovernmental organisation comprising 12 oil-producing nations. It was founded in 1960 after a US law imposed quotas on Venezuelan and Persian Gulf oil imports in favour of the Canadian and Mexican oil industries. OPEC's stated objective is 'to co-ordinate and unify the petroleum policies of member countries and ensure the stabilisation of oil markets in order to secure an efficient, economic and regular supply of petroleum to consumers, a steady income to producers and a fair return on capital to those investing in the petroleum industry'. In 2007 the OPEC countries accounted for 78 per cent of world crude oil reserves. OPEC has been heavily criticised at times for the allegedly political nature of some of its decisions. This has generally happened when the oil-rich Arab countries have wanted to put pressure on the USA and other Western countries with regard to the Israel-Palestine issue. At an OPEC meeting in November 2007, Venezuela's President Hugo Chavez urged the organisation to take a 'stronger political and geopolitical role'.

Countries endowed with other raw materials such as food products, timber, minerals and fish also figure prominently in world trade statistics. In the developed world the wealth of countries such as Canada and Australia has been built to a considerable extent on the export of raw materials in demand on the world market. LEDCs rich in raw materials, such as Brazil and South Africa, have been trying to follow a similar path. In both cases, wealth from raw materials has been used for economic diversification to produce a more broadly based economy.

Comparative advantage

The concept of **comparative advantage** is an important part of classical theory on international trade. This states that different countries will specialise in producing those goods and services for which each is best endowed. Each country will then trade a proportion of these goods and services with other nations to obtain goods and services that it needs but for which it is not favourably endowed. The concept is very easy to understand with regard to raw materials, but it also applies to manufactured goods and services. It is saying that even in the complexity of the modern global economy, countries tend to concentrate on the goods and services they are best at producing. This results in specialisation in production and employment. The evidence of this is that some countries have a global reputation for particular products. Examples include German cars, Japanese high-tech products, Scotch whisky, Belgian chocolate and Swiss watches.

Locational advantage

The location of market demand influences trade patterns. It is advantageous for an exporting country to be close to the markets for its products as this reduces transport costs, along with other advantages gained from spatial proximity. For example, the tourist industry in France benefits from the large populations of neighbouring countries that can reach France relatively quickly and cheaply. Likewise manufacturing industry in Canada benefits from the proximity of the huge American market.

Some countries and cities are strategically located along important trade routes, giving them important advantages in international trade. For example, Singapore, at the southern tip of the Malay peninsula, is situated at a strategic location along the main trade route between the Indian and Pacific Oceans. Similarly, Rotterdam in the Netherlands is located near the mouth of the River Rhine. Many goods brought in by large ocean carriers are trans-shipped onto smaller river vessels and other modes of transport at Rotterdam, or refined or manufactured in various ways in the port's industrial area.

Investment

Investment in a country is the key to it increasing its trade. Some LEDCs have increased their trade substantially. These countries have attracted the bulk of foreign direct investment. Such low-income 'globalisers' as China, Brazil, India and Mexico have increased their trade-to-GDP ratios significantly. On the other hand, 2 billion people live in countries that have become less rather than more globalised (in an economic sense) as trade has fallen in relation to national income. This group includes most African countries.

Historical factors

Historical relationships, often based on colonial ties, remain an important factor in global trade patterns. For example, the UK still maintains significant trading links with Commonwealth countries because of the trading relationships established at a time when

Figure 3.4 Lloyds of London – insurance is a vital factor in the movement of world trade

these countries were colonies. Such links are weaker than they once were, but in many cases they remain significant (Figure 3.4). Other European countries such as France, Spain, the Netherlands, Portugal and Belgium also established colonial networks overseas and have maintained such ties to varying degrees in the post-colonial period.

Colonial expansion heralded a trading relationship dictated by the European countries mainly for their own benefit. The colonies played a subordinate role that brought them only very limited benefits at the expense of distortion of their economies. The historical legacy of this **trade dependency** is one of the reasons why, according to development economists, poorer tropical countries have such a limited share of world trade.

The terms of trade

The most vital element in the trade of any country is the terms on which it takes place. If countries rely on the export of commodities that are low in price, and need to import items that are relatively high in price, they need to export in large quantities to be able to afford a relatively low volume of imports. Many poor nations are **primary product dependent**, which means they rely on one or a small number of primary products to obtain foreign currency through export. The world market price of primary products is

in general very low compared with that for manufactured goods and services. Also, the price of primary products is subject to considerable variation from year to year, making economic and social planning extremely difficult. In contrast the manufacturing and service exports of the developed nations generally rise in price at a reasonably predictable rate, resulting in a more regular income and less uncertainty for the rich countries of the world. The **terms of trade** for many LEDCs are worse now than they were two decades ago. Thus it is not surprising that so many nations are struggling to get out of poverty.

Because the terms of trade are generally disadvantageous to the poor countries of the South, many LEDCs have very high trade deficits (Figure 3.5). Among lower-income countries the average trade balance is a deficit of 12.3 per cent of GDP. Such a level is a rarity amongst MEDCs.

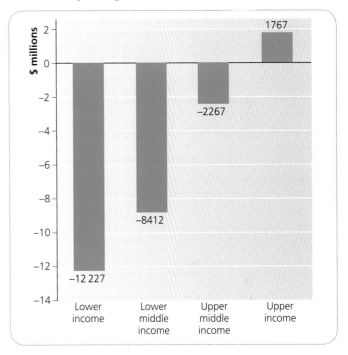

Figure 3.5 Trade balance by income group

Conventional neo-liberal economists generally welcome the large transfers of capital linked to high trade deficits. They say that trade deficits are strongly related to stages of economic development. The argument is that capital inflows swell the available pool of investment funds and thus generate future growth in the South. However, Marxist and populist writers argue that:

- If the expansion of trade volumes brings benefits to LEDCs, the accompanying expansion of trade deficits may bring considerable problems.
- Trade deficits have to be financed. One way is to borrow more money from abroad, but this will increase a country's debt. Another is to divert investment away from important areas of the economy such as agriculture, industry, education and health.
- Thus high trade deficits in the South constrain growth and produce a high level of dependency.

Changes in the global market

The rapid growth of newly industrialised countries has brought about major changes in the economic strength of countries. A recent article in *The Sunday Telegraph* entitled 'Developing nations emerge from shadows as sun sets on the West' charted the financial problems that beset the West in the first decade of the new millennium, culminating with the impact of the global recession 2008/10. It highlighted the poor decisions made by Western policy-makers, contrasting this with the powerful economic growth figures of countries such as China, India and Brazil. For example:

- China's Shanghai Composite Index of leading shares gained 140 per cent 2000–09.
- India's Sensex 30, the main index on the Mumbai stock exchange, was up 249 per cent in the same period.
- Brazil's Bovespa index of leading shares rose by 301 per cent.
- Russia's Micex index increases by a massive 802 per cent.

Together, these four formidable economies are known as the 'BRICS' (Brazil, Russia, India and China) (Figure 3.6). Their substantial growth rates are a significant threat to the established economic order. These four countries, along with other high-growth nations outside of the established core group of nations, are known as '**emerging markets**'.

While the developed world (the core) grew by an average of 2.1 per cent a year in the first decade of the twenty-first century, the emerging markets expanded by 4.2 per cent. The International Monetary Fund estimates that the figures for 2010 will be 1.3 per cent and 5.1 per cent respectively, and for 2011–14 the respective growth rates will be 2.5 per cent and 6.4 per cent a year. These are very significant differences indeed.

In 1990 the MEDCs controlled about 64 per cent of the global economy as measured by gross domestic product. This fell to 52 per cent by 2009 – one of the most rapid economic changes in history! Most of this global shift has occurred in the last decade.

Such a huge global economic change has had major political consequences, with the emerging economies exerting much more power than they had previously in international negotiations.

Many major investors are turning their backs, at least partially, on Western nations and seeking out opportunities in the faster-growing emerging markets. There have been major changes in the distribution of the world's foreign exchange reserves. The G7 countries (USA, Canada, Japan, Germany, UK, France and Italy) now hold only 17 per cent of the global total between them. Japan is the only significant creditor nation in this group. In contrast, the BRICs hold 42 per cent, with China alone holding 30 per cent. It is not so long ago that the USA was the world's biggest creditor. Today it is by far the world's biggest debtor. Much of the money borrowed by the USA and other Western economies has come from the reserves built up in emerging markets. The West no longer dominates the world's savings and as a result no longer dominates global investment and finance.

Trade agreements

A **trade bloc** is a group of countries that share trade agreements between each other. Since the Second World War there are many examples of groups of countries joining together to stimulate trade between themselves and to obtain other benefits from economic co-operation (Figure 3.7). The following forms of increasing economic integration between countries can be recognised:

- **Free trade areas:** members abolish tariffs and quotas on trade between themselves but maintain independent restrictions on imports from non-member countries. NAFTA is an example of a free trade area.
- **Customs unions:** this is a closer form of economic integration. Besides free trade between member nations, all members are obliged to operate a common external tariff on imports from non-member countries. Mercosur, established

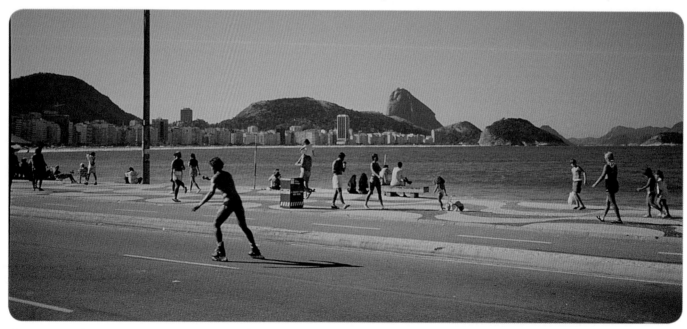

Figure 3.6 Rio de Janeiro – Brazil is one of the BRIC nations

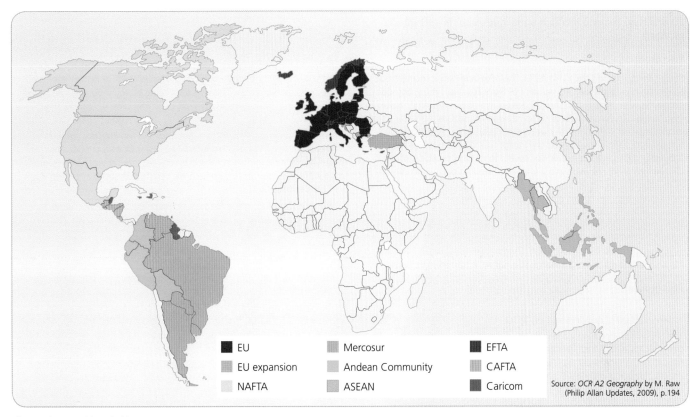

EU
EU expansion
NAFTA

Mercosur
Andean Community
ASEAN

EFTA
CAFTA
Caricom

Source: *OCR A2 Geography* by M. Raw
(Philip Allan Updates, 2009), p.194

Figure 3.7 World trade blocs

on 1 January 1995, is a customs union joining Brazil, Paraguay, Uruguay and Argentina in a single market of over 200 million people.

- **Common markets:** these are customs unions which in addition to free trade in goods and services, also allow the free movement of labour and capital.
- **Economic unions:** these organisations have all the characteristics of a common market but also require members to adopt common economic policies on such matters as agriculture, transport, industry and regional policy. The EU is an example of an economic union, although it must be remembered that its present high level of economic integration was achieved in several stages. When the UK joined in 1973 the organisation could best be described as a common market. The increasing level of integration has been marked by changes in the name of the organisation. Initially known as the European Economic Community, it later became the European Community and finally, from November 1993, the European Union.

Regional trade agreements have proliferated in the last two decades. In 1990 there were fewer than 25; by 1998 there were more than 90. The most notable of these are the European Union, NAFTA in North America, ASEAN in Asia, and Mercosur in Latin America. The United Nations (1990) refer to such organisations as 'geographically discriminatory trading arrangements'. Nearly all of the World Trade Organisation (WTO)'s members belong to at least one regional pact. All such arrangements have one unifying characteristic: the preferential terms that trade participants enjoy

over non-participating countries. Although no regional group has as yet adopted rules contrary to those of the WTO, there are some concerns:

- Regional agreements can divert trade, inducing a country to import from a member of its trading bloc rather than from a cheaper supplier elsewhere.
- Regional groups might raise barriers against each other, creating protectionist blocks.
- Regional trade rules may complicate the establishment of new global regulations.

There is a growing consensus that international regionalism is on the ascendency. The EU, NAFTA and ASEAN+ (associated agreements with other countries) triad of regional trading arrangements dominate the world economy, accounting for 67 per cent of all world trade. Whether the regional trade agreement trend causes the process of world trade liberalisation to falter in the future remains to be seen.

Apart from trade blocs there are a number of looser trade groupings aiming to foster the mutual interests of member countries. These include:

- The Asia-Pacific Economic Co-operation forum (APEC). Its 21 members border the Pacific Ocean and include Canada, the USA, Peru, Chile, Japan, China and Australia. The member countries have pledged to facilitate free trade.
- The Cairns Group of agricultural exporting nations was formed in 1986 to lobby for freer trade in agricultural products. Its members include Argentina, Brazil, Canada, New Zealand, Australia, the Philippines and South Africa.

EU and New Zealand bilateral trade agreement in agricultural products	
Background	**Agreement**
Before the UK joined the EU in 1973, New Zealand had a special trade relationship with the UK: 90 per cent of New Zealand's meat and dairy products were exported to the UK. Special trading arrangements were negotiated between the EU and New Zealand to secure the latter's main export market. Although New Zealand's major export markets have increasingly shifted to Asia and the Pacific rim, the EU remains New Zealand's second largest trading partner (for sheepmeat, dairy produce and wine). The UK remains New Zealand's most important trading partner within the EU.	Initially the EU imposed a common external tariff of 20 per cent on New Zealand imports. This was later reduced to 10 per cent and then to 0 per cent with a voluntary limit on the volume of New Zealand exports. The Uruguay round of WTO negotiations in the 1990s changed this arrangement and introduced Tariff Rate Quotas (TRQs). New Zealand's lamb exports to the EU were allocated a tariff-free quota of 227 000 t year^{-1}. Any imports exceeding the quota attracted a 12.8 per cent tariff. New Zealand has, none the less, complained that trade in lamb is unfair. Whereas New Zealand sheep farmers receive no government subsidies, EU farmers can lower their prices because they get a ewe subsidy of €21 per head.

EU and bilateral trade agreement with ACP banana growers	
Background	**Agreement**
There is a long-running dispute between the EU, ACP banana growers, Latin American banana growers and the WTO.	The 2000 Cotonou trade agreement between the EU and ACP provided a 775 000 tonne tariff-free quota for ACP bananas. At the same time Latin American producers faced a €230 t^{-1} tariff for their banana exports to the EU.
The UK and France have close political, historic and economic ties with many small countries in Africa, the Caribbean and the Pacific (ACP) which depend heavily on banana exports. The special trade agreements concluded between the UK, France and the ACP banana growers were adopted by the EU.	In 2007 WTO ruled that this agreement violated global trade rules, giving an unfair advantage to ACP growers. Although the tariff for Latin American bananas was reduced to €175 t^{-1} the WTO insists that the revised trade arrangements remain unacceptable. By the end of 2008 the dispute was still unresolved.
Meanwhile, other banana exporters, especially in Latin America (e.g. Ecuador, Nicaragua, Mexico) complained that these arrangements were unfair. They argued that they should have the same access to the EU market as ACP growers. However, growing conditions in Latin America are more favourable, the scale of production is much greater (with large plantations owned by US TNCs) and therefore costs are low. Free trade would mean that ACP growers could not compete and that most would go out of business.	

Figure 3.8 Examples of EU trade agreements

Source: *OCR A2 Geography* by M. Raw (Philip Allan Updates, 2009), p.196

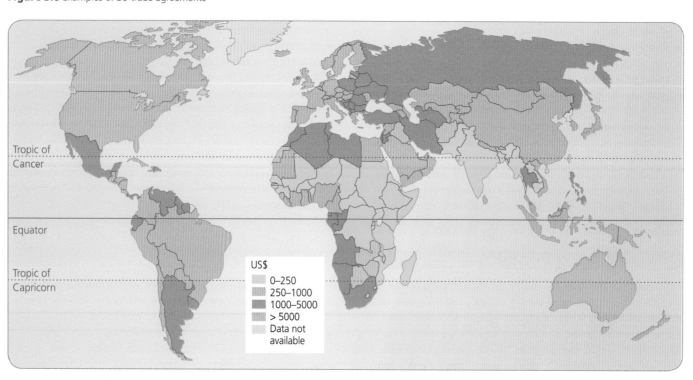

Figure 3.9 Exports of goods and commercial services per capita

Figure 3.8 details trade agreements between the EU and New Zealand, and the EU and the ACP.

Trade and development

There is a strong relationship between trade and economic development. In general, countries that have a high level of trade are richer than those with lower levels of trade. Figure 3.9 shows the value of exports of goods and commercial services per capita for 2003, and provides good evidence for this assertion. Countries that can produce goods and services in demand elsewhere in the world will benefit from strong inflows of foreign currency and from the employment their industries provide. Foreign currency allows a country to purchase from abroad goods and services it either does not produce itself or does not produce in large enough quantities.

An Oxfam report published in April 2002 stated that if Africa increased its share of world trade by just 1 per cent it would earn an additional £49 billion a year – five times the amount it receives in aid. The World Bank has acknowledged that the benefits of globalisation are barely being passed on to Sub-Saharan Africa and may actually have accentuated many of its problems.

Section 3.1 Activities

1 Explain the importance of resource endowment as a factor in world trade.

2 What do you understand by the concept of *comparative advantage*?

3 How have **a** locational advantage and **b** historical factors influenced global trade patterns?

4 Define the *terms of trade*.

5 Why have trade agreements increased significantly in recent decades?

6 Briefly examine the link between trade and development.

The World Trade Organisation

In 1947 a group of 23 nations agreed to reduce tariffs on each other's exports under the General Agreement on Tariffs and Trade (GATT). This was the first multilateral accord to lower trade barriers since Napoleonic times. Since the GATT was established there have been nine 'rounds' of global trade talks, of which the most recent, the Doha (Qatar) round, began in 2001. A total of 142 member countries were represented at the talks in Doha.

The most important recent development has been the creation of the World Trade Organisation (WTO) in 1995. Unlike its predecessor, the loosely organised GATT, the WTO was set up as a permanent organisation with far greater powers to arbitrate trade disputes. Figure 3.10 shows the benefits of the global trading system according to the WTO.

Although agreements have been difficult to broker at times, the overall success of GATT/WTO is undeniable: today average tariffs are only a tenth of what they were when GATT came into force and world trade has been increasing at a much faster rate than

GDP. However, in some areas **protectionism** is still an issue, particularly in the sectors of clothing, textiles and agriculture. In principle, every nation has an equal vote in the WTO. In practice, the rich world shuts out the poor world from key negotiations. In recent years agreements have become more and more difficult to reach, with some economists forecasting the stagnation or even the break-up of the WTO.

Relations between the USA and the EU were soured in the early 2000s by the so-called 'banana war', and by disagreements over hormone-treated beef, GM foods and steel (Figure 3.11). Leading

1 The system helps promote peace.
2 Disputes are handled constructively.
3 Rules make life easier for all.
4 Freer trade cuts the cost of living.
5 It provides more choice of products and qualities.
6 Trade raises incomes.
7 Trade stimulates economic growth.
8 The basic principles make life more efficient.
9 Governments are shielded from lobbying.
10 The system encourages good government.

Source: WTO

Figure 3.10 The ten benefits of the WTO trading system

Trade Wars: Steel

Four months after the WTO launched a new round of global trade talks in Doha, the USA imposed tariffs of up to 30% on steel imports to protect its own fragile steel industry. More than 30 US steel producers went bankrupt between 1997 and 2002. Those that remained were considered to be inefficient and high cost compared with most of their foreign counterparts. Management consultants have largely put this down to the strength of the steel unions and their demands for high wages and health insurance. The crux of the problem is that world steelmaking capacity, estimated at between 900 million and 1000 million tonnes, is 20% higher than current demand. Although restructuring has already occurred, more is bound to happen both in the USA and in other parts of the world.

The reaction of America's trading partners was not difficult to predict. Trade unionists warned that the new trade barriers could result in 5000 job losses in the UK and 18 000 in the EU as a whole. The countries affected by the new tariffs argued that the USA was in breach of WTO rules. They also announced that they would demand compensation from the USA for the effect of the tariffs. However, as it could take up to two years for the WTO to reach a judgement, significant damage could be done in the intervening period to the steel industries of those nations affected. To its credit the EU stated that any retaliatory action would be within WTO rules. Overall this dispute was the last thing that the global steel industry, worth an estimated $500 billion, wanted.

Figure 3.11 Trade war in the WTO

agricultural exporters such as the USA, Australia and Argentina want a considerable reduction in barriers to trade for agricultural products. Although the EU is committed in principle to reducing agricultural support, it wants to move slowly, arguing that farming merits special treatment because it is a 'multifunctional activity' that fulfils important social and environmental roles. Many LEDCs have criticised the WTO for being too heavily influenced by the interests of the USA and the EU.

The WTO exists to promote **free trade**. Most countries in the world are members and most of those countries that are not currently members want to join. The fundamental issue is: does free trade benefit all those concerned, or is it a subtle way in which the rich nations exploit their poorer counterparts? Most critics of free trade accept that it does generate wealth but they deny that all countries benefit from it. For example, Barry Coates, Director of the World Development Movement, wrote in the *Observer* newspaper (21 November 1999), 'Trickle-down to the poor hasn't happened. In the past 20 years, the developing countries' share of world trade has halved, income per person has fallen in 59 countries, and the number of people living on less than $1 a day has risen dramatically.' The non-governmental organisation Oxfam is a major critic of the way the present trading system operates. Figure 3.12 shows the main goals of its 'Make Trade Fair' campaign.

1 End the use of conditions attached to IMF–World Bank programmes which force poor countries to open their markets regardless of the impact.
2 Improve market access for poor countries and end the cycle of subsidised agricultural overproduction and export dumping by rich countries.
3 Change WTO rules so that developing countries can protect domestic food production.
4 Create a new international commodities institution to promote diversification and end oversupply in order to raise prices for producers and give them a reasonable standard of living.
5 Change corporate practices so that companies pay fair prices.
6 Establish new intellectual property rules to ensure that poor countries are able to afford new technologies and basic medicines.
7 Prohibit rules that force governments to liberalise or privatise basic services that are vital for poverty reduction.
8 Democratise the WTO to give poor countries a stronger voice.

Figure 3.12 Oxfam's 'Make Trade Fair' Campaign

However, others would view the data available in a different way. Over the 1985–2000 period, global inequality as measured by the Gini coefficient seems to have declined significantly (Figure 3.13). The main reason for this has been the rise in living standards in China and India. But what about the poor countries of Africa

and elsewhere in the world? Supporters of the WTO say that it is scarcely credible to argue that the poverty of these countries is the result of globalisation since they are all outside the mainstream of free trade and economic globalisation. Critics of the WTO, on the other hand, say that the WTO and other international organisations should be paying more attention to the needs of these countries, making it easier for them to become more involved in, and gain tangible benefits from, the global economic system.

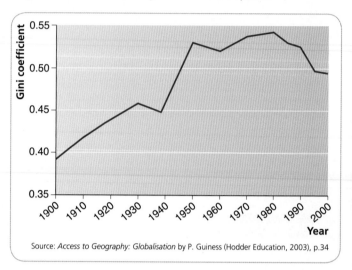

Source: *Access to Geography: Globalisation* by P. Guiness (Hodder Education, 2003), p.34

Figure 3.13 Gini coefficient of worldwide income distribution

Critics of the WTO ask why it is that MEDCs have been given decades to adjust their economies to imports of textiles and agricultural products from LEDCs, when the latter are pressurised to open their borders immediately to banks, telecommunications companies and other components of the service sector in MEDCs. The removal of tariffs can have a significant impact on a nation's domestic industries. For example, India has been very concerned about the impact of opening its markets to foreign imports (Figure 3.14).

Since India was forced by a WTO ruling to accelerate the opening up of its markets, food imports have quadrupled. Large volumes of cheap, subsidised imports have flooded in from countries such as the USA, Malaysia and Thailand. The adverse impact has been considerable and includes the following:

- Prices and rural incomes have fallen sharply. The price paid for coconuts has dropped 80 per cent, for coffee 60 per cent, and pepper 45 per cent.
- Foreign imports, mainly subsidised soya from the USA and palm oil from Malaysia, have undercut local producers and have virtually wiped out the production of edible oil.

Figure 3.14 India: the impact of the removal of agricultural tariffs

The new emphasis on exports, in order for India to compete in the world market, is also threatening rural livelihoods. For example, in Andhra Pradesh, India funding from the World Bank and the UK will encourage farm consolidation, mechanisation and modernisation. In this region it is expected that the proportion of people living on the land will fall from 70 per cent to 40 per cent by 2020.

Farmers, trade unionists and many others are against these trends, or at least the speed at which they are taking place. They are calling for the reintroduction of import controls, thus challenging the basic principle of the globalisation process – the lowering of trade barriers.

Opposition to the WTO comes from a number of sources:

- many LEDCs who feel that their concerns are largely ignored
- environmental groups concerned, for example, about a WTO ruling that failed to protect dolphins from tuna nets
- labour unions in some MEDCs, notably the USA, concerned about (a) the threat to their members' jobs as traditional manufacturing filters down to LEDCs, and (b) violation of 'workers' rights' in LEDCs.

Case Study

The trade in tea

Tea, like coffee, bananas and other raw materials, exemplifies the relatively small proportion of the final price of the product that goes to producers. The great majority of the money generated by the tea industry goes to the post-raw material stages (processing, distributing and retailing), usually benefiting companies in MEDCs rather than the LEDC producers.

A report by the Dutch Tea Institute in 2006 drew particular attention to:

- the problems of falling prices and rising input costs
- the consequent pressure to limit labour costs of tea production workers
- the urgent need for improvement of labour, social, ecological and economic conditions throughout the tea sector in the LEDCs.

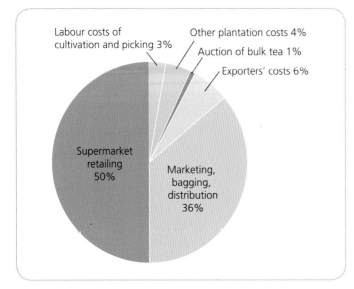

Figure 3.15 Tea value chain

The global tea market is dominated by a small number of companies including Unilever and Sara Lee. About half of all the tea produced is traded internationally. Annual export sales of tea in its raw material state are worth almost $3 billion. The retail value of the global tea business is of course much higher. The large tea companies wield immense power over the industry. As many countries now produce tea they have to compete with each other in an increasingly competitive market. Global supply is rising at a faster rate than consumption, keeping prices low.

Tea producers complain that the global trading system prevents them from moving up the value chain (Figure 3.15) by processing and packing the tea they grow. This is mainly because they would have to compete with very powerful brands, and they would find it very difficult to achieve the economies of scale of the global tea companies.

The nature and role of fair trade

Many supermarkets and other large stores in Britain and other MEDCs now stock some 'fairly traded' products. Most are agricultural products such as bananas, orange juice, nuts, coffee and tea (Figure 3.16) but the market in non-food goods such as textiles and handicrafts is also increasing. The fair trade system operates as follows:

- Small-scale producers group together to form a co-operative or other democratically run association with high social and environmental standards.
- These co-operatives deal directly with companies (cutting out 'middlemen') such as Tesco and Sainsbury in MEDCs.
- MEDC companies (through their customers) pay significantly over the world market price for the products traded. The price difference can be as large as 100 per cent. This might mean, for example, supermarket customers paying a few pence more for a kilo of bananas.
- The higher price achieved by the LEDC co-operatives provides both a better standard of living (often saving

Figure 3.16 Fair trade tea

In 1993 a group of farmers in Ghana formed a co-operative to sell their own cocoa. It was supported by SNV, a Dutch NGO, and the UK Department for International Development. The co-operative ensures farmers are paid for what they produce and are not cheated by middlemen. It includes:

- *Kuapa Kokoo Farmers' Union.* This is a national body made up of 45 000 cocoa farmers who elect representatives.
- *Kuapa Kokoo Farmers' Trust.* This is responsible for distributing money for community projects, generated from the Fairtrade Premium. Projects include providing clean water supplies and mobile health clinics, building schools and improving sanitation.

In 2008 Kuapa Kokoo sold 4250 tonnes of cocoa to the Fairtrade market. This means that the farmers receive a guaranteed price. For example, even if the world price of cocoa falls to US$1000 per tonne, the Fairtrade price remains at US$1600 per tonne. The minimum Fairtrade price is $1600 – if the world price goes higher farmers will receive the higher price, plus the social premium of $150 per tonne, and these prices have been reviewed and will be increased.

In 1998 Kuapa Kokoo came together with the NGO Twin, supported by The Body Shop, Christian Aid and Comic Relief, to found the Divine Chocolate company. As Kuapa Kokoo is part owner of Divine it not only gets a fair price for its cocoa but also has an influence on how the organisation is run and a share in the profits it has helped to create. Divine Fairtrade chocolate is sold in the UK, the Netherlands, Scandinavia and the USA.

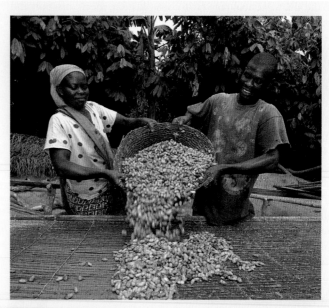

Kuapa Kokoo farmers spread cocoa beans out to dry

Like all food production, fair trade will only work as a solution if it is sustainable in the long term. Income, and therefore food security, depends on maintaining soil health and water supply through good agricultural management. In Africa, a continent riven by war, conflict and corruption, political stability is equally important. Fair trade can contribute to this stability by reducing poverty.

Figure 3.17 Kuapa Kokoo Fairtrade Co-operative

producers from bankruptcy and absolute poverty) and some money to reinvest in the farms of producers.

Advocates of the fair trade system argue that it is a model of how world trade can and should be organised to tackle global poverty. This system of trade began in the 1960s with Dutch consumers supporting Nicaraguan farmers. It is now a global market worth £315 million a year, involving over 400 MEDC companies and an estimated 500 000 small farmers and their families in the world's poorest countries. Food sales are growing by more than 25 per cent a year, with Switzerland and the UK being the largest markets. Figure 3.17 compares the prices received by plantation workers under 'normal' trading conditions with those received by workers in a fair trade scheme.

Section 3.1 Activities

1 Examine the role of the World Trade Organisation.

2 Why has the WTO been so heavily criticised?

3 Describe and explain the nature and role of fair trade.

4 Comment on the tea value chain presented in Figure 3.15.

3.2 Debt and aid and their management

Debt: causes, nature and problems

Experts from a variety of disciplines blame the rules of the global economic system for excluding many countries from its potential benefits. Many single out **debt** as the major problem for the world's poorer nations. Here debt is considered at the national scale rather than the personal level. The term *debt* generally refers to external debt (foreign debt) which is that part of the total debt in a country owed to creditors outside the country. *Unpayable debt* is a term used to describe external debt when the interest on the debt is beyond the means of a country, thus preventing the debt from ever being repaid. A country's external debt

– both debt outstanding and debt service – affects a country's creditworthiness and thus its overall economic vulnerability.

Many poor countries are currently paying back large amounts in debt repayments to banks, lending agencies and governments in MEDCs while at the same time struggling to provide basic services for their populations. An ever increasing proportion of new debt is used to service interest payments on old debts. The **debt service ratio** of many poor countries is at a very high level. While supporters of globalisation argue that economic growth through trade is the only answer, critics say that MEDCs should do more to help the poor countries through **debt relief** and by opening their markets to exports from LEDCs.

The USA owes more money to the rest of the world than any other country. Some other rich countries such as the UK and France also owe substantial amounts. However, these countries have huge assets against which they can borrow, so their debts are thought to be manageable, although the recent global financial crisis has called this into question. However, in general, debt repayment by rich countries is very different from the immense struggle that poor countries have in trying to pay their debts.

The total external debt of the poorest countries of the world (the 'low-income countries') was $375 billion in 2006. During 2006 these countries paid over $34 billion to the developed world to service their debts. These payments averaged $94 million a day. When a country has to use a high proportion of its income to service debt, this takes money away from what could have been spent on education, health, housing, transport and other social and economic priorities. Multilateral debts are obligations to international financial institutions such as the World Bank, the International Monetary Fund and regional development banks. Multilateral debt service takes priority over private and bilateral debt service.

How did the **debt crisis** come about? Development economists have pointed to a sequence of events that began in the early 1970s as the main reason for the debt problems of many poor countries. It began with the Arab-Israeli war of 1973–74 which resulted in a sharp increase in oil prices. Governments and individuals in the oil-producing countries invested so-called petrodollars (profits from oil sales) in the banks of affluent countries. Eager to profit from such a high level of investment, these banks offered relatively low-interest loans to poorer countries to fund their development. These countries were encouraged to exploit raw materials and grow cash crops so that they could pay back their loans with profits made from exports. However, periods of recession in the 1980s and 1990s led to rising inflation and interest rates in Western countries. At the same time crop surpluses resulted in a fall in prices. As a result the demand for exports from LEDCs fell and export earnings declined significantly as a result. These factors, together with oil price increases, left many LEDCs unable to pay the interest on their debts.

Loans can help countries to expand their economic activities and set up an upward spiral of development if used wisely. However, many of the loans that burden the world's poorest countries were given under dubious circumstances and at times at very high rates of interest. Critics argue that banks frequently lent irresponsibly to governments that were known to be corrupt.

The term '**odious debt**' has been used to describe debt incurred as rich countries loaned to dictators or other corrupt leaders when it was known that the money would be wasted. For example, shortly after freedom from apartheid South Africa had to pay debts incurred by the apartheid regime. Often such loans led to little tangible improvement in the quality of life for the majority for the population, but instead saddled them with long-term debt. If such countries had been companies they would have been declared bankrupt. However, international law offers no 'fresh start' to countries in such a situation.

Many development economists also focus on the legacy of **colonialism**, arguing that the colonising powers left their former colonies with high and unfair levels of debt when they became independent. Such debts were often at very high interest rates. For example:

- In 1949, Indonesia, as a condition of independence, was required to assume the Dutch colonial government's debt, much of which had been acquired fighting pro-independence rebels in the previous four years.
- In order to receive independence from France, Haiti was required to pay France 150 million francs.

In recent years much of the debt has been 'rescheduled' and new loans have been issued. However, new loans have frequently been granted only when poor countries agreed to very strict conditions under 'structural adjustment programmes' which have included:

- agreeing to free trade measures, which have opened up their markets to intense foreign competition
- severe cuts in spending on public services such as education and health
- the privatisation of public companies.

Figure 3.18 shows international lending to LEDCs by region, from 2000 to 2007. In 2000 and 2001, the highest lending went to Latin America and the Caribbean. Thereafter Europe and Central Asia became the focus of lending, with Latin America and the Caribbean in second place. Despite the disadvantages that many countries have suffered over the medium and long term from improper lending, it is a vital component of the global economic system.

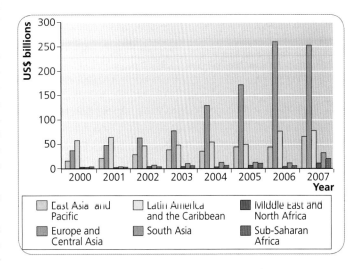

Figure 3.18 Gross cross-border bank lending to LEDCs, by region 2000–07

409

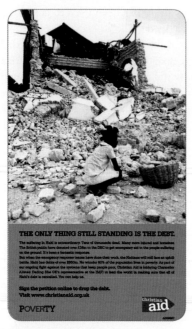

Figure 3.19 is a Christian Aid newspaper advertisement illustrating the plight of Haiti, one of the world's poorest countries, after the devastating earthquake of January 2010. Other organisations such as Oxfam, CAFOD and Islamic Relief mounted similar campaigns to cancel debt.

The **debt service ratio** is the proportion of a country's export earnings that it needs to use to meet its debt repayments. Figure 3.20 illustrates this information for a number of African countries. Some countries need to put aside 20–30 per cent of their export earnings to meet their debt repayments. A larger number of countries have a debt service ratio of between 10 and 20 per cent. These figures would be very significant for affluent countries, but can prove to be a crippling burden for nations with very low incomes.

Table 3.5 shows debt servicing as a percentage of the value of exports of goods and services. This is often taken as a measure of the affordability of debt. The figures range from 1 per cent for Ghana and Kazakhstan to 19 per cent for Brazil and 23 per cent for Argentina. While such data provides useful information it must always be remembered that some countries have a much greater capacity to handle debt than others.

Figure 3.19 Christian Aid Haiti campaign

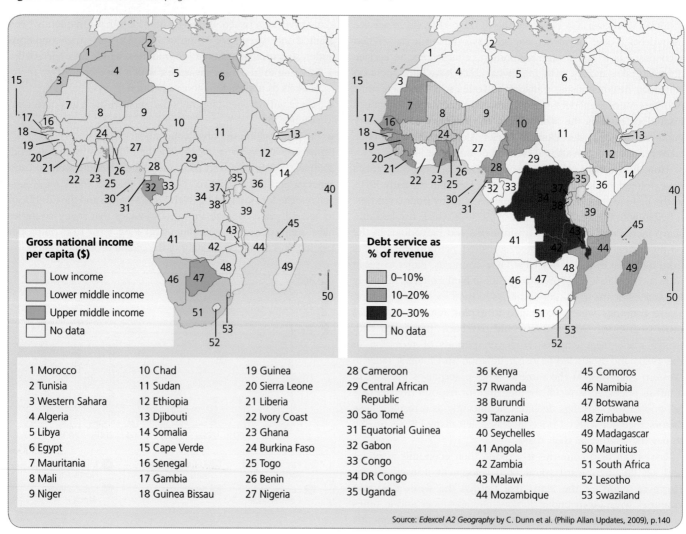

Figure 3.20 Africa's income and debt servicing, 2003

Table 3.5 Debt and debt servicing in a sample of countries, 2005

Country	Total outstanding external debt (US$ billion)	Debt servicing as % of exports of goods and services
Argentina	127.3	23
Brazil	240.5	19
Chile	58.2	14
Ghana	4.9	1
India	221.2	4
Indonesia	141.2	12
Kazakhstan	98.7	1
Kenya	6.7	7
Malawi	0.9	8
Malaysia	73.4	2
Mexico	205.3	14
Nigeria	8.0	17
Ukraine	92.5	5

Debt relief

Restructuring debt to LEDCs began in a limited way in the 1950s. In 1956 Argentina was the first country to renegotiate the repayment of its debt with bilateral creditors within the framework of the Paris Club (set up for this purpose). Attempts were made by creditor nations to tackle the 'Third World debt crisis' through the 1980s and 1990s. However, these efforts were viewed as limited in nature and often self-serving. The overall debt of poorer countries continued to rise. The rescheduling of debt repayments often brought temporary relief, but with interest added over a longer time period the overall debt simply increased. It was not until the mid-1990s that a more comprehensive global plan to tackle the debt of the poorest countries was formulated (Figure 3.21).

Strengths	Weaknesses
• Allow a country's loans to be rescheduled in order to make them more manageable	• Often accompanied by a shift from domestic food cultivation to production of cash crops or commodities for export
• Make the country's economy more competitive	• Reduce government expenditure by cutting social programmes, e.g. health and education, and abolishing food and agricultural subsidies
• Improve foreign investment potential by removing trade and/or investment restrictions	• Privatisation of state enterprises to cut government expenditure results in assets being sold to TNCs
• Boost foreign exchange by promoting exports	• Increase pressure on countries to generate exports to pay off debt. This is likely to increase deforestation, land degradation and other environmental damage
• Reduce government deficits through cuts in spending	• Some MEDCs accused of protecting their own interests

Figure 3.21 Strengths and weaknesses of debt reduction schemes

The Heavily Indebted Poor Countries (HIPC) Initiative

The Heavily Indebted Poor Countries (HIPC) Initiative was first established in 1996 by the International Monetary Fund (IMF) and the World Bank. Its aim was to provide a comprehensive approach to debt reduction for heavily indebted poor countries so that no poor country faced a debt burden it could not manage. To qualify for assistance, countries have to pursue IMF and World Bank supported adjustment and reform programmes. In 1999, a comprehensive review of the initiative allowed the fund to provide faster, deeper and broader debt relief and strengthened the links between debt relief, poverty reduction and social policies. In 2006 the Multilateral Debt Relief Initiative (MDRI) was launched to provide additional support to HIPCs to reach the Millennium Development Goals. In 2007, the Inter-American Development Bank also decided to provide debt relief to the five HIPCs in the western hemisphere.

According to a recent World Bank-IMF report, debt relief provided under both initiatives has substantially alleviated debt burdens in recipient countries. The report noted that 35 of 40 eligible countries had reached the 'decision point' by the end of June 2009. Of these countries 26 had reached the 'completion point'.

Decision point is when a country is considered eligible for HIPC Initiative assistance. To reach decision point, a country should have a track record of macro-economic stability, have prepared an interim Poverty Reduction Strategy Paper (PRSP), and cleared any outstanding arrears. Completion point means that the country can now receive full and irrevocable reduction in debt available under the HIPC Initiative and MDRI. To reach completion point, a country must maintain macro-economic stability under an IMF's Poverty Reduction and Growth Facility (PGRF)-supported programme, carry out key structural and social reforms as agreed upon at the decision point, and implement a PRSP satisfactorily for one year.

Figure 3.22 shows the status of HIPC countries. Apart from countries at decision point and completion point, the Figure also shows five countries at 'pre-decision point'. Figure 3.23 shows the financial estimates of debt relief under the HIPC Initiative and MDRI at the end of 2009. About 45 per cent of the funding comes from the IMF and other multilateral institutions, and the rest comes from bilateral creditors. The total cost of providing assistance is estimated to be about $75 billion.

Debt relief frees up resources for social spending

Debt relief is part of a much larger process, which includes international aid, designed to address the development needs of low-income countries. For debt reduction to have a meaningful impact on poverty, the additional funds made available need to be spent on programmes that are of real benefit to the poor.

Before the HIPC Initiative, eligible countries spent on average more on debt serving than on education and health combined.

Completion Point 28 countries

AFGHANISTAN	BURUNDI	ETHIOPIA	HAITI	MALI	NIGER	SIERRA LEONE
BENIN	CAMEROON	GAMBIA, THE	HONDURAS	MAURITANIA	RWANDA	TANZANIA
BOLIVIA	CENTRAL AFRICAN REPUBLIC	GHANA	MADAGASCAR	MOZAMBIQUE	SÃO TOMÉ AND PRÍNCIPE	UGANDA
BURKINA FASO	CONGO, REP. OF	GUYANA	MALAWI	NICARAGUA	SENEGAL	ZAMBIA

Countries reach the completion point if they maintain macro-economic stability under a PRGF (Poverty Reduction and Growth Facilities)-supported programme, carry out key structural and social reforms, and satisfactorily implement for a minimum of one year a Poverty Reduction Strategy. Debt relief is then provided irrevocably by the country's creditors. MDRI relief is provided upon reaching the completion point.

Decision Point 7 countries

CHAD	CONGO, DEM. REP. OF	IVORY COAST	GUINEA	GUINEA-BISSAU	LIBERIA	TOGO

Countries reach the decision point if they have a track record of macro-economic stability, have prepared a Poverty Reduction Strategy through a participatory process, and have debt burden indicators above the HIPC (Heavily Indebted Poor Country) Initiative thresholds using the most recent data for the year immediately prior to the decision point. The amount of debt relief necessary to bring countries' debt indicators to HIPC thresholds is calculated, and countries begin receiving interim debt relief on a provisional basis.

Pre-Decision Point 5 countries

COMOROS	ERITREA	KYRGYZ REPUBLIC	SOMALIA	SUDAN

Countries that have been assessed to meet the income and indebtedness criteria at end-2004 and wish to avail themselves of the HIPC initiative.

Figure 3.22 Status of HIPC countries

	World Bank group debt relief			Total debt relief		
	HIPC	MDRI	HIPC and MDRI	HIPC	MDRI	HIPC and MDRI
All HIPCs	15.0	20.0	35.0	75.6	31.0	106.5
Post-completion point HIPCs	11.0	16.9	27.9	42.0	26.6	68.6
7 interim HIPCs	2.5	2.8	5.3	16.5	3.9	20.4
Pre-completion point HIPCs	1.5	0.3	1.8	17.0	0.5	17.5

The debt stocks of the 35 post-decision-point HIPCs have been reduced by over 80%

Debt stocks of the 35 post-decision-point HIPCs, in US$ billion, end 2009

Before traditional debt relief	141
After traditional debt relief	117
After HIPC initiative debt relief	58
After additional bilateral debt relief	53
After MORI	23

Figure 3.23 HIPC Initiative and MDRI (Multilateral Debt Relief Initiative): estimates of debt relief, end 2009 (US$ billions)

Now these countries have significantly increased their spending on education, health and other social services. On average, such spending is around five times the amount of debt-service payments.

The amount of debt service paid by eligible countries fell, on average, by about two percentage points of GDP between 2001 and 2009. Their debt burden is expected to be reduced by about 80 per cent after the full delivery of debt relief.

Conclusion

There can be little doubt that the HIPC Initiative and MDRI have been more comprehensive debt relief structures than anything that had gone before. However, the initiatives have drawn criticism both in terms of the limited number of countries involved and the total extent of debt reduction. Even if all of the external debts of these countries were cancelled, most would still depend on significant levels of concessional external assistance, since their receipts of such assistance have been much larger than their debt-service payments for many years.

Since 1990 LEDCs have increased their buffer for external debt and its service. Total debt services have decreased significantly since 1999, due largely to debt relief initiates by multilateral and bilateral donors.

Section 3.2 Activities

1 Define **a** *debt* and **b** *debt service ratio*.

2 What do you understand by the term *odious debt*?

3 How has the legacy of colonialism contributed to the debts of a considerable number of poor countries?

4 Discuss the sequence of events that are generally accepted to have led to the debt crisis.

5 **a** What is *debt relief*?
   b Comment on the nature and effectiveness of the HIPC Initiative and the MDRI.

International aid

The origins of foreign aid date back to the Marshall Plan of the late 1940s. This was when the USA set out to reconstruct the war-torn economies of Western Europe and Japan as a means of containing the international spread of communism. By the mid-1950s the battle for influence between West and East in the developing world began to have a marked effect on the geography of aid. Even today bilateral aid is strongly influenced by ties of colonialism and neo-colonialism and by strategic considerations. However, it would be wrong to deny that aid is also given for humanitarian and economic reasons (Figure 3.24).

Figure 3.24 A school in North Africa – education is often a focus of international aid

Aid is assistance in the form of grants or loans at below market rates. Most LEDCs have been keen to accept foreign aid because of the:

- 'foreign exchange gap' whereby many LEDCs lack the hard currency to pay for imports such as oil and machinery which are vital to development
- 'savings gap' where population pressures and other drains on expenditure prevent the accumulation of enough capital to invest in industry and infrastructure

- 'technical gap' caused by a shortage of skills needed for development.

Many poor countries rely on a very small range of exports for foreign currency. The prices of such products are often low compared with the goods and services they need to import, and the prices for such raw materials can also be very volatile.

But why do richer nations give aid? Is it down to altruism, or self-interest? Much of the evidence suggests the latter. Contrary to popular belief, most foreign aid is not in the form of a grant, nor is famine relief a major component. A significant proportion of foreign aid is 'tied' to the purchase of goods and services from the donor country and often given for use on jointly agreed projects. However, the proportion of tied aid in relation to total international aid has been falling in recent decades.

Figure 3.25 shows how these factors combine to form the cycle of poverty.

The different types of international aid

Figure 3.26 shows the different types of **international aid**. The basic division is between official government aid and voluntary aid:

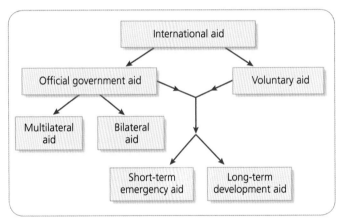

Figure 3.26 The different types of international aid

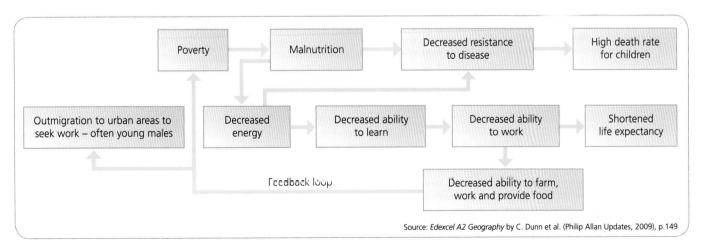

Source: *Edexcel A2 Geography* by C. Dunn et al. (Philip Allan Updates, 2009), p.149

Figure 3.25 The cycle of poverty

413

- Official government aid is where the amount of aid given and who it is given to is decided by the government of an individual country. The Department for International Development (DFID) runs the UK's international aid programme.
- Voluntary aid is run by non-governmental organisations (NGOs) or charities such as Oxfam, ActionAid and CAFOD. NGOs collect money from individuals and organisations. However, an increasing amount of government money goes to NGOs because of their special expertise in running aid programmes efficiently.

Official government aid can be divided into:

- bilateral aid, which is given directly from one country to another, and
- multilateral aid, which is provided by many countries and organised by an international body such as the United Nations.

Aid supplied to poorer countries is of two types:

- Short-term emergency aid is provided to help cope with unexpected disasters such as earthquakes, volcanic eruptions and tropical cyclones.
- Long-term development aid is directed towards the continuous improvement in the quality of life in a poorer country.

Figure 3.27 shows the types of bilateral aid provided by DFID. In 2007 the Department noted that UK bilateral aid had increased by 44 per cent compared with five years previously, and increased by 138 per cent compared with ten years previously. As Figure 3.27 shows, bilateral aid covers a number of different categories of assistance. Figure 3.28 shows how DFID can provide emergency aid to countries in need.

There is no doubt that many countries have benefited from international aid. All the countries that have developed into NICs from LEDCs have received international aid. However, their development has been due to other reasons too. It is difficult to be precise about the contribution of international aid to the development of each country. According to some left-wing economists, aid does not do its intended job because:

- too often aid fails to reach the very poorest people and when it does the benefits are frequently short-lived
- a significant proportion of foreign aid is 'tied' to the purchase of goods and services from the donor country and often given for use only on jointly agreed projects
- the use of aid on large capital-intensive projects may actually worsen the conditions of the poorest people
- aid may delay the introduction of reforms, for example the substitution of food aid for land reform
- international aid can create a culture of dependency which can be difficult to break.

Financial Aid – Poverty Reduction Budget Support (PRBS) – Funds provided to developing countries for them to spend in support of a government policy and their expenditure programmes whose long-term objective is to reduce poverty; funds are spent using the overseas governments' own financial management, procurement and accountability systems to increase ownership and long-term sustainability. PRBS can take the form of a general contribution to the overall budget – **general budget support** – or support with a more restricted focus which is earmarked for a specific sector – **sector budget support**.

Other Financial Aid – Funding of projects and programmes such as Sector Wide Programmes not classified as PRBS. Financial aid in its broader sense covers all bilateral aid expenditure, other than technical cooperation and administrative costs, but in SID we separately categorise Humanitarian Assistance, DFID Debt Relief and 'other bilateral aid' as it is a rapidly declining flow.

Technical Cooperation – Activities designed to enhance the knowledge, intellectual skills, technical expertise or the productive capability of people in recipient countries. It also covers funding of services that contribute to the design or implementation of development projects or programmes.

This assistance is mainly delivered through research and development, the use of consultants, training (generally overseas partners visiting the UK or elsewhere for training programmes) and employment of 'other Personnel' (non-DFID experts on fixed-term contracts). This latter category is becoming less significant over time as existing contracted staff reach the end of their assignments.

Humanitarian Assistance – Provides food aid and other humanitarian assistance, including shelter, medical care and advice in emergency situations and their aftermath. Work of the conflict pools is also included.

DFID Debt Relief – Includes sums for debt relief on old DFID aid loans and cancellation of debt under the Commonwealth Debt Initiative (CDI). The non-CDI DIFD debt relief is reported on the basis of the 'benefit to the recipient country'. This means that figures shown represent the money available to the country in the year in question that would otherwise have been spent on debt servicing. The CDI debt cancellation is reported on a 'lump sum' basis where all outstanding amounts on a loan are shown at the time the agreement to cancel is made.

Other Bilateral Aid – Covers support to the development work of UK and international Civil Society organisations (increasingly through partnership agreements with CSOs). It includes bilateral aid delivered through multilateral organisations including aid delivered through multi donor funds such as the Education Fast Track Initiative. 'Other bilateral aid' also includes any aid not elsewhere classified such as DFID's Development Awareness Fund.

Source: *Statistics on International Development 2008,*
Department for International Development

Figure 3.27 UK Department for International Development – types of bilateral aid

4 December 2007

On 15 and 16 November, southern Bangladesh was hit by Cyclone Sidr. So far, over 6 million people have been affected and 2997 people have been confirmed dead. Many more have been injured, and the death toll could reach 10 000 (the death toll following the cyclone in 1991 was 140 000). Also, around 300 000 houses have been destroyed, as have many crops and large tracts of agricultural land.

Following an initial DFID contribution of £2.5 million, which is being channelled through the UN for immediate relief efforts, a further £2.5 million was pledged on 23 November. On 28 November, an additional £2 million was committed to help survivors to rebuild their homes and livelihoods. DFID has also provided 12 lightweight boats to reach inaccessible parts of Bangladesh, and despatched over 100 000 blankets for people made homeless.

Already DFID money is helping to rebuild more than 16 000 homes, provide food to 70 000 families and clean water to 260 000 families. The UK's disaster relief aid in Bangladesh now totals almost £12 million (US$24 million) for this year, with £4.7 million having been provided in response to the severe floods that occurred in August.

Secretary of State for International Development, Douglas Alexander, said yesterday:

'Unless emergency relief supplies get to victims it is all too likely that more people will die needlessly. That is why the UK continues to provide funds to get more food, clean water, basic shelter and other emergency supplies to tens of thousands of survivors. With half a million animals killed, nearly two million acres of crops and more than a million homes destroyed, the next challenge is to help people rebuild their homes and livelihoods. UK support is meeting immediate and longer term needs as well. I continue to be admiring of the resilience and determination of the Bangladeshi people as they face these challenges.'

Source: UK Department for International Development (DFID)

Figure 3.28 DFID provides emergency aid towards Bangladesh cyclone

Arguments put forward by the political right-wing economists against aid are as follows:

- Aid encourages the growth of a larger than necessary public sector.
- The private sector is 'crowded out' by aid funds.
- Aid distorts the structure of prices and incentives.
- Aid is often wasted on grandiose projects of little or no benefit to the majority of the population.
- The West did not need aid to develop.

Many development economists argue there are two issues more important to development than aid:

- changing the terms of trade so that LEDCs get a fairer share of the benefits of world trade
- writing off the debts of the poorest countries.

Figure 3.29 shows official development assistance (ODA) received by world region while Table 3.6 shows the top ten recipients of ODA.

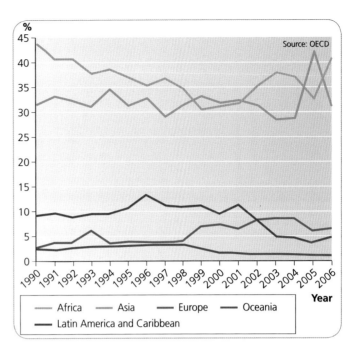

Figure 3.29 ODA by world region

Table 3.6 Top ten ODA receipts by recipient, and top ten ODA donors, 2006

a Top 10 ODA receipts by recipient

Rank	Country	US$ millions	Net disbursement %
1	Nigeria	11 434	11
2	Iraq	8 661	8
3	Afghanistan	3 000	3
4	Pakistan	2 147	2
5	Sudan	2 058	2
6	Congo, Dem. Rep.	2 056	2
7	Ethiopia	1 947	2
8	Vietnam	1 846	2
9	Tanzania	1 825	2
10	Cameroon	1 684	2
	Other recipients	68 633	65
	Total	105 292	100

b Top 10 ODA donors

Rank	Country	US$ millions	Net disbursement %
1	USA	21 162	20
2	EC	9 489	9
3	UK	8 718	8
4	France	7 919	8
5	Japan	7 313	7
6	Germany	7 034	7
7	International Development Association	5 996	6
8	Netherlands	4 282	4
9	Sweden	2 852	3
10	Canada	2 531	2
	Other recipients	27 995	27
	Total	105 292	100

Source: OECD

415

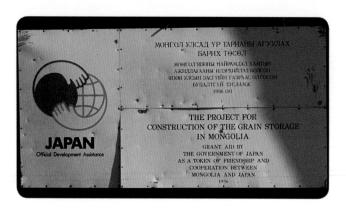

Figure 3.30 A Japanese aid project in Mongolia

The effectiveness of aid: top-down and bottom-up approaches

Over the years most debate about aid has focused on the amount of aid made available. However, in recent years the focus has shifted more towards the effectiveness of aid. This has involved increasing criticism of the traditional top-down approach to aid.

The financing of the Pergau Dam in Malaysia with UK government aid is an example of a capital-intensive government-led aid programme, set up without consulting the local people. Work began in 1991 and around the same time Malaysia bought £1 billion worth of arms from the UK, leading many people to believe that the £234 million in aid was 'tied' to the arms deal.

The Hunger Project is one of a number of organisations that have adopted a radically different approach (Figure 3.31). The Hunger

Project has worked in partnership with grassroots organisations in Africa, Asia and Latin America to develop effective bottom-up strategies. The key strands in this approach have been:

- mobilising local people for self-reliant action
- intervening for gender equality
- strengthening local democracy.

NGOs: leading sustainable development

Non-governmental organisations (NGOs) have often been much better at directing aid towards sustainable development than government agencies. The selective nature of such aid has targeted the poorest communities using **appropriate technology** and involving local people in decision-making.

Case Study

WaterAid in Mali

WaterAid was established in 1981. Its first project was in Zambia but its operations spread quickly to other countries. Mali is one of the countries WaterAid currently operates in.

Mali, in West Africa, is one of the world's poorest nations (Figure 3.32). The natural environment is harsh, and is deteriorating. Rainfall levels, already low, are falling further and desertification is spreading. Currently 65 per cent of the country is desert or semi-desert. Eleven million people still lack access to safe water. WaterAid has been active in the country since 2001.

	The conventional Top-Down, Service-Delivery Model	The Hunger Project's Bottom-up Empowerment Model
Who are hungry people?	**Beneficiaries** whose basic needs must be met.	**Principle authors and actors in development** – hardworking, creative individuals who lack opportunities.
What must be done?	**Provide services** through government or charities.	**Mobilise and empower** people's self-reliant action, and stand in solidarity with them for their success.
What's the primary resource for development?	**Money and the expertise** of consultants and programme managers.	**People:** their vision, mobilisation, entrepreneurial spirit and confidence.
Who is in charge?	**Donors**, who provide the money and hold implementers to account.	**Local people:** through elected local leaders whom they hold to account.
What are the main constraints?	**Bureaucracy:** the inefficiency of the delivery system.	**Social conditions:** resignation, discrimination (particularly gender), lack of local leadership, lack of rights.
What is the role of women?	**Vulnerable group** who must be especially targeted beneficiaries.	**Key producers** who must have a voice in decision-making.
What about social and cultural issues?	**Immutable conditions** that must be compensated for.	**Conditions** that people can transform.
How should we focus our work?	**Carefully target** beneficiaries on an objective-needs basis.	**Mobilise everyone** as broadly as possible, build spirit and momentum of accomplishment.
What is the role of central government?	**Operate** centrally managed service-delivery programmes.	**Decentralise** resources and decision making to local level; build local capacity; set standards; protect rights.
What is the role of local government?	**Implementing arm** of central programmes.	**Autonomous** leadership directly accountable to people.
What is the role of civil society?	**Implementing arm** of central programmes.	**Catalyst** to mobilise people; fight for their rights; empower people to keep government accountable.

Figure 3.31 Contrasting top-down and bottom-up aid models

Source: The Hunger Project

Figure 3.32 Mali

Figure 3.33 Sanitation is very basic in many poor countries

Its main concern is that the fully privatised water industry frequently fails to provide services to the poorest urban and rural areas. WaterAid is running a pilot scheme in the slums surrounding Mali's capital, Bamako, providing clean water and sanitation services to the poorest people. Its objective is to demonstrate to both government and other donors that projects in slums can be successful, both socially and economically.

WaterAid has financed the construction of the area's water network. It is training local people to manage and maintain the system, and to raise the money needed to keep it operational. Encouraging the community to invest in its own infrastructure is an important part of the philosophy of the project. According to Idrissa Doucoure, WaterAid's West Africa Regional Manager, 'We are now putting our energy into education programmes and empowering the communities to continue their own development into the future. This will allow WaterAid to move on and help others.'

Already there have been significant improvements in the general health of the community. The general view is that it takes a generation for health and sanitation to be properly embedded into people's day-to-day life.

WaterAid is the UK's only major charity dedicated exclusively to the provision of safe domestic water, sanitation and hygiene education to the world's poorest people. These three crucial elements provide the building blocks for all other development. Without them communities remain stuck in a cycle of disease and poverty. The combination of safe water, sanitation and hygiene education maximises health benefits and promotes development (Figures 3.33, 3.34 and 3.35). The combined benefits of safe water, sanitation and hygiene education can reduce incidences of childhood diarrhoea by up to 95 per cent. A child dies every 15 seconds from diseases associated with a lack of access to safe water and adequate sanitation.

In the longer term, communities are able to plan and build infrastructure that enables them to cope better in times of hardship. In areas with WaterAid projects, life in times of drought is eased because:

- previously in times of drought women in particular would spend hours in search of water, leaving little time to find food
- children would also miss out on education in the search for water

Figure 3.34 WaterAid's building blocks of development

Figure 3.35 WaterAid cost examples

- cattle can also be watered, rather than sold or left to die because of water shortage
- during famines, with sanitation, water and hygiene people are less sick and so are better able to fend off disease.

Microcredit and social business

The development of the Grameen Bank in Bangladesh illustrates the power of microcredit in the battle against poverty. The Grameen Foundation uses microfinance and innovative technology to fight global poverty and bring opportunities to the poorest people. The bank provides tiny loans and financial services to poor people to start their own businesses. Women are the beneficiaries of most of these loans. A typical loan might be used to buy a cow and sell milk to fellow villagers or to purchase a piece of machinery which can be hired out to other people in the community.

The concept has spread beyond Bangladesh to reach 3.6 million families in 25 countries. Muhammad Yunus highlights 'social business' as the next phase in the battle against poverty in his book *Creating a World Without Poverty*. He presents a vision of a new business model that combines the operation of the free market with the quest for a more humane world.

Section 3.2 Activities

1 Define *international aid*.

2 Explain the difference between *official government aid* and *voluntary aid*.

3 Produce a flow diagram to show how aid can speed up development.

4 Discuss two possible disadvantages of international aid.

5 Look at Figure 3.34.
  a What do you understand by the following terms?
   i *safe water* ii *sanitation* iii *hygiene education*.
  b Why is it so important to combine these three factors to maximise the health benefits to a community?

6 Explain why healthier communities are more likely to be able to improve their living standards.

7 Explain a *microcredit* and b *social business*.

3.3 The development of international tourism

Reasons for and trends in the growth of tourism

Over the past 50 years **tourism** has developed into a major global industry which is still expanding rapidly. Under one method of economic measurement it is the world's major service industry. Tourism has an economic, social and environmental impact on virtually every country in the world. In some countries it is a considerable political issue. Without doubt it is one of the major elements in the process of globalisation.

International tourist arrivals reached a record of almost 900 million in 2007. In the same year **international travel receipts** totalled over $800 billion. Between 2000 and 2007 international tourist arrivals rose over 40 per cent. This is an average of 4.5 per cent a year, marking it out as a high-growth industry. The growth in international tourism receipts was even stronger at almost 8 per cent over the same period. Tourism is an increasingly important contributor to economic growth and employment in a significant number of countries. However, the recent global recession has had a big but variable impact on the industry. Many destinations have suffered, but surprisingly some have benefited as many more people have decided to holiday in their own country rather than travelling abroad.

A range of factors have been responsible for the growth of global tourism. Figure 3.36 subdivides these factors into economic, social and political reasons and also includes factors that can reduce levels of tourism, at least in the short term. Some of these factors have been active for a longer time period than others.

Economic	Steadily rising real incomes – tourism grows on average 1.3 times faster than GDP
	The decreasing real costs (with inflation taken into account) of holidays
	The widening range of destinations within the middle-income range
	The heavy marketing of shorter foreign holidays aimed at those who have the time and disposable income to take an additional break
	The expansion of budget airlines
	'Air miles' and other retail reward schemes aimed at travel and tourism
	'Globalisation' has increased business travel considerably
	Periods of economic recession can reduce levels of tourism considerably
Social	An increase in the average number of days of paid leave
	An increasing desire to experience different cultures and landscapes
	Raised expectations of international travel with increasing media coverage of holidays, travel and nature
	High levels of international migration over the last decade or so means that more people have relatives and friends living abroad
	More people are avoiding certain destinations for ethical reasons
Political	Many governments have invested heavily to encourage tourism
	Government backing for major international events such as the Olympic Games and the World Cup
	The perceived greater likelihood of terrorist attacks in certain destinations
	Government restrictions on inbound/outbound tourism
	Calls by non-governmental organisations to boycott countries such as Burma

Figure 3.36 Factors affecting global tourism

The medical profession was largely responsible for the growth in people taking holidays away from home. During the seventeenth century doctors increasingly began to recommend the benefits of mineral waters and by the end of the eighteenth century there were hundreds of spas in existence in the UK. Bath

(Figure 3.37) and Tunbridge Wells were among the most famous. The second stage in the development of holiday locations was the emergence of the seaside resort. Sea bathing is usually said to have begun at Scarborough about 1730.

The annual holiday for the masses, away from work, was a product of the Industrial Revolution, which brought big social and economic changes. However, until the latter part of the nineteenth century only the very rich could afford to take a holiday away from home.

The first **package tours** were arranged by Thomas Cook in 1841. These took travellers from Leicester to Loughborough (UK), 19 km away, to attend temperance (abstinence from alcoholic drink) meetings. At the time it was the newly laid railway network that provided the transport infrastructure for Cook to expand his tour operations. Of equal importance was the emergence of a significant middle class who had the time and money to spare for extended recreation.

By far the greatest developments have occurred since the end of the Second World War, arising from the substantial growth in leisure time, affluence and mobility enjoyed in MEDCs. However, it took the jet plane to herald the era of international mass tourism. In 1970, when Pan Am flew the first Boeing 747 from New York to London, scheduled planes carried 307 million passengers. By 2006 the number had reached 2.1 billion.

Travel motivators are the reasons why people travel. All the major tourism organisations recognise three major categories (Figure 3.38).

Figure 3.37 The historical mineral waters in the spa town of Bath

The globalisation of international tourism

Prime reasons	Secondary subdivisions	Tertiary destination preferences	Externalities
Leisure	Holiday	Climate	Destination security
	Sport or cultural event		
	Educational trip	Attractions	
	Pilgrimage		
Business	Conference/ exhibition	Festivals and events	
	Individual meetings		
Visiting friends and relatives	Stay with family	Accommodation/ restaurants/ bars	Exchange rate
	Meet friends	Transport (to the destination and within it)	

Figure 3.38 Key travel motivators

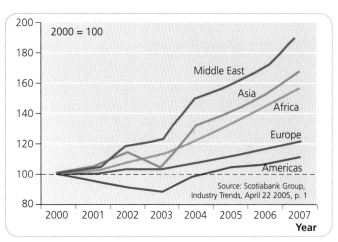

Figure 3.39 Tourist arrivals by world region 2000–07

Figure 3.39 shows international tourist arrivals by world region 2000–07. The highest rates of growth were in LEDCs:

- The Middle East led the way with an average annual growth rate of 10 per cent. Saudi Arabia and Egypt in particular showed strong growth as major resort destinations while the United Arab Emirates is attracting a growing number of leisure and business travellers.
- The next highest rate of increase was in the Asia-Pacific region with an annual average growth of 8 per cent. This was a result of (1) rapid economic expansion in the region, (2) increased marketing of tourism opportunities, and (3) improved transportation infrastructure. Inbound tourism to China is rising rapidly, but outbound travel from China is a major factor in strong tourism growth across the entire Asia-Pacific region.

- Tourism in Africa rose by an average of 6 per cent, led by the adventure tourism sector.
- In comparison with other parts of the developing world the tourism industry in Latin America and the Caribbean recorded much lower growth rates – 3 per cent over the same time period. However, in this region the average growth figure hides a wide variation. Strong growth in many South and Central American countries contrasted with lower figures in the more mature destinations of the Caribbean and Mexico.
- Although the developed regions of the world remain the largest tourism destinations, their dominance is reducing and recent growth rates have been relatively low. For example, Europe and North America accounted for 69 per cent of international arrivals in 2000, but by 2007 this had fallen to 62 per cent. Figure 3.40 shows the regional share of tourist arrivals in 2007, with Europe still accounting for 54 per cent of the global total.

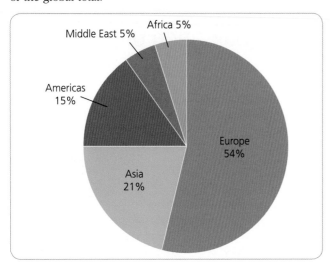

Figure 3.40 Share of tourist arrivals, 2007

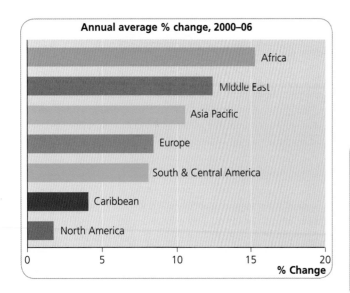

Figure 3.41 Developing markets lead growth in tourism receipts

Figure 3.41 shows the growth in tourism receipts in recent years. The trend is similar to that for tourism arrivals. However, it is not an exact relationship because:

- the average number of days spent in some destinations is longer than in others
- visitors spent more money in some destinations than others.

Table 3.7 shows international tourism arrivals by individual country. Here four countries recorded a total of over 50 million arrivals in 2007. In order of importance these were France, Spain, the USA and China. Table 3.8 shows international tourism receipts by country for the same year. The countries recording a total of over $50 billion in order of importance were the USA, Spain and France.

Table 3.7 Top ten countries – international tourism arrivals, 2007

Rank	Country	International tourist arrivals (millions)
1	France	81.9
2	Spain	59.2
3	USA	56.0
4	China	54.7
5	Italy	43.7
6	UK	30.7
7	Germany	24.4
8	Ukraine	23.1
9	Turkey	22.2
10	Mexico	21.4

Table 3.8 Top ten countries – international tourism receipts, 2007

Rank	Country	International tourist arrivals ($ billion)
1	USA	96.7
2	Spain	57.8
3	France	54.2
4	Italy	42.7
5	China	41.9
6	UK	37.6
7	Germany	36.0
8	Australia	22.2
9	Austria	18.9
10	Turkey	18.5

Source: http://en.wikipedia.org/wiki/Tourism

Many LEDCs have become more open to foreign direct investment in tourism than they were two or three decades ago. In general there are now fewer restrictions on foreign investment in tourism in LEDCs than many other economic activities. In fact many governments in LEDCs have very actively promoted a range of:

- 'soft' measures such as tourism internet sites and support for trade fairs
- 'hard' measures such as providing incentives for foreign investors.

Recent data from the World Tourism Organisation (WTO) shows that tourism is one of the top five export categories for as many as 83 per cent of countries and is the main source of foreign exchange for at least 38 per cent of countries.

Section 3.3 Activities

1 Define *tourism*.

2 Explain the terms **a** *international tourism arrivals* and **b** *international tourism receipts*.

3 Describe the changes shown in Figure 3.39.

4 Suggest reasons for the global share of tourist arrivals shown in Figure 3.40.

5 Present a brief bullet-point analysis of Figure 3.41.

Variations in the level of tourism over time and space

Unfortunately, more than many other industries, tourism is vulnerable to '**external shocks**'. Periods of economic recession characterised by high unemployment, modest wage rises, and high interest rates, affect the demand for tourism in most parts of the world. Because holidays are a high-cost purchase for most people, the tourist industry suffers when times are hard.

Tourism in individual countries and regions can be affected by considerable fluctuations caused by a variety of factors:

- **Natural disasters:** earthquakes, volcanic eruptions, floods and other natural events can have a major impact on tourism where they occur.
- **Natural processes:** coastal erosion and rising sea levels are threatening important tourist locations around the world.
- **Terrorism:** terrorist attacks, or the fear of them, can deter visitors from going to certain countries, in the short-term at least.
- **Health scares:** for example, the severe acute respiratory syndrome (SARS) epidemic in March 2003 had a considerable short-term impact on tourism in China and other countries in South East Asia.
- **Exchange rate fluctuations:** for example, if the value of the dollar falls against the euro and the pound, it makes it more expensive for Americans to holiday in Europe, but less expensive for Europeans to visit the USA.
- **Political uncertainties:** governments may advise their citizens not to travel to certain countries if the political situation is tense.
- **International image:** a 2006 US-made film called *Turistas* has caused major concern in Brazil. It depicts a group of US backpackers whose holiday in a Brazilian resort turns into a nightmare when they are drugged and kidnapped and then their organs are removed by organ traffickers.
- **Increasing competition:** as new, 'more exciting' destinations increase their market share, more traditional destinations may see visitor numbers fall considerably.

The impacts of tourism
Social and cultural impact

Many communities in LEDCs have suffered considerable adverse cultural changes, some of them through the imposition of the worst of Western values. The result has been, in varying degrees:

- the loss of locally owned land as tourism companies buy up large tracts in the most scenic and accessible locations
- the abandonment of traditional values and practices
- displacement of people to make way for tourist developments
- abuse of human rights by governments and companies in the quest to maximise profits
- alcoholism and drug abuse
- crime and prostitution, sometimes involving children

- visitor congestion at key locations, hindering the movement of local people
- denying local people access to beaches to provide 'exclusivity' for visitors
- the loss of housing for local people as more visitors buy second homes in popular tourist areas.

Figures 3.42 and 3.43 show how the attitudes to tourism of host countries and destination communities in particular can change over time. An industry that is usually seen as very beneficial initially can eventually become the source of considerable irritation, particularly where there is a big clash of cultures. Parents in particular are often fearful of the impact 'outside' cultures may have on their children.

The tourist industry and the various scales of government in host countries have become increasingly aware of these problems and are now using a range of management techniques in an attempt to mitigate such effects. Education is the most important element so that visitors are made aware of the most sensitive aspects of the host culture.

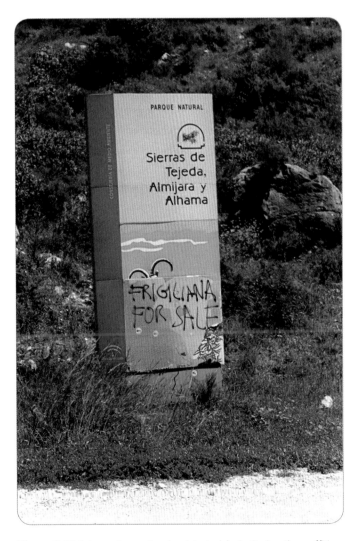

Figure 3.42 Entrance to a national park in Andalucia, Spain – the graffiti refers to the number of foreigners buying up houses in the nearby village of Frigiliana

1 **Euphoria**
- Enthusiasm for tourist development
- Mutual feeling of satisfaction
- Opportunities for local participation
- Flows of money and interesting contacts

2 **Apathy**
- Industry expands
- Tourists taken for granted
- More interest in profit making
- Personal contact becomes more formal

3 **Irritation**
- Industry nearing saturation point
- Expansion of facilities required
- Encroachment of the ways of life

4 **Antagonism**
- Irritations become more overt
- The tourist is seen as the harbinger of all that is bad
- Mutual politeness gives way to antagonism

5 **Final level**
- Environment has changed irreversibly
- The resource base has changed and the type of tourist has also changed
- If the destination is large enough to cope with mass tourism it will continue to thrive

Figure 3.43 Doxey's index of irritation caused by tourism

At its very worst the impact of tourism amounts to gross abuse of human rights. For example, the actions of the military regime in Burma – forcing people from their homes to make way for tourism developments, and using forced labour to construct tourist facilities – have brought condemnation from all over the world. The tourist industry has a huge appetite for basic resources, which often impinge heavily on the needs of local people. A long-term protest against tourism in Goa highlighted the fact that one five-star hotel consumes as much water as five local villages, with the average hotel resident using 28 times more electricity per day than a local person. In such situations tourist numbers may exceed the '**carrying capacity**' of a destination by placing too much of a burden on local resources. The concept of carrying capacity has sometime been taken beyond just the ability of the physical environment to accommodate tourists/visitors without resultant deterioration and degradation. One classification has identified four elements of the concept:

- physical – the overall impact on the physical environment, for example footpath erosion
- ecological – the number of tourists that can be accommodated without significant impact on the flora and fauna
- economic – the number of tourists a destination can take without significant adverse economic implications
- perceptual – the attitudes of the local people in terms of how they view increasing tourist numbers.

Changing community structure

Communities that were once very close socially and economically may be weakened considerably due to a major outside influence such as tourism. The traditional hierarchy of authority within the community can be altered as those whose incomes are enhanced by employment in tourism gain higher status in the community. The age and sex structure may change as young people in particular move away to be closer to work in tourist enclaves. Changing values and attitudes can bring conflict to previously settled communities. The close ties of the extended family often diminish as the economy of the area changes and material wealth becomes more important.

However, tourism can also have positive social and cultural impacts:
- Tourism development can increase the range of social facilities for local people.
- It can lead to greater understanding between people of different cultures.
- Family ties may be strengthened by visits to relatives living in other regions and countries.
- It can help develop foreign language skills in host communities.
- It may encourage migration to major tourist-generating countries.
- A multitude of cultures congregating together for major international events such as the Olympic Games can have a very positive global impact.

Section 3.3 Activities

1 Discuss three negative social/cultural aspects of tourism.

2 Comment on Doxey's index (Figure 3.43).

Economic impact

The World Travel and Tourism Council (WTTC) argues that to consider tourist receipts alone, greatly underestimates the economic importance of the industry. To rectify the situation the WTCC has developed **Travel and Tourism Satellite Accounting**. By including all the direct and indirect economic implications of tourism it is clear that the industry has a much greater impact than most people think (Table 3.9 and Figure 3.44). Under this system of measurement, global tourism was estimated to have generated $7060 billion of economic activity worldwide in 2007. The travel and tourism industry contributed 3.6 per cent to worldwide gross domestic product but the broader travel and tourism economy (which includes all the indirect benefits) contributed 10.4 per cent to world GDP. The travel and tourism industry employed 76.1 million people directly, while the wider travel and tourism economy employed 231.2 million, representing 8.3 per cent of total employment worldwide. This made it the world's largest service industry.

Tourism undoubtedly brings valuable foreign currency to LEDCs, and a range of other obvious benefits, but critics argue that its value is often overrated because:

Table 3.9 The economic impact of travel and tourism – direct method and satellite accounting

	Travel and tourism industry (direct impact)	Travel and tourism economy (satellite accounting)
Employment	76.1 million	231.1 million
% of world GDP	3.6	10.4
% of world exports	6	12

Source: J. Dove et al., *OCR AS Geography*, p308

What is commonly thought of as the 'tourism industry' is only the tip of the iceberg	Tourism economy (direct effect), accommodation, recreation, catering, entertainment, transportation
	Tourism economy (indirect effect), manufacturing, chemicals, computers, concrete, financial services, foods and beverages, furniture and fixtures, iron/steel, laundry services, metal products, mining, oil/gas suppliers, plastics, printing/publishing, rental car, resort development, sanitation services, security, ship building, suppliers, textiles, utilities, wholesalers, wood

Figure 3.44 Satellite accounting 'iceberg'

- **Economic leakages** (Figure 3.45) from LEDCs to MEDCs run at a rate of between 60 per cent and 75 per cent. With cheap package holidays, by far the greater part of the money paid stays in the country where the holiday was purchased.
- Tourism is labour-intensive, providing a range of jobs especially for women and young people. However, most local jobs created are menial, low-paid and seasonal. Overseas labour may be brought in to fill middle and senior management positions.
- Money borrowed to invest in the necessary infrastructure for tourism increases the national debt.
- At some destinations tourists spend most of their money in their hotels with minimum benefit to the wider community.
- Tourism might not be the best use for local resources which could in the future create a larger multiplier effect if used by a different economic sector.
- Locations can become overdependent on tourism.
- International trade agreements, such as the General Agreement on Trade in Services (GATS), are a major impetus to globalisation and allow the global hotel giants to set up in most countries. Even if governments favour local investors there is little they can do.

However, supporters of the development potential of tourism argue that:

- Tourism benefits other sectors of the economy, providing jobs and income through the supply chain. This is called **the multiplier effect** (Figure 3.46) because jobs and money multiply as a result of tourism development.
- It is an important factor in the balance of payments of many nations.

LEDC tourist destinations

Total money spent on tourism to this destination

Transport costs paid to airlines and other carriers

The cost of goods and services imported for the tourist industry

Foreign debt relating to tourism

Payments to foreign owners of hotels and other facilities

Remittances sent home by foreign workers

Payments to foreign companies to build tourist infrastructure

Leakages

Figure 3.45 Economic leakages

Establishment of hotels and other tourist facilities

Expansion of local job opportunities and population

Improvement of physical and cultural infrastructures

Inflow of business and capital to satisfy increased local demand

Higher business and personal tax base increases local government spending power

Substantial rise in per capita incomes

Figure 3.46 The multiplier effect of tourism

- It provides governments with considerable tax revenues.
- By providing employment in rural areas it can help to reduce rural–urban migration.
- A major tourism development can act as a growth pole, stimulating the economy of the larger region.
- It can create openings for small businesses in which start-up costs and barriers to entry are generally low.
- It can support many jobs in the informal sector, where money goes directly to local people (Figure 3.47).

Figure 3.47 Beach artist, Agadir, Morocco – an example of informal sector employment

423

Environmental impact

The type of tourism that does not destroy what it sets out to explore has come to be known as 'sustainable'. The term comes from the 1987 UN *Report on the Environment*, which advocated the kind of development that meets present needs without compromising the prospects of future generations. Following the 1992 Earth Summit in Rio de Janeiro, the WTTC and the Earth Council drew up an environmental checklist for tourist development which included waste minimisation, re-use and recycling, energy efficiency, and water management. The WTTC has since established a more detailed programme called 'Green Globe', designed to act as an environmental blueprint for its members.

The pressure group Tourist Concern defines sustainable tourism as 'Tourism and associated infrastructures that: operate within capacities for the regeneration and future productivity of natural resources, recognise the contribution of local people and their cultures, accept that these people must have an equitable share in the economic benefits of tourism, and are guided by the wishes of local people and communities in the destination areas'. This definition emphasises the important issues of equity and local control which are difficult to achieve for a number of reasons:

• Governments are reluctant to limit the number of tourist arrivals because of the often desperate need for foreign currency.
• Local people cannot compete with foreign multinationals on price and marketing.
• It is difficult to force developers to consult local people.

Negative environmental impacts

In so many LEDCs, newly laid golf courses have taken land away from local communities while consuming large amounts of scarce freshwater. It has been estimated that the water required by a new golf course can supply a village of 5000 people. In both Belize and Costa Rica, coral reefs have been blasted to allow for unhindered watersports. Like fishing and grazing rights, access to such common goods as beach front and scenically desirable locations does not naturally limit itself. As with overfishing and overgrazing, the solution to 'overtouristing' will often be to establish ownership and charge for use. The optimists argue that because environmental goods such as clean water and beautiful scenery are fundamental to the tourist experience, both tourists and the industry have a vested interest in their preservation. The fact that 'ecotourism' is a rapidly growing sector of the industry supports this viewpoint – at least to a certain extent.

Education about the environment visited is clearly the key. Scuba divers in the Ras Mohammad National Park in the Red Sea, who were made to attend a lecture on the ecology of the local reefs, were found to be eight times less likely to bump into coral (the cause of two-thirds of all damage to the reef), let alone deliberately pick a piece. However, there is huge concern about the future of many coral reefs, no more so than the Great Barrier Reef which receives 2 million visitors a year (Figure 3.48).

Figure 3.48 The Great Barrier Reef

Positive environmental impacts

The environmental impact of tourism is not always negative. Landscaping and sensitive improvements to the built environment have significantly improved the overall quality of some areas. On a larger scale tourist revenues can fund the designation and management of protected areas such as national parks and national forests.

The life cycle model of tourism

Butler's model of the evolution of tourist areas (Figure 3.49) attempts to illustrate how tourism develops and changes over time. In the first stage the location is explored independently by a small number of visitors. If visitor impressions are good and local people perceive that real benefits are to be gained then the number of visitors will increase as the local community becomes actively involved in the promotion of tourism. In the development stage, holiday companies from MEDCs take control of organisation and management, with package holidays becoming the norm. Eventually growth ceases as the location loses some of its former attraction. At this stage local people have become all too aware of the problems created by tourism. Finally, decline sets in, but because of the perceived economic importance of the industry, efforts will be made to re-package the location which, if successful, may either stabilise the situation or result in renewed growth (rejuvenation).

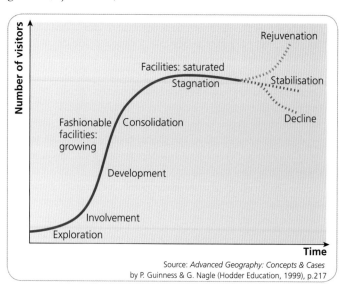

Source: *Advanced Geography: Concepts & Cases* by P. Guinness & G. Nagle (Hodder Education, 1999), p.217

Figure 3.49 Butler's model of the evolution of tourism in a region

The model provides a useful summary of the stages that a number of holiday resorts, particularly in the Mediterranean, have been through. For example, it has been applied to the Costa del Sol and the Costa Brava in Spain. However, research has shown that it does not apply well to all locations. Prosser (1995) summarised the criticisms of the model:

- doubts on there being a single model of tourism development
- limitations on the capacity issue
- lack of empirical support for the concept
- limited practical use of the model.

Also, it does not include the possible role of local and national governments in the destination country, or the impact of, say, a low-cost airline choosing to add a destination to its network.

- theme parks and holiday village enclaves
- gambling destinations
- cruising
- heritage and urban tourism
- wilderness and ecotourism
- cultural/historical interest (Figure 3.51)
- medical and therapy travel
- conflict/dark tourism
- religious tourism
- working holidays
- sports tourism.

Some aspects of special interest tourism have now reached a very significant size. For example, one in every twelve package holidays booked in early 2009 was for a cruise.

Figure 3.50 Hurgada on the Red Sea coast of Egypt

Figure 3.51 British tourists, with a local guide, visiting a First World War cemetery at Ypres, Belgium

Section 3.3 Activities

1 With the help of Table 3.9, discuss the indirect economic benefits of tourism.

2 Suggest how, by careful planning, you could minimise the economic leakage of a foreign holiday.

3 Find an example of the application of the Butler model to a particular destination. Write a brief summary of the example as a case study.

Recent developments in international tourism

The growth of special interest (niche) tourism

In the past 20 years more specialised types of tourism have become increasingly popular. An important factor seems to be a general re-assessment of the life/work balance. An increasing number of people are determined not to let work dominate their lives. One result of this has been the development of **niche tourism**. Niche market tour operators have increased in number to satisfy the rising demand for specialist holidays which include:

Ecotourism

As the level of global tourism increases rapidly it is becoming more and more important for the industry to be responsibly planned, managed and monitored. Tourism operates in a world of finite resources where its impact is becoming of increasing concern to a growing number of people. At present, only 5 per cent of the world's population have ever travelled by plane. However, this is undoubtedly going to increase substantially.

Leo Hickman, in his book *The Final Call*, claims: 'The net result of a widespread lack of government recognition is that tourism is currently one of the most unregulated industries in the world, largely controlled by a relatively small number of Western corporations such as hotel groups and tour operators. Are they really the best guardians of this evidently important but supremely fragile global industry.' Hickman argues that most countries only have a junior minister responsible for tourism rather than a secretary of state for tourism, which is what the size of the industry in most countries would justify.

Environmental groups are keen to make travellers aware of their '**destination footprint**'. They are urging people to:

- 'fly less and stay longer'
- carbon-offset their flights
- consider 'slow travel'.

Supporters of slow travel suggest that tourists should consider the impact of their activities both on individual holidays and in the longer term too. For example, they may decide that every second holiday will be in their own country (not using air transport). It could also involve using locally run guesthouses and small hotels as opposed to hotels run by international chains. This enables more money to remain in local communities.

Virtually every aspect of the industry now recognises that tourism must become more sustainable. **Ecotourism** is at the leading edge of **sustainable tourism**. An example of ecotourism in Ecuador is considered later in this topic.

A new form of ecotourism is developing in which volunteers help in cultural and environmental conservation and research. An example is the Earthwatch scientific research projects which invite members of the general public to join the experts as fully-fledged expedition members – on a paying basis, of course. Several Earthwatch projects in Australia have helped Aboriginal people to locate and document their prehistoric rock art and to preserve ancient rituals directly.

Case Study

Ecotourism in Ecuador

Ecuador's travel and tourism industry was expected to contribute 1.8 per cent to GDP in 2007, with the wider travel and tourism economy contributing 7.8 per cent. The 84 000 jobs in the industry accounted for 1.6 per cent of total employment while the 361 000 jobs in the wider travel and tourism economy made up 6.7 per cent of total employment.

International tourism is Ecuador's third largest source of foreign income after the export of oil and bananas. The number of visitors has increased substantially in recent years, both to the mainland and to the Galapagos Islands where Darwin conducted research on evolution. The majority of tourists are drawn to Ecuador by its great diversity of flora and fauna. The country contains 10 per cent of the world's plant species. Much of the country is protected by national parks and nature reserves.

As visitor numbers began to rise, Ecuador was anxious not to suffer the negative externalities of mass tourism evident in many other countries. The country's tourism strategy has been to avoid becoming a mass market destination and to market 'quality' and 'exclusivity' instead, in as eco-friendly a way as possible. Tourist industry leaders were all too aware that a very large influx of visitors could damage the country's most attractive ecosystems and harm its image as a 'green' destination for environmentally conscious visitors.

Ecotourism has helped to bring needed income to some of the poorest parts of the country. It has provided local people with a new alternative way of making a living. As such it has reduced human pressure on ecologically sensitive areas.

The main geographical focus of ecotourism has been in the Amazon rainforest around Tena, which has become the main access point. The ecotourism schemes in the region are usually run by small groups of indigenous Quichua Indians (Figure 3.52).

Galapagos islands at risk

In early 2007 the government of Ecuador declared the Galapagos Islands at risk, warning that visitor permits and flights to the island could be suspended. The Galapagos Islands straddle the equator a thousand kilometres off the coast of Ecuador. All but 3 per cent of the islands are a national park. Five of the 13 islands are inhabited. Visitor numbers are currently 100 000 a year and rising.

The volcanic islands can be visited all year round but the period between November and June is the most popular. Boat trips generally cost from £700 to over £2000. An additional national park entrance fee of £65 is payable on arrival. Among the many attractions are giant tortoises, marine iguanas and blue-footed boobies.

In signing the emergency decree to protect the islands the President of Ecuador stated: 'We are pushing for a series of

The Quichua people insist that all visitors must abide by certain rules and regulations

Exchanges of clothing or other personal items with community members are not allowed. Nor are community members allowed to accept gifts.

Avoid any displays of affection, even with close friends. In this community it is considered rude to hold hands or kiss in public.

When walking in the rainforest:
• do not touch any branches without looking carefully first – they may carry thorns, dangerous insects or even snakes
• do not pull on branches or vines – they may fall on top of you.

If you need to go to the toilet, and facilities are not immediately available, go to the side of the rainforest track, never in or near a stream or lake.

Visitors should never go off for a walk alone. It is easy to get lost in the rainforest.

All rubbish, e.g. empty bottles and tubes, must be taken away by visitors.

Do not enter people's houses without being invited in. Do not make promises you may not be able to keep. e.g. to send back photos after the visit.

Always check first before touching plants or animals. They may cause a rash, or sting you. Do not collect plants, insects or animals unless you have permission.

Figure 3.52 Example of ecotourism

actions to overcome the huge institutional, environmental and social crisis in the islands'.

The identified problems include the following:

- The local population is growing: 18 000 islanders with legal status earn a living from fishing and tourism but an additional 15 000 people are believed to live illegally in the islands.
- Illegal fishing of sharks and sea cucumbers is believed to be at an all-time high.
- The number of visiting cruise ships continues to rise.
- There are internal arguments within the management structure of the national park.
- Controversially, a hotel opened on the islands in 2006.

In mid-2007 a UN delegation visited the islands to determine whether they should be declared 'in danger'.

3.4 The management of a tourist destination

Case Study

Jamaica

Jamaica is the third largest of the Caribbean islands, and the largest English-speaking island in the Caribbean Sea. It is situated 145 km south of Cuba and 965 km south of Florida, USA. Tourism in Jamaica (Figure 3.53) originated in the latter part of the nineteenth century when a limited number of affluent people, many with medical conditions, came to Jamaica to avoid the cold winters in the UK and North America. Figure 3.54 illustrates the attractions of Jamaica's climate. The first tourist hotels were built in Montego Bay and Port Antonio. The industry expanded after the First World War with advances in transportation, although it has been estimated that only a few thousand foreign tourists visited Jamaica each year in the 1920s. By 1938 the figure had risen to 64 000 and by 1952 it had reached 104 000. Growth continued in the following decades with 345 000 visitors in 1966 and over 600 000 in 1982. Since the 1987/88 season the number of foreign tourist has exceeded one million a year, partly as a result of the significant increase in the arrivals of cruise-ship passengers.

Figure 3.54 Jamaica's climate

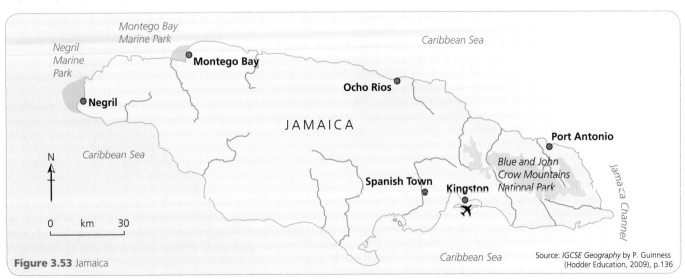

Figure 3.53 Jamaica

Source: *IGCSE Geography* by P. Guinness (Hodder Education, 2009), p.136

427

In 2005 a total of 2 614 506 visited Jamaica, comprising:
- 1 386 996 foreign nationals
- 91 667 non-resident Jamaicans
- 1 135 843 cruise passengers.

Many of the country's 2.7 million people depend on the tourist industry for all or part of their income.

Jamaica is an example of a tourist area where there has been clear evidence of growth and development. The term '**growth**' refers to the increase in numbers, while '**development**' refers to the expansion of tourism activities such as the development of adventure tourism and ecotourism. As the tourist industry has expanded, its linkages with other industries have developed as well. But as tourism develops it also has an impact on the environment, and the question of its sustainability comes to the fore. The careful management of tourism can do much to mitigate the impact. Management techniques that Jamaica has used include:

- trying to avoid the pitfalls of mass tourism, such as the construction of high-rise hotels
- creating national parks, marine parks and other protected areas
- promoting ecotourism and other environmentally friendly forms of tourism
- encouraging community tourism
- linking the profits of tourism to social development in the country.

Jamaica's north coast, with its pleasant weather and white-sand beaches, is the centre of the island's tourist industry (Figure 3.55). The main resorts are Montego Bay, Ocho Rios and Port Antonio, although many tourists also visit the capital city, Kingston. Accommodation varies between modern high-rise hotels, elegant old world style buildings, villas, apartments and guesthouses. The number of rooms available in Jamaica is approximately 30 000. Jamaica has a relatively good road network with Highway 2000 linking settlements in the south and the North Coast Highway serving the north of the island.

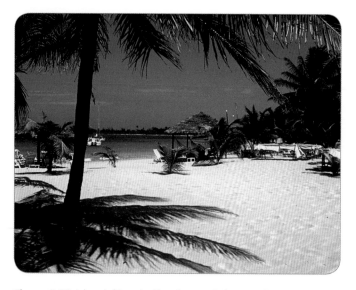

Figure 3.55 A beach fringed with palm trees in Runaway Bay

About two-thirds of visitors to the island arrive by air. Jamaica is served by two international airports, Norman Manley International in Kingston, and Sangster International in Montego Bay. There is a private jet centre in Montego Bay and four aerodromes serving small carriers for inter-island travel. Cruise passenger terminals are located in Ocho Rios, Montego Bay, Port Antonio and Kingston. In 2006, Jamaica received 350 cruise calls.

While sun and sand are the main attractions of a holiday in Jamaica, the island also has other attributes, including dolphin parks, nature reserves, museums and galleries. There is a wide variety of flora and fauna, with 252 species of birds (27 are endemic), 200 native species of orchids, 500 species of true ferns and about 50 species of coral. There are excellent facilities for a range of sports including tennis, golf and equestrian activities. Jamaica's cuisine is an attraction for many visitors. There are many festivals and entertainment events during the year, often featuring Jamaica's native music, reggae.

Among the island's protected areas are the Cockpit Country, Hellshire Hills, and Litchfield Forest Reserves. In 1992, Jamaica's first marine park, covering 15 km², was established in Montego Bay. The following year the Blue and John Crow Mountains National Park was established on 780 km² of wilderness that supports thousands of tree and fern species, rare animals, and insects, such as the Homerus swallowtail, the western hemisphere's largest butterfly. The Negril Marine Park was established in 1998. These decisions have been essential for the sustainability of the environment and the tourist industry itself. Jamaica wants to increase its tourist business, but more people will only visit if the physical environment retains its attractions and diverse attributes.

Tourism has become an increasingly vital part of Jamaica's economy in recent decades (Table 3.10). The contribution of tourism to total employment and GDP has risen substantially. Direct employment numbers 92 000, but almost 300 000 jobs depend on tourism if indirect employment is also taken into account. For example, farmers supply food to the hotels and carpenters make furniture for the industry.

The industry has brought considerable opportunities to Jamaica's population, although it has not been without its problems. During the 1970s the Jamaican government introduced 'Jamaicanisation' policies designed to attract much needed foreign investment in tourism. Policies included comparatively high wages and special industry taxes that went directly into social development, healthcare and education. These sectors are often referred to by economists as 'soft infrastructure'. However, tourism has also spurred the development of vital 'hard infrastructure' too, such as roads, telecommunications, water supply and airports. Jamaica has been determined to learn from the 'mistakes' of other countries and ensure that the population will gain real benefits from the growth of tourism.

Tourism's direct contribution to GDP in 2007 amounted to almost $1.2 billion. Adding all the indirect economic benefits increased the figure to almost $3.8 billion or 31.1 per cent of total GDP. Direct employment in the industry amounted to 92 000 but the overall figure, which includes indirect employment, is over three times as large. In the most popular tourist areas the level of reliance on the industry is extremely high.

Table 3.10 The importance of the travel and tourist industry to the Jamaican economy

2007	Travel and tourism industry	Travel and tourism economy
GDP % of total	9.6	31.1
Employment	92 000	289 000

Source: from WTTC data

Tourism is the largest source of foreign exchange for Jamaica. In terms of the relative contribution of tourism to a country's national economy, the WTTC ranks Jamaica 19th out of 176. The revenue from tourism plays a significant part in helping central and local government fund economic and social policies. Also, as attitudes within the industry itself are changing, larger hotels and other aspects of the industry have become more socially conscious. Classic examples are the funding of local social projects.

A recent paper (2007) on tourism by the People's National Party (PNP) stated that 'The momentum generated by the current round of investment in resort development has created an enormous pull factor in terms of investor confidence. This has set the stage for an even more powerful wave of investment in the next 10 years.'

The Jamaica Tourist Board (JTB) is responsible for marketing the country abroad. Recently it used the fact that Jamaica was one of the host countries for the 2007 Cricket World Cup to good effect. The JTB also promotes the positive aspects of Jamaican culture, and the Bob Marley Museum in Kingston has become a popular attraction. Such attractions are an important aid in supporting Jamaica's objective of reducing seasonality.

The high or 'winter' season runs from mid-December to mid-April when hotel prices are highest. The rainy season extends from May to November. It has been estimated that 25 per cent of hotel workers are laid off during the off-season.

Jamaica's government is working to reduce the environmental impact of tourism. Figure 3.53 shows the location of Jamaica's three national parks. A further six sites have been identified for future protection. The Jamaican government sees the designation of the parks as a positive environmental impact of tourism. Entry fees to the national parks pay for conservation. The desire of tourists to visit these areas and the need to conserve the environment to attract future tourism drives the designation and management process.

The two marine parks are attempting to conserve the coral reef environments off the west coast of Jamaica. They are at risk from damage from overfishing, industrial pollution and mass tourism. The Jamaica Conservation and Development Trust is responsible for the management of the national parks, while the National Environmental Planning Agency has overseen the government's sustainable development strategy since 2001.

Negril

Negril is a large beach resort town located on the west coast of Jamaica. The town's development as a resort location began during the late 1950s, although access to the area proved difficult as ferries were required to drop off passengers in Negril Bay, forcing them to wade to shore. When the road between Montego

Bay and Negril was improved in the early 1970s, it helped to increase Negril's position as a new resort location. A small airport was built for North American winter tourists. Europeans also came to Negril, and several hotels were built in order to cater directly to those guests. Figure 3.56 shows some of the largest hotels and the transport infrastructure of Negril.

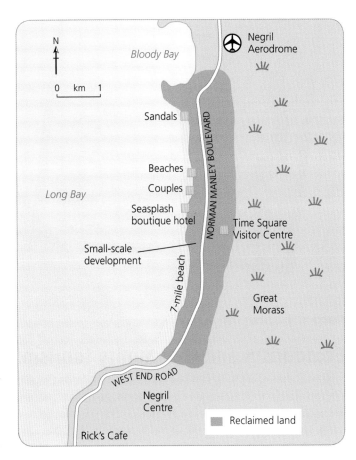

Figure 3.56 Negril

This stretch of coastline arguably has the island's best beaches. Negril's beach has been rated as one of the top ten beaches in the world by many travel magazines. To the east of the shore lies a swamp called the Great Morass, amidst which is the Royal Palm Reserve, with wetlands that are protected. In 1990, the Negril Coral Reef Preservation Society (Figure 3.57) was formed as a non-governmental organisation to address ongoing degradation of the coral reef ecosystem. This was the precursor of the Negril Marine Park, which was established in 1998. Educating people about the fragility of coral reefs (Figure 3.58) and other endangered environments is a crucial aspect of sustainability.

Figure 3.57 Negril Coral Reef Preservation Society

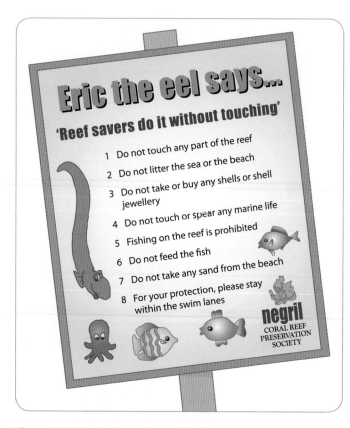

Figure 3.58 Coral reef protection society sign

- Community tourism should involve local people in decision making and ownership.
- The local community should receive a fair share of the profits from tourism ventures.
- Tour companies should try to work with communities rather than individuals to avoid creating divisions.
- Tourism should be environmentally sustainable and not put excess pressure on natural resources.
- Tourism should support traditional cultures. It should encourage people to value and respect their cultural heritage.
- Where possible, tour operators should keep groups small to minimise cultural and environmental impacts.
- Tour guides should brief tourists on what to expect and on appropriate behaviour before arriving in a community.
- Local people should have the right to say no to tourism.

Source: *Geography Review*, January 2005

Figure 3.59 Principles of community-based tourism

Ecotourism and community tourism

Ecotourism is a developing sector of the industry with, for example, raft trips on the Rio Grande river increasing in popularity. Tourists are taken downstream in very small groups. The rafts, which rely solely on manpower, leave singly with a significant time gap between them to minimise any disturbance to the peace of the forest. Ecotourism is seen as the most sustainable form of tourist activity on the island.

Considerable efforts are being made to promote **community tourism** so that more money filters down to the local people and small communities. The Sustainable Communities Foundation through Tourism (SCF) programme has been particularly active in central and south-west Jamaica. Community tourism (Figure 3.59) is seen as an important aspect of '**pro-poor tourism**'.

The Astra Country Inn in Mandeville has been recognised as a pioneer hotel in community tourism. Its work with surrounding communities has included:

- promoting bed and breakfast accommodation in private homes
- training local guides
- developing community-based tourist attractions
- encouraging the development of local suppliers.

Challenges ahead

However, tourism has not been without its problems. The behaviour of some tourists clashes with the island's traditional morals. People also have a negative image of Jamaica because of its levels of violent crime and harassment, and despite the recent initiatives of the Jamaican government to protect the environment much valuable biodiversity has already been lost. On a positive note, Jamaica is one of the few Caribbean tourist destinations that has done relatively well during the recent recession that has led to a decrease in visitor arrivals for the Caribbean region.

While Jamaica has undertaken several initiatives with regard to the sustainable development of tourism, the success of such initiatives has been mixed. A book entitled *Barriers to Sustainable Tourism Development in Jamaica* published in 2007 noted that initiatives often lacked adequate management and cohesion, and often had to work under significant financial constraints.

Section 3.4 Activities

1 With the aid of an atlas describe the location of Jamaica.

2 Produce a bullet-point analysis of Figure 3.54.

3 Explain the location of the island's main resorts.

4 Describe the transport infrastructure of Jamaica. Why is this such an important factor in the development of tourism?

5 Discuss the importance of tourism to the economy of Jamaica.

6 What measures have been taken to advance the sustainability of tourism on the island?

7 Briefly discuss the development of ecotourism and community tourism in Jamaica.

4 Economic transition

4.1 National development

Employment structure and its role in economic development

In MEDCs and an increasing number of LEDCs, people do hundreds of different jobs. All of these jobs can be placed into four broad employment sectors:

- The **primary sector** produces raw materials from the land and the sea. Farming, fishing, forestry, mining, quarrying and fishing make up most of the jobs in this sector. Some primary products are sold directly to the consumer but most go to secondary industries for processing.
- The **secondary sector** manufactures primary materials into finished products. Activities in this sector include the production of processed food, furniture and motor vehicles. Secondary products are classed either as **consumer goods** (produced for sale to the public) or **capital goods** (produced for sale to other industries).
- The **tertiary sector** provides services to businesses and to people. Retail employees, drivers, architects, teachers and nurses are examples of jobs in this sector.
- The **quaternary sector** uses high technology to provide information and expertise. Research and development is an important part of this sector. Jobs in this sector include aerospace engineers, research scientists, computer scientists and biotechnology workers. Quaternary industries have only been recognised as a separate group since the late 1960s. Before then, jobs now classed as quaternary were placed in either the secondary or tertiary sectors depending on whether a tangible product was produced or not. However, even today much of the available information on employment does not consider the quaternary sector.

Table 4.1 presents the changing employment structure in the UK over a period of 40 years.

The **product chain**, which considers the full sequence of activities needed to turn raw materials into a finished product, can be used to illustrate the four sectors of employment. The food industry provides a good example (Figure 4.1). Some companies are involved in all four stages of the food product chain. Research and development (the quaternary sector) can improve the performance of all the other three sectors.

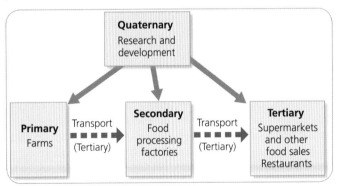

Figure 4.1 The food industry's product chain

Table 4.1 Employment structure in the UK, 1964–2005

| | 1964 | | 1973 | | 1979 | | 1983 | | 1990 | | 2005 |
	Thousands	% of total employment	Thousands	% of total employment	Thousands	% of total employment	Thousands	% of total employment	Thousands	% of total employment	Thousands	% of total employment
Total primary	1 201	5.1	773	3.4	692	3.0	672	3.0	476	2.1	297	1.1
Total secondary	10 978	46.9	9573	42.4	8911	38.5	7 748	35.4	6 093	26.6	4 437	16.6
Total tertiary	11 178	47.8	12 320	54.4	13 556	58.5	13 465	61.4	16 351	71.3	21 916	82.2
Total employment	23 357		22 664		23 158		21 891		22 920		26 650	

Source: Office for National Statistics, Crown Copyright 2006

How employment structures vary
LEDCs

People in the poorest countries of the world (LEDCs) are heavily dependent on the primary sector for employment. Most of these people work in agriculture and many are **subsistence farmers**. In some densely populated areas where the amount of land is very limited, there will not be enough work available for everyone to work a full week. The work available is often shared and people are said to be **underemployed**.

In some regions of LEDCs, mining, quarrying, forestry or fishing may dominate the economy. Work in mining in LEDCs is often better paid than jobs elsewhere in the primary sector, but the working conditions are often very harsh. In poor countries, higher-paid jobs in the secondary, tertiary and quaternary sectors are usually very few in number. The tertiary jobs that are available are often in the public sector. Public sector jobs such as teaching, nursing and refuse collection are paid by the government. However, wages in these jobs are usually low as the funds available to the governments of LEDCs are very limited.

Many of the world's poorest countries are **primary product dependent**, meaning that they rely on one or a small number of primary products for most of their export earnings. This makes them very vulnerable to changes in world markets. For example, if a country relies on coffee for most of its export earnings and the price of coffee falls substantially, that country will have far less money to pay for the imports it needs and less to invest in health, education and other important aspects affecting the quality of life of its people.

NICs

In newly industrialised countries (NICs) employment in manufacturing has increased rapidly in recent decades. NICs have reached the stage of development where they attract foreign direct investment from transnational corporations in both the manufacturing and service sectors. The business environment in NICs is such that they also develop their own domestic companies. Such companies usually start in a small way, but some go on to reach a considerable size. Both processes create employment in manufacturing and services.

The increasing wealth of NICs allows for greater investment in agriculture. This includes mechanisation which results in a falling demand for labour on the land. So, as employment in the secondary and tertiary sectors rises, employment in the primary sector falls. Eventually, NICs may become so advanced that the quaternary sector begins to develop. Examples of NICs where this has happened are South Korea, Singapore and Taiwan.

MEDCs

Developed countries (MEDCs) are often referred to as **post-industrial societies** because far fewer people are now employed in manufacturing industries than in the past. Most people work in the tertiary sector, with an increasing number in the quaternary

sector. Jobs in manufacturing industries have fallen for two reasons:
- Many manufacturing industries have moved to take advantage of lower costs in NICs and LEDCs. Cheaper labour is often the main attraction, but many other costs are also lower.
- Investment in robotics and other advanced technology has replaced much human labour in many manufacturing industries that remain in MEDCs.

Table 4.2 compares the employment structure of an MEDC, an NIC and an LEDC.

Table 4.2 Employment structure of an MEDC, an NIC and an LEDC

Country	% primary	% secondary	% tertiary
UK (MEDC)	1	17	82
China (NIC)	43	25	32
Bangladesh (LEDC)	63	11	26

A graphical method often used to compare the employment structure of a large number of countries is the triangular graph (Figure 4.2). One side (axis) of the triangle is used to show the data for each of the primary, secondary and tertiary sectors. Each axis is scaled from 0 to 100%. The indicators on the graph show how the data for the UK can be read.

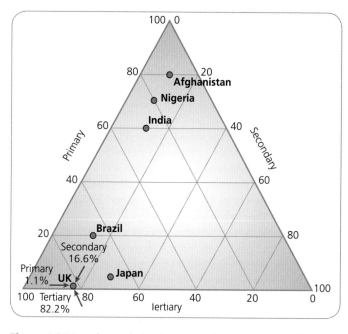

Figure 4.2 Triangular graph showing the employment structure of six countries

How employment structures have changed over time and may change in the future

As an economy advances, the proportion of people employed in each sector changes (Figure 4.3). Countries such as the UK and the USA are 'post-industrial societies' where most people work in the tertiary sector. Yet in 1900, as much as 40 per cent of employment in the USA was in the primary sector. However, the mechanisation of farming, mining, forestry and fishing drastically reduced the demand for labour in these industries. As these jobs disappeared, people moved to urban areas where jobs in the secondary and tertiary sectors were expanding. Less than 4 per cent of employment in the USA is now in the primary sector.

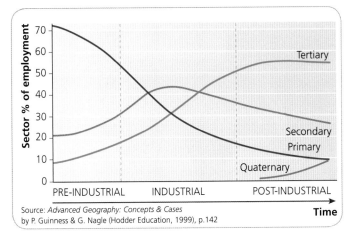

Source: *Advanced Geography: Concepts & Cases* by P. Guinness & G. Nagle (Hodder Education, 1999), p.142

Figure 4.3 The sector model

Human labour has been replaced in manufacturing too. In more and more factories, robots and other advanced machinery handle assembly-line jobs which once employed large numbers of people. Also, many manufacturing jobs once done in America are now done in NICs. In 1950 the same number of Americans were employed in the secondary and tertiary sectors. By 1980 two-thirds were working in services. Today 78 per cent of Americans work in the tertiary sector.

The tertiary sector is also changing. In banking, insurance and many other types of business, computer networks have reduced the number of people required. But elsewhere service employment is rising, such as in health, education and tourism.

Outsourcing

A major change in employment has been the increase in **outsourcing**. Companies do this to save money. Work can be outsourced to companies in the same country or it can go abroad where labour and other costs are much lower. For example, many British and American companies have outsourced their call centres to India. It has been the revolution in information and communications technology that has enabled outsourcing to develop so rapidly into a major global industry. As higher-level ICT has spread down the global economic hierarchy from core to periphery, more and more countries have been competing for this valuable business.

Employment structure: the future

The nature of work in the UK and other MEDCs has changed markedly over the past 50 years. It will continue to change in the future as the process of globalisation continues. The key questions are:

- Will even fewer people work in the primary sector and which tasks will be performed by those who remain?
- How much further will manufacturing employment fall and which products will MEDCs still produce?
- Which service sector jobs will decline and which will increase in importance?
- Which totally new services will begin to provide employment in the future?
- How many people will be unemployed at various stages in the future and what status and standard of living will they have?
- What changes will occur in, (a) the working week, (b) paid holidays, (c) retirement age, (d) pensions, (e) the school leaving age, (f) working conditions, (g) the location of employment?
- What control will national governments have over these issues?

Employment is one of the most important factors in most people's lives. It is the income from employment that influences so many aspects of an individual's quality of life. The world of 2025 is likely to be very different from its present state.

With further advances in ICT there will be a greater opportunity for more people to work from home. This is often referred to as **teleworking**. ICT will allow many people to perform the same tasks from home that they now do in their office. However, a decade ago it was thought that higher technology home working would be more important now than it has actually turned out to be. It seems that the physical clustering of people in organisations has proved more difficult to break down than many commentators thought.

It seems likely that international commuting and employment migration (geographical mobility) will increase as economic and psychological barriers to movement recede. The degree of occupational mobility should also increase as the pace of change quickens.

Section 4.1 Activities

1 Describe the changes in the employment structure of the UK shown in Table 4.1.

2 Explain the product chain illustrated by Figure 4.1.

3 Why does the primary sector dominate employment in the poorest countries of the world?

4 Explain the changes in employment structure that have occurred in NICs.

5 On a copy of Figure 4.2, plot the positions of China and Bangladesh using the data in Table 4.2.

6 Explain the changes shown in Figure 4.3.

7 Why does outsourcing occur on such a large scale?

8 Discuss the changes that are likely to occur in the future, in employment in the country in which you live.

Global inequalities in social and economic well-being

Development and its traditional income measures

Development, or improvement in the quality of life, is a wide-ranging concept. It includes wealth, but it includes other important aspects of our lives too. For example, many people would consider good health to be more important than wealth. People who live in countries that are not democracies, where freedom of speech cannot be taken for granted, often envy those who do live in democratic countries. Development occurs when there are improvements to individual factors making up the quality of life. Figure 4.4 shows one view of the factors that comprise the quality of life (Figure 4.5). For example, development occurs in a low-income country when:

- the local food supply improves due to investment in machinery and fertilisers
- the electricity grid extends outwards from the main urban areas to rural areas
- a new road or railway improves the accessibility of a remote province
- levels of literacy improve throughout the country.

The traditional indicator of a country's wealth has been the **gross domestic product (GDP)**. The gross domestic product is the total value of goods and services produced by a country in a year. A more recent measure, gross national income, has to some extent taken over from GNP as a preferred measure of national wealth. **Gross national income (GNI)** comprises the total value of goods and services produced within a country – that is, its gross domestic product – together with its income received from other countries (notably interest and dividends), less similar payments made to other countries.

To take account of the different populations of countries the **gross national income per capita** is often used. Here, the total GNI of a country is divided by the total population. Per capita figures allow for more valid comparisons between countries when their total populations are very different. However, 'raw' or 'nominal' GNI data does not take into account the way in which the cost of living can vary between countries. For example, a dollar buys much more in China than it does is the USA. To account for this the GNI at 'purchasing power parity' (PPP) is calculated. Figure 4.6 shows how **GNI at purchasing power parity per capita** varied globally in 2007. The lowest GNI figures are concentrated in Africa and parts of Asia. The highest figures are in North America, the EU, Japan, Australia and New Zealand.

Table 4.3 shows the top 20 and bottom 20 countries in GNI per capita (PPP) for 2006/07. The **development gap** between the world's wealthiest and poorest countries is huge. However, a major limitation of GNI and other national data is that these are 'average' figures for a country, which tell us nothing about:

- the way in which wealth is distributed within a country – in

Figure 4.4 Factors comprising the quality of life

Figure 4.5 An open-pit toilet – this is as far as sanitation goes in many LEDCs, and is an indicator of quality of life there

some countries the gap between rich and poor is much greater than in others
- how government invests the money at its disposal – for example, Cuba has a low GNI per capita but high standards of health and education because these have been government priorities for a long time.

Development not only varies between countries, it can also vary significantly within countries. Most of the measures that can be used to examine the contrasts between countries can also be used to look at regional variations within countries.

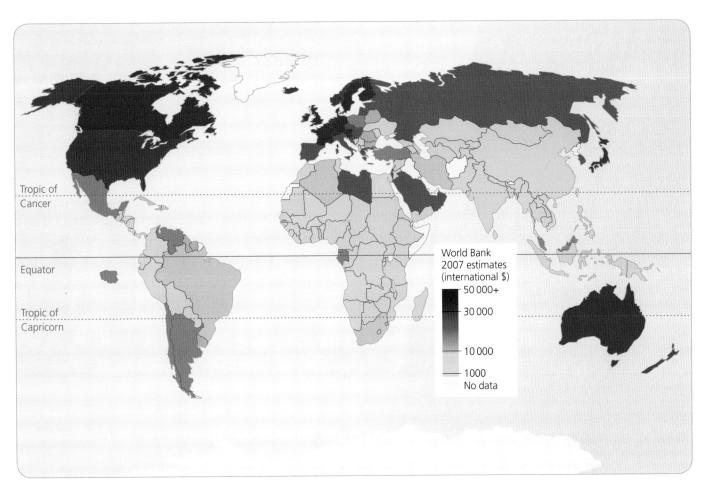

Figure 4.6 Worldwide GNI PPP per capita in 2007

Table 4.3 Top 20 and bottom 20 countries in GNI (PPP) per capita

Top 20 countries		Bottom 20 countries	
Luxembourg	65 320	Comoros	1 170
Norway	58 500	Burkina Faso	1 160
Kuwait	52 610	Chad	1 160
Macau	52 260	Uganda	1 140
Brunei	50 200	Nepal	1 120
Singapore	47 940	Mali	1 090
USA	46 970	Madagascar	1 040
Switzerland	46 640	Rwanda	1 010
Hong Kong	43 960	Ethiopia	870
Netherlands	41 670	Malawi	830
Sweden	38 180	Togo	820
Austria	37 680	Mozambique	770
Ireland	37 350	Sierra Leone	750
Denmark	37 280	Central African Rep.	730
Canada	36 220	Niger	680
UK	36 130	Eritrea	630
Germany	35 940	Guinea-Bissau	530
Finland	35 660	Burundi	380
Japan	35 220	Liberia	300
Belgium	34 760	Congo, Dem. Rep.	290

Source: Wikipedia

Broader measures of development: the Human Development Index

The way that the quality of life has been measured has changed over time. In the 1980s the Physical Quality of Life Index (PQLI) was devised. The PQLI was the average of three development factors: literacy, life expectancy and infant mortality. However, in 1990 the **Human Development Index (HDI)** was devised by the United Nations (UN) as a better measure to show the disparities between countries. The HDI contains three variables:

- life expectancy
- educational attainment (adult literacy and combined primary, secondary and tertiary enrolment)
- GDP per capita (PPP$).

The actual figures for each of these three measures are converted into an index (Figure 4.7) each of which has a maximum value of 1.0. The three index values are then combined and averaged to give an overall HDI value. This also has a maximum value of 1.0. Every year the UN publishes the *Human Development Report* which uses the HDI to rank all the countries of the world in their level of development. Table 4.4 shows the top 25 countries listed in the *Human Development Report* for 2009.

435

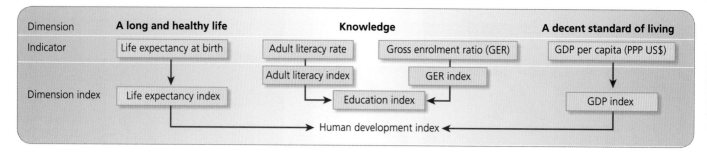

Figure 4.7 Constructing the Human Development Index

Every measure of development has merits and limitations. No single measure can provide a complete picture of the differences in development between countries. This is why the UN combines three measures of different aspects of the quality of life to arrive at a figure of human development for each country. Although the development gap can be measured in a variety of ways it is generally taken to be increasing (Figures 4.8 and 4.9).

Figure 4.8 The Waterfront, Vancouver – Canada has a very high level of human development

Table 4.4 Top 25 countries, *Human Development Report 2009*

Human Development Index rank	Human Development Index value	Life expectancy at birth (years)	Adult literacy rate (% age and above)	Combined gross enrolment ration in education	GDP per capita (PPP US$)	Life expectancy index	Education index	GDP index	GDP per capita rank minus HDI rank
	2007	2007	1999–2007	2007	2007	2007	2007	2007	
1 Norway	0.971	80.5	–	98.6	53 433	0.925	0.989	1.000	4
2 Australia	0.970	81.4	–	114.2	34 923	0.940	0.993	0.977	20
3 Iceland	0.969	81.7	–	96.0	35 742	0.946	0.980	0.981	16
4 Canada	0.966	80.6	–	99.3	35 812	0.927	0.991	0.982	14
5 Ireland	0.965	79.7	–	97.6	44 613	0.911	0.985	1.000	5
6 Netherlands	0.964	79.8	–	97.5	38 694	0.914	0.985	0.994	8
7 Sweden	0.963	80.8	–	94.3	39 712	0.930	0.974	0.986	9
8 France	0.961	81.0	–	95.4	33 674	0.933	0.978	0.971	17
9 Switzerland	0.960	81.7	–	82.7	40 658	0.945	0.936	1.000	4
10 Japan	0.960	82.7	–	86.6	33 632	0.961	0.949	0.971	16
11 Luxembourg	0.960	79.4	–	94.4	79 485	0.906	0.975	1.000	-9
12 Finland	0.959	79.5	–	101.4	34 526	0.908	0.993	0.975	11
13 USA	0.956	79.1	–	92.4	45 592	0.902	0.968	1.000	-4
14 Austria	0.955	79.9	–	90.5	37 370	0.915	0.962	0.989	1
15 Spain	0.955	80.7	97.9	96.5	31 560	0.929	0.975	0.960	12
16 Denmark	0.955	78.2	–	101.3	36 130	0.887	0.993	0.983	1
17 Belgium	0.953	79.5	–	94.3	34 935	0.908	0.974	0.977	4
18 Italy	0.951	81.1	98.9	91.8	30 353	0.935	0.965	0.954	11
19 Liechtenstein	0.951	–	–	86.8	85 382	0.903	0.949	1.000	–18
20 New Zealand	0.950	80.1	–	107.5	27 336	0.919	0.993	0.936	12
21 UK	0.947	79.3	–	89.2	35 130	0.906	0.957	0.978	–1
22 Germany	0.947	79.8	–	88.1	34 401	0.913	0.954	0.975	2
23 Singapore	0.944	80.2	94.4	–	49 704	0.920	0.913	1.000	–16
24 Hong Kong	0.944	82.2	–	74.4	42 306	0.953	0.879	1.000	–13
25 Greece	0.942	79.1	97.1	101.6	28 517	0.902	0.981	0.944	6

Source: Human Development Report 2009

Overall, inequality has been getting worse, though trends in inequality are complicated. Basically:

If you compare *individuals* – average incomes per head of the world's richest and poorest people – the gap has narrowed, largely because China and India made immense reductions in poverty.

If you compare *countries* – the average income of one country and another – the gap has widened: more countries are lagging behind the rich nations than are catching up.

If you compare incomes *within countries* – between the richest people and the poorest – then again the gap is widening: from within China to the USA, the rich are pulling away from the poor.

One review of the literature looked at inequality from a variety of angles. It concluded that people round the centre of income distribution worldwide have been drawing together to some extent, yet the extremes have been flying apart.

The gap between the richest and the poorest has been widening, but income difference for those in the middle has slightly narrowed. 'There is no sign at all that either the extreme impoverishment at the bottom or the extreme enrichment at the top of the world distribution are coming to an end.'

Source: The Tomorrow Project

Figure 4.9 Globalisation: will the gap between the rich and poor narrow?

Figure 4.10 shows the variation in human development in 2007. Countries are divided into three categories – high, medium and low human development. The 'high' category also includes those countries with 'very high' human development (Table 4.5).

Table 4.5 HDI values

Level of human development	HDI value	Number of countries 2007
Very high	0.900 and over	38
High	0.800–0.899	45
Medium	0.500–0.799	75
Low	Below 0.500	24

The *Human Development Report*

The Human Development Index is published annually. It is a key part of the *Human Development Report* (*HDR*). According to a recent edition of the *Human Development Report*, 'Human development is about putting people at the centre of development. It is about people realising their potential, increasing their choices and enjoying the freedom to lead lives they value. Since 1990, annual *Human Development Reports* have explored challenges including poverty, gender, democracy, human rights, cultural liberty, globalisation, water scarcity and climate change.'

In assessing the progress made in reducing global poverty, the *Human Development Report* has noted that:

- in the past 60 years poverty has fallen more than in the previous 500 years
- poverty has been reduced in some respects in almost all countries

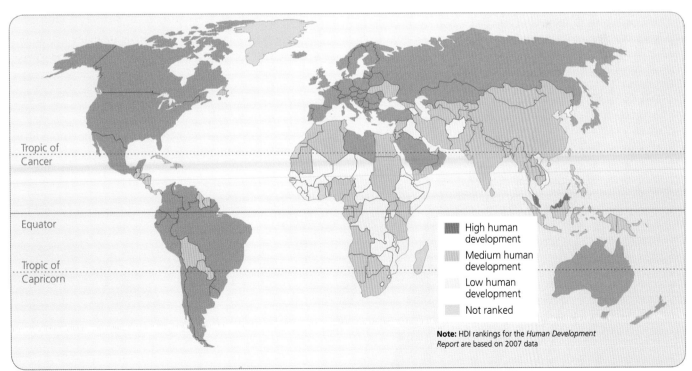

High human development

Medium human development

Low human development

Not ranked

Note: HDI rankings for the *Human Development Report* are based on 2007 data

Figure 4.10 Countries with high, medium and low human development, according to the *Human Development Report 2009*

Figure 4.11 Rural Mongolia – a part of the world where many people still live in poverty

- child death rates in developing countries have been cut by more than half since 1960
- malnutrition rates have declined by almost a third since 1960
- the proportion of children not in primary education has fallen from more than half to less than a quarter since 1960
- the share of rural families without access to safe water has been cut from nine-tenths to about a quarter since 1960.

These are just some of the achievements made during what the HDR calls the 'second Great Ascent from poverty', which started in the 1950s in the developing world, Eastern Europe and the former Soviet Union. The first Great Ascent from poverty began in Europe and North America in the late nineteenth century in the wake of the Industrial Revolution.

However, although the global poverty situation is improving, approximately one in six people worldwide struggle on a daily basis in terms of:

- adequate nutrition
- uncontaminated drinking water
- safe shelter
- adequate sanitation
- access to basic healthcare.

These people have to survive on $1 a day or less and are largely denied access to public services for health, education and infrastructure. The UN estimates that 20 000 people die every day of dire poverty, for want of food, safe drinking water, medicine and other vital needs. (Figure 4.11.)

Individual measures of development

There are many individual measures of socio-economic development, some of which have already been mentioned. Indicators not mentioned above include:

- the number of people per doctor
- energy use per capita
- number of motor vehicles per 1000 people
- per capita food intake in calories
- televisions/refrigerators per 1000 population
- per capita export and import volumes
- environmental protection expenditure as a percentage of GDP.

Some of the most important indicators of development are considered in more detail here.

Infant mortality rate

The **infant mortality rate** is regarded as one of the most sensitive indicators of socio-economic progress. It is an important measure of health equity both between and within countries.

There are huge differences in the infant mortality rate around the world, despite the wide availability of public health knowledge.

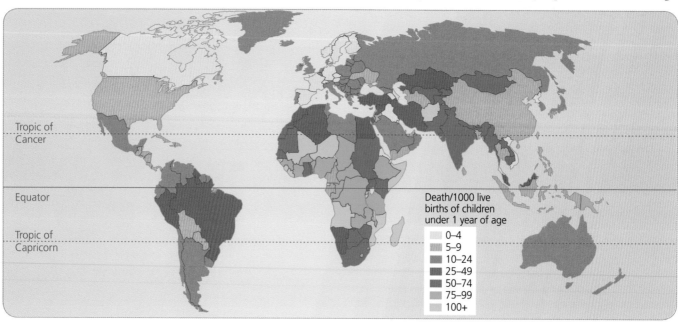

Figure 4.12 Global variations in the infant mortality rate

Differences in material resources certainly provide a large part of the explanation for how international populations can share the same knowledge but achieve disparate mortality rates. Differences in the efficiency of social institutions and health systems can also enable countries with similar resource levels to register disparate mortality levels. Figure 4.12 shows the extent of global variations in infant mortality. The highest rates are clearly concentrated in Africa and southern Asia. Infant mortality generally aligns well with other indicators of development.

However, many countries have significant intranational disparities in infant mortality, where populations share similar resource levels and health technology but achieve different health outcomes in various regions of the same country.

Education

Education is undoubtedly the key to socio-economic development. It can be defined as the process of acquiring knowledge, understanding and skills. Education has always been regarded as a very important individual indicator of development and it has figured prominently in aggregate measures. Quality education generally, and female literacy in particular, are central to development (Figure 4.13). The World Bank has concluded that improving female literacy is one of the most fundamental achievements for a developing nation to attain, because so many aspects of development depend upon it. For example, there is a very strong relationship between the extent of female literacy and infant and child mortality rates. People who are literate are able to access medical and other information that will help them towards a higher quality of life compared with those who are illiterate.

Figure 4.13 A secondary school in Morocco

The UN sees education for **sustainable development** as being absolutely vital for the future of the planet. Sustainable development seeks to meet the needs of the present without compromising those of future generations. The year 2005 was the beginning of the United Nations Decade for Sustainable Development, which will run until 2014.

Nutrition

Undernourishment is concentrated in the least developed countries, particularly in Sub-Saharan Africa and South Asia. The remaining problem areas are found in former Soviet Union countries. However, transitory areas of undernourishment can be caused by natural or human-made disasters.

Hunger may be defined as a condition resulting from chronic under-consumption of food and or nutritious food products. It can be a short-term or long-term condition. If long-term it is usually described as chronic hunger. Malnutrition is the condition that develops when the body does not get the right amount of the vitamins, minerals and other nutrients it needs to maintain healthy tissues and organ function. Malnutrition occurs in people who are undernourished. Undernutrition is a consequence of consuming too few essential nutrients or using or excreting them more rapidly than they can be replaced. The leading cause of death in children in LEDCs is protein-energy malnutrition. This type of malnutrition is the result of inadequate intake of calories from proteins, vitamins and minerals. Malnutrition is not confined to LEDCs – it can also be a condition of the very poor in more affluent nations.

The global recession of 2008/09 increased malnutrition for many of the most vulnerable people in LEDCs. A paper published by the UN Standing Committee on Nutrition found that:

- In many countries the hours of work needed to feed a household of five increased by 10–20 per cent during 2008.
- The nutritional consequences of food price increases were likely to be considerable.
- Currently some 50 million, or 40 per cent, of pregnant women in LEDCs are anaemic. This number is likely to rise because of the current economic situation. Nutritional problems very early in pregnancy will influence later foetal and infant growth.

Increased and diversified agricultural production is one of the most reliable, sustainable interventions to improve nutrition and reduce infant and child malnutrition and mortality (Figure 4.14).

Figure 4.14 Food market in Agadir, Morocco

1 Look at Figure 4.4. Select what you think are the four most important aspects of the quality of life. Justify your selections.

2 Define **a** *GNI per capita*, **b** *GNI at purchasing power parity* and **c** *the development gap*.

3 Describe the global distribution of GNI per capita (PPP) shown in Figure 4.6.

4 Why are organisations such as the UN increasingly using GNI data at purchasing power parity?

5 Discuss the extent of the development gap shown in Table 4.3.

6 Describe the global distribution of human development shown in Figure 4.10.

7 a Define the *infant mortality rate*.
b Why is it judged to be a prime indicator of socio-economic development?

8 Why is the level of education considered to be such an important measure of a country's development?

9 Discuss the importance of nutrition as a measure of development.

Different stages of development

Although the global development picture is complex, a general distinction can be made between the developed 'North' and the developing 'South'. These terms were first used in *North–South: A Programme for Survival* published in 1980. This publication is generally known as the 'Brandt Report' after its chairperson Willy Brandt.

Other terms used to distinguish between the richer and poorer nations are:

• developed and developing
• more economically developed countries (MEDCs) and less economically developed countries (LEDCs).

Over the years there have been a number of descriptions and explanations of how countries moved from one level of development to another. A reasonable division of the world in terms of stages of economic development is shown in Figure 4.15.

The concept of **least developed countries (LDCs)** was first identified in 1968 by the United Nations Conference on Trade and Development (UNCTAD). These are the poorest of the developing countries. They have major economic, institutional and human resource problems. These are often made worse by geographical handicaps and natural and human-made disasters. *The Least Developed Countries Report 2009* identified 49 countries as LDCs. With 10.5 per cent of the world's population, these countries generate only one-tenth of 1 per cent of its income (0.1%). The list of LDCs is reviewed every three years by the UN. When countries develop beyond a certain point they are no longer considered to be LDCs.

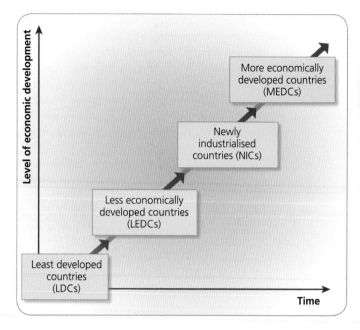

Figure 4.15 Stages of development

Many of the LDCs are in Sub-Saharan Africa. Others are concentrated in the poverty belt of Asia (including Nepal and Afghanistan) or are small island nations in the South Pacific. As the gap between the richest and poorest countries in the world widens, LDCs are being increasingly **marginalised** in the world economy. Their share of world trade is declining and in many LDCs national debt now equals or exceeds GDP. Such a situation puts a stranglehold on all attempts to halt socio-economic decline.

Least developed countries are usually dependent on one or a small number of exports for their survival. Figure 4.16 shows a classification of LDCs according to their export specialisation.

The first countries to become **newly industrialised countries (NICs)** were South Korea, Singapore, Taiwan and Hong Kong. The media referred to them as the 'four Asian tigers'. A 'tiger economy' is one that grows very rapidly. This group is now often referred to as the first generation of NICs. The reasons for the success of these countries were:

• a good initial level of infrastructure
• a skilled but relatively low-cost workforce
• cultural traditions that revere education and achievement
• governments welcoming foreign direct investment from transnational corporations
• all four countries having distinct advantages in terms of geographical location
• the ready availability of bank loans, which were often extended at government behest and at attractive interest rates.

The success of these four countries provided a model for others to follow, such as Malaysia, Brazil, China and India. In the last 15 years the growth of China has been particularly impressive. South Korea and Singapore have developed so much that many people now consider them to be developed countries.

The relative wealth of countries has a big impact on their use of resources. Table 4.6 shows the huge gap in energy consumption per capita for high, medium and low-income countries.

Oil exporters	Agricultural exporters	Mineral exporters	Manufactures exporters	Services exporters	Mixed exporters
Angola	Afghanistan	Burundi	Bangladesh	Cape Verde	Lao People's Dem. Republic
Chad	Benin	Central African Republic	Bhutan	Comoros	Madagascar
Equatorial Guinea	Burkina Faso	Dem. Republic of the Congo	Cambodia	Djibouti	Myanmar
Sudan	Guinea-Bissau	Guinea	Haiti	Eritrea	Senegal
Timor-Leste	Kiribati	Mali	Lesotho	Ethiopia	Togo
Yemen	Liberia	Mauritania	Nepal	Gambia	
	Malawi	Mozambique		Maldives	
	Solomon Islands	Niger		Rwanda	
	Somalia	Sierra Leone		Samoa	
	Tuvalu	Zambia		São Tomé and Principe	
	Uganda			United Republic of Tanzania	
				Vanuatu	

Source: The Least Developed Countries Report 2008; UNCTAD

Figure 4.16 Classification of LDCs

Table 4.6 Energy consumption per capita for high, middle and low-income countries

Total energy consumption per capita 2003 (kg of oil equivalent per person)	
High-income countries	5435
Middle-income countries	1390
Low-income countries	494

Explaining the development gap

There has been much debate about the causes of the development gap. Detailed studies have shown that variations between countries are due to a variety of factors (Figure 4.17).

Figure 4.18 shows how such factors have combined in LEDCs to produce higher and lower levels of development. In diagram (a) the area where the three factors coincide gives the highest level of development. In contrast, in diagram (b) the area where the three factors combine gives the lowest level of development.

Consequences of the development gap

The development gap has significant consequences for people in the most disadvantaged countries. The consequences of poverty

Physical geography

- Landlocked countries have generally developed more slowly than coastal ones.
- Small island countries face considerable disadvantages in development.
- Tropical countries have grown more slowly than those in temperate latitudes, reflecting the poor health and unproductive farming in the tropical regions. However, richer non-agricultural tropical countries such as Singapore do not suffer a geographical deficit of this kind.
- A generous allocation of natural resources has spurred economic growth in a number of countries.

Economic policies

- Open economies that welcomed and encouraged foreign investment have developed faster than closed economies.
- Fast-growing countries tend to have high rates of saving and low spending relative to GDP.
- Institutional quality in terms of good government, law and order and lack of corruption generally result in a high rate of growth.

Demography

- Progress through demographic transition is a significant factor, with the highest rates of growth experienced by those nations where the birth rate has fallen the most.

Figure 4.17 Factors affecting rates of development

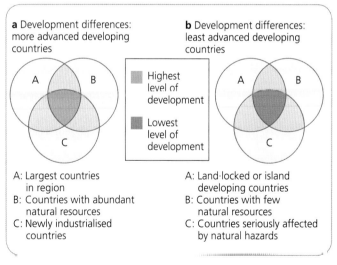

Figure 4.18 Fast and slow development LEDCs

can be economic, social, environmental and political (Figure 4.19). Development may not bring improvements in all four areas at first, but over time all four categories should witness advances.

Economic	Global integration is spatially selective: some countries benefit, others it seems do not. One in five of the world's people lives on less than $1 a day, almost half on less than $2 a day. Poor countries frequently lack the ability to pay for food, agricultural innovation, and investment in rural development.
Social	More than 850 million people in poor countries cannot read or write. Nearly a billion people do not have access to clean water and 2.4 billion do not have even basic sanitation. Eleven million children under 5 die from preventable diseases each year. People in these countries do not have the ability to combat the effects of HIV/AIDS.
Environmental	Poor countries have increased vulnerability to natural disasters. They lack the capacity to adapt to climate change or deal with consequent droughts. Poor farming practices lead to environmental degradation. Often, raw materials are exploited with very limited economic benefit to poor countries and little concern for the environment. Landscapes can be devastated by mining, vast areas of rainforest felled for logging and clearance for agriculture, and rivers and land polluted by oil exploitation.
Political	Poor countries that are low on the development scale often have a non-democratic government or they are democracies that function poorly. There is usually a reasonably strong link between development and improvement in the quality of government. In general, the poorer the country the worse the plight of minority groups.

Figure 4.19 Consequences of poverty

Section 4.1 Activities

1 Suggest three countries for each stage of development shown in Figure 4.15.

2 Draw a graph to illustrate the data presented in Table 4.6.

3 With reference to Figure 4.18, suggest why some poorer countries have been able to develop into NICs while many have not.

4 Review the physical, economic and demographic factors responsible for the development gap.

4.2 The globalisation of industrial activity

Global patterns of resources, production and markets

Globalisation is the increasing interconnectedness and interdependence of the world economically, culturally and politically. There are many aspects of globalisation, which are summarised in Figure 4.20. The word 'globalisation' did not come

Dimension	Characteristics
Economic	Under the auspices of first GATT and latterly the WTO, world trade has expanded rapidly. Transnational corporations have been the major force in the process of increasing economic interdependence, and the emergence of different generations of NICs has been the main evidence of success in the global economy. However, the frequency of 'anti-capitalist' demonstrations in recent years shows that many people have grave concerns about the direction the global economy is taking. Many LEDCs and a significant number of regions within MEDCs feel excluded from the benefits of globalisation.
Urban	A hierarchy of global cities has emerged to act as the command centres of the global economy. New York, London and Tokyo are at the highest level of this hierarchy. Competition within and between the different levels of the global urban hierarchy is intensifying.
Social/cultural	Western culture has diffused to all parts of the world to a considerable degree through TV, cinema, the internet, newspapers and magazines. The international interest in brand-name clothes and shoes, fast food and branded soft drinks and beers, pop music and major sports stars has never been greater. However, cultural transmission is not a one-way process. The popularity of Islam has increased considerably in many Western countries, as has Asian, Latin American and African cuisine.
Linguistic	English has clearly emerged as the working language of the 'global village'. Of the 1.9 billion English speakers, some 1.5 billion people around the world speak English as a second language. In a number of countries there is great concern about the future of the native language.
Political	The power of nation states has been diminished in many parts of the world as more and more countries organise themselves into trade blocs. The European Union is the most advanced model for this process of integration, taking on many of the powers that were once the sole preserve of its member nation states. The United Nations has intervened militarily in an increasing number of countries in recent times, leading some writers to talk about the gradual movement to 'world government'. On the other side of the coin is the growth of global terrorism.
Demographic	The movement of people across international borders and the desire to move across such borders has increased considerably in recent decades. More and more communities are becoming multicultural in nature.
Environmental	Increasingly, economic activity in one country has had an impact on the environment in other nations. The long-range transportation of airborne pollutants is the most obvious evidence of this process. The global environmental conferences in Rio de Janeiro (1992) and Johannesburg (2002) is evidence that most countries see the scale of the problems as so large that only co-ordinated international action can bring realistic solutions.

Figure 4.20 The dimensions of globalisation

into common usage until about 1960. In 1961 Webster became the first major dictionary to give a definition of globalisation. However, the word was not recognised as academically significant until the early to mid-1980s. Since then its use has increased dramatically.

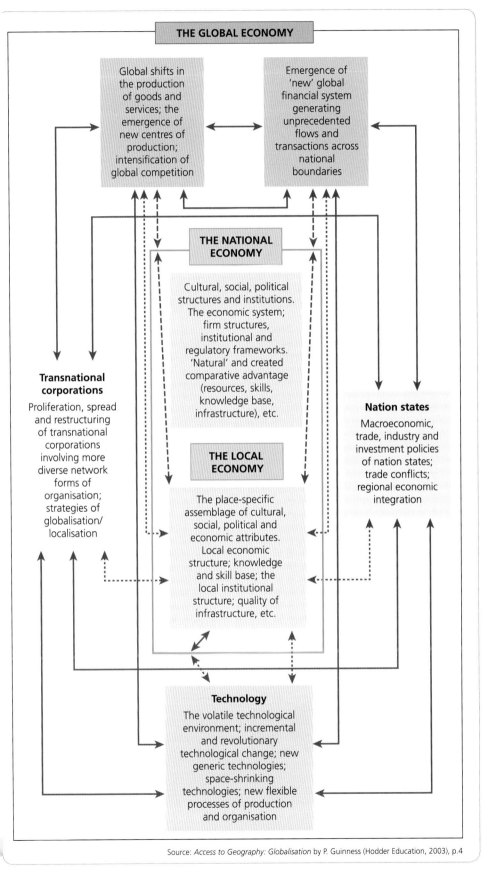

Source: *Access to Geography: Globalisation* by P. Guinness (Hodder Education, 2003), p.4

Figure 4.21 The global economy

Figure 4.21 shows Peter Dicken's view of the global economy. Transnational corporations and nation states are the two major decision-makers. Nation states individually and collectively set the rules for the global economy but the bulk of investment is through TNCs which are the main drivers of **global shift**. This is the movement of economic activity, particularly in manufacturing, from MEDCs to NICs and LEDCs. It is this process that has resulted in the emergence of an increasing number of NICs since the 1960s.

The development of globalisation

Globalisation is a relatively recent phenomenon (post-1960) which is very different from anything the world had previously experienced. It developed out of **internationalisation**. A key period in the process of internationalisation occurred between 1870 and 1914 when:

- transport and communications networks expanded rapidly
- world trade grew significantly, with a considerable increase in the level of interdependence between rich and poor nations
- there were very large flows of capital from European companies to other parts of the world.

International trade tripled between 1870 and 1913. At this time the world trading system was dominated and organised by four nations: Britain, France, Germany and the USA. However, the global shocks of the First World War and the Great Depression (1929 to late 1930s) put a stop to this period of phenomenal economic growth. It was not until the 1950s that international interdependence was back on track. Since then, world trade has grown consistently faster than world GDP. However, even by 1990 the level was unremarkable compared with that of the late nineteenth and early twentieth centuries. It is not surprising, therefore, that some writers argue that the level of integration before 1914 was similar to that of today.

443

However, today's globalisation is very different from the global relationships of 50 or 100 years ago. Peter Dicken makes the distinction between the 'shallow integration' of the pre-1914 period and the 'deep integration' of the present period. The global economy is more extensive and complicated than it has ever been before.

Economic globalisation

Figure 4.22 shows the main influences on the globalisation of economic activity. This is not a definitive list and you may be able to think of others. The factors responsible for economic globalisation can be stated as follows:

- Until the post-1950 period the production process itself was mainly organised within national economies. This has changed rapidly in the past 50 years or so with the emergence of a **new international division of labour** (NIDL) reflecting a change in the geographical pattern of specialisation, with the fragmentation of many production processes across national boundaries.
- International trade flows have become increasingly complex as this process has developed.
- There have been major advances in trade liberalisation under the World Trade Organisation.
- There was an emergence of fundamentalist free-market governments in the USA (Ronald Reagan) and the UK (Margaret Thatcher) around 1980. The economic policies developed by these governments influenced policy-making in many other countries.
- An increasing number of NICs emerged.
- The old Soviet Union and its Eastern European communist satellites merged into the capitalist system (Figure 4.23). Now, no significant group of countries stands outside the free market global system.
- Other economies opened up, notably those of China and India.

- The world financial markets were deregulated.
- The 'transport and communications revolution' has made possible the management of the complicated networks of production and trade that exist today.

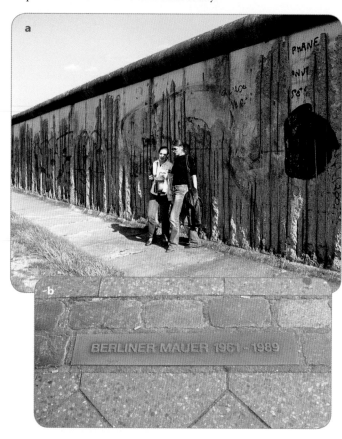

Figure 4.23 The fall of the Berlin Wall signalled the beginning of the integration of eastern Europe into the free-market system

a A part of the wall that still exists

b A plaque showing where the wall used to be

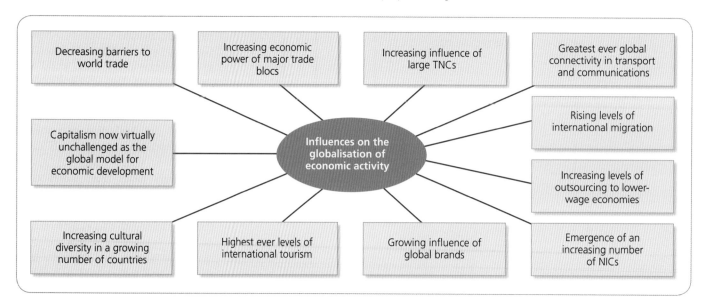

Figure 4.22 Globalisation trends

The advantages for economic activity in working at the global scale

Large companies in particular recognise many advantages in working at the global scale as opposed to at national or continental scales:

- Sourcing of raw materials and components on a global basis reduces costs.
- TNCs can seek out the lowest-cost locations for labour and other factors.
- High-volume production at low cost in countries such as China helps to reduce the rate of inflation in other countries and helps living standards to rise.
- Collaborative arrangements with international partners can increase the efficiency of operations considerably.
- Selling goods and services to a global market allows TNCs to achieve very significant economies of scale.
- Global marketing helps to establish brands with huge appeal all around the world.

Which are the most globalised countries?

Figure 4.24 shows the most globalised countries in the world according to the 2007 AT Kearney/Foreign Affairs Index of Globalisation. The 2007 index ranked 72 countries according to their degree of globalisation. These countries accounted for 97 per cent of the world's GDP and 88 per cent of the global population. The AT Kearney Index of Globalisation comprised four key elements of global integration:

- economic integration
- personal contact
- technological connectivity
- political engagement.

Economic integration brings together data on trade and foreign direct investment. The latter includes both inflows and outflows. International travel and tourism is also included in this category. Personal contact encompasses international telephone calls and cross-border remittances. As countries become more globalised, personal contacts increase accordingly. The average community today will have far more former members living abroad than was the case 30 years ago. International telephone calls are a good way of comparing countries at one point in time and also recording changes over time. Remittances have become an increasingly important source of money flowing between countries because of the growing number of migrant workers (Figure 4.25).

Figure 4.25 Post Office – Tiananmen Square, Beijing

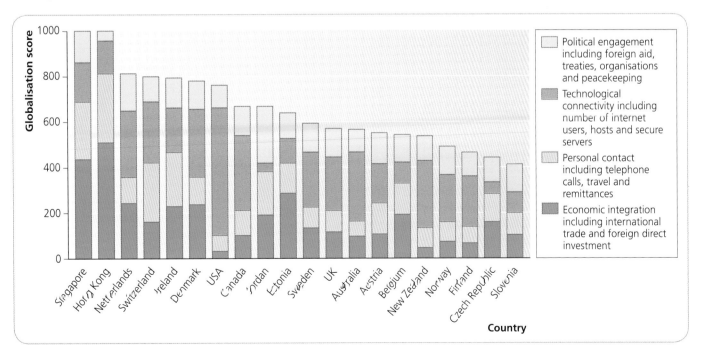

Figure 4.24 AT Kearney Globalisation Index 2007

Technological connectivity concerns the number of internet users and internet hosts. The internet has arguably been the single most important advance in the globalisation process.

Political engagement considers a country's membership of a variety of international organisations. International contacts are vital to virtually all aspects of the development process.

Figure 4.24 shows that the most globalised countries in rank order are Singapore, Hong Kong, Netherlands, Switzerland, Ireland, Denmark, and the USA. However, the composition of their total globalisation scores is markedly different in some cases. Economic integration is the most important factor for Singapore and Hong Kong. It is much less important for the other five most globalised countries, and its contribution is particularly low for the USA. It can be argued that large economies like the USA are able to satisfy far more of their economic needs from within their own borders than small countries with limited land areas and resources in general.

For the USA, technological connectivity is by far the most dominant of the four elements of globalisation. This reflects the high level of affluence in the USA and the eagerness to embrace new technology at the business and individual levels.

Section 4.2 Activities

1 Define **a** *globalisation* and **b** *global shift*.

2 Discuss two of the dimensions of globalisation covered in Figure 4.20.

3 Write a brief summary of Figure 4.21.

4 Explain the *new international division of labour*.

5 Briefly discuss the factors responsible for economic globalisation.

6 Explain the advantages for economic activity in working at the global scale.

7 Discuss the factors used by the AT Kearney Index to measure globalisation.

Transnational corporations and foreign direct investment
Major TNCs and FDI flows

Investment involves expenditure on a project in the expectation of financial (or social) returns. **Transnational corporations (TNCs)** are the main source of **foreign direct investment (FDI)**. TNCs invest to make profits and are the driving force behind economic globalisation. They are capitalist enterprises that organise the production of goods and services in more than one country. As the rules regulating the movement of goods and investment have been relaxed in recent decades, TNCs have extended their global reach. As the growth of FDI has expanded, the sources and destinations of that investment have become more and more diverse. FDI is not dominated by flows from core to periphery in the same way that it was even 20 years ago.

Investment flows from NICs such as South Korea, Taiwan, China, India and Brazil have increased markedly. The investment flow network is more complex today than it has ever been.

There are now few parts of the world where the direct or indirect influence of TNCs is not important. In some countries and regions their influence on the economy is huge. Apart from their direct ownership of productive activities, many TNCs are involved in a web of collaborative relationships with other companies across the globe. Such relationships have become more and more important as competition has become increasingly global in its extent.

TNCs have a substantial influence on the global economy in general, and in the countries in which they choose to locate in particular. They play a major role in world trade in terms of what and where they buy and sell. A not inconsiderable proportion of world trade is intra-firm – that is, taking place within TNCs. The organisation of the car giants exemplifies intra-firm trade with engines, gearboxes and other key components produced in one country and exported for assembly elsewhere. Table 4.7 shows the world's largest TNCs by revenue, according to Global 500 published by Fortune in July 2009. The list is led by Royal Dutch Shell, Exxon Mobil and Wal-Mart Stores. All three companies recorded revenue in excess of $400 billion. Exxon Mobil recorded the largest profit of any company in the world at $45 billion. However, it should be noted that 7 of the top 24 corporations actually made a loss.

Table 4.7 The world's 24 largest corporations

Rank	Company	Revenues ($ million)	Profits ($ million)
1	Royal Dutch Shell	458 361	26 277
2	Exxon Mobil	442 851	45 220
3	Wal-Mart Stores	405 607	13 400
4	BP	367 053	21 157
5	Chevron	263 159	23 931
6	Total	234 674	15 500
7	ConocoPhillips	230 764	–16 998
8	ING Group	226 577	–1 067
9	Sinopec	207 814	1 961
10	Toyota Motor	204 352	–4 349
11	Japan Post Holdings	198 700	4 208
12	General Electric	183 207	17 410
13	China National Petroleum	181 123	10 271
14	Volkswagen	166 579	6 957
15	State Grid	164 136	664
16	Dexia Group	161 269	–4 868
17	ENI	159 348	12 917
18	General Motors	148 979	–30 860
19	Ford Motor	146 277	–14 672
20	Allianz	142 395	–3 577
21	HSBC Holdings	142 049	5 728
22	Gazprom	141 455	29 864
23	Daimler	140 328	1 973
24	BNP Paribas	136 096	4.422

Source: http://money.cnn.com

Figure 4.26 The financial district, Chicago

economies to full members of the capitalist global economy. In 2008, FDI inflows into developing and transitional economies reached record levels, accounting for 37 per cent and 7 per cent respectively of global FDI.

FDI flows increased to structurally weak economies in 2008, by 29 per cent to least developed countries, by 54 per cent to landlocked developing countries and by 32 per cent to small island developing states. This has been a very welcome trend, but there are concerns that the global financial crisis will wipe out the benefits gained from this trend.

Figure 4.28 shows the shares of the three major groups of economies in global FDI inflows for the period 1990–2008. The developed economies recorded the highest share for the entire period but the gap has been narrowing. Three distinct periods of convergence can be recognised on Figure 4.28. In 1990, the developed economies accounted for over 80 per cent of global FDI inflows. By 2008, this had fallen below 60 per cent. The developing economies accounted for only about 16 per cent of global FDI inflows in 1990, but have got up to or close to 40 per cent during the three periods of convergence. The share of the transition economies was extremely low until the new millennium, but it is now rising at a significant rate.

Capital flow can help LEDCs with economic development by furnishing them with necessary capital and technology. However, capital flow from MEDCs to LEDCs has been skewed, with some countries far more favoured than others. Most Sub-Saharan African countries, which urgently needed foreign capital for economic betterment, have been largely excluded from globalised investment in the past, although there is evidence that this is beginning to change. While controlling for other social and economic factors, democratised LEDCs appear to attract more foreign capital than undemocratic countries because their democratic institutions can provide secure and profitable environments for investment with protection of property rights and social spending on human capital.

According to the *World Investment Report 2009*, there are 82 000 TNCs worldwide, with 810 000 foreign affiliates. The 100 largest TNCs represent a significant proportion of total global production. Over the three years from 2006 to 2008, they accounted for, on average, 9 per cent of estimated foreign assets, 16 per cent of sales and 11 per cent of employment of all TNCs. Their combined value-added accounted for about 4 per cent of global GDP.

Global FDI inflows reached a historic high of $1979 billion in 2007 (Figure 4.27), although this declined by 14 per cent in 2008 with the onset of the global financial crisis. The crisis has changed the geography of investment, with the share of developing and 'transition economies' in global FDI flows rising sharply to 43 per cent in 2008. The transition economies are those in south-east Europe and the Commonwealth of Independent States (CIS). They have been given the term 'transition economies' by the *World Investment Report* to recognise that they are still in the process of change from centrally planned communist

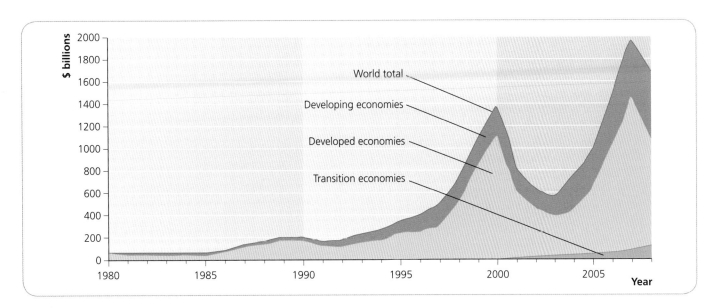

Figure 4.27 FDI inflows, global and by groups of economies, 1980–2008

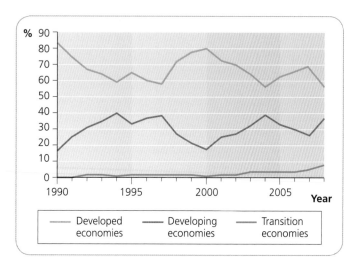

Figure 4.28 Shares of the three major groups of economies in global FDI inflows, 1990–2008

Figure 4.29 Japanese investment in the UK: Suzuki in Crawley

The development of TNCs over time

Figure 4.30 shows the main stages in the historical evolution of TNCs. Although the first companies to produce outside their home nation did not emerge until the latter half of the nineteenth century, by 1914 US, British and mainland European firms were involved in substantial overseas manufacturing production. Prior to the First World War, the UK was the major source of overseas investment, the pattern of which was firmly based on its empire. Between the wars TNC manufacturing investment, particularly American, increased substantially. By 1939 the USA had become the main source of foreign investment in manufacturing. The USA was to become even more powerful in the global economy after the Second World War, for it was the only industrial power to emerge from the conflict stronger rather than weaker.

However, the USA does not dominate the global economy today in the way it did in the immediate post-war period. The reconstruction of the Japanese and German economies resulted in both countries playing a significant transnational role by the 1970s, which was to expand considerably in the following

Figure 4.30 Stages in the evolution of TNCs

Period	Type	Characteristics
1500–1800	Mercantile capitalism and colonialism	Government-backed chartered companies
1800–75	Entrepreneurial and financial capitalism	Early development of supplier and consumer markets Infrastructural investment by financial houses
1875–1945	International capitalism	Rapid growth of market-seeking and resource-based investments
1945–60	Transnational capitalism	FDI dominated by USA TNCs expand in size
1960–present	Globalisation capitalism	Expansion of European and Japanese FDI Growth of inter-firm alliances, joint ventures and outsourcing

decades. In fact the large Japanese TNCs were to become models for their international competitors as they revolutionised business organisation. Other MEDCs such as the UK, France, Italy, the Netherlands, Switzerland, Sweden and Canada also played significant roles in the geographical spread of FDI. More recently, NICs such as South Korea and Taiwan have expanded their corporate reach, not just to lower wage economies but also into MEDCs. Figure 4.31 illustrates the sequential development of a transnational corporation, which begins with operation in the domestic market only. Large companies often reach the stage when they want to produce outside of their home country and take the decision to become transnational. The benefits of such a move include:
- using cheaper labour, particularly in LEDCs
- exploiting new resource locations

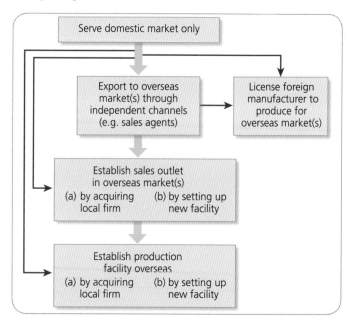

Figure 4.31 Sequential development of a transnational corporation

- circumventing trade barriers
- tapping market potential in other world regions
- avoiding strict domestic environmental regulations
- maximising exchange rate advantages.

Contrasting spatial and organisational structures

TNCs vary widely in overall size and international scope. Variations include:

- the number of countries
- the number of subsidiaries
- the share of production accounted for by foreign activities
- the degree to which ownership and management are internationalised
- the division of research activities and routine tasks by country
- the balance of advantages and disadvantages to the countries in which they operate.

Large TNCs often exhibit three organisational levels: headquarters, research and development, and branch plants. The headquarters of a TNC will generally be in the MEDC city where the company was established. Research and development is most likely to be located here too, or in other areas within this country. It is the branch plants that are the first to be located overseas. However, some of the largest and most successful TNCs have divided their industrial empires into world regions, each with research and development facilities and a high level of independent decision making. Figure 4.32 shows the locational changes that tend to occur as TNCs develop over time.

Figure 4.33 shows four simplified models which illustrate major ways of organising the geography of TNC production units. Toyota and the other global car manufacturers are closest to model (c), a system often referred to as a horizontal organisational structure. In contrast, Nike is a good example of model (d), illustrating a vertical organisational structure. However, Nike is not integrated

in the traditional sense – it does not own the various stages of production because it subcontracts the manufacturing stages of its product range.

a Globally concentrated production

All production at a single location. Products are exported to world markets.

b Host-market production

Each production unit produces a range of products and serves the national market in which it is located. No sales across national boundaries. Individual plant size limited by the size of the national market

c Product specialisation for a global or regional market

Each production unit produces only one product for sale throughout a regional market of several countries. Individual plant size very large because of scale economies offered by the large regional market.

d Transnational vertical integration

Each production unit performs a separate part of a production sequence. Units are linked across national boundaries in a 'chain-like' sequence – the output of one plant is the input of the next plant

Each production unit performs a separate operation in a production process and ships its output to a final assembly plant in another country.

Figure 4.33 Ways of organising TNC production units

Figure 4.32 The development of TNCs – locational changes

① Export-led development

② Overseas location of branch plants

③ Shift of R&D and HQ functions

④ Rationalisation

Increasing globalisation

Age
Number of plants/facilities
Time

Activities concentrated in home country where labour and sourcing are established. However, exports may be subject to tariffs and other restrictions

Incentives include cheaper labour, access to markets, and financial assistance from host governments

New locations become semi-autonomous as products are more carefully tailored to new markets

Increasing competition or recession necessitates concentrating activities in the best locations

Source: *Advanced Geography: Concepts & Cases* by P. Guinness & G. Nagle (Hodder Education, 1999), p.167

Nike is the world's leading supplier of sports footwear, apparel and equipment, and one of the best-known global brands. It was founded in 1972 and the company went public in 1980. The company is an example of a vertical organisational structure across international boundaries, characterised by a high level of subcontracting activity. Nike does not make any shoes or clothes itself, but contracts out production to South Korean and Taiwanese companies. Nike employs 650 000 contract workers in 700 factories worldwide. The company list includes 124 plants in China, 73 in Thailand, 35 in South Korea and 34 in Vietnam. More than 75 per cent of the workforce is based in Asia. The majority of workers are women under the age of 25.

The subcontracted companies operate not only in their home countries but also in lower-wage Asian economies such as Vietnam, the Philippines and Indonesia. One hundred and fifty Asian factories employing 350 000 workers manufacture products for Nike. The company has a reputation for searching out cheap pools of labour. Nike's expertise is in design and marketing. Figure 4.34 shows Nike's 'commodity circuit'. It is a clear example of the New International Division of Labour (NIDL).

Nike illustrates both 'Fordist' and 'Flexible' characteristics. An example of its Fordist nature is the Air Max Penney basketball shoes consisting of 52 component parts from five different countries. The shoes pass through 120 people during production, on a clearly demarcated global production chain.

However, Nike also exhibits Flexible characteristics. The company aims to produce new shoes on a regular basis to cater for niche markets. To achieve this objective it utilises a just-in-time innovation structure, buying in necessary expertise at short notice. This involves short-term subcontracts, often allocated to firms based close to Nike's research and development headquarters near Beaverton in the state of Oregon, USA.

Section 4.2 Activities

1 Define **a** *transnational corporations* and **b** *foreign direct investment*.

2 Write a 100-word report on the information in Table 4.7.

3 Describe the FDI inflow trends shown in Figure 4.27.

4 Comment on the trends shown in Figure 4.28.

5 Describe and explain the development of TNCs over time.

6 Comment on the different forms of TNC organisation shown in Figure 4.33.

7 Produce a brief bullet-point summary of the Nike case study.

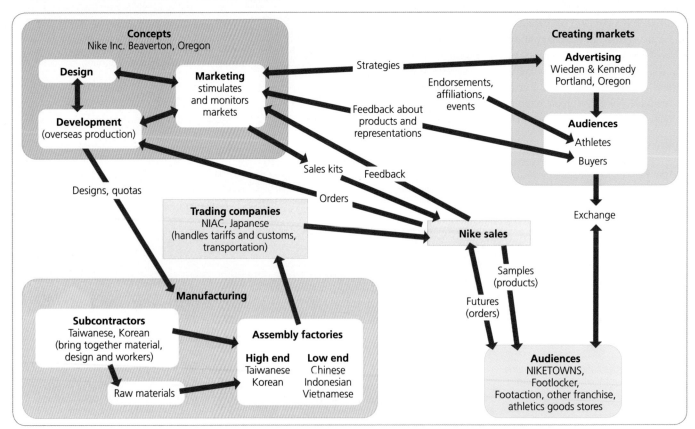

Figure 4.34 Nike's commodity circuit

The emergence and growth of NICs

In Asia, four generations of NIC can be recognised in terms of the timing of industrial development and their current economic characteristics. Within this region, only Japan is at a higher economic level than the NICs (Table 4.8) but there are a number of countries at much lower levels of economic development. The latter group are the least developed countries in the region.

Table 4.8 NICs and their level of development

Level	Countries	GNP per capita 2005 ($)
1	Japan: an MEDC	38 984
2	First generation NICs, e.g. Taiwan	16 764
3	Second generation NICs, e.g. Malaysia	4 963
4	Third generation NICs, e.g. China	1 735
5	Fourth generation NICs, e.g. Vietnam	623
6	Least developed countries, e.g. Mongolia	380

Nowhere else in the world is the filter-down concept of industrial location better illustrated. When Japanese companies first decided to locate abroad in the quest for cheap labour, they looked to the most developed of their neighbouring counties, particularly South Korea and Taiwan. Most other countries in the region lacked the physical infrastructure and skills levels required by Japanese companies. Companies from elsewhere in MEDCs, especially the USA, also recognised the advantages of locating branch plants in such countries. As the economies of the first generation NICs developed, the level of wages increased resulting in:

- Japanese and Western TNCs seeking locations in second generation NICs where improvements in physical and human infrastructures now satisfied their demands but where wages were still low
- indigenous companies from the first generation NICs also moving routine tasks to their cheaper-labour neighbours such as Malaysia and Thailand.

With time, the process also included the third generation NICs, a significant factor in the recent very high growth rates in China and India. The least developed countries in the region, nearly all hindered by conflict of one sort or another at some time in recent decades, are now beginning to be drawn into the system. The recent high level of FDI into Vietnam makes it reasonable to think of the country as an example of a fourth generation Asian NIC.

First generation NICs

What were the reasons for the phenomenal rates of economic growth recorded in South Korea, Taiwan, Kong Hong and Singapore from the 1960s? What was it that set this group of 'Asian tigers' apart from so many others? From the vast literature that has appeared on the subject the following factors are usually given prominence:

- A good initial level of hard and soft infrastructure provided the preconditions for structural economic change.

- As in Japan previously, the land-poor NICs stressed people as their greatest resource, particularly through the expansion of primary and secondary education but also through specialised programmes to develop scientific, engineering and technical skills.
- These countries have cultural traditions that revere education and achievement.
- The Asian NICs became globally integrated at a 'moment of opportunity' in the structure of the world system, distinguished by the geostrategic and economic interests of core capitalist countries (especially the USA and Japan) in extending their influence in East and South East Asia.
- All four countries had distinct advantages in terms of geographical location. Singapore is strategically situated to funnel trade flows between the Indian and Pacific Oceans, and its central location in the region has facilitated its development as a major financial, commercial and administrative/managerial centre. Hong Kong has benefited from its position astride the trade routes between north-east and south-east Asia, as well as acting as the main link to the outside world for south-east China. South Korea and Taiwan were ideally located to expand trade and other ties with Japan.
- The ready availability of bank loans, often extended at government behest and at attractive interest rates, allowed South Korea's *chaebol* in particular to pursue market share and to expand into new fields.

As their industrialisation processes have matured, the NICs have occupied a more intermediate position in the regional division of labour between Japan and other less developed Asian countries.

Deindustrialisation

In the USA and the UK the proportion of workers employed in manufacturing has fallen from around 40 per cent at the beginning of the twentieth century to less than half that now. Even in Japan and Germany, where so much industry was rebuilt after 1945, manufacturing's share of total employment has dropped below 25 per cent. Not a single MEDC has bucked this trend, known as **deindustrialisation**. The causal factors of deindustrialisation are:

- technological change enabling manufacturing to become more capital-intensive and more mobile
- the filter-down of manufacturing industry from MEDCs to lower wage economies, such as those of South East Asia
- the increasing importance of the service sector in the MEDCs.

There can be little surprise in the decline of manufacturing employment, for it has mirrored the previous decline in employment in agriculture in MEDCs. So if the decline of manufacturing in MEDCs is part of an expected cycle, the consequence of technological improvement and rising affluence, why is so much concern expressed about this trend? The main reasons would appear to be:

- The traditional industries of the Industrial Revolution were highly concentrated, so the impact of manufacturing decline has had severe implications in terms of unemployment and other social pathologies in a number of regions.

451

- The rapid pace of contraction of manufacturing has often made adjustment difficult.
- There are defence concerns if the production of some industries falls below a certain level.
- Some economists argue that over-reliance on services makes an economy unnecessarily vulnerable.
- Rather than being a smooth transition, manufacturing decline tends to concentrate during periods of economic recession.

The filter-down process of industrial relocation

The filter-down process, detailed by W.R. Thompson and others, operates at both global and national scales. Economic core regions have long been vulnerable to the migration of labour-intensive manufacturing to lower-wage areas of the periphery, as exemplified in the USA by the historical drift of the textile and shoe industries from New England, and apparel manufacture from New York, to North and South Carolina. The filter-down process is based on the notion that corporate organisations respond to changing critical input requirements by altering the geographical location of production to minimise costs and thereby ensure competitiveness in a tightening market.

The economic core (at national and global levels) has monopolised invention and innovation, and has thus continually benefited from the rapid growth rates characteristic of the early stages of an industry's life cycle (the product life cycle), one of exploitation of a new market. Production is likely to occur where the firm's main plants and corporate headquarters are located. Figure 4.35, illustrating the **product life cycle**, indicates that in the early phase scientific-engineering skills at a high level and external economies are the prime location factors.

In the growth phase, methods of mass production are gradually introduced and the number of firms involved in production generally expands as product information spreads. In this stage, management skills are the critical human inputs. Production technology tends to stabilise in the mature phase. Capital investment remains high and the availability of unskilled and semiskilled labour becomes a major locating factor. As the industry matures into a replacement market, the production process becomes rationalised and often routine. The high wages of the innovating area, quite consistent with the high-level skills required in the formative stages of the learning process, become excessive when the skill requirements decline and the industry, or a section of it, 'filters-down' to smaller, less industrially sophisticated areas where cheaper labour is available, but which can now handle the lower skills required in the manufacture of the product.

On a global scale, large transnational companies have increasingly operated in this way by moving routine operations to LEDCs since the 1950s. However, the role of indigenous companies in developing countries should not be ignored. Important examples are the *chaebols* of South Korea, such as Samsung and Hyundai, and Taiwanese firms such as Acer. Here the process of filter-down has come about by direct competition from LEDCs rather than from

the corporate strategy of huge North American, European and Japanese transnationals.

It has been the revolution in transport and communications that made such substantial filter-down of manufacturing to LEDCs possible. Containerisation and the general increase in the scale of shipping have cut the cost of the overseas distribution of goods substantially, while advances in telecommunications have made global management a reality. In some cases whole industries have virtually migrated, as shipbuilding did from Europe to Asia in the 1970s. In others the most specialised work is done in MEDCs by skilled workers, and the simpler tasks elsewhere in the global supply chain.

Although the theory of the product life cycle was developed in the discipline of business studies to explain how the sales of individual products evolve, it can usefully be applied at higher

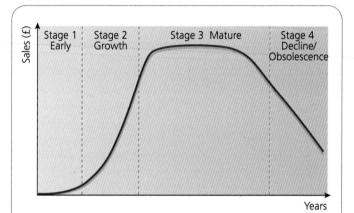

Requirements	Product–Cycle Phase		
	Early	Growth	Mature
Management	2	1	3
Scientific-engineering know-how	1	2	3
Unskilled and semi-skilled labour	3	2	1
External economies	1	2	3
Capital	3	1a	1a

Source: Based on Oakey 1984 and Erickson & Leinbach 1979

Figure 4.35 The product life cycle

scales. A firm with a range of ten products, half in stage 3 and half in stage 4, would have no long-term future. A healthy multi-product firm will have a strong research and development (R&D) department ensuring a steady movement of successful products onto the market to give a positive distribution across the four stages of the model. Likewise, the industry mix of a region or a country can be plotted on the product life cycle diagram. Regions with significant socio-economic problems are invariably over-represented in stages 3 and 4. In contrast, regions with dynamic economies will have a more even spread across the model, with particularly good representation in the first two stages.

Figure 4.36 summarises the positive and negative effects of globalisation on (a) MEDCs and (b) NICs and LEDCs, including the impact of deindustrialisation on more affluent countries. Economists have recognised two types of deindustrialisation: positive and negative:

- Positive deindustrialisation occurs when the share of employment in manufacturing falls because of rapid productivity growth but where displaced labour is absorbed into the non-manufacturing sector. In such a situation the economy is at or near full-employment and GDP per capita is rising steadily.

- Negative deindustrialisation results from a decline in the share of manufacturing in total employment, owing to a slow growth or decline in demand for manufacturing output, and where displaced labour results in unemployment.

Unfortunately in the UK and many other MEDCs the deindustrialisation experienced has been predominantly of the negative kind. Regional development policies in the UK and other countries have tried to address these problems with varying degrees of success.

Section 4.2 Activities

1 Describe and explain the information shown in Table 4.8.

2 Discuss the reasons for the development of the first generation of TNCs.

3 With reference to Figure 4.35, explain the product life cycle.

4 Examine the connection between industrial growth in NICs and some LEDCs, and deindustrialisation in MEDCs.

5 With reference to Figure 4.36, discuss the positive effects of deindustrialisation in MEDCs.

	Positive	Negative
In MEDCs	• Cheaper imports of all relatively labour-intensive products can keep cost of living down and lead to a buoyant retailing sector. • Greater efficiency apparent in surviving outlets. This can release labour for higher productivity sectors (this assumes low unemployment). • Growth in LEDCs may lead to a demand for exports from MEDCs. • Promotion of labour market flexibility and efficiency, greater worker mobility to area with relative scarcities of labour should be good for the country. • Greater industrial efficiency should lead to development of new technologies, promotion of entrepreneurship and should attract foreign investment. • Loss of industries can lead to improved environmental quality (e.g. Consett).	• Rising job exports leads to inevitable job losses. Competition-driven changes in technology add to this. • Job losses are often of unskilled workers. • Big gaps develop between skilled and unskilled workers who may experience extreme redeployment differences. • Employment gains from new efficiencies will only occur if industrialised countries can keep their wage demands down. • Job losses are invariably concentrated in certain areas and certain industries. This can lead to deindustrialisation and structural unemployment in certain regions. • Branch plants are particularly vulnerable as in times of economic recession they are the first to close, often with large numbers of job losses.
In NICs and LEDCs	• Higher export-generated income promotes export-led growth – thus promotes investment in productive capacity. Potentially leads to a multiplier effect on national economy. • Can trickle down to local areas with many new highly paid jobs. • Can reduce negative trade balances. • Can lead to exposure to new technology, improvement of skills and labour productivity. • Employment growth in relatively labour-intensive manufacturing spreads wealth, and does redress global injustice (development gap).	• Unlikely to decrease inequality – as jobs tend to be concentrated in core region of urban areas. May promote in-migration. • Disruptive social impacts, e.g. role of TNCs potentially exploitative and may lead to sweatshops. Also branch plants may move on in LEDCs too, leading to instability (e.g. in Philippines). • Can lead to overdependence on a narrow economic base. • Can destabilise food supplies, as people give up agriculture. • Environmental issues associated with over-rapid industrialisation. • Health and safety issues because of tax legislation.

Source: Sue Wam, 'The Global Shift', *Geo Factsheet*, Curriculum Press

Figure 4.36 The positive and negative impacts of global shift

4.3 Regional development

The extent of income disparities within countries

The scale of disparities within countries is often as much an issue as the considerable variations between countries (Figure 4.37). The **Gini coefficient** is a technique frequently used to show the extent of income inequality. It allows:

- analysis of changes in income inequality over time in individual countries
- comparison between countries.

Figure 4.38 shows global variations in the Gini coefficient for 2007/08. It is defined as a ratio with values between 0 and 1.0. A low value indicates a more equal income distribution while a high value shows more unequal income distribution. A Gini coefficient of 0 would mean that everyone in a country had exactly the same income (perfect equality). At the other extreme a Gini coefficient of 1 would mean that one person had all the income in a country (perfect inequality). Figure 4.38 shows that in general more affluent countries have a lower income gap than lower-income countries. In 2007/08 the global gap ranged from 0.232 in Denmark to 0.707 in Namibia.

Figure 4.39 shows income disparity within a number of countries over a period of more than four decades. In countries like France and Mexico there has been a clear decline in income

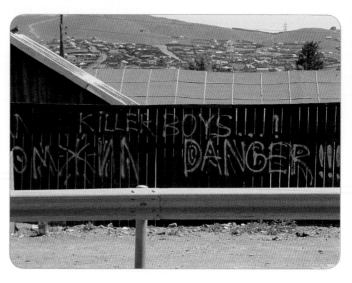

Figure 4.37 Graffiti on a fence in a lower-income part of Ulaanbaatar, Mongolia

inequality whereas China and Brazil show a significant increase. The abrupt changes that have occurred from time to time for some countries are often related to economic recessions which generally have the greatest impact on people on low incomes.

The Lorenz curve is a graphical technique that shows the degree of inequality between two variables. It is often used to show the extent of income inequality in a population. The diagonal line represents perfect equality in income distribution. The further the curve is away from the diagonal line the greater the degree of income inequality. Thus in Figure 4.40 income inequality in Brazil was less in 2005 than in 1996. However, the significant gap between the 2005 curve and the diagonal line indicates that income inequality in Brazil remains very substantial indeed.

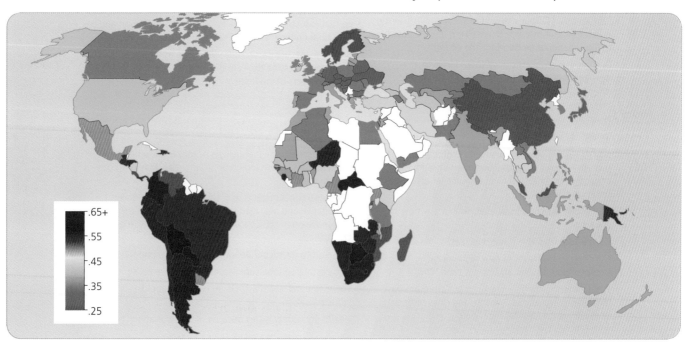

Figure 4.38 Worldwide variations in the Gini coefficient, 2007/08

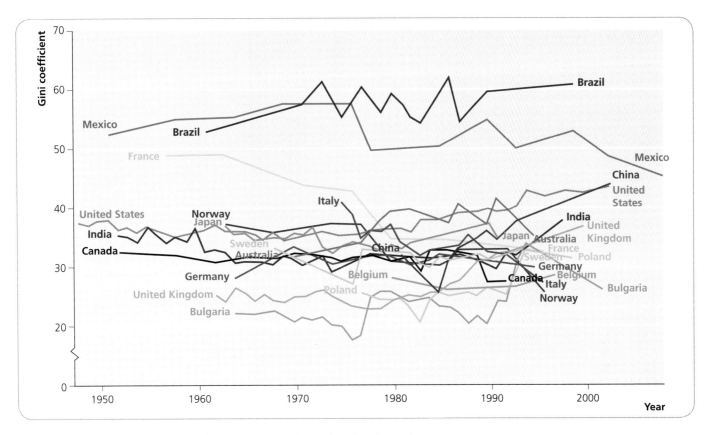

Figure 4.39 Gini index – income disparity since the Second World War for selected countries

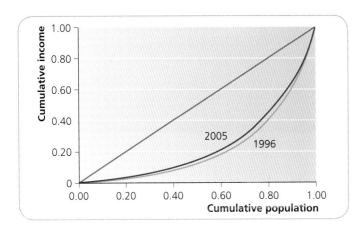

Figure 4.40 Lorenz curve for Brazil

A report published in October 2008 entitled 'Growing Unequal? Income Distribution and Poverty in OECD (Organisation for Economic Cooperation and Development) Countries' found that:

- the gap between rich and poor has grown in more than three-quarters of OECD countries over the past two decades
- the economic growth of recent decades has benefited the rich more than the poor; in some countries, such as Canada, Finland, Germany, Italy, Norway and the USA, the gap also increased between the rich and the middle class
- countries with a wide distribution of income tend to have more widespread income poverty
- social mobility is lower in countries with high inequality,

such as Italy, the UK and the USA, and higher in the Nordic countries where income is distributed more evenly.

Disparities within countries are rarely uniform throughout countries and thus a significant regional component usually exists. In China, the income gap between urban residents and the huge farm population reached its widest level ever in 2008 as rural unemployment in particular rose steeply. The ratio between more affluent urban dwellers and their rural counterparts reached 3.36 to 1, up from 3.33 to 1 in 2007. This substantial income gap is a very sensitive issue in China as more and more rural people feel they have been left behind in China's economic boom. The size of the income gap is not just a political problem, it is also causing considerable national economic concern. Falling purchasing power in rural areas is hindering efforts to boost domestic consumer spending. The government wants to do this to help compensate for declining exports caused by the global recession.

Section 4.3 Activities

1 What is the *Gini coefficient*?

2 Describe the global variation in the Gini coefficient shown in Figure 4.38.

3 How has the Gini coefficient varied over time for the countries shown in Figure 4.39?

4 What does the Lorenz curve in Figure 4.40 show?

5 Comment on the findings of the 2008 OECD report.

Theory of regional disparities

The Swedish economist Gunnar Myrdal produced his **cumulative causation** theory in 1957. Figure 4.41 is a simplified version of the model Myrdal produced. Cumulative causation theory was set in the context of LEDCs but the theory can also be applied reasonably to more advanced nations. According to Myrdal a three-stage sequence can be recognised:

- the pre-industrial stage when regional differences are minimal
- a period of rapid economic growth characterised by increasing regional economic divergence
- a stage of regional economic convergence when the significant wealth generated in the most affluent region(s) spreads to other parts of the country.

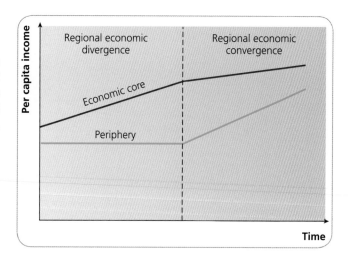

Figure 4.42 Regional economic divergence and convergence

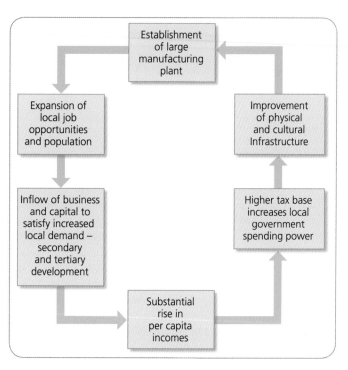

Figure 4.41 Simplified model of cumulative causation

Figure 4.42 shows how the regional economic divergence of the earlier stages of economic development can eventually change to regional economic convergence.

In Myrdal's model, economic growth begins with the location of new manufacturing industry in a region with a combination of advantages greater than elsewhere in the country. Once growth has been initiated in a dominant region, spatial flows of labour, capital and raw materials develop to support it and the growth region undergoes further expansion by the cumulative causation process. A detrimental 'backwash effect' is transmitted to the less developed regions as skilled labour and locally generated capital is attracted away. Manufactured goods and services produced and operating under the scale economies of the economic 'heartland' flood the market of the relatively underdeveloped 'hinterland', undercutting smaller-scale enterprises in such areas (Figure 4.43).

Figure 4.43 A village in eastern Siberia – the standard of living in most parts of Asiatic Russia (the periphery) is lower than in European Russia

However, increasing demand for raw materials from resource-rich parts of the hinterland may stimulate growth in other sectors of the economy of such regions. If the impact is strong enough to overcome local backwash effects, a process of cumulative causation may begin leading to the development of new centres of self-sustained economic growth. Such 'spread effects' are spatially selective and will only benefit those parts of the hinterland with valuable raw materials or other significant advantages.

The American economist Hirschman (1958) produced similar conclusions to Myrdal although he adopted a different terminology. Hirschman labelled the growth of the **economic core region** (heartland) as 'polarisation', which benefited from 'virtuous circles' or upward spirals of development, whereas the **periphery** (hinterland) was impeded by 'vicious circles' or downward spirals. The term 'trickle-down' was used to describe the spread of growth from core to periphery. The major difference between Myrdal and Hirschman was that the latter stressed to a far greater extent the effect of counterbalancing forces overcoming polarisation (backwash), eventually leading to economic equilibrium being established. The subsequent literature has favoured the terms *core* and *periphery* rather than Myrdal's alternatives.

Section 4.3 Activities

1 Suggest reasons why income disparities are narrowing in some countries but getting wider in others.

2 Define the terms **a** *economic core region* and **b** *periphery*.

3 Explain in your own words the process shown in Figure 4.41.

4 Describe and explain the trends shown in Figure 4.42.

5 What is the evidence in Figure 4.43 that this region is part of the economic periphery of Russia?

Factors affecting internal disparities
Residence

Where people are born and where they live can have a significant impact on their quality of life (Figure 4.44). The focus of such study has been mainly on:

- regional differences within countries
- urban/rural disparities
- intra-urban contrasts.

Figure 4.44 Manholes in Ulaanbaatar, Mongolia. People in poverty sometimes live down these manholes because they provide access to the underground hot-water pipes that can provide warmth in the harsh winters.

Case Study
Regional contrasts in Brazil

South East Brazil (Figure 4.45) is the economic core region of Brazil. Over time the South East region has benefited from spatial flows of raw materials, capital and labour (Figure 4.46a). Capital and labour have come from abroad as well as from internal sources. The region grew rapidly through the process of cumulative causation. This process not only resulted in significant economic growth in the core, but also had a considerable negative impact on the periphery. The overall result was widening regional disparity. However, more recently some parts of the periphery, with a combination of advantages above the level of the periphery as a whole, have benefited from spread effects (trickle-down) emanating from the core (Figure 4.46b). Such spread effects are spatially selective and may be the result of either market forces or regional economic policy or, as is often the case, a combination of the two. The South region has been the most important recipient of spread effects from the South East, but the other regions have also benefited to an extent. This process has caused the regional gap to narrow at times, but often not for very long (Figure 4.39). However, in Brazil income inequality still remains very wide.

Figure 4.45 South East Brazil

Table 4.9 The population of Brazil's five regions, Census 2000 (millions)

South East	72.4
North East	47.7
South	25.1
North	12.9
Centre West	11.6

The South East's primary, secondary, tertiary and quaternary industries generate large amounts of money for Brazil. The natural environment of the South East provided the region with a number of advantages for the development of primary industries:

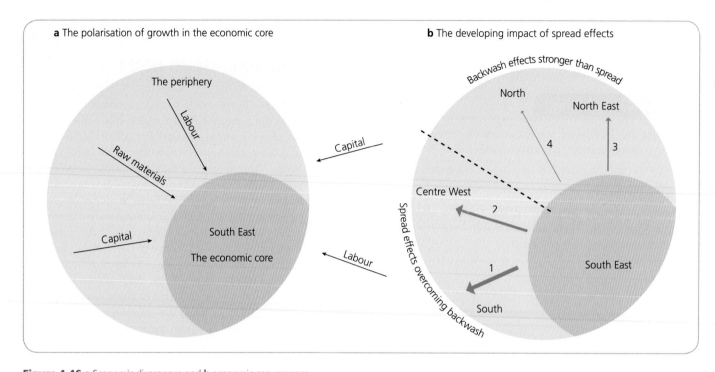

a The polarisation of growth in the economic core

The periphery

Labour

Raw materials

Capital

Capital

South East

The economic core

Labour

b The developing impact of spread effects

Backwash effects stronger than spread

North

North East

4

3

Centre West

2

Spread effects overcoming backwash

1

South East

South

Figure 4.46 a Economic divergence and **b** economic convergence

- The warm temperature, adequate rainfall and rich terra rossa soils (weathered from lava) have provided many opportunities for farming. The region is important for coffee, beef, rice, cacao, sugar cane and fruit.
- Large deposits of iron ore, manganese and bauxite have made mining a significant industry. Gold is still mined.
- The region is energy-rich, with large deposits of oil and gas offshore. Hydro-electric power is generated from large rivers flowing over steep slopes.
- The temperate rainforest provides the raw material for forestry.
- Fishing is important for many of the coastal settlements.

The South East is the centre of both foreign and domestic investment in manufacturing industry. In the 1950s and 1960s the government wanted Brazil to become an NIC. Because the South East had the best potential of all Brazil's five regions, investment was concentrated here. The region is the focus of the country's road and rail networks. It has the country's main airports and seaports. It also has a significant pipeline network for oil and gas. More TNCs are located in the South East than in the rest of Brazil. With the highest population density in Brazil, the labour supply is plentiful. The region also has the highest educational and skill levels in the country (Table 4.9).

The car industry is a major activity in the region. Most of the world's large car makers are here, including Ford, GM, Toyota, VW and Fiat. Other manufacturing industries include food processing, textiles, furniture, clothing, printing, brewing and shoemaking. The raw materials located in the region and the large market have provided favourable conditions for many of these industries. However, cheaper imports of shoes, clothes and textiles from Asia have led to a number of companies in the region closing.

São Paulo is by far the largest financial centre in South America. The headquarters of most Brazilian banks are in São Paulo. Most major foreign banks are also located there. This is not surprising as Brazil dominates the economy of South America and São Paulo is the largest city in South America. The South East is the centre of research and development in both the public and private sectors. Eighty km from São Paulo is São Jose dos Campos, where

+20 000
+15 000
+10 000
+5000
+1000

Figure 4.47 Brazilian states by GDP per capita (Brazilian reais), 2007

the Aerospace Technical Centre is located. It conducts teaching, research and development in aviation and outer space studies. Many people would be surprised to know that aircraft and aircraft parts make up Brazil's largest export category.

The success of the first large wave of investment by foreign TNCs in the South East encouraged other TNCs to follow suit. For the past 50 years the South East has experienced an upward cycle of growth (cumulative causation).

Figure 4.47 shows variations in GDP per capita by state in 2007. The highest figure of 40 696 reals (RS) was recorded in the Federal District, followed by São Paulo (RS22 667) and Rio de Janeiro (RS19 245). The lowest figures were in Alagoas (RS5858), Maranhao (RS5165) and Piaui (RS4661).

Intra-urban variations: the growth of slums and urban poverty

Residence as a factor in inequality within countries can also be examined at a more detailed scale (Figures 4.48 and 4.49). The focus of such analysis has been on intra-urban variations and the large number of people living in slum housing. Thirty-two per cent of the world's urban population – almost 1 billion people – are housed in slums, with the great majority living in LEDCs. A **slum** is a heavily populated urban area characterised by substandard housing and squalor. However, virtually all large cities in MEDCs also have slum districts. The UN recognises that the focus of global poverty is moving from rural to urban areas, a process known as the '**urbanisation of poverty**'. Without significant global action, the number of slum dwellers will double over the next 30 years. The urban poor live in inner city slums, peripheral shanty towns and in almost every other conceivable space, such as on pavements, traffic roundabouts, under bridges, and in sewers.

The numbers of people living in urban poverty are increased by a combination of economic problems, growing inequality and population growth, particularly growth due to in-migration

Figure 4.48 Favela in São Paulo

Figure 4.49 The middle-income Jardins district of São Paulo

(Figure 4.50). As *The Challenge of Slums* (2003) states: 'Slums result from a combination of poverty or low incomes with inadequacies in the housing provision system, so that poorer people are forced to seek affordable accommodation and land that become increasingly inadequate.' The report identifies women, children, widows and female-headed households as the most vulnerable among the poor. In urban African slums, women head over 30 per cent of all households.

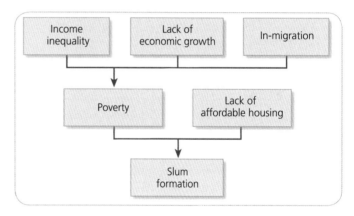

Figure 4.50 Diagram of slum formation

The Challenge of Slums groups the dimensions of urban poverty as follows:
- **Low income:** consisting of those who are unable to participate in labour markets and lack other means of support, and those whose wage income is so low that they are below a nominal poverty line.
- **Low human capital:** low education and poor health. Health 'shock' in particular can lead to chronic poverty.
- **Low social capital:** this involves a shortage of networks to protect households from shocks; weak patronage on the labour market; labelling and exclusion. This particularly applies to minority groups.
- **Low financial capital:** lack of productive assets that might be used to generate income or avoid paying major costs.

Figure 4.51 sums up the constituents of urban poverty. The

complexities of urban poverty indicate how difficult it is for individuals to improve their socio-economic situation. In many countries social mobility has become more difficult rather than easier in recent times.

- Inadequate income (and thus inadequate consumption of necessities including food and, often, safe and sufficient water; often problems of indebtedness, with debt payments significantly reducing income available for necessities).

- Inadequate, unstable or risky asset base (non-material and material including educational attainment and housing) for individuals, households or communities.

- Inadequate shelter (typically poor quality, overcrowded and insecure).

- Inadequate provision of 'public' infrastructure (e.g. piped water, sanitation, drainage, roads, footpaths) which increases the health burden and often the work burden.

- Inadequate provision for basic services such as daycare/schools/vocational training, healthcare, emergency services, public transport, communications, law enforcement.

- Limited or no safety net to ensure basic consumption can be maintained when income falls; also to ensure access to shelter and healthcare when these can no longer be paid for.

- Inadequate protection of poorer groups' rights through the operation of the law, including laws and regulations regarding civil and political rights, occupational health and safety, pollution control, environmental health, protection from violence and other crimes, protection from discrimination and exploitation.

- Voicelessness and powerlessness within political systems and bureaucratic structures, leading to little or no possibility of receiving entitlements.

Source: Paul Guinness, 'Slum Housing Global Patterns Case Studies' *Geo FactSheet* No 180, Curriculum Press

Figure 4.51 The constituents of urban poverty

Section 4.3 Activities

1 Explain the processes illustrated in Figure 4.46.

2 Produce a graph to illustrate the regional breakdown of Brazil's population (Table 4.9).

3 Examine the factors that lead to the formation of slums in developing countries (Figure 4.50).

4 Compare Figures 4.48 and 4.49, which show different residential districts in São Paulo.

5 Discuss the constituents of urban poverty shown in Figure 4.51.

Ethnicity and employment

The development gap often has an ethnic and/or religious dimension whereby some ethnic groups in a population have income levels significantly below the dominant group(s) in the same population. This is often the case with **indigenous populations**. It is invariably the result of discrimination, which limits the economic, social and political opportunities available to the disadvantaged groups. Examples include South Africa (Table 4.10), Indonesia and Bolivia. Because of such obvious differences in status, tensions can arise between majority and minority groups resulting in:
- social unrest
- migration
- new political movements.

In South Africa the wide gap in income originated in the apartheid era, but since then it has proved extremely difficult to close for a variety of reasons. Political change often occurs well in advance of significant economic and social change. Table 4.10 shows the 2005 mean per capita income for the white population at 7646 Rand. In contrast the mean for the African population was only 775 Rand. The Asian population occupies an intermediate position with a 2005 figure of 2785 Rand.

Table 4.10 South Africa – per capita income differences (rand) by ethnic group, 2007

	1995	2000	2005
African: mean	615.36	575.64	775.46
African: median	333.23	278.46	406.95
Coloured: mean	935.65	1141.80	1384.95
Coloured: median	583.72	655.11	651.47
Asian: mean	2299.15	2021.84	2785.50
Asian: median	1596.02	1306.92	1583.09
White: mean	4436.18	5129.21	7645.56
White: median	3442.72	3544.50	5331.61
Total: mean	1101.48	1074.29	1514.81
Total: median	428.74	356.27	483.87

Source: *South African Development Indicators 2008*, p23

Inequality of wealth distribution is higher in Latin America than in any other part of the world. Indian and black people make up a third of the population, but have very limited parliamentary representation. Figure 4.52 shows the situation in five Latin American countries in 2005, prior to political transformation in Bolivia. The changes that have occurred in Bolivia have given hope to indigenous peoples elsewhere in Latin America. Such ethnic differences often have a strong regional component, as ethnic groups tend to concentrate in certain rural and urban areas.

Indians and blacks – poorly represented in parliament

In Ecuador, Guatemala and Peru, indigenous people make up 34–60 per cent of the population but have had few seats in parliament. Even in Bolivia the majority Indian population only has 26 per cent of seats – though its power to change government policy through mass protest has been growing, an alarming development for governments fearful of 'mob rule'. Part of the popular enthusiasm for Hugo Chávez – and the fear and loathing he inspires in traditional elites – arises from the fact that he is part Indian and part black, thus representing two of the most disadvantaged groups in Latin American history.

Country (ethnic group)	% of population	% representation in lower house
Bolivia (indigenous)	61	26
Ecuador (indigenous)	34	3
Guatemala	60	12
Peru (indigenous)	43	1
Brazil (African descent)	44	3

Figure 4.52 Indians and black people in South America – poorly represented in parliament

Education

Education is a key factor in explaining disparities within countries. Those with higher levels of education invariably gain better-paid employment. In LEDCs there is a clear link between education levels and family size, with those with the least education having the largest families. Maintaining a large family usually means that saving is impossible and varying levels of debt likely. In contrast, people with higher educational attainment have smaller families and are thus able to save and invest more for the future. Such differences serve to widen rather than narrow disparities. Educational provision can vary significantly not just by social class, but also by region.

Brazil has a greater disparity in income levels than most other countries. An important research study in the late 1990s concluded that the main cause was the huge variation in access to education. One of the authors of the study, Ricardo Paes de Barros, stated: 'There are not two Brazils. The poor and the rich live together in the same cities. They often work in the same multinational companies. The problem is that their educational background is absurdly unequal, and this results from the very poor quality of the public basic education system.' The report concluded that educational attainment explains 35–50 per cent of income inequality.

Figure 4.53 shows the population of secondary education or higher by region. The highest percentage is in the South East and the lowest in the North East. In the SAEB (Portuguese and mathematics) scores for students completing secondary education, the scores for 2005 had a regional ranking of:

1 South		**2** South East	
3 Centre West		**4** North East	
5 North.			

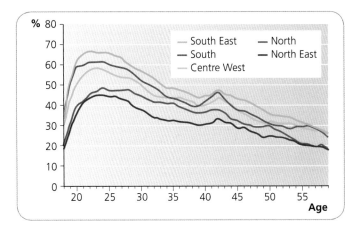

Figure 4.53 Percentage population of secondary education or higher in Brazil, by region

Land ownership (tenure)

The distribution of land ownership has had a major impact on disparities in many countries. It can have a significant regional component. The greatest disparities tend to occur alongside the largest inequities in land ownership. The ownership of even a very small plot of land provides a certain level of security that those in the countryside without land cannot possibly aspire to.

Case Study

Brazil: inequities in land ownership

The distribution of land in Brazil in terms of ownership has been a divisive issue since the colonial era. Then the monarchy rewarded those in special favour with huge tracts of land, leaving a legacy of highly concentrated ownership. For example, 44 per cent of all arable land in Brazil is owned by just 1 per cent of the nation's farmers (Figure 4.54), while 15 million peasants own little or no land. Many of these landless people are impoverished roving migrants who have lost their jobs as agricultural labourers due to the spread of mechanisation in virtually all types of agriculture.

Figure 4.54 Crop production in Brazil

461

BRAZIL: MARCHING FOR REAL LAND REFORM

By Fabiana Frayssinet

RESENDE, Brazil, Aug 12 (IPS) – After 10 years of waiting for secure title to the land they occupy and farm, 35 families in Resende, in the southeastern Brazilian state of Rio de Janeiro, have joined a huge march organized by the Landless Workers Movement (MST) in Brasilia to demand effective agrarian reform.

Mario Laurindo knows all about protest demonstrations. Some 14 years ago, he and others in the MST set up a roadside camp and were evicted. For the past 10 years he and his family have lived in the "Terra Libre" (Free Land) settlement, 176 kilometres from the city of Rio de Janeiro, the state capital.

"We may grow old in the attempt, but we will continue the struggle," Laurino told IPS. A long time ago, he left the 'favela' (shantytown) where he lived, because he had no job, food or health care, and wanted to escape the high levels of urban violence.

Now, at least, he has plenty of food. With his wife and two children – they had two more, but they died – the family produces enough to subsist on, from honey to bananas. They also keep chickens and a few dairy cows.

Like other families in the settlement, Laurindo sells his surplus produce at a nearby town where he goes every day, crossing a river on boats built by another neighbour. Barter with other settlers complements the family diet.

"I'll never work for someone else again. Now I'm my own boss," says Laurindo, who has taken up the way of life of a small farmer and ekes out the family income with odd jobs such as bricklaying, but always on a self-employed basis, he stresses.

Like Osvaldo Cutis, a teacher and the spokesman for Terra Libre, Laurindo shares the goals of the settlements and of the MST, which is mobilizing 3,000 of its activists in Brasilia from Aug. 10–19.

The demonstration in the capital, which included marches, debates, cultural events and other activities, is an effort by the MST to put pressure on the government of leftwing President Luiz Inàcio Lula da Silva to distribute land within the next six months to at least 90,000 families who have been squatting in different parts of the country since 2003, many of them camping by the roadside.

The landless movement has carried out land occupations for the past 25 years "calling for fulfillment of law," Cutis told IPS. It also seeks better living conditions for another 45,000 families "who have been resettled on paper only," and are "suffering hardship" because they are still waiting for resources for housing, infrastructure and production, he said.

People in the Terra Libre settlement are all too familiar with this situation, The state Institute for Agrarian Reform (INCRA) has not legalized their ownership of the land where they have lived "on a temporary basis" for over a decade because of red tape and endless battles over inheritance and compensation for expropriation in the courts.

Terra Libre occupies 460 hectares of an old estate, which was deemed unproductive according to official criteria set out in the law on agrarian reform, and which owed its workers the equivalent of one million dollars before it was taken over by the MST.

The problem is that until they have legal title to the land, the settlers do not have access to credits and tools from INCRA. But according to MST, many families to whom the government has already granted title deeds have not yet received this assistance.

"It's hard to convince some farmers to put effort and work into a plot of land that they might be forced to leave tomorrow," Curtis said.

Figure 4.55 Marching for real land reform

At least a partial solution to the problem is **land reform** (Figure 4.55). This involves breaking up large estates and redistributing land to the rural landless. Although successive governments have vowed to tackle the problem, progress has been limited due to the economic and political power of the big 'fazenda' or farm-owners, who have not been slow to use aggressive tactics (legal or otherwise) to evict squatters and delay expropriation.

In the mid-1990s land reform clearly emerged as Brazil's leading social problem, highlighted by a number of widely publicised squatter invasions. Such land occupations have occurred in both remote regions and established, prosperous farmlands in the South and South East. Each year in April, the Landless Rural Workers' Movement (known as the MST) organises a series of land invasions, takeovers of buildings and other protests. The purpose is twofold:

- to keep the issue high on the national political agenda
- to commemorate the killing 11 years ago of 19 landless protestors by police in the state of Para.

Section 4.3 Activities

1 Produce a graph to show selected data from Table 4.10.

2 Describe the data presented in Figure 4.52.

3 With reference to Figure 4.53, explain how variations in educational attainment affect regional development.

4 Write a 100-word summary of the article on land reform in Brazil (Figure 4.55).

5 Suggest how land tenure can have an impact on regional disparities.

4.4 The management of development

Case Study

Bolivia: managing the impact of globalisation

Bolivia (Figure 4.56) has recently introduced a **resource nationalisation** policy to regain an important aspect of its sovereignty and to use the expected increase in national income to combat inequality and poverty. Along with Cuba and Venezuela it forms the so-called 'radical block' of nations in Latin America which are concerned about US economic power in the region and the exploitative action of TNCs in general.

Figure 4.56 Bolivia

Bolivia is South America's poorest country, with a gross national income per capita of only $1260 in 2007 (Table 4.11). It is one of only two South American countries that are landlocked – the other being Paraguay. Bolivia has a population of just under 10 million. The majority of the population are of indigenous origin, mainly Aymara and Quechua, accounting for at least 60 per cent of the population. Following decades of military coups and short-lived governments, Bolivia has been under civilian rule since the 1980s.

Table 4.11 Bolivia factfile

Total population 2007	9.5 million
Crude birth rate 2007	28/1000
Crude death rate 2007	8/1000
Life expectancy 2007	65 years
Infant mortality rate 2007	48/1000
Adult literacy rate 2007	90%
GNI per capita 2007	$1260
% of population using improved drinking water sources, 2006	86%
Debt services as a % of exports of goods and services, 2006	8%
ODA inflow, 2006	$581 million

Source: UNICEF

In the 1980s and 1990s the Bolivian government introduced free market reforms. Such reforms were required by the World Bank if Bolivia was to continue to receive aid. **Privatisation** was at the heart of this agenda. Investors, usually foreign, were allowed to acquire 50 per cent ownership and management control of public sectors such as electricity, telecommunications and the state oil corporation, in return for an agreed level of capital

463

investment. Although the Bolivian government had little choice, it also wanted to link economic growth with equity so that poorer people would gain more benefit from Bolivia's participation in the global economy. The measures to achieve this included:

- a type of decentralisation called Popular Participation
- education reform to improve access to opportunities for the poor.

These two strategies were mainly targeted at improving the lives of the indigenous and mestizo (mixed race) populations. These population groups scored significantly below the national average on virtually every indicator of the quality of life. However, very limited progress with these objectives led to frequent changes in government due to public disquiet. A significant change occurred in December 2005 when Evo Morales of the Movement Toward Socialism (MAS) was elected as the country's first indigenous president. He was elected on a pledge to challenge the free market reforms that most people felt the country had been pressurised into adopting. There was widespread concern that these policies benefited large TNCs and the rich in Bolivia, to the detriment of the poor and of the environment. These were concerns voiced in a number of other countries which were in a similar situation. Bolivia has the highest income inequality in Latin America and is the sixth most unequal in the world (Figure 4.57). This is a situation that will take time to change.

The **indigenous population** of Bolivia has always had to endure a much lower quality of life than the people of Spanish descent. Two-thirds of Bolivia's population are indigenous, the largest number of any country within the region. However, the advent of 'participative democracy' in the last decade or so has resulted in a startling transformation of political power in the country. The key to this change was the indigenous population organising itself in an increasingly sophisticated manner. An important staging post was the success of Bolivia's poor in major protests over water and gas privatisation.

The indigenous population has been particularly susceptible to:

- lack of economic opportunities in rural areas where there are particularly high concentrations of indigenous peoples – this has resulted in large-scale migration to urban areas
- low employment rates in the formal sector and thus heavy reliance on the informal sector
- lack of access to land
- lack of access to basic social services (education, health, energy)
- continued discrimination and stereotyping
- higher adjustment costs to the economic reforms of the 1990s (privatisation etc.).

Table 4.12 shows the indigenous/non-indigenous schooling gap for Bolivia and four other Latin American countries. The smallest gap for these five countries is 2.3 years in Peru, rising to a very significant high of 3.7 years in Bolivia. Figure 4.58 shows the considerable gap between incomes achieved in the formal and informal sectors. The indigenous population are heavily over-represented in the latter sector.

Table 4.12 The indigenous/non-indigenous schooling gap

Country	Non-indigenous	Indigenous	Schooling gap in years
Bolivia	9.6	5.9	3.7
Ecuador	6.9	4.3	2.6
Guatemala	5.7	2.5	3.2
Mexico	7.9	4.6	3.3
Peru	8.7	6.4	2.3

Source: Bjorn-Soren Gigler, 'Missing Dimensions of Poverty Data', OPHI 29 May 2007,

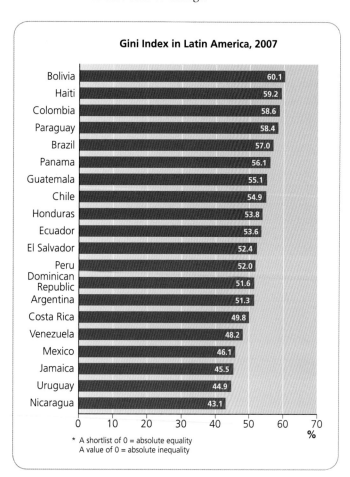

Figure 4.57 Income inequality in Latin America

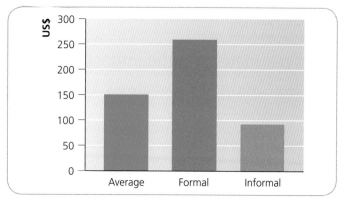

Figure 4.58 The income gap between the formal and informal economy

In May 2006 President Morales nationalised the country's gas and oil industry. Bolivia has the second largest natural gas reserves (13.8 trillion m³) in Latin America, but produces only a small amount of oil for domestic use. The foreign energy companies were told they had six months to sign new operating contracts or leave the country. All agreed to sign new contracts which will result in higher revenues for the government. Now, all foreign energy companies have to deliver all their production to the state-run YPFB for distribution and processing.

Overall, Bolivia has taken control of 82 per cent of the oil and gas in the country, leaving the remainder to foreign companies. Although Bolivia suffered much international criticism for its action, many aspects of Bolivia's resource nationalisation actually replicate Norway's oil management policies. Norway is very much a 'respected' member of the international community. The new government in Bolivia saw that regaining control of the country's natural resources was a vital first step towards generating the revenue to achieve much needed development.

The process of resource nationalisation has not only affected TNCs from MEDCs, but also its South American neighbour Brazil. Brazil's state-controlled oil company Petroleo Brasileiro SA produces 70 per cent of Bolivia's natural gas. Bolivia argues that Brazil gets the gas at a very low rate which is about half of what gas costs in the USA. Brazil feels that the price is fair given the fact that it built the gas pipeline between the two countries at a cost of $2.5 billion.

In 2006 President Morales said: 'Nationalisation will not stop at oil and gas resources, we'll extend it to land.' Brazilians grow more than a third of the soya beans in Bolivia and the concerns of these farmers about losing their land has led to discussions between the two governments. Bolivia has stated that its main concern is illegal or undocumented occupation of Bolivian land, especially land within 50 km of the Brazilian border, territory that Bolivia's constitution prohibits foreigners from owning.

Bolivians hold a certain resentment against some of their South American neighbours. Since the middle of the nineteenth century, Bolivia has lost about half its territory in natural resource disputes, the largest amount going to Brazil. Bolivia lost its Pacific coastline as a result of the 1879–84 War of the Pacific against Chile. This war was largely fought over guano (bird dung) which is used as a fertiliser.

Bolivia is adopting a socialist model of regional commerce and co-operation as opposed to what it sees as 'US-backed free trade'. Bolivia views the concept of the Free Trade Area of the Americas as an attempt by the USA to 'annex' Latin America. The government is trying to attract foreign investment while at the same time giving the state a larger role in managing the economy.

The privatisation of water has been a major issue. The resulting large increases in water bills provoked huge demonstrations such as those in Cochabamba, Bolivia's third largest city (Figure 4.59). The Bolivian government withdrew its water contract with Bechtel and its operating partner Abengoa. As a result the companies sued the Bolivian government for $50 million. However, in 2006 the companies agreed to abandon their legal action in return for a token payment.

Figure 4.59 Protest against water privatisation in Bolivia

Bolivia has a problem with the USA's drug war in South America. The USA wants to end the production of coca and thus reduce cocaine production to zero. Although Bolivia is against the trade in illegal drugs, it wants to preserve the legal market for coca leaves and promote the export of legal coca products. The reduction in the coca crop has hit many people on low incomes.

The Bolivian government is concerned by the number of people moving abroad to find work to earn money for their families. Limited employment in Bolivia is a major problem. In many cases children are left behind with no-one to care for them. In 2007 the Bolivian government announced that it was to create 360 000 jobs by 2010, but it has fallen well short of this target, due at least partly to the global financial crisis.

The actions of the USA in 'pressurising' Colombia and Peru into free-trade agreements have damaged Bolivian exports to these countries. Sixty per cent of Bolivia's main farm export, soya, goes to Colombia. Now Bolivia is concerned that cheap, subsidised US food will undercut much of Bolivia's market in Colombia.

In April 2006 Bolivia signed the people's trade agreement with Venezuela and Cuba. These two countries have agreed to take all of Bolivia's soya production as well as other farm products at market prices or better. Venezuela will also send oil to Bolivia to meet domestic shortages in production. Cuba has agreed to supply doctors.

In September 2008, President Morales ordered the US Ambassador to Bolivia, Philip Goldberg, to leave the country. The US Ambassador was accused of 'conspiring against democracy' and encouraging rebel groups who were protesting in eastern Bolivia. In November 2008, the USA suspended duty-free access for Bolivian exports and President Morales suspended US Drug Enforcement Administration operations, accusing its agents of espionage.

Like many countries that rely heavily on the export of raw materials to earn foreign currency, Bolivia has a sizeable foreign debt. At the end of 2006, Bolivia owed $3.2 billion to foreign creditors.

In December 2009 Evo Morales was re-elected as President of Bolivia, winning more than 60 per cent of the vote. His left-of-centre Movement Toward Socialism party gained majorities in both the 36-seat Senate and the 130-member Lower House. Supported strongly again by the largely poor indigenous population, Morales promises to push through further social and economic reforms. Before Morales came to power in 2005, Bolivia had had five Presidents in five years. There seems to be a perception amongst a majority of Bolivians that the country is moving towards a fairer society with a government determined to ensure a better balance of benefits from foreign investment than was the case in the past.

A UN human rights report on Bolivia, published in 2008, welcomed the positive advances made by the government in the areas of economic, social and cultural rights. The report highlighted programmes like the 'dignity pension' for the elderly and the Juancito Pinto voucher for schoolchildren in poor rural areas, as well as the 'yes I can' literacy campaign.

Figure 4.60 shows how the National Development Plan is attempting to move Bolivia away from the dominant influences of Colonialism and Neo-liberalism to Interculturalism and Egalitarianism. Figure 4.61 shows in more detail how Bolivia is doing this.

Figure 4.60 Reconstructing the state

The media in the USA generally portrays Evo Morales in an unfavourable light because he is seen as a threat to US interests. However, in much of Latin America he is favourably regarded because he is perceived to have stood up to the USA and big business in the interests of the ordinary people of Bolivia. Even amongst very intelligent people, perceptions can vary widely. It is often difficult for us to be totally impartial in our views.

Strategic goals	Indicators
Transformation of productive sector	Industrial transformation
	Strengthen domestic markets
	Redistribution of income
	Promote traditional economic sector
Economic stability	Redistribution of wealth
	State-led growth
	Trade surplus
Economic growth	Increase GDP
	Increase productivity
Social change and ethno-development	Regional development plans for most vulnerable regions (ethnic, cultural and social factors)
	Improved well-being of most vulnerable social groups
Empowerment	Promote 'Territorialización' (communal land rights/land-reform)
	Towards a more egalitarian society
	Transparency and participation
Equity	Equity (gender, age, cultural and social)
	Access, development and transfer of technologies
	Justice
	Promote harmony with the environment
Employment	Long-term employment with dignity
	Full employment

Figure 4.61 Strategic goals

Section 4.4 Activities

1 Using atlas maps, describe the general physical and human geography of Bolivia.

2 Comment on the information presented in Table 4.11. Find out some other facts that illustrate the quality of life in Bolivia.

3 Discuss the range of income inequality in Latin America shown by Figure 4.57.

4 Describe and explain the indigenous/non-indigenous schooling gap shown in Table 4.12.

5 What is the extent of the income gap between the formal and informal economy in Bolivia (Figure 4.58)?

6 a What is *resource nationalisation*?
  b Why has Bolivia pursued this policy?
  c How in the long term could this policy prove to be
    i of benefit to Bolivia   **ii** a disadvantage to Bolivia?

7 Why have Bolivia's recent policies to cope with globalisation created tension with the USA?

Index

Index

Index

Index

Index

Index

Acknowledgements

The publishers would like to thank the following for permission to reproduce copyright material:

Photo credits

Garrett Nagle: **p.9**, **p.10**, **p.16**, **p.22**, **p.25**, **p.27**, **p.40**, **p.44**, **p.45**, **p.47** *all*, **p.50**, **p.57**, **p.61**, **p.62**, **p.68** *both*, **p.75**, **p.78**, **p.79** *all*, **p.85**, **p.86** *both*, **p.204**, **p.206**, **p.207**, **p.211** *all*, **p.212**, **p.215**, **p.216** *both*, **p.218**, **p.219**, **p.220**, **p.221**, **p.235**, **p.238**, **p.242** *both*, **p.244**, **p.248** *both*, **p.251** *both*, **p.253** *all*, **p.254**, **p.259**, **p.269** *both*, **p.270** *all*, **p.272**, **p.274** *both*, **p.275**, **p.279**, **p.284**, **p.290**, **p.297**, **p.298** *both*, **p.299** *both*, **p.300**, **p.307**, **p.312**, **p.319**, **p.324** *all*, **p.325**, **p.326**

Paul Guinness: **p.90**, **p.92**, **p.95**, **p.96**, **p.99** *both*, **p.102**, **p.107** *both*, **p.109**, **p.114**, **p.116**, **p.117**, **p.119**, **p.122**, **p.124**, **p.125**, **p.127** *top left*, **p.129**, **p.131**, **p.132**, **p.135**, **p.139**, **p.141**, **p.142** *both*, **p.150**, **p.154** *top left*, **p.156**, **p.158**, **p.159**, **p.160**, **p.162**, **p.163**, **p.164**, **p.166**, **p.168**, **p.169**, **p.170**, **p.172** *both*, **p.175** *both*, **p.180**, **p.182**, **p.184**, **p.186**, **p.188**, **p.189**, **p.190**, **p.329** *top right*, **p.331**, **p.333**, **p.337**, **p.345**, **p.346**, **p.347**, **p.352**, **p.364** *both*, **p.365**, **p.367**, **p.368**, **p.369**, **p.371**, **p.382** *both*, **p.384**, **p.386**, **p.388**, **p.397**, **p.399**, **p.401**, **p.402**, **p.407**, **p.413**, **p.416**, **p.417**, **p.419**, **p.421**, **p.423**, **p.424**, **p.425** *both*, **p.434** *bottom right*, **p.436**, **p.439** *both*, **p.444**, **p.445**, **p.447**, **p.448**, **p.454**, **p.456**, **p.457**, **p.459** *both*, **p.461**
Chris Guinness: **p.87**, **p.93**, **p.97**, **p.105**, **p.112**, **p.121**, **p.127** *bottom right*, **p.154** *bottom right*, **p.329** *top left*, **p.355**, **p.379**, **p.387**, **p.438**

p.144 © Dabrowski/Keystone/Rex Features; **p.197** *both* © NASA; **p.222** © Schafer & Hill/Getty Images; **p.273** © Guardian News & Media Ltd 2010; **p.278** © United States Geological Survey Publications; **p.334** © Paul Nevin/Photolibrary; **p.335** © Frédéric Soltan/Sygma/Corbis; **p.339** © Eye Ubiquitous/Alamy; **p.340** © Ariana Cubillos/AP/Press Association Images; **p.343** © C Goodwin/Courtesty of Wikipedia; **p.356** © Bloomberg via Getty Images; **p.408** © Kim Naylor/Divine Chocolate; **p.410** © Mirrorpix; **p.428** © International Photobank/Alamy; **p.429** © Negril Coral Reef Preservation Society; **p.434** *top right* © aberenyi/Fotolia.com; **p.465** © Thomas Kruse

Artwork credits

Artwork: **p.12** A. Goudie and R. Gardner, Waterfall formation, from *Discovering Landscapes in England and Wales* (Chapman & Hall, 1992), reproduced by permission of the publisher; **p.14** A. Goudie, River delta shapes related to river, wave and tidal processes, from *The Nature of the Environment* (Blackwell, 1993), reproduced by permission of the publisher; **p.31** *right* G. Nagle, Latitudinal contrasts in insolation, from *Geography Through Diagrams* (Oxford University Press, 1998), © Garrett Nagle, reproduced by permission of the publisher; **p.32** R. Barry & R. Chorley, Contrasts in insolation by season and latitude, from *Atmosphere, Weather and Climate* (Routledge, 1998), reproduced by permission of the publisher; **p.33** D. Briggs et al., Seasonal temperature patterns, from *Fundamentals of the Physical Environment* (Routledge, 1997), reproduced by permission of the publisher; **p.34** *left* R. Barry & R. Chorley, Variations in pressure, from *Atmosphere, Weather and Climate* (Routledge, 1998), reproduced by permission of the publisher; **p.34** *right* E. Linacre & B. Geerts, Surface winds, from *Climates and Weather Explained* (Routledge, 1997), reproduced by permission of the publisher; **p.36** *top* G. Nagle, The effects of the North Atlantic Drift/Gulf Stream, from *Geography Through Diagrams* (Oxford University Press, 1998), © Garrett Nagle, reproduced by permission of the publisher; **p.40** D. Briggs et al., Maximum vapour pressure, from *Fundamentals of the Physical Environment* (Routledge, 1997), reproduced by permission of the publisher; **p.45** G. Nagle, Types of precipitation, from *Geography Through Diagrams* (Oxford University Press, 1998), © Garrett Nagle, reproduced by permission of the publisher; **p.53** *top* D. Briggs et al., The urban heat island (Chester), from *Fundamentals of the Physical Environment* (Routledge, 1997), reproduced by permission of the publisher; **p.53** *bottom* D. Briggs et al., The effect of terrain roughness on wind speed, from *Fundamentals of the Physical Environment* (Routledge, 1997), reproduced by permission of the publisher; **p.134** *top* City of Toronto Planning & Development Department, Toronto – changing social structure, from *Toronto in Transition* (April 1980); **p.149** P. J. Cloke, An index of rurality for England and Wales, from *Regional Studies, Volume 11* (1977); **p.187** *bottom right* Hugh Matthews, The cycle of deprivation, from *British Inner Cities* (Oxford University Press, 1991), © Hugh Matthews 1991, reproduced by permission of the publisher; **p.192** D. Briggs et al., Air masses, from *Fundamentals of the Physical Environment* (Routledge, 1997), reproduced by permission of the publisher; **p.193** *right* E. Linacre & B. Geerts, ITCZ and surface winds, from *Climates and Weather Explained* (Routledge, 1997), reproduced by permission of the publisher; **p.198** R. Barry & R. Chorley, Köppen's climate classification, from *Atmosphere, Weather and Climate* (Routledge, 1998), reproduced by permission of the publisher; **p.201** E. Linacre & B. Geerts, El Niño events, from *Climates and Weather Explained* (Routledge, 1997), reproduced by permission of the publisher; **p.203** *top* D. Briggs et al., A model of succession, from *Fundamentals of the Physical Environment* (Routledge, 1997), reproduced by permission of the publisher; **p.203** *top left* D. Briggs et al., Community changes through succession, from *Fundamentals of the Physical Environment* (Routledge, 1997), reproduced by permission of the publisher; **p.205** *top* D. Briggs et al., Tropical rainforest types, from *Fundamentals of the Physical Environment* (Routledge, 1997), reproduced by permission of the publisher; **p.206** D. Briggs et al., Vegetation structure in a rainforest, from *Fundamentals of the Physical Environment* (Routledge, 1997), reproduced by permission of the publisher; **p.209** D. Briggs et al., Types of savanna, from *Fundamentals of the Physical Environment* (Routledge, 1997), reproduced by permission of the publisher; **p.210** *top* D. Briggs et al., Savanna soils, from *Fundamentals of the Physical Environment* (Routledge, 1997), reproduced by permission of the publisher; **p.234** Human activity and longshore drift…, from *New Scientist*; **p.236** *bottom left* A. Goudie, Evolution of wave-cut platforms, from *The Nature of the Environment* (Blackwell, 1993), reproduced by permission of the publisher; **p.239** *bottom* A. Goudie, Beach deposits, from *The Nature of the Environment* (Blackwell, 1993), reproduced by permission of the publisher; *p.254* Relative sea-level change in the USA, from *New Scientist*; **p.317** A. S. Goudie, A model of desertification, from *The Human Impact on the Natural Environment* (Blackwell, 1993), reproduced by permission of the publisher; **p.347** Charles Whynne-Hammond, Transport costs and distance, from *Elements of Human Geography* (George Allen & Unwin, 1979); **p.410** Cameron Dunn et al., Africa's income and debt servicing (IDA and IMF sources), from *Edexcel A2 Geography* (Philip Allan, 2009)

Tables: **p.54** J. Tivy, Average changes in climate caused by urbanisation, from *Agricultural Ecology* (Longman, 1990); **p.80** *top left* A. Goudie, Examples of methods of controlling mass movement, from *The Nature of the Environment* (Blackwell, 1993); **p.82** *left* I. Simmons, Major direct environmental impacts of coal use (excluding human health), from *Changing the Face of the Earth: Culture, Environment, History* (Blackwell, 1989), reproduced by permission of the publisher; **p.82** *right* I. Simmons, Effluents from a coal-fired power station, from *Changing the Face of the Earth: Culture, Environment, History* (Blackwell, 1989), reproduced by permission of the publisher; **p.89** *left* Population Reference Bureau, Birth rate, death rate and rate of natural change by world region, 2010, from *2010 World Population Data Sheet*, reproduced by permission of the publisher; **p.89** *right* Population Reference Bureau, Variations in total fertility rate and the percentage of women using contraception by world region, 2010, from *2010 World Population Data Sheet*, reproduced by permission of the publisher; **p.92** Population Reference Bureau, Death rate, infant mortality rate and life expectancy at birth by world region, 2010, from *2010 World Population Data Sheet*, reproduced by permission of the publisher; **p.95** Population Reference Bureau, Dependency ratio calculations, from *2010 World Population Data Sheet*, reproduced by permission of the publisher; **p.99** Population Reference Bureau, The percentage of total population aged 65 years and over, 2010, from *2010 World Population Data Sheet*, reproduced by permission of the publisher; **p.116** The Risk Institute, Demographic changes in China, 1950-2005, from http://eng.newwelfare.org/wp-content/uploads/2008/03/strangestab1.gif, reproduced by permission of The Geneva Association; **p.128** *top* Reasons for migration from rural areas in Peru and Thailand, from J. Laite The migrant response in central Peru, in *The Urbanization of the Third World*, edited by J. Gugler (Oxford University Press, 1988), reproduced by permission of the publisher; **p.128** *bottom* M. Parnwell, Reasons for migration from rural areas in Peru and Thailand, from *Population Movements and the Third World* (Routledge, 1993), reproduced by permission of the publisher; *p.143* Population Reference Bureau, Factors encouraging migration from Mexico, by type of migrant, from *Population Bulletin, Volume 63, No. 1 (2003)*; **p.144** Mexican guest workers in the USA under H-2 visas, 1998–2006, from www.globalworkers.org, reproduced by permission of Global Workers Justice Alliance; **p.157** Rural facilities in the Isle of Purbeck, 2004, reproduced by permission of Dorset County Council; **p.167** Research Network, Loughborough University, Beta and gamma global cities. Globalisation and World Cities (GaWC); **p.213** *left* S. Nortcliff, Distribution of the main types of soil in the humid tropics, in The clearance of the tropical rainforest, from *Teaching Geography, 12, 3, pp.110–113 (1987)*, reproduced by permission of the Geographical Association; **p.295** C. Park, Monitoring for earthquake prediction, from *The Environment* (Routledge, 1997), reproduced by permission of the publisher; **p.329** Main types of irrigation, from *The Water Crisis: A Matter of Life and Death*, from *Understanding Global Issues*; **p.341** Area in farming in Jamaica, 1996 and 2007, from www.statinja.gov.jm, reproduced by permission of the Statistical Institute of Jamaica; **p.342** Exports of traditional and non-traditional commodities, January–December 2009, reproduced by permission of the Statistical Institute of Jamaica; **pp.353–4** ILO, Export processing zones – types of zones, from www.ilo.org, reproduced by permission of the International Labour Organization; **p.364** Oil reserves to production ratio 2009, from *BP Statistical Review of World Energy 2010*, reproduced by permission of BP p.l.c.; **p.366** Gas – Billion cubic metres, from *BP Statistical Review of World Energy 2010*, reproduced by permission of BP p.l.c.; **p.367** Proved coal reserves 2009, from *BP Statistical Review of World Energy 2010*, reproduced by permission of BP p.l.c.; **p.393** NACSO, Update 'Scaling up Namibia's community conservancies', p.32, MET 2005; NEEN 2004a, b, c; Weaver 2007; Jones 2008; **p.416** The Hunger Project, *Contrasting top-down and bottom-up aid models*; **p.423** J. Dove et al., The economic impact of travel and tourism – direct method and satellite accounting, from *OCR AS Geography* (Heinemann, 2008); **p.429** *The importance of the travel and tourist industry to the Jamaican economy*, reproduced by permission of the World Travel & Tourism Council; **p.446** The world's 24 largest corporations, from http://money.cnn.com; **p.453** Sue Warn, The positive and negative impacts of global shift , in *The Global Shift*, from Geo Factsheet, reproduced by permission of Curriculum Press; **p.464** Bjorn-Soren Gigler, The indigenous/non-indigenous schooling gap, from *Missing Dimensions of Poverty Data* from http://commons.wikimedia.org/wiki/File:Infant_mortality_rate_world_map.PNG

Text extracts: **p.118** Chen Weihua, extract from *China Daily*, 28 July 2009; **p.137** Website item on an African conflict, from www.insidesomalia.org, 7 August 2009; **p.148** C. Bull, P. Daniel & M. Hopkinson, Principal characteristics of traditional rural society, from *The Geography of Rural Resources* (Oliver & Boyd, 1984); **p.181** Earthscan, extract from *The Challenge of Slums*, from *Global Report on Human Settlement 2003*; **p.460** Paul Guinness, extract from The constituents of urban poverty, in *Slum Housing Global Patterns Case Studies*, from Geo FactSheet, No. 180, reproduced by permission of Curriculum Press.

Crown copyright material is reproduced under Class Licence Number C02P0000060 with the permission of the Controller of HMSO.

Every effort has been made to trace and contact all copyright holders. The Publishers will be pleased to rectify any omissions brought to their attention at the earliest opportunity.